LEGAL METHOD
AND WRITING

LEGAL METHOD AND WRITING

SECOND EDITION

CHARLES R. CALLEROS

PROFESSOR OF LAW
ARIZONA STATE UNIVERSITY

LITTLE, BROWN AND COMPANY
BOSTON   NEW YORK   TORONTO   LONDON

LIBRARY OF CONGRESS CATALOG CARD NO. 94-75305

ISBN 0-316-12505-9

SECOND EDITION

Third Printing

ICP

Published simultaneously in Canada
by Little, Brown & Company (Canada) Limited

PRINTED IN THE UNITED STATES OF AMERICA

TO MOM, DAD, AND JIM,
WITH LOVE

SUMMARY OF CONTENTS

vii

CONTENTS

PART

I

INTRODUCTION TO THE LEGAL SYSTEM

CHAPTER

1

Overview of the Case Method of Study

CHAPTER

2

Statutory and Common Law Analysis

‖ C H A P T E R ‖
3

The Role of Precedent   33

‖ C H A P T E R ‖
4

An Approach to Legal Method   51

C H A P T E R

5

Introduction to Writing Style   79

P A R T

II

WRITING IN LAW SCHOOL—FROM CASE BRIEFS TO EXAMINATIONS   87

C H A P T E R

6

Case Analysis   89

CHAPTER

7

Reorganization, Summary, and Inductive Reasoning in Outline Form 117

CHAPTER

8

Essay Examinations 137

‖ CHAPTER ‖
10

Organization of Office Memoranda and Briefs 199

‖ C H A P T E R ‖
11

Legal Writing Style in the Office Memorandum 227

CHAPTER

12

Introduction to Advocacy   293

‖ C H A P T E R ‖

13

Pleadings — 321

‖ C H A P T E R ‖
14

Motion for Summary Judgment   343

‖ C H A P T E R ‖
15

Motion to Exclude Evidence Before Trial   367

‖ C H A P T E R ‖
16

Appellate Briefs   377

PART

V

WRITING TO PARTIES: CONTRACTS AND CORRESPONDENCE

CHAPTER

17

Contracts

CHAPTER

18

Advice and Demand Letters — 453

TABLE OF CHARTS AND SAMPLE DOCUMENTS

SAMPLE DOCUMENTS

‖ PREFACE ‖

The activities of practicing attorneys speak volumes about the importance of legal writing classes in law school. Although analytic skills and a general knowledge of legal principles will form the intellectual foundation of your practice of law, legal analysis is only as effective as the quality with which it is expressed. In your practice, you undoubtedly will devote a substantial proportion of your time and effort to drafting legal documents such as office memoranda, letters, pleadings, motions, briefs, contracts, and wills. Moreover, techniques of expression are closely linked to the underlying substantive analysis; indeed, problems in writing style often betray confusion in the analysis.

Unfortunately, as a first-semester law student, you may have difficulty seeing the relationship between your efforts in legal writing classes and your short-term objectives for success in law school. Certainly the grades you earn on final exams are one clear measure of your success in law school. But you may be tempted to view your first-year writing courses, which may be ungraded, as a means of achieving a wholly distinct goal of preparing for successful performance in summer clerkships and in post-graduate practice. The extreme academic pressures of law school may stimulate you to place primary emphasis on your short-term goals of success on final examinations in graded courses and perhaps to resent an ungraded legal writing course as an inconvenient distraction.

With this book, I hope to reassure you that your work in your first-year legal writing courses will directly contribute to your success with law school exams as well as with legal documents that you draft in a summer clerking position or in post-graduate employment. I attempt to achieve that objective in two ways. First, I hope to eliminate any mystery in the study of law by comprehensively examining the three critical components for success in law school: (1) briefing and synthesizing cases, (2) reorganizing and summarizing course materials in course outlines, and (3) analyzing and answering essay examinations. Second, I demonstrate in Parts I–III that the skills you develop in analyzing a client's legal problem and drafting an office memorandum are directly transferable to your task of analyzing an essay exam and writing the exam answer.

Additionally, this book examines techniques of advocacy and client representation that should appeal to a broad spectrum of readers: participants in a first-year moot-court program, students in an advanced writing seminar, student law clerks, and practicing attorneys. For example, Part IV examines written advocacy in the context of pleadings, pretrial motions, and appellate briefs. Moreover, it thoroughly examines principles of writing and persuasion that apply generally to any litigation document. Part V provides a step-by-step approach to drafting simple contracts, advice letters, and demand letters. Finally, the extensive citations in footnotes, most of which first-year law students can pass over, will provide attorneys with a valuable source of authorities.

Chapters 5 and 10–12 of this book address matters of style. They use problems and examples to outline a general approach to style that focuses on the policies underlying conventions of composition and presentation of legal authority. In these chapters, I encourage you to adopt the following philosophy: We should not memorize and mechanically apply rules of composition any more than we would mechanically apply "black letter" rules of law. Instead, we must understand the goals and purposes of the conventions of legal writing, and we should apply them flexibly to satisfy those goals and purposes.

Of course, this book reflects my own style quirks and biases: I freely split infinitives but always use the serial comma, and I dislike sexism in language. While writing this book, I encountered the problem of sexism in language most often in the form of personal pronouns in the third person. If I constantly resorted to an ostensibly generic pronoun normally associated with the male gender, such as "his" or "him," I would offend those readers who do not view the pronoun as gender generic and who believe that the increasing number of female attorneys and judges deserves specific recognition. On the other hand, multiple pronouns such as "his or her" often needlessly clutter already complex sentences, and plural pronouns such as "they" are not always consistent with content. As a provocative response to the problem, I have alternated between male and female pronouns, for example by referring to an associate in a law firm with the pronoun "he" and to his supervising attorney with the pronoun "she." This approach may distract readers at one time or another, perhaps because it catches readers assuming that a judge or a senior partner is male. If so, perhaps the distraction is constructive: It may help us to envision a profession so well integrated that feminine pronouns and ethnic names will sound natural and commonplace.

Charles R. Calleros

March 1994

‖ ACKNOWLEDGMENTS ‖

My interest and enthusiasm for legal writing stem largely from the inspiration and training that I received as a court law clerk at the Office of Central Staff Attorneys for the United States Court of Appeals for the Ninth Circuit. In particular, I am grateful to my primary supervisors, Peter Shaw and Gregory Hughes, now practicing in California law firms. I am equally grateful to United States Court of Appeals Judge Procter Hug, Jr., who sowed the seeds of my current views on flexible, policy-oriented approaches to legal writing.

Other attorneys, judges, and colleagues contributed to my first edition with their comments on early drafts. In particular, I thank Thomas Gordon, who is a staff attorney for the Arizona Court of Appeals, fellow legal writing instructor, and former classmate at University of California at Davis School of Law. Mr. Gordon's keen analytic insights into the art of legal writing have contributed greatly to this book. Other important contributors include the rigorous reviewers for Little, Brown and Company, who strongly influenced the organization and content of the book, and Janet Wagner, an attorney who skillfully and artfully critiqued my writing style. Several colleagues contributed to selected portions of the book. They include Fred Cole, Amy Gittler, Mark Hielman, William Monahan, Roger Perry, Frank Placenti, Thomas Quarelli, Paul Ulrich, Judge Noel Fidel, and Professors Jane Aiken, Rebecca Berch, Betsy Grey, Mark Hall, David Kader, Robert Misner, Cathy O'Grady, Mary Richards, Bonnie Tucker, James Weinstein, and Larry Winer.

The truly indispensable contributors to this book, however, are the students and attorneys who accepted my instruction and used the early versions of the teaching materials from which this book is derived. I especially acknowledge the Phoenix law firm of Streich, Lang, Weeks & Cardon for its dedication to continuing education in legal writing. I also thank the hard-working student writing instructors who helped me direct an experimental first-year writing program at the College of Law in the 1985–1986 academic year. The continuing success of that program is a tribute to their early efforts.

I must also thank staff and student research assistants for their contributions to the first and second editions: Donna Blair and Gail Geer provided word-processing; Janice Fuller, Mark Burgoz, and Michael Rutledge checked citations; Virginia Vasquez evaluated the original manuscript for readability from the perspective of a first-year student; and Mark Burgoz, Toby Schmich, and Victoria Stevens provided other editorial work. Finally, I am indebted to Arizona State University College of Law, and especially to Dean Richard Morgan, who fully supported my efforts to produce this second edition.

LEGAL METHOD
AND WRITING

P A R T

I

INTRODUCTION TO THE LEGAL SYSTEM

1

Overview of the Case Method of Study

In your first-year contracts course, you probably will study the case of *Hadley and Another v. Baxendale and Others*.[1] By examining the history of this case now, you can become acquainted with the methods by which you will study law in most of your classes.

The dispute between the Hadleys and Baxendale began as a business transaction during an economic boom in the midst of England's industrial revolution. Operators of a flour mill in Gloucester entered into a contract with a carrier for the transportation of a broken engine shaft to a manufacturer in Greenwich, on the other side of England.

The operators of the mill, the Hadleys, were anxious to transport the broken shaft to the manufacturer as quickly as possible; the failure of the shaft had halted the milling of corn, and the broken shaft would serve as a model for the manufacture of a new shaft. An employee of the carrier, Pickford and Co., promised that the shaft would be delivered to the manufacturer within two days after the date that the carrier took possession of the shaft. For this, the mill operators paid £2 4s. The carrier could have transported the shaft as promptly as promised had it immediately used available means of land transportation. Presumably to reduce costs, however, it held the shaft for several days in London before loading it onto a canal barge along with a shipment of iron that was bound for the same manufacturer. As a consequence, the carrier delivered the shaft to the manufacturer on the seventh day after the carrier received it, resulting in an additional delay of five days during which the mill was stopped.

The mill operators demanded that the carrier compensate for an estimated £300 in lost profits that the mill suffered because of the additional delay. The carrier refused, and the mill operators sued the carrier's managing director, Baxendale, in a trial court in Gloucester, claiming approximately £200 in damages. Although the carrier offered to settle the dispute for £25, the mill operators rejected the offer, and the case went to trial before a jury. The mill operators presented witnesses who testified to £120 in damages,

---

1. 9 Ex. 341, 156 Eng. Rep. 145 (1854).

and the jury awarded the mill operators £50 in a compromise verdict that became the judgment of the trial court.

The carrier appealed to the Court of Exchequer. It ultimately persuaded a panel of three judges on that court to reverse the judgment of the trial court and to grant a new trial on the ground that the trial judge had given the jury excessive latitude in awarding damages for lost profits.

In the appellate court's written opinion, the authoring judge explained that a jury may award only those damages that would flow naturally from the breach of such a contract or that would be reasonably within the contemplation of the parties because of special circumstances communicated at the time of contracting. Because the appellate judges assumed that the mill would ordinarily have spare shafts with which to keep running, they concluded that lost profits stemming from an idle mill would not be the natural consequence of the breach of the contract for prompt carriage. Whether the possibility of lost profits would nonetheless have been in the contemplation of the parties would depend on whether, at the time of contracting, the mill operators had communicated to the carrier the special circumstances that the broken shaft was the mill's only shaft and that the mill would be idle in its absence.

The appellate court concluded that the mill operators had informed the carrier only that they operated a mill and that the article to be transported was the broken shaft of a mill.[2] On this premise, the appellate court held that the trial judge should not have allowed the jury to consider any lost profits in its calculation of damages.

The case of *Hadley v. Baxendale* illustrates both how a case makes its way through the legal system and how you typically will encounter the case only at the final destination in its legal journey. Reacting to a pressing

---

2. Interestingly, this represents a departure from the summary of the trial proceedings prepared by the court reporter, who had reported at the beginning of the appellate opinion that the mill operators had informed the carrier that the mill was stopped. See Richard Danzig, The Capability Problem in Contract Law 80 (1978) (characterizing the finding of the Court of Exchequer as "remarkable").

commercial need, the mill operators entered into an agreement with the carrier to exchange money for certain services. Disappointed with the services rendered, the mill operators demanded compensation. Failing to secure the compensation through less formal means, they filed an action in a trial court to obtain a judgment compelling the carrier to pay compensation.

At trial, the parties discovered that their claims and defenses were limited by their ability to present credible supporting evidence to the jury, to whom the court had delegated the task of finding facts. Hence, the mill operator's original demand dropped first from £300 to £200, and then to the £120 of losses for which it could produce testimony. Relying on centuries of development of law and custom, the court recognized the contractual relationship as one deserving of the protection of the Queen's courts, and it permitted the jury to award damages for the carrier's breach of the contract. The jury awarded less in damages than the trial court's instructions and the testimony would have allowed, but more than the carrier thought the law should permit. Accordingly, the carrier took the dispute before a court of higher authority, which ordered a new trial that would exclude lost profits from any recovery. The higher court explained its decision in a written judicial opinion.

In only a tiny percentage of disputes do the parties complete this process of full trial followed by review of the trial court's judgment in one or more appellate courts. Countless people become entangled in disputes that arguably give rise to legal claims, yet they seldom take the formal step of filing lawsuits to test their claims. In even fewer cases do they fully try their disputes in the trial court. In most lawsuits, the parties manage to "settle" their disputes before trial by agreeing to a compromise, thus avoiding the expense and risks of full trial. In many others, a full trial of the facts is unnecessary to resolve the dispute, and the trial court grants judgment for one of the parties before trial.

In cases that result in judgment after a full trial, only a small percentage of losing parties seek review of the adverse judgment in an appellate court. Still fewer seek further review in a higher appellate court when one is available. Thus, the proportions of disputes that proceed to various levels of dispute resolution roughly describe a pyramid:

Appeals to
the appellate
court of last resort

Appeals to an intermediate
court of appeals

Full trials in a trial court

Lawsuits filed but resolved before full trial

Disputes that give rise to plausible legal claims
but are not the subject of formal legal actions

It is primarily to the decisions of the appellate courts that law school courses will direct your attention. In nearly all first-year courses in law school, students encounter the law in casebooks, each of which presents judicial opinions on various topics that relate to a general field of law such as property, contracts, crimes, procedure, or torts.

The "cases" in a casebook are the disputes that parties bring to courts for resolution. Most of the judicial opinions that analyze the cases are the opinions of appellate courts. The edited appellate opinions published in casebooks often summarize the facts of the dispute and the proceedings in lower courts in the most economical way possible,[3] sometimes providing no more than a bare outline of the human drama that has preceded the appellate litigation. Most appellate opinions focus instead on using the cases before them as vehicles for developing and articulating general legal rules or principles. These rules not only resolve the dispute before the court, they also provide guidance to courts and litigants in future disputes of a similar nature, as well as to persons who desire to conform their actions to the law so as to avoid disputes.

Judicial opinions may mystify you in your first weeks at law school. They are peppered with legal terminology that will incrementally become part of your working vocabulary only after weeks and months of study. Even worse, some of the judicial language, particularly in the older cases, will be antiquated or overly formal and will have no place in your own writing; yet you must immerse yourself in the language to understand the opinions.

Moreover, the opinions assume a knowledge of the legal system and of the legal method that courts use when working within that system. For example, you might wonder how an early English decision such as *Hadley v. Baxendale* is relevant to your study of American law. Also confusing to some new law students is the relationship between "common law" and "statutory law," both of which may be addressed in the same judicial opinion.

Part I of this book seeks to answer these and many other questions by introducing you to our legal system and to fundamental principles of legal method. This foundation should better prepare you to develop skills in studying law in first-year courses, in analyzing legal problems in a law office or judge's chambers, and in advocating a client's position to a court, all of which are discussed in Parts II-V. Chapter 2 begins building the foundation with an introduction to the American legal system.

You undoubtedly must prepare cases for class discussion beginning with the first day of class. Accordingly, before your first week of classes, you may wish to glance through Sections I and III of Chapter 6. As the introduction and conclusion of the chapter, these sections provide an overview to the process of briefing cases for class discussion. After you later complete Part I, you can study Chapters 6-8 more thoroughly to develop a comprehensive, three-point plan for success in your substantive courses: (1) briefing and synthesizing cases, (2) outlining course materials, and (3) applying effective examination techniques.

---

3. Indeed, many of the details of Hadley v. Baxendale described in this book do not appear in the report of the Court of the Exchequer, much less in a casebook's edited version of that report. The source of this book's more detailed recounting of the case is Richard Danzig, The Capability Problem in Contract Law 68-105 (1978).

EXERCISE 1-1

Examine the chart on page 5, which uses a pyramid to represent the tiny proportion of disputes that reach an appellate court. In class discussion or in a written essay, discuss the factors that likely determine whether a dispute will reach an appellate court. Do you think that those factors affect the kinds of issues that are addressed by the courts? Is it possible that they affect the nature of the law expressed in judicial opinions?

2

Statutory and Common Law Analysis

I. SOURCES OF LAWMAKING POWERS

The United States Constitution allocates powers between the state and national governments and thus establishes the framework for our federal system of government. In turn, each state's constitution establishes the framework for that state's government. A fundamental tenet of these state and federal constitutions is the separation of powers between the legislative, judicial, and executive branches of government. Although lawmaking functions rest primarily with the legislative branch, all three branches exercise some form of lawmaking power.

The state and federal legislatures create law by enacting statutes within the authority granted to them by the state and federal constitutions. Although the primary function of the executive branch is enforcement of laws, the executive branch often leads in policy development by proposing legislation to a legislature. Conversely, a legislature may delegate some of its lawmaking power to the executive branch by statutorily authorizing an executive agency to issue rules and regulations designed to help implement a statutory scheme.

For example, in the exercise of its federal constitutional authority to regulate commerce, the United States Congress has enacted comprehensive labor relations statutes, such as the National Labor Relations Act.[1] It has also created the National Labor Relations Board, an agency of the United States, and it has authorized the board to issue administrative rules and regulations necessary to help the board enforce the labor relations statutes.[2]

---

1. 49 Stat. 449 (1935).
2. 29 U.S.C. §§153, 156 (1988); American Hosp. Ass'n v. NLRB, 499 U.S. 606, 609 (1991).

Legislatures cannot amend a constitution in the same way that they enact statutes. For example, Article V of the United States Constitution authorizes Congress to propose constitutional amendments, but such proposals do not become effective until ratified by the legislatures or constitutional conventions of three-fourths of the states.

The judicial branch of government develops law in two ways, both of them in the context of particular disputes. First, state and federal courts contribute to the development of constitutional and statutory law by interpreting the necessarily general terms of such law and applying those terms to the facts of disputes. Second, as an offspring of the English judicial system, American courts have adopted and continue to develop a substantial body of common law, judge-made law that applies to issues not addressed by constitutional or statutory law. State courts are the primary source of common law, because federal courts no longer create and develop "federal general common law."[3] Nonetheless, the federal courts retain the power in a few restricted fields, such as admiralty law, to develop "specialized federal common law."[4]

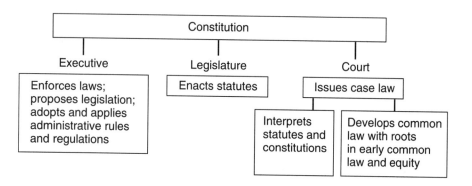

An example of the interplay between statutory law and common law is provided in the first-year contracts course. Many principles of contract law, such as consideration, offer and acceptance, performance and breach, and remedies, find their source in a substantial body of common law, developed by judges, first in England and later in America. This common law forms a backdrop against which state legislatures have enacted statutes, such as commercial codes, that supersede some of the common law rules. In the resulting hybrid system, the statutes provide the rule of law on issues to which they apply, while common law applies to gaps within and between statutes.

These fundamental principles of state and federal lawmaking apply only in limited fashion to two other kinds of governments in the United States: (1) local governments of political subdivisions of the states, such as cities and counties, and (2) American Indian tribal governments.

Local governments come in a variety of models. Although many of

---

3. Erie R.R. v. Tompkins, 304 U.S. 64, 78 (1938).
4. Henry J. Friendly, In Praise of Erie—And of the New Federal Common Law, 39 N.Y.U. L. Rev. 383, 405 (1964).

them exercise legislative, executive, and judicial powers, they do not always practice the same degree of separation of these powers as do state and federal governments. In many states, the state constitution and statutes at least partially define the legal structure that a local government can adopt and the powers that it can exercise.

More nearly autonomous are American Indian tribes. Although their powers may be limited by federal law, they are otherwise sovereign governments with inherent powers to exercise tribal authority. Not all of the tribes have chosen to adopt every fundamental tenet of the state and federal governments. For example, the Navajo Nation of the southwestern United States has no constitution, and it has not always recognized complete separation of legislative, judicial, and executive powers. Nonetheless, its legal system is similar to the Anglo-American system in several important respects. The tribe elects the members of the Navajo Tribal Council, which enacts statutory law in the form of tribal codes. The executive power rests primarily in the President, an elected official. Finally, the Navajo tribal trial courts and the Navajo Supreme Court apply federal law and tribal codes, and they develop and apply a tribal common law based on tribal custom and cultural values.

This book primarily addresses state and federal common law and statutes. This chapter separately discusses first common law analysis and then statutory analysis before further addressing the relationship between the two.

II. COMMON LAW

The common law that American courts develop and apply has its roots in the English common law, which was dispensed in the courts of the English king. This English law came to be known as the "common law" because it applied generally throughout medieval England and thus replaced a less uniform system of customary law dispensed in local or regional courts and in the private courts of feudal lords. The English Court of Chancery, representing a separate system of law, competed with the early common law courts for jurisdiction by applying a system of "equity law" that provided relief when common law remedies were inadequate.

Distinctions between some common law and equitable claims, defenses, and remedies continue to have substantive significance.[5] Most American jurisdictions, however, have eliminated the dual court system by merging law and equity procedure.[6] Accordingly, this book will use the term "common law" to refer generally to laws created and developed by the courts, regardless whether the principles have their roots in early common law or equity law.

Oliver Wendell Holmes traced the origins of some English and American

---

5. Dan B. Dobbs, Remedies §2.6 (1973); cf. 5A Arthur L. Corbin, Corbin on Contracts §1136 (1964) (procedural merger of law and equity has resulted in partial substantive merger of legal and equitable principles of remedies).

6. See, e.g., Fed. R. Civ. P. 2 ("There shall be one form of action to be known as 'civil action.' "); Dobbs, supra note 5, §2.6 app., at 81-82 (1973).

common law to early Germanic and Roman law.[7] Other common law principles simply reflect judicial recognition of community needs, habits, or customs, and are "accounted for by their manifest good sense."[8] More generally, common law is "the embodiment of broad and comprehensive unwritten principles . . . inspired by natural reason and an innate sense of justice."[9]

The term "common" may be misleading when applied to American common law: The courts in each state are free to develop the common law of that state in a manner that reflects local policies; therefore, variations in common law among the states are inevitable. Nonetheless, to a surprising degree, courts in different states share common views on general principles of law. For example, a federal appellate court has noted that "the principles of contract law do not differ greatly from one jurisdiction to another."[10] Perhaps more important for law students and practitioners, the legal method employed by courts in deciding disputes and developing common law does not vary substantially among the states.

The early common law crime of burglary, which was punishable by death, illustrates the judicial development of common law rules to serve particular needs of the community. In imposing capital punishment for this crime, the common law courts sought to deter a serious invasion of the right of habitation during hours of darkness, when the inhabitants were most vulnerable to attack and the invader most likely to escape recognition. Efforts by the common law courts to narrowly address that evil are reflected in the general definition of common law burglary, which separates the crime into distinct elements: (1) the breaking and (2) entering (3) of the dwelling house (4) of another (5) in the night (6) with the intent to commit a felony.

In defining and applying these elements of common law burglary in the context of successive cases, the courts exhibited a reluctance to extend the crime beyond the minimum reach necessary to achieve the underlying purposes of the crime, probably because of the severity of punishment. For example, the courts viewed an intruder as less culpable if the occupant of a dwelling encouraged the intrusion by failing to properly secure the dwelling. Accordingly, many courts held that a trespasser who gained entry by further opening a partially open door or window had not committed the "breaking" necessary for a burglary.[11]

The history of another common law crime, murder, illustrates the manner in which courts gradually developed common law doctrine "over several centuries of time as a parade of cases, involving different fact situations, came before the judges for decision."[12] The common law decisions generally define murder as the unlawful killing of another human being with malice aforethought. Early decisions defined "malice aforethought" narrowly by requiring proof of a premeditated intent to kill. As subsequent cases pre-

---

7. Oliver W. Holmes, Jr., The Common Law 2, 18, 34, 340-344, 360 (1923).
8. Id. at 2, 337-339.
9. Stanley Mosk, The Common Law and the Judicial Decision-Making Process, 11 Harv. J.L. & Pub. Pol'y 35 (1988) (citing Rodriguez v. Bethlehem Steel Co., 525 P.2d 669, 682-683 (Cal. 1974)).
10. E.g., In re Cochise College Park, Inc., 703 F.2d 1339, 1348 n.4 (9th Cir. 1983).
11. Wayne R. LaFave & Austin W. Scott, Jr., Criminal Law §8.13, at 792-793 (2d ed. 1986).
12. Id. §1, at 605.

sented unpremeditated or even unintentional killings that warranted classification as murder, courts effectively expanded the definition of "malice aforethought" by recognizing other circumstances that would justify conviction for murder: intentional but unpremeditated killing without sufficient provocation; unintentional killing during the commission of another felony; unintentional killing through conduct that reflects a reckless disregard for the lives of others; and killing during the course of conduct engaged in with the intent to do serious bodily harm short of death.[13]

This process of incremental development of the common law does not always proceed in an unbroken line. Courts sometimes abandon previously adopted lines of authority to chart new courses that better reflect current social, economic, and technological realities:

> The inherent capacity of the common law for growth and change is its most significant feature. It is constantly expanding and developing to keep up with the advancement of civilization and the new conditions and progress of society, and adapting itself to the gradual changes in trade, commerce, arts, inventions, and the needs of the country. . . . The vitality of the common law can flourish if the courts remain alert to their obligation and have the opportunity to change it when reason and equity so demand. The common law requires that each time a rule of law is applied, it must be carefully scrutinized to make sure that the conditions and needs of the times have not so changed as to make further application of the rule an instrument of injustice. Although the legislature may speak to the subject, in the common law system the primary instruments of legal evolution are the courts.[14]

A change in conditions is not the only possible inspiration for abandonment of existing common law. A court will occasionally conclude that a previous decision was flawed from its inception. Hindsight may show that the previous court premised its decision on erroneous factual assumptions about conditions existing at that time. Alternatively, the current court, which itself may have changed in political or intellectual composition, may simply reject the reasoning of the previous decision.[15] This process of evolution, however, is restricted by the doctrine of stare decisis, explored in Chapter 3.

═══════ E X E R C I S E   2 - 1 ═══════

1. Wrongful Conception, Wrongful Life

In general, the common law of torts imposes civil liability upon a physician who breaches a duty of care to a patient. By applying this general common law rule to new medical procedures, courts and juries necessarily refine the content of the rule. In the following problem, you should assume that the common law of the jurisdiction has not previously addressed the issues that are raised by the facts. You must decide how you would fashion the common law that applies to the issues if you were a judge preparing to instruct a jury on the applicable legal rules. Specifically, you must decide to

---

13. Id. at 605-606.
14. Mosk, supra note 9, at 36.
15. See generally Geoffrey R. Stone, Precedent, the Amendment Process, and Evolution in Constitutional Doctrine, 11 Harv. J.L. & Pub. Pol'y 67, 71 (1988).

what extent you think the common law should impose liability on a physician for negligently permitting a child to be conceived.

Problem

When Sandra Gonzalez and her husband, Miguel, had their third child, they agreed that they desired no further children and that Miguel should undergo sterilization. They consulted Dr. Leonard, who performed a vasectomy. Although Dr. Leonard pronounced the operation a success, he in fact performed the vasectomy carelessly and neglected to order routine follow-up tests. Miguel impregnated Sandra within four months after the failed sterilization procedure.

a. In the process of developing the state's common law of torts, should a state court permit Sandra and Miguel to sue Dr. Leonard on a negligence theory of "wrongful conception"? If so, should the damages include only the medical expenses and other costs associated with the childbirth, or should they more broadly include the costs of raising the fourth child?

b. Suppose that the fourth child was born with severe mental retardation, but that the failed sterilization procedure did not contribute to the retardation. Should these facts affect the court's evaluation of the parents' claims based on wrongful conception? Should the court recognize a cause of action on the behalf of the fourth child for "wrongful life," permitting the child herself to collect damages on the theory that she would have been better off had she not been conceived?

c. Should the analysis of any of these questions be affected by the fact that Sandra could have legally aborted her fetus soon after discovering her pregnancy?

2. *Punitive Damages for Breach of a Marriage Agreement*

A contract may be partially defined as a legally enforceable private agreement in which parties have exchanged promises to engage in some performance in the future. The law of contracts governs the formation, interpretation, and enforcement of contracts. A party to a contract who fails to perform its contractual promise is said to have "breached" the contract. The victim of such a breach may bring an action in court to enforce the contract. In most cases, a court will award money damages as remedy for a breach. Specifically, it will order the breaching party to pay to the victim of the breach "compensatory damages" in the amount of the value of the expected performance.

As a general principle of the common law of contracts, an award of damages for breach of contract is limited to such compensatory damages. Absent proof of an independent civil wrong known as a "tort," most courts will not grant additional "punitive damages" designed to punish the breaching party and to discourage other parties from breaching contracts.

An early exception to this general rule is the traditional willingness to award punitive damages for breach of a contract to marry. Contracts scholar Arthur L. Corbin discussed the kinds of jury instructions that might permit a jury in such cases to award damages that have punitive elements:

Thus, where, under promise of marriage, *A* is seduced by *B* and then cast off in disgrace, it is proper to tell the jury that they may consider these facts and may increase the damages even though there is no evidence of pecuniary loss. Again, where *A* is jilted by *B*, who marries another without first notifying *A* that the engagement is broken and denies that there has been an engagement, *A*'s hurt feelings, wounded pride, the length of the engagement, the loss of opportunity to marry others, *B*'s wealth and social standing may all be considered by the jury in awarding damages.[16]

Assume that an 1898 decision of a state's highest court permits an award of punitive damages for breach of any marriage agreement, even if the breach is not accompanied by an independent tort or elements of a tort. Does such a "marriage contract" exception find support in contemporary public policy and social mores?

Those who doubt the continued vitality of actions for breach of marriage agreements should consult the complaint in Appendix VI. Drafted in 1984, it alleges breach of a promise to marry. In reviewing proposed instructions to a jury on the proper measure of damages in such an action, should a court today abandon this traditional exception to the rule against awarding punitive damages? Conversely, can you think of other kinds of contracts of more recent origin that are so exceptional in nature that they should inspire a new exception to the general rule against punitive damages for breach of contract?

III. STATUTORY ANALYSIS

A. ROLE OF CONSTITUTIONAL AND STATUTORY LAW

"The Constitution states the framework for all our law. Legislation is one great tool of legal change and readaptation."[17] As expressed by a state supreme court, constitutional and statutory law reflect collective expressions of public policy, or social values:

> As the expressions of our founders and those we have elected to our legislature, our state's constitution and statutes embody the public conscience of the people of this state.[18]

Consistent with its role as the paramount policymaking body, a legislature often enacts statutes to address problems that it concludes are not adequately addressed by the common law. For example, the early common law crime of theft was defined as a trespassory taking and carrying away of

---

16. 5 Arthur L. Corbin, Corbin on Contracts §1077, at 441 (1964).
17. Karl N. Llewellyn, The Bramble Bush 10 (7th prtg. 1981).
18. Wagenseller v. Scottsdale Memorial Hosp., 710 P.2d 1025, 1033 (Ariz. 1985).

personal property of another with intent to steal.[19] The requirement of a trespassory taking excluded the conduct of one who took possession of another's property lawfully, but who subsequently converted the property to his own use with the intent to permanently deprive the owner of it. Aware that the common law did not impose criminal liability for such a misappropriation and determined to criminalize such conduct, English and American legislators created the statutory crime of embezzlement, generally defined as the fraudulent conversion of another's property by one who is already in lawful possession of it.[20] Had the legislatures not acted, the courts might have eventually achieved the same result through further development of the common law, but legislative action sometimes provides a quicker and more certain change of course.

A more contemporary example deals with the process of reaching a legally binding agreement through the process of offer and acceptance. Under the common law of contracts, a department store's newspaper advertisement typically amounts to an invitation to negotiate rather than an offer to enter into a binding contract; in most cases, a customer makes the first offer by entering the store and requesting to purchase the advertised goods. Under common law, the store owner is free to reject the customer's offer without incurring any contractual liability.[21] Unfortunately, this allocation of legal rights and obligations has encouraged some sellers to use "bait-and-switch" tactics: They lure customers into their stores with the "bait" of goods advertised at spectacularly reduced prices; then they "switch" goods by resisting the customer's desire to purchase the advertised goods and by persuading the customer to purchase a more expensive item. In response, state legislatures have promoted public policy favoring consumer protection by enacting legislation that restricts or prohibits such bait-and-switch tactics.[22] These state laws have altered rights and obligations as they were defined under the common law of contracts.

Common Law of Contracts: If store's ad is not an offer, Customer makes first offer. Store can reject that offer and can "switch" Customer to more expensive item.	**Consumer-Protection Legislation:** Legislature concludes that common law is deficient and enacts protective legislation to address the "bait and switch" problem.

Early English and American legislatures tended not to replace common law wholesale with a comprehensive system of statutes. Instead, they typically enacted statutes to correct specific defects or fill gaps in a well-developed

---

19. Wayne R. LaFave & Austin W. Scott, Jr., Criminal Law §8.2, at 706 (2d ed. 1986).
20. Id. at §8.6.
21. 1 Arthur L. Corbin, Corbin on Contracts §25 (1963); John D. Calamari & Joseph M. Perillo, Contracts §2-6(e), at 36-37 (3d ed. 1987).
22. See, e.g., Unif. Consumer Sales Practices Act §3(b)(6); Cal. Bus. & Prof. Code §12024.6 (West Supp. 1987); Note, State Control of Bait Advertising, 69 Yale L.J. 830 (1960).

body of common law. Thus, until this century, statutory law assumed a role of secondary importance in American law, inspiring one scholar to characterize them as "warts on the body of the common law."[23] However, state and federal legislation has so proliferated in this century that "most American jurisdictions now are Code states."[24] This new prominence of statutory law in the American legal system warrants an examination of methods of statutory analysis.

B. JUDICIAL INTERPRETATION AND APPLICATION OF STATUTES

A statute imposes liability on certain employers for discrimination against any individual in the "terms" or "conditions" of employment "because of such individual's . . . sex." Would the statute impose liability on an employer who fired your clients, male and female homosexuals, because of their sexual orientation? Would it impose liability on an employer who made sexual advances toward only female employees, thus adversely affecting their working environment, but who did not condition tangible job benefits on acquiescence to his demands? The answers to these questions depend on the intended meaning of the statutory language "because of . . . sex" and "terms" or "conditions" of employment.

The questions arise because statutory language sometimes is vague or ambiguous. An ambiguous term has multiple meanings, although each of the meanings may be precise and all of the meanings may be easily identified. A vague term is uncertain in its meaning and indefinite in its scope, making it difficult to identify the meaning or meanings that it encompasses.[25]

As discussed more fully below, statutory language sometimes is necessarily vague because of deliberate generality or is avoidably ambiguous because of unintended imprecision. Consequently, the way in which statutory language applies to the facts of a particular dispute may be subject to reasonable dispute. Courts give greater specificity and precision to the statutory language by interpreting and applying the statute in the context of the dispute.

A court does not engage in a wholly creative process when it interprets a vague or ambiguous statute. Rather, it seeks to determine and to give effect to the intent of the enacting legislature by analyzing the statutory language, the stated or apparent purpose of the statute, and the legislative activities related to enactment of the bill.[26]

This search for the intended meaning of a statute is governed by a separate layer of judicially developed rules of interpretation and construction. Although the terms "interpretation" and "construction" are often used interchangeably, this book will recognize the following distinction: "Interpretation" refers to the process of determining legislative intent; "construc-

---

23. Llewellyn, supra note 17, at 89; see also Roscoe Pound, Common Law and Legislation, 21 Harv. L. Rev. 383 (1908).
24. Mosk, supra note 9, at 35.
25. See generally W. Quine, Word and Object 85, 129 (1960).
26. E.g., Jackson Transit Auth. v. Local Div. 1285, Amalgamated Transit Union, 457 U.S. 15, 22-29 (1982); Mohasco Corp. v. Silver, 447 U.S. 807, 815 (1980).

tion" refers to the process of reconciling statutory language with public policy in the absence of conclusive evidence of legislative intent.

Evidence of legislative intent may be intrinsic to the statute, extrinsic to it, or both. Intrinsic evidence of legislative intent is the statutory text itself. This includes the statutory language in question and other portions of the statute that state or imply the statutory purpose or otherwise provide a context within which to interpret the language in question. Some statutes include a section of defined terms, which may provide partial guidance even when it does not conclusively resolve a dispute over the proper interpretation of the language in question.

Extrinsic evidence of legislative intent includes other information about the social or legal context of the legislation in question. For example, contemporaneous case law or companion legislation may provide insights into the nature of the social problem that the statutory language in question was meant to address.

However, the primary source of extrinsic evidence of legislative intent is the legislative history of the statute in question. This includes the text of legislative debates, preliminary drafts of the legislation, and hearings or reports of legislative committees. Under the "plain meaning" rule of interpretation, if the statutory language in question has a plain meaning on its face, a court may be reluctant to consider legislative history supporting a less obvious interpretation.[27] However, it arguably is not precluded from doing so,[28] as when a federal court of appeals engaged in an exhaustive analysis of legislative history and statutory policy to interpret the statutory term "or" to mean the conjunction "and," rather than the disjunctive "either/or."[29]

Unfortunately, misuse of legislative history may mislead more than enlighten. The search for legislative intent is an attempt to reconstruct the collective intent of numerous legislators whose views on the wisdom or scope of the statute may conflict. Opposing advocates often can draw on different portions of legislative history to support conflicting views on the proper interpretation of a statute: They simply invoke isolated statements of legislators taken out of the context of the complete debate on a bill. Indeed, a court may then justify the result that it wants to reach by selectively drawing on portions of legislative history that support that result. These and other pitfalls have led one Supreme Court Justice to decry the "level of unreality that our unrestrained use of legislative history has attained."[30]

If a court cannot obtain clear evidence of legislative intent through intrinsic or extrinsic evidence, it may use other means to resolve vagueness or ambiguity in statutory language. For example, if an administrative agency has developed expertise in administering the statute, the court may simply

---

27. See, e.g., Connecticut Nat'l Bank v. Germain, 112 S. Ct. 1146, 1149-1150 (1992) (giving priority to the plain language of the statute over legislative history and canons of construction).

28. See Maine v. Thiboutot, 448 U.S. 1, 13-14 (1980) (Powell, J., dissenting).

29. Unification Church v. INS, 762 F.2d 1077, 1083-1090 (D.C. Cir. 1985); see also Mountain States Tel. & Tel. Co. v. Arizona Corp. Comm'n, 773 P.2d 455, 465 (Ariz. 1989) (supp. opinion) (courts have consulted legislative history to determine whether "shall" means "must" or "may" in various statutes).

30. Blanchard v. Bergeron, 489 U.S. 87, 98 (1989) (Scalia, J., concurring).

defer to that agency's interpretation of the statutory language.[31] Otherwise, the court may resort to a judicial rule of construction, such as the general rule that ambiguities in criminal statutes "should be resolved in favor of lenity."[32] Such a rule may reflect general policies with which the legislature is likely to agree, but it does not necessarily reflect the legislative purpose of the particular statute in question.[33] Accordingly, a court will resort to a general rule of construction only if a "statute's language, structure, purpose, and legislative history leave its meaning genuinely in doubt."[34]

In the following subsections, analyses of two kinds of uncertainty in statutory language provide vehicles for examining techniques that the courts use to clarify the scope and effect of statutes. First, an analysis of ambiguous statutory language illustrates general rules of statutory interpretation and construction. Second, an analysis of vague statutory language illustrates the manner in which courts gradually give concrete meaning to abstract statutory language by applying general terms to particular disputes.

1. Imprecision Leading to Ambiguity

Ambiguity may result from avoidable imprecision in the words or phrases selected by the drafter. The question raised at the beginning of Section B above addresses the proper interpretation of a federal statute popularly known as Title VII of the Civil Rights Act of 1964. Section 703(a) of the Act prohibits certain kinds of employment discrimination:

> It shall be an unlawful employment practice for an employer . . . to discriminate against any individual with respect to his compensation, terms, conditions, or privileges of employment, because of such individual's race, color, religion, sex, or national origin. . . .[35]

It is unclear from the quoted language whether §703(a) prohibits an employer from discriminating against gay and lesbian employees because of their sexual orientation. Perhaps Title VII's reference to "sex" as a protected classification would prohibit such an employment policy. It would most clearly do so if Congress used the term "sex" to refer broadly to any sexual characteristic, including an individual's sexual orientation, rather than only to the characteristic of being male or female.

Judicial interpretation of a statute should start with the most direct intrinsic evidence of legislative intent: the statutory language in question.[36]

---

31. See, e.g., Young v. Community Nutrition Inst., 476 U.S. 974, 979-984 (1986).
32. Bell v. United States, 349 U.S. 81, 83 (1955); Johnson v. State, 602 So. 2d 1288, 1290 (Fla. 1992).
33. See, e.g., Bell v. United States, 349 U.S. 81, at 83-84 (1955).
34. United States v. Otherson, 637 F.2d 1276, 1285 (9th Cir. 1980), cert. denied, 454 U.S. 840 (1981); cf. EEOC v. Arabian Am. Oil Co., 499 U.S. 244, 260-261 (1991) (Marshall, J., dissenting) (arguing that majority of the Court gave undue weight to a rule of construction disfavoring extraterritorial application of congressional legislation).
35. 42 U.S.C. §2000e-2(a) (1982).
36. See, e.g., Laurence H. Tribe, Judicial Interpretation of Statutes: Three Axioms, 11 Harv. J.L. & Pub. Pol'y 51 (1988) ("Axiom one is: *Language first.*"); Unification Church v. INS, 762 F.2d 1077, 1083 (D.C. Cir. 1985).

INTERPRETATION: EVIDENCE OF LEGISLATIVE INTENT

Intrinsic Evidence:

Start with Statutory Language

including the clause in question, defined terms, statements of purpose, related statutory provisions, and statute as a whole.

If the statutory language is ambiguous, or if extrinsic evidence would otherwise be helpful, consult extrinsic evidence of legislative intent:

Extrinsic Evidence:

Primarily, Legislative History

including preliminary drafts, committee hearings and reports, and legislative floor debates.

If legislative intent remains unclear, seek guidance from general rules of construction:

CONSTRUCTION: GENERALIZATIONS ABOUT PROBABLE LEGISLATIVE INTENT

Examples:

Construe criminal statutes narrowly, in favor of lenity.
Construe remedial statutes liberally to provide an adequate remedy for the full range of problems that inspired the legislation.
Avoid a construction that would render a statute invalid or a clause superfluous.
If a statute specifically lists some items for statutory treatment, the legislature likely intended to exclude other items that are not listed.

An analysis of the language of Title VII §703(a), however, provides only limited guidance. Dictionaries commonly define "sex" as, among other things, either (1) the division of species between male and female or (2) more general sexual behavior and characteristics:

> 1: either of two divisions of organisms distinguished respectively as male or female   2: the sum of the structural, functional, and behavioral peculiarities of living beings that subserve reproduction by two interacting parents and distinguish males and females   3a: sexually motivated phenomena or behavior   b: SEXUAL INTERCOURSE.[37]

Other provisions of Title VII may provide intrinsic evidence of the intended meaning of "sex" in §703(a). In Subsection h of §703, Congress probably used the term in the narrow sense of the division of species between male and female.[38] There it used "sex" in a reference to the Equal Pay Act of 1963, which more clearly prohibits only certain kinds of discrimination based on the status of an employee as male or female.[39] If Congress consciously used "sex" in that sense in §703(h), the obvious virtues of consistency in statutory drafting suggest the likelihood, though not the certainty, that Congress ascribed the same meaning to "sex" when it used that term in §703(a) of the same act.

Thus, intrinsic evidence of Congress's intended meaning in §703(a) of the word "sex" is helpful but inconclusive. Therefore, a court interpreting "sex" would likely seek guidance from extrinsic evidence, such as legislative history. The original House bill did not include sex as a prohibited basis of discrimination. Instead, Southern Democrat and Chair of the House Rules Committee Howard Smith proposed the addition of "sex" as a protected classification in a last-minute amendment on the House floor. He apparently hoped that the amendment would spark sufficient controversy to cause the defeat of the entire bill.[40]

Smith's unsuccessful strategy left the courts with "little legislative history to guide us in interpreting the Act's prohibition against discrimination based on 'sex'."[41] However, the few statements made on the House floor about the proposed amendment, both by Smith and by Representatives who more sincerely favored equality of the sexes, suggest that the speakers interpreted

---

37. Webster's Seventh New Collegiate Dictionary 347 (1970) (as quoted in Holloway v. Arthur Andersen & Co., 566 F.2d 659, 662 n.4 (9th Cir. 1977)).

38. Section 703(h) incorporates limitation set forth in the Equal Pay Act:

> . . . It shall not be . . . unlawful . . . to differentiate upon the basis of *sex* . . . if such differentiation is authorized by the provisions of [the Equal Pay Act].

42 U.S.C. §2000e-2(h) (1988) (emphasis added).

39. The Equal Pay Act refers to members of the "opposite sex":

> No employer . . . shall discriminate . . . between employees on the basis of *sex* by paying wages to employees . . . at a rate less than the rate at which he pays wages to employees of the *opposite sex* . . . for equal work. . . .

29 U.S.C. §206(d) (1988) (emphasis added). The phrase "opposite sex" is commonly used to refer only to distinctions between males and females. Therefore the Equal Pay Act is nearly unambiguous in its classifying only on the basis of employees being male or female.

40. Charles Whalen & Barbara Whalen, The Longest Debate 84, 115-116 (1985).

41. Meritor Sav. Bank, FSB v. Vinson, 477 U.S. 57, 64 (1986).

"sex" to refer narrowly to the characteristic of being male or female.[42] That interpretation is supported by post-enactment evidence of congressional intent. First, the House report on the 1972 Amendments to Title VII clearly shows that Congress was primarily concerned with putting women on equal economic footing with men. Second, successive congressional rejections of several bills proposing to amend Title VII by adding "sexual preference" as a protected classification suggest that members of Congress probably had never collectively intended the statutory term "sex" to encompass sexual preference.[43]

Relying on this legislative history, courts have interpreted the word "sex" in §703(a) to refer only to male or female status and not also to sexual orientation.[44] Interpreted in that way, Title VII does not clearly prohibit an employer from discriminating against employees because of their homosexuality, provided that the employer applies the same policy to gay males as it does to lesbian females.[45]

Had the evidence of specific congressional intent been less convincing, the interpreting court might have applied the general rule of construction that "remedial" statutes should be liberally construed. Title VII is remedial in its purpose of redressing the pervasive social and economic problem of employment discrimination.[46] Therefore, the rule of construction would favor a liberal construction of the term "sex," which might encompass sexual orientation. However, this general rule of construction is subordinate to evidence of more specific congressional intent relating to the statute in question.[47]

Congress might have avoided the ambiguity in §703(a) by selecting a more precise term, such as "gender," which more clearly refers only to classifications based on one's status as male or female. Although "gender" refers to classifications in grammar as well as in animal species, that ambiguity would not likely cause confusion in the context of §703(a).

2. Generality Resulting in Vagueness

Even if the legislature chooses its words carefully, most statutory language is necessarily general, because almost all legislation addresses broad categories of activities or disputes rather than particular cases. Legislators simply do not possess the stamina and prescience required to consider every potential dispute within the scope of legislation and to provide a specific resolution for each. Instead, courts provide greater specificity in statutory

---

42. Whalen & Whalen, supra note 40, at 116-117.
43. Holloway v. Arthur Andersen & Co., 566 F.2d 659, 662 (9th Cir. 1977).
44. E.g., id. at 662-663.
45. E.g., De Santis v. Pacific Tel. & Tel. Co., 608 F.2d 327 (9th Cir. 1979). But cf. Gay Law Students Ass'n v. Pacific Tel. & Tel. Co., 595 P.2d 592 (Cal. 1979) (different result under California constitutional and statutory law); Sam Marcosson, Harassment on the Basis of Sexual Orientation: A Claim of Sex Discrimination Under Title VII, 81 Geo. L.J. 1, 3-10 (1992) (critiquing *Desantis*).
46. E.g., Bell v. Brown, 557 F.2d 849, 853 (D.C. Cir. 1977).
47. See Mohasco Corp. v. Silver, 447 U.S. 807, 818-819 (1980) (Title VII is remedial legislation, but also is the product of legislative compromise).

language by applying the general terms of the statute to the facts of particular disputes, thus adding precision to statutory law in much the same way that they develop common law—gradually and in the context of successive disputes.

For example, §703(a) of Title VII of the Civil Rights Act of 1964 prohibits discrimination only with respect to an individual's "compensation, terms, conditions, or privileges of employment."[48] That statutory phrase is necessarily general, because Congress could not practically describe in more specific terms all of the possible kinds of discrimination that have a sufficient relationship to employment to trigger congressional concern about equal opportunity in the workplace. That generality results in a vagueness that promotes disputes over the interpretation and application of the statute in particular cases.

For instance, parties may reasonably dispute whether sexual advances made by an employer's agent to an employee affect the employee's "terms, conditions, or privileges of employment" if the agent does not make tangible benefits of employment contingent on acquiescence to the demands.[49] Courts have given more specific meaning to the statutory phrase by adopting a more specific legal standard for determining the circumstances in which the statute is satisfied: To give effect to Title VII's remedial purpose, courts have decided that sexual advances by an employer's agent may affect "terms, conditions, or privileges of employment" if they create "a substantially discriminatory work *environment,* regardless of whether the complaining employees lost any tangible job benefits as a result of the discrimination."[50]

Although the "discriminatory work environment" standard adds a judicial gloss to the statutory language by identifying a specific subset of employment relations within the scope of the statute, the judicial standard is itself abstract and suffers from its own problems of vagueness. The United States Supreme Court provided a small measure of guidance by approving liability only if the harassment is "sufficiently severe or pervasive 'to alter the conditions of . . . employment and create an abusive working environment.' "[51] However, the precise parameters of the judicial standard, and thus of the statutory language that it seeks to effectuate, will take form only when courts repeatedly apply the standard to the facts of different disputes.

In one case, for example, a federal trial court found that an employer's chief executive created a discriminatory work environment for an employee by giving her a pornographic magazine, leaving an article on her desk about extramarital affairs, and subjecting her to unwelcome sexual advances on at least seven occasions.[52] In contrast, in another case, a federal trial court

---

48. 42 U.S.C. §2000e-2(a) (1988).

49. Such conduct constitutes sex discrimination if the harasser would not have engaged in the conduct but for the employee's gender; that requirement normally is satisfied in the case of a heterosexual or homosexual harasser, but not necessarily in the case of a bisexual harasser. See Barnes v. Castle, 561 F.2d 983, 990 n.55 (D.C. Cir. 1977). That analysis, however, does not answer the question whether the discrimination satisfies Title VII's requirement of a nexus to employment.

50. Bundy v. Jackson, 641 F.2d 934, 943-944 (D.C. Cir. 1981).

51. Meritor Sav. Bank, FSB v. Vinson, 477 U.S. 57, 67 (1986) (quoting Henson v. Dundee, 682 F.2d 897, 904 (11th Cir. 1982)).

52. Ross v. Twenty-four Collection, Inc., 681 F. Supp. 1547, 1551 (S.D. Fla. 1988), *aff'd,* 875 F.2d 873 (11th Cir. 1989).

found that a supervisor did not create a discriminatory work environment by displaying a condescending and impatient attitude toward an employee and by teasing her about her personal relationship with a co-worker.[53] If you examine those and other decisions addressing the same issue in different factual contexts, you can gain a better understanding of the intended reach of the statute than is provided by the general statutory language, "terms, conditions, or privileges of employment," or even the more specific judicial interpretation, "discriminatory work environment."

Unfortunately, you should be prepared to encounter cases at the margin that tend to add to your confusion rather than your understanding. For example, a federal appellate court has held in two cases that supervisors and co-workers did not create a discriminatory work environment by subjecting employees to conduct and lewd comments that were relatively "isolated," even though the conduct included physical contact, such as a hand on an employee's shoulder or a slap on an employee's buttocks.[54] A federal trial court in a different geographic jurisdiction, however, found that a supervisor created a discriminatory work environment by subjecting an employee to a single slap on her buttocks and by threatening to repeat that conduct.[55] You could reasonably interpret such cases as reflecting disagreement among the courts about the proper interpretation and application of the legal standard, a phenomenon addressed in succeeding chapters in this book, particularly Chapter 6, Section II.B.7.

EXERCISE 2-2

1. *Statutory Policy and Classification*

The Highway Patrol of State X informed legislators of State X that motorists were causing accidents by consuming soft drinks while driving. The Highway Patrol was not overly concerned that drivers could keep only one hand on the wheel while consuming soft drinks. Instead, they were concerned that drivers often obstructed their vision, and thus lost partial control of their automobiles, when they tilted their heads back and tipped their soft drink containers upward to consume the last of their soft drinks. In response, state legislators amended the State X Vehicle Code to make it a misdemeanor "to operate a motor vehicle while consuming any beverage from a can or bottle." Should the new law apply to:

a. a driver who tilts her head back to drink water from a metal, canvas-covered canteen?

b. a driver who keeps his head level while he sips a soft drink through a straw from a bottle?

c. a driver who eats a submarine sandwich in a way that distracts her and obstructs her vision?

---

53. Saxton v. American Tel. & Tel. Co., 785 F. Supp. 760, 765 (N.D. Ill. 1992).

54. Weiss v. Coca-Cola Bottling Co., 990 F.2d 333, 337 (7th Cir. 1993); Scott v. Sears, Roebuck & Co., 798 F.2d 210, 211-214 (7th Cir. 1986).

55. Campbell v. Kansas State Univ., 780 F. Supp. 755, 761-762 (D. Kan. 1991).

2. *Legislative History*

The current codification of a Reconstruction era civil rights act prohibits certain kinds of discrimination:

> *All persons* within the jurisdiction of the United States shall have the same right in every State and Territory to make and enforce contracts . . . *as is enjoyed by white citizens.* . . .

42 U.S.C. §1981 (emphasis added). The original predecessor to this statute contained similar language:

> [C]itizens of the United States . . . , of every race and color, without regard to any previous condition of slavery or involuntary servitude, . . . shall have the same right, in every State and Territory in the United States, to make and enforce contracts . . . *as is enjoyed by white citizens.* . . .

Civil Rights Act of 1866 §1, 14 Stat. 27 (1866) (emphasis added); see also Civil Rights Act of 1870 §§16, 18, 16 Stat. 144 (1870). The "immediate impetus" for the original statute was "the necessity for further relief of the constitutionally emancipated former Negro slaves."[56] However, to allay fears among some legislators that the proposed bill would favor nonwhites, proponents of the bill defended it at several stages of the legislative process as one that would protect *all* citizens.[57] More than a century after the initial enactment, the United States Supreme Court applied the modern version of this statute to prohibit private, commercially operated, nonsectarian schools from discriminating against African-Americans in admission to the schools.[58]

a. Should a court apply the statute to protect nonwhites other than African-Americans from race discrimination in contractual relations?

b. Should a court apply the statute to protect white citizens from race discrimination? See *McDonald v. Santa Fe Trail Transportation Co.,* 427 U.S. 273 (1976).

c. If the statute applies to protect racial groups other than African-Americans, how does one define race for purposes of finding prohibited discrimination? Would the statute apply to prohibit discrimination against a person because he is Arab rather than Anglo-American? See *St. Francis College v. Al-Khazraji,* 481 U.S. 604 (1987) (looking to racial classifications recognized at time of enactment of predecessors to §1981). Would it apply to discrimination because one is Jewish? See *Shaare Tefila Congregation v. Cobb,* 481 U.S. 615 (1987) (same analysis under companion statute, 42 U.S.C. §1982).

---

56. McDonald v. Santa Fe Trail Transp. Co., 427 U.S. 273, 289 (1976).
57. Id. at 289-295.
58. Runyon v. McCrary, 427 U.S. 160 (1976), *reaff'd in part,* Patterson v. McLean Credit Union, 491 U.S. 164 (1989).

C. LEGISLATIVE CHANGE

As a serious student of the law, you should not be content to simply interpret statutory law but should reflect on the political wisdom of the legislative purpose. A legislature that has the power to enact legislation also has the power to repeal or amend it, and a constant critique of statutory law helps to fuel the dynamic process of the growth and development of legislation.

For example, the discussion in the previous section shows that Congress probably intended Title VII's prohibition of "sex" discrimination to apply to discrimination on the basis of gender but not on the basis of sexual orientation. The first exercise below asks you to consider whether the policies underlying Title VII's current prohibitions apply as well to discrimination because of sexual orientation, and whether Congress should amend Title VII to prohibit such discrimination.

You may question some statutes not for the policies they reflect but for the manner in which they express policy. Many students have done this after struggling with alternative interpretations of Uniform Commercial Code §2-207. As originally drafted, the first of three subsections of §2-207 provides that a response to an offer may be an acceptance even though it varies the terms of the offer:

> (1) A definite and seasonable expression of acceptance or a written confirmation which is sent within a reasonable time operates as an acceptance even though it states terms additional to or different from those offered or agreed upon, unless acceptance is expressly made conditional on assent to the additional or different terms.

The second subsection provides that, between merchants, some of the new terms in the acceptance may be added to the contract without the express assent of the original offeror:

> (2) The additional terms are to be construed as proposals for addition to the contract. Between merchants such terms become part of the contract unless:
> > (a) the offer expressly limits acceptance to the terms of the offer;
> > (b) they materially alter it; or
> > (c) notification of objection to them has already been given or is given within a reasonable time after notice of them is received.

If you have ever explored the puzzles raised by these subsections of §2-207, you may be ready to agree with one commentator that

> the section is a mess. It is confusing, susceptible to different and inconsistent interpretations, and nigh well impossible to apply to solve a specific fact situation.[59]

---

59. Morris G. Shanker, Contract by Disagreement!? (Reflections on UCC 2-207), 81 Com. L.J. 453 (1976).

As this book goes to press, the American Law Institute is considering proposals to redraft §2-207 of the Uniform Commercial Code.

═══════ E X E R C I S E   2 - 3 ═══════

1. *Invidious Discrimination*

Thirty years after the 1963 civil rights march in Washington, D.C., for racial equality, hundreds of thousands of lesbian and gay Americans rallied in the nation's capital to demand freedom from discrimination.[60] Consider the bases of discrimination covered by Title VII of the Civil Rights Act of 1964: race, color, religion, sex, and national origin. Other federal statutes prohibit discrimination based on age or handicap. What characteristics do these classifications have in common? Why are these classes entitled to special protection? Should Congress amend Title VII to include sexual orientation as a protected characteristic? Of what significance are recent studies suggesting that homosexuality is at least in part biologically determined?[61] Do you support legislation banning discrimination on the basis of positive testing for the AIDS virus?

2. *Mandatory Safety Rules*

Do you support state legislation requiring a person to wear a protective helmet while driving or riding as a passenger on a motorcycle on a public street or highway? What policy arguments support or oppose such legislation?

3. *Surrogate Motherhood*

    a. Legislative Authorization or Prohibition

Many states have recently enacted legislation specifically addressing "surrogate mother contracts." Pursuant to such contracts, a woman charges a fee to carry to full term a fetus that either is the product of artificial insemination of the woman's own ovum or is the implanted, fertilized ovum of another woman. Technically, the woman bearing the child is a "surrogate mother" only if she is carrying the fertilized ovum of another woman. If she is carrying her own artificially inseminated ovum, she is the biological mother. However, the term "surrogate mother" is frequently used to refer to both roles. In either case, on birth of the child, the "surrogate mother" is obligated under the contract to relinquish custody of the child to the biological parent or parents who contracted with her.

    (1) What public policies are implicated in a legislative decision to approve, prohibit, or otherwise regulate such contracts?

---

60. Jeffrey Schmalz, Gay Americans Throng Capital in Appeal for Rights, N.Y. Times, Apr. 26, 1993, at A1.
61. See William A. Henry III, Born Gay?, Time, July 26, 1993, at 36; Natalie Angier, Study Suggests Strong Genetic Role in Lesbianism, N.Y. Times, Mar. 12, 1993, at A8.

(2) If called on to draft legislation on the subject, how would you balance the conflicting policies?

b. Specific Enforcement and Punitive Damages

In enforcing ordinary commercial contracts, a court may in limited circumstances remedy a breach of promise by "specifically enforcing" the promise, or ordering the breaching party to perform precisely as promised. In most cases, however, specific enforcement is impracticable or otherwise inappropriate, and the court will award "substitutional relief" by ordering the breaching party to pay money damages.

(1) As a legislator, would you vote for a statute that would authorize or mandate specific enforcement of a surrogate mother contract, thus compelling the surrogate mother to relinquish custody of her newborn child, as promised in the contract?

(2) After reviewing Exercise 2-1(2), supra pages 14-15, would you vote for a statute that would authorize a court to award punitive damages against a surrogate mother who failed to relinquish custody?

IV. INTERPLAY BETWEEN STATUTORY AND COMMON LAW ANALYSIS

A. RELATIONSHIP BETWEEN STATUTORY LAW AND COMMON LAW

Although the legislature and the judiciary each exercise lawmaking powers, the legislature is the paramount lawmaking authority, and legislative enactments supersede inconsistent common law. The Supreme Court's following statement about the federal system applies as well to the state governments:

> [W]e consistently have emphasized that the federal lawmaking power is vested in the legislative, not the judicial, branch of government; therefore, federal common law is "subject to the paramount authority of Congress."[62]

Accordingly, the legislature may enact statutes that modify, overrule, or codify existing common law. For example, under the common law of contracts, parties may form a contract through a process of agreement that culminates in an offer and an acceptance. A recipient who is dissatisfied with an offer may decline to accept it and may instead convey a counteroffer to the other party. Indeed, under the traditional common law "mirror-image rule," a party who significantly varies the terms of an offer in a purported acceptance conveys a counteroffer rather than an effective acceptance.[63] However, all states have enacted some version of Article 2 of the Uniform Commercial Code, which rejects and supersedes this common law rule for

---

62. Northwest Airlines, Inc. v. Transport Workers Union, 451 U.S. 77, 95 (1981) (quoting New Jersey v. New York, 283 U.S. 336, 348 (1931)).
63. E.g., 1 Arthur L. Corbin, Corbin on Contracts §82 (1963).

transactions in goods. As set forth in the immediately preceding Section III.C, §2-207 of the Code recognizes, in some circumstances, an acceptance that includes a nontrivial variance of the terms of the offer.

Even if no statute currently applies to a dispute, a court may decline to extend common law principles to the area if it concludes that the matter is better left to legislative action.[64] Moreover, if the court decides to develop and apply the common law, it nonetheless may look to statutory law for expressions of public policy that help the court formulate the common law rule. In one case, for example, a court addressed the question whether, under the common law of torts, retailers should assume liability for injuries stemming from their sales of guns without regard to the care that they exercised in the sales. The court looked to the policy of federal and state gun control legislation to apply this doctrine of "strict liability" to the sale of some, but not all, kinds of guns.[65] Another court drew guidance from an enacted, but not yet effective, commercial code to develop a common law doctrine of unconscionability in sales contracts.[66]

Although statutory law supersedes common law, the common law at the time of a statute's enactment may provide contextual background that is helpful in analyzing legislative intent.[67] If a statute overrules a common law rule or seeks to address a problem left untouched by the common law, a court can better understand the statute's intended scope if it appreciates the deficiencies of the common law to which the legislature responded.[68] Conversely, if a statute codifies existing common law, cases that developed the common law rule obviously will provide guidance in interpreting the statute.

For example, under the common law of contracts an offeror is the "master of his offer" and, with some limitations, is free to prescribe the manner in which the offeree can accept his offer.[69] Even in the absence of an express limitation by the offeror on the means of accepting his offer, some courts adopted relatively technical rules of common law that required the offeree to communicate acceptance in the same mode in which the offeror had communicated the offer, such as by telegram.[70] The Uniform Commercial Code has embraced the first common law principle and rejected the second:

> Unless otherwise unambiguously indicated by the language or circumstances
> (a) An offer to make a contract shall be construed as inviting acceptance in any manner and by any medium reasonable in the circumstances.[71]

---

64. E.g., City & County of San Francisco v. United Ass'n of Journeymen etc. of United States & Canada, 726 P.2d 538 (Cal. 1986).

65. Kelley v. R.G. Indus., 497 A.2d 1143 (Md. 1985).

66. Williams v. Walker Thomas Furniture Co., 350 F.2d 445 (D.C. Cir. 1965).

67. See 2A C. Dallas Sands, Sutherland Statutory Construction, §50.01 (4th ed. 1984); Wayne R. LaFave & Austin W. Scott, Jr., Criminal Law §2.2, at 79-80 (2d ed. 1986) (interpretation of criminal statutes in light of common law); City of Oklahoma City v. Tuttle, 471 U.S. 808, 835-838 (1985) (Stevens, J., dissenting).

68. See, e.g., Heydon's Case, 76 Eng. Rep. 637, 638 (1584) (*quoted in* C. Dallas Sands, supra note 67, §45-05, at 21).

69. See, e.g., E. Allan Farnsworth, Contracts §3.14, at 153 (2d ed. 1990).

70. See, e.g., U.C.C. §2-206 comment 1 (1990).

71. U.C.C. §2-206(1)(a) (1990).

Although subsection (a) substitutes a more flexible standard for some of the more technical common law rules of acceptance, the clause preceding this subsection retains the common law principle that the offeror is the master of the offer and may restrict the means of acceptance, so long as the restriction is clearly indicated. If a court is sensitive to the arbitrariness of the common law rules rejected by the Code, and if it is familiar with the common law principle embraced by the Code, it can better appreciate the intended scope of the Code.[72]

Moreover, a statute often addresses only selected issues within the general subject matter touched by the statute, thereby creating gaps that common law may fill. In some cases the statute itself provides for reference to common law, as in the Uniform Commercial Code:

> Unless displaced by the particular provisions of this Act, the principles of law and equity, including the law merchant and the law relative to capacity to contract, principal and agent, estoppel, fraud, misrepresentation, duress, coercion, mistake, . . . or other validating or invalidating cause shall supplement its provisions.[73]

In other cases, statutes only implicitly incorporate common law principles. For example, a federal statute imposes liability for certain conduct without any express qualifications or limitations. Yet, courts have assumed that Congress intended the statute to implicitly incorporate common law defenses of immunity from liability for money damages:

> It is by now well settled that the tort liability created by [42 U.S.C.] §1983 cannot be understood in a historical vacuum. In the Civil Rights Act of 1871, Congress created a federal remedy against a person who, acting under color of state law, deprives another of constitutional rights. . . . One important assumption underlying the Court's decisions in this area is that members of the 42d Congress were familiar with common-law principles, including defenses previously recognized in ordinary tort litigation, and that they likely intended these common-law principles to obtain, absent specific provisions to the contrary.[74]

B. JUDICIAL POWER AND LIMITATIONS REGARDING LEGISLATION

Although the legislature can modify or overrule common law principles developed by the court, the courts retain an important role in the development of statutory law. Courts may review statutes for consistency with constitutional requirements and will refuse to enforce unconstitutional legis-

---

72. See Empire Mach. Co. v. Litton Business Tel. Sys., 566 P.2d 1044, 1048 (Ariz. App. 1977).
73. U.C.C. §1-103 (1990).
74. City of Newport v. Fact Concerts, Inc., 453 U.S. 247, 258 (1981).

lation.[75] Additionally, as discussed in Section III above, courts determine the scope and effect of legislation by interpreting statutes and applying them to particular disputes.

Nonetheless, courts have less flexibility in interpreting statutory law than in developing common law. If a court changes its previous analysis of legislative intent, it may overrule its earlier interpretation of a statute, just as it sometimes overrules its previous application of a principle of common law.[76] However, the court may not ignore a statute or modify its terms to reflect judicial views that are inconsistent with legislative intent. In contrast, a court may directly reject the substance and reasoning of a common law principle that is announced and applied in a prior decision: "[W]e have not hesitated to change the common law . . . where . . . such course was justified."[77]

Interestingly, some American Indian tribal court judges have boldly hinted that they may challenge the conventional hierarchy of laws in tribal governments. Under Anglo-American assumptions, tribal codes should have priority over tribal common law, because the tribal council has adopted the codes, just as a federal or state legislature enacts statutes. However, even though tribal codes are formally enacted by tribal councils, many were conceived and drafted by Anglo-Americans and may reflect a poor understanding of tribal culture. In contrast, some tribal courts more consciously seek to promote tribal culture and policies when they develop and apply tribal common law.

This phenomenon may justify a departure from Anglo-American legal method in tribal courts. For example, the Navajo Supreme Court has hinted that it may simply refuse to give effect to outdated tribal code sections that fail to promote Navajo values or are inconsistent with longstanding Navajo custom. In gestures acknowledging the role of the legislative branch of government, it has explicitly recommended in its opinions that the Navajo Tribal Council amend tribal codes that do not promote Navajo culture and policies.[78] This kind of communication between branches of government is not foreign to the Anglo-American legal system. However, not content to wait for action from its legislative branch, the Navajo Supreme Court has considered a more radical legal method. When necessary to preserve important values of tribal culture or sovereignty, the Navajo Supreme Court appears willing to elevate Navajo common law or custom above otherwise applicable tribal codes.[79]

That such legal method is generally viewed as remarkable[80] simply illus-

---

75. Marbury v. Madison, 5 U.S. (1 Cranch) 137 (1803) (federal system).

76. E.g., Monell v. Department of Social Servs., 436 U.S. 658 (1978) (overruling the Court's previous decision that the term "person" in 42 U.S.C. §1983 does not include municipalities); Wayne R. LaFave & Austin W. Scott, Jr., Criminal Law §2.2, at 88-90 (2d ed. 1986); see also infra Chapter 3, Section III.

77. Kelley v. R.G. Indus., 497 A.2d 1143, 1150-1151 (Md. 1985).

78. See, e.g., In re: Validation of Marriage of Francisco, 16 Indian L. Rep. 6113, 6115 (Navajo S. Ct. 1989).

79. See id. ("This court . . . does not rely on [the tribal code], but instead on Navajo custom.").

80. But see Guido Calabresi, A Common Law for the Age of Statutes 163-166 (1982) (recommending that Anglo-American courts refuse to enforce outdated statutes unless reaffirmed by the legislature).

trates the rigidity of the Anglo-American hierarchy of laws: A constitution defines the reach of statutory authority, and statutes can limit the application of common law.

V. SUMMARY

Legislatures enact statutes within the authority granted to them by state and federal constitutions. Courts create case law in the context of individual disputes by (1) interpreting and applying the provisions of constitutions and statutes and (2) developing and applying a separate body of judge-made common law. A state or federal legislature is the primary policymaking body within a jurisdiction, and it can modify or overrule common law by enacting a superseding statute.

3

The Role of Precedent

I. INTRODUCTION TO STARE DECISIS

In American law, previous court decisions may influence, or even dictate, the result in a dispute currently before a court. The legal effect of the previous decisions is governed by a complex set of conventions for which the Latin phrase "stare decisis" is often used as convenient shorthand.

As defined in Black's Law Dictionary, "stare decisis" means "[t]o abide by, or adhere to, decided cases." Under the doctrine of stare decisis, a court endeavors to decide each case consistently with its own previous decisions, sometimes called "precedent." Moreover, the court is strictly bound by the precedent of a higher court that reviews the decisions of the subject court.

Judicial adherence to the doctrine of stare decisis serves several significant goals:

(1) it promotes efficiency in judicial administration by relieving judges of the burden of revisiting settled legal questions in each case;

(2) it facilitates private and commercial transactions by ensuring a degree of certainty and predictability in the law that regulates such transactions; and

(3) it satisfies the common moral belief that persons in like circumstances should be treated alike.[1]

You can explore the third justification for stare decisis on a simple level by examining familiar decisions such as parental decisions on simple family

---

1. Edgar Bodenheimer, Jurisprudence: The Philosophy and Method of the Law 425-428 (rev. ed. 1974); Sol Wachtler, Stare Decisis and a Changing New York Court of Appeals, 59 St. John's L. Rev. 445, 447-452 (1985).

matters. Imagine that two parents, Gerald and Janice, formulated rules to impose on their two children, Tanya and Jamal, both of whom were excellent students. When the children entered their teen years, Gerald and Janice required them to "use good sense" in restricting their hours away from home at night.

When Jamal, the older child, entered his junior year of high school, he began to attend evening social and athletic events frequently. After he had stayed out past 11:00 P.M. three nights in a single week, his parents admonished him. In justifying their admonishment, Gerald and Janice explained that Jamal had not used the requisite good sense for a student of his age and responsibilities. The parents worried that excessively late hours would hamper their son's studies and even endanger his health. To avoid such evils, they announced a refinement of their previous "good sense" rule: Jamal can stay out at night on nonfamily outings no more than twice in a week. Furthermore, despite Jamal's arguments that midnight was a more reasonable curfew, Gerald and Janice announced that Jamal must come home by 11:00 P.M. on such occasions.

A year later, Tanya entered her junior year of high school and also began to attend evening social and athletic events frequently. When Tanya stayed out one night past 10:30 P.M., Gerald and Janice admonished her about her hours. Both parents initially held the opinion that Tanya should not stay out at night on nonfamily outings more than once in a week and that she must come home by 10:00 P.M. on such occasions. Asked for her reaction to these restrictions, Tanya protested that the proposed rule would treat her unfairly: Although she and Jamal were engaged in nearly identical activities, she would be subject to greater restrictions than those that her parents had imposed on Jamal.

On reflection, Gerald and Janice realized that they had justified the difference in treatment by distinguishing between their two children on the basis of gender: They had assumed that Tanya needed extra protection because she is female. Tanya persuaded them, however, that Jamal and Tanya were indeed similarly situated because of their activities and that gender was not relevant to the policies and purposes of the curfew rule. Accordingly, Janice and Gerald applied the same restrictions to Tanya that they had earlier devised for Jamal.

Throughout months of applying their general curfew rule to Jamal and Tanya, Gerald and Janice developed exceptions to meet special circumstances. For example, both Tanya and Jamal were members of high school basketball teams, both of which occasionally traveled by bus to night games at competing schools in a neighboring county. On such nights, the team bus often did not return the team members to school in time to enable them to return home before 11:00 P.M. Because they valued their children's participation in athletic events, Gerald and Janice permitted late hours on such nights pursuant to one of a growing number of special exceptions to their general rule.

Midway through Jamal's senior year at high school, Gerald and Janice concluded that their general curfew rule was unworkable for two reasons. First, their rule had been excessively mechanical and inflexible from its inception: It required the formulation of numerous exceptions to meet special circumstances, and it completely failed to address questions about activities that should be prohibited rather than merely restricted in their hours and frequency. Second, circumstances had changed: Both Tanya and Jamal had increased their participation in worthy organizations and activities that occasionally required late hours or even overnight stays. The general rule now required so many exceptions to meet legitimate needs that it ceased to have significant meaning.

Gerald and Janice were initially reluctant to abandon a rule that they had so thoughtfully developed and applied. After a year and a half, however, they abandoned their original curfew rule and substituted a new, more flexible one. They announced that they would evaluate any proposed activity primarily on the basis of the nature of the activity rather than solely on the frequency and degree to which it required late hours.

Thus, Gerald and Janice strove for consistency in applying their rules to specific events, but they departed from past practice when new information or changes in circumstances suggested that their previous decisions no longer provided the best guide for satisfying their policy objectives. Specifically, they initially announced a general rule for Jamal that satisfied general policy concerns about Jamal's health and academic performance. They applied the same rule to Tanya, rather than a more restrictive rule, because Tanya persuaded them that her case was indistinguishable from that of Jamal. Gerald and Janice later developed special exceptions to their general rule to meet the needs of specific events. Eventually, they grew dissatisfied with their general rule, and they abandoned it. They replaced it with a new rule that used different criteria for evaluating their children's activities.

This parental decisionmaking illustrates some of the ways in which courts develop case law within and without the framework of stare decisis. However, most courts would not be quite as casual as were Gerald and Janice in departing from stare decisis and abandoning their original rules in favor of new ones. Separate opinions by different Justices in a decision of the United States Supreme Court illustrate judicial concern for at least the appearance of adherence to the doctrine of stare decisis. In *Pennhurst State School & Hospital v. Halderman*,[2] the Supreme Court held that the eleventh amendment to the United States Constitution prohibited a federal trial court from exercising a certain kind of "jurisdiction," or judicial power. In reaching that result, a majority of the Court found a way to avoid the decisionmaking restrictions imposed by stare decisis. It concluded that its prior decisions reaching a contrary result had not specifically addressed the issue and therefore created no precedent on the issue:

> These cases thus did not directly confront the question before us. "[W]hen questions of jurisdiction have been passed on in prior decisions *sub silentio*,[3] this Court has never considered itself bound when a subsequent case finally brings the jurisdictional issue before us." [Citation omitted] We therefore view the question as an open one.[4]

---

2. 465 U.S. 89 (1984).

3. "Sub silentio" is a Latin phrase meaning "[u]nder silence; without any notice being taken." Black's Law Dictionary 1281 (5th ed. 1979).

4. *Pennhurst*, 465 U.S. at 119.

Other Justices on the Supreme Court complained in a separate "dissenting opinion" that the majority had mischaracterized the holdings of the prior decisions and thus had failed to accord them the deference demanded by stare decisis:

> None of these cases contain only "implicit" or *sub silentio* holdings; all of them explicitly consider and reject the claim that the Eleventh Amendment prohibits federal courts from issuing injunctive relief based on state law. There is therefore no basis for the majority's assertion that the issue presented by this case is an open one. . . .[5]

Indeed, the dissenters implicitly accused the majority of analyzing the prior decisions disingenuously:

> The majority incredibly claims that *Greene* contains only an implicit holding on the Eleventh Amendment question the Court decides today. . . . In plain words, the *Greene* Court held that the Eleventh Amendment did not bar consideration of the pendent state-law claims advanced in that case. The Court then considered and sustained those claims on their merits.[6]

Similarly sharp comments punctuated the 1987 hearings of the Senate Judiciary Committee on Judge Robert Bork's unsuccessful bid for confirmation to the United States Supreme Court. Judge Bork's nomination sparked heated debate about the extent to which Bork would adhere to stare decisis if confirmed.[7]

Any governing principle that engenders such controversy is worth further exploration. The strength of an authority as precedent depends in part on the relationship between the court that created the precedent and the court that may subsequently apply it. Therefore, our exploration should begin with an introduction to the court system.

II. THE COURT SYSTEM

A. STRUCTURE OF STATE AND FEDERAL COURTS

Most state court systems include courts of "limited jurisdiction," which hear disputes on limited matters such as domestic relations, traffic violations, and civil suits with small amounts in controversy. All other disputes are

---

5. Id. at 137 (Stevens, J., dissenting).
6. Id. at 137 n.14.
7. Compare The White House Report: Information on Judge Bork's Qualifications, Judicial Record & Related Subjects (July 31, 1987) (Statement on "General Judicial Philosophy" of Judge Bork), *reprinted in* 9 Cardozo L. Rev. 187, 191 (1987), with The United States Senate Judiciary Committee Chairman's Consultants, Response Prepared to White House Analysis of Judge Bork's Record §VI (Sept. 2, 1987), *reprinted in* 9 Cardozo L. Rev. 219, 287-296 (1987).

tried in branches of a trial court of "general jurisdiction," typically named "Superior Court," "Circuit Court," or "District Court."

In most states, final decisions of this trial court may be reviewed in appellate courts at two different levels: A disappointed litigant may appeal from a trial court judgment to an intermediate court of appeals; further appeals are taken to a court of last resort, often known as the "Supreme Court" of the state. Some court systems have no intermediate appellate court. Instead, a single state court of last resort hears appeals directly from judgments of the trial courts of general jurisdiction.[8] Under either model, a disappointed litigant in state court may seek further review on questions of federal law in the United States Supreme Court.[9]

The state court system in California is representative of the four-tier model:

California Supreme Court
State court of
last resort

California Courts of Appeal

1st App. District	3d App. District	5th App. District
2d App. District	4th App. District	6th App. District

California Superior Court
Primary trial court
in 58 counties

Municipal and Justice Courts
Limited jurisdiction

In California, two courts of limited jurisdiction, Justice Courts and Municipal Courts, hear restricted classes of cases. The trial court of general jurisdiction is the Superior Court, which serves each of 58 counties throughout the state. The Superior Court hears appeals from the courts of limited jurisdiction, and it entertains original actions in a wide variety of civil and criminal cases. Disappointed litigants in a criminal or civil case may appeal from a judgment of the Superior Court to the California Courts of Appeal. This intermediate appellate body consists of six courts, each of which hears

---

8. In 1991, those court systems included those of the District of Columbia and the following states: Delaware, Maine, Mississippi, Montana, Nevada, New Hampshire, North Dakota, Rhode Island, South Dakota, Vermont, West Virginia, and Wyoming. Kamla J. King & Judith Springberg, BNA's Directory of State and Federal Courts, Judges, and Clerks ("BNA's Directory of Courts") *ix-xii* (4th ed. 1992). The intermediate court of appeals in North Dakota was a temporary court as of 1991. Id. at 251.

9. 28 U.S.C. §1257 (1988).

civil and criminal appeals from departments of the Superior Court in counties assigned to the appellate court's district. A disappointed litigant in the Courts of Appeal may appeal to the California Supreme Court in certain kinds of cases and may petition for discretionary review in others.[10]

For example, California's Second Appellate District includes the counties of Los Angeles, San Luis Obispo, Santa Barbara, and Ventura. The California Court of Appeal for the Second Appellate District would hear appeals from the decisions of the California Superior Court in those counties. A litigant disappointed by a decision of the Court of Appeal for the Second Appellate District could appeal to the California Supreme Court or petition it for discretionary review.

The structure of the federal court system is similar to that of the California court system:

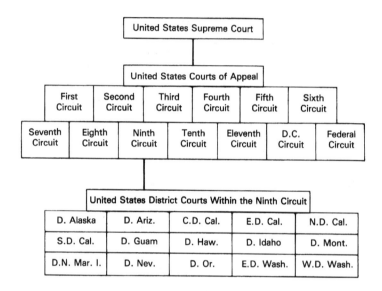

The primary federal trial courts are the United States District Courts. With few exceptions, disappointed litigants appeal from a judgment of a district court to the appropriate one of 13 United States Circuit Courts of Appeals. Further appeals, most of them discretionary, are taken to the United States Supreme Court. The chart above shows the line of review from judgments of the United States District Courts that serve the geographical area within the jurisdiction of the United States Court of Appeals for the Ninth Circuit.

The Ninth Circuit encompasses the states and territories of Alaska, Arizona, California, Guam, Hawaii, Idaho, Montana, Nevada, the Northern Mariana Islands, Oregon, and Washington. Each of those states and territories has at least one district court; California and Washington have more.

---

10. BNA's Directory of Courts, supra note 8, at 55.

For example, California is divided into four district courts: the United States District Courts for the Central, Eastern, Northern, and Southern Districts of California.

B. COURT STRUCTURE AND STARE DECISIS

Precedent has only limited stare decisis effect on the decisionmaking of the court that created the precedent: Although it will do so only in unusual circumstances, a court can depart from its own prior rulings. For lower courts within the same court system, stare decisis is less flexible: Precedent is binding on the lower courts for which the creating court acts as a court of review. As discussed further in Section III below, the lower court must either distinguish the precedent or apply it as controlling authority.

Stare decisis generally does not require a court to follow the precedent of coequal, autonomous courts, of lower courts within the same court system, or of any courts outside that system, although the court may consider such nonbinding precedent as persuasive authority. For example, the Arizona Supreme Court is not bound by the decisions of the other Arizona courts or by those of the California Supreme Court. Similarly, the United States Court of Appeals for the First Circuit is not bound by the decisions of either the United States Court of Appeals for the Second Circuit or any United States District Courts. Precedent of the United States Supreme Court, however, is binding on all federal courts and, on matters of federal law, on all state courts.

In some courts, a judicial unit of fewer than all members of the court may create precedent for the entire court. For example, the United States Court of Appeals for the Ninth Circuit has more than two dozen judges, but most appeals in the circuit are heard by panels of three judges each. Each three-judge panel creates precedent that must be followed by all other three-judge panels in the circuit. Within the circuit, a decision of a three-judge panel can be overruled only by a limited en banc panel of 11 members of the court.[11]

III. SCOPE AND APPLICATION OF STARE DECISIS

Some form of stare decisis is justified in any society that values efficiency, certainty, and at least those notions of fairness predicated on equal treatment for similarly situated parties. On the other hand, unquestioning adherence to precedent may extend the rule of previous decisions beyond the rationale and policy of the original decision, or it may retain outdated or otherwise unsound precedent.

---

11. See, e.g., United States v. McLennan, 563 F.2d 943, 948 (9th Cir. 1977); U.S. Ct. App. Ninth Cir. R. 35-3 (1992).

Two limits to stare decisis help to strike the proper balance between consistency and rigidity in the law:

(1) A court may distinguish a prior decision if it concludes that the prior decision addressed a significantly different dispute from the one presently before the court. If so, even under stare decisis, the prior decision does not dictate the result in the case before the court.

(2) Alternatively, even though a prior decision of a court would otherwise be binding in a dispute presently before the same court, the court may reject its own precedent as authority for the present dispute. Specifically, it can directly depart from its previous decision after giving it the deference required by stare decisis.

A. ANALOGIZING AND DISTINGUISHING PRECEDENT

Few disputes are so similar in their facts and legal issues that resolution of the first dispute provides a clear basis for resolving the second. In those relatively rare cases, the prior decision is "controlling" precedent in the sense that it dictates the result of the subsequent case under stare decisis.[12]

More often, differences between two cases in the facts and in the nature of the legal claims and defenses raised by the litigants are sufficiently substantial that the prior decision does not clearly dictate the resolution of the second. Whether the differences meet this standard often is a question of degree on which reasonable jurists may disagree.[13]

Assuming that the precedent is not strictly controlling, the differences between the cases may be such that the reasons for the result in the prior decision do not apply to the current case. If so, the distinctions between the two cases justify a different result in the current case, or at least an analysis free of deference to the prior decision. Conversely, even though a prior decision does not provide a clear resolution of the current case because of differences between the two cases, the reasons for the legal result in the prior decision may apply equally to the current case. If so, the prior case is analogous to the current case in a way that justifies the same legal result in both.

Of course, this process of either restricting or extending the application of precedent in relation to a new dispute is far from an exact science. The determination whether a prior decision supports a proposed outcome in a new case may implicate the most deeply held values of those who must interpret and apply the precedent:

> Like the antebellum judges who denied relief to fugitive slaves . . . the Court today claims that its decision, however harsh, is compelled by existing legal doctrine. On the contrary, the question presented by this case is an open one, and our Fourteenth Amendment precedents may be read more broadly or narrowly depending upon how one chooses to read them. Faced with the

---

12. See generally Hutto v. Davis, 454 U.S. 370 (1982).

13. Compare id. at 372-375 (majority opinion) and id. at 375-381 (Powell, J., concurring) with id. at 381-388 (Brennan, J., dissenting).

choice, I would adopt a "sympathetic" reading, one which comports with dictates of fundamental justice and recognizes that compassion need not be exiled from the province of judging.[14]

Although uncertainty about the reasons for a prior decision often complicates the analysis, courts regularly engage in the processes of distinction and analogy to limit, extend, refine, and clarify the rules of prior decisions. Indeed, the precise parameters of the rule of a decision typically do not become clear until courts analyze the decision in subsequent decisions in the context of other disputes. This inquiry is largely one of defining, limiting, and extending the "holdings" of prior decisions; you will revisit it when you study the discussion in Chapter 6 of techniques of briefing cases.

Supreme Court decisions interpreting and applying the fourth amendment to the United States Constitution[15] illustrate the techniques of analogy and distinction. In *Carroll v. United States*,[16] the Supreme Court held that the fourth amendment permitted federal officers to search an automobile without first obtaining a warrant. The Court reasoned that, although a suspect may have privacy interests in the contents of an automobile, the ready mobility of the automobile makes it impracticable for officers to obtain a warrant before searching.[17] Seven months later, in *Agnello v. United States*,[18] the Supreme Court held that the fourth amendment prohibited the warrantless search of the home of a suspect who had been arrested in another location.[19] In disapproving the warrantless search, the *Agnello* Court distinguished *Carroll* on the bases of the immobility of the house and the particularly great privacy interests the owner has in the contents of a house.[20]

Sixty years after *Carroll* and *Agnello*, in *California v. Carney*,[21] the Court considered whether the fourth amendment prohibited law enforcement officers from engaging in a warrantless search of a fully mobile motor

---

14. DeShaney v. Winnebago County Dep't of Soc. Serv., 489 U.S. 189, 212-213 (1989) (Blackmun, J., dissenting).

15. The fourth amendment prohibits unreasonable searches and seizures by government officials:

> The right of the people to be secure in their persons, houses, papers, and effects, against unreasonable searches and seizures, shall not be violated, and no Warrants shall issue, but upon probable cause, supported by Oath or affirmation, and particularly describing the place to be searched, and the persons or things to be seized.

U.S. Const. amend. IV.

16. 267 U.S. 132 (1925).

17. Id. at 153; California v. Carney, 471 U.S. 386, 390 (1985) (quoting and interpreting *Carroll*). Under *Carroll*, even if a warrant is not required, the searching officers must have probable cause to believe that the car contains contraband before they can search it. *Carroll*, 267 U.S. at 153-162. Discussion of the issue of probable cause, however, is not necessary to the analysis in the text above.

18. 269 U.S. 20 (1925), *overruled in part*, United States v. Havens, 446 U.S. 620 (1980).

19. Long before Carroll v. United States, the Supreme Court had assumed that police generally could not search a house without a warrant, unless the search was incidental to a lawful arrest in the house. *Agnello*, 269 U.S. at 32 (interpreting Boyd v. United States, 116 U.S. 616 (1886)). The Court did not directly decide that question, however, until *Agnello*, a few months after *Carroll*. *Agnello*, 269 U.S. at 32.

20. *Agnello*, 269 U.S. at 31-33; see also Payton v. New York, 445 U.S. 573, 585-590 (1980).

21. 471 U.S. 386 (1985).

home. Neither *Carroll* nor *Agnello* clearly controlled, because a motor home arguably combines the mobility of an automobile and the privacy interests associated with a house.[22] Consequently, the result in *Carney* under the doctrine of stare decisis depended on whether the Court found the facts of the case to be more nearly analogous to those of *Carroll* or to those of cases like *Agnello*.

The California Supreme Court had disapproved the search on two grounds. First, it analogized *Carney* to cases like *Agnello*, reasoning that the nature of the contents of a motor home creates similarly high expectations of privacy in those contents as the privacy expectations that one has in the contents of a house. Second, it distinguished *Carroll* on the basis of the comparatively low expectation of privacy that an owner has in the contents of an automobile.[23]

On review, the United States Supreme Court reversed the decision of the California Supreme Court. It analogized the case to *Carroll*, reasoning that an automobile and a motor home are not only similarly mobile but are similar in the reduced expectations of privacy in their contents. The expectations of privacy in a motor home are low partly because of the pervasive governmental regulation applicable to all licensed motor vehicles.[24] The two appellate courts applied the precedent differently because they differed in their analyses, primarily factual, of the expectations of privacy that one has in the contents of a motor home.

The processes of analogy and distinction may be applied to the selection or refinement of legal rules as well as to factual analysis. For example, suppose that you represent the plaintiff in an action against a tailor who agreed to make gowns for a wedding ceremony and who misrepresented the state of

Carroll v. United States (1925)

Automobile:

Fully mobile;
low expectation of privacy
in its contents.

Warrant not required.

Agnello v. United States (1925)

House:

Not mobile;
high expectation of privacy
in its contents.

Warrant required.

California v. Carney (1985)

Motor Home:

Fully mobile, but expectation of privacy
in contents arguably higher than in
contents of automobile.

Warrant required?

---

22. See id. at 395 (Stevens, J., dissenting).
23. People v. Carney, 668 P.2d 807, 810-814 (Cal. 1983).
24. *Carney*, 471 U.S. at 390-394; see also New York v. Class, 475 U.S. 106 (1986).

readiness of the gowns at the time of delivery. To prevail on a claim under a state consumer fraud statute, you must establish that the statute applies to fraud during the delivery of goods under a preexisting agreement and is not limited to fraud during bargaining, fraud that induces the contract. The statute itself prohibits various kinds of fraud during the "advertisement or sale" of goods. The term "advertisement" does not help you on this question, because it normally refers to representations made before an agreement is reached. Although the term "sale" might refer to performance of an existing contract, the statute doesn't specifically define "sale" in a way that resolves the question whether "sale" refers to the moment of contracting or to the subsequent transfer of goods. A commercial statute of the same state, however, specifically defines sale as "the passing of title from the seller to the buyer for a price," an event that could coincide with the delivery of goods under a preexisting contract. The remedial purposes of the consumer fraud statute suggest that it should have at least the breadth of application of the state's commercial statutes. Therefore, as counsel for the plaintiff in the fraud action, you could argue by analogy to the commercial statute that the consumer fraud statute prohibits fraud during the delivery of goods under a preexisting contract.[25]

In contrast, the common law requirement of proof of fraud by the elevated standard of "clear and convincing evidence" may not apply by analogy to an action under the consumer fraud statute. In enacting the statute, the legislature intended to increase consumer protection beyond that afforded by an action for common law fraud. Therefore, the statute should require proof by the normal standard of a "preponderance of the evidence" rather than the more demanding common law standard.[26]

Although these examples involve interpretation and application of constitutional and statutory law, they also illustrate the manner in which common law develops, case by case, through analogy and distinction in the context of stare decisis.

B. OVERRULING PRECEDENT

Precedent that is indistinguishable in any material way from the dispute before the court is "controlling." In most court systems, a lower court is absolutely bound by the controlling precedent of the appellate courts that review its decisions.[27] However, the doctrine of stare decisis is more flexible in the courts that created the precedent.[28] In exceptional circumstances, a court may depart from a strict application of stare decisis and refuse to follow its own precedent that otherwise would be controlling. In so doing, it "overrules" the prior decision and substitutes new precedent in its place.

---

25. Cf. Schmidt v. American Leasco, 679 P.2d 532, 534-535 (Ariz. Ct. App. 1983) (fraud during performance of lease).
26. See, e.g., Dunlap v. Jimmy GMC of Tucson, Inc., 666 P.2d 83, 89 (Ariz. Ct. App. 1983) (applying Arizona consumer fraud statute).
27. E.g., Hutto v. Davis, 454 U.S. 370, 375 (1982).
28. E.g., Jaffree v. Wallace, 705 F.2d 1526, 1532 (11th Cir. 1983), aff'd, 472 U.S. 38 (1985).

An early Supreme Court decision was surprisingly liberal in its approval of such departures from stare decisis:

> The rule of *stare decisis,* though one tending to consistency and uniformity of decision, is not inflexible. Whether it shall be followed or departed from is a question entirely within the discretion of the court, which is again called upon to consider a question once decided.[29]

A more recent statement of the Court is more cautious: "[A]ny departure from the doctrine of stare decisis demands special justification."[30]

More specifically, "informed by a series of prudential and pragmatic considerations," the Supreme Court may feel justified in overruling a prior decision if

(1) "a prior judicial ruling should come to be seen so clearly as error that its enforcement was for that very reason doomed";

(2) "the rule has proved to be intolerable simply in defying practical workability";

(3) "related principles of law have so far developed as to have left the old rule no more than a remnant of abandoned doctrine"; or

(4) "facts have so changed or come to be seen so differently, as to have robbed the old rule of significant application or justification."[31]

In accordance with the third and fourth justifications, a court may overrule a previous decision that was sensible in light of its original social, economic, technological, and legal context but that fails to serve important policies in current conditions.[32] Under the early English common law, for example, an employment contract that provided for an annual salary was interpreted as providing a one-year term of employment absent a clear expression of contrary intent. The original impetus for the one-year rule was a desire to protect seasonal farm workers from the insecurity of shorter and unpredictable terms of employment. Nonetheless, English courts extended the rule to a new population of factory workers created by the industrial revolution.

Some American jurisdictions adopted a form of the English one-year rule, perhaps because of the early American tradition that a master was responsible for the well-being of his servants. Employer paternalism, however, declined with the industrialization of the United States in the late nineteenth century. Partly to facilitate efficient allocation of resources in developing industries subject to business cycles, American courts abandoned the English rule. In its place, they created the "at will" doctrine, which

---

29. Hertz v. Woodman, 218 U.S. 205, 212 (1910).

30. Arizona v. Rumsey, 467 U.S. 203, 212 (1984); see also Patterson v. McLean Credit Union, 491 U.S. 164, 172-173 (1989).

31. Planned Parenthood of S.E. Penn. v. Casey, 112 S. Ct. 2808, 2809 (1992).

32. See, e.g., Amadio v. Levin, 501 A.2d 1085 (Pa. 1985) (to recognize right on behalf of deceased fetus under wrongful death and survival statutes, court relied partly on intervening advances in medical knowledge and on changes in the laws of other states to overrule precedent).

raised a presumption that an employment contract for an indefinite term was terminable by either party at any time and for any reason or no reason at all.

The at-will rule was consistent with developing contract doctrine, which imposed obligations based on voluntary agreement rather than on status such as that of an employer in the master-servant relationship.[33] In this century, however, American industry has outgrown its need for protection from labor costs that cannot vary perfectly with business needs. Concern has shifted to the need for greater security for nonunion employees, whose bargaining power is typically much inferior to that of their employers. As a reflection of this shift in concern, courts have begun to depart from their traditionally rigid application of the at-will rule and have recognized exceptions to the rule in the form of new tort and contract theories.[34]

Even absent an intervening change in conditions, a court may overrule one of its prior decisions simply because it thinks that the prior decision was poorly reasoned at the outset or has proved to be unworkable in light of experience.[35] For example, in *Maryland v. Wirtz*,[36] the Supreme Court held that the principles of state sovereignty in the tenth amendment[37] did not prohibit Congress from regulating the compensation of state employees by applying the Fair Labor Standards Act of 1938 to selected state institutions. The Court relied heavily on dicta[38] from a previous decision of the Court, *United States v. California*.[39] Eight years later, in *National League of Cities v. Usery*,[40] a closely divided Supreme Court overruled *Maryland v. Wirtz*: A plurality of four Justices explained that the dicta from *United States v. California* on which the *Maryland* Court had relied was "simply wrong."[41] Eight years after *National League of Cities*, the Supreme Court in a 5-4 decision overruled *National League of Cities* on the ground that *it* was wrongly decided:

---

33. Gary E. Murg & Clifford Scharman, Employment at Will: Do the Exceptions Overwhelm the Rule?, 23 B.C. L. Rev. 329, 332-336 (1982).

34. See, e.g., Wagenseller v. Scottsdale Memorial Hosp., 710 P.2d 1025, 1030-1041 (Ariz. 1985); Petermann v. International Bhd. of Teamsters Local 396, 344 P.2d 25 (Cal. Ct. App. 1959); Modern status of rule that employer may discharge at-will employee for any reason, Michael A. Di Sabatino, Annotation, 12 A.L.R.4th 544 (1982).

35. Geoffrey R. Stone, Precedent, the Amendment Process, and Evolution in Constitutional Doctrine, 11 Harv. J.L. & Pub. Pol'y 67, 71 (1988).

36. 392 U.S. 183 (1968).

37. The tenth amendment to the United States Constitution reserves power to the states:

> The powers not delegated to the United States by the Constitution, nor prohibited by it to the States, are reserved to the States respectively, or to the people.

38. "Dicta" are statements in a judicial opinion that are not necessary to the court's resolution of the dispute before it. Dicta may give some insight into the court's views about the proper resolution of other disputes, but they do not form part of the decision's binding precedent.

39. 297 U.S. 175, 184-185 (1936) (quoted in *Wirtz*, 392 U.S. at 198).

40. 426 U.S. 833 (1976).

41. Id. at 854-855. Justice Blackmun wrote a separate opinion concurring with the plurality opinion and providing the fifth vote necessary to overrule Maryland v. Wirtz. Id. at 856.

We do not lightly overrule recent precedent. We have not hesitated, however, when it has become apparent that a prior decision has departed from a proper understanding of congressional power under the Commerce Clause.[42]

The Supreme Court's double reverse on the proper interpretation of the tenth amendment may simply exemplify a more general relationship between the Supreme Court and the United States Constitution. Article V of the Constitution provides that an amendment to the Constitution is not effective unless approved by two-thirds of each house of Congress and ratified by three-fourths of the states. Thus, Congress cannot easily amend the Constitution to reflect changing social or economic conditions or to overrule judicial interpretations with which Congress disagrees. In recent history, for example, Congress marshaled sufficient votes to propose the Equal Rights Amendment and even to extend the time within which the states could ratify it, but fewer than the requisite number of states ratified.[43] Consequently, some scholars and judges believe that the Supreme Court should "keep [constitutional] law in accord with the dynamic flow of the social order," with less than the normal restraints of stare decisis,[44] and with less than complete deference to the immediate concerns of Congress when it enacted the constitutional provision or amendment in question.[45]

Nonetheless, countervailing considerations may justify deference to precedent in some cases, even when fundamental constitutional rights are at issue. First, people may have so substantially relied on an established proposition of law that overruling the prior decision would result in "special hardship" and "inequity."[46] Second, an extraordinarily divisive issue may call for a ruling that is sufficiently durable to erase all doubts about its vulnerability to continuing political pressures. This consideration is present

> whenever the Constitution calls the contending sides of a national controversy to end their national division by accepting a common mandate rooted in the Constitution.
>
> The Court is not asked to do this very often, . . . But when the Court does act in this way, its decision requires an equally rare precedential force to counter the inevitable efforts to overturn it and to thwart its implementation. . . . [O]nly the most convincing justification under accepted standards of precedent could suffice to demonstrate that a later decision overruling the first was anything but a surrender to political pressure. . . .[47]

---

42. Garcia v. San Antonio Metro. Transit Auth., 469 U.S. 528, 557 (1985).

43. John E. Nowak, Ronald D. Rotunda & J. Nelson Young, Constitutional Law App. B, at 1105-1106 (2d ed. 1983). In an exceptional reaction to a particular ruling of the Supreme Court, Congress proposed, and the states ratified, the eleventh amendment as a way of overruling Chisholm v. Georgia, 2 U.S. (2 Dall.) 419 (1793). Nowak, Rotunda & Young, supra, at 52-53.

44. Edgar Bodenheimer, Jurisprudence: The Philosophy and Method of the Law 430 (rev. ed. 1974); see also Patterson v. McLean Credit Union, 491 U.S. 164, 172-173 (1989).

45. See generally Nowak, Rotunda & Young, supra note 43, at 14 n.13 (comparing value-oriented theory of judicial review to others); Raoul Berger, New Theories of "Interpretation": The Activist Flight from the Constitution, 47 Ohio St. L.J. 1 (1986).

46. Planned Parenthood of S.E. Penn. v. Casey, 112 S. Ct. 2791, 2808 (1992).

47. Id. at 2815.

In *Planned Parenthood of Southeastern Pennsylvania v. Casey*,[48] the Supreme Court invoked both of these considerations in declining to abandon the central rule of *Roe v. Wade*,[49] which established a woman's limited constitutional right to terminate a pregnancy.

The Court conceded that the reliance factor weighs most heavily in commercial contexts, "where advance planning of great precision is most obviously a necessity."[50] However, even in the noncommercial contexts of reproduction and sexual equality, reliance could not be discounted:

> [F]or two decades of economic and social developments, people have organized intimate relationships and made choices that define their views of themselves and their places in society, in reliance on the availability of abortion in the event that contraception should fail. The ability of women to participate equally in the economic and social life of the Nation has been facilitated by their ability to control their reproductive lives. . . . The Constitution serves human values, and while the effect of reliance on *Roe* cannot be exactly measured, neither can the certain cost of overruling *Roe* for people who have ordered their thinking and living around that case be dismissed.[51]

Moreover, in the context of extraordinary national division over abortion rights, a dramatic change in the course of constitutional law might fan the flames of controversy by suggesting that continued strife could inspire further changes in course:

> The court's duty in the present case is clear. In 1973, it confronted the already-divisive issue of governmental power to limit personal choice to undergo abortion, for which it provided a new resolution based on the due process guaranteed by the Fourteenth Amendment. Whether or not a new social consensus is developing on that issue, its divisiveness is no less today than in 1973, and pressure to overrule the decision, like pressure to retain it, has grown only more intense. A decision to overrule *Roe*'s essential holding under the existing circumstances would address error, if error there was, at the cost of both profound and unnecessary damage to the Court's legitimacy, and to the Nation's commitment to the rule of law.[52]

Moreover, the central rule of *Roe* had not proved unworkable and had not been eroded by changes in facts or in related principles of law. Accordingly, although the Court departed from *Roe* in other respects, it reaffirmed *Roe*'s "central holding."[53]

IV. SUMMARY

Under the doctrine of stare decisis, a court endeavors to decide each case consistently with its previous decisions, sometimes called precedent.

---

48. 112 S. Ct. 2791 (1992).
49. 410 U.S. 113 (1973).
50. *Casey*, 112 S. Ct. at 2809.
51. Id.
52. Id. at 2816.
53. Id. at 2804, 2817.

This policy of consistency permits a court to depart from precedent if the precedent is distinguishable from the current dispute. Even if the precedent is not distinguishable, a court may depart from stare decisis and overrule its own prior case law if a different rule of law would better respond to current social and economic conditions. Stare decisis is less flexible with respect to the precedent of a higher court in the same jurisdiction: A trial court or intermediate court of appeals is strictly bound to apply the precedent of a higher court. A court is never bound to apply the precedent of a lower court or any court in another jurisdiction.

═══════ E X E R C I S E   3 - 1 ═══════

Review Exercise 2-1(2) on pages 14-15 and analyze the following problems based on decisions of the fictitious Calzona Supreme Court:

PRECEDENT: *Smith v. Collier,* 47 Calz. 78 (1891)

On February 1, Smith and Collier agreed to marry before the end of the year. They later set a wedding date of December 1. In November, Smith complained about Collier's habit of playing poker on Saturday nights. In retaliation, Collier announced that Collier would not marry Smith. Smith sued Collier for breach of contract, requesting compensatory and punitive damages. Smith did not allege that Collier committed a tort.

The opinion of the Calzona Supreme Court includes the following excerpt:

> We affirm the trial court's factual findings that Collier breached the marriage contract with the malicious intent to cause Smith injury. Although the courts of this state recognize a general rule against punitive damages for breach of contract, the trial court correctly instructed the jury that it could award punitive damages as well as compensatory damages in this case.

1. Distinguishing *Smith v. Collier*

In the following cases, you represent the defendant. Identify the facts in *Smith v. Collier* that appear to have motivated the court to permit an award of punitive damages. Identify factual differences in your case that might motivate the Calzona Supreme Court to distinguish *Smith v. Collier* and to rule that punitive damages cannot be awarded against your client. Explain why those factual differences justify a different result from the ruling in *Smith v. Collier.* Identify any factual similarities between your case and *Smith v. Collier.* Explain why those similarities do not justify the same result as in *Smith v. Collier.* Which of the following cases is easiest to distinguish from *Smith v. Collier?*

a. *White v. Strunk*

White agreed to pay Strunk $100,000 for construction of a house on White's property. Strunk agreed to complete construction by August 1, regardless of weather or labor conditions. Unfortunately, abnormally frequent rainfall and faulty workmanship by subcontractors delayed Strunk's work. Despite Strunk's best efforts, he failed to complete construction by August 1, causing White to suffer economic losses.

b. *Roget v. Webster*

Roget agreed to pay Webster $100,000 in exchange for Webster's promise to construct a house on Roget's property. Before either Roget or Webster began performance, Ballentine offered to pay Webster $150,000 to build a similar house on Ballentine's property. Because he could not perform both jobs at once, and because a contract with Ballentine was more profitable, Webster repudiated his contract with Roget and accepted Ballentine's offer.

c. *White v. Benkowski*

White's property had no water supply. White agreed to pay Benkowski a monthly fee in exchange for fresh water supplied through pipes from Benkowski's well. After personal animosity developed between White and Benkowski, Benkowski maliciously shut off the water supply to White's property.

2. Overruling *Smith v. Collier*

You represent the defendant in *Statler v. Corbin*, a case that is factually and procedurally indistinguishable from *Smith v. Collier*. Explain why the Calzona Supreme Court should overrule *Smith v. Collier* and disallow punitive damages for breach of a marriage agreement.

3. Distinguishing *Statler v. Corbin*, 305 Calz. 219 (1990)

In *Statler v. Corbin*, the Calzona Supreme Court overruled *Smith v. Collier* and held that punitive damages are not available to remedy even a malicious breach of a marriage contract. In the following case, you represent the plaintiff. Identify factual or procedural differences between *Statler v. Corbin* and your case, and explain why those differences justify an award of punitive damages in your case.

Jones v. Marsh

In July, Jones and Marsh agreed to marry on November 1. At a family reunion in August, Marsh broke off the engagement in a public statement in which he cruelly humiliated Jones. In addition to proving breach of contract, you have alleged and proved that Marsh intentionally inflicted emotional distress on Jones, conduct that is actionable as a tort in Calzona. In opposing Jones's request for punitive damages, Marsh relies on *Statler v. Corbin*.

4

An Approach to Legal Method

I. OVERVIEW—SOLVING LEGAL PROBLEMS

Attorneys perform many tasks for clients that may not directly relate to litigation of legal disputes, including estate and tax planning, business counseling, and legislative lobbying. Even these tasks, however, may be inspired partly by the desire to avoid or influence future litigation. Moreover, relatively few clients seek legal counseling to avoid potential legal problems; instead, most people consult an attorney only after they have become embroiled in a legal dispute in which litigation has commenced or is imminent. With a little luck and skill, the parties or their attorneys may still avoid formal litigation in court by using "alternative dispute resolution" such as negotiation, mediation, or informal arbitration.[1] However, these methods of "ADR" still require the parties to evaluate or present their cases within a general legal framework. Consequently, legal method relating to litigation of legal disputes is an important component of nearly every attorney's practice.

As explored in detail in Chapter 13, a lawsuit is formally commenced with the filing of "pleadings": The plaintiff brings suit by filing a "complaint" against the defendant, and the defendant responds by filing an "answer." If you represent a party in the early stages of such litigation, you must evaluate the strengths and weaknesses of your client's claims or defenses to help you prepare for various stages of advocacy, from the pleadings and settlement negotiations to trial and appeal. In a large or medium-sized law firm, the typical means of communicating your evaluation to other members of the firm is an office memorandum of law, discussed in detail in Part III

---

1. See, e.g., Stephen G. Goldberg, Frank E. A. Sander & Nancy H. Rogers, Dispute Resolution (1992).

of this book. The principal means of persuading a judge or other adjudicatory body to accept your client's legal claims or defenses is a written brief, discussed in detail in Part IV. To prepare either kind of document, you must apply fundamental skills of legal method that you develop in the first year of law school, as discussed in Part II.

This chapter will examine methods of legal problem-solving in the context of litigation of legal disputes. It builds on the groundwork laid in Chapters 2 and 3, and it provides an overview for more detailed discussions of legal method found throughout the remaining chapters.

II. IDENTIFYING ISSUES FOR ANALYSIS

A. DEFINING ISSUES

A legal issue is a question that a judge, jury, agency hearing officer, arbitrator, or other adjudicator must resolve to determine the outcome of a legal dispute. Whenever an event creates the conditions for a legal dispute, you can identify potential legal issues immediately after the event, even though no party has yet begun to litigate a claim or has even made any demands on another. Constitutions, statutes, case law, and perhaps even the private law of an agreement between the parties impose duties on some parties and correlative rights on others in the context of the event. Armed with at least a general knowledge of the law and of the facts of the event, you can address the question whether any party is liable to another for breach of a legal duty. At the least, you can advance arguments in support of either a potentially wronged victim or a potentially liable party. If the arguments for both parties have potential merit, you have identified a legal issue.

1. Issues and Subissues

A general issue may encompass discrete subissues. For example, case law establishes that a defendant generally will be liable to the plaintiff for damages caused by breach of contract if (1) the parties formed an enforceable contract and (2) the defendant failed to perform his contractual promises, thus breaching the contract. At the broadest level, the facts of a dispute might raise the general issue of whether the defendant is liable for breach of contract. More specifically, the facts may raise separate subissues about (A) contract formation and (B) performance and breach.

You may want to further subdivide these subissues to recognize multiple legal elements associated with each. For example, case law establishes two primary requirements for contract formation: (1) an agreement reached through a process of offer and acceptance and (2) "consideration" in the form of a mutually induced exchange. These elements are distinct, because parties are capable of agreeing to a transaction that does not satisfy the consideration requirement. Depending on the circumstances of the dispute, the facts may raise separate subissues regarding (1) offer and acceptance and (2) consideration. Similarly, within the subissue of performance and breach, the law and the facts may raise a second level of subissues regarding, for example, (1) interpretation of the defendant's contractual promises and (2) possible discharge of the defendant's obligations because unforeseen circumstances made his performance impossible.

2. Continuing Development of Issues

At the inception of a dispute, incomplete knowledge of the facts and vagueness or ambiguity in the arguably applicable legal rules make the eventual outcome of the dispute particularly uncertain. At that stage, you can identify the issues only tentatively. As the dispute proceeds through stages of litigation, the issues will become increasingly well defined.

For example, a demand letter or complaint may reveal which of numerous potential legal claims a claimant has decided to advance, thus raising some questions of liability and eliminating others. Under modern rules of civil procedure, each party to a civil lawsuit must disclose some kinds of information to the opposing party, and each party may use various "discovery" devices to obtain certain other kinds of information from witnesses and from the opposing party.[2] This court-supervised discovery and disclosure process or other investigation may reveal that some claims or defenses are meritless and may raise new questions about others. Moreover, as explored in Chapters 14 and 15, a litigant may request the court to rule before trial that certain evidence will be excluded from trial or even that the litigant is entitled to judgment without trial. Thus, pretrial motions may raise issues under applicable rules of evidence or procedure concerning the admissibility of evidence or the proper application of standards for summary disposition. Finally, if the dispute goes to trial, the nature of the disposition in the trial court and the factual record developed in the trial court will help determine which issues the losing party might reasonably raise on appeal.

As illustrated by these examples, the parties help to define the issues by making strategic decisions about what claims and defenses to assert and about which procedural vehicles should be used to assert them. With few exceptions, courts will decline to address questions that are not raised by either party to a dispute.[3]

---

2. See, e.g., Fed. R. Civ. P. 26-37 (as amended 1993).

3. E.g., Jones v. City of Somerville, 735 F.2d 5, 7 (1st Cir. 1984) (appellate waiver of legal theory for failure to present it to trial court); Hershinow v. Bonamarte, 735 F.2d 264, 266 (7th Cir. 1984) (waiver of claim presented to appellate court in perfunctory manner). But cf. Giannakos v. M/V Bravo Trader, 762 F.2d 1295, 1297 (5th Cir. 1985) (federal trial and appellate courts must address questions of federal subject-matter jurisdiction on their own motions); In re Pizza of Hawaii, Inc., 761 F.2d 1374, 1377-1378 (9th Cir. 1985) (appellate court must determine appellate jurisdiction on its own motion); In re Pacific Trencher & Equip., Inc., 735 F.2d 362, 364 (9th Cir. 1984) (discretionary appellate consideration of pure question of law not raised in the trial court).

3. Materiality

Not every potential disagreement about the facts or the law amounts to a legal issue. Even a hotly disputed question of fact or law would not be "in issue" if it were immaterial. A disputed point is immaterial if it could not affect the outcome of the lawsuit in light of other facts and rules of law.

To take an obvious example, suppose that evidence shows that the defendant drove his car through an intersection and struck the plaintiff in a pedestrian crosswalk. The defendant's liability for negligence would not be affected by even a heated disagreement over the color of the socks that the defendant wore that day. Assuming that the identity of the driver of the car is conclusively established through some means other than the color of the socks he wore, the issues of law and fact would include such material questions as the following:

(1) Which party had the green light?
(2) What injuries did the plaintiff sustain?
(3) Does the law permit the jury to reduce the plaintiff's recovery if her own negligence combined with that of the defendant to cause her injuries?

Of course, many cases raise closer questions of materiality than that in the example above. As discussed in the next section, some questions of materiality may be a matter of degree requiring the exercise of judgment in selecting issues for discussion or argument in a legal document.

═══════ E X E R C I S E 4 - 1 ═══════

Although American jurisdictions have enacted criminal codes that largely supersede the early criminal common law, imagine a state that still applies the common law definition of the crime of burglary: the breaking and entering of a dwelling of another at night with the intent to commit a felony. As stated in Chapter 2, the law relating to this crime reflected a concern about a serious invasion of the right of habitation during hours of darkness, when the inhabitants were most vulnerable to attack and the invader most likely to escape recognition.

Armed only with this general knowledge of the law, identify the issues relating to the common law crime of burglary raised by the following facts:

In June, Leona Rosal left her San Francisco apartment and drove her VW bus down the coast for a three-week vacation in Monterey Bay. Although she occasionally ate at restaurants or stayed with friends, she mostly slept in the back of the bus and prepared simple meals in the bus with groceries that she purchased at local stores.

On the evening of June 20, Leona parked her bus in an overnight recreational-vehicle parking space at Seacliff State Beach. She prepared dinner from an ice chest in the back of the bus, leaving the driver's window in the cab completely open and an expensive portable stereo radio and cassette player on the driver's seat. She fell asleep in the back of her bus at 11:00 P.M. A curtain separated the sleeping area of the bus from the driver's cab. At 5:15 A.M., just as the first hints of a sunrise glowed from the hilltops opposite the ocean, Michael Glass, a local surfer, approached Leona's van. Through the open window next to the driver's seat, Michael spied the stereo equipment lying on the seat. Hoping to add it permanently to his own home system, Michael opened the closed but unlocked driver's door and placed his hand on the stereo equipment. At that moment, a patrolling police officer drove up to Leona's VW bus and arrested Michael for burglary and attempted larceny. Leona awoke only when the officer knocked on her bus after the arrest.

You may assume that theft of the stereo equipment would constitute felony larceny in the jurisdiction. In the prosecution of Michael Glass on the burglary charge, what elements of the common law crime of burglary would the prosecutor and defense attorney likely dispute? What elements of burglary are not reasonably in dispute? Would further facts help define or resolve the issues? Would case law that refines the law of burglary help define or resolve the issues? If you were assigned the task of preparing an office memorandum on this problem, what facts or law would you desire to investigate further?

B. SCOPE OF ANALYSIS

Any dispute of at least moderate complexity presents a range of potential legal theories and arguments that you might raise in litigation. At the near end of the spectrum are persuasive and conventional legal theories or arguments that a court would almost certainly address in analyzing the dispute. At the far end are legal theories or factual analogies of such doubtful merit or applicability that a court might view them as frivolous or immaterial to the outcome of the dispute.

The extent to which you discuss topics toward the far end of the spectrum is a question of "scope of analysis" and depends partly on the nature of your document. The scope of analysis typically is quite broad in a law school essay examination answer, somewhat narrower in an office memorandum addressed to a supervising attorney, and narrower still in a good brief addressed to a judge.

You will often touch on a broad range of issues in an examination answer because most law professors will specifically test your ability to spot issues. Indeed, on many examinations, you will earn a higher grade if you identify and briefly discuss all possible issues, including the less obvious and more exotic ones, than if you thoroughly analyze only the most obvious.

In comparison, your supervising attorney may expect a slightly narrower scope of analysis in your office memorandum. She probably will want detailed discussion of significant issues and she will generally encourage creative and aggressive analysis, but she may not have time to thoroughly examine more exotic theories or approaches if they are unlikely to have an effect on the outcome of the dispute. Unfortunately, you may be tempted to convey to your supervisor the long hours that you have spent in the library by describing in detail every legal theory or authority that made its way into your library notes. Your supervisor will not be impressed. She realizes that you will regularly investigate leads that bear no useful fruit, and she expects the final draft of your memorandum to shield her from the burden of retracing your steps down paths that led only to distracting tangents.

On the other hand, the materiality of a fact or theory may be difficult to assess in the early stages of litigation and fact investigation. Accordingly, if you draft an office memorandum at the early stages of a dispute, you should consider discussing close questions of scope of analysis with your supervising attorney before beginning to write. Absent specific direction from your supervisor, you probably should at least mention any argument of potential significance, even if only in a sentence or two. You can distinguish between a major theory and a less significant one in the depth of your analysis of each. Then, if later developments in the litigation establish the significance of an issue of previously questionable importance, you can analyze that issue in greater depth in a supplemental memorandum.

When drafting a brief, you often must exercise even stricter control on the scope of analysis. Although creative and novel arguments often win appeals by inspiring changes in the law, some arguments are so clearly marginal that they may simply detract from the cumulative persuasiveness of the entire brief. If you add a nearly frivolous argument to one with greater merit, you reduce the number of pages within the maximum allowed that you can devote to the meritorious argument. Even worse, you may lose credibility on the whole brief.

III. DEDUCTIVE REASONING

A. THE LEGAL SYLLOGISM—ORIENTATION AND LIMITATIONS

Once you have identified legal issues and have determined the appropriate scope of analysis, you must analyze the issues. Most essay examinations, office memoranda, and briefs require more than purely abstract legal analysis: They require you to apply legal standards to specific facts to reach a conclusion. In many cases, the analysis follows a pattern of deductive reasoning known as the syllogism, which derives a conclusion from a major premise and a minor premise:

> Minor Premise: All men are mortal.
> Major Premise: Socrates is a man.
> Conclusion: Therefore, Socrates is mortal.[4]

In a legal argument, the major premise is a legal rule. It may represent the terms of a statute, the holding of a single judicial decision that acts as

---

4. See generally Irving M. Copi, Introduction to Logic §1.4, at 23-24 (4th ed. 1972).

precedent, or a general principle derived from a series of previous decisions. The minor premise of a legal argument generally is a set of facts taken from the dispute that you are analyzing. The conclusion represents your resolution of the question whether the facts stated in the minor premise satisfy the legal standard stated in the major premise.

A deductive argument is valid if its conclusion follows necessarily from its premises; the correctness or truth of the conclusion of a valid argument depends on the truth of its premises.[5] For example, the fourth amendment to the United States Constitution ordinarily requires a police officer to obtain a search warrant from a judicial officer before searching an enclosed structure such as a house. However, under the "automobile exception," an officer may search an automobile without a warrant if he has probable cause to believe that it contains evidence of a crime. Suppose that a police officer searched Jack Greenberg's motor home without a warrant and found illegal drugs. In the state's criminal prosecution of Greenberg for possession of the illegal drugs, the state might advance the following valid deductive argument:

Major Premise—The automobile exception to the fourth amendment's warrant requirement applies to all vehicles with mobility similar to that of an automobile on a street or highway.

Minor Premise—Even while parked in Greenberg's backyard, Greenberg's motor home was a vehicle with mobility similar to that of an automobile on a street or highway.

Conclusion—The automobile exception to the fourth amendment's warrant requirement applied to Greenberg's motor home while it was parked in Greenberg's backyard.

Although the conclusion of this valid argument follows necessarily from the premises, the conclusion is not true if either of the premises is untrue. The attorney for each party will attempt to persuade the judge to reach a certain conclusion by accepting particular formulations of the major and minor premises and by rejecting others. For example, Greenberg's attorney could raise the fourth amendment issue by asking the judge to exclude the evidence obtained in the warrantless search of Greenberg's motor home. In response, the state prosecutor would advance the deductive argument above to demonstrate that the fourth amendment did not require the police to obtain a warrant to search Greenberg's motor home. Greenberg's attorney could attack this argument either by arguing as a matter of law that the prosecutor's major premise exaggerates the scope of the automobile exception or by establishing as a matter of fact that the prosecutor's minor premise exaggerates the mobility of the motor home parked in Greenberg's backyard.

A deductive argument is not valid if its conclusion does not follow necessarily from its premises. For example, if Greenberg's attorney proved that Greenberg's motor home was significantly less mobile than an automobile on the street or highway, the judge would undoubtedly replace the

---

5. Id. at 23.

prosecutor's untrue minor premise with the minor premise established by Greenberg's attorney. As reconstructed, the deductive argument would no longer be valid, because the prosecutor's conclusion would not follow from the original major premise and the new minor premise.

Deductive reasoning provides at least a rough organizational framework for most legal analyses in office memoranda, answers to essay examinations, and briefs. The usefulness of the syllogism in legal reasoning, however, is limited by the flexibility and uncertainty inherent in legal analysis. For example, to establish the major premise of your argument, you may state your interpretation of the holding of a previous decision or your synthesis of the holdings of a series of decisions. Until a judge expresses her opinion on the matter, however, you cannot be certain whether she will agree with your interpretation of previous decisions and thus with your statement of the major premise.

Indeed, the dominant description of legal method in this century, known as "legal realism," rejects the notion that the law is external to the judges and other officials who apply and enforce it. Instead, the law is simply a prediction about what such officials will do in the face of a dispute. Moreover, their decisions will be based on a complex set of motivations, including personal values and prejudices not explicitly accounted for in the formal abstract rule of law. Thus, judges or juries can take advantage of uncertainty in law or facts by manipulating them to justify results that they reach on other than purely logical grounds.[6]

In short, legal disputes cannot be analyzed with mathematical certainty:

> The life of the law has not been logic: it has been experience. The felt necessities of the time, the prevalent moral and political theories, intuitions of public policy, avowed or unconscious, even the prejudices which judges share with their fellow-men, have had a good deal more to do than the syllogism in determining the rules by which men should be governed.[7]

Nonetheless, the syllogism provides a useful starting point for discussing general techniques of presenting legal analyses.

B. IRAC

Most law students use the acronym IRAC to help them remember the elements of deductive reasoning. IRAC stands for Issue, Rule, Application, and Conclusion. Thus, after identifying an **Issue**, you should

---

6. See J. W. Harris, Legal Philosophies 93-98 (1980). The more recent Critical Legal Studies movement goes beyond legal realism to broadly attack contemporary legal method, scholarship, and education as a system that legitimizes and perpetuates an oppressive socio-economic order. See generally Critical Legal Studies Symposium, 36 Stan. L. Rev. 1 (1984); Mark Kelman, A Guide to Critical Legal Studies (1987); Roberto M. Unger, The Critical Legal Studies Movement (1986). Scholars of the Critical Race School and the Feminist School of legal theory more specifically charge that traditional legal reasoning is grounded in, and helps to perpetuate, racist and sexist institutions and attitudes. See generally Richard Delgado & Jean Stefancic, Critical Race Theory: An Annotated Bibliography, 79 Va. L. Rev. 461 (1993); Deborah L. Rhode, Justice and Gender (1989).

7. Oliver W. Holmes, Jr., The Common Law 1 (1923); see also id. at 312 ("The distinctions of the law are founded on experience, not on logic. It therefore does not make

(1) state the legal **Rule** that will help resolve the issue,
(2) **Apply** the rule to the relevant facts, and
(3) reach a **Conclusion** on the question of whether the facts satisfy the legal rule.

For example, the following excerpt of an answer to an essay examination discusses the availability of punitive damages in a tort action. Although the examination answer itself should not explicitly refer to IRAC, the margin notes below represent the elements that a student should keep in mind when formulating a complete response. In this example, after raising an issue about punitive damages, the student has summarized general legal rules regarding the availability of punitive damages, has applied them to the facts of the examination, and has reached a conclusion.

Punitive Damages—In addition to compensation for his actual losses, Ling may request punitive damages, designed to punish the tortfeasor and to deter others from engaging in similar wrongdoing.	Issue
A jury has the discretion to award punitive damages if the tortfeasor acted with the malicious intent to cause harm. In many jurisdictions, punitive damages are also permitted if the tortfeasor acted with reckless disregard for the risk of harm to others. Unless exceptional circumstances justify the risky conduct, a person acts recklessly if he consciously engages in conduct that he knows or should know poses a great risk of harm to others.	Rules
In this case, Con Motor Co. did not maliciously intend to cause injury when it designed its Firebird sports car. In fact, the discussion at the May meeting shows that the board of directors genuinely hoped that the risky design would not cause accidents. However, Con's chief engineer informed the board of directors of her opinion that placement of the gas tank near the rear exterior of the car would create a risk of deadly explosion in even minor rear-end collisions. Yet, the directors approved that design solely because it would save production costs of $100/car. In so doing, Con's directors knowingly created a great risk of death or terrible injury to consumers without any socially significant justification.	Application to facts
Con Motor Co. thus acted recklessly, permitting a jury in many jurisdictions to assess punitive damages against it. Indeed, in a jurisdiction that requires proof of malicious intent to injure, this case	Conclusion

---

the dealings of men dependent on a mathematical accuracy."); Neil MacCormick, Legal Reasoning and Legal Theory 65-72 (1978) (discussing "the limits of deductive justification").

would be a good vehicle for arguing for a liberaliza-
tion of the standards to include recklessness as a
basis for an award of punitive damages.

To help you avoid the oversimplification that may result from an excessively mechanical application of IRAC, later chapters of this book explore
some sophisticated techniques of analysis that build on the general framework
of deductive reasoning. Chapter 7, Section II introduces two variations of
inductive reasoning, and Chapter 10, Section III.E tackles problems of
organization that arise when an issue or subissue presents different layers or
levels of syllogisms.

IV. DEVELOPMENT OF LEGAL PRINCIPLES

A. OVERVIEW—SOURCES OF AUTHORITY

Consistent with the general pattern of deductive reasoning, your first
step in discussing a legal issue is to identify and analyze applicable legal
rules. You will seldom find these rules clearly set forth in a single source of
authority; the law that an adjudicator will apply to resolve a legal issue may
be a combination of rules, any one of which may represent a synthesis of
several sources of law. The relative importance of legal authorities to the
analysis of the issue depends on such factors as

(1) the primary or secondary nature of the authority;
(2) the jurisdiction, in the sense of the political or geographical body,
    in which primary authority is controlling; and
(3) if the primary authority is case law, the strength of the case law as
    precedent.

1. Primary and Secondary Authority

So far, this book has addressed only "primary" legal authority: direct
statements of law issued by lawmaking bodies. Primary authority includes
constitutions, statutes and local ordinances, administrative rules and regulations, and case law. Subject to limitations discussed in Sections 2 and 3
below, a primary authority or combination of primary authorities will supply
the applicable rule in any legal dispute.

"Secondary" authorities, such as treatises, restatements of the law, and
articles, do not directly supply the rule of law in a legal dispute. Instead,
they express a commentator's explanation of the law or her opinions about
what the law should be. A secondary authority has persuasive value only: It
may influence a court or legislature to act in a particular way, but it has no
mandatory or binding effect.

An example of a popular treatise is Prosser and Keeton on Torts. This secondary authority generally describes tort law in American jurisdictions and examines the relevant policies supporting competing approaches in the tort law of different states.

Another frequently cited example of secondary authority is the collection of Restatements of Law issued by the American Law Institute. The Institute has drafted two restatements of contract law, the Restatement of Contracts (1932) and the Restatement (Second) of Contracts (1979). Each of these is divided into numerous sections and subsections, most of which attempt to summarize rules of the common law of contracts generally accepted when the restatement was drafted. A few sections, however, are meant to influence the law by promoting trends that had not yet been widely accepted at the time of drafting. Section 90 of each restatement, for example, represents an innovative view of a theory of recovery based on reliance, commonly known as promissory estoppel. Although no court is required to follow the approach of either restatement, §90 has in fact influenced many courts. Indeed, some courts have quoted approvingly the precise language of §90 of the first restatement, thus incorporating it into its own case law and giving it the quality of primary authority.[8]

Unless a secondary authority has been thus incorporated into primary authority, you should use it only as a starting point in your analysis. You may use secondary authorities to help you locate and understand primary authority or to help develop an argument not fully addressed or supported by primary authority. However, you should not base your legal analysis or argument on a secondary authority when supporting primary authority is available.

2. Jurisdiction in Which Authority Controls

Some federal constitutional, statutory, and special common laws apply broadly to all jurisdictions. For example, the thirteenth amendment to the United States Constitution abolishes the institution of slavery, whether practiced by a government or private entity, within the United States.

In contrast, the constitutional, statutory, and common laws of a state apply only within that state. For example, the Civil Code of California and the case law of the California courts interpreting that code do not have any binding effect on the law of torts or contracts in New York. Similarly, the courts of one state are free to develop the common law of that state independently of the judicial development of common law in other states.

Even though the laws of one state do not directly apply to activities in another state, in some circumstances those laws may have at least persuasive influence in the other state. For example, in developing the Arizona common law tort of wrongful discharge of an employee, the Arizona Supreme Court

---

8. See, e.g., Corbit v. J. I. Case Co., 424 P.2d 290, 300-301 (Wash. 1967) (en banc) (quoting §90 as a "useful guideline").

has drawn guidance from the emerging common law of California and of other states.[9]

Indeed, even case law from one state interpreting a statute of that state could have persuasive effect on the application of a statute of a different state, if the statutes in both states have similar or identical language and purposes. For example, the New York and New Hampshire legislatures have adopted identical versions of Uniform Commercial Code §2-302, which authorizes a court to deny enforcement of a contract provision that is "unconscionable."[10] A New York trial court interpreting §2-302 of New York's commercial code drew support from, though was not bound by, a decision of the New Hampshire Supreme Court interpreting the identical language in §2-302 of New Hampshire's commercial code.[11]

3. Strength of Case Law as Precedent

The binding or persuasive force of case law will depend on its strength as precedent under the doctrine of stare decisis. Section 2 above has already examined one aspect of this relationship: the relationship of the authority to the forum jurisdiction. The strength of case law as precedent also depends on

(1) the relative levels of the court that created the precedent and the one applying it, and

(2) the degree to which the precedent is directly applicable, rather than merely analogous, to the current dispute.

a. Level of Court

A trial court or intermediate court of appeals is bound by squarely applicable precedent of a higher court within its court system. Moreover, although a court can overrule its own precedent, it will do so only in exceptional circumstances warranting departure from the doctrine of stare decisis. On the other hand, it need not defer at all to the decisions of a lower court within the same state; at most, those decisions would have persuasive effect.

Thus, whenever possible, you obviously should support your analyses or arguments with case law from an appellate court in your jurisdiction that is higher than the court in which your dispute is currently being adjudicated. The basis for a helpful illustration is provided by the description of the United States Courts of Appeals for the Ninth Circuit on pages 38-39. When writing a brief to that Court of Appeals, you should try to support your

---

9. Wagenseller v. Scottsdale Memorial Hosp., 710 P.2d 1025, 1030-1031 (Ariz. 1985).

10. N.H. Rev. Stat. Ann. §382-A: 2-302 (1961); N.Y. [U.C.C.] Law §2-302 (McKinney 1964).

11. Jones v. Star Credit Corp., 59 Misc. 2d 189, 298 N.Y.S.2d 264 (1969) (citing American Home Improvement, Inc. v. MacIver, 201 A.2d 886 (N.H. 1964), for the proposition that §2-302 applies to "price unconscionability").

argument with United States Supreme Court precedent, which is binding on the Court of Appeals. If no Supreme Court authority applies, you can strongly support your argument with a previous decision of the Ninth Circuit Court of Appeals itself. Although a special 11-member panel of the Court can overrule such precedent, it will do so only in unusual circumstances. If no higher authority is available, you can derive some support for your argument from a published decision of the United States District Court for the Northern District of California, a federal trial court. However, because decisions of the District Court have only persuasive value in the Court of Appeals, you will then assume the burden of persuading the Court of Appeals that the District Court's decision represents the best legal approach, the approach that the Court of Appeals should adopt as its own.

b. Controlling, Analogous, and Distinguishable Authority

The strength of case law as binding or persuasive authority also depends on the degree to which it squarely applies to the current dispute. Even precedent of a higher court within the jurisdiction will not control the outcome of the dispute if it is distinguishable; the more significant the distinctions, the less nearly analogous is the precedent, thus decreasing the likelihood that the precedent will influence the outcome. Similarly, the persuasiveness of nonbinding authority from lower courts within the jurisdiction or from courts of other jurisdictions will depend in part on the degree of similarity between the precedent and the current dispute.

When evaluating the legally significant similarities or distinctions between precedent and the current dispute, you should resist the temptation to overemphasize superficial factual similarities that appear in legally distinct contexts. Consider, for example, a current dispute in which the plaintiff's new television set spontaneously generated an electrical fire, causing major damage to the plaintiff's home. In this dispute, the parties may raise the issue of whether the retailer is liable to the plaintiff on a claim of breach of the warranty of merchantability implied in the sales contract under the state's version of the Uniform Commercial Code (UCC).[12] Suppose further that an appellate opinion in the state, decided in 1957, holds only that the plaintiff in that action, a consumer, failed to file his complaint within the time prescribed by the state's statute of limitations, thus barring his action for negligent manufacture of a television set that spontaneously burst into flames, setting fire to the plaintiff's home.

At first glance, the prior decision might appear significant because of the factual similarities of the events giving rise to the actions. In fact, however, the prior decision may be completely inapplicable. It does not interpret the UCC's warranty of merchantability in a contract for a sale of goods because it addresses a legally distinct cause of action in tort; indeed, the prior decision was issued before state enactment of the UCC and before the widespread

---

12. The UCC's warranty of merchantability implies a promise on the part of a merchant that goods are generally nondefective. U.C.C. §2-314 (1990).

adoption of more contemporary tort doctrines of products liability. Most important, the prior decision discusses only the bar of the statute of limitations; it does not directly address the elements of any claim for relief other than timely filing. More helpful to the current dispute would be analogous precedent that addresses the scope of the warranty of merchantability, even if in the context of different goods causing different kinds of accidents and injuries.

4. Summary

Only primary authority within the forum jurisdiction is potentially binding. Primary authority from other jurisdictions and secondary authority are persuasive only.

If the primary authority is case law within the forum jurisdiction, its strength as precedent will depend partly on the relative levels of the court that created the precedent and the court that will apply it. It will depend also on how closely analogous the precedent is to the current dispute.

═══════ E X E R C I S E 4 - 2 ═══════

The Hazardous Materials Transportation Act (HMTA) of State *X* makes it a criminal offense to transport certain hazardous materials, such as toxic chemicals, except with statutorily specified safeguards. For example, the statute requires a transporter of regulated materials to first confine the materials in steel drums and then secure the drums within a cargo bay that is enclosed on all sides with material of specified strength. Leek Chemical Co. violated the HMTA by transporting highly toxic chemicals in steel drums secured to an open flatbed truck. The truck overturned on a slick highway, causing several of the barrels to roll across lanes of oncoming traffic. An automobile driven by Daniel Stein collided with one of the barrels, bursting the barrel and spreading the toxic chemical onto and into Stein's automobile. Stein was not seriously injured by the initial impact with the barrel; however, he was permanently injured by contact with the toxic chemical.

Stein sues Leek Chemical Co. in tort for damages. In State *X*, Leek Chemical Co. will be liable for negligence if it engaged in a negligent act or omission through breach of a duty of care owed to Stein, causing Stein to suffer injury. Stein hopes to establish the element of negligent act through the doctrine of negligence per se, which other states recognize but which the Supreme Court of State *X* has never squarely adopted. Under the strongest version of the doctrine of negligence per se, proof of Leek Chemical Co.'s violation of the HMTA, a safety statute, would conclusively establish the element of negligent act.

To help her evaluate proposed jury instructions at the close of the trial in Stein's lawsuit, the trial judge requests briefing and oral argument on the question of whether State *X* recognizes the doctrine of negligence per se. Stein has the following authority at his disposal:

(1) abundant case law from other states recognizing the doctrine of negligence per se in a variety of contexts;

(2) an opinion from the highest appellate court of neighboring State Y approving application of the doctrine of negligence per se to a violation of a similar hazardous materials transportation statute in State Y;

(3) an opinion of the State X intermediate court of appeals holding that evidence of violation of the State X speed limit laws, proximately causing injury, supported a jury verdict of negligence, even in the absence of any other evidence of lack of due care;

(4) an opinion of the Supreme Court of State X holding that a transporter of regulated hazardous materials may be criminally liable under the HMTA for violations of that act, even if the illegal transportation does not result in any accident or injury.

Discuss the relative strength of these authorities to Stein's position. How should Stein's attorney use each authority, if at all?

B. ANALYSIS OF LEGAL STANDARDS

In some legal disputes, formulation of the applicable legal rules is a simple task: The applicable laws are easily identified and their general content is clear, at least in the abstract. For example, a dispute over the jury's authority to grant punitive damages in a tort action may be governed by clearly defined rules in the forum state's case law. If so, you could summarize those rules directly and concisely in an office memorandum:

In this state, a jury may award punitive damages against a person who has committed a tort with either (1) intent to cause injury or (2) reckless disregard for the risk of harm to others. Unless exceptional circumstances justify the risky conduct, a person acts recklessly if he consciously engages in conduct that he knows or should know poses a great risk of harm to others. *Ray v. Bradbury* . . .

In such a dispute, once the facts are found, any significant uncertainty about the outcome of the dispute typically derives from a mixed question of fact and law: Do the particular facts of the case satisfy the legal rule? Although analysis of such a mixed question necessarily involves refinement of the content of the legal rule, it also requires careful evaluation of the facts. Thus, assuming that *Ray v. Bradbury* reflects current policy in the jurisdiction, the tortfeasor will not likely dispute the abstract rule governing the availability of punitive damages. More substantially in issue is a mixed question of fact and law: Do the facts of the case reflect recklessness or an intent to injure and thus satisfy the legal rule?

In other disputes, however, the parties may raise substantial issues about the fundamental content of applicable legal rules, such as the issue of whether the word "sex" in Title VII refers narrowly to gender or more broadly to gender and sexual orientation. Compared to the dispute described in the preceding paragraph, resolution of this question requires less comprehensive fact analysis and more thorough analysis of the content of the rule at a fairly general level. An even more extreme example is provided by the question of whether a court should change the course of the common law by adopting a new theory of tort liability for wrongful discharge of an employee. Although such a question would arise in the context of the facts of a particular dispute, the question of whether to adopt a new common law theory of liability would be analyzed as a nearly pure question of law.

If an issue in a brief, office memorandum, or answer to a law school essay examination raises a question about the fundamental content of a legal rule at a general level, you should analyze the legal rule thoroughly before engaging in substantial fact analysis. The discussion of common law and statutory law in Chapter 2 provides a foundation for the development of techniques of legal analysis. Three techniques are particularly important: (1) recognition of the hierarchical nature of authority, (2) consideration of policy concerns, and (3) synthesis of incremental authority.

1. Hierarchy of Authority

Constitutional law, statutory law, and common law form a hierarchy in descending order of priority: Assuming that the applicable state or federal constitution authorizes the exercise of state or federal power, a legislature can overrule or modify the common law by enacting statutory law. Accordingly, rather than assume that an issue is governed by common law, you should first consider the possible applicability of constitutional or statutory law.

If a statute applies, you should begin your research and analysis with the relevant language of the statute, even though it may be insufficiently narrow to clearly resolve the issue by itself. Only after you have studied the letter of the statute and its context within an act or a code system can you fully appreciate interpretive case law on the matter. The following passage from an office memorandum illustrates the hierarchy of authority and the focus on statutory language.

The Arizona Constitution grants municipalities the right to engage in industrial activities:

Constitution

The State of Arizona and each municipal corporation within the State of Arizona shall have the right to engage in industrial pursuits.

Ariz. Const. art. 2, §24. The Arizona Public Utilities statute more specifically grants municipal corporations the power to acquire water utility corporations "within or without its corporate limits":

Statute

[Municipal corporations may] engage in any business or enterprise which may be engaged in by persons by

virtue of a franchise from the municipal corporation, and may construct, purchase, acquire, own
and maintain within or without its corporate limits
any such business or enterprise.

Ariz. Rev. Stat. Ann. §9-511.

The statutory reference to corporate limits appears without qualification to permit a municipal
corporation to acquire utilities that provide service
outside the municipality's corporate limits. Arizona
case law, however, hints at a narrower interpretation
that recognizes two limitations on the acquisition
power.

First, it is unclear whether a city may acquire a   **Interpretive case
water company's property outside the city corporate   law**
limits unless the city has shown that it genuinely
and reasonably anticipates future growth into that
area. See *Sende Vista Water Co. v. City of Phoenix*,
617 P.2d 1158 (Ariz. Ct. App. 1980). In *Sende*,
. . .

In theory, the principle of analyzing statutory language before turning
to interpretive case law also applies to constitutional provisions, as illustrated
in the example above. As a practical matter, however, some constitutional
provisions are so general that their actual language may provide quite limited
guidance, and interpretive case law takes on special significance. For example,
the reference to "equal protection" in the fourteenth amendment to the
United States Constitution is purposefully vague; its generality invites the
courts to shape its contours in a way that best satisfies its underlying policies.
The mass of case law interpreting the Equal Protection Clause has embel-
lished this simple clause with rich detail. Accordingly, when researching
and analyzing an equal protection problem, you should not begin with a
grammatical analysis of the words "equal protection." Instead, after identifying the fourteenth amendment as the source of the clause, you could
appropriately turn immediately to interpretive case law.

Conversely, the eleventh amendment to the Constitution is actually too
specific to provide a good starting point for analysis. The actual language
of the eleventh amendment appears to bar federal suits against a state, but
only if brought by a noncitizen of that state:

> The Judicial power of the United States shall not be construed to extend
> to any suit in law or equity, commenced or prosecuted against one of the
> United States by Citizens of another State, or by Citizens or Subjects of any
> Foreign State.

Many scholars and court decisions, however, interpret this amendment to
simply express part of a more general common law principle of sovereign
immunity that applies with equal force to a suit against a state brought by

a citizen of that state.[13] Thus, your analysis of state sovereign immunity in federal courts should not dwell too long on the language of the eleventh amendment, but should turn quickly to interpretive case law.[14]

2. Policy Analysis

Almost by definition, policy analysis lies at the heart of most lawmaking. A legislature pronounces public policy when it enacts public legislation within the framework of applicable constitutions. Any such enactment represents elected officials' choice among alternative means to address the socio-economic needs of the jurisdiction. Not surprisingly, the search for legislative intent typically does not end with a conclusive grammatical analysis of language or with a reference to specific and definitive legislative history. Instead, statutory interpretation most often takes the form of a multifaceted analysis reconciling the statutory language, legislative history, and general rules of construction with the apparent policies or purposes on which the legislation is based. Constitutions are less specific than most statutes and are not so easily amended; consequently, analysis of policy and general purpose often is even more important in constitutional interpretation.

Similarly, because common law rules are largely a reflection of judicial recognition of community needs, habits, or customs, they constitute the judiciary's pronouncement of public policy within the framework of constitutional and statutory law. Any question about further development of the common law, such as adoption of a new theory of common law liability or elimination of a common law basis for damages, necessarily raises policy questions about the effect that the new rule will have on the community and about the relationship of the new rule to legislative policies.

The arguments and conclusions that you develop in response to a policy question depend in part on the values that you apply to the problem. A policy argument may be based on moral, economic, political, institutional, or other social values.[15] When developing or evaluating a legal argument, you should identify the values underlying the legislative purpose and judicial policy of applicable authorities, and you should determine which policy arguments would best advance your client's position.[16]

---

13. See, e.g., Hans v. Louisiana, 134 U.S. 1 (1890); Theodore Eisenberg, Civil Rights Legislation 224 (1981).

14. One author has warned:

> Although the eleventh amendment provides something to read when contemplating a state's immunity from suit in federal court . . . , it is a trap for those who dig no further.

Eisenberg, supra note 13, at 221.

15. P. S. Atiyah & Robert S. Summers, Form and Substance in Anglo-American Law 5 (1987) (defining "substantive reasons" for legal decisions); see also Robert S. Summers, Two Types of Substantive Reasons: The Core of a Theory of Common-Law Justification, 63 Cornell L. Rev. (1978).

16. See generally J. M. Balkin, The Crystalline Structure of Legal Thought, 39 Rutgers L. Rev. 1 (1986).

=========== E X E R C I S E   4 - 3 ===========

1. *Surrogate Motherhood and Baby Selling*

State *X* has a criminal "baby selling" statute making it a felony "to relinquish custody of one's child to another for payment, or to pay or offer to pay another to relinquish custody of the other's child." What is the likely policy behind this statute, and what kind of conduct should be its primary concern? In light of your understanding of the statutory policy, should a court interpret the statute to prohibit a surrogate mother from charging a fee for carrying the fertilized ovum of another couple to full term and surrendering custody of the child to the couple after birth? Does the analysis change if the one charging the fee agrees to artificial insemination of her own ovum, thus making her the biological mother? Should the state enact new legislation more specifically addressing surrogate mother contracts?

2. *Job Security*

State *X* has long recognized the common law "at-will" rule, which permits an employer to discharge an employee for any reason, or for no reason at all, so long as the employment contract does not provide the employee with job security. Unionized employees in State *X* have used the collective bargaining process to negotiate labor agreements that include a promise by the employer not to fire any employee except for "just cause." Almost all nonunion employees, however, lack the bargaining power to negotiate such agreements; their employment contracts are terminable at the will of either party and therefore do not restrict the employer's discretion to discharge employees. Most employers' discretion to discharge is limited by labor and nondiscrimination statutes, but those laws prohibit a fairly narrow range of conduct.

What are the policy implications of a new law that would further restrict the right of an employer to discharge employees, even in the absence of a contractual provision for job security? Assume that two laws are under consideration: One would prohibit an employer from discharging any employee except for "good cause"; the other would prohibit an employer more narrowly from discharging an employee for a reason that contravenes an important public policy reflected in existing legislation or case law. Does either proposed law express a desirable public policy? Should a court adopt one of these standards as a new theory of common law tort liability? Should such lawmaking be left to the legislature? Which of the laws is the best vindication of public policy? If the first law is adopted, how should "good cause" be defined? If the second law is adopted, how would it expand existing legal rights and duties?

---

3. *Synthesis of Incremental Law*

In few research problems is the legal standard set forth in a single, clearly controlling authority. More often, the legal rules that apply to a dispute are the products of a synthesis of multiple authorities. For example, a Reconstruction era civil rights statute imposes liability for racial discrimination in private contractual relations,[17] but its application is tempered by constitutional interests in privacy and free association.[18] Thus, the true reach of the statute is defined both by the language of the statute and by the first amendment to the federal Constitution.

Synthesis of authority is particularly important in case analysis. Whether it interprets statutory law or develops common law, case law is inherently incremental. Courts express their legal analyses in the context of individual controversies, and an isolated holding in a judicial opinion is often too narrow to support an accurate prediction about how the decision will influence subsequent cases. Instead, as discussed further in Chapter 7, a series of cases addressing a topic in a variety of factual contexts will support a generalization about the case law. The generalization can then be applied more broadly to a wide range of cases.

4. Developing Arguments for Both Sides

With few exceptions, essay examinations and office memorandum assignments call on you to present a balanced discussion of legal issues. Although one party may be identified as your client, your professor or supervising attorney expects you to explore the weaknesses of the client's claims and defenses as well as the strengths.

When writing a brief, you should not take such a balanced approach; instead, you must advocate your client's position and discredit your opponent's arguments. Nonetheless, to maximize your own advocacy, you must anticipate and evaluate the arguments of your opponent. You might express that more balanced analysis in an office memorandum, or you might simply contemplate it as you outline the arguments for your brief.

Thus, to analyze a legal dispute effectively, you must develop arguments for both sides of the dispute. In synthesizing case law, you should consider alternative formulations of the general principles that emerge from individual holdings. Similarly, in analyzing statutory language, you should consider intrinsic and extrinsic aids that support alternative interpretations.

For example, the common law of negligence imposes tort liability on a person who proximately causes injury to another by breaching a duty of care owed to the injured person. As a specific application of this tort law, physicians in most circumstances are liable for injuries caused by their failure to exercise reasonable skill and care in their practices. Suppose that the courts of State *X* have also developed a common law doctrine of strict liability for injuries resulting from ultrahazardous activities, but they have refused to apply this doctrine even to experimental medical practices. Against this background of common law, State *X* might enact a statute that makes

---

17. 42 U.S.C. §1981 (1988) (as interpreted in Runyon v. McCrary, 427 U.S. 160 (1976)).

18. See id.; cf. Board of Directors of Rotary Int'l v. Rotary Club of Duarte, 481 U.S. 537 (1987) (application of state antidiscrimination statute to Rotary Club did not violate club members' rights to free association).

any "commercial enterprise strictly liable" for injuries caused by its use "of any toxic material."

Now suppose that a medical patient in this state died from a reaction to general anesthesia triggered by the patient's rare disorder of the nervous system. Much of the legal dispute in a malpractice action brought by the patient's estate might center around the applicability of the statute. Assuming that anesthesiology is "a commercial enterprise," if the anesthetic is "a toxic material" within the meaning of the statute, the anesthesiologist or her employer would be statutorily liable without regard to the care that she exercised. In contrast, a companion claim based on common law negligence would require an inquiry into the duty of care that the anesthesiologist owed and the degree of care she actually exercised.

In preparing for advocacy, counsel for either side of this dispute would want to evaluate arguments for both sides on the question of the applicability of the statute. For example, without going beyond the face of the statute, counsel for the estate could argue that the statutory requirement of "toxic materials" is satisfied in this case because the ordinary meaning of "toxic" is "poisonous," and the anesthetic acted like a poison on the nervous system of the patient. Counsel for the estate would also want to anticipate a strong counterargument: It is doubtful that the legislature intended to inhibit physicians' use of substances that produce medically beneficial results in almost all cases in which they are administered; rather, the statutory term "toxic materials" is likely intended to apply only to materials that are generally harmful to all persons, such as potent acids or pesticides. After formulating and evaluating the anesthesiologist's probable counterargument, counsel for the estate should try to present the estate's argument in a way that will reduce the impact of the counterargument.

V. FACT ANALYSIS—APPLICATION OF LAW TO FACTS

A. BASIC PATTERNS

At trial, the critical issues often are questions of purely historical fact, such as the question whether the party with the burden of persuasion has proved that an employer exclaimed "Women can't perform this job!" when he rejected a woman's application for employment. As explored in later chapters, appellate courts will defer to some degree to the factual findings of a jury or trial judge; therefore, issues on appeal inevitably contain a more substantial element of law. However, even nearly pure questions of law are developed in the context of particular disputes and with an appreciation for the probable facts of future disputes. More importantly, most disputes present nontrivial questions about whether the facts satisfy the applicable legal standards, such as whether certain acts of preparation leading up to a murder satisfy the "premeditation" requirement of a first-degree murder statute.

A pattern should emerge from your treatment of facts in an office memorandum or brief. First, you will state all the important facts of the dispute at or near the beginning of the document. Second, you will separately analyze groups of facts as the minor premises of deductive arguments in the discussion section of a memorandum or the argument section of a brief. In that section, after discussing the legal rule applicable to a particular issue, you will discuss or argue whether the relevant facts satisfy the legal rule. You and your professor will follow a similar pattern in an essay examination: Your professor will state all the facts in the essay question, and you will analyze groups of facts as the minor premises of deductive arguments in your examination answer.

If your assignment does not call for great depth of analysis, you might directly explain why particular facts support or undermine the application of a legal rule. Suppose, for example, that you are writing an office memorandum analyzing the claims of a client seeking punitive damages, as introduced in previous examples in this chapter. After stating the legal rule that a malicious or reckless tortfeasor may be liable for punitive damages, you could identify the facts relevant to this issue and explain how each supports or defeats application of the legal rule:

Facts showing no intent	We have no evidence that Con Motor Co. maliciously intended to cause injury when it designed the Firebird sports car. In fact, our notes of the May meeting of the board of directors shows that the board members genuinely hoped that the risky design would not cause accidents.
Facts showing recklessness	However, we do have evidence of recklessness. Con's Chief Engineer informed the board of directors of her opinion that placement of the gas tank near the rear exterior of the car would create a risk of deadly explosion in even minor rear-end collisions. Yet, the directors approved that design solely because it would save production costs of $100/car. In so doing, Con's directors knowingly created a great risk of death or terrible injury to consumers without any socially significant justification.

B. DEVELOPING ARGUMENTS FOR BOTH SIDES

As with your analysis of more abstract legal rules, your fact analysis in an essay examination answer or in an office memorandum ought to explore arguments for both sides of the dispute. Similarly, when writing a brief, you should consider your opponent's factual arguments as you develop your own. In the typical dispute, some facts will support application of the legal rule and others will suggest that the legal rule is not satisfied. Still other facts may be used in different ways to support both positions. By balancing and weighing the facts, you can reach at least a qualified conclusion about whether the legal rule is satisfied.

This can be illustrated by extending one of the examples in the previous section on analysis of legal rules. If the parties dispute an anesthesiologist's liability on a claim of common law negligence, an office memorandum might call for analysis of the following facts:

1. The anesthesiologist informed a patient scheduled for heart surgery of the advantages and risks associated with the three most appropriate anesthetics. On the basis of relative costs, the patient rejected the safest anesthetic in favor of a generally safe and more widely used anesthetic.
2. The anesthesiologist administered general anesthesia without assistance, before the surgical team had arrived and while the circulating nurse was occupied with another patient.
3. While administering general anesthesia, the anesthesiologist concentrated intensely on gauges on her equipment that measured the patient's intake of the anesthetic.
4. The anesthesiologist did not maintain visual contact with the patient or with equipment monitoring the patient's vital signs; as a consequence, she failed to terminate the intake of anesthetic until ten seconds after the first visible signs of an adverse reaction.
5. The patient suffered from a rare disorder of the nervous system that produced the fatal reaction to the anesthetic.
6. The patient died within a minute of the administration of general anesthesia.

The facts in the first paragraph suggest that the anesthesiologist followed a reasonable procedure in prescribing the anesthetic. Indeed, the facts in paragraph 5 suggest that the patient's unusual disorder, rather than the anesthesiologist's conduct, precipitated the fatal reaction. Moreover, the facts in paragraph 3 support an argument that the anesthesiologist used at least reasonable care in administering the anesthetic, because she concentrated intensely on an obviously important function.

In addition to providing some support for a finding of reasonable care, however, the facts of paragraph 5 emphasize the need for special care in administering the anesthetic. Moreover, the facts of paragraph 2 support an argument that the anesthesiologist breached a duty of care in administering the anesthetic without assistance. Although the facts of paragraph 3 reflect the anesthesiologist's genuine concern about the patient's potential sensitivity to anesthesia, they also raise a question about the appropriate focus of the anesthesiologist's attention. Finally, the facts of paragraph 4 support an argument that the anesthesiologist acted carelessly in focusing her attention so narrowly on the intake gauge.

To complete your deductive reasoning in an office memorandum, you must discuss whether the facts establish a breach of the applicable duty of care, thus satisfying the legal rule that defines an element of the cause of action. Because the facts in this case support opposing arguments, different legal analysts might reasonably reach different conclusions, depending on the significance the analysts assign to particular facts. Regardless of the author's conclusion, however, the office memorandum should present the best factual arguments for both sides of the dispute. Of course, an advocate writing a brief would emphasize the facts supporting her argument and would develop her argument in a way that lessened the impact of anticipated counterarguments.

VI. REACHING CONCLUSIONS

The final element of deductive reasoning is a conclusion derived from the law of your major premise and the facts of your minor premise. When writing a brief, you obviously must state a firm conclusion for each argument that you present. Your conclusions represent the critical points that the court must accept before granting your client the relief that he seeks.

You may hesitate to state conclusions in the more nearly neutral analysis of an office memorandum or essay examination answer, particularly if the dispute presents close questions. Nonetheless, most supervising attorneys and professors will want you to take a position and to reveal your best judgment about the probable outcome of each issue. If necessary, you may hedge your conclusions with qualifiers such as "probably," but you should remember to complete your deductive reasoning by stating a conclusion for each issue:

> On these facts, a jury likely will find that Con Motor Co. acted recklessly, permitting the jury to award punitive damages.

In some cases, you may find it appropriate to make your conclusion contingent on your ability to establish critical facts or law:

> Assuming that we can prove that most hospitals require a team of at least two personnel to administer anesthesia, a jury will almost certainly find that Humana Hospital was negligent in this case.

VII. SUMMARY

To analyze a legal problem, you should

(1) identify the **issue**,
(2) state the legal **rule** or rules that will help you resolve the issue,
(3) **apply** the rule to the relevant **facts**, and
(4) reach a **conclusion** on the question of whether the facts satisfy the legal rule.

A single dispute between two parties may present several issues. To achieve an appropriate scope of analysis, you must judge which issues and subissues are sufficiently significant and material to warrant discussion and which are sufficiently tangential to warrant exclusion or summary treatment.

Whenever the law or fact analysis is in doubt, you must evaluate arguments for both sides of the dispute. To evaluate arguments about the applicable legal rules, you should consider

(1) the hierarchy of primary authority,
(2) synthesis of authorities,
(3) policy analysis, and
(4) the relative strength of different kinds of case law as precedent.

Always state a conclusion for each issue, even in the analysis in an office memorandum or examination answer.

═══════ E X E R C I S E   4 - 4 ═══════

This and later chapters of this book will introduce you to an integrated process of

(1) case analysis,
(2) synthesis of cases in an outline, and
(3) flexible application of deductive reasoning in applying principles to new sets of facts, such as those in examination questions.

The following exercises are designed to introduce you to these processes on a level that should require no formal training or knowledge of special legal rules. Follow the directions of the exercises, use your common sense, and express your answers in simple, concise language.

1. *Case Analysis*

In each of the three cases below, try to derive a lesson or a rule from the case that would help guide the central character, Vihn Ly, in his future actions regarding speed limits on streets and highways. State this point in a simple sentence or two, including a brief statement of the probable policy justifications for the rule. If you wish, you may also briefly describe special facts that help illustrate the rule. In the second and third cases, you may also consider commenting briefly on ways in which the case compares or contrasts with the preceding case or cases.

In this exercise, do not concern yourself with the question of whether Mr. Ly obeyed or violated the speed limit. Instead, focus on the facts and policies that justify the establishment of different speed limits in different settings.

In the first case analysis below, the exercise is completed as an example.

a. The Case of the School Zone

Vihn Ly recently immigrated to the United States, enrolled in a community college in Phoenix, Arizona, and obtained a driver's permit. While driving throughout the state, he carefully surveyed his surroundings so that he could quickly learn the customs and rules of American driving.

When approaching an elementary school on a two-lane residential street at 8:15 on Monday morning, Ly noticed dozens of children laughing and running in the schoolyard, as well as a few children walking on the sidewalk toward the school. He also noticed a sign stating "15 mph when school is in session." Before Ly could slow down, however, a police officer pulled him over and cited him for driving 25 miles per hour.

Sample Statement of Lesson: The speed limit in an elementary school zone in a residential neighborhood is 15 mph when school is in session, probably because the risk of children running into the road is particularly great at that time and place. In this case, that risk was underscored by presence of numerous children in the playground and on the sidewalk.

b. The Case of the Urban Freeway

Later that morning, Ly entered the interstate freeway from the center of Phoenix. Within the city limits, the divided freeway meandered through the city in gentle curves, varying in width from three to four lanes in each direction. It was heavily traveled, with cars and trucks frequently changing lanes and merging near the numerous freeway entrances and exits, some of which were only one mile apart from the next set of entrances and exits.

Ly was traveling 60 miles per hour and noticed that many cars were passing him. Nonetheless, he slowed down when he noticed a sign stating "55 mph." He was not anxious to repeat his experience in the school zone.

Lesson?

c. The Case of the Rural Freeway

As Ly proceeded south on the freeway toward Tucson, he left the Phoenix city limits and passed through nearly 100 miles of rural, nonresidential desert. The freeway was mostly straight and level, varying in width from two to three lanes in each direction. Traffic was light, and several consecutive freeway entrances and exits were separated by ten to fifteen miles. Ly noticed a sign posting a speed limit of 65 miles per hour, and he increased his speed accordingly.

Lesson?

2. *Synthesis and Outlining*

Use the three cases in problem 1 above to generalize about legislative policy in setting speed limits on different roads. As an example of one approach, try the following:

First, think about the factors that seem to influence the setting of speed limits. Your stated policy justifications in each of the cases should help you here. Then, try to make a single statement that helps to explain all of the speed limits described in the cases. As an example, you might complete the following sentences:

> Speed limits on streets and freeways range from 15 mph to 65 mph, depending upon such factors as . . . . These factors reflect general policy concerns for . . . .

For this exercise, you should not concern yourself with the question whether Ly obeyed or violated the speed limits in each of the cases. To keep this exercise simple, focus your attention only on the speed limits and the justifications for them. Of course, quite apart from Ly's obeying or violating the speed limits, the particular circumstances of each case will help you identify the justifications for the speed limits.

Once you have constructed your statement, illustrate it with a series of three examples. Each example should be a brief summary of the critical information in each of the three cases. The information is critical if it helps to illuminate the point that you make in your general statement.

For example, your series of illustrations could take the following form:

Speed limits on streets and freeways range from 15 mph to 65 mph, depending upon such factors as . . . . These factors reflect an overarching policy concern for . . . .

1. *Example*—In The Case of the School Zone, the speed limit in a residential elementary school zone was set at 15 mph while school was in session, because . . . .

2. *Example*—In contrast, in The Case of the Rural Freeway, ...

3. *Example*—In The Case of the Urban Freeway, ...

3. *Predicting the Outcome of a New Case*

Just before reaching Tucson, Ly exited the freeway and drove on a straight, level two-lane undivided highway through desert. Side roads intersected the highway every few miles. The traffic was light, and the area was sparsely populated, but several homes bordered the highway over a 10-mile stretch.

One hundred yards ahead, a police officer sat in his car at a stop sign where a side road intersected the highway. Ly was traveling 50 mph. He was eager to obey the speed limit, but he had forgotten to note the posted speed limit a few miles back.

In the face of uncertainty about the speed limit, Ly prudently slowed down as he approached the officer. However, the incident stimulated his curiosity about the speed limit.

Place yourself in Ly's position. Use your general statement in problem 2 above as a guide for guessing the speed limit for the highway. Apply the factors that you derived from each of the previous cases to the facts of this new case. Then, reach some reasonable conclusion about the probable speed limit. Do not look for some magic number as the single correct answer. Simply make a reasonable estimate based on the other cases, and support your estimate with good analysis of the policies and the facts.

CHAPTER
5

Introduction to Writing Style

I. GENERAL APPROACH

The two most important characteristics of good legal writing style are clarity and conciseness. The importance of clarity in legal writing should be obvious: Your legal memorandum will not enlighten, nor will your brief persuade, unless the reader of each can understand it. To appreciate the significance of conciseness, you need only consider the time pressures that a supervising attorney or a judge faces; neither has time to glean from 20 pages ideas that you could have clearly expressed in 10.[1]

The dual goals of clarity and conciseness are often compatible: Making a draft more concise by omitting surplus words and by organizing your points more efficiently likely will enhance clarity as well. At the margin, however, further conciseness may come only at the expense of clarity; in those circumstances, you must give priority to clarity.

II. THE PERSPECTIVE OF THE LEGAL WRITER

Law students often complain that the emphasis on clarity and conciseness in legal writing courses compels them to abandon the literary eloquence

---

1. See, e.g., Reliance Ins. Co. v. Sweeney Corp., Maryland, 792 F.2d 1137, 1139 (D.C. Cir. 1986) ("this court encourages short, tightly argued briefs in all cases, regardless of their complexity"); Morgan v. South Bend Community School Corp., 797 F.2d 471, 480 (7th Cir. 1986) ("A [page] limitation induces the advocate to write tight prose, which helps his client's cause."); Westinghouse Elec. Corp. v. NLRB, 809 F.2d 419, 424-425 (7th Cir. 1987) (imposing $1,000 penalty on counsel for evading federal rule limiting the number of pages of its opening brief).

that they strove so hard to develop in college and to replace it with a dry, uniform style. They may overstate their complaint; effective legal writing reflects application of principles of good writing generally. Nonetheless, as an inevitable consequence of the substance and purpose of legal documents, the substance and style of legal writing does indeed differ from other kinds of writing.

For example, consider how different writers might treat the subject of a male employer's sexual harassment of a female subordinate. A poet might try to create an image of the pain and frustration of the victim of the harassment, so vivid an image that readers who had never experienced sexual harassment could appreciate the victim's plight.[2] A writer for a political journal might describe the specific incident as a symptom of more general oppression within a sexist society. A novelist might describe the harassment in particularly dramatic prose, perhaps as a vehicle of character development or perhaps purely to engage or shock the reader.

On the other hand, an associate for the firm representing the victim of the harassment is understandably preoccupied with the legal significance of the employer's actions. In preparing an office memorandum, the associate will analyze whether the harassment constituted "extreme and outrageous conduct," thus satisfying an element of a claim under the tort of intentional infliction of emotional distress. The extent of the injury suffered by the victim will interest the associate mainly as an indication of the damages that the victim can recover. Moreover, the associate may discuss events or circumstances that other writers would ignore completely. For example, the associate may note that the employer employs only 12 employees and therefore is not a covered "employer" for purposes of Title VII of the Civil Rights Act of 1964.[3]

The different perspectives of these writers necessarily influence their writing styles. The poet's meaning may be obscured in the interest of "avoiding dull exposition" and of gaining dramatic effect through rhythm and metaphor.[4] Similarly, the novelist may seek to entertain or stimulate the reader by resorting to elegant variation or other deliberate ambiguity.[5] But the legal writer can seldom afford to entertain at the expense of communicating clearly. On occasion, legal writers may have legitimate reasons for ambiguity, but deliberate ambiguity should be the exception, not the rule. A supervising attorney is not interested in dwelling on each sentence of an office memorandum to divine its meaning as he might dwell on each line of a poem. Similarly, a judge will not likely be persuaded by a brief that she doesn't fully comprehend, even though it entertains her.

This does not mean that lawyers must always write from a legal perspective. If you desire to retain or develop literary eloquence, you may write poetry by night and easily adapt your writing style to the requirements of

---

2. Cf. Elisabeth W. Schneider, Poems and Poetry 3 (1964) (discussing the difficulty of transferring an "experience whole and alive into the mind, emotions, and sensations of another person").

3. See 42 U.S.C. §2000e(b) (1988).

4. See Schneider, supra note 2, at 25-26.

5. See William Strunk, Jr. & E. B. White, The Elements of Style 79 (3d ed. 1979) ("There are occasions when obscurity serves a literary yearning, if not a literary purpose. . . .").

the law office by day. Nor does it mean that legal writing must be dull and dry. Clear, concrete, concise writing can and should be active, vivid, and engaging. Indeed, the persuasive effect of a brief may be enhanced with a telling metaphor or an unusually dramatic phrase.

Moreover, the legal perspective does not doom legal writers to absolute uniformity of style. The goals of clear communication or persuasion leave room for individuality. Indeed, you should approach rules of writing style in much the same way that you approach legal rules: You should extend the application of the rules no further than necessary to serve the policies that support the rules. Even seemingly inflexible conventions of punctuation or sentence structure may simply reflect a desire for clarity or proper emphasis, leaving room for writers' discretion in how best to achieve those objectives.

III. A POLICY-ORIENTED APPROACH

Many rules of composition are nothing more than conventions that reflect generalities about the best way to achieve clear, concise writing with effective emphasis and flow. Even the traditional rule against splitting infinitives appears to have given way to a more flexible discretionary approach: "Some infinitives seem to improve on being split, just as a stick of round stovewood does."[6] You will do well to familiarize yourself with rules of composition, including the recommendations summarized in Chapter 11, as general guides to achieving the objectives of clarity and conciseness rather than as ends in themselves.

For example, many writers believe that they may never start a sentence with "However," because teachers or editors told them of a rule against such placement. But it is difficult to justify an inflexible rule to that effect; instead, the placement of transitional words such as "however" likely is influenced by considerations of emphasis and flow in the sentence. Those considerations often call for placement of "however" at a natural breaking point in mid-sentence, because it subordinates "however" as a parenthetic transition guide, and it permits more substantive parts of the sentence to enjoy the prominence of the position at the beginning of the sentence:

The statute of frauds does not apply, however, because Vasquez could have performed the contract within one year.

However, if you wish to draw immediate attention to the change of direction signaled by the transition word or phrase, placement at the beginning of the sentence, as in this one, is perfectly appropriate.

The history of the debate about the "serial" comma rule further illustrates the benefits of understanding the justifications for rules or conventions of composition. According to the traditional rule, you should use a comma to separate each element of a series of three or more things, as in "meat,

---

6. Id. at 58, 78.

vegetables, and dairy products." During the "new English" and "new math" movements of the 1960s, grade schoolteachers began teaching a discretionary trend to omit the last comma of the series on the ground that the conjunction "and" or "or" adequately separates the last two elements of the series. The trend never permanently displaced the traditional rule: Strunk and White continued to advocate use of the final comma,[7] and many grade schools eventually returned to the traditional teachings. Unfortunately, many students had in the meantime adopted an inflexible practice of always omitting the final comma.

In fact, omitting the final comma may hamper clarity in a series in which some elements have multiple subelements, such as "fish, fruits or grains and dairy products." Depending on the location of a final comma, this could mean either:

(1) {fish}, {fruits or grains}, and {dairy products}, or
(2) {fish}, {fruits}, or {grains and dairy products}.

Subtle, temporary ambiguities in structure sometimes arise even if the series uses only the conjunction "and" and not the disjunctive conjunction "or."[8]

Armed with these insights, you can choose either of two approaches to the comma controversy, depending on the emphasis that you place on different policies of composition. If you value consistency as well as clarity, you could reasonably adopt the traditional convention of always using the final comma, because you know that it will sometimes be necessary for clarity and will never cause confusion.[9] Alternatively, if you prefer to restrict punctuation to the necessary minimum, you could exercise stylistic discretion to insert the final comma when it is necessary for clarity and to omit it otherwise.

When widely accepted, this flexible, policy-oriented approach to composition could end countless hours of office arguments over the proper "rule" governing the final comma in a series. Until then, you should be prepared to explain your reasoning to reviewers who dogmatically insist either that the final comma is either incorrect or mandatory in every context.

IV. AUDIENCE AND PURPOSE

In every legal document, you should adapt your writing style to achieve the purpose of the document and to suit the needs of your intended audience. Many of the chapters in this book thoroughly examine this feature of writing style in the context of essay examinations, office memoranda, briefs, and letters. An overview here will serve to introduce some fundamental principles.

---

7. Id. at 1-2 (1st ed. 1959); id. at 2 (2d ed. 1972); id. at 2 (3d ed. 1979).
8. See, e.g., Bryan A. Garner, The Elements of Legal Style 18 (1991) (providing illustrations).
9. Id. at 17 ("Always Use the Serial Comma"). This author adopts this approach.

A. PURPOSE

Many legal documents can be classified as having either of two essential purposes: (1) to communicate a balanced analysis, or (2) to persuade. With few exceptions, essay examination answers, office memoranda, and advice letters to clients fall into the first category. Ordinarily, the purpose of each is to help your reader understand the strengths and the weaknesses of a legal claim or defense. Briefs to a court and demand letters to an opposing party, on the other hand, fall into the second category. The purpose of a brief is to persuade a judge or panel of judges to make a ruling that favors your client. The purpose of a demand letter is to persuade another party to take some practical action, such as pay a debt, drop a claim, or cease some activity that is causing injury to your client.

You should adapt the content and style of the writing in each of your documents to suit these distinct purposes. For example, in an office memorandum and an advice letter, you must communicate to your supervising attorney and to your client the strengths as well as the weaknesses of your client's claims or defenses. Thus, if your client seeks to prove that her employer breached an employment contract by discharging her without good cause, you should candidly reveal to her and to your supervisor that the contract language is ambiguous on that point:

> Each of the five grounds for discharge specifically listed in section IX of the employment contract describes some kind of misconduct or unsatisfactory performance by the employee. However, the prefatory phrase "such as" suggests that the list is not exhaustive, but illustrative. If so, the employer may argue that he retained the right to fire an employee for any reason and that he listed only the most obvious reasons in the contract.
>
> To establish that the contract requires just cause for dismissal, we should. . . .

In contrast, in your brief to a court, you will attempt to persuade a judge or panel of judges to interpret the contract language in a way that limits grounds for discharge. Accordingly, you should adopt a writing style that reflects confidence in your client's position:

> Section IX of the contract limits grounds for discharge to employee misconduct or poor performance. Even if the five grounds listed in section IX are illustrative rather than exhaustive, as argued by the defendant, they all illustrate cases in which the employer has good cause for terminating the employment contract. Thus, section IX describes a limited category of grounds for discharge that does not justify the arbitrary discharge in this case. . . .

B. AUDIENCE

Even when you seek to achieve similar purposes with different documents, you may need to adapt your writing style to the needs of each audience. For example, in both an office memorandum and an advice letter, your purpose is to present a balanced analysis of your client's claims and defenses. However, the readers of each document may vary greatly in legal sophistication. The experienced attorney who reads your office memorandum will appreciate your use of fundamental legal terminology and legal authority, as in this excerpt from an analysis of a client's defense in a civil rights action:

> Even if the district court denies Officer Tippett's motion for summary judgment, he can file an interlocutory appeal on the issue of qualified immunity. See *Mitchell v. Forsyth*, 472 U.S. 511, 524-530 (1985).

On the other hand, your client, Police Officer Tippett, presumably has little or no legal training in pretrial and appellate civil procedure. Accordingly, in an advice letter to Officer Tippett on the same issue, you should explain your analysis in nonlegal terms:

> Even if the trial court denies your request to dismiss the action against you before trial, you need not face a trial immediately. Under federal law, you can immediately appeal the trial court's rejection of your immunity defense. In the meantime, the trial will be delayed while the appellate court determines whether your asserted conduct was indeed sufficiently reasonable to warrant granting you immunity from liability for damages.

In some cases, your task is complicated by the presence of multiple purposes and audiences. You can best explore these matters further in later chapters, in the context of thorough examination of particular documents.

V. CONCLUSION

This introduction to writing style completes the discussion in Part I of method in legal analysis and writing. This chapter and Chapters 10-12 develop and describe a method of approaching and resolving problems of composition, much as Chapters 2-4 describe a method of approaching legal problems.

Chapters 10-12 thoroughly examine problems of organization and writing style in the context of office memoranda and briefs. You may benefit by glancing at selected topics in those chapters before moving on to Part II of this book. However, because problems in writing style are often closely linked with problems in legal method and analysis, you can profitably delay close examination of Chapters 10-12 until you have studied both Parts I and II.

E X E R C I S E   5 - 1

Examine your previous education and experiences in writing. Consider whether the special characteristics of legal writing will require you to depart from writing styles that you have successfully used in other contexts. Use this self-examination to help prepare you for constructive criticism from your writing instructors.

WRITING IN LAW SCHOOL—FROM CASE BRIEFS TO EXAMINATIONS

6

Case Analysis

I. STUDY OF CASES

When preparing for law school classes or researching an office memorandum, you must engage in case analysis: the study of judicial decisions, mostly appellate, that resolve particular disputes. Although you will encounter case law differently in a law firm than in law school, you ultimately will perform similar analytic functions with it.

In a law firm, your supervising attorney typically will request a memorandum that addresses the rights and liabilities of parties to an actual pending dispute, and you will research and analyze case law with that dispute in mind. The reported judicial decisions that you find in the library are unedited opinions that often address multiple issues, some of which may be irrelevant to the dispute that is the subject of your office memorandum.

In one way, your task at law school is simpler: Rather than search for unedited opinions in the library, you will read opinions that are grouped in some logical fashion in a casebook and are edited to isolate selected issues. Just as you typically will analyze case law in a law firm to determine its applicability to a new dispute, you should analyze case law in law school with an appreciation for the way in which newly discovered legal principles might apply to facts other than those presented in the opinions. Professors will routinely test that facility with classroom hypotheticals and essay examinations.

II. PREPARING A CASE BRIEF

A. GENERAL APPROACH AND FORMAT

Both when researching a memorandum problem and when preparing for class, you should prepare "case briefs," written, analytic summaries of appellate opinions. Although you will eventually develop shorthand techniques for taking notes on cases that you find in the library or that are assigned in a casebook, you should prepare formal, thorough case briefs in the first semester to ensure that you develop skills of case analysis.

You should not be troubled if your instructors and textbooks recommend a variety of different formats for case briefs. All the formats include essentially the same information; they vary chiefly in emphasis and organization. Below are outlines of two sample formats. If necessary, you can modify either one of them to suit the particular requirements of a classroom instructor who might ask students to recite parts of a case in a different order.

A	B
1. Identification	1. Identification
2. Issue(s) and Holding(s)	2. Facts
3. Facts	3. Procedural History
4. Procedural History	4. Issue(s) and Holding(s)
5. Reasoning	5. Reasoning
6. Evaluation	6. Evaluation
7. Synthesis	7. Synthesis

Although format B is probably the more conventional of the two, format A has the advantage of forcing you to frame the legal issue before stating the facts, thus ensuring that you state the facts with an appreciation for their legal significance. The issue and holding also provide an effective overview of the case brief.

Whatever format you select, your first step in briefing a case is to read it completely before beginning to write. To state some elements of a case brief, you must first understand other elements, and the organization of an appellate opinion may differ from that of either case brief format outlined above. Indeed, some elements of the case brief may not appear explicitly anywhere in the opinion. Instead, the precise issue and holding of a decision may be only implicit in the court's statement of the facts, legal reasoning, and disposition. Consequently, before beginning to brief a case, you should read the entire opinion as many times as is necessary to understand all the elements of the case.

B. ELEMENTS OF A CASE BRIEF

1. Identification of the Case

Your case brief should begin with

(1) the name of the case, which is usually taken from the names of two adversary parties;[1]

---

1. In some *in rem* actions, a named party may be an object, such as money, a plot of land, or a ship. E.g., United States v. $129,374 in U.S. Currency, 769 F.2d 583 (9th Cir. 1985); Winooski Hydroelectric Co. v. Five Acres of Land, 769 F.2d 79 (2d Cir. 1985); Giannakos v. M/V Bravo Trader, 762 F.2d 1295 (5th Cir. 1985); see Oliver W. Holmes, Jr., The Common Law 28-30 (1923). In other cases, the case name will refer not to adversary parties but to events, relationships, or other subjects of proceedings. E.g., In re Garland Corp., 6 Bankr. 456 (Bankr. 1st Cir. 1980) (bankruptcy proceeding); In re: Validation of

(2) the jurisdiction, in the sense of the geographical and political body, within which the court sits;

(3) the level of the deciding court; and

(4) the date of decision.

For example, the following notes identify a 1904 decision of the Supreme Court of the State of Rhode Island:

Davis v. Smith (R.I. S. Ct. 1904)   ‖

You may also wish to jot down

(5) the citation to the reporters in which the full opinion appears in the library, to develop familiarity with citation form; and

(6) the page on which the case appears in the casebook (CB), to facilitate quick cross-reference between notes and casebook:

Davis v. Smith, 26 R.I. 129, 58 A. 630 (S. Ct. 1904), CB 387   ‖

These examples all identify the authoring court in *Davis v. Smith* as the court of last resort in Rhode Island. That information is significant: It shows that the court is not bound by lower court decisions within Rhode Island or by decisions in other states, although such decisions might provide persuasive authority.

The early date of the *Davis v. Smith* decision, 1904, helps identify the decision's place in Rhode Island law. As discussed in Chapter 3, any aging decision is vulnerable to changes in economic conditions, political and social attitudes, and the legal context over the years. Just such changes prompted the Rhode Island Supreme Court to overrule *Davis v. Smith* in 1967.[2]

The name of a case does not always clearly identify the original parties to the underlying dispute. A named party may be a representative of one of the original disputants or an assignee of its rights and obligations. For example, the dispute in *Hamer v. Sidway*[3] concerned the contract rights and obligations of William E. Story, Sr., and his nephew, William E. Story, 2d. The case name is taken from the parties to the lawsuit: the executor of the senior Story's estate and a person who acquired the nephew's contract rights through assignment.

Identifying the court may be problematic as well. *Hamer v. Sidway* is a decision of the Court of Appeals of New York, the court of last resort in New York. "Court of Appeals" is a label more commonly associated with an intermediate court of appeals, rather than the court of last resort. To add to the confusion, the decision in *Hamer v. Sidway* indicates that the Court of Appeals reviewed the judgment of the "general term" of the New York "Supreme Court," which had reversed the judgment of the "special term" of the Supreme Court. "Supreme Court" is a name that in most states would signify the court of last resort. In fact, the opening paragraph of its opinion in *Hamer v. Sidway* reveals that different terms of the New

---

Marriage of Francisco, 16 Indian L. Rep. 6113 (Navajo S. Ct. 1989) (marriage validation proceeding).

2. Rampone v. Wanskuck Bldgs., Inc., 227 A.2d 586 (R.I. 1967).

3. 27 N.E. 256 (N.Y. 1891).

York Supreme Court acted as the trial court and the intermediate appellate court.[4] Fortunately, most court systems use the more familiar labels "Court of Appeals" to refer to the intermediate appellate court and "Supreme Court" to refer to the court of last resort.

2. Issue and Holding

a. Issue

An "issue" is a material question of fact or law that arises from the claims, defenses, and arguments of the parties. An issue may be a question of law, such as whether Congress intended the term "sex" in §703(a) of Title VII of the Civil Rights Act of 1964 to encompass sexual orientation as well as gender. Except at the trial level, an issue rarely presents only a question of fact, such as whether the evidence shows that an employer exclaimed "Women can't perform this job!" when he rejected a woman's application for employment.

Perhaps most commonly, the issue before a trial or appellate court requires a combination of legal and factual analysis in the determination of whether the facts of a dispute satisfy a general legal rule. An example of such a question is whether certain conduct by an employer in fact created a discriminatory work environment, thus satisfying Title VII's rule regarding discrimination in "conditions . . . of employment." By applying the rule to the facts and reaching a conclusion, the court not only resolves the immediate dispute before it, it also refines the rule by adding more concrete substance to its abstract terms.

If you look for a concise statement of the issues in an appellate opinion, you may find only frustration. Courts do not always state the issues in simple terms before resolving them. When a court does formally state the issues, it may not state them with the narrowness and specificity required for development of analytic skills in the first semester. You may find clues to the precise question addressed by the court in the court's description of the trial court decision that it is reviewing, in its summary of the parties' arguments on appeal, in the emphasis it places on particular facts, and in its discussion of the law.

At a minimum, you should state an issue sufficiently narrowly that it identifies a substantive legal question that distinguishes the case from the bulk of case law in the casebook. In addition, you should specifically incorporate the facts of the case that are critical to the court's analysis and that therefore help to define the precedential effect of its decision.

For example, consider the following case summary, which is loosely

---

4. A recent guide identifies the current structure of the New York court system: The trial courts of general jurisdiction are the Supreme Court and the County Court. The intermediate appellate courts are the Appellate Divisions of Supreme Court and the Appellate Terms of Supreme Court. The Court of Appeals is the court of last resort. Kamla J. King & Judith Springberg, BNA's Directory of State Courts, Judges, and Clerks 232 (4th ed. 1992).

based on the procedural history and appellate disposition of a tort claim in *Wagenseller v. Scottsdale Memorial Hospital*:[5]

> Catherine Wagenseller (the employee) worked for Scottsdale Memorial Hospital (the employer) as a staff nurse under an employment contract of indefinite term. She alleged that her supervisor discharged her partly because she refused to participate in a humorous skit in which the participants "mooned" fellow hospital employees. The trial court found that the parties did not dispute any material facts and that the employer was entitled to summary judgment, which is judgment before trial, because the indefinite term of the employment contract made it terminable at the will of either party. Such a contract is terminable at any time and for any reason, or for no reason at all. The intermediate court of appeals affirmed.
>
> The state supreme court reversed and remanded to the trial court, deciding that an employer is liable in tort to an employee if it discharges the employee for a reason that contravenes a clear mandate of public policy. The state supreme court found such a mandate in a state criminal statute that prohibited certain acts of "indecent exposure." In discussing the sources of public policy, the court compared criminal statutes to other sources, such as common law: "Although we do not limit our recognition of the public policy exception to cases involving a violation of a criminal statute, we do believe that our duty will seldom be clearer than when such a violation is involved."

The following statement of the issue in *Wagenseller* is obviously too general:

Did the trial court correctly grant summary judgment for the defendant? ‖

This issue statement describes the trial court's disposition and the stage of the proceedings at which it made the disposition, facts that are within the procedural history of the case. Unfortunately, if your statement of the issue does no more than identify elements of the procedural history, you will not distinguish the case from hundreds of others in first-year casebooks. The procedural facts will certainly help you understand the decision. Moreover, the standards for summary judgment may even be the central issue in a case raising a dispute about rules of civil procedure. However, this case presents substantive questions of tort and perhaps contract law, and the issue statement should identify them.

The following statement of the issue is an improvement, because it identifies a substantive legal dispute:

Is an employer liable in tort for discharging an at-will employee for a ‖ ‖
reason that violates public policy?

This statement of the issue identifies (1) a legally significant relationship between the parties (employer/employee), (2) the nature of the claim (tort), (3) the basis for the claim (public policy), and (4) the obstacle to relief on a contract claim (the at-will nature of the employment contract).

---

5. 710 P.2d 1025 (Ariz. 1985).

Though the second statement of the issue is much more informative, it still leaves room for improvement. Your issue statement will better define the effect of the decision as precedent if you more specifically refer to the critical facts of the case.

For example, the court discusses the sources of public policy. That discussion suggests that a subsequent case may raise the question of the legal significance of public policy that is expressed in a judicial opinion analyzing common law, rather than in a criminal statute. To help determine whether *Wagenseller* would be controlling on, distinguishable from, or persuasively analogous to the subsequent dispute, your statement of the issue in *Wagenseller* could incorporate material facts that provide a potential basis for analogy and distinction:

> Is the employer liable in tort for discharging an at-will employee because of her refusal to participate in a public "mooning," a discharge that contravened the public policy against indecent exposure reflected in a criminal statute?

This statement of the issue identifies the source of public policy, and it gives sufficient factual details to permit an assessment of the importance of that policy.

The point at which the disadvantages of increased complexity begin to outweigh the benefits of enhanced specificity in the issue statement is a matter for your judgment and personal style. As discussed in Subsection b below, you can reduce the complexity of the issue statement by transferring some of the critical information to the statement of the holding.

Finally, although you should incorporate facts into your issue statement, you should not assume matters that are in dispute and that are thus themselves issues considered by the court. For example, the previous statement of the issue assumes that (1) the employment contract was terminable at will, and (2) the criminal statute reflected a public policy against compelled "mooning" and therefore against an employer's discharging an at-will employee for refusing to engage in "mooning." The statement questions only whether state law recognizes a claim in tort for such retaliation against an at-will employee. Suppose instead that the employee had alleged breach of contract and had disputed that the employment contract was terminable at will. Suppose further that the employer had disputed that the criminal statute reflected a public policy against compelled "mooning." In those circumstances, you should add an issue relating to contract law and should divide the tort issue into two subissues:

> 1. Did the employee establish a genuine factual dispute on the question of whether the employer made a binding promise in its personnel manual to give the employee job security, thus entitling the employee to a trial on her contract claim?
> 2. Even if the employment contract was terminable at will, is the

employer liable to the employee for discharging her for a reason that violates public policy?
a. Should the court recognize a new exception to the at-will rule by imposing tort liability for such a discharge?
b. Does a state criminal statute prohibiting public exposure of one's anus or genitalia reflect a public policy against compelled public exposure of bare buttocks?[6]

Issue #1 achieves specificity in procedural facts, as well as historical facts, by identifying the employee's burden on a motion for summary judgment.

b. Holding

The "holding" is simply the court's answer to the question presented in the issue. If you state the issue sufficiently narrowly and specifically to provide a basis for evaluating the effect of the decision as precedent, you may state the holding with a simple "yes" or "no." Of course, if a professor asks you during class discussion for the holding of a case without first asking for the issue, she expects you to offer more than "yes" or "no." In those circumstances, you should transform the issue into a detailed holding in the form of a statement:

The employee was entitled to a trial on her contract claim because she established a genuine factual dispute on the question of whether the employer made a binding promise in its personnel manual to give the employee job security.

Even when coupling the holding to a detailed statement of the issue, you may wish the holding to convey further information than "yes" or "no." For example, if a fully descriptive statement of the issue would be unwieldy, you can move some of the critical information to the holding:

Issue: Did the employer discharge the employee for a reason that violates public policy, thus rendering the employer liable in tort for wrongful discharge?

Holding: Yes. By discharging the employee because she refused to partici- pate in public "mooning," the employer violated public policy reflected in a criminal statute prohibiting indecent exposure.

The holding and the issue obviously are simply the opposite sides of the same coin. Therefore, the following examination of the appropriate scope of statements of holding is simply a continuation and refinement of the preceding discussion of narrowness and specificity in issues.

Because narrowly drafted statements of the issue and holding represent an attempt to identify the effect of the decision under stare decisis, from a

---

6. See id. at 1035 n.5 (admitting to "little expertise in the techniques of mooning").

practical standpoint the precise contours of the issue and holding may not become clear until subsequent decisions interpret and apply them as precedent. Through that process of determining whether the prior decision is controlling, analogous, or distinguishable, subsequent decisions can refine the judicial understanding of the relative importance of various facts and policies to the prior decision and consequently to the resolution of subsequent disputes as well.

For example, in *Monge v. Beebe Rubber Co.*[7] the New Hampshire Supreme Court held an employer liable for discharging a female employee because she had engendered hostility in her foreman by refusing his sexual advances. The court's own statement of its holding is reasonably consistent with a broad theory of liability that encompasses a wide range of employer actions:

> We hold that a termination by the employer of a contract of employment at will which is motivated by bad faith or malice or based on retaliation is not in the best interest of the economic system or the public good and constitutes a breach of the employment contract.[8]

Six years later, in *Howard v. Dorr Woolen Co.*,[9] however, the same court adopted one of the narrowest of the possible interpretations of *Monge*'s holding. The *Howard* court clearly required (1) a link to public policy beyond a general interest in good faith and fair play in a private employment relationship, and (2) retaliation for a specific act or refusal to act on the part of the employee:

> We construe *Monge* to apply only to a situation where an employee is discharged because he performed an act that public policy would encourage, or refused to do that which public policy would condemn.[10]

Without explaining which of the two requirements was missing, the *Howard* court applied its view of the holding in *Monge* to refuse to impose liability for an employer discharging an employee because of sickness and age.[11]

This process of refining the holding of a prior decision may permit a court to interpret precedent in a way that was not intended by the court establishing that precedent. In most subsequent decisions, however, courts faithfully attempt to identify the considerations that were essential to the decision that acts as precedent and to evaluate the precedent's effect on the subsequent disputes.

If the holding of a decision is thus defined in terms of the way in which courts make use of the decision as precedent in subsequent cases, the issue and holding of the decision cannot be identified with perfect certainty when analyzing that decision in isolation. Rather, each decision presents a range

---

7. 316 A.2d 549 (N.H. 1974).
8. Id. at 551 (the unofficial reporter omits the word "in" in the quoted passage).
9. 414 A.2d 1273 (N.H. 1980).
10. Id. at 1274.
11. Id. (interpreted in Wagenseller v. Scottsdale Memorial Hosp., 710 P.2d 1025, 1032 n.3 (Ariz. 1985)).

of possible statements of the issue and holding.[12] When preparing for class, you should try to state an issue and holding that falls somewhere within a plausible range and to appreciate how other statements nearer to either end of the plausible range would aid in the advocacy of either side of a subsequent dispute.

For example, if you had argued on behalf of one of the parties in the *Howard* case, you would have addressed the holding of *Monge,* a previous decision of the state court of last resort in the forum jurisdiction. If you had represented the plaintiff in *Howard,* you might have argued for the broadest plausible interpretation of the *Monge* precedent, so that it would strongly support liability for your client. Specifically, you might have interpreted *Monge* to approve tort liability whenever an employer discharges an employee for a reason that would be viewed by the average person as unfair, because such a discharge would be both unfair to the discharged employee and harmful to the morale and productivity of all employees. Conversely, if you had represented the employer in *Howard,* you might have argued for a narrower interpretation of *Monge,* so that you could more easily distinguish it from the *Howard* case. Specifically, you might have interpreted *Monge* to impose liability only if an employer discharges an employee in retaliation for resisting a demand specifically prohibited by statute, a particularly strong source of public policy.

Finally, as a student analyzing *Monge* without the benefit of the appellate decision in *Howard,* you should formulate some reasonable statement of the *Monge* holding within the range defined by plausible arguments of advocates. You should also be prepared to play the role of advocate and discuss the narrowest and broadest plausible interpretations of *Monge.* Of course, the *Howard* court in fact adopted a quite narrow interpretation of the holding in *Monge.* Such an interpretation was not inevitable, however, and you could reasonably have interpreted the holding of *Monge* more broadly until *Howard* came to your attention.

3. Facts

Pressed for time, you may be tempted to skim over the facts of a case and rush to the middle of the opinion, searching for succinct statements of law that you can preserve in your notes. In the final analysis, however, legal rules are nothing more than statements of the legal consequences of special facts:

> Wherever the law gives special rights to one, or imposes special burdens on another, it does so on the ground that certain special facts are true of those individuals. In all such cases, therefore, there is a twofold task. First, to determine what are the facts to which the special consequences are attached; second, to ascertain the consequences. The first is the main field of legal argument.[13]

---

12. See Karl N. Llewellyn, The Bramble Bush 75-76 (7th prtg. 1981).
13. Oliver W. Holmes, Jr., The Common Law 289 (1923).

Whether case law is based on statutory interpretation or common law, it generally develops gradually, with each new opinion adding refinements in the law through its application of legal standards to the facts of a new dispute. A court's statements about the law are fully meaningful only when read in light of the facts of the dispute that the court resolves. Consequently, you should master the facts of a case with the same intensity that you devote to appreciating the court's discussion of legal principles.

Your statement of facts should include all "material" facts, facts that have legal significance and therefore directly influence the court's holding and reasoning. Identification of material facts is not an exact science; rather, it is a matter of judgment that requires an appreciation of the factors that the court considered in reaching its decision. In your statement of facts, you should also refer in general terms to any additional background facts that, although legally unimportant, are helpful to a full understanding of the dispute and to class discussion. At the least, your statement of facts should identify

(1) the principal parties to the underlying dispute that gave rise to the legal proceedings,
(2) the relationships among those parties, and
(3) the events that led to the dispute.

You may wish to refer to such facts as "historical facts" to distinguish them from "procedural facts," which are discussed in Subsection 4 below.

For purposes of discussion, this book will often use the procedural term "plaintiff" to refer to the party who initiates a lawsuit, and the term "defendant" to refer to the one against whom suit is brought. You can create a more concrete image of the underlying dispute, however, if you identify the parties with their more specific, formal names.

In addition, you should consider supplementing the formal names with labels that have substantive, rather than merely procedural, significance. Because statutes generally address broad categories of activities rather than individual cases, they often create rights and obligations in broad but carefully defined classifications of persons, such as "employers" and "employees," or "buyers" and "sellers."[14] Similarly, although courts interpret statutes and develop common law in the context of individual disputes, a series of judicial decisions on closely related points may create case law that allocates rights and obligations according to membership within general classes of persons, such as "landowners" and "trespassers."[15] Therefore, you can more clearly reveal the legal significance of material facts in your case brief if you identify the named parties or other important actors with labels that reflect undisputed and legally significant classifications, such as employer, buyer, seller, merchant, landlord, tenant, landowner, or invitee.

When you assign a label to a party or otherwise characterize a factual matter, you should not prematurely state a conclusion on an issue that is

---

14. See, e.g., Title VII of the Civil Rights Act of 1964, 42 U.S.C. §§2000e(b), 2000e-2(a) (1988) (defining and imposing obligations on "employers").
15. See, e.g., W. Page Keeton et al., Prosser and Keeton on the Law of Torts §58, at 393 (5th ed. 1984) (duties owed by landowner to trespassers, licensees, and invitees).

disputed by the parties and that is later analyzed in the opinion. For example, your statement of facts should not refer to a seller as a "merchant" if the parties dispute whether the seller is a merchant for purposes of determining the seller's warranty obligations under the Uniform Commercial Code.[16] Similarly, your statement of facts should not state that the defendant in a criminal burglary prosecution "broke into" a "dwelling" if "breaking" and "dwelling" are elements of the charged offense and if the parties dispute those elements.[17]

Rather than state disputed legal conclusions in your statement of facts, you should summarize the subsidiary facts that the court analyzes in reaching its conclusion on the issue. For example, in the first case in the preceding paragraph, you might state that the seller of a computer system did not normally buy or sell goods, and that her sale of the computer system was an isolated transaction, but that the seller's occupation as a computer repairperson led the buyer to believe that the seller had special knowledge of the performance capabilities of different computer systems. In other parts of your case brief, you can discuss whether those subsidiary facts satisfy the legal definition of "merchant."[18]

In most cases the appellate judge who wrote the opinion has already sifted and condensed the facts that were presented to the trial court. Nonetheless, you should try to be even more discriminating in your identification of material facts and helpful background facts, and you should try to summarize them further. You should also reorganize the opinion's facts if its organization is not satisfactory; chronological order is often the most logical.

To truly master the facts, however, you should go beyond simply summarizing or reorganizing the opinion's fact statement. Otherwise, you may find yourself simply transferring words and phrases from the casebook to your case brief without truly comprehending their meaning. Instead, you should seek a conceptual understanding of the facts, one that creates concrete images of the parties and transactions. If necessary to attain that goal, you should prepare charts, time lines, or other graphics that vividly represent the relationships among multiple parties and events.

To fully appreciate this point, return briefly to the discussion of *Hadley v. Baxendale* in Chapter 1. Notice how the charts summarize the transactions and legal proceedings in a rough time line. Did those charts help you form a vivid image of the events? If so, imagine how your own charts or other graphics can help you visualize complex transactions or relationships among parties. As a practical matter, moreover, they will enhance your class performance in at least three ways. First, by preparing graphics, you will force yourself to thoroughly study and comprehend the facts, because you will

---

16. See U.C.C. §2-314 (1990) (implying a warranty of merchantability in a contract for the sale of goods "if the seller is a merchant with respect to goods of that kind").

17. See Wayne R. LaFave & Austin W. Scott, Jr., Criminal Law §8.13 (2d ed. 1986).

18. The U.C.C. definition focuses on regular practices and on representations of expertise:

> Merchant means a person who deals in goods of the kind or otherwise by his occupation holds himself out as having knowledge or skill peculiar to the practices or goods involved in the transaction. . . .

U.C.C. §2-104 (1990).

not be able to represent the facts in a graphic form unless you truly understand what happened in the case. Second, by referring to your graphic representation in class, you can quickly recall the facts at a glance. Third, by relying primarily on such a representation in your class recital of the facts, you will tend to describe the facts more naturally and spontaneously than if you mechanically read your summary of the facts verbatim from your notes.

4. Procedural History

In your statement of the procedural history of a case on appeal, you should identify

(1) which party or parties initiated legal action against which others,
(2) the legal claims and defenses and the relief sought,
(3) the trial court's disposition along with the stage of the proceedings at which the trial court rendered its decision,
(4) the dispositions of any intermediate courts below the authoring court, and
(5) the authoring court's disposition.

In some cases, it may also be helpful to summarize the arguments that the parties made to the trial or appellate courts.

The case name on appeal does not always reveal which party initiated the legal action in the trial court. Although the case name as it appears in the trial court begins with the plaintiff's name, the case name in the appellate courts of some jurisdictions begins with the name of the party who is dissatisfied with the trial court's decision and has thus appealed (the "appellant") or petitioned for review (the "petitioner").[19]

The nature of the plaintiff's legal claim and request for relief in the trial court may provide a key to the appellate court's analysis. For example, classification of a plaintiff's legal claim as one in tort rather than in contract may determine whether the claim is barred by a statute of limitations[20] or whether the plaintiff is entitled to punitive damages.[21] Similarly, whether a contract is sufficiently definite to enforce may depend on whether the plaintiff seeks enforcement through an award of damages or through injunctive relief granting specific enforcement.[22]

As with the statement of facts, you should not reach a premature conclusion in your statement of the procedural history regarding the nature of a legal claim if that is one of the issues disputed by the parties and analyzed by the court. For example, the parties may dispute whether a claim is properly

---

19. See, e.g., Fiege v. Boehm, 123 A.2d 316 (Md. 1956) (Hilda Boehm had sued Louis Fiege in the trial court).
20. See, e.g., Salmon Rivers Sportsman Camps, Inc. v. Cessna Aircraft Co., 544 P.2d 306, 310 (Idaho 1975).
21. John D. Calamari & Joseph M. Perillo, Contracts §14-3 (3d ed. 1984).
22. See E. Allan Farnsworth, Contracts §3.28, at 215 (2d ed. 1990); cf. 5A Arthur L. Corbin, Corbin on Contracts §1174, at 278-279 (1964) ("It is believed, however, that the required degree of definiteness and certainty [for specific enforcement] is seldom much greater than is required for enforcement by other remedies.").

classified as tort or contract, because that classification may determine the applicable statute of limitations or the availability of punitive damages.[23] In many cases, however, the nature of the legal claim will be undisputed and easily identifiable.

By stating the dispositions of all the courts that rendered decisions in the case, you can identify precisely the ruling that the authoring court has reviewed. The "disposition" is the practical, procedural effect of the court's holding on the litigation. In an opinion of a trial court, it might be "action dismissed," "summary judgment for the plaintiff," or "judgment on the jury verdict for the defendant." In an opinion of an appellate court, it might be "affirmed," "reversed," or "reversed and remanded for further proceedings."

In stating the trial court's disposition, you should try to identify the stage of the proceedings at which the trial court rendered judgment. An appellate court gives varying degrees of deference to different kinds of trial court decisions. Therefore, the likelihood of reversal by an appellate court depends partly on the stage of the proceedings at which judgment is rendered and, in some cases, on the classification of critical issues as ones of fact or law.[24]

For example, although appellate courts review without restriction the legal rules formulated by trial courts, they restrict their review of the factual findings made by a trial judge or jury after a full trial, overturning such findings only in unusual circumstances.[25] On the other hand, a trial judge does not resolve disputes of fact when he uses summary judgment to dispose of claims before trial, and an appellate court will reverse summary judgment if it determines, without deference to the analysis of the trial court, that the parties genuinely dispute material facts.[26] Further, on a motion to dismiss an action for failure of the complaint to state a claim for relief, both the trial court and appellate courts simply assume the truth of the allegations of fact in the complaint and analyze the legal significance of those allegations.[27]

5. Reasoning

a. Rule and Rationale

In part, published appellate judicial decisions serve the function of ensuring the "correct" result in a particular case. However, their primary

---

23. See, e.g., Woodward v. Chirco Constr. Co., 687 P.2d 1275, 1278 (Ariz. App. 1984), *approved as supplemented,* 687 P.2d 1269 (Ariz. 1984) (en banc) (implied warranty claim arose out of a written contract and therefore was governed by six-year limitations period rather than by shorter limitations period for tort claims); Gates v. Life of Montana Ins. Co., 668 P.2d 213, 215 (Mont. 1983) (breach of implied duty of good faith and fair dealing in employment contract gives rise to a tort, thus permitting award of punitive damages).

24. See Chapter 16, Section II.

25. See, e.g., Fed. R. Civ. P. 52(a) (federal appellate court may not set aside trial judge's findings of fact unless they are "clearly erroneous"); 2 Fed. Proc., L. Ed. §2:233, at 195-196 (1981) (reviewing court cannot overturn the fact findings of a jury unless they are not supported by substantial evidence).

26. See Fed. R. Civ. P. 56 (summary judgment standards); Heiniger v. City of Phoenix, 625 F.2d 842, 843-844 (9th Cir. 1980) (standards for appellate review of summary judgment).

27. See, e.g., Experimental Eng'g, Inc. v. United Technologies Corp., 614 F.2d 1244,

purpose is to serve the "institutional function" of "developing and declaring legal principles that will have application beyond the case that serves as the vehicle for expression of the principles."[28] The reasoning set forth in a judicial opinion should guide others in predicting how the court will apply its decision to subsequent, analogous cases. Because certainty in the law is not the only criterion for judicial rulemaking, courts should hesitate to extend a previous decision beyond the reasons that supported it.

By carefully studying the reasoning of opinions, you will gradually develop a "feel" for the way in which judges decide cases. With that acquired knowledge, you can develop the ability not only to analyze a problem and predict its likely outcome in court, but also to persuade a court to reach a conclusion favorable to your client.

Unfortunately, published opinions provide only an imperfect guide to the decisionmaking process. The reasons for an individual judge's vote on an appellate panel may be complex, and some of her reasons may be subconscious.[29] Of the reasons on which the judge consciously relies, the judge may not express all of them to fellow panel members in panel discussions and memoranda. Finally, the published opinion of the panel may exclude some of the more pragmatic reasons privately expressed by panel members to one another and may focus instead on more conventional legal analysis. Because an opinion thus only imperfectly communicates a court's actual reasoning, you should not hesitate to "read between the lines" and attempt to identify facts or policy considerations that likely contributed to the court's decision, even though the court did not expressly identify them as critical factors.

On the most fundamental level, when stating a court's reasoning, you should note whether the court is interpreting and applying a constitution or statute or is developing common law. Many judicial opinions deal with a combination of different sources of law. Beyond that, you should summarize the court's reliance on precedent, its analysis of policy considerations, its explanation of the significance of critical facts, and its adoption or recognition of a legal rule of general application.

Some opinions do not formulate or restate a general legal rule that controls the analysis. Instead, they simply define a dispute on particular facts, reach a decision, and provide a justification that is fairly narrowly tailored to the dispute before the court. Such an opinion leaves you only with a "holding" in the narrowest sense. Using techniques described in the next chapter, however, you can synthesize several such cases addressing similar issues and derive your own rule of general application.

b. Holding and Dictum

One of your most challenging tasks is to distinguish the holding of a decision from dicta. Narrowly defined, a "holding" is the court's resolution

1246 (9th Cir. 1980) (dismissal is appropriate only if court is convinced that the plaintiff can prove no set of facts in support of a claim that would warrant relief).

28. Charles R. Calleros, Title VII and Rule 52(a): Standards of Appellate Review in Disparate Treatment Cases—Limiting the Reach of *Pullman-Standard v. Swint*, 58 Tul. L. Rev. 403, 420-421 (1983).

29. See generally id. at 424 & n.97.

of an issue before it, limited to the particular facts of the dispute. It does not include statements in the opinion about the probable outcome of disputes not before the court.

"Dictum," on the other hand, is a statement in the opinion that helps explain the court's reasoning but that addresses questions not squarely presented in the dispute before the court. Courts make and apply law in the context of individual disputes; however, as a natural consequence of the uniformity of treatment demanded by stare decisis, courts have developed general rules that apply to whole categories of disputes.[30] As a means of explaining the reasons supporting its holding, a court may in dicta compare its rule of decision with other rules that it does not apply to the dispute, or it may discuss in dicta how its rule of decision would apply to facts other than those presented in the dispute before it.

As illustrated by the following excerpt, the issue and holding of a previous decision limits its effect as precedent under stare decisis. Even a lower court that is absolutely bound by the holdings of the previous decision may choose not to follow the dicta of the decision. In this example from civil rights litigation, a United States Court of Appeals extended the same immunity defense to judges of limited jurisdiction state courts, such as traffic courts, as had been applied to judges of general jurisdiction state courts, such as general trial courts. In doing so, it departed from United States Supreme Court dictum:

> The district court held that judges of courts of limited jurisdiction may be sued for judicial acts done merely in excess of jurisdiction. . . . Although the Supreme Court cases relied upon by the district court contain language supporting such a view, . . . we hold that judges of courts of limited jurisdiction are entitled to absolute immunity for their judicial acts unless they act in the clear absence of all jurisdiction.
>
> First, we emphasize that since the [Supreme Court] cases involved suits against judges of courts having general jurisdiction, any statements made by the Supreme Court about judges of courts having only limited or inferior jurisdiction were *dicta*.[31]

Dictum in an opinion is not meaningless; it may in fact help you accurately predict the authoring court's action in a subsequent case that squarely presents the issue addressed in the dictum.[32] Nonetheless, because dictum does not have the force of precedent, you should take care to read all of the court's reasoning in light of its narrow, fact-specific holding. You should not confuse what a court *says*, or even what it *says it is doing*, with what it actually *does* in a case.

6. Evaluation

You should resist any tendency to defer to the reasoning of a judicial decision as the expression of the single "correct" analysis of a dispute. Many

---

30. See generally Karl N. Llewellyn, The Bramble Bush 40-41 (1978).
31. King v. Love, 766 F.2d 962, 966 (6th Cir. 1985), *cert. denied*, 474 U.S. 971 (1985).
32. Robert E. Keeton, Venturing to Do Justice 30-31 (1969).

disputes present close questions that are reasonably susceptible to alternative, inconsistent resolutions. You should read a decision critically to determine whether you agree with the result and the reasoning. Constant practice in critically examining judicial opinions will help you develop the ability later to persuade a court to adopt or reject the rule or reasoning of nonbinding authority.

On one level, you should examine an opinion for doctrinal integrity by asking such questions as

(1) whether the court analogized or distinguished precedent in a convincing manner,

(2) whether it applied the appropriate standard of review,

(3) whether it analyzed a statute under accepted principles of statutory interpretation and construction, or

(4) whether the court placed excessive emphasis on certainty in a general rule at the expense of equitable considerations in the context of peculiar facts.

On another, closely related level, you should examine the policy and practical implications of an opinion. For example, you might ask such questions as

(1) whether a decision that promotes economic security for employees unwisely reduces economic efficiency at the expense of producers and consumers, or

(2) whether a court-developed tort standard allocates risks among parties in a way that encourages them to conduct themselves in a manner that avoids harm to others yet encourages socially productive ventures.

7. Synthesis

Perhaps the most important and the most challenging element of a case brief is the "synthesis," in which you explore the relationships among two or more cases that address the same issue or closely related ones. After comparing the critical elements of each in a series of cases, you can refine your view of the holding of each case in the series. With synthesis, you can either (1) formulate a general principle that explains each decision or (2) compare and evaluate the inconsistent approaches of different courts or of the same court over time. By synthesizing cases, you take a critical step in legal analysis that will have special significance when you look ahead to final examinations: Synthesis forms a bridge between daily briefing of isolated cases and periodic preparation of course outlines.

The process of synthesizing cases reveals that the study of case law is analogous in some ways to the study of a foreign language. After a brief introduction to the basic structure of a language and its rules of pronunciation, you typically proceed to study the language by gaining familiarity with a succession of words and phrases that gradually grow into a working vocabulary. The learning process is complicated by the relationship of parts to the whole: You cannot fully appreciate the nuances of meaning of a word or phrase without a working knowledge of its role in a larger body of the language; yet you cannot attain a working knowledge of the larger body of the language without first gaining at least a preliminary understanding of individual words and phrases. As you gradually add to your vocabulary and to your understanding of the relationship of words and phrases to one another, you continually refine your understanding of the individual words and phrases that you studied earlier, and you come closer to attaining fluency in the whole language.

Similarly, when studying law, you cannot fully appreciate the legal significance of a single judicial decision without examining its role within a larger body of case law; yet, you cannot master the larger body of case law without first gaining at least an imperfect grasp of its parts, first one case in isolation and then a growing group of cases. As you brief a series of cases, you will gain new insights by examining the cases' relationships to one another. Those insights may cause you to modify your early, less sophisticated understanding of a case standing alone or standing with fewer cases in the series. Additionally, they may enable you to identify a general legal principle, or at least a set of accepted criteria, that helps to explain the decisions.[33]

The first step in synthesizing cases is to compare the cases' substantive results as conveyed by their holdings, regardless of the procedural dispositions of the appellate courts. For example, assume that two appellate decisions from different jurisdictions, States X and Y, have addressed the question of whether a particular newspaper advertisement meets the following definition of an offer: An "offer" is an expression of willingness to enter into a contract that empowers the offeree to create a contract by accepting the offer. In Case A, an appellate court of State X affirmed a trial court judgment that a particular newspaper advertisement amounted to an offer to sell the advertised goods. In Case B, an appellate court of State Y affirmed a trial court judgment that another newspaper advertisement communicated only an invitation to negotiate rather than an offer to sell.[34] If you are not yet prepared to abandon hope of finding at least limited uniformity among the states in their application of common law, you should be curious about the reasons for the difference in results.

In the next step of the synthesis, you should determine whether Cases A and B are materially distinguishable and therefore warrant different results on application of the same legal principles, or whether they are legally inconsistent and simply represent different views of the law adopted by courts in different states. As a general approach, you should first attempt to reconcile the cases by searching for distinctions in facts, procedure, or both that support a conclusion that the cases are legally consistent. For

---

33. For a critical evaluation of the method with which case synthesis is taught in American law schools, see Richard K. Greenstein, Teaching Case Synthesis, 2 Ga. St. U. L. Rev. 1 (1985-1986).

34. Compare Lefkowitz v. Great Minneapolis Surplus Store, 86 N.W.2d 689 (Minn. 1957) (offer) and Craft v. Elder and Johnston Co., 38 N.E.2d 416 (Ohio App. 1941) (no offer), *reprinted in part in* E. Allan Farnsworth & William F. Young, Cases and Materials on Contracts 145-148 (4th ed. 1988).

example, unusually specific and detailed language of commitment in the advertisement in Case *A* might clearly communicate a willingness to conclude a contract for sale on a customer's assent. In contrast, more general language in the advertisement in Case *B* might leave important terms of sale unaddressed, suggesting a need for further bargaining before the advertiser is willing to commit itself to a contract for sale.

In these circumstances, you could compose a single, narrow legal rule that is consistent with the reasoning of each case and that produces different results on application to the facts of both cases:

> A newspaper advertisement is an offer only if it is so clear and definite that it leaves no important detail for future negotiation.

With such a synthesis, you will better understand the holdings of Cases *A* and *B*, more firmly grasp otherwise abstract legal principles, and improve your ability to predict the outcome of a new case that presents the same issue on novel facts.

If you fail to find material distinctions in facts or procedure between Cases *A* and *B*, you can safely conclude that the appellate decisions are legally inconsistent. In that event, you should analyze the reasons for the different views of the law. Perhaps States *X* and *Y* apply different legal approaches because they emphasize different policies. Such a synthesis helps you to put conflicting case law into perspective and to develop the ability to persuade a court in a future case to adopt one line of conflicting authority over another.

Different results in cases decided by the same court present particularly interesting questions of synthesis, because the court cannot depart from a prior decision without departing also from stare decisis and overruling the prior decision. If the cases are not obviously distinguishable but the court does not explicitly overrule the prior decision, you should search with particular care for possible distinguishing features before concluding that the court has implicitly overruled the prior decision. Of course, the proper synthesis may lie in middle ground: A decision may limit the range of possible interpretations of a prior holding without completely overruling it.

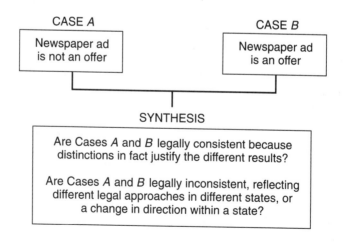

If two cases reach the same result, a synthesis should compare the facts and reasoning of the two cases to determine whether the courts were influenced by similar factors. For example, suppose that, in Case *B,* a court in State *Y* held that a particular newspaper advertisement constituted an offer to sell the advertised goods. Suppose further that, in Case *C,* a court in State *Z* found a different newspaper advertisement to constitute an offer. Although both decisions find offers, a comparison of the facts may suggest that Case *C* represents a significant extension of the holding of Case *B.* Similarly, the reasoning of Case *B* might suggest that the court in State *Y* would not have reached the same result if presented with the facts on which the court in State *Z* found an offer in Case *C.*

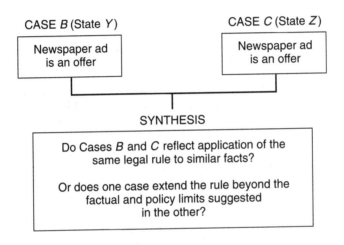

When you synthesize, you compare two or more cases, of course. There-fore, when you prepare a single case brief in isolation, you will not include a synthesis, except perhaps in the form of a prediction of the questions that may arise later from uncertainty in the breadth of the holding of the case. The late Professor Llewellyn went so far as to state that

> a case read by itself is meaningless, is nil, is blank, is blah. Briefing should begin *at the earliest* with the second case of an assignment. Only *after* you have read the second case have you any idea what to do with the first.[35]

Thus, in a perfect world, you could read all in a series of cases relating to a particular problem area before briefing any of them. You would then brief each case with an eye to the problems raised in the others, and finally prepare a single synthesis of the entire series of cases.

Unfortunately, class assignments and library research techniques seldom permit that luxury. As a more practical procedure, you should prepare a synthesis for each case in a series beginning with the second case. Each succeeding synthesis will reflect the addition of a case to the group of

---

35. Karl N. Llewellyn, The Bramble Bush 55 (7th prtg. 1981).

cases among which you can make comparisons, thus adding new insights to previous syntheses.

III. SUMMARY

After thoroughly reading the entire case at least once, follow these steps:

(1) Identify the case. Include details that help identify the case's place in the overall case law of the jurisdiction and the case's value as precedent.

(2) State the issue and the holding as narrowly as possible without making your question cumbersome and unwieldy; tailor your statement of the issue to the facts.

(3) Summarize the material facts and the helpful background facts.

(4) Summarize the procedural history, including the dispositions in the trial court and on appeal.

(5) Summarize the reasoning of the court. Distinguish holding from dictum. Identify general rules recognized by the court, and pay particular attention to the authority, policy analysis, and logic on which the court relies.

(6) Critically evaluate the court's holding and reasoning.

(7) Synthesize the case with others that present the same or a similar issue. Attempt to explain apparently conflicting results among the cases.

========= E X E R C I S E   6 - 1 =========

1. Case Brief

Using the techniques described in this chapter, read the following excerpt of the appellate opinion in *White v. Benkowski,* and prepare a case brief. Do not be satisfied with the court's statement of the issue; try to improve on it. Critically evaluate the court's holding and dicta regarding the availability of punitive damages; ask yourself whether you can defend the court's views on the grounds of economic efficiency, certainty in legal rules, equity in individual cases, the proper roles of compensation and deterrence, or any other policy considerations. You should not yet attempt to synthesize this case with any others, although you may comment on possible extensions of, or limitations on, its holding that subsequent cases could introduce. After completing your case brief, compare it with the sample set forth in Exercise 6-1(2) below.

WHITE v. BENKOWSKI
Supreme Court of Wisconsin
37 Wis. 2d 285, 155 N.W.2d 74 (1967)

This case involves a neighborhood squabble between two adjacent property owners.

Prior to November 28, 1962, Virgil and Gwynneth White, the plaintiffs, were desirous of purchasing a home in Oak Creek. Unfortunately, the particular home that the Whites were interested in was without a water supply. Despite this fact, the Whites purchased the home.

The adjacent home was owned and occupied by Paul and Ruth Benkowski, the defendants. The Benkowskis had a well in their yard which had piping that connected with the Whites' home.

On November 28, 1962, the Whites and Benkowskis entered into a written agreement wherein the Benkowskis promised to supply water to the Whites' home for 10 years or until an earlier date when either water was supplied by the municipality, the well became inadequate, or the Whites drilled their own well. The Whites promised to pay $3 a month for the water and one-half the cost of any future repairs or maintenance that the Benkowski well might require. As part of the transaction, but not included in the written agreement, the Whites gave the Benkowskis $400 which was used to purchase and install a new pump and an additional tank that would increase the capacity of the well.

Initially, the relationship between the new neighbors was friendly. With the passing of time, however, their friendship deteriorated and the neighbors actually became hostile. In 1964, the water supply, which was controlled by the Benkowskis, was intermittently shut off. Mrs. White kept a record of the dates and durations that her water supply was not operative. Her record showed that the water was shut off on the following occasions:

(1) March 5, 1964, from 7:10 P.M. to 7:25 P.M.
(2) March 9, 1964, from 3:40 P.M. to 4:00 P.M.
(3) March 11, 1964, from 6:00 P.M. to 6:15 P.M.
(4) June 10, 1964, from 6:20 P.M. to 7:03 P.M.

The record also discloses that the water was shut off completely or partially for varying lengths of time on July 1, 6, 7, and 17, 1964, and on November 25, 1964.

Mr. Benkowski claimed that the water was shut off either to allow accumulated sand in the pipes to settle or to remind the Whites that their use of the water was excessive. Mr. White claimed that the Benkowskis breached their contract by shutting off the water.

Following the date when the water was last shut off (November 25, 1964), the Whites commenced an action to recover compensatory and punitive damages for an alleged violation of the agreement to supply water. . . .

The jury returned a verdict which found that the Benkowskis maliciously shut off the Whites' water supply for harassment purposes. Compensatory damages were set at $10 and punitive damages at $2,000. On motions after verdict, the court reduced the compensatory award to $1 and granted defendants' motion to strike the punitive-damage question and answer.

Judgment for plaintiffs of $1 was entered and they appeal.

WILKIE, Justice.
Two issues are raised on this appeal. . . .
2. Are punitive damages available in actions for breach of contract? . . .

PUNITIVE DAMAGES

"If a man shall steal an ox, or a sheep, and kill it, or sell it; he shall restore five oxen for an ox, and four sheep for a sheep."[3]

Over one hundred years ago this court held that, under proper circumstances, a plaintiff was entitled to recover . . . punitive damages.[4]

Kink v. Combs[5] is the most recent case in this state which deals with the practice of permitting punitive damages. In *Kink* the court relied on *Fuchs v. Kupper*[6] and reaffirmed its adherence to the rule of punitive damages.

In Wisconsin compensatory damages are given to make whole the damage or injury suffered by the injured party.[7] On the other hand, punitive damages are given

> . . . on the basis of punishment to the injured party not because he has been injured, which injury has been compensated with compensatory damages, but to punish the wrongdoer for his malice and to deter others from like conduct.[8]

Thus we reach the question of whether the plaintiffs are entitled to punitive damages for a breach of the water agreement. The overwhelming weight of authority supports the proposition that punitive damages are not recoverable in actions for breach of contract.[9] In Chitty on Contracts, the author states that the right to receive punitive damages for breach of contract is now confined to the single case of damages for breach of a promise to marry.[10]

Simpson states:

> Although damages in excess of compensation for loss are in some instances permitted in tort actions by way of punishment . . . in contract actions the damages recoverable are limited to compensation for pecuniary loss sustained by the breach.[11]

Corbin states that as a general rule punitive damages are not recoverable for breach of contract.[12]

In Wisconsin, the early case of *Gordon v. Brewster*[13] involved the breach of an employment contract. The trial court instructed the jury that if the nonperformance of the contract was attributable to the defendant's wrongful act of discharging the plaintiff, then that would go to increase the damages sustained. On appeal, this court said that the instruction was unfortunate and might have led the jurors to suppose that they could give something

---

3. Exodus 22:1.
4. McWilliams v. Bragg (1854), 3 Wis. 377 (*424).
5. (1965), 28 Wis. 2d 65, 135 N.W.2d 789.
6. (1963) 22 Wis. 2d 107, 125 N.W.2d 360.
7. Malco, Inc. v. Midwest Aluminum Sales (1961), 14 Wis. 2d 57, 66, 109 N.W.2d 516, 521.
8. Id.
9. Annot. (1933), 84 A.L.R. 1345, 1346.
10. 1 Chitty, Contracts, (22d ed. 1961), p.1339.
11. Simpson, Contracts, (2d ed. hornbook series), p.394, sec. 195.
12. 5 Corbin, Contracts, p.438, sec. 1077.
13. (1858), 7 Wis. 309 (*355).

more than actual compensation in a breach of contract case. We find no Wisconsin case in which breach of contract (other than breach of promise to marry)[14] has led to the award of punitive damages.

Persuasive authority from other jurisdictions supports the proposition (without exception) that punitive damages are not available in breach of contract actions.[15] This is true even if the breach, as in the instant case, is willful.[16]

Although it is well recognized that breach of a contractual duty may be a tort,[17] in such situations the contract creates the relation out of which grows the duty to use care in the performance of a responsibility prescribed by the contract.[18] Not so here. No tort was pleaded or proved.

Reversed in part by reinstating the jury verdict relating to compensatory damages and otherwise affirmed.

2. Sample Case Brief

Compare the case brief that you prepared in Exercise 6-1(1) with the following sample. Remember that the sample is only an example of a reasonable reaction to the opinion; it is not necessarily the best interpretation and evaluation of the opinion, and it certainly is not the only reasonable one. In particular, the "evaluation" is a matter of individual opinion.

White v. Benkowski, 37 Wis. 2d 285, 155 N.W.2d 74 (1967), CB 12.

Issue and Holding: Is Buyer entitled to an award of punitive damages for Supplier's malicious breach of a contract to supply water, even though Buyer established no independent tort? No.

Facts: The Whites (Buyer) and Benkowskis (Supplier) are neighbors. By written agreement Supplier promised to supply Buyer's house with water from Supplier's well for 10 years, unless the well became inadequate or unnecessary. The relationship deteriorated, and Supplier maliciously shut off Buyer's water supply partially or completely on nine occasions for the purpose of harassing Buyer.

Procedural History: Buyer sued Supplier for compensatory and punitive damages, alleging only breach of contract. On a finding of malicious breach of contract, the jury awarded Buyer $10 in compensatory damages and $2,000 in punitive damages. On motions after verdict, the trial court disal-

---

14. Simpson v. Black (1870), 27 Wis. 206.

15. White, Inc. v. Metropolitan Merchandise Mart (1954), 48 Del. 526, 9 Terry 526, 107 A.2d 892; Thompson v. Mutual Ben. Health & Acc. Ass'n of Omaha, Neb. (D.C. Iowa 1949), 83 F. Supp. 656; Cain v. Tuten (1950), 82 Ga. App. 102, 60 S.E.2d 485; Mabery v. Western Casualty & Surety Co. (1952), 173 Kan. 586, 250 P.2d 824; Bland v. Smith (1955), 197 Tenn. 683, 277 S.W.2d 377, 49 A.L.R.2d 1212.

16. McDonough v. Zamora (Tex. Civ. App. 1960), 338 S.W.2d 507; Holt v. Holt (Tex. Civ. App. 1954), 271 S.W.2d 477; Chelini v. Nieri (Cal. App. 1948), 188 P.2d 564.

17. Colton v. Foulkes (1951), 259 Wis. 142, 47 N.W.2d 901; Presser v. Siesel Construction Co. (1963), 19 Wis. 2d 54, 119 N.W.2d 405; Peterson v. Sinclair Refining Co. (1963), 20 Wis. 2d 576, 123 N.W.2d 479.

18. 38 Am. Jur., Negligence, p.661, sec. 20.

lowed punitive damages and reduced the compensatory-damage award from $10 to $1. Buyer appealed. The appellate court reversed the trial court's reduction of the award for compensatory damages, but it affirmed the trial court's elimination of the award for punitive damages.

Reasoning: Prior Wisconsin case law, persuasive authority from other jurisdictions, and the views of three commentators support the following common law principle: Even an intentional and malicious breach of contract will not support an award of punitive damages. In dictum, the court suggests that punitive damages could be awarded if the breach of contract also constituted an independent tort; however, Buyer failed to plead and prove an independent tort. The court did not explicitly overrule a 19th century decision in which it had approved punitive damages for breach of a marriage contract, thus leaving open the possibility of exceptions to the rule of the current case for breaches of extraordinary contracts.

Evaluation: In light of the maliciousness of Supplier's behavior, this decision is too restrictive. To deter such egregious conduct, I would allow punitive damages on a contract claim if the breaching party breached to maliciously injure the other party rather than to reallocate its resources to a more profitable and efficient use.

3. *Case Briefs with Synthesis*

Contracts are formed through a process of offer and acceptance. An offer is an expression of a willingness to enter into a contract. It gives to the party to whom it is addressed, the "offeree," the power to create the contract by assenting to the offer in a manner authorized by the offer. To constitute an offer, an expression must lead a reasonable person in the position of the offeree to understand that she has such power.

With that background, prepare a case brief for each of the following two cases. End the second case brief with a synthesis of the two cases.

CRAFT v. ELDER & JOHNSTON CO.
38 N.E.2d 416 (Ohio App. 1941)

BARNES, Judge. . . .

. . . On or about January 31, 1940, the defendant, the Elder & Johnston Company, carried an advertisement in the Dayton Shopping News, an offer for sale of a certain all electric sewing machine for the sum of $26 as a "Thursday Only Special." Plaintiff . . . alleges that the above publication is an advertising paper distributed in Montgomery County and throughout the city of Dayton; that on Thursday, February 1, 1940, she tendered to the defendant company $26 in payment for one of the machines offered in the advertisement, but that defendant refused to fulfill the offer and has continued to so refuse. The petition further alleges that the value of the machine offered was $175 and she asks damages in the sum of $149 plus interest from February 1, 1940. . . .

The trial court dismissed plaintiff's petition as evidenced by a journal entry, the pertinent portion of which reads as follows: "Upon consideration the court finds that said advertisement was not an offer which could be accepted by plaintiff to form a contract, and this case is therefore dismissed with prejudice to a new action, at costs of plaintiff." . . .

We will now briefly make reference to some of the authorities. "It is clear that in the absence of special circumstances an ordinary newspaper advertisement is not an offer, but is an offer to negotiate—an offer to receive offers—or, as it is sometimes called, an offer to chaffer." Restatement of the Law of Contracts, Par. 25, Page 31.

Under the above paragraph the following illustration is given, " 'A,' a clothing merchant, advertises overcoats of a certain kind for sale at $50. This is not an offer but an invitation to the public to come and purchase."

"Thus, if goods are advertised for sale at a certain price, it is not an offer and no contract is formed by the statement of an intending purchaser that he will take a specified quantity of the goods at that price. The construction is rather favored that such an advertisement is a mere invitation to enter into a bargain rather than an offer. So a published price list is not an offer to sell the goods listed at the published price." Williston on Contracts, Revised Edition, Vol. 1, Par. 27, Page 54.

"The commonest example of offers meant to open negotiations and to call forth offers in the technical sense are advertisements, circulars and trade letters sent out by business houses. While it is possible that the offers made by such means may be in such form as to become contracts, they are often merely expressions of a willingness to negotiate." Page on the Law Contracts, 2d Ed., Vol. 1, Page 112, Par. 84. . . .

"But generally a newspaper advertisement or circular couched in general language and proper to be sent to all persons interested in a particular trade or business, or a prospectus of a general and descriptive nature, will be construed as an invitation to make an offer." 17 Corpus Juris Secundum, Contracts, Page 389, §46, Column 2. . . .

We are constrained to the view that the trial court committed no prejudicial error in dismissing plaintiff's petition.

The judgment of the trial court will be affirmed and costs adjudged against the plaintiff-appellant.

Entry may be prepared in accordance with this opinion.

GEIGER, P. J., and HORNBECK, J., concur.

LEFKOWITZ v. GREAT MINNEAPOLIS SURPLUS STORE
251 Minn. 188, 86 N.W.2d 689 (1957)

MURPHY, Justice

This is an appeal from an order of the Municipal Court of Minneapolis. . . . The order for judgment awarded the plaintiff the sum of $138.50 as damages for breach of contract.

This case grows out of the alleged refusal of the defendant to sell to the plaintiff a certain fur piece which it had offered for sale in a newspaper advertisement. It appears from the record that on April 6, 1956, the defendant published the following advertisement in a Minneapolis newspaper:

Saturday 9 A.M. Sharp
3 Brand New
Fur
Coats
Worth to $100.00
First Come
First Served
$1
Each

On April 13, the defendant again published an advertisement in the same newspaper as follows:

Saturday 9 A.M.
2 Brand New Pastel
Mink 3-Skin Scarfs
Selling for $89.50
Out they go
Saturday, Each. . . . $1.00
1 Black Lapin Stole
Beautiful,
worth $139.50. . . . $1.00
First Come
First Served

The record supports the findings of the court that on each of the Saturdays following the publication of the above-described ads the plaintiff was the first to present himself at the appropriate counter in the defendant's store and on each occasion demanded the coat and the stole so advertised and indicated his readiness to pay the sale price of $1. On both occasions, the defendant refused to sell the merchandise to the plaintiff. . . .

The defendant relies principally on *Craft v. Elder & Johnston Co.* . . . On the facts before us we are concerned with whether the advertisement constituted an offer, and, if so, whether the plaintiff's conduct constituted an acceptance.

There are numerous authorities which hold that a particular advertisement in a newspaper or circular letter relating to a sale of articles may be construed by the court as constituting an offer, acceptance of which would complete a contract. [citations omitted]. . . .

The authorities above cited emphasize that, where the offer is clear, definite, and explicit, and leaves nothing open for negotiation, it constitutes an offer, acceptance of which will complete the contract. The most recent case on the subject is *Johnson v. Capital City Ford Co.,* La. App., 85 So. 2d 75, in which the court pointed out that a newspaper advertisement relating to the purchase and sale of automobiles may constitute an offer, acceptance of which will consummate a contract and create an obligation in the offeror to perform according to the terms of the published offer.

Whether in any individual instance a newspaper advertisement is an offer rather than an invitation to make an offer depends on the legal intention of the parties and the surrounding circumstances. Annotation, 157 A.L.R. 744, 751; 77 C.J.S., Sales, §25b; 17 C.J.S., Contracts, §389. We are of the view on the facts before us that the offer by the defendant of the sale of the Lapin fur was clear, definite, and explicit, and left nothing open for negotiation. The plaintiff having successfully managed to be the first one to appear at the seller's place of business to be served, as requested by the advertisement, and having offered the stated purchase price of the article, he was entitled to performance on the part of the defendant. . . .

Affirmed.

7

Reorganization, Summary, and Inductive Reasoning in Outline Form

I. REORGANIZATION—MAPPING THE FOREST

When preparing for final examinations or preparing to write a legal memorandum, a law student or an associate in a law firm must make a significant transition from analysis of individual cases to the final expression of a completed legal analysis of the assigned problem. That transition begins with the synthesis of cases and continues with further analysis and reorganization, often leading to a transfer of the information in library notes or class notes to an outline.

An associate researching and analyzing a simple problem may not need to reorganize her modest library notes before expressing her analysis in a short memorandum. On the other hand, long hours of researching a complex, multiple-issue problem may produce a mass of disorganized notes dealing with several issues and lines of authority. In those circumstances, the associate may need to summarize and reorganize the notes in some manner before writing or even outlining the memorandum, and perhaps even before completely analyzing the problem.

Such a process is facilitated by taking library notes on note cards and limiting the notes on each card to discussion of a single statute, case, or other authority. Indeed, if a single case separately discusses more than one issue relating to the assignment, the associate should note the discussion of each issue on separate note cards:

The associate can use these cards to help her prepare an outline of the fruits of her research. As an initial step, she can devise categories for the note cards that identify distinct legal issues and can assign each card to one of the groups:

If the associate has used a note pad rather than note cards, she may wish to prepare an index of the cases, and perhaps even of distinct issues within a case, by assigning consecutive numbers to her case briefs:

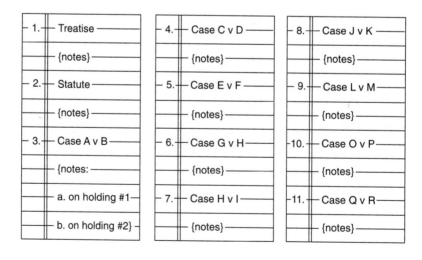

When reorganizing the product of her research in an outline, she can refer to her notes on a case or other authority by its number on the note pad:

```
            C.    Issue 3
                  Case A v B #3b
                  Case O v P #10
                  Case I v J #7
                  Case Q v R #11

      IV.    DISCUSSION

          A.    Issue 1

                  Case A v B #3a
                  Case C v D #4
                  Case K v L #8
                  Case G v H #6

          B. Issue 2

                  Statute #2
                  Treatise #1
                  Case M v N #9
                  Case E v F #5
```

With either technique, the associate can more easily analyze her notes because she has divided them into manageable portions, each of which relates to a distinct legal problem. If she takes her notes on a portable computer, she can reorganize the information even more easily.

A law student preparing for final examinations has a special need to summarize, reorganize, and reanalyze his notes in outline form. In the course of a semester, a typical law student will amass several notebooks full of case briefs and notes of class discussion. Although these notes represent a summary of the thousands of pages of reading and hundreds of hours of class discussion and lecture for several courses, they are still too massive and disorganized to permit effective review and analysis for exam preparation. A well-organized summary of those notes in outline form can enable the student to stand back from the trees formed by cases and to see the broad outline of the legal forest.

The real value of a course outline, however, is not in the final product as a study aid, but in the student's activities of reviewing and synthesizing material and of drafting the outline. These tasks develop important skills of organization, analysis, and expression. A method of reasoning essential to the entire process of outlining is inductive reasoning.

II. INDUCTIVE REASONING

Through two variations of inductive reasoning, you can use information from a series of specific cases to reach a conclusion about either

(1) the outcome of another specific case, or
(2) the likelihood of the truth of a general proposition.[1]

A. ANALOGY

The process of using inductive reasoning to predict the outcome of a specific case by comparing it to other cases is one of analogy. For example, a series of cases has permitted warrantless searches of automobiles and similar vehicles, if the searches were supported by probable cause, because (1) the mobility of the vehicles created exigent circumstances that made it impracticable to obtain a warrant before searching, and (2) the owner of each vehicle had only limited expectations of privacy in its contents because the vehicle was subject to extensive administrative regulation. From those cases, you could use inductive reasoning to conclude that police may search a motor home without a warrant because (1) the motor home is similar in mobility to the vehicles that were the subjects of the prior cases, and (2) government regulation of all licensed motor vehicles gives the owner of the motor home reduced expectations of privacy similar to those of the owners of the vehicles in the prior cases:

Four cases permitted warrantless searches of the following kinds of vehicles, because each vehicle was mobile and subject to administrative regulation:

Case #1: car on highway
Case #2: delivery truck in a private driveway
Case #3: family van in a shopping center parking lot
Case #4: four-wheel drive truck on unpaved desert

One reasonable conclusion from the prior cases:

In Case #5, a warrant should not be required to search a motor home parked on the street in a residential neighborhood, because it is mobile and subject to administrative regulation, as were the vehicles in Cases 1-4.

As with all inductive reasoning, this conclusion about the motor home does not necessarily follow from the outcomes of the previous cases. Rather, the strength of the supporting cases simply makes the truth of the conclusion

---

1. See, e.g., Irving M. Copi, Introduction to Logic 23-26, 351-353 (4th ed. 1972).

more or less likely. Indeed, you might argue that government regulation of licensed vehicles is less significant to the scope of privacy expectations than is the range and nature of activities for which a vehicle is designed. If that argument were accepted, you might use inductive reasoning to generalize from a different series of cases, each of which held that police could not search a house, apartment, or other dwelling without a warrant even if they had probable cause to search. From those cases, you could conclude that the occupant of a motor home would enjoy protection from warrantless searches similar to that enjoyed by the occupant of a house, because each structure is designed for residential uses such as sleeping, eating, and storing personal effects:

Four cases required a warrant to search the following kinds of dwellings, partly because the expectation of privacy in the contents of dwellings is so high:

Case #1: unattached house on its own lot
Case #2: rented unit of apartment complex
Case #3: weekend cabin in the mountains
Case #4: natural cave on private land used as a dwelling

One reasonable conclusion from the prior cases:

In Case #5, a warrant should be required to search a motor home parked on the street in a residential neighborhood, because it is used as a dwelling during vacation travel and contains the kinds of personal items normally stored in a fixed dwelling.

Thus, depending on the relative weight that you assigned to competing factors and values, you would find one of the two competing lines of authority more nearly analogous to your case. This flexibility in inductive reasoning explains why judges can reasonably differ on the proper application and extension of precedent.[2]

B. GENERALIZING FROM PARTICULARS

The second variation of inductive reasoning allows you to construct a general proposition from specific cases. By using this process to prepare a course outline, you can begin making the transition from daily briefing of cases to solving problems on a final examination. With this type of reasoning, you attempt to construct a general rule that is consistent with the facts and outcomes of past cases. You can then apply the general rule to other cases with similar facts.

---

2. See, e.g., California v. Carney, 471 U.S. 386 (1985) (rejecting the California Supreme Court's conclusion that a warrant was required to search a motor home).

For example, you may have briefed four cases in which courts denied punitive damages on claims for various breaches of contract: innocent breach of a construction contract, intentional breach of a contract for the sale of real estate, malicious breach of a contract to supply water, and intentional breach of an employment contract. Although the rule would not necessarily follow from the cases, you could reasonably induce from the cases a general rule that punitive damages are not available for breach of contract. You could then apply that rule to a new case, such as the intentional breach of a lease, that is not identical to any of the prior cases but is nonetheless encompassed by the general rule derived from the prior cases through inductive reasoning:

Four cases denied punitive damages for the following kinds of breach of contract:

Case #1: innocent breach of a construction contract
Case #2: intentional breach of a realty contract
Case #3: malicious breach of a water-supply contract
Case #4: intentional breach of a lease

General rule derived from the prior cases:

Punitive damages are not available for breach of contract, regardless of the breaching party's state of mind.

Application of general rule to new case:

In Case #5, punitive damages will not be available for intentional breach of an employment contract.

The degree of confidence that you have in the general rule will depend on the strength of the supporting cases. If one of the previous decisions had awarded punitive damages for breach of a marriage contract, the general rule stated above would be a less reliable guide to the outcome of other kinds of disputes within its terms, and you would apply the rule with caution. You could improve the reliability of the rule by modifying it to achieve consistency with all the previous cases: Punitive damages are not available for breach of contract, except for breach of marriage contracts.

=========== E X E R C I S E   7 - 1 ===========

Review the illustration in Chapter 3, pages 34-35, regarding the family rules developed by Gerald and Janice for their children, Tanya and Jamal. Assume that Gerald and Janice did not clearly articulate their rules but provided guidance to Jamal simply by admonishing him when they disapproved of his actions. Imagine how Jamal might use inductive reasoning to infer rules from the following events:

1. On Friday, October 1, Jamal attended a high school football game, which ended at 9:45 P.M. He then joined some friends for pizza and arrived home at 11:30 P.M. Gerald and Janice scolded him for being late, saying "next time, come home right after the game."

2. On Friday, October 8, Jamal attended a high school football game, which ended at 9:45 P.M. He then joined some friends for pizza and arrived home at 10:55 P.M. His parents greeted him at the door cheerfully and asked, "How was your evening?"

3. On Saturday, October 9, Jamal took a friend out to a movie and returned home by 11:00 P.M. His parents expressed no disapproval of his actions.

4. During the Week of October 11-17, Jamal attended a special meeting of the high school debate club on Tuesday night, a football game on Friday night, and a high school musical production on Saturday night, returning home by 11:00 P.M. on each night. On Sunday morning, Gerald and Janice admonished him that he was "taking too much time away from his studies" and that he should not go out at night so often.

5. During the week of December 1-7, Jamal went to a musical concert on Thursday night and saw a movie on Friday night, returning home by 11:00 P.M. on each night. On Saturday night, Gerald and Janice took Tanya and Jamal to a relative's wedding and reception, returning home with the family by 10:45 P.M. Gerald and Janice expressed no disapproval of Jamal's actions during that week.

C. RELATIONSHIP TO DEDUCTIVE REASONING

Both forms of inductive reasoning described in Sections A and B above can be applied to the broad framework of deductive reasoning described in Chapter 4, pages 56-60. In that framework, after identifying an issue, you state the applicable rule and apply it to the relevant facts to reach a conclusion:

Issue	
Rule	{Major Premise}
Application to Facts	{Minor Premise}
Conclusion	

1. Formulating the Rule

Through the inductive process of constructing a general proposition from a series of cases, you can identify the rule that forms the major premise of your deductive analysis. In an office memorandum or a brief, you could represent this process comprehensively in several paragraphs or pages of in-depth analysis of case law that shows how you arrived at your understanding of the current form of a developing legal principle.[3] The discussion of law in the first sample memorandum in Chapter 9, pages 186-187, illustrates such analysis.

Alternatively, you could state the rule as simply as a proposition in a single sentence, followed by citation to a couple of cases from which you derived the rule:

> A promise does not satisfy the consideration requirement if it allows the promisor to refrain from performing according to his unfettered discretion rather than to external constraints. *See Strong v. Sheffield,* 144 N.Y. 392, 39 N.E. 330 (1895); *see also Di Benedetto v. Di Rocco,* 372 Pa. 302, 93 A.2d 474 (1953).

Because of time limitations and other constraints, when you state a rule in an examination answer, you will tend toward this simpler example, almost always without any citation to authority.[4]

2. Applying the Rule to the Facts

To help you apply the legal rule to the facts of your dispute, you can invoke the inductive process of analogizing between previous cases and your own. In an office memorandum or brief, you may represent this process comprehensively in several paragraphs or pages in which you compare the facts and reasoning of previous cases to the facts of your own case. Again, the fact analysis in the first sample memorandum in Chapter 9, page 187, illustrates such explicit analogy and distinction.

Alternatively, you could analyze the facts more simply by directly explaining why the facts of your case do not satisfy the legal rule:

> In this case, the lender's promise to forbear until he "needs" the money appears to condition the length of his forbearance on financial events that are at least partly outside his control. As long as his income and expenses create no need for the money, the lender has committed himself to forbear from demanding payment. Therefore, the lender's promise satisfies the consideration requirement, and the guarantor's promise is enforceable.

As with the statement of the legal rule, your fact analysis in an exam answer will often tend toward this simpler example. In developing even a simple fact analysis, however, you may implicitly compare the facts of your case with the facts and reasoning of the cases that you have earlier analyzed. Thus, although you may not always have time during an examination to

---

3. One author refers to this process as a separate step of analysis, which he calls "rule proof." Richard K. Neumann, Jr., Legal Reasoning and Legal Writing §7.1, at 111-112 (1990).

4. See id. §7.3, at 124 (characterizing this lesser depth of analysis as absence of "rule proof").

express the details of your comparison, the inductive process of analogizing and distinguishing cases nonetheless informs your fact analysis.

3. Role of the Course Outline

By preparing a course outline, you can use inductive reasoning to help bridge the gap between your case briefs and the deductive analysis called for in a law school examination. As discussed more fully below, your outline should be organized around general legal rules, some of which you have constructed through inductive reasoning from groups of cases. These are rules that you can later recall and restate in an examination answer.

Moreover, your outline should illustrate these rules with brief summaries of the cases from which you derived the rules. Your familiarity with the facts and reasoning of these cases will help you apply the general rules to the facts of your examination questions, even if you do not always have time during the examination to fully express your process of analogizing and distinguishing cases.

III. TECHNIQUES OF OUTLINING COURSE MATERIALS

To transform your case briefs and class notes to a useful outline, you must reorganize, analyze, and summarize. The finished product will be an infinitely more useful study guide than your original notes, but the real value of a course outline is in the process of constructing it rather than in the finished product. Expressing your understanding of the law in outline form forces you to identify and resolve lingering areas of confusion that a less rigorous form of review might conceal. Moreover, outlining develops skills of organization and expression that you must summon and apply in the examination room and the law office. A commercial outline might contain information that you can understand and even remember, but it does not provide an effective means of developing important skills.

A. FUNDAMENTAL PRINCIPLES OF OUTLINING

The format for a course outline is largely a matter of personal style for each student. The techniques of outlining described in this chapter are not the only ones that you might find helpful. The techniques described here, however, have the benefit of developing skills that can be readily employed in drafting office memoranda and briefs, as well as exam answers. These outlining techniques require you to

(1) classify cases to facilitate a reorganization that focuses on general principles rather than on individual cases, and

(2) display the proper relationships among points in the outline.

1. Classification

Your course outline should not simply present a series of case briefs or even of case brief summaries. Instead, it should emphasize general rules of law and should subordinate the case briefs to the role of illustrating the rules.

The first step in organizing such a course outline is to classify the kinds of problems or rules addressed in the case briefs and class notes and to recognize which kinds of problems are subsets of more general topics. Depending on the volume and complexity of the material to be outlined, you may identify several levels of classifications of problem areas or principles. If so, the most logical way to proceed is first to identify the classifications that have the broadest scope, and then to identify the subsidiary classifications that form subsets of the major classifications.

For example, the remedies portion of a contracts course might encompass two broad categories of relief: (1) specific relief, in the form of an injunction to perform as promised, and (2) substitutional relief, or money damages. Within each of those two major topics, the course material would undoubtedly present subsidiary problem areas, each of which encompasses another set of subsidiary problem areas, and so on. The following sequence of headings traces a single, descending line of such classifications leading to the topic of the availability of punitive damages in tort and contract actions.

> I. Specific Relief
>   • • • •
> II. Substitutional Relief—Money Damages
>   A. Nominal Damages
>   • • • •
>   B. Compensatory Damages
>   • • • •
>   C. Punitive Damages
>   1. Purpose and Measure
>   • • • •
>   2. Availability
>   a. Torts
>   • • • •
>   b. Contracts
>   • • • •

Each of the classifications in this outline identifies a subset of the area of law encompassed by the subject of remedies and identifies the subject matter of disputes that have required the application of legal rules to facts. Moreover, each major classification in the outline first addresses a topic at the most general level and then separately examines more specific problems within the topic.

To clearly signal the organizational procession from the general to the

specific, you may wish to begin each significant section and subsection with
a brief paragraph or a separate introductory section that presents an overview
of the subsections that follow:

    I. Overview
       A successful claimant may be entitled to either or both of two
       basic kinds of relief: (1) specific relief, in the form of an injunction
       that orders the defendant to take, or refrain from taking, some
       action, (2) substitutional relief, in the form of an award of money
       damages.
   II. Specific/Injunctive Relief
      • • • •
  III. Substitutional Relief
       Depending on the circumstances, courts may award any of three
       kinds of money damages: nominal, compensatory, or punitive.
       A. Nominal Damages
         • • • •
       B. Compensatory Damages
         • • • •
       C. Punitive Damages
         • • • •

2. Proper Relationships Among Points

By displaying the proper relationships among points in your outline,
you demonstrate a full understanding of its analytic content. For example,
the excerpts presented above accurately identify some topics as subsets of
more general topics. In contrast, the following outline erroneously classifies
compensatory damages as an element of specific relief. It also misleadingly
suggests that the topics of the availability and measure of punitive damages
are no more closely related to one another than either is to questions about
nominal damages:

    I. Specific Relief
       A. Compensatory Damages
         • • • •
   II. Substitutional Relief—Money Damages
       A. Nominal Damages
       B. Availability of Punitive Damages
       C. Measure of Punitive Damages

If you have trouble getting your outline started, you might set organizational considerations aside until you clearly identify the points that you later
will display in logical structure. For example, you might start by glancing
through your notes and the table of contents of your coursebook and
by making a "laundry list" of rules or problem areas that the cases have
presented:

injunctions   expectation interest   nominal damages
adequacy of remedy at law   compensatory damages
mitigation of damages   punitive damages   unique goods
specific performance of personal services

Once you have identified the topics that you want to address in the outline, you can classify the problems presented in the list and can determine their proper relationships to one another.

My two sons use a remarkably similar process when they clean their playroom. Scattered throughout the room are such things as stuffed animals and dolls, fiction and nonfiction books, and toy dinosaurs and cars. They know that the stuffed animals and dolls belong on the window box, the dinosaurs belong in the red toy bin, the cars belong in a special box, and the books belong on one of two shelves. Their nonfiction reference books, such as those on science and nature, belong on a shelf in their bedroom closet. All other books are stored between book ends on top of a bedroom dresser. When putting away these belongings, they typically wade through the scattered objects, picking out all the objects within a single category or subcategory, such as all cars, and putting them in their proper place before gathering objects from another category or subcategory. The organizational structure of their activity could be represented in the following way:

I. Proper Places for Dolls, Toys, and Books
   A. Dolls and Stuffed Animals
      {together as single category on window box}
   B. Toys
      1. Dinosaurs
         {red toy bin}
      2. Cars
         {special box}
   C. Books
      1. Nonfiction Reference Books
         {bedroom closet shelf}
      2. All Other Children's Books
         {between bookends on dresser}

Of course, my children's chore is relatively simple. Their playthings are concrete, simple, and readily distinguished from one another. Moreover, my wife and I devised the categories and the corresponding storage areas.

As a law student, however, you must work with more abstract principles and must devise your own categories and subcategories. Your casebook's table of contents may provide some hints on categories and organization, but you should not hesitate to depart from it. A casebook will occasionally adopt an unusual organizational structure for pedagogical purposes, and you may prefer a more straightforward structure that will translate more readily to a guide for problem-solving.

Organizing an outline of legal points is not an exact science. The flexibility and uncertainty inherent in the analysis of much of the material that you encounter in the first year of law school make it impossible to identify a single "correct" method of organizing an outline of that material. Nonetheless, your diligent efforts leading to a reasonable outline will develop skills of organization that you can transfer directly to more formal legal documents such as briefs, memoranda, and contracts.

B. CONTENT OF THE OUTLINE

1. Identifying, Constructing, and Stating Rules

As a means of preparing to apply general legal rules to the facts of an exam problem, you should identify or even construct legal rules from the statutes and cases that you have studied. This process does not compel an unduly simplistic and mechanical approach to the law. The legal rules are simply shorthand representations of more complex sets of information that are explored in greater detail in references to the case law from which the rules are drawn. Consider, for example, one scholar's views on identifying and stating general principles relating to the doctrine of consideration in contract law:

> Here, as elsewhere, it is our function to construct working rules and definitions. The process and the result are made no different by the admission that the rules and definitions are not absolute but relative, not eternal but changeable. They will be useful if they are based on judicial history down to date, if they clearly indicate the facts and transactions to which they apply, and if they are in accord with the prevailing judicial action of modern time. At the least, we can review and classify the facts that have been held to be (or not to be) a "sufficient consideration" to make an informal promise enforceable. If we find a high degree of uniformity and agreement, rules can be stated and definitions attempted. We can consider the rules and definitions of the past, show the extent to which they have worked, and indicate the variation and progress that require a new restatement.[5]

On some topics, a legislature supplies a statutory rule, or a court states a general rule derived from earlier case law. Even dictum from a judicial opinion may provide a reliable guide to a tentative statement of a general rule. Although you must identify the narrow holding of a decision to evaluate the effect of the case as precedent, you may safely look to dictum for aid in constructing general rules that you can profitably apply in an examination.

In many instances, however, you will not find concise statements of general rules on a particular legal topic in statutes or in the holdings or dicta of judicial decisions. Instead, you must identify the cases that address issues related to the topic, and you must use synthesis and inductive reasoning to construct a general rule from the individual cases. To use the example presented in the previous section, you might study the holdings in a series of decisions denying punitive damages in different kinds of contracts cases and construct a general rule that punitive damages are not available for

---

5. 1 Arthur L. Corbin, Corbin on Contracts §109, at 489-490 (1963).

breach of contract, even though none of the decisions stated such a rule of general application. Indeed, your synthesis and inductive reasoning at the outline stage may lead you to revise your earlier, more tentative generalizations about a series of cases.

2. Illustrating Rules with Examples

Regardless of the method that you use to identify a general legal rule, your statement of the rule should not stand alone. You should illustrate and give more definite shape to the rule by summarizing the case law from which the rule was derived and by identifying competing rules or exceptions to the rule:

> V. Punitive Damages
>   A. Purpose and Measure
>   • • • •
>   B. Availability
>   1. Torts— . . .
>   2. Contracts—Courts generally do not award punitive damages for breach of contract.
>   a. Example: In *White v. Benkowski,* CB at 12, the court affirmed a trial court's denial of punitive damages for even a malicious breach of an agreement to supply water.
>   b. Exception to Rule: In dictum, the *White* court suggested that it might retain a traditional exception allowing punitive damages for breach of a marriage agreement.
>   c. Minority Approach: A few jurisdictions have followed the lead of *Jordan v. Ash,* CB at 16, which granted punitive damages for an employer's "malicious and oppressive" breach of an employment agreement, even though the employee had not proved all the elements of an independent tort.

The concise statement of the general rule in Subsection 2 of the outline above represents the kind of information that you must recall and express on a law school examination. To apply that rule to the facts of an exam question, however, you must have a more concrete understanding of the law than is reflected in the abstract statement of the general rule. For this, you must analyze individual cases, as illustrated in Subsections a, b, and c in the above example.

Subsections a and b illustrate a student's understanding of the parameters of the rule in most jurisdictions: Some courts might award punitive damages in the exceptional case of breach of a marriage agreement; otherwise, even a finding of malice on the part of the breaching party will not move a court to depart from the general rule. Subsection c reflects the student's judgment that *Jordan* represents a minority approach that departs from the general view that malice is not significant to the availability of punitive damages for breach of contract. By identifying the factual context of *Jordan*, the student can remain sensitive to the possibility that the minority approach is limited to employment contracts or other contracts in which the parties have disparate bargaining power.

A more sophisticated outline of the same material might incorporate a policy analysis of the rule and the cases that illustrate it, perhaps reflecting the student's evaluation, as well as her synthesis, of the cases:

> 2. Contracts—Courts generally do not award punitive damages for breach of contract.
>
> a. Possible policy justifications—A breach of a private contract may not injure community interests as much as would a tort or a crime. Indeed, in some instances a breach may benefit the community by permitting reallocation of the freed resources to more productive uses. Compensatory damages would permit this reallocation while making the victim of the breach whole, but punitive damages would discourage the reallocation.
>
> b. Example: In *White v. Benkowski*, CB at 12, the court affirmed denial of punitive damages for even a malicious breach of a contract to supply water. This decision doesn't seem to further any important policy, however, because the supplier did not reallocate the water to a more urgent use.
>
> c. Exception: In dictum, the *White* Court suggested that it might retain a traditional exception allowing punitive damages for breach of a marriage agreement, presumably because, according to Corbin, "community resentment" may once have been greater in such cases.
>
> d. Minority Approach: In *Jordan v. Ash*, CB at 16, the court approved punitive damages for an employer's "malicious and oppressive" breach of an employment agreement, even though the employee had not proved all the elements of an independent tort. Deterrence through punitive damages is appropriate in such cases, because the injurious conduct is designed to harm others rather than to reallocate resources or serve any other business needs.

In this example, illustration c does more than simply identify possible limitations to the rule. It also implicitly raises questions about the continued viability of an exception that arguably is rooted in outdated values. Similarly, illustration d does more than identify a minority approach as a different kind of qualification to the general rule. In conjunction with illustration b, it implicitly compares the merits of maintaining certainty in a broad rule of general application (illustration b) with the case-specific fairness achieved by narrowly shaping rules so that they apply no further than the reasons that support them (illustration d).

The policy analysis may be suggested in the opinions themselves, may be the topic of class discussion, or may be the product of your original analysis. If time permits, you may wish to consult a treatise for clarification or for ideas that enrich your outline. However, you will develop skills best by preparing outlines from course materials and class notes with little or no reference to study aids and with only occasional reference to respected treatises to help clear up areas of confusion.

When you outline course material, your single-sentence summaries of the cases should represent a substantial condensation of your case briefs and notes of class discussion. Nonetheless, they should include a sufficient reference to the facts of those cases to bring each case to life and to place statements about the legal results of the cases in their factual context. Indeed, you may find that you can analyze some exam questions best by directly analogizing the exam problem to, or distinguishing it from, a particular case summarized in your outline rather than by recalling a general and abstract principle that you have constructed from several cases.

In preparing the outline, however, you should maintain a basic structure that organizes the subject matter around legal rules and that subordinates the cases to illustrations of those rules. For example, a case that addresses distinct issues relating to the proper measure of compensatory damages and to the availability of punitive damages might appear in summarized form in two places in the outline: (1) A summary of the court's first holding would illustrate a rule about compensatory damages, and (2) a summary of the second holding would illustrate a rule about punitive damages stated in a different section of the outline.

Often, you can best illustrate the parameters of a rule by comparing two factually distinguishable, legally consistent cases that reach different results. By identifying a set of facts that satisfies the legal rule and by contrasting them with a set of facts that does not, the outline helps to bring concrete meaning to an otherwise abstract rule.

For example, an outline of statutory liability for civil rights violations might address the subtopic of a judge's defense of absolute immunity from money damages. More particularly, it could compare cases that address the principle that a judge is protected only for acts performed in a "judicial function":

VI. Immunity Defenses
   [overview]
   A. Absolute Immunities—Legislators, judges, and prosecutors must make sensitive policy decisions on controversial matters and are conspicuous targets for retaliatory suits. Absolute immunity allows them to exercise discretion without fear of reprisal.
      1. Legislators—. . .
      2. Judges—A state judge is absolutely immune from liability for money damages, even for allegedly malicious unconstitutional acts, if the judge (i) had subject-matter jurisdiction, and (ii) was acting in a judicial function.

Rule

         a. Subject-matter Jurisdiction—. . .
         b. Judicial Function—A judge enjoys immunity only for actions taken within a judicial function, as contrasted with the judge's administrative function.

(1) Example: In *Forrester v. White,* CB 423 (7th Cir. 1986),[6] a judge enjoyed absolute immunity from liability for alleged discrimination in firing a probation officer. Because the probation officer's duties included advising the judge on substantive matters, hiring or firing the officer was a judicial function that "directly implicated the exercise of the judge's discretionary judgment."

Facts that satisfy the rule

(2) Example: In *McMillan v. Svetanoff,* CB 425 (7th Cir. 1986), a judge was not absolutely immune from liability for alleged race discrimination in firing a court reporter, who recorded proceedings but did not perform legal analysis. Hiring and firing such employees was an administrative task because it did not require exercise of the judge's legal knowledge or experience.

Facts that do not satisfy the rule

In this outline, subsections b(1) and b(2) give concrete meaning to the abstract rule stated in subsection b by providing examples of (1) facts that satisfy the rule stated in subsection b and (2) facts that fail to satisfy the rule.

C. THE OUTLINE AS A STUDY TOOL

Although the process of preparing an outline is more valuable than the finished product, a thoughtful outline makes an excellent study tool. When reviewing for exams, you can put your voluminous notes aside and use the brief references to cases in the outline to trigger your memory about the fuller case analysis that you performed earlier in the semester.

In the few hours before an exam, you may want to take a broader view of the course by skimming the legal rules stated in the major sections and subsections of your outline. The factual context provided by case summaries will easily come to mind if you have earlier analyzed those cases, expressed the analysis in the outline, and read the entire outline once or twice after preparing it. Indeed, you may find it helpful to prepare a brief outline of the outline by writing down the major headings of the outline on a separate sheet of paper.

---

6. *Rev'd,* 484 U.S. 219 (1988). Although the circuit decision was reversed in 1988, the state of the law in the Seventh Circuit in 1986 provides a good vehicle for illustrating factually contrasting decisions in the same jurisdiction.

IV. SUMMARY

To outline course material:

(1) Analyze and synthesize by briefing the cases and reflecting on class discussion.
(2) Identify topics that you intend to address in the outline. You should identify significant general rules that are stated in the course materials or that you can construct from the course materials through a process of synthesis and inductive reasoning.
(3) State those rules in an organized fashion that shows the proper relationships among the rules.
(4) Finally, illustrate the general rules with brief summaries of the cases from which the rules are derived.

════════ E X E R C I S E   7 - 2 ════════

1. *Outlining Exercise—Rules of the House*

Imagine that parents, Gerald and Janice, are teaching their infant son, Reggie, good habits and behavior. Reggie can't fully understand abstract rules, so Gerald and Janice teach him through positive or negative feedback in specific situations. In the last few weeks, Reggie remembers the following experiences for which he received praise or admonishment:

The Case of the Hand in the Cookie Jar: Reggie reached into a cookie jar and helped himself to a cookie shortly before dinner. Janice and Gerald admonished Reggie that the cookie would spoil his appetite for dinner.

The Case of the Broken Vase: Reggie climbed onto a chair, reached a vase on a table top, and threw the vase to the floor, breaking it. Janice and Gerald sent Reggie to his room, admonishing him that he should not play with his parent's possessions.

The Case of the Chocolate Ice Cream: After dinner one night, Reggie asked for some chocolate ice cream. To his surprise, his parents served him a dish of ice cream, praising him for having finished his vegetables.

The Case of the Mistreated Teddy Bear: Anxious to test his parents' limits one evening, Reggie climbed onto a chair with his favorite teddy bear and threw the teddy bear onto the living room carpet. Reggie's parents saw this event but had no reaction; they continued reading the newspaper and watching TV.

The Case of the Bouncing Ball: Emboldened by the teddy bear incident, Reggie brought out his favorite rubber ball and began kicking it around the living room, causing it to bounce off the TV set and to narrowly miss

Janice's glass of wine sitting on the coffee table. Janice flashed Reggie an angry glance, and Gerald sternly said, "Outside with that ball, young man!"

Assignment: From these cases, derive at least two general rules governing Reggie's behavior in his home. Illustrate each of your rules with brief summaries that show what kinds of behavior either satisfy or violate the rules. If appropriate, draft an overview statement that captures the essence of all the rules and examples. When you have completed your outline, compare it with the sample outline in Chapter 8, pages 148-149.

2. Outlining Exercise—Advertisements as Offers

Review the case briefs that you prepared for Exercise 6-1(3), pages 112-115. Prepare an excerpt of a contracts outline that addresses the question of whether a store's newspaper advertisement amounts to an offer. Derive a general legal rule from the two cases, and use summaries of the cases as illustrations of the rule.

8

Essay Examinations

I. OVERVIEW—PERSPECTIVE AND GENERAL FORMAT

The answer to a law school essay examination is generally similar to the discussion section of an office memorandum, which is discussed in detail in Chapter 9. When you reach Chapter 9, you should reflect on these parallels. To better prepare you for the comparison, this chapter will occasionally pause to note which facets of examination answers have counterparts in office memoranda and to point out the differences in styles appropriate to each document.

A. PERSPECTIVE

Most essay examinations ask for a balanced analysis of a problem with a direction such as the following: "Discuss the claims and defenses that the parties may reasonably assert. Be sure to discuss arguments on both sides of each issue." Like an actual office memorandum assignment, the exam problem may identify one of the parties as your client. Nonetheless, the exam obviously requests that you adopt an objective perspective rather than advocate only your client's claims and defenses. In addition to developing arguments for your own client, you must anticipate and demonstrate an understanding of the counterarguments that the opposing party likely will raise.

Indeed, many exam problems do not even identify one of the parties as your client. Your perspective then will be even more strictly neutral than it would be for an office memorandum, which at least anticipates advocacy on behalf of an identified client.

Finally, a few exam problems may ask you to advocate only the claims and defenses of an identified client. If so, your answer will take the partisan approach of a brief to a court. Such exams, however, are rare.

B. GENERAL FORMAT

As introduced in Chapter 4, an answer to an essay examination and the discussion section of an office memorandum typically share a general structure: After (1) identifying the issue, you should (2) summarize the applicable legal rule or rules, (3) apply the rule to the relevant facts to determine whether the facts satisfy the legal rule, and (4) state a reasonable conclusion.

Some of the more formal components of other legal documents are notably missing from a good exam answer. For example, professors normally do not require you to formally state all the issues at or near the beginning of your answer, as you would in an office memorandum or in some briefs. Even more important, you should never waste time drafting an introduction that separately restates all the facts of the problem. In all but the most unusual examinations, the problem will state the facts for you. Accordingly, your professor will test your ability to analyze groups of those facts in the context of specific issues, but not your ability to restate all the facts at the outset.

II. ELEMENTS OF THE ANSWER

A. ISSUES

1. Identifying Issues

Occasionally, a professor will identify examination issues by asking you to respond to specific questions, such as "Did Seller make an offer to Buyer?". More commonly, the exam problem will end with a very general question about the rights and obligations of the party, and it requires you to identify the relevant issues.

To identify the issues, you must apply the skills and knowledge that you have acquired from briefing cases and outlining course material throughout the semester. By briefing countless cases, you have learned to sift through complicated fact patterns and to recognize the kinds of facts that have potential legal significance. Moreover, by briefing and synthesizing cases and by outlining the course material, you have armed yourself with a general knowledge of relevant legal rules and policies. With this preparation, by carefully studying the facts of the exam problem, you can determine what claims and defenses the parties can reasonably assert and which elements of those claims and defenses are placed in doubt.

For example, suppose that an exam problem asks you to assume that the relevant jurisdiction has retained the common law definition of burglary. Part of the problem describes Michael Glass just before dawn opening the door of the cab of a VW van and reaching inside to steal stereo equipment lying on the driver's seat. It also states that the owner of the van, Leona Rosal, is sleeping in the back of the van while on a road trip, with curtains drawn between her and the cab of the van. The problem also asks you to assume that theft of the stereo equipment would constitute felony larceny in the jurisdiction.

You know from your studies that the common law crime of burglary requires proof of the breaking and entering of a dwelling of another at night with the intent to commit a felony. Armed with this knowledge, you can see that the facts provide a nonfrivolous basis for prosecuting Michael Glass for common law burglary. Specifically, Michael's opening the cab door and reaching into the van to steal the stereo equipment are almost certainly a "breaking and entering" with an "intent to commit a felony." These elements of the crime probably do not raise issues warranting substantial discussion.

Other elements of the crime, however, are in doubt. The moments "just before dawn" are only arguably "during the night," and the cab of Leona's van is not clearly part of "a dwelling." Thus, whether Michael committed a burglary is subject to some debate and is a general issue in the problem.

Moreover, each element of the crime that is in doubt forms the basis of a subissue. For example, the VW van may be unlike the more conventional houses that satisfied the "dwelling" requirement in the common law cases that you have studied. Although Leona is temporarily using the van as sleeping quarters, the van is arguably primarily a means of transportation, and the cab is physically separated from the sleeping quarters. Because you can reasonably argue either side of this topic, whether Leona's van is a "dwelling" for purposes of common law burglary is a subissue warranting discussion. Other elements of the crime and possible defenses may be placed in issue by the facts summarized above or by other facts in the problem.

2. Scope of Analysis

Because the process of identifying issues requires you to exercise judgment, you can never determine with complete certainty which questions your professor thinks are sufficiently clearly raised by the facts to warrant discussion. Moreover, some professors directly examine your ability to identify as many issues as possible, including those related to novel or particularly creative legal theories. When in doubt, therefore, you should identify and at least briefly discuss even marginal issues. If the professor expects some discussion of a marginal issue, you will earn valuable points even with a conclusory discussion. On the other hand, if the professor disagrees that a particular matter warrants analysis, you will have minimized the lost time by keeping the discussion brief.

3. Expressing Your Identification of Issues

You need not state each of the issues and subissues of an examination problem in polished detail. However, your answer should leave no doubt about which issue you are analyzing in any passage in the answer. To guide your reader through your analysis, you can use the same techniques that help convey organization to the reader of an office memorandum. You should discuss major issues in separate sections and should precede each discussion with a section heading that generally identifies the issue analyzed in that section.

A section heading introducing an issue or subissue can simply be a brief word or phrase that refers to a claim, a defense, or one element of a claim or defense. Unless the question raises the possibility of claims of only one party against one other, section headings also should identify which party is bringing a claim against which other in each section.

For example, an examination problem might raise issues about various tort claims among three parties: Smith, Jones, and King. A student might display the general organization of his answer with section headings such as the following:

I. Smith v. Jones
   A. Battery
      • • • •
   B. Infliction of Emotional Distress
      • • • •
II. Smith v. King
   A. Negligence
      • • • •
   B. Strict Products Liability
      • • • •
III. Jones v. Smith—Defamation
      • • • •

In some cases, you may wish to illuminate the issue that is denoted by a section heading by referring briefly to a potential argument of one of the parties, to facts that raise the issue, or to a preliminary legal conclusion that sets up the issue. For example, under section II.A in the example above, you might provide this orientation: "Smith may claim that King negligently hired Jones, proximately causing Smith's injuries at Jones's hands."

Alternatively, you can replace the word or phrase in the section heading with a question stated in a full sentence: "Is King liable to Smith for negligently hiring Jones, proximately causing Smith to suffer injury at Jones's hands?" If you adopt this approach, however, remember that the professor reading the examination answer typically will not expect the precision and specificity appropriate for the formal statement of issues in a case brief, office memorandum, or brief to a court. Therefore, you should not waste valuable time trying to meet those standards in framing your issue.

If your analysis of an issue is lengthy or complex, you may want to use subsection headings to identify your discussions of subissues:

I. Smith v. Jones
   A. Battery
      • • • •
   B. Infliction of Emotional Distress
      [overview of elements of claim]
      1. Extreme and Outrageous Conduct
         • • • •
      2. Intent or Recklessness
         • • • •
      3. Severe Emotional Distress
         • • • •

In simpler cases, however, subtler guides to the reader often will be sufficient for subissues. You can separate your discussions of distinct subissues into separate paragraphs, and you can use a topic sentence to identify the subissue addressed in each paragraph:

B. Infliction of Emotional Distress

[overview of elements of claim]
"Extreme and outrageous" conduct is limited to . . . Viewed in isolation, Principal Jones's method of questioning Schoolboy Smith about illegal drugs . . .
Reckless disregard for the risk of causing severe distress can be established through . . . In this case, Principal Jones was aware . . .
Severe emotional distress means more than . . .

In response to a complex essay question that raises multiple issues, you may help orient the reader by beginning your response with an introductory paragraph that briefly identifies all the major issues that you plan to discuss. However, you should not compose a lengthy introduction that makes the subsequent discussion redundant.

B. LEGAL RULE

1. Presentation of Legal Rules

At the broadest level, the statement of a legal rule may be a summary of the elements of a claim that a party in the examination problem may reasonably pursue:

Intentional Infliction of Emotional Distress

Principal Jones may be liable to Schoolboy Smith for intentional infliction of emotional distress if he engaged in extreme and outrageous conduct that caused Smith severe emotional distress, and if Jones either intended to cause such distress or recklessly disregarded the near certainty of causing such distress.

If you divide the discussion of this claim into subsections or paragraphs to address separate subissues, you might state a subrule in the form of a definition or other illumination of one of the elements of the claim:

> "Extreme and outrageous" conduct is limited to shocking conduct that is beyond all possible bounds of decency. The defendant's conduct is more likely to satisfy this standard if he occupies a position of power or authority over the plaintiff.

Some examination problems may raise questions about choice of law or the precise formulation of the applicable rule. For example, a problem in a contracts examination may raise the question of whether the Uniform Commercial Code or the common law applies to a transaction.[1] Other examination problems may raise questions about the choice between traditional rules and progressive trends, or between majority rules and minority approaches. If you have time to discuss such problems, you should consider briefly discussing each of the competing rules. Then, in the fact analysis that follows, you can discuss the likelihood of success of a claim or defense under each legal rule.

2. Depth and Formality of Analysis

When writing an office memorandum, you normally must discuss specific statutes and case law from a particular jurisdiction that apply to the dispute, and you must carefully cite to the authority on which you rely. Moreover, you often will present the in-depth case analysis and synthesis from which you derive a legal rule.

In contrast, most law school examinations will require you to discuss general legal principles, primarily common law rules, that you must memorize for a closed-book examination. Additionally, you ordinarily will not have time to describe the process of synthesizing cases from which you have derived legal rules. Instead, you may simply present the kind of concise statements of law that you have constructed for your outlines.

Moreover, in an examination answer, you ordinarily need not cite to authority in your discussion of legal rules. You may earn an extra point or two by identifying the names of particular cases that illustrate issues or rules, but that practice is productive only if you remember the case name quickly and with certainty. The extra point or two is not worth a significant investment of time, and the possibility of losing points by naming an irrelevant case reduces the appeal of guessing.

Your professor's expectations may be greater if she gives an open-book examination or provides statutory materials for the examination. If you have legal authority at your disposal during the examination, you can more easily cite to statutes and cases, quote relevant portions of statutes, and explain

---

1. Article 2 of the Uniform Commercial Code applies "[u]nless the context otherwise requires . . . to transactions in goods." U.C.C. §2-102 (1990).

how two or more cases combine to contribute to the development of a legal principle.

C. FACT ANALYSIS—APPLICATION OF LAW TO FACTS

1. Presentation of Fact Analysis

In each section or subsection devoted to an issue or subissue, you should identify facts relevant to the issue and should briefly explain whether the facts satisfy the legal rule that you have summarized. In most cases, you have identified a matter as an issue because the facts of the problem suggest uncertainty about whether a legal rule is satisfied. Therefore, you usually can find some facts that support each side of the dispute, and you should take care to argue both sides:

> *Intentional Infliction of Emotional Distress*
>
> Principal Jones may be liable. . . .
> Viewed in isolation, Principal Jones's method of questioning School-boy Smith about illegal drugs probably was not "extreme and outrageous" in itself, because Jones "addressed Smith politely" and "never raised his voice." On the other hand, Jones was inherently intimidating to Smith, a 10-year-old child, because of Jones's status as an adult and as the highest authority at the elementary school. Moreover, it was common knowledge in the school that Jones had suspended two other students that semester for forging false notes excusing absences. By asking Smith to empty his pockets and to reveal the contents of his desk and locker, Jones implicitly accused Smith of lying when Smith denied any involvement with illegal drugs. In light of Jones's position of authority, his request to search Smith may have been unusually shocking and intimidating, particularly because the request immediately followed Smith's sincere denials.

2. Depth and Formality of Analysis

In an office memorandum, you will explore in depth the application of legal rules to facts by carefully comparing the facts and reasoning of previous cases to the facts of your own case. Through this process of analogizing and distinguishing precedent, you can thoroughly analyze the facts of your case to determine whether they satisfy the applicable legal rules.

In contrast, few professors will expect you to describe particular cases studied in class and to expressly analogize them to, or distinguish them from, the dispute presented in an exam problem. If you have conscientiously briefed your cases throughout the semester, you will recall cases that help you to spot issues and to analyze the problem, and you may mentally draw direct distinctions and analogies. However, you will seldom have sufficient time to express those distinctions and analogies in thorough case analysis in your examination answer. Instead, you should directly explain how relevant facts support or undermine the application of a legal rule.

Again, those professors who give open-book examinations may have higher expectations. If class materials are readily available to you during the exam, you may be expected to compare cases in your fact analysis. This may be true also for a closed-book exam in an exceptional area of law dominated by a manageable number of conspicuous cases, such as the Supreme Court case law governing personal jurisdiction. If you have mastered a relatively small number of important cases that define an area of law, you can feasibly refer to them by name and develop analogies and distinctions, even if you do not have access to your course materials during the examination.

D. THE CONCLUSION

1. Taking a Position

Just as your supervising attorney will expect you to reach conclusions on even close questions in an office memorandum, most law professors will expect you to state a conclusion for each issue that you discuss in an examination answer. On close questions, you can hedge the conclusion with qualifying terms, such as "probably." More important, the professor may accept any of several reasonable positions as an acceptable conclusion. Nonetheless, she will expect some resolution of each issue and subissue:

> *Intentional Infliction of Emotional Distress*
>
> Principal Jones may be liable to Schoolboy Smith . . .
>
> *Extreme Conduct—*
> • • • •

Subsidiary conclusion

> Principal Jones's questioning and request to search constituted extreme and outrageous conduct.
>
> *Intent or Recklessness—*
> • • • •

Subsidiary conclusion

> Although Principal Jones may not have intended to inflict severe emotional distress, he probably acted recklessly.
>
> *Severe Distress—*
> • • • •

Subsidiary conclusion

> Schoolboy Smith's transitory fear probably did not amount to severe emotional distress.
>
> *Conclusion—*

General conclusion

> Because Schoolboy Smith probably did not suffer extreme emotional distress, I conclude that Principal Jones is not liable for intentional infliction of emotional distress.

2. Comprehensive Conclusions

In an office memorandum, you should not only state conclusions at the end of your discussion of each issue or subissue, you should also summarize and evaluate all your major conclusions in a separate conclusion section.

In contrast, few law professors will expect you to summarize all previous major conclusions in a general summary of claims and defenses at the end of your answer to an exam problem. Such a consolidated restatement of conclusions ordinarily will score few points in an examination unless it adds new information or enhances the clarity of the discussion that precedes it. Accordingly, in most cases you will benefit by using the last few minutes allocated to a problem to look for additional issues that you might have missed rather than to summarize conclusions that you have already clearly communicated in your discussions of individual issues.

III. TECHNIQUES FOR WRITING EXAM RESPONSES

A. EFFECTIVE USE OF TIME

At the beginning of the examination, you should determine how much time you will allocate to each problem, and you should adhere to that schedule. Adequate discussions of all the problems in an examination will score more points than unusually thorough discussions of some of the problems at the cost of inadequate treatment of others. The same holds true for treatment of issues within a problem: Adequate discussions of all the major issues will score more points than an unusually thorough discussion of only half the issues. Thus, if an exam problem raises an unusual number of issues, the professor may expect only superficial discussion of each.

Although law school examinations require quick thinking, uninterrupted concentration, and rapid writing, you should not begin writing prematurely. You are more likely to write sensible responses and to avoid wasted effort if you spend up to a quarter or even a third of the time allotted for each problem in mastering the assignment and in "prewriting."

B. MASTERING THE ASSIGNMENT

You should read an exam problem once at a moderately quick pace to get a general picture of the events described, to classify the general nature of the probable claims and defenses, and to discover the particular question or questions stated by the professor, usually at the end of the problem. You should then read the problem at least once again, this time at a much more deliberate pace, to spot specific issues and to make marks or margin notes that highlight important facts.

C. PREWRITING

A few students have such well-developed skills of organization, such good memories, and such powers of concentration that they can write their examination answers without first outlining their analyses. The rest of us, however, will benefit greatly if we devote a few minutes to analysis and outlining before beginning to write.

The outline on scratch paper should be nothing more than a skeletal construction of the issues that you intend to address and the significant facts relating to each of those issues. The outline becomes the primary vehicle for analysis and organization. Before you begin writing, you can use it to decide which issues you will address, what order of presentation is most logical or efficient, and what facts support each side of the dispute in each section:

Q1—
Smith v. Jones

   I. Intent. Inflic. of Emot. Distress
     Extreme Conduct—Jones—polite, but great authority.—Request to search suggests disbelief and possibility of discipline
     Intent or Reckless— . . .
  II. Defamation
    • • • •

If the legal rules associated with an issue are unusually complex, or if you desire to discuss alternative legal theories, you may wish to include some reference to the law in the outline as well.

By scribbling a quick outline, you can examine your complete analysis at a glance and can determine whether it makes sense. If the analysis appears to be faulty, incomplete, or illogically organized, you can easily change your plans at the outlining stage. Changing your approach after writing half of your response would be much more difficult.

Finally, after completing your outline, you should quickly read the problem once again before beginning to write. Because you have fully analyzed the problem in the outline, you can then more effectively recognize the legal significance of facts in the problem. Indeed, facts that appeared to be insignificant in early readings may now reveal themselves as material.

D. WRITING THE ANSWER

If you have prepared an outline of your answer, writing the answer in the answer booklet should be a fairly mechanical process. Your task is simply that of expressing in full sentences the ideas that are represented in your examination outline, taking care to cover all the elements discussed in Section I. above: issue, rule of law, application of law to facts, and conclusion. The outline provides a guide that will keep you on track even when you momentarily lose sight of the main issues because of nervousness or temporary devotion to the details of a subissue.

Because of the intense time pressures of most exams, law professors do not expect polished writing or perfect organization, and you should not waste precious time thinking about the best possible way to express your ideas. Nonetheless, you will have an advantage if you have developed skills of organization and clear, concise writing: You will score more points by clearly expressing a great number of material ideas than will students whose writing is verbose and repetitious or is so unclear that the professor simply cannot understand it.

If you discover near the end of an exam that you have insufficient time to complete your analysis in full prose, you should simply outline the remainder of your response in your examination answer booklet. Most professors will give more points for a clear overview of all the remaining issues than for a fuller development of only one of several remaining issues.

IV. SUMMARY AND REVIEW

To develop skills of legal analysis and writing in law school,

(1) brief and synthesize cases;
(2) prepare a course outline by further synthesizing cases, reorganizing materials to highlight legal principles, and illustrating the principles with summaries of the case briefs; and
(3) analyze examination problems and express the answer in a clear, well-organized fashion.

Below is a progression of study and exam materials that illustrate the process of studying law, from briefing cases to taking an exam. Because this example is taken from a family setting, the summary of cases is much less formal than a series of briefs of judicial opinions. With a bit of imagination, however, you can draw an analogy between these sample materials and those that you will prepare in law school.

Notice that the legal rules stated in the exam answer are taken directly from the student's outline, which the student has committed to memory. Moreover, the student's knowledge of the case illustrations in the outline helps the student engage in the fact analysis in the examination answer. Finally, one issue in the exam requires the student to develop new rules by extrapolating from the familiar rules and the policies that support them.

CASE SUMMARIES WITH SYNTHESES

The case of the Hand in the Cookie Jar: Baby Reggie reached into a cookie jar and helped himself to a cookie shortly before dinner. Janice and Gerald admonished Reggie that the cookie would spoil his appetite for dinner.

The case of the Broken Vase: Reggie climbed onto a chair, reached a vase on a table top, and threw the vase to the floor, breaking it. Janice and Gerald sent Reggie to his room, admonishing him that he should not play with his parents' possessions.

The case of the Chocolate Ice Cream: After dinner one night, Reggie asked for some chocolate ice cream. To his surprise, his parents served him a dish of ice cream, praising him for having finished his vegetables. Unlike in the cookie jar case, Reggie did not spoil his appetite by eating the ice cream.

The case of the Mistreated Teddy Bear: Anxious to test his parents' limits one evening, Reggie climbed onto a chair with his favorite teddy bear and threw the teddy bear onto the living room carpet. Reggie's parents saw this event but had no reaction; they continued reading the newspaper and watching TV. Unlike in the broken vase case, Reggie's actions here did not jeopardize his parents' possessions.

The case of the Bouncing Ball: Emboldened by the teddy bear incident, Reggie brought out his favorite rubber ball and began kicking it around the living room, causing it to bounce off the TV set and to narrowly miss Janice's glass of wine sitting on the coffee table. Janice flashed Reggie an angry glance, and Gerald sternly said, "Outside with that ball, young man!" This is more similar to the broken vase case than to the teddy bear case, because Reggie's bouncing ball threatened to cause harm to his parents' television set and wine glass.

OUTLINE

Rules for Reggie

I. Overview—Reggie's parents try to restrict Reggie's activities to those that are beneficial to his health and that protect his parents' possessions from harm.

II. Dietary Rules—Reggie is permitted to eat sweets, but only at times that won't spoil his appetite for more healthful foods.

A. Example: In *the case of the Chocolate Ice Cream,* Reggie's parents gladly served him ice cream after dinner, because he had eaten all his vegetables.

B. Example: In *the case of the Hand in the Cookie Jar,* Reggie was not permitted to eat a cookie shortly before dinner, because it would ruin his appetite for dinner.

III. Rules about Toys—Reggie is permitted to play only with his own toys, and not in a way that will endanger his parents' possessions.

A. Example: In *the case of the Broken Vase,* Reggie was disciplined for breaking his parents' vase.

B. Example: In *the case of the Bouncing Ball,* Reggie was admonished for playing with his own rubber ball in a way that endangered his parents' possessions, such as the TV set and wine glass.

C. Example: In *the case of the Mistreated Teddy Bear,* Reggie was permitted to play with his own teddy bear, even by throwing it onto the floor, apparently because such conduct did not harm any of his parents' possessions.

EXAMINATION PROBLEM

On Saturday morning, Reggie began coloring in his coloring book with a box of crayons. He soon expanded his artistic activity to drawing a multicolored mural on one of the walls of his room. Displeased with the quality of his drawing, Reggie broke each of his 24 crayons in half and threw them into his waste basket. Indeed, he was so displeased with his artistry that he decided to wash his drawing off the wall. To that end, Reggie opened the cupboard under the kitchen sink and took a bottle of liquid drain cleaner, which he thought was a form of soap but was in fact a toxic chemical capable of burning his eyes and skin. At that moment, Reggie's parents intercepted him and discovered each of his activities during the day. Fully discuss whether Reggie has violated any rules of his house.

EXAMINATION ANSWER

I. Harm to Parents' Possessions

Issue[2]

Reggie's parents permit him to use and even abuse his own toys, but they do not allow Reggie to harm their possessions.

Rule

Reggie did not harm his parents' property by drawing in his coloring book. Nor did he harm their property by breaking his crayons, because those presumably were his own toys. However, Reggie almost certainly violated his parents' rules by drawing on his bedroom wall. Although the wall was in his room, his parents probably view it as part of their possessions, because they undoubtedly are responsible for maintaining it. Reggie did not physically break the surface of the wall as he might break a vase. However, a crayon drawing on the wall might require vigorous scrubbing or even repainting. Therefore, it probably represents actual harm to the wall.

Application

---

2. The margin labels are designed to remind you that a complete legal analysis should include four basic elements. Those labels should not appear in the margins of an actual examination answer; some professors may be offended by such a mechanical approach.

Conclusion	Reggie has violated his parents' rule against harming their possessions.
Issue	*II. Promotion of Reggie's Health and Safety of Parents' Possessions*
Rule	In addition to prohibiting Reggie from harming their possessions, Reggie's parents forbid him to eat sweets if they will spoil his appetite for more healthful foods.
Application	Reggie has not tried to eat sweets at an inappropriate time. However, he has endangered his health by carrying a dangerous chemical, the drain cleaner, with the intention of opening the bottle and using the chemical to clean his wall. The policy behind the dietary rule is apparently to help maintain Reggie's health. Therefore, Reggie's parents likely would disapprove of other activities that endanger his health, particularly activities that would cause more serious harm than simply eating unhealthful foods.
	Similarly, Reggie's parents may admonish him under an extension of their rule prohibiting harm to their possessions. Reggie is unlikely to do any harm to the drain cleaner. On the other hand, the drain cleaner is one of his parents' possessions rather than one of Reggie's toys. Moreover, if Reggie spilled the drain cleaner, he would waste it, and he might harm other possessions of his parents that came in contact with the chemical. Therefore, Reggie's parents are likely to disapprove of Reggie's taking the drain cleaner out of concern for their possessions as well as concern for Reggie's safety.
Conclusion	Because the chemical could cause serious harm to Reggie and to his parents' possessions, I conclude that his parents will admonish him and will adopt a general rule prohibiting him from taking such bottles from cupboards.

=== **S A M P L E S** ===

1. *Sample Examination Answer*

Read the Sample Memorandum 1 on page 185. Imagine that an exam problem raises several issues, one of which is similar to the consideration issue discussed in that sample memorandum. The general structure of the discussion of that issue in the examination answer would be similar to that of the discussion section of the sample memorandum. Nonetheless, even a thorough examination answer would be less formal than the memorandum. For example, the examination answer would omit citations and in-depth case analysis:

Q1

Lender v. Borrower

• • • •

Lender v. Guarantor

• • • •

Consideration—Illusory Promise

Issue

This lender's promise to refrain from asserting his claim and demanding payment until he "needs the money" arguably is illusory, thus creating doubt whether the guarantor's promise is enforceable.

Rule

An enforceable contract requires a bargained-for exchange in which a promisor exchanges his own promise for a return promise or performance. The requirement of an exchange is not satisfied if one party gives only an illusory promise, which does not commit the promisor to any future performance. Even if a promise leaves open the possibility that the promisor will escape obligation, however, the promise is valid if the promisor does not have complete control over the events on which the promisor's obligation is conditioned.

Application

The lender's promise to forbear until he "needs" the money appears to condition the length of his forbearance on financial events that are at least partly outside his control: As long as his income and expenses created no need for the money, the lender had a commitment to forbear from demanding payment. In an effort to escape obligations, the guarantor could argue that the word "need" refers to a subjective perception of deprivation that is inseparable from one's desires, which are subject to the promisor's unfettered discretion. However, "need" is distinguishable from "want."

Conclusion

Because the formality of the written agreement suggests that the parties must have intended to create binding obligations, a court probably would interpret the word "need" to impose objective restrictions on the lender's rights and conduct, thereby satisfying the consideration requirement and making the guarantor's promise enforceable.

2. Sample Examination Problem and Response

Examine the following contracts problem and response. Although the fact analysis is fairly simple, the internal organization is more complex than that in the sample answer in Problem 1 above, because the issue of recovery under quasi-contract invites discussion of two subissues in separate paragraphs, each with its own subrule, fact analysis, and preliminary conclusion.

Problem

While jogging one morning, realtor Maria Reyes came upon the victim of an auto accident that had occurred a few minutes earlier. The victim was unconscious and was bleeding profusely from a severed artery. Reyes easily saved the victim's life by flagging down a passing motorist and by applying direct pressure to the severed artery, a service for which a paramedic unit would have charged $300. Reyes later demanded compensation from the victim. Discuss the potential liability and remedies.

Sample Answer

Liability for unjust enrichment[3]

The unconscious victim could not expressly or through conduct communicate a promise to pay Reyes. Therefore, Reyes cannot recover on the basis of contract or promissory estoppel.[4]

Reyes likely will bring an action in quasi-contract for restitution of the reasonable value of the benefit that she conferred on the victim. To recover on this theory, she must prove that she unjustly enriched the victim.[5]

Enrichment is a measurable benefit. Reyes enriched the victim by rendering tangible first aid services and summoning help, thus saving the victim's life.[6]

Reyes must prove that it would be unjust for the victim to retain the benefits of the first-aid services without compensating Reyes for them. Reyes could prove this by showing that she had some relationship with the victim that led Reyes reasonably to expect compensation. However, the courts ordinarily presume that emergency services at the scene of an accident are provided gratuitously. Reyes could overcome that presumption if she could show that she acted in a professional capacity when rendering the services or that the services she rendered were unusually burdensome or hazardous. She likely will not succeed, because she is a realtor and is not in the business of charging for medical services, and because she "easily saved the victim's life" without risk to herself.[7]

Because the facts suggest that Reyes could not reasonably have expected

---

3. This heading reflects the exam writer's decision to discuss issues of liability separately from those of remedies. Within the section addressing liability, the writer introduces the elements of quasi-contract and unjust enrichment, and she analyzes each separately. She could have begun each of those analyses with a subsection heading, but good paragraphing appears to be a sufficient guide to organization within the two major sections.

4. This paragraph makes an introductory point by stating the facts and conclusion and leaving the rule implicit. It is not absolutely necessary for a good answer, but it might be good for an extra point or two because it explains how the student selected some issues for discussion and excluded others.

5. This paragraph identifies the main issue and states the applicable rule on the broadest, most general level.

6. This paragraph introduces a minor subissue, "enrichment," states the applicable rule, and reaches a conclusion on that subissue by applying the rule to the facts. Because this element of the claim is not seriously in doubt, it does not warrant fuller discussion. The brief discussion of this subissue serves primarily to introduce a more substantial issue in the next paragraph.

7. Like the preceding paragraph, this one identifies a subissue, states the law applicable to that subissue, and reaches a conclusion on that subissue by applying the law to the facts.

compensation for her emergency services, I conclude that Reyes cannot recover.[8]

Remedies

Assuming that Reyes could prove a claim for quasi-contract, she would be entitled to restitution measured by the reasonable value of the benefit that she bestowed on the victim. The purpose of such relief would be to deny the unjust enrichment to the recipient of the benefit; therefore, whenever feasible, damages ought to be measured by the value that the recipient places on the benefit. If that is not feasible, a court may award damages based on the general market value of the benefit or on the out-of-pocket costs incurred by the provider of the benefit.[9]

In this case, from the perspective of the victim, the value of the benefit bestowed by Reyes arguably is the value of the victim's life. A court would not likely use this value as the measure of the restitutionary relief, because it is relatively difficult to fix and because it is disproportionally greater than the effort expended by Reyes. Instead, the court probably would award the damages based on the general market value of Reyes's services. That measure is more nearly proportionate to Reyes's efforts, and it can easily be established by reference to the $300 fee that would have been charged by a paramedic unit. Alternatively, a court might award damages based on the actual costs incurred by Reyes, as measured by such things as inconvenience to Reyes and possible damage to her jogging clothes. However, because the market-value remedy is more consistent with restitution, I conclude that a court would award $300 in damages if Reyes could establish a claim based on quasi-contract.[10]

EXERCISE 8-1

1. *The Bait*

Review the case briefs that you prepared for Exercise 6-1(3), page 112, and the outline that you prepared for Exercise 7-2(2), page 135. Then, put away your notes, treat the following problem as a closed-book examination question, and write a response in essay form that identifies the issue, summarizes the law, applies the law to the facts relevant to the issue, and arrives at a conclusion on the issue.

Problem

Billy Anaya read the following advertisement for Matt's Bedroom Furniture Mart in his town's primary newspaper:

---

8. This paragraph states a conclusion on the entire issue of liability.
9. This paragraph discusses the legal standards for computing damages.
10. This paragraph reaches a conclusion on the question of damages by applying the legal standards to the facts.

THIS SATURDAY ONLY—NOON TO 9 PM

Specially marked floor models up to ½ off! Beds, headboards, dressers, and lamp tables, in all styles, sizes, finishes. Come in and browse around. But hurry, all items are subject to prior sale.

Billy visited Matt's Bedroom Furniture Mart at 8 P.M. on Saturday and saw a beautiful hardwood bedframe and headboard marked ½ off from $600 to $300. He told a saleswoman that he wanted to purchase it, but the saleswoman replied, "I'm sorry, but my manager just informed me that we are ending the sale early. I'm afraid that we cannot take any further purchases at the sales prices. However, you really ought to consider purchasing this at the regular price; it's more than worth it."

Does Billy have an enforceable contract with Matt's Bedroom Furniture Mart for sale of the bedframe and headboard for $300? You can assume that the saleswoman is an authorized representative for the store. Also assume that no statutes apply to the facts; analyze this problem under the common law of contracts only.

2. *The Surfing Burglar*

Review Exercise 4-1 on page 54. Treat it as a closed-book examination question and write a response in essay form that identifies the issues, summarizes the law, applies the law to the facts relevant to each issue, and arrives at a conclusion on each issue. You may supplement the statements of law in Exercise 4-1 with any common law of burglary that you have studied in your criminal law course. Otherwise, base your analysis on the general legal rules provided in Exercise 4-1. In this introductory exercise, permit yourself 45 minutes to complete your examination response; be prepared for greater time pressures later in the semester.

WRITING IN THE LAW OFFICE—NEUTRAL ANALYSIS

9

The Office Memorandum
of Law

I. PURPOSE AND PERSPECTIVE

An office memorandum of law is one of the most effective means with which a new associate or a summer law clerk can directly help a supervising attorney represent a client. The supervising attorney may be preparing a more formal document, such as a pleading or brief to a court, an opinion letter to a client, or a demand letter to an opposing party, for which she may use the office memorandum as a source of information, or even as a partial rough draft. In other cases, the supervising attorney may use the information in an office memorandum to develop a tax strategy for a business client or a settlement strategy for negotiations on behalf of a litigation client.

An office memorandum informs rather than advocates. To effectively represent the client, the supervising attorney must know both the weaknesses and the strengths of the client's claims and defenses. If you present a balanced analysis of the dispute in your office memorandum, you will enable your supervising attorney to focus her attention on her strongest arguments, to anticipate the counterarguments of the opposing party, and to develop an effective strategy. On the other hand, if you selectively bear only good news to your supervising attorney, you will mislead her and perhaps cause her embarrassment when further proceedings expose holes in her client's case that she might have avoided or at least anticipated had the law firm confronted them at an earlier stage.

On the other hand, an office memorandum is not entirely neutral; in most cases, it anticipates advocacy on behalf of a client. Therefore, even though you explore arguments on both sides of a dispute in your memorandum, you should not convey a detached indifference to the outcome.

Many supervising attorneys complain that student law clerks and recent graduates of law school tend to treat office memoranda as purely academic exercises and to abandon a client's cause too readily after identifying obstacles to the client's claims or defenses. Accordingly, not only should you identify weaknesses in a client's case, you should recommend the best means of overcoming them. You must neither conceal such weaknesses nor surrender to despair over them. Instead, you should identify the best means to exploit the strengths of the client's case, and you should suggest creative solutions to the problems raised by the weaknesses.

II. GENERAL FORMAT FOR AN OFFICE MEMORANDUM

Like alternative formats for student case briefs, a number of formats for office memoranda have earned popularity. If your law firm or individual supervising attorney expresses a preference for a particular format, you should respect the wishes of your intended audience. Otherwise, you can choose any reasonable format, such as any of the following:

Format A	Format B	Format C
I. Issue(s)	I. Overview	I. Issue(s)
II. Brief Answer(s)	II. Facts	II. Conclusion
III. Facts	III. Issue(s) & Brief Answer(s)	III. Facts
IV. Discussion	IV. Discussion	IV. Discussion
V. Conclusion	V. Conclusion	

Format A presents the issues first so that the reader can appreciate the legal significance of the facts when she reads them. Following the statement of issues are brief answers that tersely preview the final conclusion. As discussed below, the brief answers and the conclusion serve different purposes.

In some cases, complex multiple transactions and confusing relationships between multiple parties may make the statement of the issues incomprehensible to one who has not first read the facts. Format B provides an alternative format for such cases: In a paragraph or two, a brief overview identifies the general nature of the dispute and the issues, and it summarizes the writer's conclusions. Such an introduction enables the reader to appreciate the legal significance of the facts, and it may eliminate the need for anything more than one or two words in the brief answers. In turn, the statement of facts gives the reader sufficient information to comprehend a detailed statement of the issues, permitting the author of the memorandum to follow the facts with a more formal, specific statement of the issues than was feasible in the overview.

Format C is quite common in law offices. Because it deletes the brief answers and moves the main conclusion forward, however, it is less effective than the other formats for two reasons. First, a full conclusion that summarizes the analysis and offers strategic recommendations may be premature if placed before the discussion section: The reader is better able to appreciate a sophisticated conclusion after first digesting the discussion. Second, a multi-issue memorandum that ends with the discussion of a single issue tends to produce a feeling of anticlimax: The reader typically feels much more satisfied if the memorandum concludes with a section that ties all of the issues together.

III. ELEMENTS OF AN OFFICE MEMORANDUM

The following subsections examine the content of the substantive elements of Format A.

A. ISSUES—IDENTIFICATION AND EXPRESSION

Your task of identifying issues for analysis in an office memorandum is similar to that of identifying issues on a law school examination: You must have at least a general knowledge of the law governing the dispute so that you can recognize the legal problems raised by the facts. In many cases, courses that you have taken in law school will enable you to identify the general nature of the issues and to direct your research efforts; if not, a secondary source such as a good treatise may provide the necessary background information.

You should not finally identify and express the issues until the final stages of drafting. When you prepare a case brief for class discussion, you ordinarily cannot state with particularity the issues discussed in the judicial decision until you have completed your analysis of the entire opinion. Similarly, when preparing an office memorandum, you ordinarily cannot state with particularity the issues raised by the facts of the dispute until you have finished your research and have fully analyzed the problem. At that time, you must decide which elements of a claim or defense are sufficiently in doubt that they warrant identification and discussion as issues.

For example, Title VII of the Civil Rights Act of 1964 imposes liability on employers for engaging in "unlawful employment practices," and it defines "employer" in part as "a person engaged in an industry affecting commerce."[1] Although engagement "in an industry affecting commerce" is always an element of employer liability, in many cases the facts known to all parties leave no doubt that the employer's activities satisfy the statutory rule under any reasonable interpretation. In such a case, the party charged

---

1. 42 U.S.C. §§2000e(b) (definition of "employer"), 2000e-2(a) (unlawful employer practices) (1988); see also id. at §§2000e(g) and (h) (definitions of "commerce" and "industry affecting commerce").

with discrimination could not credibly dispute its status as an "employer" on grounds relating to commerce, and you should not identify that matter as an issue in your memorandum. At most, you might briefly state this conclusion in an introduction to the discussion of a substantial issue.

In the same case, however, unusual facts and uncertainty in the applicable legal standards might raise doubts about whether the employer has committed an "unlawful employment practice." Because the employer likely will deny committing an unlawful employment practice, and because the parties can reasonably dispute that matter, you should identify it as an issue and discuss it.

Once you have identified and analyzed issues for discussion in your memorandum, you should state them with the same specificity and attention to facts that would be appropriate in the statement of issues in a case brief prepared for class discussion. To review these techniques, you may want to return briefly to Chapter 6, pages 92-95.

For example, you should not state the issue in such general terms as whether the employer committed an unlawful employment practice. Instead, after researching the law and analyzing the facts, you can more precisely identify the contours of the dispute likely to be raised by the parties:

> Did Salerno create a hostile or offensive working environment for his female employees by repeatedly asking them for dates, thus making Salerno liable for sex discrimination with respect to terms or conditions of employment?

B. BRIEF ANSWER

Each brief answer should be a succinct response to the question presented in each issue. The precise form of the answer may depend on the degree of specificity that you have achieved in the statement of the issue, just as the appropriate form for the statement of the holding in a case brief may depend on the degree of specificity of the issue statement.

In some cases, the issue may be sufficiently simple and the statement of the issue sufficiently specific to justify limiting the brief answer to a word or two, such as "yes," "no," "probably yes," or "probably no." If so, each brief answer can appear immediately after the statement of the corresponding issue without any separate section heading.

In many cases, however, you may find it difficult to state all the elements of a complex issue in a single, graceful sentence. In those cases, you can supply additional information in a brief answer of one or more sentences under a separate section heading. Even so, you should not use the brief answer to explore analytic justifications in great depth; the reader can more easily absorb a complex summary of the analysis after she has read the discussion section of the memorandum. For example, the medical malpractice dispute discussed on pages 70-71 might raise the following issues and brief answers:

I. ISSUES

A. Does the phrase "any toxic material" in New Maine's strict liability statute encompass a generally safe anesthetic that produced a fatal reaction in a patient with a rare nerve disorder?

B. Is Humane Hospital liable to Souza's estate for negligent administration of the anesthetic?

1. Did Humane's anesthesiologist breach a duty of care by administering the anesthetic without assistance and by failing to monitor Souza's reactions to anesthesia?

2. Did Souza's nerve disorder constitute a supervening cause that broke the chain of causation between the anesthesiologist's conduct and Souza's death?

II. BRIEF ANSWERS

A. Probably not. A restrictive interpretation is supported by the legislative history and by a general public policy in New Maine encouraging the provision of affordable medical services. The legislature probably did not intend the statutory phrase "toxic material" to include medically prescribed substances that ordinarily produce a beneficial result or otherwise facilitate medical treatment.

B. Probably yes.

1. Probably yes. Under generally accepted hospital procedures, at least two trained medical personnel must monitor the administration of anesthesia, with at least one person monitoring the patient's reactions. A jury likely will find that the anesthesiologist breached a duty of care to the patient by administering the anesthesia alone.

2. No. The jury likely will also find that the patient's nerve disorder was not a supervening cause and that the anesthesiologist's negligence proximately caused the patient's death.

C. FACTS

Some new associates in a law firm regularly omit statements of facts in their legal memoranda. The associates often explain that a supervising attorney obviously knows the facts of an assigned case because she gives the facts to the associate in some oral or written form when she assigns the memorandum.

For several reasons, however, you should include at least a brief statement of facts in a legal memorandum unless your supervising attorney specifically authorizes you to omit it. The supervising attorney may have been familiar with the facts when she assigned the memorandum, but she may need a brief review to refresh her memory when she later reads your memorandum. Alternatively, she may simply want reassurance that you share her understanding of the facts. Furthermore, the memorandum should be a self-contained document that is helpful to any member of the firm who may be called on to take over the file, including an attorney who knows nothing about the case and does not have time to glean the facts from the file. Finally, a statement of the factual premises on which you based your legal analysis protects you from criticism if that analysis later becomes obsolete or misleading in light of newly discovered facts.

In selecting facts for statement, you should focus on material facts and background facts with attention to the considerations that you would apply in preparing a case brief for class. However, you should hesitate less in an office memorandum than in a case brief to mention a marginally significant fact. When briefing a case, you must rely on the court's summary of the facts as a complete record on which the court based its decision; moreover, you can test your analytic abilities by attempting to isolate the material facts and helpful background facts and by omitting the others. In contrast, when preparing an office memorandum at an early stage of a dispute, you know that the facts on which you rely for your analysis are incomplete. Subsequent proceedings may reveal other facts that support new claims, defenses, or arguments. Moreover, previously known facts that appeared to be unimportant when you drafted the memorandum may take on new legal significance as a consequence. In your statement of facts, therefore, you should recite all material facts in detail, and you should summarize any other information that either provides helpful background material or appears to have the potential to take on new significance as the litigation proceeds.

D. DISCUSSION

1. Introducing Your Analysis

In the discussion section of your legal memorandum, you will express your complete legal analysis of each issue stated at the beginning of the memorandum. If your memorandum addresses a single issue that you have formally stated at or near the beginning of the memorandum, your discussion of the issue need not begin with any descriptive heading beyond the major section heading "Discussion."

However, if you address multiple issues, you should separately analyze each issue under a descriptive section heading. Although the heading need not restate the issue in full detail, it should link your analysis to an issue that is more formally and narrowly stated earlier in the memorandum:

> IV. Discussion
>   A. Strict Liability for Use of Toxic Materials
>   • • • •
>   B. Negligence
>   • • • •
>   1. Negligent Act
>   • • • •
>   2. Proximate Cause
>   • • • •

Immediately after you identify an issue with a section heading, you may want to illuminate the issue in an introductory sentence or two that refers briefly to facts, arguments, or theories that help to explain the significance of the issue. For example, the following opening sentence expands on the section heading by explaining the significance of the theory of strict liability:

A. Strict Liability for Use of Toxic Materials

If a statute or the common law imposes strict liability for Souza's death, then Souza's estate can establish liability without proving negligence.

In some cases, the opening paragraph of a section may even draw subsidiary legal conclusions as a means of pinpointing the narrow question in dispute. For example, the following paragraph concludes that a proposed transaction would include a sale of goods. Coupled with other observations, that subsidiary conclusion leads to the primary issue of the section:

A. Choice of Law — U.C.C. or Common Law

Whether Maldonado accepted Weinstein's offer depends in part on whether the common law of contracts or the Uniform Commercial Code (U.C.C.) applies to the transaction. The U.C.C. applies only to "transactions in goods." U.C.C. §2-102 (1990). Weinstein's offer to supply specifically identified, separately priced, movable plumbing parts clearly contemplates a sale of goods as part of the transaction. *See* U.C.C. §2-105(1) (1990). His proposed transaction, however, also involves the service of installing the fixtures, raising a question about the applicability of the U.C.C. to mixed transactions for both services and the sale of goods.

The U.C.C. applies to such a mixed transaction only if . . .

Of course, if an issue is adequately represented in a section heading and needs no further elaboration, the discussion can proceed immediately to an analysis of the legal standards:

A. Applicability and Satisfaction of the Statute of Frauds

The Arizona statute of frauds bars enforcement of "an agreement which is not to be performed within one year from the making thereof," unless it, "or some memorandum thereof, is in writing and signed by the party to be charged." Ariz. Rev. Stat. Ann. §44-101(5) (West 1967) (copy of full text attached). . . .

2. Analyzing the Law and the Facts

After you have drafted the section heading and the optional elaboration of the issue, you ordinarily should follow the pattern of deductive reasoning developed in Chapter 4: Analyze the law and apply the law to the facts to reach a conclusion. The nature of the analysis in a discussion section obviously will vary with each issue. If the clearly applicable abstract legal rule is simple, you can present the rule and supporting authority directly and concisely, permitting you to direct most of your attention to fact analysis. Other issues may require a choice among competing rules or a clarification of the content of the applicable legal rule. If so, you may need to discuss the abstract legal rule in depth before applying it to the facts. Of course, determining the content of the rule and applying it to the facts are often related tasks: Your discussion of the question of whether particular facts satisfy the legal standard may help to clarify the content of a vague or uncertain rule.

a. Example: Statutory Analysis

Below is a portion of the discussion section of a sample office memorandum set in the fictitious state of New Maine. It analyzes the issue of statutory liability for administering anesthesia. The statutory analysis in the passage focuses on defining the legal rule in a simple factual context, thus requiring relatively little independent fact analysis. After refining the issue in an introduction, the author of the discussion presents the statutory analysis on three levels in descending order of priority: the language of the statute, its legislative history, and general policy considerations. In this example, the author has applied the law to the relevant facts at each level of the statutory analysis rather than in a single consolidated fact analysis at the end of the discussion.

IV. DISCUSSION

A. Strict Liability for Use of Toxic Materials

Introduction

If a statute or the common law imposes strict liability for Souza's death, then Souza's estate can establish liability without proving negligence. New Maine's common law doctrine of strict liability for injuries caused by ultrahazardous activities does not apply to noncriminal medical practices engaged in by licensed physicians. *Stanislaus v. Good Samaritan Hospital*, 212 N. Me. 113, 115 (1979). New Maine has recently enacted a statute, however, that imposes strict liability for injuries stemming from the use of "any toxic material":

A commercial enterprise is liable for injuries proximately caused by its use of any toxic material, without regard to the degree of care exercised by the enterprise.

12 N. Me. Rev. Stat. §242 (1988). As a profit-making hospital, Humane presumably is a "commercial enterprise" within the meaning of the statute. It is less certain, however, that the anesthetic administered to Souza would qualify as a "toxic" material. | **Narrow issue**

The common meaning of the word "toxic" is "poisonous." *See, e.g., The Random House Dictionary of the English Language* 1500 (unabridged) (1970). Souza's estate might plausibly argue that the anesthetic was a toxic material because it was poisonous to Souza, even though it would not have been poisonous to most others. The word "toxic," however, applies more naturally to substances that are universally harmful to humans, such as cyanide, DDT, or sulfuric acid. It strains the common meaning of "toxic" to apply it to an anesthetic that might occasionally be harmful to persons with unusual allergies or other extraordinary conditions. | **Analysis of statutory language** ... **Fact analysis**

Legislative history also supports a restrictive interpretation of the statutory term "any toxic material." The report of the New Maine Senate Committee on Health and Welfare suggests that the legislature was concerned only with the most deadly of substances: | **Legislative history**

> The purpose of this bill is to reallocate the cost of unavoidable accidents from victims to industry and its consumers, to discourage unnecessary use of deadly chemicals and other hazardous materials, and to encourage the development and use of substitute materials that are generally safe for human contact.

N. Me. Sen. Rep. No. 112, 1987-1988 Sess. 2 (1988). The anesthetic in this case probably is closer to the materials "generally safe for human contact" condoned by the legislature than it is to the "deadly chemicals and other hazardous materials" condemned by it. | **Fact analysis**

Finally, general state policy appears to support an interpretation that excludes medically prescribed substances from the reach of the statute. The legislature and judiciary of New Maine have recognized a policy of restricting the liability of physicians to encourage the ready availability of affordable medical services. For example, under the New Maine "Good Samaritan" statute, physicians who provide | **Policy analysis** certain emergency medical services are not liable for adverse consequences unless they engage in culpable conduct amounting to at least gross negligence. 12 N. Me. Rev. Stat. §229 (1985). This protective policy is also reflected in the courts' refusal to extend common law strict liability for ultrahazardous activities to even experimental medical practices. *Stanislaus*, 212 N. Me. at 115. The legislature presumably was aware of these legal developments when it enacted the toxic materials statute in 1988.

Souza's estate may argue that the legislature intended to partially overrule *Stanislaus* by imposing strict liability on a limited segment of the activities of commercial medical practices. However, absent more specific evidence of legislative intent to alter the course of existing common law, it is probably more likely that the legislature retained its protective attitude and assumed that the term "toxic material" would not include routinely prescribed medicines or anesthetics.

Fact analysis

In this case, the prescribed anesthetic, ethane, was not the safest available at the time of Souza's operation. Nonetheless, it is a frequently prescribed substance that produces beneficial results with only minor side effects in all but the most unusual cases.

Conclusion

The strict liability statute almost certainly does not apply to Souza's death.

b. Example: Established Common Law

In contrast to the previous example, the sample discussion below briefly summarizes noncontroversial legal standards and places greater emphasis on fact analysis. After illuminating the issue of negligence and summarizing general principles, the discussion separately addresses distinct subissues in different subsections. Within the first of those subsections, devoted to "negligent act," the author has consolidated the relatively simple legal standards in a single paragraph, leading to a single, uninterrupted line of fact analysis. She has divided the fact analysis itself into two paragraphs, presenting opposing factual arguments.

IV. DISCUSSION

A. Strict Liability for Use of Toxic Materials

• • • •

B. Negligence

Assuming that Humane Hospital is not strictly liable for Souza's death, it may nonetheless be liable to Souza's estate if its agent caused the death through negligence. *See Kityama v. Mercy Hospital,* 183 N. Me. 752, 759-760 (1974) (hospital liable for negligence of its nurse). An action for negligence requires proof of a negligent act or omission that proximately causes injury. *Baker v. Bruce,* 153 N. Me. 817, 820 (1967).

In our case, the injury to Souza is obvious. In greater doubt are the elements of negligent act and proximate cause.

1. Negligent Act

A negligent act or omission consists of the breach of a duty of care owed to another. *Id.* at 821. A medical specialist owes a duty to patients to exercise at least the ordinary skill and care that is reasonable and customary nationwide in that medical specialty. *Kityama,* 183 N. Me. at 760. Furthermore, under the "thin-skulled plaintiff" rule, that duty of care encompasses the special care necessary to address increased risks created by a patient's unusual susceptibility to injury. *Id.* In this case, Humane's anesthesiologist, Unger, may have breached duties of care in her unassisted administration of general anesthesia in the face of Souza's known nervous condition.

Unger exercised care in determining Souza's disorder of the nervous system and in informing her of the risks presented by each of the most suitable anesthetics. Moreover, when administering the anesthetic selected by Souza, Unger took care to provide the prescribed dosage by monitoring the anesthetic intake gauge.

However, Unger's intense concentration on the anesthetic intake gauge may have been an act of carelessness, rather than enhanced care, because it diverted Unger's attention from Souza and from equipment monitoring Souza's vital signs. Faced with Souza's known nervous disorder, Unger probably had a duty to follow the standard medical practice of summoning a nurse to assist her in administering the anesthesia. Had she done so, the team could have monitored both Souza's vital signs and the intake gauge, and a team member undoubt-

(marginal annotations)

Introduction

Narrow issues

Legal rules

Fact analysis favoring Humane

Fact analysis favoring Souza's estate

Conclusion

edly would have detected signs of distress at least 10 seconds before death, arguably enough time to cease anesthesia and take corrective measures.

On these facts, a jury could find that Unger was negligent in her administration of the anesthetic.

2. Proximate Cause

• • • •

E. THE CONCLUSION

Even though the questions addressed in an office memorandum may be close, and even though your supervising attorney will not feel bound by your advice, she will expect you to take a position by stating your conclusions. A thorough memorandum will include both (1) a brief resolution of each issue within the part of the discussion section devoted to that issue, and (2) a more general summary of conclusions in a separate section at the end of the memorandum.

In the conclusion section, you can summarize the individual conclusions that you have reached in the discussion section of the memorandum. In addition, you may wish to summarize the analytic support for the conclusions in a depth that would have been inappropriate in the brief answers stated earlier.

Finally, you should use the "Conclusion" section to express any strategic recommendations that your analysis inspires. For example, you may recommend that the law firm file a complaint, settle a weak case, investigate certain facts, or concentrate its efforts on a particular legal theory.

Although you may express more information in the conclusion section than in the brief answers, your conclusion should nonetheless represent a selective summary of your analysis and recommendations. In a simple case, a few sentences may suffice; even moderately complex cases require no more than a few paragraphs.

For example, the following passage concisely synthesizes the conclusions previewed above in Section B as brief answers, and it adds strategic recommendations:

Summary of analyses

V. CONCLUSION

In light of legislative and judicial policies favoring limits on physicians' liability, the strict liability statute regulating toxic materials probably will not apply to the administration of anesthetic in this case. The courts will be even less likely to retreat from precedent by applying the common law doctrine of strict liability for ultrahazardous activities. A jury may find, however, that Humane's anesthesiologist was negligent in failing to summon assistance to administer the anesthesia or to monitor the patient closely. We can try to characterize Souza's nervous condition as a supervening cause, but *Rainbow Landscaping* will not be easy to distinguish.

Because the risk of substantial liability is great, I recommend that we advise Humane to settle. Souza's estate may be willing to compromise: their negligence claim is not appropriate for summary disposition, and they may want to avoid the unpredictability of a jury.

Strategic recommendation

IV. TECHNIQUES FOR PREPARING OFFICE MEMORANDA

The techniques you use to master an assignment, research the problem, and prepare a memorandum for a supervising attorney are partly a matter of office policies and your personal style. The following suggestions provide a foundation on which you may build to suit your particular needs.

A. MASTERING THE ASSIGNMENT

The surest way to disappoint a supervising attorney is to misunderstand the assignment. Even a thoroughly researched and beautifully written memorandum will fall flat if it fails to address the matters that the supervisor wanted the associate to analyze.

Unfortunately, many supervising attorneys are too busy to communicate their assignments clearly and thoroughly. Even worse, most will not accept blame for confusion about the assignment. Instead, they expect you to assume responsibility for clarifying vague or confusing points. Consequently, you should not be shy about demanding additional information from the supervising attorney. Indeed, you should aggressively dig out the information that you need to master your assignment so that you can draft a memorandum that precisely meets the needs of your supervising attorney.

Confusion about the topics that your supervising attorney expects you to address may take various forms. In some cases, your inability to identify narrow, precise issues may stem from necessary abstractness in the assignment that is only partially avoidable. Supervising attorneys occasionally request office memoranda on general, abstract questions of law, such as the likely scope and effect of a new statute. Although they are not yet working on any disputes relating to the assigned issues, they expect that the general legal analyses developed in such memoranda will help them counsel clients who are concerned about their rights or obligations under the new law. You can tailor such a memorandum to your supervisor's needs by requesting clarification on (1) the kinds of topics that your supervisor deems to be essential and on (2) the kinds of disputes in which the firm's clients likely would become embroiled.

In many cases, abstraction in the assignment is unnecessary because the supervising attorney intends to use the legal analysis in the memorandum to help represent a client in a currently active, concrete dispute. In such a case, if your supervising attorney does not provide you with sufficient information to enable you to thoroughly understand the factual context, you should take steps to acquire that information. By anticipating the application of legal standards to facts, you can frame the issues precisely and narrowly, and you can tailor the research and analysis to your supervisor's real needs.

Vagueness in an assignment often is attributable to precisely the analytic uncertainty on which the memorandum is intended to shed light. Therefore, you may benefit from secondary meetings with the supervising attorney after the initial assignment but before writing the memorandum. In some cases, your supervising attorney will not even attempt to identify issues but will instead supply the factual context and ask you to define and analyze the issues. In other cases, the supervisor may state the issues in general and preliminary form, expecting you to refine and supplement them. Even if the supervisor has no such expectation, you may acquire information that allows you to focus the issue statement more sharply. With a thorough knowledge of the factual context, you can clarify the essential issues as your research deepens your understanding of the legal standards.

As you do so, questions may arise about appropriate limits on the range of topics that you should address or about the depth to which the supervisor would like you to analyze a tangential issue. If so, you should determine whether the supervisor can conveniently give brief guidance on these questions before you begin writing. Although you should not become dependent on such guidance, neither should you give credence to a popular assumption on the part of clerks and associates that supervisors are universally hostile to such contacts. Most supervisors will recognize the benefit of a brief follow-up meeting, and many will make the time for it.

B. RESEARCH TOOLS AND STRATEGY

Effective research skills are the product of long hours in the library, for which no primer on research techniques can substitute. Nonetheless, a few tips on research strategy may help you avoid duplicative or unproductive activity. The following discussion provides a preliminary guide to selected research tools available in virtually any law library.[3]

1. Basic Research Tools

As suggested in Chapter 2, most research assignments require research of primary law in state or federal constitutions, statutes, or judicial decisions. The judicial decisions establish case law, some of which develops common law principles, and some of which interprets and applies constitutional or statutory provisions.

Official code services reproduce the text of state and federal constitutions, statutes, and rules governing judicial proceedings. For example, the multi-volume United States Code reproduces the text of the United States Constitution, federal statutes enacted by Congress, and rules governing federal judicial proceedings, such as the Federal Rules of Civil Procedure and the Federal Rules of Evidence.

For example, the following excerpt from Title 18 of the United States Code sets forth the one-sentence text of §3290. That statute states an exception to the general rule that the government must prosecute a federal crime, if at all, within a certain period of time after the commission of the crime. The statutory text is followed by notes on historical background and by statutory cross references:

248; Aug. 30,
'99; Nov. 18,
'081(b), 102

§ 3290. Fugitives from justice

No statute of limitations shall extend to any person fleeing from justice.

(June 25, 1948, ch. 645, 62 Stat. 829.)

ЭТES

'56a, 588, 589
'ay 10, 1934,

'89 of title
.ance. The
.ince to time
.rous changes
consolidation,
b)(2), (3), (5)
'e.
.d and "regu-
.onize with sec-

HISTORICAL AND REVISION NOTES

Based on Title 18, U.S.C., 1940 ed., § 583 (R.S. § 1045).

Said section 583 was rephrased and made applicable to all statutes of limitation and is merely declaratory of the generally accepted rule of law.

CROSS REFERENCES

Absence from district as tolling limitation for prosecution for internal revenue violations, see section 6531 of Title 26, Internal Revenue Code.

SECTION REFERRED TO IN OTHER SECTIONS

.hline substitut-
dismissed after

This section is referred to in title 26 section 6531.

---

3. This discussion does not address computer research, legislative history, agency rules and regulations, local ordinances, or special services for certain subject areas, such as tax, labor law, and American Indian tribal codes and case law. For more comprehensive guides to research tools and techniques, you can consult guides such as Christina L. Kunz, Deborah A. Schmedemann, Ann L. Bateson, Matthew P. Downs & C. Peter Erlinder, The Process of Legal Research (3d ed. 1992); Christoper G. Wren & Jill Robinson Wren, Using Computers in Legal Research: A Guide to LEXIS and WESTLAW (1994).

An annotated code service, such as United States Code Annotated or United States Code Service, is a particularly useful research tool. In addition to the information provided by the official code, it cites to and briefly summarizes judicial decisions that interpret the statute.

For example, the excerpts on page 173 from West Publishing Co.'s United States Code Annotated supplement the text of §3290 with an indexed summary of cases in which the statute has been interpreted and applied. Under category 9, entitled "Constructive Flight," an annotation cites to and describes a holding of *United States v. Catino*[4] regarding the theory of "constructive flight."

Using the citation in the annotated codebook as a guide, you can find the full text of the judicial decision that interprets the constitution, statute, or rule. Normally, you will find the decision in a multi-volume service known as a "reporter" system, such as Federal Reports 2d. In a reporter published by West Publishing Co., the text of the judicial decision is preceded by consecutively numbered "headnotes," which summarize critical points of law or application of fact in the opinion. To help you find the portion of the text of the opinion that corresponds to a particular headnote, the West reporter inserts within the text a bracketed number that matches the corresponding headnote number. More important for further research purposes, each headnote refers to one or more topics with "key numbers" that refer to a section of a West case digest that collects other cases addressing the same issue.

An example is on page 174, where excerpts of the court's opinion in *United States v. Catino* are from pages 718, 719, and 722 of volume 735 of West's Federal Reporter 2d. The text of the opinion begins immediately after the designation of the authoring judge: "LUMBARD, Circuit Judge:". After a review of the facts and a discussion of preliminary points of law, the opinion states a rule about intent to flee, immediately after the numbers "4, 5" within brackets. The number "4" within the brackets corresponds to the fourth headnote preceding the opinion itself. That headnote not only summarizes the point about intent to flee stated in the opinion, it assigns that point to a category that it has designated "Criminal Law 153."

The designation "Criminal Law 153" includes a representation of a key and is called a "Digest Topic" with a "Key Number." It corresponds to a section of the multi-volume West's Federal Practice Digest 4th, which is essentially an enormous outline of federal case law, similar in form and design to the kind of course outline described in Chapter 7. By pulling the appropriate volume on "Criminal Law" in the West Federal Practice Digest 4th and turning to §153, you can find citations to *United States v. Catino*, as shown in the excerpts on page 175. More important to your continuing search, you can find other cases addressing the same or similar issues. In

---

4. The annotation cites to the case in an unconventional manner. A more widely accepted citation form would read "United States v. Catino, 735 F.2d 718 (2d Cir. 1984), *cert. denied*, 469 U.S. 855 (1984)."

§ 3290. Fugitives from justice

No statute of limitations shall extend to any person fleeing from justice. (June 25, 1948, c. 645, 62 Stat. 829.)

Historical and Revision Notes

Reviser's Note. Based on Title 18, U.S.C., 1940 ed., § 583 (R.S. § 1045).

Said section 583 was rephrased and made applicable to all statutes of limitation and is merely declaratory of the generally accepted rule of law.

Cross References

Internal revenue criminal prosecutions, presence outside United States or status of fugitive from justice as affecting periods of limitations, see section 6531 of Title 26, Internal Revenue Code.

Library References

Criminal Law ⊕153.
C.J.S. Criminal Law § 230.

Notes of Decisions

Absence from jurisdiction 8
Authorities, flight from 10
Burden of proof 16
Construction 1
Constructive flight 9
Escapees, persons within section 4
Extradition 2
Flight from
　Authorities 10
　Unrelated charges 11
Good faith effort to surrender 13
Motive and intent 14
Persons entitled to plead limitations 15
Persons within section
　Gene～～　3

Ship's personnel, persons within section 6
Sufficiency of evidence 17
Termination of fugitive status 12
Unrelated charges, flight from 11
Visitors, persons within section 7
Waiver 19
Weight and sufficiency of evidence 17

1. Construction

Congressional policies underlying thi～ chapter and the "fleeing from jus～～～ tion to it are harmoniz～d by i～

～ 583 ～ [now this ～.
th～ ～ is not ne～ ～ry that the party charged should have left jurisdiction in which crime was allegedly committed, after an indictment found, or for purpose of avoiding a prosecution anticipated or begun, but simply that, having within the jurisdiction committed that which by its laws constituted a crime, he had left its jurisdiction. McGowen v. U.S., 1939, 105 F.2d 791, 70 App.D.C. 268, 124 A.L.R. 1047, certiorari denied 60 S.Ct. 98, 308 U.S. 552, 84 L.Ed. 464. See, also, King v. U.S., C.C.A.Ark.1944, 144 F.2d 729, certiorari denied 65 S.Ct. 711, 324 U.S. 854, 89 L.Ed. 1413.

"Fugitive from justice" is person who, having committed a crime in violation of laws of United States, flees from jurisdiction of court

residen～ ～ace th～ trict, or a ～oncealing ～ ～. therein, avoid detection or punis～ ～t for some o～ fense against the United States, to constitute a "fleeing from justice." U.S. v. O'Brian, C.C. Kan.1873, Fed.Cas.No.15,908.

9. Constructive flight

Fact that defendant, who was in French prison awaiting trial on french charges, actively resisted extradition request throughout proceedings instead of consenting to return to United States, coupled with his letter expressing a desire to resist all further extradition requests, constituted a constructive flight from justice, thereby tolling limitations period under section 3282 of this title. U.S. v. Catino, C.A.N.Y.1984, 735 F.2d 718, certiorari denied, 105 S.Ct. 180, 83 L.Ed.2d 114.

677

ᴊın jurisᴅ.. where an ᴏffense ᴜᴀ.. been committed with intent of avoiding arrest or prosecution. 18 U.S. C.A. §§ 3282, 3290.

3. Criminal Law ⚖︎153

A person can be "fleeing from justice" in one jurisdiction for purposes of tolling provision for five-year limitations period, even though in prison in another. 18 U.S. C.A. §§ 3282, 3290.

4. Criminal Law ⚖︎153

Intent to flee from prosecution or arrest may be inferred from a person's failure to surrender to authorities once he learns that charges against him are pending, whether defendant leaves jurisdiction intending to avoid prosecution or, having learned of charges while legally outside jurisdiction, constructively flees by deciding not to return. 18 U.S. C.A. §§ 3282, 3290.

5. Criminal Law ⚖︎153

that authoᴏ. knew of ᴅᴀnd-ho..

UNITED STATES of America, Appellee,

v.

Alfred CATINO, Defendant-Appellant.

No. 956, Docket 83–1419.

United States Court of Appeals, Second Circuit.

Argued March 22, 1984.

Decided May 24, 1984.

Certiorari Denied Oct. 1, 1984.
See 105 S.Ct. 180.

Defendant was convicted in the United States District Court for the Southern District of New York, Lee P. Gagliardi, J., for failin�. to beginᴏ. ᴀ a senᴏ. ᴏᴘort

ᴄ., ..ᴍply proᴠᴏ ..ᴏssfuᴜ. C.A. §§ 3282, 3290.

9. Criminal Law ⚖︎113

The term "first brought" within meaning of statute providing that for offense alleged to have been committed outside jurisdiction of any district, venue lies only in the district where offender is arrested or first brought applies only in situations where offender is returned to United States already in custᴏ. 18 U.S.C.A § 32ᴏᴏ

ᴏes la.. ᴜᴏited States . ᴀls he losᴜ protection of Speedy Trial Act). However, he argues that a non-fugitive cannot *become* a fugitive by virtue of his resistance to extradition. We disagree.

Beᴏ ᴀRD, ᴜAN anᴏ PRATT, . ᴏᴜt Judges.

LUMBARD, Circuit Judge:

Alfred Catino appeals from his conviction entered June 4, 1983, in the Southern District of New York, Gagliardi, J., following his conditional guilty plea. Catino pleaded guilty to two counts: failing to arᴏ. ᴏn ᴏ.rch 1975 ᴏegin servᴏ ᴏe impᴏ ᴏor ᴏ. ᴏf

ᴠᴀnᴀ. ıl.

[4, 5] The intent to flee from prosecution or arrest may be inferred from a person's failure to surrender to authorities once he learns that charges against him are pending. *Matter of Assarsson,* 687 F.2d 1157, 1161–62 (8th Cir.1982); *United States v. Ballesteros-Cordova,* 586 F.2d 1321, 1324 (9th Cir.1978). This is true whether the defendant leaves the jurisdiction intending to avoid prosecution, or, having learned of charges while legally outside the jurisdiction, "constructively flees" by deciding not to return. *Jhirad v. Ferrandina,* 536 F.2d 478, 483–84 (2d Cir.), *cert. denied,* 429 U.S. 833, 97 S.Ct. 97, 50 L.Ed.2d 98 (1976) (*Jhirad II*). The fact that the authorities know of the defendant's whereabouts outside of the jurisdiction doesᴏot of itself start the sᴏᴏte runniᴏ ᴏ II, ᴏ

ᴏes ᴏo (statᴏᴜth effort to ᴏ Catino had ᴏguendo that extradition in ᴏake a factual ts view, the ᴏnced by his ᴏno obviously ᴏt returning to ᴏas new charges December 14, ᴏdition request ᴏ and continᴏ was denied ᴏourt reasoned ᴏtus from March his resistance to ᴏ District made ᴏ justice" with ᴏeast until the Since toᴏ

...90, ...8

...itation period for
...personal income
...ning false cor-
...'uring 60–day
...mmons en-
...een taken,
... 26 U.S.C.A.
...).
...304.

...ing to enforce
...il full compli-
...until 60–day
...of judicial en-
...so that six-year
...led and IRS could
...ully making and
...eturns. 26 U.S.
...7609(a)(1), (b),
...R.A.P. Rule

1283, certiorari
...482 U.S. 927, 96

...ough nuclear
...employees
...iod for
...stat...

...w...
...culative ... ...that
...nt to avoid bei...g contin-
...agent was insufficient to
...stimony lacked circumstan-
...ustworthiness. Fed.Rules
U.S.C.A.
...6 F.2d 896.

...ception stating that
...eriod in criminal cases
...or of any person fleeing
...rehensive, in that a person
...in one jurisdiction loses
...of limitations for all
...sdictions. 18 U.S.C.A.

...d 718, certiorari
...469 U.S. 855, 83

...five-year limitations
...a person absents him-
...ere an offense has
...of avoiding arr...t
...§ 3282

⬅153. —— Fugitives from justice.

C.A.D.C. 1983. U.S. v. Singleton, 702 F.2d 1159, 226 U.S.App.D.C. 422, appeal after remand 759 F.2d 176, 245 U.S.App.D.C. 156, rehearing denied 763 F.2d 1432, 246 U.S.App.D.C. 171.

C.A.Cal. 1982. U. S. v. Gonsalves, 675 F.2d 1050, certiorari denied 103 S.Ct. 83, 459 U.S. 837, 74 L.Ed.2d 78, appeal after remand 731 F.2d 1409.

C.A.7 (Ill.) 1988. Defendant's intent to avoid arrest or prosecution must be proven to trigger tolling of applicable statute of limitations because defendant was a fugitive from justice. 18 U.S.C.A. § 3290.
U.S. v. Marshall, 856 F.2d 896.

To invoke fugitive from justice tolling statute, Government must demonstrate that defendant fled jurisdiction with intent to avoid arrest or prosecution by a preponderance of the evidence. 18 U.S.C.A. § 3290.
U.S. v. Marshall, 856 F.2d 896.

District court's determination that defen-
...nt fled juri... ...to avoid pr... ...tion was
...lear... ...d al... ...of

...an... ...rom
ed State... ...al on crim... ...ue
was not re... ...d of a duty to do a... ...could to
return.
U.S. v. Catino, 735 F.2d 718, certiorari denied 105 S.Ct. 180, 469 U.S. 855, 83 L.Ed.2d 114.

Fact that defendant, who was in French prison awaiting trial on French charges, actively resisted extradition request throughout proceedings instead of consenting to return to United States, coupled with his letter expressing a desire to resist all further extradition requests, constituted a constructive flight from justice, thereby tolling statute of limitations period. 18 U.S.C.A. §§ 3282, 3290.
U.S. v. Catino, 735 F.2d 718, certiorari denied 105 S.Ct. 180, 469 U.S. 855, 83 L.Ed.2d 114.

Tolling statute of limitations period on ground that defendant's resistance to extradition request constituted a constructive flight from justice did not impermissibly penalize defendant for asserting his right to oppose extradition, On theory that to claim benefit of statute of limitations, he would ... ...e had to give up his right to resist unl... ...on, ...that ther... ...othing... ...ath...

addition to the citations, the digest often summarizes the point in each opinion that relates to the Key Number topic.

Even without the annotated codebook that cited to *United States v. Catino,* you could find that case and others on point by searching through the index of the West Federal Practice Digest 4th. Under the heading "FUGITIVES FROM JUSTICE" and the subheading "LIMITATION of prosecution, suspension," the index refers you to Digest Topic and Key Number "Crim Law 153," which will lead you directly to the relevant cases:

FRIENDLY

98 F P D 4th—76

References are to Digest Topics and Key Numbers

FRIENDLY SUIT
SUBMISSION of controversy, see this index Submission of Controversies

FRIENDSHIP
CONSIDERATION for contract. Contracts 60

FRIGHT
DAMAGES, fright as element. Damag 51, 52

FRINGE BENEFITS
WORKERS' compensation, computation of wages, see this index Workers' Compensation

FRISK
⌐OP and frisk ⌐rally, see this index Stop and Frisk

FUGITIVES
DETAINERS. Extrad 54
SLAVES. Slaves 9

FUGITIVES FROM JUSTICE
EXTRADITION in general. Extrad 30, 37
HARBORING or concealing. Comp Off 3.5
LIMITATION of prosecution, suspension. Crim Law 153

FULL FAITH AND CREDIT
APPELLATE jurisdiction of cases involving Federal Constitution. Courts 219.8(4)
JUDGMENT, foreign judgments, see this index Foreign Judgments
STATE court judgment, affect in Federal court—
Child⌐   ⌐ Judgm 828(3.2)
S⌐   ⌐ts, records, et⌐ ⌐f every other st⌐

Reprinted with permission from Federal Practice Digest 4th. Copyright © by West Publishing Company.

Alternatively, if you had sufficient experience to identify "Criminal Law" as the digest topic, you might find Key Number 153 by glancing through the table of contents at the beginning of the Criminal Law section in the digest, as shown in the excerpt on page 177.

If you proceeded in this manner, you would find *United States v. Catino* through the digest and only then discover the statute by reading the case. In those circumstances, you should also find the statutory text in the annotated codebook. Although the codebook annotations and the West digest entries will inevitably refer to many of the same cases, the overlap may not be perfect, and the two services often organize and categorize their case summaries differently. You will not unreasonably duplicate your efforts by looking for helpful cases in both services.

Of course, if you are researching a question governed exclusively by common law, you can bypass the legislative materials and focus your attention on case law. You might initially find a case in the West digest, perhaps after consulting its index or the table of contents preceding a major topic in the digest. Alternatively, you might find citation to a helpful case while studying a secondary authority, such as an article or treatise. Although such secondary authorities are not sources of primary law that directly bind any government official, they may help you understand the contours of a legal topic and find citations to cases that can act as a springboard for further research.

CRIMINAL LAW   27 F P D 4th—350

Reprinted with permission from Federal Practice Digest 4th. Copyright © by West Publishing Company.

Finally, you must check the subsequent history of any judicial decision on which you rely in your analysis. Using a computer citation checking program, or using Shepard's multi-volume citation service, you should determine whether the decision has been affirmed, overruled, followed, distinguished, or questioned, or simply whether it has been accepted or rejected for future appellate review. Secondarily, you can use such a citation service as you would a case digest to find other cases on point. The service will identify subsequent decisions that have cited to the decision you are checking, and some of those subsequent decisions will offer useful holdings or discussions.

Unless an issue is tightly controlled by a seminal decision and its progeny, however, a citation checking service is a relatively clumsy means of finding helpful case law and should not be your tool of first resort. Aside from revealing subsequent history on a decision, it may be useful primarily as a method of cross-checking your previous research in annotated codebooks and case digests; on rare occasions it will turn up a useful subsequent decision that you missed with your primary case-finding tools. To use Shepard's most efficiently for such cross-checking, pay attention to a superscript number set within the citation to a subsequent decision. It refers to a West headnote number in the decision whose citation you are checking.

Such a superscript in a Shepard's subsequent citation means that the subsequent decision cites the earlier decision on a particular issue. The superscript is the same as the headnote number in the earlier decision corresponding to that issue. If you intend to use the earlier decision in your analysis only with respect to the issue corresponding to a particular headnote number, you can limit your search in Shepard's to subsequent decisions whose citations contain the same superscript in their Shepard's citation.

For example, in this excerpt from Shepard's Federal Cases citation service, the entries below the designation "Vol. 735" identify decisions that have cited to cases published in volume 735 of the Federal Reports 2d. More specifically, the entries below the number 718 identify subsequent decisions that cite to *United States v. Catino*, which appears in volume 735 of Federal Reports 2d, starting on page 718. Many of those subsequent citations cite to *United States v. Catino* for different points. However, the ones with the superscript "4" after the "F2d" designation cite to *United States v. Catino* on the topic corresponding to headnote 4 in *Catino*, the general definition of intent to flee from prosecution. If you were interested in researching that proposition only, you could examine only those cases cited in Shepard's with the supernumeral "4."

Of course, you should not forget to note the subsequent history of *United States v. Catino*. The Shepard's notation "U.S. cert den" shows that the United States Supreme Court rejected an invitation to review the federal appellate court's decision in *Catino*.

Vol. 735

```
827F2d²1570
827F2d⁴1573
j827F2d1577
836F2d¹⁹539
848F2d1574
23ARF691s

—488—
US cert den
in469US1018
⌐105S⌐

6υ.
63Bʌ w¹540
64BRW²835

—718—
US cert den
in469US855
in105SC180
    Cir. 2
739F2d⁴796
635FS¹²766
638FS⁴620
686FS²85
686FS⁴85
    Cir. 4
787F2d949
    Cir. 5
f809F2d¹²248
628FS⁴1476

    Cir. 11
765F2d⁴1050
765F2d⁷1050
24ARF365s
33ARF716s

—725—
US cert den
in469US1110
10⌐⌐⌐288
```

2. Research Strategy

Before setting your sights on specific primary authority, you should acquire a general grasp of the fundamental legal principles in the relevant subject areas so that you can more effectively identify issues and exclude unproductive lines of inquiry. A general survey course on the subject in law school should be sufficient to enable you to define issues and to delve immediately into specific, primary authority such as statutes or case law. If you have not taken a course on the subject matter of the assignment, you should consider beginning your research with a secondary source that provides necessary general background information. As their labels suggest, primary authority within the relevant jurisdiction takes analytic precedence over secondary authority. Nonetheless, you will often find and use the primary authority more effectively if you first consult a secondary source, such as a reputable treatise, to enhance your understanding of the broad outlines of the subject.

Once you have begun to explore primary authority, you should look for relevant legislation before digging too deeply into case law. A single statute can diminish or even destroy the authoritative value of a whole line of case law that developed obsolete common law doctrines or interpreted previously effective legislation. Thus, you can avoid hours of marginally productive reading by immediately finding the latest applicable legislation.

Even when you know that a body of case law interprets currently effective legislation, you should turn first to the statute itself. At least a glance at the statutory language will provide valuable context for the case law that interprets the statute. Moreover, an annotated codebook may help you dig up interpretive case law that you missed with other case-finding tools.

Of course, if you find no statute or constitutional provision on point, you may safely turn to case law as primary authority for applicable common law. In the absence of any relevant primary authority in the jurisdiction, you can rely on the persuasive authority provided by secondary sources or by primary authority from other jurisdictions.

C. USE OF THE LIBRARY

1. Taking Notes

You should take thorough notes on any authority that may be helpful. Even marginally applicable cases may warrant note; their relevance may become clear only after further research and analysis. To avoid the need for frequent returns to the library, your notes should include any information that you may later need in drafting the office memorandum, including

(1) the full citation,
(2) the specific page on which relevant material appears,
(3) a sufficient summary of the facts to provide necessary context and to define the holding,
(4) a careful summary of the holding and reasoning, including helpful dictum, on any issues relevant to your research assignment, and
(5) the verbatim language of any passage that you think might be worth quoting. You may want to photocopy any part of an opinion that warrants special or extended study.

Moreover, to facilitate further research, you should record data provided by the publisher designed to be used with formal research tools. For example, an opinion that is reproduced in a reporter published by West Publishing Company will begin with West "headnotes," each of which includes at least one key number. As discussed in Section B above, these headnote and key numbers are worth recording in your notes, because they will help you find other cases on point. Accordingly, the following library notes incorporate these West features:

Osterholt v. St. Charles Drilling Co., 500 F. Supp. 529 (E.D. Mo. 1980).

pp. 530-32. Landowner sued drilling company for damages stemming from installation of defective well and water system. pp. 534-35—Judgment for P on K.

pg. 536 [9] (Fraud 61)—punitive damages denied for alleged misrepresentation, because of absence of "aggravating circumstances" such as willful, wanton, reckless, or malicious conduct.

   Court refers to 582 F.2d at 1087.

In this example, the researcher is particularly interested in the passage on page 536 discussing punitive damages. The shorthand citation at the end of the notes refers to an opinion cited in *Osterholt* that the researcher will examine. The phrase "(Fraud 61)" refers to a West key number that will help the researcher use the West digest system to find other cases discussing the same issue. Indeed, that key number may lead to other cases reported in the West system that will supply the researcher with other West key numbers that are productive on the topic of punitive damages. The number nine in brackets refers to the headnote number associated with the relevant passage. As illustrated in Section B above, that headnote number will help the researcher use Shepard's citation service as a tool for finding subsequent cases that cite *Osterholt* on the issue of punitive damages for tort.

2. Library Courtesy

In light of the scarcity of resources in any law library, discourtesy in the library can lead to frustration and wasted time for all. Rather than pile three dozen books on a table for an afternoon's reading, you should take only one or two books off the shelves at a time, take notes, and immediately reshelve the books. If you follow a methodical approach, you can efficiently exhaust the research possibilities with a minimum duplication of effort.

For example, after finding an applicable statute in an annotated codebook, you may use the annotations to find interpretive case law. Because the descriptive paragraphs in the annotations provide only general guidance, you may not be able to determine whether a reported opinion contains noteworthy information until you have glanced at the opinion itself. You can do that while standing at the stacks. If the opinion warrants close reading, you can take the reporter to a library carrel for note-taking. If the opinion appears to be unhelpful, you can return the reporter to the shelves without having taken it from the vicinity.

D. REORGANIZATION AND OUTLINING

As summarized at the beginning of Chapter 7, the process of transforming library notes into a well-organized office memorandum is similar to that of summarizing and reorganizing case briefs in a student course outline. Both processes require you (1) to synthesize cases to arrive at general principles and (2) to classify cases to show which of them illustrates each principle. With this synthesis and reorganization, you can highlight ideas and illuminate them with illustrative cases, rather than simply present a laundry list of individual cases whose relationships to one another are unclear.

If you produce voluminous library notes for a complex assignment, you may wish to begin the process of reorganization by indexing your notes in the manner described at the beginning of Chapter 7. For example, a researcher has assigned a number to each authority summarized in the following library notes:

1. Statute of frauds—Ariz. Rev. Stat. Ann. §44-101 (1967).

"No action shall be brought in any court in the following cases unless the promise or agreement upon which the action is brought . . . is in writing and signed by the party to be charged . . . 5. Upon an agreement which is not to be performed within one year from the making thereof."

2. *Tiffany Incorporated v. W.M.K. Transit Mix, Inc.*, 16 Ariz. App. 415, 493 P.2d 1220 (1972).

P.2d at 1221-22—Tiffany prepared a bid to state agency to complete work on highway project; before bidding, it received oral price quote from Transit Mix for the supply of sealcoat chips for the project. Tiffany used that quote in its bid, the state awarded the bid to Tiffany, Transit refused to perform, Tiffany sues, and Transit raises statute of frauds as defense.

1222-23—UCC statute of frauds applies

a. 1224-25 [5-7] (Estoppel 52, 85, 99)—distinction between equitable and promissory estoppel: equitable—reliance on misrepresentation of fact; used as a "shield" or defense against some claim. Promissory—reliance on a promise; used as a defense or as basis for cause of action for damages.

b. 1225 [8, 9] (Estoppel 85)—If proved at trial, following facts would support application of promissory estoppel: Transit promised to supply sealcoat chips at certain price in event that Tiffany got the main bid; Tiffany relied by using quote in its own bid; Transit should have foreseen that Tiffany would use its quote if it were the lowest. (dictum?)

1225-26 [10] (Frauds, stat. of 144)—nonetheless, statute of frauds bars enforcement of promise. Court recognizes estoppel to avoid statute if promisee relies on misrepresentation about requirements of statute (equitable estoppel?) or on promise to satisfy or not to rely on statute—but can't avoid statute by relying on other party's underlying oral promise to perform.

3. *Mac Enterprises v. Del E. Webb Development Co.*, 132 Ariz. 331, 645 P.2d 1245 (Ct. App. 1982).

P.2d at 1250 [6] (Frauds, stat. of 144)—no estoppel to avoid statute of frauds, because Webb made no promise upon which Mac could reasonably rely.

4. *Kiely v. St. Germain*, 670 P.2d 764 (Colo. 1983) (en banc).

768-69—[7] (Frauds, stat. of 119(1))—good discussion of liberal Rest.

2d use of promissory estoppel to avoid statute of frauds and case law that prompted it—*Tiffany* cited as example of narrower approach.

• • • •

After analyzing the problem, the researcher then developed a rough outline to express a proposed organization for each office memorandum. As illustrated at the beginning of Chapter 7, the outline of the discussion section is organized around legal principles and identifies which authority supports and illustrates each principle:

III. DISCUSSION

A. Applicability and Satisfaction of Statute of Frauds

Rules: requires writing signed by party to be charged if can't be performed in 1 year [ARS 44-101(5), #1]

Facts: K is for 2 years, and no writing at all

Conclusion: statute applies & is not satisfied

B. Estoppel to Avoid Statute

1. Misrep. or Promise about Statute's Requirements

Rules: equitable estoppel and promissory estoppel relating to requirements of statute [*Cress*, #6; and *Johnson*, #10, or *Tiffany*, #2a]

Facts: no representation or promise about statute's requirements

Conclusion: trad. forms of avoidance through estoppel not available

2. Reliance on Underlying Promise to Perform

Rules: Introduce liberal doctrine [Rest. 2d, #5, *Kiely*, #4]. Discuss whether AZ likely to adopt liberal rule [*Cf. Fremming*, #9, with *Tiffany*, #2b]

—Some cases have assumed theory, but found elements not satisfied [*Trollope*, #8, and *Mac*, #3]

—Distinguish *Tiffany*? [Wallach, #13 and UCC sections it cites; *Trollope*, #8; *Dean*, #7, and *Johnson*, #10]

Facts: Williams' actions probably constitute detrimental, foreseeable reliance

Conclusion: If AZ court adopts liberal view of avoidance of statute through promissory estoppel, facts probably support claim for damages.

Some authorities appear more than once and in different parts of the outline because those authorities contain information relevant to more than one topic or subtopic in the discussion. Each shorthand reference to an authority is followed by the index number to the place in the author's library notes where that authority is summarized. As illustrated at the beginning of Chapter 7, the index number helped the author quickly locate the authority in his notes when he drafted the memoranda.

When researching a problem, you should avoid the temptation to include every idea and authority that you have encountered in the library. The outlining stage provides a good opportunity to exclude marginally relevant material as well as to reorganize and analyze.

E. WRITING THE MEMORANDUM

Once you are satisfied with the organization and analysis reflected in your outline, you can use the outline as a general guide when writing the memorandum. Many law firms encourage their attorneys to dictate their first drafts into handheld tape recorders, but many new associates find it difficult to display good style in dictation. Consequently, if you dictate the first draft, you may want to work from a particularly detailed written outline so that you can focus your attention on sentence structure rather than on organizational matters.

═══════════ S A M P L E S ═══════════

1. *Sample Memorandum 1*

Imagine that an attorney from the fictitious state of Calzona drafted the following office memorandum using only authority from the Calzona Supreme Court. Study the memorandum and consider the questions that follow it.

MEMORANDUM
TO: Susan Elias
FROM: James Nelson
RE: Enforceability of Julie Week's Promise to Act as Guarantor for her Cousin's Loan Obligation; File 85-87
DATE: September 16, 1985

I. ISSUE AND BRIEF ANSWER

By stating that he would refrain from demanding payment from the Borrower on a loan obligation until he "needs the money," did the Lender state a promise that bound him to a future performance, thus providing consideration for the Guarantor's promise to pay the obligation in the event that the Borrower failed to pay on demand? Probably yes.

II. FACTS

One of our regular business clients, Julie Week (Guarantor), asserted the following facts in an interview.

On December 15, 1993, Guarantor's cousin, Don Caslin (Borrower), purchased a used Mercedes Benz sports coupe from a private owner, Thomas Beatty (Lender), for $20,000. In a self-financing arrangement, Borrower paid $8,000 on delivery and agreed in writing to pay the remainder of the purchase price in 12 monthly installments of $1,000 each, beginning January 1, 1994.

From January to June 1994, Borrower timely paid Lender a total of $6,000 in monthly installments. In late June, however, Borrower suffered unusual losses in his private business, and he failed to pay the installments due on July 1 and August 1. After Lender threatened to sue for the return of the automobile, Guarantor negotiated a written agreement (the Guarantee Agreement) with Lender designed to give Borrower time to recover from his temporary financial difficulties. Dated August 5, 1994, the Guarantee Agreement refers to the agreement between Lender and Borrower as the "CREDIT/SALE AGREEMENT," and it contains the following statement of mutual obligations:

> 1. LENDER will refrain from asserting his claim against BORROWER and from demanding payment on the CREDIT/SALE AGREEMENT until LENDER needs the money.
> 2. In the event that BORROWER fails to pay all amounts due under the CREDIT/SALE AGREEMENT upon demand by LENDER, GUARANTOR will pay those amounts immediately and will pay further installments as they become due under the CREDIT/SALE AGREEMENT.

On August 25, 1994, Lender demanded payment from Borrower, and Borrower explained that he could not yet pay. On September 2, 1994, Lender demanded immediate payment of $3,000 from Guarantor; he also stated that he expects either Borrower or Guarantor to pay the remaining three installments as they become due on the first of each month.

We do not yet have any evidence that Lender engaged in fraud during formation of the Guarantee Agreement or that he did not in fact have a "need" for the money on August 25. You have asked me to analyze the question whether the Guarantee Contract is unenforceable on its face for lack of consideration.

III. DISCUSSION

Lender's promise to refrain from asserting his claim and demanding payment until he "needs the money" arguably is illusory. If so, Guarantor's promise is not supported by consideration and is unenforceable.

An enforceable contract requires a bargained-for exchange in which a promisor exchanges his own promise for a return promise or performance. *Smith v. Newman*, 161 Calz. 443, 447, 667 P.2d 81, 84 (1984); *Barney v. Johnson*, 93 Calz. 127, 312 P.2d 550 (1961); *see also* Restatement (Second) of Contracts §71 (1981). The requirement of an exchange is not satisfied if one party gives only an illusory promise, which does not commit the promisor to any future performance. *See Atco Corp. v Johnson*, 155 Calz. 1211, 627 P.2d 781 (1980).

In *Atco Corp.*, the manager of an automobile repair shop purportedly promised to delay asserting a claim against the owner of an automobile for $900 in repairs. Specifically, he promised to forbear from asserting the claim "until I want the money." In exchange, a friend of the owner promised to act as guarantor of the owner's obligation. *Id.* at 1212, 627 P.2d at 782. The word "want" stated no legal commitment because it permitted the manager at his own discretion to refuse to perform any forbearance at all. Because the manager incurred no obligation, the guarantor's promise was gratuitous and unenforceable. *Id.* at 1213-1214, 627 P.2d at 782-784.

On the other hand, even if a promise leaves open the possibility that the promisor will escape obligation, the promise is valid if the promisor does not have complete control over the events on which the promisor's obligation is conditioned. *See Bonnie v. DeLaney*, 158 Calz. 212, 645 P.2d 887 (1982). In *Bonnie*, an agreement for the sale of a house provided that the buyer could cancel the agreement if the buyer "cannot qualify for a 30-year mortgage loan for 90% of the sales price" with any of several banks listed in the agreement. *Id.* at 213, 645 P.2d at 888. In enforcing the agreement against the seller, the court distinguished *Atco Corp.* on the ground that the word "cannot" referred to the buyer's *ability* to obtain a loan rather than to his *desire*. Because his ability to obtain a loan was partly controlled by events and decisions outside his control, the promises in the sale agreement were nonillusory and binding. *Id.* at 214-215, 645 P.2d at 889-891.

Our client's case probably is more nearly analogous to *Bonnie* than it is to *Atco Corp.* Lender's promise to forbear until he "needs" the money appears to condition the length of his forbearance on financial events that are at least partly outside his control: As long as his income and expenses create no need for the money, Lender has a commitment to forbear from demanding payment. To convince a court to draw an analogy to *Atco Corp.* rather than to *Bonnie*, we should argue that the word "need" refers to a subjective perception of deprivation that is inseparable from one's desires. Lender arguably can control his financial needs through his personal spending decisions, subject only to his own discretion.

Unfortunately, the analogy to *Bonnie* is stronger because financial needs are almost certainly controlled partly by external factors. Lender's promise probably is not illusory.

IV. CONCLUSION

The promises stated in the Guarantee Agreement appear to satisfy the consideration requirement because Lender assumed a legal obligation by promising to refrain from asserting his claim and demanding payment until he "needs" the money. Unless we discover other serious defects in the Guarantee Agreement, the Guarantor's defenses will not be worth litigating. We should urge Guarantor to settle the claim, and we should try to persuade Borrower to indemnify Guarantor and to assume responsibility for further payments.

Questions on Sample Memorandum 1

a. Did the substantive labels assigned to the parties serve as helpful reminders of the respective roles of the parties, or would you have retained the parties' last names as less distracting references?

b. Is the statement of the issue sufficiently detailed to justify a brief answer of only two words, or would you have preferred a more detailed brief answer under a separate heading?

c. Does the statement of facts include any facts that you would omit or summarize further? Does it omit any important facts to which the author likely had access?

d. Identify the parts of the "Discussion" section that illuminate the issue, discuss the legal standards, analyze the facts, and state a conclusion.

e. Do you agree with the author's analysis? Does it adequately explore both sides of the dispute? Is it too pessimistic?

2. *Sample Memorandum 2*

The following memorandum, which is set in a fictitious jurisdiction, borrows from examples set forth in previous sections of this chapter addressing individual elements of office memoranda.

MEMORANDUM
TO: James Clapton
FROM: Ginger Jackson
RE: *Souza v. Humane;* strict liability and negligence—File No. 88-117
DATE: September 10, 1988

I. ISSUES

A. Does the phrase "any toxic material" in New Maine's strict liability statute encompass a generally safe anesthetic that produced a fatal reaction in a patient with a rare nerve disorder?

B. Is Humane Hospital liable to Souza's estate for negligent administration of the anesthetic?

1. Did Humane's anesthesiologist breach a duty of care by administering the anesthetic without assistance and by failing to monitor Souza's reactions to anesthesia?

2. Did Souza's nerve disorder constitute a supervening cause that broke the chain of causation between the anesthesiologist's conduct and Souza's death?

II. BRIEF ANSWERS

A. Probably not. A restrictive interpretation is supported by the legislative history and by a general public policy in New Maine encouraging the provision of affordable medical services. The legislature probably did not intend the statutory term "toxic material" to include medically prescribed substances that ordinarily produce a beneficial result or otherwise facilitate medical treatment.

B. Probably yes.

1. Probably yes. Under generally accepted hospital procedures, at least two trained medical personnel must monitor the administration of anesthesia, with at least one person monitoring the patient's reactions. A jury likely will find that the anesthesiologist breached a duty of care to the patient by administering the anesthesia alone.

2. No. The jury likely will also find that the patient's nerve disorder was not a supervening cause and that the anesthesiologist's negligence proximately caused the patient's death.

III. FACTS

On February 17, 1988, our client, Humane Hospital, Inc. (Humane), admitted 22-year-old Teresa Souza to its facility in Greenville, New Maine, for surgery to correct a bone deformity in her foot. Souza's bone deformity was not life-threatening, but it severely hampered her mobility. The planned surgery required general anesthesia.

Dr. Roberta Unger, an anesthesiologist for Humane, studied Souza's medical history and discovered that she suffered from a rare nerve disorder that slightly increased the risk that she would suffer an adverse reaction from anesthesia. Unger carefully informed Souza of the advantages and risks associated with each of the three safest and most effective general anesthetics. Souza decided to proceed with the operation and with the administration of general anesthesia. Unger and Souza ultimately agreed that Unger would administer ethane, a widely used and generally safe form of ether. Unger had initially recommended Forane, a potent muscle relaxant that maintains a stable heart rate. Souza, however, rejected Forane because of its greater cost.

At 10:00 A.M. on February 18, Souza was prepared for surgery. While the circulating nurse was occupied with another patient, and before the surgical team arrived, Unger began administering the prescribed anesthetic to Souza. Unger and Souza were alone in the room. Apparently because she was concerned that an overdose might trigger an adverse reaction, Unger concentrated intensely on the anesthetic intake gauge, which monitored the flow of anesthetic. As a consequence, she failed to watch either Souza or the equipment monitoring Souza's reactions. Approximately one minute after Unger began administering the anesthetic, the monitoring equipment sounded an alarm, and Souza died. Efforts to revive her failed. According to computer records, the monitoring equipment reflected growing signs of distress in Souza beginning approximately 10 seconds before her death and before the alarm sounded.

An autopsy showed that the anesthetic combined with Souza's nerve disorder to trigger a reaction that caused cardiac arrest. Mary L. Richards, Ph.D., a professor at the University of New Maine School of Nursing, has told us that hospitals throughout the nation ordinarily require the anesthesiologist to be accompanied by a nurse during the administration of anesthesia. Both the nurse and the anesthesiologist are expected to continuously assess the patient's reaction to anesthesia by reading monitoring equipment and by observing the patient directly. Although she cannot be certain, Richards guesses that the fatal reaction was triggered largely by the final 10 seconds of Unger's administration of anesthesia.

Souza's estate has sued Humane in tort for wrongful death. It advances two theories of tort liability: (1) statutory strict liability for use of toxic materials, and (2) negligence in the administration of the anesthetic.

IV. DISCUSSION

A. Strict Liability for Use of Toxic Materials

If a statute or the common law imposes strict liability for Souza's death, then Souza's estate can establish liability without proving negligence. New Maine's common law doctrine of strict liability for injuries caused by ultrahazardous activities does not apply to noncriminal medical practices engaged in by licensed physicians. *Stanislaus v. Good Samaritan Hospital*, 212 N. Me. 113, 115 (1979). New Maine has enacted a statute, however, that imposes strict liability for injuries stemming from the use of "any toxic material":

A commercial enterprise is liable for injuries proximately caused by its use of any toxic material, without regard to the degree of care exercised by the enterprise.

12 N. Me. Rev. Stat. §242 (1987) (effective Jan. 1, 1988). The New Maine courts have not yet had an opportunity to interpret the strict liability statute in a published opinion. As a profit-making hospital, Humane presumably is a "commercial enterprise" within the meaning of the statute. It is less certain, however, that the anesthetic administered to Souza would qualify as a "toxic" material.

The common meaning of the word "toxic" is "poisonous." *See, e.g., The Random House Dictionary of the English Language* 1500 (unabridged) (1970). Souza's estate might plausibly argue that the anesthetic was a toxic material because it was poisonous to Souza, even though it would not have been poisonous to most others. The word "toxic," however, applies more naturally to substances that are universally harmful to humans, such as cyanide, DDT, or sulfuric acid. It strains the common meaning of "toxic" to apply it to an anesthetic that might occasionally be harmful to persons with unusual allergies or other extraordinary conditions.

Legislative history also supports a restrictive interpretation of the statutory term "any toxic material." The report of the New Maine Senate Committee on Health and Welfare suggests that the legislature was concerned only with the most deadly of substances:

> The purpose of this bill is to reallocate the cost of unavoidable accidents from victims to industry and its consumers, to discourage unnecessary use of deadly chemicals and other hazardous materials, and to encourage the development and use of substitute materials that are generally safe for human contact.

N. Me. Sen. Rep. No. 112, 1987-1988 Sess. 2 (1988). The anesthetic in this case probably is closer to the materials "generally safe for human contact" condoned by the legislature than it is to the "deadly chemicals and other hazardous materials" condemned by it.

Finally, general state policy appears to support an interpretation that excludes medically prescribed substances from the reach of the statute. The legislature and judiciary of New Maine have recognized a policy of restricting the liability of physicians to encourage the ready availability of affordable medical services. For example, under the New Maine "Good Samaritan" statute, physicians who provide certain emergency medical services are not liable for adverse consequences unless they engage in culpable conduct amounting to at least gross negligence. 12 N. Me. Rev. Stat. §229 (1985). This protective policy is also reflected in the courts' refusal to extend common law strict liability for ultrahazardous activities to even experimental medical practices. *Stanislaus*, 212 N. Me. at 115. The legislature presumably was aware of these legal developments when it enacted the toxic materials statute in 1988. Souza's estate may argue that the legislature intended to partially overrule *Stanislaus* by imposing strict liability on a limited segment of the activities of commercial medical practices. However, absent more specific evidence of legislative intent to alter the course of existing common law, it is probably more likely that the legislature retained its protective attitude and assumed that the term "any toxic material" would not include routinely prescribed medicines or anesthetics.

In this case, the prescribed anesthetic, ethane, was not the safest available at the time of Souza's operation. Nonetheless, it is a frequently prescribed substance that produces beneficial results with only minor side effects in all but the most unusual cases. The strict liability statute probably does not apply to Souza's death.

B. Negligence

Assuming that Humane is not strictly liable for Souza's death, it may nonetheless be liable to Souza's estate if its agent caused the death through negligence. *See Kityama v. Mercy Hospital,* 183 N. Me. 752, 759-760 (1974) (hospital liable for negligence of its nurse). An action for negligence requires proof of a negligent act or omission that proximately causes injury. *Baker v. Bruce,* 153 N. Me. 817, 820 (1967).

In our case, the injury to Souza is obvious. In greater doubt are the elements of negligent act and proximate cause.

1. Negligent Act

A negligent act or omission consists of the breach of a duty of care owed to another. *Id.* at 821. A medical specialist owes a duty to patients to exercise at least the ordinary skill and care that is reasonable and customary nationwide in that medical specialty. *Kityama,* 183 N. Me. at 760. Furthermore, under the "thin-skulled plaintiff" rule, that duty of care encompasses the special care necessary to address increased risks created by a patient's unusual susceptibility to injury. *Id.* In this case, Humane's anesthesiologist, Unger, may have breached duties of care in her unassisted administration of general anesthesia in the face of Souza's known nervous condition.

Unger exercised care in determining Souza's disorder of the nervous system and in informing her of the risks presented by each of the most suitable anesthetics. Moreover, when administering the anesthetic selected by Souza, Unger took care to provide the prescribed dosage by monitoring the anesthetic intake gauge.

However, Unger's intense concentration on the anesthetic intake gauge may have been an act of carelessness, rather than enhanced care, because it diverted Unger's attention from Souza and from the equipment monitoring Souza's vital signs. Faced with Souza's known nervous disorder, Unger probably had a duty to follow the standard medical practice of summoning a nurse to assist her in administering the anesthesia. Had she done so, the team could have monitored both Souza's vital signs and the intake gauge, and a team member undoubtedly would have detected signs of distress at least 10 seconds before death, arguably enough time to cease anesthesia and take corrective measures.

On these facts, a jury could find that Unger was negligent in her administration of the anesthetic.

2. Proximate Cause

Even if its agent was negligent, Humane will not be liable to Souza's estate unless the negligence proximately caused Souza's death. *See, e.g., Baker v. Bruce,* 153 N. Me. 817, 821 (1967). Proximate cause is a flexible doctrine that precludes liability if the relationship between negligence and an injury is so attenuated that it would be unfair to hold the negligent party responsible for the injury. *Id.* at 821-822.

In this case, we can argue that the 10-second warning appearing on the monitoring equipment would not have given even two observant medical personnel sufficient time to reverse Souza's fatal reaction. If so, even careful administration of anesthesia would have resulted in death, suggesting that Souza's reaction was truly an unforeseeable accident rather than the proximate result of any negligent act. Unfortunately, the factual premise of this argument may be unsound: According to our own expert, the marginal effects of the final 10 seconds of anesthesia probably were critical. We may want to investigate this further with other experts.

As a fall-back position on proximate cause, we could try to characterize Souza's rare nervous condition as a supervening cause. Such an intervening cause may break the chain of causation between the negligence and the injury, particularly if the intervening event was unexpected. *Safehouse Insurance Co. v. Rainbow Landscaping Co.,* 223 N. Me. 29, 31, 35 (1987) (dictum). Unfortunately, a court may be reluctant to analyze this issue within the framework of supervening cause. Under the more conventional approach, a court would simply apply the "thin-skulled plaintiff" rule to expand Unger's duty of care to encompass responsibility for increased risks of injury created by Souza's known nervous condition. However, if we can persuade the court to depart from the conventional approach and to analyze the increased risk within the less clearly applicable framework of supervening cause, we will gain the opportunity to develop an additional argument to avoid liability.

To develop a supervening-cause argument, we must distinguish *Rainbow Landscaping,* which liberally allocates the risks of some intervening causes to the tortfeasor. In *Rainbow Landscaping,* a landscaping company agreed in writing with a general contractor to install a sprinkler system in the yards surrounding a new house in its final stages of construction. The written contract specifically obligated the landscaper to perform its work "in a manner that does not interfere with the ongoing work of other subcontractors or deface their finished product." *Id.* at 32. On the day that the landscaper began its work, its employees knew that another subcontractor was painting the interior of the house. While welding a sprinkler pipe to a house water line, an employee of the landscaper ignited paint fumes that had accumulated in a room recently painted by the painting subcontractor. The resulting fire entirely destroyed the nearly completed house.

In a suit brought against the landscaper by the owner's insurer, the landscaper argued on its motion for a directed verdict that, even if the landscaper had acted negligently, the paint fumes constituted an intervening cause that precluded a finding of proximate cause. The trial court denied the motion, and the jury returned a verdict for the insurer. The New Maine Supreme Court affirmed: It held that the landscaper was responsible for the consequences of the combustion of paint fumes that it had triggered because its employee should have been aware of the paint fumes and the danger they posed. *Id.* at 35. In dictum, the court stated that it might have reached a different result had the landscaper reasonably failed to foresee that the welding could trigger such a blaze. *Id.*

We can try to distinguish our case from *Rainbow Landscaping* by arguing that the landscaper's agreement to accommodate the work of other subcontractors justified the finding that the landscaper should have known of the hazard. Under this reasoning, the agreement was critical to the allocation of responsibility to the landscaper for the consequences of igniting the paint. That contract has no direct counterpart in this case. Moreover, in light of New Maine's policy of limiting the liability of medical care providers, a court might be willing to apply the doctrine of proximate cause more stringently in a hospital setting than in a construction setting.

On the other hand, although Souza's adverse reaction to the anesthetic was not highly probable, it was certainly foreseeable as a possible consequence; Unger's intense concentration on the intake gauge shows that she indeed specifically anticipated such a reaction. The absence of a contract such as the one in *Rainbow Landscaping* might be viewed as a technical and only marginally material distinction.

Therefore, even if we can persuade a court to analyze Souza's nervous condition within the framework of supervening cause, the court probably will not find the doctrine satisfied on the facts of this case. If Souza can prove that Unger was negligent, she can probably show proximate cause as well.

V. CONCLUSION

In light of legislative and judicial policies favoring limits on physicians' liability, the strict liability statute regulating toxic materials probably will not apply to the administration of the anesthetic in this case. The courts will be even less likely to retreat from precedent by applying the common law doctrine imposing strict liability for ultrahazardous activities. A jury may find, however, that Humane's anesthesiologist was negligent in failing to summon assistance for the administration of the anesthesia and to monitor Souza more closely. We can try to characterize Souza's nervous condition as a supervening cause, but *Rainbow Landscaping* will not be easy to distinguish.

Because the risk of substantial liability is great, I recommend that we advise Humane to settle. Souza's estate may be willing to compromise; their negligence claim is not appropriate for summary disposition, and they may want to avoid the unpredictability of a jury.

Questions on Sample Memorandum 2

a. Distinguish between the statutory and common law claims discussed in Sample Memorandum 2. How does the legal method of analyzing one claim differ from that of the other?

b. Review the statutory analysis in section IV.A of Sample Memorandum 2. Its original analysis of language, legislative history, and policy is indispensable precisely because no court had yet interpreted the statute. Imagine instead that the author of the memorandum had found a New Maine case that discusses the applicability of the strict liability statute to a restaurant that sold raw oysters infected with the *Vibrio vulnificus* bacteria. Most oysters naturally absorb this bacteria, and almost all persons who ingest the bacteria after eating raw oysters suffer no ill effects. However, in a tiny percentage of persons, particularly those with liver or kidney problems, the bacteria can lead to septicemia, which often results in death. In the New Maine case, *Spratt v. Shuck,* a man developed a bacterial infection and died after eating raw oysters served in a restaurant.[6]

Imagine that the New Maine Supreme Court examined the language, legislative history, and policy of the New Maine statute governing strict liability for toxic materials. Imagine further that it found that a raw oyster infected with the *Vibrio vulnificus* bacteria is not a "toxic material" within the meaning of the statute. Would the author of the memorandum discuss the issue of statutory liability in the same manner if a case like *Spratt v. Shuck* were available? Would she rely as heavily on her own analysis of language, legislative history, and policy? How would the analysis differ if it focused on case law such as *Spratt v. Shuck?*

c. Review the subsection discussing the element of proximate cause in a negligence action. Note how the author of the memorandum seeks to manipulate the analytic framework within which to address the legal consequences of Souza's unusual nervous condition. Is this a fair method of argument? Can it be used in other contexts? Most professors of tort law readily conclude that a court would analyze Souza's nervous condition within the "thin-skulled plaintiff" rule regarding the scope of duties, and not within the framework of proximate cause. In that light, is the argument in the memorandum a welcome exercise in creative argument, or is it a misleading waste of time for the reader?

d. Notice the frequent use of the word "we" in the section on proximate cause. Should the author of a memorandum avoid using such first-person pronouns in a legal analysis? Are first-person pronouns appropriate when referring to the law firm's development of facts or legal theories? Are they better than passive voice or other abstractions?

3. *Review—Sample Examination Answer*

Review Sample Memorandum 1 above. The following single-issue examination problem is roughly based on the dispute analyzed in that memorandum. Study the sample answer that follows the problem and compare its sparer, leaner style with the more thorough analysis in the memorandum. Note also the function of each of the four paragraphs in the answer:

---

6. See Simeon v. Doe, 618 So. 2d 848 (La. 1993).

¶1 identifies the issue and explains why other matters are not in issue;
¶2 discusses the applicable legal rule;
¶3 applies the rule to the facts; and
¶4 states a conclusion.

Problem

On December 15, pursuant to an enforceable agreement, Lender sold his used Mercedes Benz car to Borrower for $20,000. Under the terms of the agreement, Borrower paid $8,000 in cash and agreed to pay the remaining $12,000 to Lender in 12 monthly installments of $1,000 each, beginning January 1.

Borrower paid the first six monthly installments, but failed to pay the next two installments on July 1 and August 1. When Lender threatened to sue Borrower, Borrower's cousin (Guarantor) entered into the following Guarantee Agreement with Lender to give Borrower time to recover from temporary financial difficulties. This Guarantee Agreement refers to the original contract between Lender and Borrower as the "CREDIT/SALE AGREEMENT."

GUARANTEE AGREEMENT

Parties . . .

Recitals . . .

Mutual Rights and Obligations
The parties agree to the following exchange:
1. LENDER will refrain from asserting his claim against BORROWER and from demanding payment on the CREDIT/SALE AGREEMENT until LENDER needs the money.
2. In the event that BORROWER fails to pay all amounts due under the CREDIT/SALE AGREEMENT upon demand by LENDER, GUARANTOR will pay those amounts immediately and will pay further installments as they become due under the CREDIT/SALE AGREEMENT.

Guarantor and Lender signed this agreement on August 5. On August 25, Lender demanded payment of past due installments from Borrower. Borrower responded that he couldn't pay. Accordingly, on August 26, Lender demanded payment of past due installments from Guarantor and stated that he expected either Borrower or Guarantor to pay the remaining installments as they came due.

You represent Guarantor, who does not want to perform on her promise to pay Borrower's debt. In a balanced discussion addressed to your supervising attorney, fully address the rights and liabilities of Lender and Guarantor under the Guarantee Agreement. Do not discuss promissory estoppel, quasi-contract, or other theories of liability aside from conventional contract.

Sample Answer

Guarantor's performance under paragraph 2 of the Guarantee Agreement is due because Borrower has failed to pay on Lender's demand. The issue is whether the Guarantee Agreement is enforceable. The Guarantee Agreement appears to be reasonably definite and to have resulted from a valid offer and acceptance. Moreover, Lender had a perfectly valid claim under the original sale agreement; therefore, a promise by him to forbear from filing suit on that claim could be good consideration for Guarantor's conditional promise to pay. However, Lender's promise to refrain from asserting his claim and demanding payment only until he "needs the money" arguably is illusory, thus creating doubt whether Guarantor's promise is supported by consideration.

An enforceable contract requires a bargained-for exchange in which a promisor exchanges his own promise for a return promise or performance. The requirement of an exchange is not satisfied if one party gives only an illusory promise, which does not commit the promisor to any future performance. A promise is illusory if it leaves the promisor free to perform or not according to his unfettered whim or discretion, such as a promise to refrain from asserting a claim "until I want the money." On the other hand, even if a promise leaves open the possibility that the promisor will escape obligation, the promise is valid if the promisor does not have complete control over the events on which the promisor's obligation is conditioned, such as a promise to buy land "if I can qualify for a loan."

Guarantor should argue that Lender's promise to forbear until he "needs" the money permits Lender to decide at his own whim and unfettered discretion when to demand payment, because he has some control of his own needs. However, that argument would prevail only if the word "need" refers to a subjective perception of deprivation that is inseparable from Lender's purely personal wants or desires. Lender can argue that the word "need" conditions the length of his forbearance on financial events that are at least partly outside his control: As long as his income and expenses create no need for the money, Lender has a commitment to forbear from demanding payment.

Unfortunately for our client, Lender's promise in the Guarantee Agreement probably is not illusory, because the word "need" provides some substance to Lender's commitment to forbear. Therefore, Guarantor's promise probably is supported by consideration and is enforceable.

V. SUMMARY

Before drafting an office memorandum, you should

(1) master the assignment,
(2) research and analyze the problem,

(3) outline your memorandum, and

(4) choose a suitable format.

Before writing your answer to a law school examination, reflect on the parallels between an essay exam answer and the discussion section of an office memorandum.

10

Organization of Office Memoranda and Briefs

One of the most important features of effective legal analysis and writing is good organization. Techniques of organization are also among the most difficult to develop and to teach. With a few months of practice, however, you can steadily improve your skills. Regular outlining of course material in law school is an excellent way to build basic skills.

Although the focus of Part III is objective analysis in office memoranda, the techniques of organization described in this chapter apply directly to both office memoranda and legal briefs. Accordingly, this chapter uses examples from both memoranda and briefs. The following sections explore problems of organization on four different levels, progressing from broader problems of (1) format and (2) relationships among multiple issues, to narrower problems of (3) progression within sections and (4) effective paragraphing.

I. FORMAT

Before drafting any legal document, you must select an appropriate format for the document. The format will determine the essential content of the document and the order in which you present the different parts of that content.

Rules of procedure and local court rules prescribe formats for appellate briefs. With somewhat less detail, they also prescribe or suggest formats for trial pleadings, motions, and briefs. You should take care to follow these rules, because they presumably reflect the court's views about effective content and administrative efficiency. If you depart from the prescribed format, you may irritate the judge or judges who must read the document. Indeed, you may even lead the judge or the clerk's office to reject the document for filing or to impose other sanctions.[1]

The most appropriate format for other documents, such as a contract or office memorandum, is partly a matter of judgment or style for you or your law firm. For example, Chapter 9, page 158, outlines three different formats for an office memorandum; whether one is more appropriate to an assignment than the others will depend on such factors as the complexity of the memorandum, the preferences of your supervising attorney, and your own personal style. Before beginning to write such a document, you should take a few moments to determine which format will best suit your audience, your personal style, and the purposes of the document.

II. RELATIONSHIPS AMONG MULTIPLE ISSUES AND SUBISSUES

Your statement of the issues and your discussion or argument section of an office memorandum or legal brief should reflect the proper relationships among multiple issues and subissues. Good organization at this broad level requires a thorough understanding of the substantive analysis as well as attention to techniques of effective writing. Therefore, if you experience unusual difficulty with this level of organization, you may wish to supplement your research before proceeding further. By reviewing basic principles in a secondary source, you can gain a broad perspective that will help you organize your material.

A. PROPER RELATIONSHIPS AMONG TOPICS

Stated most simply, the section headings of the discussion or argument section of a document should show which topics are distinct and independent, and which are subsets of a more general topic. The statement of the issues should show the same relationships. These relationships are a function of the elements of the legal claims or defenses in question.

For example, suppose that you are preparing an office memorandum to discuss the following theories of employer liability for the discharge of an employee: (1) violation of a promise expressed in the company policy manual to invoke specified hearing procedures before terminating any employee; (2) wrongful discharge for a reason that violates public policy; and (3) intentional infliction of emotional distress.

The following information about the legal content of these claims under Arizona law will help you devise an appropriate organizational structure.

---

1. See, e.g., McGoldrick Oil Co. v. Campbell, Athey & Zukowski, 793 F.2d 649, 653 (5th Cir. 1986) (ordering a brief "stricken"); Westinghouse Elec. Corp. v. NLRB, 809 F.2d 419, 424-425 (7th Cir. 1987) (imposing $1,000 penalty on counsel for evading federal rule limiting the number of pages of its opening brief).

The elements of a contract action for breach of promise in a policy manual are (1) a promise in the manual by the employer to restrict the circumstances justifying discharge of the employee; (2) a basis for enforcing the promise, such as incorporation of the manual into the employment contract; and (3) breach of the promise.[2] The elements of the tort of wrongful discharge of an at-will employee in violation of public policy are (1) discharge of the employee (2) for a reason that contravenes a public policy that is clearly mandated by constitution, statute, or case law.[3] Finally, the elements of the tort of intentional infliction of emotional distress are (1) extreme and outrageous conduct (2) that is taken with the intent to cause emotional distress or with reckless disregard for the possibility of those consequences and (3) that causes (4) severe emotional distress.[4]

Although organization of these topics is a matter of judgment rather than an exact science, most legal writers will agree that the following section headings of the discussion section of the memorandum leave some room for improvement:

IV. DISCUSSION
    A. Wrongful Discharge—Violation of Public Policy or Breach of Promise in Employee Manual
    B. Intentional Infliction of Emotional Distress
       1. Remedies

First, section A inappropriately encompasses two distinct kinds of claims. True, both claims represent common law theories of liability in an emerging field known generically as wrongful discharge. However, wrongful discharge in violation of public policy is a tort whose elements have little in common with those of a claim for breach of a contractual promise to restrict the circumstances of terminating the employment contract.

Second, section B inappropriately includes a single subsection on remedies. If remedies were the only topic in section B, a subsection designation would be unnecessary. On the other hand, if section B discusses a theory of liability as well as remedies, both subtopics should be represented in subsection headings if either is. Finally, if the topic of remedies encompasses all of the theories of liability, it should not be buried within a section that addresses only the theory of intentional infliction of emotional distress.

These considerations suggest an improved organizational structure such as the following:

A. Breach of Contract
B. Wrongful Discharge in Violation of Public Policy
C. Intentional Infliction of Emotional Distress
D. Remedies

---

2. E.g., Wagenseller v. Scottsdale Memorial Hosp., 710 P.2d 1025, 1036-1038 (Ariz. 1985); Leikvold v. Valley View Community Hosp., 688 P.2d 170 (Ariz. 1984).
3. *Wagenseller*, supra note 2, at 1031-1036.
4. E.g., Watts v. Golden Age Nursing Home, 619 P.2d 1032 (Ariz. 1980).

Of course, this sample outline represents only one of many reasonable organizational structures for the memorandum in question. Other organizational structures may reflect different ways of presenting the analyses of remedies. For example, you might recognize that sections A through C present various theories of liability and could be consolidated in a section that is on the same level as the separate topic of remedies. Because the remedies for breach of contract are significantly different from those available for either of the tort claims, the section on remedies could discuss them separately:

> A. Theories of Liability
>   1. Breach of Contract
>   2. Wrongful Discharge in Violation of Public Policy
>   3. Intentional Infliction of Emotional Distress
> B. Remedies
>   1. Contract
>   2. Tort

Alternatively, you might decide to discuss remedies within each of the sections that introduces a theory of liability, rather than in a separate comprehensive section devoted to remedies. Under this organizational scheme, you might consolidate the two tort theories into a single section if you concluded that the remedies for each would be governed by the same tort principles. Depending on the depth of discussion in the memorandum, you could discuss remedies either in a paragraph at the end of each major section or, as shown below, in separate subsections.

> A. Breach of Contract
>   1. Breach of Promise in an Employee Manual
>   2. Remedies
> B. Tort
>   1. Wrongful Discharge in Violation of Public Policy
>   2. Intentional Infliction of Emotional Distress
>   3. Remedies

B. ORDER OF TOPICS

In an office memorandum, you should organize your topics in a logical order that permits early topics to build a foundation for subsequent topics. The clearest example of this is a multiple-issue discussion in which some issues are "threshold issues" in the sense that the resolution of those issues affects the analysis of other issues. Logically, you should discuss the threshold issues before you discuss the issues that are dependent on the outcome of the threshold issues.

For example, suppose that Maya Tortilla Co. alleges that Bakeway Supermarkets (1) formed a contract with Maya; (2) breached its contractual obligations, at least under Maya's interpretation of the contract; (3) and is liable to Maya for $20,000 in damages. If Bakeway disputes each of these allegations, the parties have raised three entirely separate issues.

Logically, you should discuss issue 1 first because contract formation is a threshold issue: Bakeway did not assume any contractual obligations and consequent potential liability if it did not form a contract with Maya. Similarly, you should discuss issue 2 before issue 3 for two reasons. First, Bakeway is not liable in damages unless it breached. Second, to determine whether Bakeway breached, you must interpret the contract and define Bakeway's obligation; in turn, the scope of Bakeway's obligation will determine Maya's expectation interest, on which damages will be based.

If you are drafting a brief rather than an office memorandum, you might organize your arguments differently: Strategic considerations may lead you to depart from a purely logical ordering of arguments. Like other people, judges are strongly influenced by first impressions. In many cases, the first arguments in a brief influence the judge more strongly than later ones. Also, if pressed for time, a busy trial judge may not reach the last few pages of a pretrial motions brief before oral argument. Accordingly, if one of your arguments is much stronger than the others, you might exercise discretion to present it first in your brief, even though another issue is logically prior.

Finally, you should apply all these considerations only to order your topics effectively, not to cut off discussion of any of the issues. In a close case, you cannot predict with certainty how a court will resolve a threshold issue. Accordingly, if a threshold issue raises a question sufficiently doubtful to warrant full discussion in an office memorandum or a brief, you should address all of the other substantial issues, even if you tentatively resolve the threshold issue in a way that logically would cut off discussion. In an office memorandum, for example, if you conclude that Bakeway did not breach the contract, you should nonetheless discuss the question of the amount of damages for which Bakeway would be liable if it had breached.

C. TECHNIQUE

By far the most efficient way to organize the topics of a memorandum or brief is to outline them after you have researched and analyzed the problem but before you begin to write. Even when you are working under severe time pressure, you should take a few minutes to organize your notes, think deeply and creatively about the analysis, and explore the relationships among topics by comparing different outlines of the discussion or argument. You can much more easily modify your analytic approach and writing strategy at the outline stage than you can midway through the first draft.

If you do not prepare an outline before writing the first draft, and if the first draft appears hopelessly disorganized, you can still derive benefits from outlining techniques, albeit with less efficiency than at the prewriting stage. By writing out the section and subsection headings of your first draft in outline form, you can expose and evaluate the organization of your draft and can improve the organization by modifying the outline.

Finally, once you have chosen an organizational structure, you should clearly communicate that structure to the reader with descriptive section and subsection headings that are at least roughly parallel to the structure of the statement of issues. In an answer to a law school examination, such headings may even take the place of more formal statements of the issues.

III. PROGRESSION WITHIN SECTION OR SUBSECTION

Once you have divided your topics into separate sections, you are ready to organize the discussion or argument within each section. At the most general level, your analysis should follow the familiar pattern of deductive reasoning: After introducing the issue or argument with a heading and perhaps with a brief introduction in the text, you should discuss or argue the law, apply that law to the facts, and reach a conclusion.

Effective progression within a section also requires attention to one or more of five considerations:

(1) hierarchy of authority,
(2) progression from general to specific,
(3) progression from fundamental to uncertain,
(4) historical development, and
(5) separation or consolidation of logical discussions or arguments.

The first four of these considerations deal mainly with the development of legal standards. The fifth deals with methods of combining legal and factual analysis.

A. HIERARCHY OF AUTHORITY

In statutory analysis, the hierarchy of authority leads to a convention of organization. You should analyze, or at least present, the language in question before analyzing cases that either interpret the statute or that discuss supplemental common law:

> ### C. Commercial Impracticability
>
> The Uniform Commercial Code (U.C.C.) provides that, in limited circumstances, a seller's failure to deliver goods is not a breach of contract
>
>> if performance as agreed has been made impracticable by the occurrence of a contingency the non-occurrence of which was a basic assumption on which the contract was made . . .
>
> U.C.C. §2-615(a) (1990). The U.C.C.'s use of the term "impracticable" suggests a more liberal standard for discharging obligations than the traditional common law standard of "impossibility of performance." *See Bjorn v. Borg* . . .

The normal convention of starting with the statutory language will occasionally apply with less force in the analysis of some of the more commonly litigated provisions of a constitution. Because constitutional provisions are typically even more general than statutory provisions, the enormous body of case law interpreting some provisions may take on a life of its own, overshadowing the actual words of the provision. Thus, you need not quote the language of the fourth amendment before asserting a well-established proposition about the need to obtain a warrant before searching a dwelling; reference to case law interpreting the fourth amendment in most cases will be sufficient. Nonetheless, you should begin the analysis by at least identifying the fourth amendment as the source of the restriction on searches. Moreover, some constitutional issues, like most issues of statutory interpretation, will be sufficiently novel to require original analysis, in which case you should begin the analysis with the language of the constitutional provision.

B. PROGRESSION FROM GENERAL TO SPECIFIC

Reading a legal analysis or argument should be like viewing a large painting that covers a third of the wall of a museum exhibit room. As the viewer enters, he sees the general outlines of the whole painting, and he becomes curious about a few provocative parts of the whole. He then moves closer to the painting to separately examine each of these parts. Finally, when he steps back to view the painting again as a whole, he may appreciate it more fully than he did when he had not yet explored some of the details. Similarly, a legal document should

(1) provide an overview to the document,
(2) separately explore important matters in some detail, and
(3) conclude with a summary or with general insights that are easier to appreciate after the discussion of details.

On a broad level, a memorandum or brief performs these functions with (1) the statement of issues or other introduction, (2) the discussion or argument, and (3) the conclusion. On a narrower level, this kind of progression is often appropriate within a section of the discussion or argument.

For an example of progression within a section, suppose that the plaintiff in a tort action alleges that the defendant intentionally inflicted emotional distress. If the defendant, your client, contends that the facts in the record fail to satisfy two of the elements of that tort, your brief for the defendant might address each of those elements separately, either in separate paragraphs or separate subsections of the argument. If so, you can orient the reader by beginning with a paragraph that introduces each of the elements:

II. ARGUMENT

    A. Lew's Allegations in Count II Fail to
    State a Claim for Intentional Infliction
    of Emotional Distress.

To establish a right to relief for intentional infliction of emotional distress, Lew must plead and   **General overview** prove that (1) Smith engaged in extreme and outrageous conduct (2) with the intent to cause severe emotional distress or with reckless disregard for the possibility of those consequences, and that (3) his actions caused Lew to suffer (4) severe emotional distress. *See Watts v. Golden Age Nursing Home,* 127 Ariz. 255, 619 P.2d 1032 (1980). Even assuming the truth of Lew's allegations about the manner in which Smith terminated Lew's employment contract, the complaint does not properly allege either the extreme conduct or the severe distress required for liability. Therefore, Lew has failed to state a claim for relief in Count II.

Specific argument

1. Smith's Alleged Conduct Was Not "Extreme and Outrageous."

Only the most deplorable and shocking conduct satisfies the narrow definition of "extreme and outrageous conduct." *See* . . .

In this case, the allegations that Smith . . .

2. Lew's Alleged "Depression" Does Not Amount to Severe Emotional Distress.

Proof of severe emotional distress . . .

The introduction in the first paragraph above not only provides an overview of the legal standards, it summarizes the overall argument of the section. That argument appears elsewhere as well: (1) It is stated concisely in the heading for section A; (2) it is developed in greater detail in each of the subsections; and (3) it should be repeated in general terms at the end of section A, in a separate conclusion section at the end of the document, or both.

At a different level within a section, you might introduce a general principle in a topic sentence before exploring it in greater detail within the same paragraph:

Topic sentence

Specific case analysis

Even if a promise leaves open the possibility that the promisor will escape obligation, however, the promise is valid if the promisor does not have complete control over the events on which the promisor's obligation is conditioned. *See Bonnie v. DeLaney,* 158 Calz. 212, 645 P.2d 887 (1982). In *Bonnie,* an agreement for the sale of a house provided that the buyer could cancel the agreement if the buyer "cannot qualify for a 30-year mortgage loan for 90% of the sales price" with any of several banks listed in the agreement. *Id.* at 213, 645 P.2d at 888. In enforcing the agreement against the seller, the court distinguished *Atco Corp.* on the ground that the word "cannot" referred to the buyer's ability to obtain a loan rather than to his desire. Because his ability to obtain a loan was partly controlled by events and decisions outside his control, the promises in the sale agreement were nonillusory and binding. *Id.* at 214-15, 645 P.2d 889-91.

In the preceding example, the opening sentence of the paragraph summarizes the general point that the *Bonnie* decision illustrates. That introduction prepares the reader for the detailed analysis of *Bonnie* that follows.

C. PROGRESSION FROM FUNDAMENTAL TO COMPLEX POINTS

Some legal discussions or arguments may lend themselves to a related method of organization within a section or subsection: progression from fundamental or undisputed points to complex or disputed points. In some cases, the preliminary points may address matters that are not even ultimately in issue; they may simply provide helpful background information or establish legal premises to the main topic of discussion.

For example, the following passage from a brief provides background information about statutory policies. That information helps support the ultimate argument that a contractual provision attempting to fix damages for breach is not enforceable:

C. The Liquidated Damages Clause Is Void as a Penalty

The contract for the sale of the engine parts is a "transaction in goods" and thus is covered by the Uniform Commercial Code. U.C.C. §§2-102, 2-105 (1990). U.C.C. remedies for breach of contract are designed to compensate the victim of the breach for the loss of the value of the expected performance. *See* U.C.C. §1-106(1) (1990). They do not permit imposition of a penalty that is designed to discourage breach or to punish the breaching party. *Id.*; U.C.C. §2-718(1) (1990).

[margin note: Fundamental premises]

Within limited parameters, the U.C.C. permits parties to agree to fix damages for breach in advance by including a provision for "liquidated damages" in their sales contract. However, such damages must be limited to

[margin note: Transition to disputed point]

an amount which is reasonable in the light of the anticipated or actual harm caused by the breach,

> the difficulties of proof of loss, and the inconve-
> nience or nonfeasibility of otherwise obtaining an
> adequate remedy. A term fixing unreasonably large
> liquidated damages is void as a penalty.
>
> U.C.C. §2-718(1) (1990). In this case, section 5.4
> of the contract attempts to fix damages at an amount
> that is disproportionate to any anticipated or actual
> harm. Thus, it is an unenforceable penalty clause.

The first paragraph of the preceding passage addresses fundamental matters of statutory policy that are technically not in issue because the opposing party will not dispute them. It provides a general orientation, however, that will help to place in perspective the argument relating to the hotly disputed question: Does the liquidated damages clause constitute an impermissible penalty under the UCC?

D. HISTORICAL DEVELOPMENT

You may help your audience understand the current contours of a legal rule by outlining the historical context from which the rule emerged. In rare cases, by chronologically describing the metamorphosis of a rule, you can help your reader appreciate the current state of the law without distracting her from the issue at hand. In most cases, however, you will develop your points more efficiently and gracefully if you (1) adopt one or more of the methods of organization discussed in Sections A-C above, (2) begin your analysis with current authority, and (3) incorporate the historical analysis into the discussion of that authority.

1. Chronological Development

A strictly chronological account of the development of a legal rule might be helpful if the current rule arguably retains vestiges of earlier forms of the rule:

> *A. Tippett's Qualified Immunity Defense*

Statute

> Federal civil rights legislation imposes liability for deprivation of constitutional rights by agents of the state:
>
> Every person who . . .
>
> 42 U.S.C. §1983.

Chronology of interpretive case law

> Although section 1983 does not expressly limit its remedies, it implicitly incorporates a variety of traditional immunity defenses. *E.g., Tenney v. Brandhove,* 341 U.S. 367, 376 (1951) (absolute

immunity for state legislators). The Supreme Court has recognized a qualified immunity for executive officials, such as police officers, acting in discretionary functions. *Pierson v. Ray*, 386 U.S. 547 (1967). In *Pierson*, the Court held that police officers who illegally arrested protesting clergymen could escape liability for money damages under section 1983 if "they reasonably believed in good faith that the arrest was constitutional." *Id.* at 557.

In an action under section 1983 alleging constitutional deprivations by school board officials, the Supreme Court further developed its test for qualified immunity. *Wood v. Strickland*, 420 U.S. 308 (1975). In *Wood*, the court emphasized that the test for qualified immunity included both objective and subjective elements:

> The official himself must be acting sincerely and with a belief that he is doing right, but an act violating a student's constitutional rights can be no more justified by ignorance or disregard of settled, indisputable law on the part of one entrusted with supervision of students' daily lives than by the presence of actual malice. . . . [A] school board member . . . must be held to a standard of conduct based not only on permissible intentions, but also on knowledge of the basic, unquestioned constitutional rights of his charges.

Id. at 321-22.

The qualified immunity doctrine took an abrupt turn in *Harlow v. Fitzgerald*, 457 U.S. 800 (1982). To facilitate summary judgment on a defense of qualified immunity, the Court abandoned much of the subjective element of the test, increasing its reliance on objective reasonableness. The *Harlow* test protects government officials if "their conduct does not violate clearly established statutory or constitutional rights of which a reasonable person would have known." *Id.* at 818. *Harlow* involved a suit against federal officials, but courts have extended the *Harlow* modifications of the qualified immunity test to section 1983 actions. *E.g.,* . . .

Although the *Harlow* test contemplates that qualified immunity defenses in many cases will present questions only of objective reasonableness, the test arguably retains some remnants of the subjective element of *Wood v. Strickland. See Harlow*, 457 U.S. at 821 (Brennan, J., concurring). . . .

1951

1967

1975

1982

Unfortunately, you may be tempted to chronologically develop the law even when it is unnecessary or ineffective as a method of organization. Every legal rule has a history, and most have steadily changed shape over time as courts and legislatures have modified, supplemented, and refined them. When writing a comprehensive law review article, you might choose to trace the chronological development of a significant legal rule in your scholarly analysis. Such a deliberate approach, however, may tend to impede the swifter flow of a legal memorandum or brief. Therefore, when writing a memorandum or brief, you ordinarily should adopt a method of organization that emphasizes the current state of the law. You should chronologically trace the development of a legal rule only when other methods of organization would inadequately convey the current form of the rule.

2. Current State of the Law as Focal Point

Thus, even when the current law is comprehensible only in the context of earlier developments, you often can focus on current case law and can explore the historical context within your analysis of contemporary cases:

B. Interlocutory Appeal

Currently applicable case law

Federal law vests the federal courts of appeals with jurisdiction over appeals only from "final decisions" of the federal district courts. 28 U.S.C. §1291 (1988). Nonetheless, Officer Tippett probably can immediately appeal the district court's denial of his motion for summary judgment based on the defense of qualified immunity. *See Mitchell v. Forsyth*, 472 U.S. 511, 524-30 (1985).

Earlier source of controlling principle

In *Mitchell*, a person whose conversation had been intercepted in an illegal F.B.I. wiretap sued the U.S. Attorney General for authorizing the warrantless wiretap. The trial court denied the attorney general's motion for summary judgment based on absolute and qualified immunity, and the attorney general filed an interlocutory appeal. *Id.* at 513-17. The Supreme Court held that the court of appeals had jurisdiction over the interlocutory appeal under the "collateral order" doctrine established in *Cohen v. Beneficial Industrial Loan Corp.*, 337 U.S. 541 (1949).

Earlier source of related principles

In applying the collateral-order doctrine to a qualified immunity defense, the *Mitchell* Court considered two attributes of the defense, each of which stems from the objective nature of the test as established in *Harlow v. Fitzgerald*, 457 U.S. 800, 815-19 (1982). First, the test fashioned in *Harlow* is designed to permit the dismissal of insubstantial claims on summary judgment, thus protecting government officials from the burdens of trial. *Mitchell,* 472 U.S. at 526. Second, the *Harlow* test normally permits the appellate court to decide the interlocutory appeal as a matter of law. *Id.* at 528.

In our case, Crawford has asserted that Tippett maliciously . . .

Under this approach, you can focus your discussion on the current authority, *Mitchell,* and you can convey the historical significance of *Cohen* and *Harlow* within your discussion of *Mitchell.* This approach permits you to present much of the analysis of *Mitchell* within one or more of the organizational structures discussed in Sections A-C above.

E. SEPARATION OR CONSOLIDATION OF ANALYSES

1. Overview

In analyzing an issue in a memorandum or a brief, you ordinarily should follow the general structure of the syllogism of deductive reasoning:

(1) major premise—rule of law
(2) minor premise—application of law to facts
(3) conclusion

At the simplest level, you can present all the elements of a single syllogism in a single, undivided section of your discussion or argument:

A. *Topic*
   Introduction
   Legal Rule
   Application to Facts
   Conclusion

Many topics of discussion or argument, however, are not so simple. If a topic is unusually complex, you might separately present the elements of a single syllogism in several subsections:

A. *Topic*
   Introduction
   1. Legal Rule
      a. Analysis of Persuasive Authority
      b. Policy Analysis

2. Application to Facts
    a. Analysis of Category A Facts
    b. Analysis of Category B Facts
3. Conclusion

Conversely, if your main topic of discussion or argument encompasses closely related subtopics that do not warrant separation into formal subsections, you might exercise discretion to discuss more than one topic within an undivided section or subsection. If so, you can present your analysis in either of two ways. First, you can separate the topics into several smaller syllogisms within the section, each syllogism with its own legal and factual analyses:

B. *Topic*
    Introduction
    Legal Rule 1
    Facts 1
    Conclusion 1
    Legal Rule 2
    Facts 2
    Conclusion 2

Alternatively, you can consolidate the related topics into a single syllogism:

A. *Topic*
    Introduction
    Legal Rules 1 & 2
    Application to Facts 1 & 2
    Conclusions

Most writers tend to react to these problems of organization on a subconscious, intuitive level. However, the decision to separate or consolidate is sufficiently important to warrant conscious analysis.

2. Single Syllogism in Undivided Section

At the broadest level, if a topic or argument is sufficiently important and discrete to warrant a separate section or subsection heading, you ordinarily should develop it completely and resolve it within that section or subsection. In the following excerpts from a brief, an advocate divides the arguments about two elements of a tort into subsections. In each of these subsections, the advocate analyzes an element in a single, complete syllogism. For example, in subsection A.1 below, she presents her view of the law for that element, applies the law to the facts relating to that element, and states a conclusion about the sufficiency of the allegations relating to that element:

II. ARGUMENT

    A. Lew's Allegations in Count II Fail to State a Claim for Intentional Infliction of Emotional Distress.

    To establish a right to relief . . .

        1. Smith's Alleged Conduct Was Not "Extreme and Outrageous."

    Only the most deplorable and shocking conduct satisfies the narrow definition of "extreme and outrageous conduct." *See* . . . Conduct that simply reflects normal social and economic adversities is not extreme or outrageous. *See, e.g., Frank v. Boswell,* . . .

    In *Frank,* a landlord's eviction notice did not reflect extreme and outrageous conduct, even though it was "rude, threatening, and intimidating." *Id.* at 289. The court reasoned that . . .

    In this case, Lew's complaint alleges conduct that is even less extreme than the conduct in *Frank.* It alleges that Smith "fired Lew without severance pay and with full knowledge that Lew's family was facing a desperate financial crisis." Plaintiff's Second Amended Complaint ¶7. It further alleges that Smith communicated his decision in a "terse, unfriendly, and unsympathetic conversation, without advance notice." *Id.* at ¶8.

    These allegations state only that Lew was the victim of his own economic distress and that Smith acted to protect the interests of his business. Although some business owners might take it upon themselves to offer personal counseling and financial aid to their employees or ex-employees, Smith has no legal duty to do so.

    Thus, the complaint does not allege circumstances that could establish the requisite "extreme and outrageous conduct."

        2. Lew's Alleged "Depression" Does Not Amount to Severe Emotional Distress.

    Proof of severe emotional distress . . .

Annotations (right margin):

- Major argument
- First subargument
- General rules of law
- In-depth analysis of case law
- Facts of current dispute
- Analysis of facts
- Conclusion
- Second subargument

3. Separation of Elements of Single Syllogism into Multiple Subsections

In a particularly complex analysis, you might depart from the most basic organizational structure by developing only one element of a complete analysis within a section or subsection. For example, you could develop the legal rules in one section and analyze the facts in a separate section, perhaps dividing the fact analysis into subsections:

	A. Officer Bates Could Not Lawfully Arrest Jones Without Probable Cause to Believe That Jones Had Committed a Felony.
Legal rules	Although a police officer may arrest a suspect without a warrant in some circumstances, he may not place a suspect under full arrest without probable cause to believe that the suspect has committed a crime. *See* . . . A police officer does not have probable cause unless . . .
	B. Officer Bates Did Not Have Probable Cause.
Application to facts	At the suppression hearing, Officer Jones asserted that Jones matched the description of the burglar and that Jones volunteered incriminating statements. Whether taken separately or together, however, these factors did not create probable cause.
	1. Jones Did Not Match the Description of the Burglar.
First subset of facts	A written transcript of the radio report shows that Officer Bates received the following description of the burglary suspect: white male, six feet tall, 180 lbs., short brown hair, wearing a navy blue windbreaker. . . .
	2. Jones's Statements Did Not Create Probable Cause.
Second subset of facts	The combined testimony of Jones and Officer Bates creates a clear and consistent picture of their conversation on Washington Street. . . .

Under this approach, the discussion of the law appears primarily in section A of the brief, and section B addresses the fact analysis. It would not be uncommon, however, for the author of such a passage to refer briefly to legal authority within section B when helpful to support the fact analysis.

4. Multiple Syllogisms Within Single, Undivided Section

Conversely, you may have occasion to present more than one complete analysis in a discrete section or subsection. If so, you can either (1) fully develop and resolve one syllogism before analyzing the next, or (2) combine the related legal rules of arguably distinct syllogisms and apply them to all the relevant facts.

a. Separation of Multiple Syllogisms

Within an undivided section, you may occasionally address several closely related topics, none of which is sufficiently important and discrete to warrant further subdivision into subsections. In many such cases, you can develop these related topics separately within the section or subsection.

For example, you can completely develop and resolve an introductory analysis before moving on to the main topic, as in the following excerpt from a legal memorandum:

I. OPTION CONTRACT UNDER UCC

In some circumstances, a merchant's promise not to revoke an offer to buy or sell goods is enforceable even if gratuitous:

> An offer by a merchant to buy or sell goods in a signed writing which by its terms gives assurance that it will be held open is not revocable, for lack of consideration . . . ; but any such term of assurance on a form supplied by the offeree must be separately signed by the offeror.

General statutory rules

U.C.C. §2-205 (1990).

"Merchant" includes "a person who deals in goods of the kind." U.C.C. §2-104 (1990). Stillwell regularly sells computers as part of her wholesale office supply business. Therefore, she is a merchant of the goods that she offered to supply to Azoulay, and §2-205 thus governs the revocability of her offer.

Complete syllogism on preliminary matter

A more difficult question is whether Stillwell "separately signed" the promise not to revoke contained in the form supplied by Azoulay, the offeree. The purpose of the statutory requirement for a separate signing is . . .

Transition to main topic of discussion

The second paragraph of this example quickly resolves the question of merchant status in a complete syllogism, with a statement of the law, an analysis of the facts, and a conclusion. Because that issue is simple and noncontroversial, it does not warrant presentation in a separate subsection with its own heading. On the other hand, it is sufficiently independent from the analysis of the requirement for a separate signing that you should develop and resolve it in a separate paragraph before analyzing other topics raised by the general standards in the first paragraph.

Some legal writers strain this form of separation when using it within a section that features in-depth case analyses of a series of cases. Rather than synthesize these cases and apply the synthesized law in consolidated form to the facts, the writer pauses briefly after each case analysis and applies the holding of that case to the relevant facts. Although this is a popular form of argument, it sometimes results in repetition and a rambling, piecemeal effect. You should not use it as a substitute for effective expression of synthesis of authority.

b. Consolidation of Multiple Syllogisms

In other cases, you may prefer to combine closely related legal standards and apply them as a group to all the relevant facts. This approach is illustrated by the second and third paragraphs of the following excerpt of a brief:

II. ARGUMENT

> A. *Bennett Will Prove That Tippett Is Liable Under 42 U.S.C. §1983 for Violating Bennett's Civil Rights.*

General statutory rules

Federal law imposes civil liability on a person who acts under the color of state law to deprive another of a federal right:

> Every person who, under the color of any [state law or custom], subjects, or causes to be subjected, any citizen of the United States or other person within the jurisdiction thereof to the deprivation of any rights, privileges or immunities secured by the Constitution and laws, shall be liable to the party injured . . .

42 U.S.C. §1983 (1988).

Consolidated discussion of rules for three subarguments

A private party acts "under the color of state law" if he acts in concert with a state official acting in his official capacity. *Dennis v. Sparks,* 449 U.S. 24, 27-29 (1980). State action denying a litigant a fair and impartial hearing in civil litigation constitutes a deprivation of due process under the four-teenth amendment. *Cf. Cross v. Georgia,* 581 F.2d 102, 104 (5th Cir. 1978) (criminal prosecution). Although section 1983 implicitly incorporates the common law doctrine of absolute immunity for judges, that immunity does not protect private parties who conspire with the judge. *Dennis,* 449 U.S. at 29-32.

In this case, Bennett will prove all the elements of his claim under section 1983. First, the evidence will show that Tippett conspired with Judge Bell by bribing Judge Bell to rule against Bennett on his motion for a preliminary injunction; Tippett therefore acted under the color of state law. Second, Tippett's bribe denied Bennett an impartial hearing and therefore deprived Bennett of his federal right to due process. Finally, even though Tippett acted under the color of state law, he has no official state function and therefore does not enjoy the protection of any official immunity.

Consolidated application of three rules to facts

Thus, the evidence will show that Tippett is liable to Bennett for violating Bennett's due process rights.

Conclusion

c. Discretion to Separate or Consolidate

The decision to separate or consolidate legal analyses often is a matter of judgment on which reasonable writers can disagree. As a general rule, a more superficial treatment of the topics lends itself to consolidation, as in the example above. On the other hand, if you analyze closely related topics in greater depth, you could divide the same discussion of a brief into separate syllogisms that are fully developed and resolved in separate paragraphs within the section:

II. ARGUMENT

A. Bennett Will Prove That Tippett Is Liable Under 42 U.S.C. §1983 for Violating Bennett's Civil Rights.

Federal law imposes civil liability on a person who acts under the color of state law to deprive another of a federal right:

General statutory rules

Every person who, under the color of any . . .

Full syllogism on first subargument

42 U.S.C. §1983 (1988). In this case, Bennett will prove all the elements of his claim under section 1983.

A private party acts "under the color of state law" if he acts in concert with a state official acting in his official capacity. *Dennis v. Sparks,* 449 U.S. 24, 27-29 (1980). In *Dennis,* a state judge . . . Similarly, the evidence in this case will show that Tippett conspired with Judge Bell by bribing Judge Bell to rule against Bennett on his motion for a preliminary injunction. Therefore, Tippett acted under the color of state law.

Full syllogism on second subargument

The fourteenth amendment's guarantee of due process in state proceedings is a federal substantive right, the deprivation of which is remediable under section 1983. *See generally Carey v. Piphus,* 435 U.S. 247 (1978). State conduct denying a litigant a fair and impartial hearing in civil litigation constitutes a deprivation of due process under the fourteenth amendment. *Cf. Cross v. Georgia,* 581 F.2d 102, 104 (5th Cir. 1978) (criminal prosecution). In this case, Tippett's bribing the judge directly affected the outcome of the hearing on Bennett's request for a preliminary injunction; therefore, Tippett caused a deprivation of Bennett's right to due process.

Full syllogism on third subargument

Finally, Tippett is not immune from liability for money damages. Bennett agrees that state judges are absolutely immune from liability for damages for their judicial acts taken within their jurisdiction. *Stump v. Sparkman,* 435 U.S. 349 (1978). However, such immunity does not extend to a private party who conspires with a state judge, even though by so conspiring the private party acts under the color of state law. *Dennis,* 449 U.S. at 29-32 (1980). In this case, Tippett has no official status as an officer of the court; instead, he is a private party who therefore enjoys no official immunity.

General conclusion

Thus, the evidence will show that Tippett is liable to Bennett for violating Bennett's due process rights.

Of course, if the topics are truly independent and warrant extended discussion, you may wish to adopt the conventional approach of presenting each analysis in a separate subsection and under a separate heading:

II. ARGUMENT

A. Bennett Will Prove That Tippett Is Liable Under 42 U.S.C. §1983 for Violating Bennett's Civil Rights.

Federal law imposes civil liability . . . . 42 U.S.C. §1983. In this case, Bennett will prove all the elements of his claim under section 1983.

General statutory rules

1. Tippett Acted Under the Color of State Law.

A private party acts "under the color of state law" if he acts in concert . . .
In *Dennis*, . . .
In this case, the evidence will show that Tippett conspired with Judge Bell . . .
Therefore, Tippett acted under the color of state law.

Full syllogism in several paragraphs within first subsection

2. Tippett Denied Bennett Due Process.

The Fourteenth Amendment's guarantee of due process in state proceedings is a federal substantive . . .
In *Cross*, . . .
In this case, Bennett will prove that Tippett bribed Judge Bell to rule against Bennett on his motion for a preliminary injunction. . . .
Therefore, Tippett violated Bennett's rights to due process.

Full syllogism in several paragraphs within second subsection

3. Tippett Is Not Immune From Suit.

Bennett agrees that . . .

Third subsection

d. Separate Analysis of Adverse Authority in Responsive Brief

A special organizational structure is sometimes appropriate for responsive briefs. In the ordinary three-stage briefing procedure, the answering brief will respond directly to the opening brief, and the reply brief will respond to the answering brief. In responding to an argument in a preceding brief, you can affirmatively develop a legal theory and apply it to the facts, and you can then separately address authority on which the preceding brief relies. You should analyze each adverse authority and discredit or distinguish it. You can use the same technique in an opening brief that anticipates a counterargument.

For example, in the following sample passage, the brief writer has affirmatively and confidently argued that Tippett denied Bennett due process under a mainstream legal theory. Only after completing that argument does he seek to persuade the judge to reject an approach based on *Parratt v. Taylor*, on which the opposing party relied in a previous motion:

II. ARGUMENT

    A. Bennett Will Prove That Tippett Is Liable Under 42 U.S.C. §1983 for Violating Bennett's Civil Rights.

    1. Tippett Acted Under . . .

    2. Tippett Denied Bennett Due Process.

Full syllogism in several paragraphs within second subargument

    The Fourteenth Amendment's guarantee of due process in state proceedings is a federal substantive . . .
    In *Cross*, . . .
    In this case, Bennett will prove that Tippett bribed Judge Bell to rule against Bennett on his motion for a preliminary injunction. . . . Therefore, Tippett violated Bennett's rights to due process.

Separate paragraphs distinguishing adverse authority

    Tippett argued in the reply brief to his motion to dismiss that Bennett has an adequate remedy under state tort law and that section 1983 therefore affords him no relief, citing *Parratt v. Taylor*, 451 U.S. 527 (1981). *Parratt* is distinguishable . . .

In this example, *Parratt v. Taylor* does not clearly address a distinct topic; instead, it helps define the limits of due process in certain contexts. Thus, in a neutral analysis, you might consolidate your discussion of *Parratt* with your discussion of other authorities that establish the legal rule, even though you ultimately distinguish *Parratt* from your case.

In a responsive brief, however, you can invite the judge to analyze your case initially without the distraction of distinguishable adverse authority. By delaying your analysis of the adverse case law in this manner, you are free to develop the initial argument strongly and positively, without the qualifications inherent in the subsequent discussion of adverse authority.

5. Summary

These examples have primarily illustrated two issues of organization: (1) whether to present topics in separate sections or within a single, undivided section and (2) whether to separate or consolidate analyses within a section. These issues illustrate the role of judgment in legal writing and particularly in developing organizational structures. Many problems of this nature have no single, clearly correct solution; your resolution will depend on the nature and the depth of the analyses or arguments and on your personal style preferences.

IV. PARAGRAPHS

Some scholars of legal method and writing use the topic heading "Paragraphs" to classify a surprisingly broad range of writing techniques, from topic sentences to more general techniques of presenting a legal discussion or argument. This book addresses all such topics in substantial detail, but not all of them under the heading "Paragraphs." More narrowly, this section on paragraphs introduces techniques of (1) using paragraphing to signal changes of topics within a discussion, (2) analyzing the appropriate content of paragraphs, and (3) effectively ordering sentences within a paragraph.

A. THE ROLE OF PARAGRAPHS WITHIN A SECTION

Just as descriptive headings and subheadings communicate the division of a discussion or argument into sections or subsections, good paragraphing helps to communicate the organizational structure within a section or subsection. For instance, the paragraphing in the following passage signals the transition from (1) an analysis of the statutory requirements of conduct "under the color of" state law to (2) an analysis of fourteenth amendment guarantees:

A private party acts "under the color of state law" if he acts in concert with a state official acting in his official capacity. *Dennis v. Sparks,* 449 U.S. 24, 27-29 (1980). In *Dennis,* a state judge . . . Similarly, the evidence in this case will show that Tippett conspired with Judge Bell. . . .	**Statute**
The fourteenth amendment's guarantee of due process in state proceedings is a federal substantive right. . . .	**Constitution**

A second presentation of the same arguments assumes a greater depth of analysis. Imagine that each of five topic sentences begins a new paragraph. The five topic sentences represented by the phrases and clauses in the following example signal the transitions between (1) general legal rules, (2) in-depth case analysis, (3) fact analysis, (4) conclusion, and (5) analysis of potentially adverse authority.

Law	The fourteenth amendment's guarantee of due process in state proceedings is a federal substantive right . . . *Cf. Cross v. Georgia,* . . .
	In *Cross,* . . .
Facts	In this case, Bennett will prove . . .
Conclusion	Thus, Tippett is liable to Bennett . . .
Adverse authority	Tippett has argued . . . , citing *Parratt v. Taylor,* 451 U.S. 527 (1981). *Parratt* is distinguishable . . .

B. PARAGRAPH CONTENT AND DEVELOPMENT

To say that each paragraph should present a single topic or idea oversimplifies the matter, for the appropriate scope of the subject matter of each paragraph may depend on the relationship between the paragraph and the remainder of the discussion. For example, the following analysis of merchant status is superficial, conclusory, and preliminary to the main topic for discussion. Accordingly, you could combine the legal standard, fact analysis, and conclusion in a single paragraph:

> "Merchant" includes "a person who deals in goods of the kind." U.C.C. §2-104(1) (1990). Jones regularly sells computers as part of her wholesale office supply business. Therefore, she is a merchant of the goods that she offered to supply to Azoulay, and section 2-205 thus governs the revocability of her offer.

In contrast, the reader can most easily absorb the typically more thorough analysis of the main topic if you divide the statement of legal rules and the fact analysis into at least two separate paragraphs. At the simplest level, each paragraph could correspond to one of the three elements of deductive reasoning. For example, after it explains the issue, a sample exam answer analyzes a problem in three paragraphs that (1) summarize the applicable legal rules, (2) apply the rules to the facts, and (3) state a conclusion:

Legal rules	An enforceable contract requires a bargained-for exchange in which a promisor exchanges his own promise for a return promise or performance. The requirement of an exchange is not satisfied if one party gives only an illusory promise, which does not commit the promisor to any future performance. A promise is illusory if it leaves the promisor free to perform or not according to his unfettered whim or discretion, such as . . .
Application to facts	Guarantor should argue that Lender's promise to forbear until he "needs" the money permits Lender to decide at his own whim and unfettered discretion when to demand payment, because he has some control of his own needs. However, that

argument would prevail only if the word "need" refers to a subjective perception of deprivation that is inseparable from Lender's purely personal wants or desires. Lender can argue . . .

Unfortunately for our client, Lender's promise in the guarantee agreement probably is not illusory, because the word "need" provides some substance to Lender's commitment to forbear. Therefore, Guarantor's promise probably is supported by consideration and is enforceable. | **Conclusion**

In more complex analyses, the development of legal standards alone may progress through several paragraphs, perhaps beginning with an overview of general standards in one paragraph, followed by two or more additional paragraphs, each of which explores a significant case or a policy argument. Similarly, the fact analysis may progress through several paragraphs, perhaps displaying different levels of fact analysis or different categories of facts. For example, the five paragraphs represented by the following phrases and clauses help to signal the transitions between (1) general legal standards, (2) in-depth case analysis, (3) identification of relevant facts, (4) analysis of those facts, and (5) conclusion:

A. Smith's Alleged Conduct Was Not "Extreme and Outrageous."

. . . Conduct that simply reflects normal social and economic adversities is not extreme or outrageous. *See, e.g., Frank v. Boswell,* . . . | **Law**

In *Frank,* . . .

In this case, Lew's complaint alleges conduct that is even less extreme than the conduct in *Frank.* . . . | **Facts**

These allegations state only that . . .

Thus, the complaint does not allege circumstances that could establish the requisite "extreme and outrageous conduct." | **Conclusion**

C. THE ROLE OF SENTENCES WITHIN A PARAGRAPH

A paragraph does not contain some magic number of sentences. The appropriate number of sentences depends in part on the relationship between the paragraph and the topics addressed in surrounding paragraphs.

Of course, if you find that you have set off a single sentence as a separate paragraph, you should always question whether the isolated sentence would better serve as the concluding sentence of the previous paragraph or the topic sentence of the next one. As illustrated by the concluding paragraph of the previous section, however, a single sentence may stand by itself as a separate paragraph if it completely addresses a discrete topic or if presentation in a separate paragraph achieves important goals of clarity or emphasis. If you blindly adhere to a "rule" against single-sentence paragraphs, you may find yourself composing an unnecessary, empty sentence to accompany an informative sentence that could have stood alone.

Whenever possible, your first sentence in a multiple-sentence paragraph should communicate your strategy by introducing the topic of the paragraph, expressing a transition, or both. For example, the first sentence in the following example signals the transition from the analysis of precedent to the identification of the relevant facts of the current dispute, and it provides an overview of the case comparison:

> In this case, Lew's complaint alleges conduct that is even less extreme than the conduct in *Frank*. It alleges that Smith "fired Lew without severance pay and with full knowledge that Lew's family was facing a desperate financial crisis." Plaintiff's Second Amended Complaint ¶7. It further alleges . . .

In this sample paragraph, the topic sentence introduces fact analysis. Topic sentences or thesis statements are at least as important in introducing discussions of legal authority. To effectively present legal authority, you must use such topic or transition sentences or paragraphs to introduce statutes and case law and to express your syntheses of authority.

After you have composed an effective topic sentence, you should organize other sentences within a paragraph to develop information in a logical, organized fashion. For example, the paragraph below is designed to define the limits of the scope of the Uniform Commercial Code and to raise a question about the applicability of the Code to a particular transaction. The awkward placement of the second and third sentences of the paragraph disrupts continuity by stating an intermediate conclusion before establishing its premise:

General issue	Whether Maldonado accepted Weinstein's offer depends in part on whether the common law of contracts or the Uniform Commercial Code (U.C.C.) applies to the transaction. Weinstein's
Application to facts	offer to supply specifically identified, separately priced, movable plumbing parts clearly contemplates a sale of goods as part of the transaction. *See*
Legal premise	U.C.C. §2-105(1) (1990). The U.C.C. applies only to "transactions in goods." U.C.C. §2-102 (1990). His proposed transaction, however, also involves the
Specific issue	service of installing the fixtures, raising a question about the applicability of the U.C.C. to mixed transactions for both services and the sale of goods.

Reversing the order of the second and third sentences develops points in a more logical order and retains the coherence of transitions:

. . . whether the common law of contracts or the Uniform Commercial Code (U.C.C.) applies to the transaction.	**General issue**
The U.C.C. applies only to "transactions in goods." U.C.C. §2-102 (1990).	**Legal premise**
Weinstein's offer to supply specifically identified, separately priced, movable plumbing parts clearly contemplates a sale of goods as part of the transaction. *See* U.C.C. §2-105(1) (1990).	**Application to facts**
His proposed transaction, however, also involves the service of installing the fixtures, raising a question about . . .	**Specific issue**

Many organizational approaches may result in a logical and coherent presentation of information in a paragraph. Nonetheless, one simple technique is worth highlighting: You can lead a reader from familiar to new information in a paragraph by beginning each sentence with a previously established idea and linking it to a new idea. For example, the phrases in bold typeface in the following passage represent new information, and the italicized phrases represent previously introduced information. In each sentence after the first one, previously introduced information is linked to a new idea.

An enforceable contract requires a **bargained-for exchange** in which a promisor **exchanges** his own promise for a return promise or performance. The requirement of an *exchange* is not satisfied if one party gives only an **illusory promise,** which does not commit the promisor to any future performance. A *promise is illusory* if it leaves the promisor free to perform or not according to his **unfettered whim or discretion,** such as . . .

This technique of consistently linking a familiar idea with a new one is only one of many approaches that you may use in developing a paragraph. You should always retain maximum flexibility to adapt your organizational approach to the particular characteristics of a passage. The next chapter provides further guidance. It (1) continues to explore paragraphing and paragraph content in the context of presentation of authority and (2) addresses good organization of words and clauses within a sentence to enhance the clarity or persuasive force of the sentence.

V. SUMMARY

When organizing the topics or arguments in an office memorandum or brief, you should

(1) with few exceptions, discuss separate issues in separate sections or subsections,

(2) arrange your sections and subsections so that they reflect the proper relationships among topics and subtopics, and

(3) present your topics or arguments in a logical order, subject to considerations of strategy.

Within a section or subsection, you should

(1) explain the legal rule,
(2) apply the rule to the facts, and
(3) reach a conclusion.

If the topic or argument within a section or subsection is governed by several closely related rules, you should exercise judgment to either

(1) consolidate your statement of all the rules before applying them to all the relevant facts or

(2) separately apply some preliminary legal rules to facts before progressing to other rules within the section or subsection.

When organizing material within a section or subsection, you should consider:

(1) the hierarchy of authority and
(2) progression from general to specific and from fundamental to uncertain.

You should not describe the chronological development of a legal rule except as necessary to clarify the current state of the law.

Legal Writing Style in the Office Memorandum

Chapter 5's introduction to writing style identified clarity and conciseness as the principal characteristics of effective legal writing. This chapter more comprehensively examines those topics as well as special problems of using authority and quotations.

This chapter uses selected writing problems as vehicles for developing a method for legal writing, a flexible approach that provides general guidance in any legal writing assignment. It seeks to show you that effective legal writing style to a great extent is analogous to the sound practices of legal method and analysis discussed in the preceding chapters. Accordingly, it invites you to treat rules and conventions of writing very much like legal rules: To use them well, you must understand their purposes and policies.

Although this chapter primarily addresses writing style for office memoranda, most of the principles discussed apply equally to briefs, and some of the examples are taken from briefs. Special techniques of persuasive writing are explored in the next chapter.

I. CLARITY

You cannot write clearly unless you first develop clear ideas. In many cases, muddled legal writing reflects an incomplete understanding of the substantive legal analysis and suggests the need for further research and reflection. Only when you have fully mastered your analysis can you clearly communicate the analysis to a comprehending reader.

Beyond sound analysis, an important element of clarity in any legal document is effective organization on all the levels discussed in Chapter 10.

Other elements of clarity, discussed below, are simplicity, effective sentence structure, and precision in word selection.

A. SIMPLICITY AND PLAIN ENGLISH

For centuries, the public has complained about lawyers' fondness for legal jargon: stuffy, peculiar, archaic legal terminology. People have good reason to complain. For example, some lawyers still refuse to end a witness's sworn and notarized written statement with the perfectly descriptive word "signed." Instead, they insist on inserting the archaic phrase "Further affiant sayeth not."

Although the extent to which you stray from plain and simple terms is partly a matter of personal style, you should tend toward simplicity. If a simple, familiar word will clearly express your idea, your reader may find that a peculiar, complex, or unfamiliar word or phrase in its place is distracting or even unintelligible.

Moreover, simplicity in writing does not condemn you to expressing only simple ideas. Rather, it helps you to express even complex and abstract ideas in such clear, concrete, and simple terms that your reader easily grasps your ideas on first reading.

You can best appreciate the virtues of simplicity by recognizing the ultimate purpose of your document. A legal memorandum should efficiently communicate ideas, and a brief should persuade. A document cannot perform either of these functions if the reader must pause at every sentence to ponder its meaning.

Unfortunately, unnecessary abstraction, complexity, and peculiarity found in some legal writing suggests that the writer's objective is to "sound like a lawyer" or to impress his supervising attorney or a judge with the breadth of his vocabulary. For example, I heard once that a summer associate at a major law firm boasted that his first office memorandum contained unusually sophisticated language that twice compelled his supervising attorney to resort to a dictionary. The busy supervisor did not appreciate the distraction, and the law firm did not offer permanent employment to the boastful associate. The summer associate would have made a better impression if he had clearly and simply expressed ideas that reflected good, creative legal analysis.

As an advocate, you may be tempted someday to resort to peculiar legal jargon if the doubtful merit of your client's claims or defenses leaves you with little of value to say. You may consider using the jargon to distract the judge from the substantive emptiness of your arguments or to intimidate opposing parties when plain English would betray the emptiness of your threats. You should resist the temptation. If you fulfill your ethical duty to refrain from advancing frivolous claims and defenses, you can advance arguments that you are not ashamed to spell out in plain English.

Occasionally, a peculiar word or phrase earns its place in legal writing as a shorthand term for an unavoidably complex or unfamiliar concept. For example, Chapter 3 uses the term "stare decisis" to refer to a complex set of principles that help to define American legal method. Although this Latin term is unfamiliar to most students entering law school, it qualifies as a useful "term of art" because it is widely accepted among trained lawyers as convenient shorthand for a set of ideas that the more familiar term "precedent" does not fully convey. Surprisingly few forms of peculiar legal language, however, are justified as necessary terms of art. Therefore, you should critically evaluate any unusual language in your writing to ensure that it informs more than distracts.[1]

This advice applies as well to nonlegal cliches, such as frequently repeated metaphors. Occasionally, a metaphor will succinctly and richly convey an idea by creating a vivid image or drawing upon the reader's experience. For example, Martin Luther King, Jr., stated shortly before his assassination that he had "been to the mountain-top" and had "seen the promised land." Aside from being tragically prophetic, this metaphor powerfully conveyed King's vision that his followers would someday enjoy equality even though he might not live long enough to experience such a society himself.

On the other hand, few legal writers display King's gift for effective use of metaphor, and legal documents seldom equal civil rights oratory as appropriate vehicles for metaphor.[2] Yet, some legal writers overestimate the communicative power of metaphor and use it when a straightforward explanation would convey an idea more clearly. Even worse, they sometimes resort to cliche by substituting an overused metaphor for more rigorous thinking and precise writing.

For example, suppose that a defendant in a civil suit argued persuasively in a brief that the statutory limitations period had expired on the plaintiff's tort claim. In his answering brief, the plaintiff shifted emphasis from his tort claim to his claim on a written contract, which claim was subject to a longer limitations period. In her reply, the defendant argued that the written contract was unenforceable under the statute of frauds because the defendant had not signed it. In attacking the plaintiff's futile shift in emphasis from the tort to the contract claim, the defendant might be tempted to gloat that "the plaintiff has jumped out of the frying pan and into the fire." However, more than a few judges might find such a cliche trite or distracting. It would not advance the defendant's argument any more clearly or effectively than a direct explanation:

By relying on the contract claim, the plaintiff appears to concede that the limitations period has expired on his tort claim. However, his contract claim fares no better because enforcement of the alleged contract is barred by the statute of frauds.

When you resort to cliches, you also risk retelling them incorrectly, thus distracting the reader further and damaging your credibility. Particularly embarrassing are mixed metaphors that inject unintended humor in a serious legal argument. In one of his popular workshops on legal writing, Gary

---

1. See Richard C. Wydick, Plain English for Lawyers 53-55 (2d ed. 1985).
2. See, e.g., Barbara Child, What Does "Plain Language" Mean These Days?, 3 Scribes J. Legal Writing 1, 14 (1992) ("Of course poetry is the realm of metaphor. Statutes are not.").

Kinder revealed some of the more outrageous mixed metaphors that he has collected from clients and colleagues over the years:

Your Honor, I'm beating my head against a dead horse.
Sometimes you just have to sit in the other guy's shoes.
That's water under the belt.
I'm just going to have to shoot from the seat of my pants.
We're going to grab the bull by the horns and let the chips fall where they may.[3]

Granted, few legal writers will let gems like these creep into their final drafts. Nonetheless, they illustrate the point that both legal jargon and nonlegal cliches should earn their places in a legal document. When you see them in your writing, you should critically examine them to determine whether they truly convey your ideas more effectively than direct, simple explanations.

Finally, legal jargon is particularly inappropriate in a document that is addressed to a layperson, perhaps a client, who may be unfamiliar with even rudimentary legal terminology. When addressing such an audience, not only should you exercise special care to avoid unnecessary jargon, you should explain in plain English the meanings of legal terms of art that other attorneys would easily recognize.

═══════ E X E R C I S E 1 1 - 1 ═══════

A simple contract should (1) introduce the parties to the contract, (2) recite any background facts that explain the motivations of the parties and thus help to explain their bargain, (3) define the parties' rights and obligations by setting forth their mutual promises, and (4) signify each party's agreement to the terms of the contract.

The following contract is written in antiquated jargon. Parts of the contract are taken from the contract interpreted in *McMichael v. Price*, 58 P.2d 549 (Okla. 1936). Contract language from formbooks provided further inspiration.

Simplify all or part of the structure and language of the contract so that it expresses the terms of the parties' agreement in plain English. Feel free to use subject headings, section numbers, and paragraphing. Compare your revision with the sample contracts in Chapter 17, pages 450-452.

Requirements Contract

This contract for the purchase and sale of sand entered into on this, the _____ day of _____, by and between Sooner Sand Co., a general partnership of which Harley T. Price and W. M. McMichael are partners, hereinafter known as the party of the first part, and Bassi Distribut-

---

3. Gary Kinder, Getting the Judge to Say "Yes!", Lecture at Writing Workshop (Phoenix, Ariz., June 4, 1993).

ing Co. a joint venture of Bassi Trucking Co. and Hardcore Rock & Gravel, Inc., hereinafter known as the party of the second part, Witnesseth:

Whereas, the party of the first part is engaged in the business of selling and shipping sand from Phoenix to various customers in the State of Arizona but has not developed markets outside of Arizona and desires to supply sand wholesale to a distributor with customers outside the state; and

Whereas, the party of the second part has an established business in Phoenix selling and shipping sand to various customers in several states outside Arizona, including California, Nevada, Utah, and Colorado, and desires a stable source of supply of sand for that business;

Now, therefore, in consideration of the mutual covenants herein contained, and other good and valuable consideration the receipt of which is hereby acknowledged, the parties hereby represent, warrant, affirm, promise, covenant, and agree that the said party of the first part will, upon receipt of periodic written orders submitted by the said party of the second part, furnish all of the sand which the said party of the second part requires for shipment to various and sundry points outside of the State of Arizona, for a period of five (5) years from the date hereinabove, said sand to be of a grade and quality at least equal in quality and comparable with the sand of various grades sold by other sand companies in the City of Phoenix, Arizona; furthermore, the said party of the second part agrees to pay as payment and compensation for said sand so furnished a sum per ton which represents sixty percent (60%) of the current market price per ton of concrete at the place of destination of said shipment.

In witness whereof, the said parties have hereunto set their hands and seals the day and year first above written.

———————————————
Sooner Sand Co.—Authorized Agent

———————————————
Bassi Distributing Co.—Authorized Agent

B. SENTENCE STRUCTURE

1. Structuring and Punctuating Long or Complex Sentences

Short, crisp sentences can be powerful:

Jenkins lived to tell his side of the story. Roberts did not. ‖

On the other hand, a succession of very short sentences may sound stilted or may require empty or repetitive transitional phrases to link the sentences together:

It was 1:00 A.M. John left the party. He went home. He drove his BMW. ‖

Moreover, long sentences that convey numerous thoughts in multiple clauses are not necessarily problematic; if punctuated and constructed sensibly, they may be clear and readable.

Unfortunately, however, legal writing often suffers from unnecessarily long and complex sentences that are poorly constructed. The reader of such a sentence is called upon to assimilate too much information at once and to guess at the proper relationships of the ideas.

Two characteristics of the process of legal writing may account for many excessively long and complex sentences. First, the writer has researched and pondered his analysis before verbalizing it, and he may have forgotten the difficulty that another lawyer encounters when exposed to the concepts for the first time. If so, he may attempt to convey a greater number of difficult concepts in a single sentence than the reader is prepared to digest. Second, many lawyers dictate their first drafts on a tape recorder and neglect to revise the transcribed draft adequately. Dictation may encourage long and complex sentences, because the speaker is deceived into believing that his inflection, dynamics in volume, and pauses provide adequate guides to sentence structure. In fact, transcripts of trials and presidential press conferences reveal that such oral guides to structure often do not transcribe adequately to the written page.

a. Closure and Visual Guides to Structure

You can use two devices to avoid or revise unmanageable sentences: closure and visual guides to structure.

Closure usually refers to punctuation that allows a reader to pause to assimilate one or more ideas before moving to the next. For example, the following passages illustrate three levels of closure. The first presents at least three distinct ideas in a single sentence punctuated only by commas:

> Although punitive damages are designed to punish the wrongdoer rather than compensate the victim for actual injury, many courts will award punitive damages only if the plaintiff proves actual injury, and some courts will limit punitive damages to an amount that bears a reasonable relationship to the award of compensatory damages.

The sentence above is constructed reasonably well. However, the commas in the sentence invite only brief pauses between ideas, leaving the reader breathless if she is unfamiliar with the subject matter. Periods dividing the passage into three sentences encourage the reader to pause more substantially and to digest each idea before facing the next:

> Punitive damages are designed to punish the wrongdoer rather than compensate the victim for actual injury. Nonetheless, many courts will award punitive damages only if the plaintiff proves actual injury. Moreover, some courts will limit punitive damages to an amount that bears a reasonable relationship to the award of compensatory damages.

If you desire to link the second and third ideas to one another more closely than to the first idea in the paragraph, you can replace the second period with a semicolon. The semicolon provides such a conceptual link with nearly the same level of closure as provided by a period:

> Punitive damages are designed to punish the wrongdoer rather than compensate the victim for actual losses. Nonetheless, many courts will award punitive damages only if the plaintiff proves actual injury; moreover, some courts will limit punitive damages to an amount that bears a reasonable relationship to the award of compensatory damages.

In some passages, visual guides to the structure of a long sentence may effectively substitute for the closure provided by multiple short sentences. The following passages illustrate both techniques. The first sample passage takes advantage of closure by limiting each sentence to a single idea:

> The evidence supports three critical factual conclusions. First, the marijuana, cocaine, and heroin all belonged to Carson and Klein. Second, Rivers was unaware of the presence of those drugs in the house when he entered the living room. Third, when Klein offered to sell the marijuana to Rivers, Rivers declined and attempted to leave the house.

The closure is welcome in this example, because two of the factual conclusions set forth in separate sentences are sufficiently complex to require punctuation within those conclusions.

In the next sample passage, the series of conclusions in the first passage progresses through a single sentence without the disruption of substantial closure. It retains some of the qualities of closure by using numbers as the equivalent of road signs[4] to identify the end of one element of the series and the beginning of the next:

> The evidence supports three critical factual conclusions: (1) the marijuana, cocaine, and heroin all belonged to Carson and Klein; (2) Rivers was unaware of the presence of those drugs in the house when he entered the living room; and (3) when Klein offered to sell the marijuana to Rivers, Rivers declined and attempted to leave the house.

If the elements of the series are less complex, you can provide a subtler guide to sentence structure by repeating an introductory word or phrase, such as "that" in the following example:

> Top Notch Co. is not liable on this contract theory unless Jackson can prove that the personnel manual was part of Jackson's employment contract, that the manual contained a promise of job security, and that Top Notch breached such a promise when it discharged Jackson for refusing to shave his beard.

---

4. Professor Richard Wydick calls this technique "tabulation." Richard C. Wydick, Plain English for Lawyers 42-43 (2d ed. 1985).

Some writers balk at repeating "that" in this manner, or even at using it in the first instance. In some sentence structures, their point is well taken. For example, the word "that" is unnecessary in the following sentence:

‖ I knew that he would come back.

Although the sentence above does not display any errors of grammar or syntax, a writer could exercise discretion to omit the word "that," thus adopting a more concise style with no appreciable loss of clarity:

‖ I knew he would come back.

In other cases, however, the word "that," although unnecessary, may help the reader to distinguish quickly between two possible sentence structures. Consider, for example, the following sentences:

‖ The court held two principles above all others.
‖ The court held the defendant in custody without bail.[5]
‖ The court held the defendant had not consented to the search.

In the first two sentences, the word "held" is used, at least figuratively, in the sense of possessing, retaining, or raising some thing, abstract or concrete. In those two sentences, the word "that" has no place; the writer could not insert it without adding other words. In the third sentence, however, the word "held" is used in a different sense and syntax. Like the word "said" or "concluded" in similar contexts, it introduces a holding or ruling of the court. In this context, a writer could exercise discretion to insert "that" after "held":

‖ The court held that the defendant had not consented to the search.

Indeed, although not necessary, the word "that" in the final sample sentence helps the reader to instantly change gears from the structure of the first two sample sentences to the different structure of the third. Without the "that" as a guide to the structure of the third sentence, the reader might momentarily assign the same meaning to "held" that it had in the first two sentences, relying later on context to dispel the confusion.

Thus, one should not too quickly adopt an inflexible rule against inserting "that" in such contexts. The decision whether to employ such a guide to structure is a matter of judgment, style, and context in these examples. In other contexts, the insertion of a word, such as a preposition, as a guide to sentence structure may be more critical.

For example, suppose that a will provides for the distribution of $1 million in stocks and other personal property in the following manner:

---

5. This sentence would be more precise if it stated that the court ordered the sheriff to hold the defendant without bail, but it suffices to illustrate the point under consideration.

> I leave all my personal property in equal shares per capita to the issue of my brother, Steve Lee, and my daughter, Cathy Chin, then living at the time of my death.

The testator is survived by Cathy Chin, by Cathy Chin's three daughters, and by Steve Lee's son, Kirby.

You know from your research that "equal shares per capita" means that all the ultimate beneficiaries will receive equal shares. However, the will is ambiguous in its identification of the ultimate beneficiaries. Under one interpretation, it leaves the property in two equal shares to Kirby Lee and Cathy Chin. Suppose, however, that you represent Cathy Chin's daughters. You could reasonably argue that the will leaves the personal property to the surviving issue of Steve Lee and the surviving issue of Cathy Chin, so that Kirby Lee and Cathy Chin's three daughters each take one-fourth of the property.

This second interpretation assumes that the phrase "the issue of" applies equally to the phrases "my brother, Steve Lee" and "my daughter, Cathy Chin." If the testator had intended such a distribution, however, she could have stated her will more clearly by repeating a single preposition. By inserting a second "of" before "my daughter," she could have related both "brother" and "daughter" back to "issue," ensuring that Cathy's daughters each receive a per capita distribution equal to that of Steve's son:

> . . . in equal shares per capita to the issue *of* my brother, Steve Lee, and *of* my daughter, Cathy Chin . . .

You probably could eliminate the ambiguity more gracefully or more completely in other ways. Nonetheless, this example serves to illustrate the tension between clarity and conciseness, even when nothing more than a two-letter word lies in the balance.

b. Complex Series

Chapter 5 examined the serial comma rule and its relationship to the goal of clarity in writing. To ensure clarity in complex as well as simple contexts, adherents to the traditional approach consistently insert the final comma in any series of two or more things:

We encountered high winds, driving rain, and dense fog.

The elements of a series, however, need not be limited to simple nouns, such as "wind, rain, and fog." They may be verb phrases, such as "washed the car, mowed the lawn, and repaired the roof." They may even be independent clauses, each of which could stand alone as a complete sentence with a subject and verb.

Particularly troublesome is a series in which at least one element contains a subsidiary series presenting subelements. The first challenge in such a sentence is to clearly distinguish among the elements and subelements at various levels in the series and subsidiary series. Unfortunately, legal writers frequently confuse these relationships:

> The defendant took his car to a garage for repairs, repainting, other maintenance, and lacked money for public transportation to another city.

The writer has punctuated this sentence as a single series with four elements: repairs, repainting, other maintenance, and lacked money. The series is not parallel in structure because the first three elements are objects and the fourth is a verb with an object. Along with the content of the sentence, that lack of parallelism helps to reveal the intended sentence structure. If retained as a single sentence, the passage is best structured as a compound sentence with two independent clauses as the major elements and with a series of three subelements within the first major element:

(1) The defendant took his car to a garage for
    (a) repairs,
    (b) repainting, **and**
    (c) other maintenance, and
(2) **he** lacked money for public transportation to another city.

The seemingly minor revisions in the corrected sentence are significant. The addition of the conjunction "and" between the second and third element of the subsidiary series signals the end of that series. Moreover, the addition of the subject "he" in the second major element of the compound sentence transforms that element into an independent clause, parallel with the first major element.

Further complexity in the sentence raises discretionary matters of style:

> The defendant stands accused of murdering Mr. Yakamoto in San Francisco on June 10. On that day, however, the defendant was seen at his home 75 miles away in Santa Cruz, his only car was in the shop for repairs, repainting, and other maintenance, and he had no money for public transportation to another city.

As in a compound sentence that presents two independent clauses joined by a simple conjunction, the commas suffice to separate the three independent clauses in the second sentence above. However, a writer could exercise discretion to achieve greater closure after each major element of such a series by replacing the appropriate commas with semicolons. Semicolons separating the major elements of a series are particularly helpful in this example because one of the elements includes a series of subelements separated by commas:

> . . . the defendant was seen at his home 75 miles away in Santa Cruz; his only car was in a garage awaiting repairs, repainting, and other maintenance; and he had no money for public transportation to another city.

Of course, you could separate the major elements even more clearly by dividing them into separate sentences. Depending upon their context within a larger passage, however, you may occasionally wish to link the elements of a complex series together in a single sentence. If so, your sentence structure and punctuation should guide your reader through the elements of each series or subsidiary series.

c. Toward a Flexible, Policy-Oriented Approach to Punctuation

Many routine conventions of punctuation provide guides to sentence structure and should be applied flexibly to achieve that goal. For example, the insertion of a comma to separate independent clauses joined by a conjunction[6] is not arbitrary; it often avoids temporary confusion in sentence structure, as illustrated by the following unpunctuated sentence:

Coastal Bank breached its loan commitment to the owner and the contractor threatened to terminate its performance.

Halfway through the sentence, many readers assume that the conjunction "and" joins "owner" to "the contractor." Thus, on encountering "the contractor," those readers conclude for a fraction of a second that the bank owed its loan commitment to the contractor as well as to the owner. By the time they reach the verb "threatened," they realize from context that "the contractor" is the subject of a new independent clause rather than the second in a series of two objects of the prepositional phrase "to the." By that time, however, the ambiguity in sentence structure has caused readers to hesitate for a moment and perhaps even to regress by rereading the sentence. This momentary confusion may be even more pronounced in a more complicated compound sentence.

A comma inserted before the conjunction more quickly identifies "the contractor" as the beginning of a new independent clause:

Coastal Bank breached its loan commitment to the owner, and the contractor threatened to terminate its performance.

This example illustrates two general principles of style. First, the reader of a brief or memorandum may be able to glean the meaning of the first sample sentence from context; however, if multiplied in the course of a document, the additional labor and frequent instances of momentary confusion can leave the reader weary. Some conventions of punctuation or other matters of style may not be critical to the reader's ultimate comprehension, but they enhance the efficiency and ease with which the reader comprehends.

Second, you should apply rules or conventions of writing style the way that you apply rules of law: Apply and extend them as far as necessary to vindicate their underlying purposes or policies, but no further. For example, the following compound sentence is perfectly readable without a comma separating the independent clauses:

---

6. See William Strunk, Jr. & E. B. White, The Elements of Style 5 (3d ed. 1979).

‖ The robber ran and the police gave chase.

Because this sentence is short and simple, the reader can recognize its structure at a glance, arguably making the comma unnecessary as a guide to structure.

You can avoid the comma question and raise others by placing a period after the first independent clause:

‖ The robber ran. And the police gave chase.

This punctuation gives special emphasis to the action in each clause, but many writers recoil at the idea of beginning a sentence with the simple conjunction "and" or "but." Such usage is not grammatically incorrect; it is simply stylistically questionable in many cases. If the clauses are simple and short, they will normally flow more smoothly if combined in a single sentence with a conjunction in the middle of the sentence. On the other hand, if you want to divide the clauses into two sentences to emphasize each clause or to provide your reader with closure after a long clause, you probably will prefer a stronger transition word than "and" or "but." Particularly in legal documents, most writers prefer to begin a sentence with a more substantial conjunctive adverb, such as "Moreover," "Furthermore," "In contrast," or "However":

‖ Mr. Blumquist survived the initial explosion. However, he died a short time later of smoke inhalation.

Thus, you will seldom need to begin a sentence with "and" or "but" to achieve important objectives in legal writing. But you should not conclude that this construction is universally incorrect. It will simply be a rare passage in legal writing that benefits from such construction. In this entire book, only a handful of sentences begin with "and" or "but." And the two in this paragraph are included primarily to underscore the theme of this subsection: Many rules of composition should be viewed as general guides to style rather than absolute prohibitions on unconventional usage.

A few more examples will underscore this point. Consider, for example, the question whether to insert a comma after a subordinate phrase or clause to separate it from the main clause that follows it:

‖ After reviving the victim at poolside{,} the paramedic transported her to the hospital emergency room.

Some writers, including this author, normally insert such a comma, even after a relatively short and simple introductory phrase or clause. By analogy to the justification for the traditional serial comma rule, we reason that the comma almost never hurts and that it may be a helpful guide to sentence structure if the introductory phrase or clause is long or complex.

Other writers, however, prefer to avoid unnecessary punctuation. They may prefer to insert a comma after an introductory phrase or clause only when necessary for clarity. Such an exercise of discretion is perfectly legitimate, although it requires the writer to determine the degree of complexity or length that would cause a reader to stumble in the absence of a comma.

For example, each of the following five sentences or excerpts begins with a subordinate word, phrase, or clause. The word or phrase beginning the main clause is printed in bold. In which of the examples would you insert a comma before the main clause?

(i) Later **he** mowed the lawn.
(ii) On January 1, 1987 **he** resolved to quit smoking.
(iii) After she examined the patient **Dr. Ong** requested a conference with the chief surgeon.
(iv) Based on Hart's conduct and oral representations and on the plain language of the policy manual **the manual** appears . . .
(v) Although few courts have addressed the question whether a member of a city council enjoys the absolute immunity conferred on state legislators **the policy** of protecting the legislative process from . . .

As stated above, a writer could reasonably choose to insert a comma in each of the five examples. Others might exercise discretion to withhold further punctuation from example (i) and perhaps example (ii) because readers can recognize the relatively simple structures of those examples at a glance. Even those inclined to preserve ink, however, should begin adding a comma at the level of complexity of example (iii) or (iv). The dependent clause at the beginning of example (iii) includes a subject, verb, and object. Moreover, the object, "the patient," might be confused with the subject of the main clause, "Dr. Ong," unless separated by a comma:

After she examined the patient, Dr. Ong requested a conference . . .   ‖

In examples (iv) and (v), the introductory phrases or clauses are sufficiently long and complex that readers will appreciate a comma, because it invites them to pause to assimilate the information in the introduction before proceeding to the main clause.

Example (ii) invites a separate exploration of commas within and after dates. Varying approaches to this topic have gained favor among editors and authorities. No approach is satisfying, however, unless it finds support in some consistent reasoning; it must be more than a set of arbitrary rules committed to memory.

To derive a consistent approach to commas in and around dates, you should first justify the comma that is beyond debate. Americans universally insert a comma after the day when stating the month, day, and year: "January 12, 1994." The justification for this comma is not a need to set off parenthetic information; neither the day nor the year display the properties of parenthetic information. Instead, we seem to insert the comma to avoid the jumble of numbers that would result if the day and year were not separated: "January 12 1994." This rationale is consistent with the practice of the Europeans, who appropriately omit the comma because they place the month between the day and the year: "12 January 1994."

From this reasoning, you can derive answers to any problem regarding commas and dates. For example, you need no comma when stating the month and year, because the year is not parenthetic and because the date does not contain two sets of numerals that require separation: "January 1994." Moreover, you normally need no comma after a date in the middle of a clause:

∥ The document dated June 10, 1986 represents a modification of an earlier agreement.

In this example, the writer directs the reader's attention to one document out of several, all of which have different dates. As discussed more fully in Section B.4 below, the date should not be set off with commas in this example, because it is "restrictive" in the sense that it defines which of several documents represents the modification.

Conversely, you should insert a comma before or after the date if it falls in a position that would require a comma after any word or phrase. For example, the entire date may be parenthetic, calling for commas before and after:

∥ His driver's license expired on his 34th birthday, July 27, 1993, when he was still in prison.

In other cases, you might insert a comma after a date that ends an introductory phrase or clause, as discussed at the beginning of this subsection. For example, the comma may help the reader recognize the point of separation between a long introductory phrase or clause and the main clause:

∥ Although the parties negotiated throughout the month of March 1992, they failed to reach agreement on two critical terms.

In other cases, a comma after an introductory date may not be necessary for clarity but may still be acceptable as a matter of discretionary style:

∥ On October 10, 1991, the parties agreed to modify their contract.

A final example will serve to emphasize the role of style and judgment in punctuation and to illustrate the limits of inflexible rules. In the following sentence, a common convention of punctuation justifies each of the commas, viewed in isolation:

∥ The contract is written, signed, and dated, and, therefore, the statute of frauds does not apply.

The first two commas appropriately separate three elements of a series. The third comma appropriately separates the two independent clauses joined by the conjunction "and." The last two commas at least represent a defensible judgment that "therefore" is parenthetic and should be set apart from the rest of the clause with commas.

Nonetheless, most writers would be dissatisfied with the sentence, because the concentration of five commas within six words of text is distracting. In response, many writers simply omit one or more commas without changing the structure of the sentence:

The contract is written, signed, and dated and, therefore the statute of ‖ frauds does not apply.

This revision simply makes matters worse. Although it is less cluttered, it omits commas that served important functions.

An honest appraisal of the original sentence should reveal structural flaws. None of the five commas are incorrect; however, the sentence structure concentrates the commas in a manner that is stylistically displeasing. You can directly respond to this problem by changing the location of "therefore," thus decreasing the need for commas around it by lessening its parenthetic qualities:

The contract is written, signed, and dated, and the statute of frauds ‖ therefore does not apply.

Alternatively, you can replace one of the commas with a semicolon by omitting the conjunction "and" between the two independent clauses:

The contract is written, signed, and dated; therefore, the statute of frauds ‖ does not apply.

In sum, if you understand the policy justifications for conventions of punctuation, you can more confidently recall them, apply them, and even depart from them when the context justifies an unconventional approach. Conversely, even technically correct writing may display problems of style that invite you to exercise judgment and to consciously choose among alternative sentence structures.

Appendix V describes other common conventions of punctuation and asks you to analyze them.

========= E X E R C I S E   1 1 - 2 =========

1. *Preposition Power*

Review the discussion in Section B.1.a above (page 235) regarding the distribution of property under a will. Suppose the testator had intended to leave one-half to Kirby Lee and one-half to Cathy Chin in the circumstances described. How could the testator have unambiguously achieved that distribution? Try to achieve that result first by (i) inserting a single preposition in the ambiguous sentence, and alternatively by (ii) moving one or more parts of the sentence to another position within the sentence. Explain how your revisions remove ambiguity from the sentence.

2. Care with Commas

Which of the following sentences requires further punctuation? How would you correct it? Should you address these sentences with an inflexible rule of punctuation or with attention to principles of good writing underlying conventions of punctuation?

a. Two pieces of evidence link Jones to the crime: A witness observed Jones strike the victim with his fist and a glove recovered from the crime scene matches the one found in Jones's car.

b. The court dismissed the action and Romero appealed.

c. The judge dismissed the action because the limitations period had expired.

d. Because the limitations period had run the court dismissed the action.

e. In some cases even perfectly relevant evidence should be excluded if it would seriously confuse the jury because the prejudicial effect of such evidence outweighs its probative value.

3. Closure and Road Signs

Redraft the following sentence to improve its readability. Break it into multiple sentences or clauses, or use any other device to lead the reader gracefully through the ideas it expresses.

> Plaintiff American Continental Can Co. brought this action against Defendants Conco Sheet Metal Co., Bassi Distributing Co., and Miller Trucking Co., alleging that Conco Sheet Metal Co. had sold it defective sheet metal, that Bassi Distributing Co. had fraudulently misrepresented the description and quality of Conco Sheet Metal Co.'s products, and that Miller Trucking Co. had negligently damaged sheet metal that it agreed to transport from the warehouse of Conco Sheet Metal Co. to the factory of American Continental Can Co., and requesting compensatory and punitive damages.

4. The Ambiguous Series

Identify the major elements of the series in the sentence set forth below. Where does the last element of the series begin? What different interpretations does the sentence permit? How would you use a comma to advance either interpretation over the other?

> In the event of default, the lessee must vacate the premises, forfeit the security deposit and pay Lessor's actual damages or pay liquidated damages under section 12 of this Lease.

2. Concrete Verbs and Active Construction

a. Concrete Verbs

Lawyers often sacrifice vigor and clarity in their legal writing by employing vague and abstract verbs such as "involve," "exist," or "occur":

‖ A modification to the contract occurred on July 1.

Even more frequently, lawyers drain the strength from verbs by building sentences around a form of the phrase "there is":

There was a modification to the contract on July 1.   ‖

The author of the preceding sentence has converted the active verb "modify" into the noun "modification," creating a need for the verb "was," a form of the relatively abstract and passive infinitive "to be." Unless you really intend to focus attention on the mere existence or absence of modification, you could improve this sentence by identifying the actors, abandoning the "be" verb, and focusing on the real action word in the sentence, "modify":

Nelson and Kubichek modified their contract on July 1.   ‖

In some cases, replacing abstract wording such as "there is" with a more concrete, active verb will enable you to add new meaning as well as vigor. For example, the following sentence abstractly comments on the absence of critical evidence:

There is no evidence in the record that Robert Emery intended to kill ‖
the bank teller.

A more concrete verb can emphasize the absence not only of direct evidence of intent but also of circumstantial evidence from which a factfinder might infer intent:

No evidence in the record even suggests that Robert Emery intended to ‖
kill the bank teller.

b. Active and Passive Construction

Avoidance of forms of "there is" in legal writing is simply a special branch of a more general preference for active voice in sentence structure. A clause in active voice presents its principal parts in the normal order of actor, verb, and object of the action, such as "curiosity killed the cat."

In contrast, the following sentence features three clauses in passive voice, each of which places the object before the verb and dispenses with the actor altogether:

The *Allen* doctrine has been criticized, but it continues to be applied ‖
because it has been approved in dictum.

The following revision identifies the actors associated with each verb, but it still uses passive voice throughout, as revealed by the inverted order of object, verb, and actor:

The *Allen* doctrine has been criticized by dozens of commentators and ‖

a handful of appellate judges, but it continues to be applied by trial judges because it has been approved in dictum by the Supreme Court.

Active voice is more informative than the first example above, and it more directly and concisely conveys all the information presented in the second example:

Dozens of commentators and a handful of appellate judges have criticized the *Allen* doctrine, but trial judges continue to apply it because the Supreme Court has approved it in dictum.

The vigor of active construction can be especially useful in composing strong statements in persuasive writing. For example, the following sentence in passive voice fails to assign responsibility for the repair of the air conditioning:

Passive

The air conditioning was not repaired until 60 days after the tenant gave written notice of the defect.

In contrast, the next sentence uses active voice to identify the landlord as the responsible party and to characterize the landlord's inaction as a culpable omission:

active

The landlord neglected to repair the air conditioning until 60 days after the tenant gave written notice of the defect.

Although active voice generally is more direct, concise, or informative than passive voice, you may occasionally have reason to prefer passive voice. For example, you may use passive voice to deliberately omit reference to an actor or actors whose identities are unknown or unimportant:

‖ The bridge was erected in 1923.

Even in this case, some writers so strongly prefer active voice that they refer to the actor or actors generically:

‖ Workers built the bridge in 1923.

However, most writers would reasonably adopt the passive construction to avoid diverting the reader's attention to unimportant information.

In some cases, you may be aware of the identity of the actor but use passive construction to avoid drawing attention to that identity. For example, a defense attorney might desire to emphasize mitigating factors in a crime while avoiding any reminder to the jury that her client stands accused of the wrongdoing:

‖ The hostage was not harmed in any way.

Conversely, you may deliberately use passive voice to place unusual emphasis on the actor by placing the actor at the end of the sentence, as in the second of the following sentences:

> The defense wants you to believe that Mr. Cass committed suicide by injecting himself with a lethal dose of heroin. To the contrary, the evidence shows that the heroin was injected by the defendant, Ms. Borden.

In some sentences, if you place the actor or actors at the beginning of the sentence, you will unduly delay introducing the verb:

> Ms. Williams, the firm's top expert in tax law, and Mr. Scales, an eloquent oral advocate with 20 years of experience before the state appellate courts, argued the case.

With passive voice, you can introduce the simple object and verb early in the sentence:

> The case was argued by Ms. Williams, the firm's top expert in tax law, and by Mr. Scales, an eloquent oral advocate with 20 years of experience before the state appellate courts.

In summary, you should prefer vigorous, concrete verbs in active construction unless you have a specific purpose for a vague, abstract, or passive verb.

═══════ E X E R C I S E   1 1 - 3 ═══════

1. *Benefits of Active, Concrete Verbs*

Replace the passive, abstract verbs in the following sentences with more active, concrete verbs.
   a. There are only two Supreme Court decisions that address this issue.
   b. It was argued by government counsel that the tax regulation was applicable to the land exchange.
   c. The landlord was ordered by the court to achieve completion of the repairs within 30 days.
   d. There was a conspiracy among four distributors to effect an immediate price increase.

2. *Benefits of Passive Construction*

By replacing the active verb with a passive verb, restructure the following sentence to minimize the number of words separating the subject, verb, and object and to emphasize the "clearly erroneous" standard.

Federal Rule of Civil Procedure 52(a), which provides that a federal trial court's findings of fact in a nonjury trial "shall not be set aside unless clearly erroneous," governs this appeal.

---

3. Effective Placement of Modifiers

For clarity, you should place a modifying word, phrase, or clause close to the part of the sentence that it modifies. On the other hand, to ensure a smooth flow in your writing, you should avoid interrupting important parts of a sentence with a lengthy modifier. The following sample sentences illustrate how these principles relate to one another.

The first sample sentence below attempts to describe the effects of cross-examination on a witness. Unfortunately, it subjects the reader to a classic dangling modifier:

‖ Withering under relentless cross-examination, the prosecutor forced the witness to recant his earlier testimony.

The first five words of this sample sentence form a subordinate phrase. It is subordinate because, unlike the clause that follows it, it cannot stand alone as a full sentence; rather, it provides further information about an element of the clause. The subject of the independent clause, "the prosecutor," is positioned next to the modifying phrase and thus receives the impact of that phrase. But it is the witness, not the prosecutor, who withered under the cross-examination. You can remedy this defect in the sentence by changing the modifying phrase so that it addresses the action of the prosecutor:

‖ With relentless cross-examination, the prosecutor forced the witness to recant his earlier testimony.

But this alters the focus of the sentence. If you want to retain the focus on the witness, you can restructure the sentence so that the original modifying phrase is adjacent to the object that it modifies, "the witness":

‖ The witness, withering under the prosecutor's relentless cross-examination, recanted his earlier testimony.

That sentence structure leaves no doubt that the witness is the one who has withered. Unfortunately, it places the modifying phrase between the subject and the verb, separating important parts of the sentence. This separation will not be objectionable if the modifier is very short and simple and if it creates only a minor inconvenience in the sample sentence above. However, a longer, more complex modifier in that position can be distracting:

‖ The witness, who had testified on direct examination that he was walking toward the intersection and therefore was in a position to see the signal,

admitted on cross-examination that he had his back to the intersection ‖
at the time of the accident.

To eliminate the separation of subject and verb in the shorter sample
sentence, you might consider gathering all the parts of the main clause and
moving them to the beginning of the sentence:

The witness recanted his earlier testimony, withering under the prosecu- ‖
tor's relentless cross-examination.

In other sentences, this structure is often quite successful. Unfortunately,
in this sample sentence, it introduces the reader to the recantation before the withering, producing a sense of anticlimax. More important, it
creates ambiguity about whether the witness or his earlier testimony was
withering.

Perhaps the best revision of the sample sentence places the modifying
phrase or clause at the beginning of the sentence, paving the way for an
uninterrupted main clause:

Withering under the prosecutor's relentless cross-examination, the witness ‖
recanted his earlier testimony.

Some might object to this structure on the ground that a long subordinate
phrase or clause at the beginning of a sentence unduly delays introduction
of the main clause. That objection is valid with the following qualification:
A moderately long or complex subordinate phrase or clause ordinarily will
be less distracting if it is placed at the beginning of the sentence than if it
appears in the middle of the sentence and separates important parts of the
main clause.

The following passages are sample revisions of a sentence with long and
multiple subordinate clauses. When compared to the previous examples,
these alternative revisions suggest that the best solutions to the problems
discussed above sometimes differ with the circumstances of each sentence.

Unlike the more moderate introduction in the last sample revision
above, the subordinate clauses in the following sentence inconveniently delay
introduction of the main clause:

Because the consumer fraud statute applies to misrepresentations in either ‖
the "advertisement or sale" of merchandise, and because the "sale" of ‖
merchandise normally is associated with the passing of title from the seller ‖
to the buyer, *see* U.C.C. §2-106(1), the statute appears to apply to a ‖
seller's misrepresentations made during the delivery of merchandise under ‖
a preexisting contract. ‖

You would only increase the reader's frustration by moving the subordinate clauses to the middle of the sentence, between the subject and the
verb:

> The consumer fraud statute, because it applies to . . . , and because the "sale" of merchandise normally is . . . , appears to apply to a seller's misrepresentations . . .

You could reveal the information in the sentence more gracefully by starting with the main clause:

> The consumer fraud statute appears to apply to a seller's misrepresentations made during the delivery of merchandise under a preexisting contract, because the statute applies to misrepresentations in either the "advertisement or sale" of merchandise, and because the "sale" of merchandise normally is associated with the passing of title from the seller to the buyer, *see* U.C.C. §2-106(1).

In the context of this sample sentence, this structure does not produce the ambiguity or inappropriate sense of anticlimax that it produced in one of the revisions of the first sample sentence above.

Of course, this revised sentence is nonetheless too long and complex. You can solve all the problems in this passage simply by breaking it into shorter sentences, as recommended in the discussion of closure in Section B.1.a above:

> The consumer fraud statute applies to misrepresentations in either the "advertisement or sale" of merchandise. The "sale" of merchandise normally is associated with the passing of title from the seller to the buyer. *See* U.C.C. §2-106(1). Therefore, the statute appears to apply to . . .

═══════ E X E R C I S E 11 - 4 ═══════

1. *Precise Placement of Modifiers*

Consider the different positions into which you could insert the word "only" in the following sentence:

Officer Jones fired his gun three times at the suspect.

Which of the positions is most consistent with the information in each of the following?

a. Officer Jones fired his gun three times, not five times as reported by a witness.

b. Officer Jones fired his gun three times, but no other officer fired his gun more than once.

2. *Modifying Clauses and Sentence Structure*

Revise the following sentences. Which of several possible revisions do you prefer, and why?

a. The trial judge, after reviewing the evidence and considering the arguments of the parties, ruled that the contraband was the product of an illegal search.

b. Protesting that he had not finished his testimony, the bailiff escorted the witness from the courtroom.

4. Restrictive and Nonrestrictive Clauses

Most writers confess to difficulty in identifying restrictive and nonrestrictive clauses and in choosing between the relative pronouns "that" and "which" once they have identified the clause. One noted scholar has offered the following introductory advice:

> A defining relative clause [a restrictive clause] is one that identifies the person or thing meant by limiting the denotation of the antecedent: *Each made a list of books that had influenced him*; not books generally, but books as defined by the *that*-clause. Contrast with this: *I always buy his books, which have influenced me greatly*; the [nonrestrictive] clause does not limit *his books*, which needs no limitation; it gives a reason . . . , or adds a new fact . . .
>
> (A) of *which* and *that*, *which* is appropriate to nondefining [nonrestrictive] and *that* to defining [restrictive] clauses; . . .[7]

a. The Role of the Comma

To illustrate the distinction between restrictive and nonrestrictive clauses, imagine that you and a friend are conversing in a room with three paintings hanging on the nearest wall. As your conversation turns to the weather, your friend makes a statement that is reproduced below without internal punctuation:

My hair *which I just washed and styled an hour ago* goes completely limp ‖ in this humid weather.

Now, imagine the inflection and timing of your friend's oral statement. She probably stressed the main clause: "My hair goes completely limp in this humid weather." On the other hand, you can imagine that her voice lowered in pitch and volume when she interjected the italicized clause: "which I just washed and styled an hour ago." You can imagine her pausing after "hair" and "ago," lending a parenthetic quality to the information between the pauses.

The italicized clause is parenthetic because it is not needed to identify the subject, "my hair." Your friend has only one head of hair, and she has directed your attention to that unique object simply by referring to "my hair." Her statement about recently washing and styling her hair helps to reinforce her point about the effects of humidity, but that statement is not

---

7. H. W. Fowler, Modern English Usage 626, 699 (2d ed. 1965). Fowler also addresses the relationship between "who," "which," and "that":

> (B) of *which* and *who*, *which* belongs to things, and *who* to persons; (C) of *who* and *that*, *who* suits particular persons, and *that* generic persons.

Id. at 699.

needed to identify her head of hair and distinguish it from all others within the range of your perception. Thus, you could naturally treat the italicized clause as an "aside," an interruption of the main clause. The clause provides interesting additional information, but the rest of the sentence would coherently stand alone without it. The italicized clause is "nondefining" because it is not necessary to define the subject. Stated otherwise, it is "nonrestrictive" because it is not necessary to restrict the universe of heads of hair to the one head of hair belonging to your friend; the phrase "my hair" had already accomplished that task.

In an oral statement, you would normally pause before and after such a nonrestrictive clause. In a written statement, you achieve the same effect by setting the clause apart with commas:

‖ My hair, which I just washed and styled an hour ago, goes completely limp in this humid weather.

Imagine now that your conversation turns to the three paintings hanging on the nearest wall. You would undoubtedly experience confusion if your friend made the following statement without pointing to a particular painting:

‖ The painting was donated by my cousin.

The subject "the painting" is not sufficiently precise to distinguish among the three paintings on the wall and to identify the one to which your friend is referring. She could avoid the confusion by adding a clause that directs your attention to a single painting. Each of the following revisions contains such a clause:

‖ The painting *hanging in the middle* was donated by my cousin.
The painting *which is hanging in the middle* was donated by my cousin.
The painting *that is hanging in the middle* was donated by my cousin.

Regardless which version your friend spoke, she did not pause before the italicized passage; instead, she plowed straight through the sentence at least until she had singled out one of the paintings. The italicized information is not parenthetic; rather than interrupting the main clause, it is a direct continuation of the subject, necessary to identify or to define the painting to which she is referring. In that sense, it is a "defining" or "restrictive" clause because it restricts the universe of three paintings on the wall to the single painting to which your friend intends to refer. Just as such a clause would not inspire a pause in an oral statement, it would not require commas in a written statement.

So far, your reaction to these examples is probably a resounding "Who cares?". The following sample sentences, however, illustrate that the distinction between a restrictive and nonrestrictive clause occasionally materially affects the content of a sentence in legal writing. The construction of the first sample sentence suggests that all reckless driving constitutes a felony and that a new statute therefore applies to all reckless driving:

The new statute mandates a jail term only for reckless driving, which ‖ constitutes a felony violation of the vehicle code.

The meaning of this sentence is primarily conveyed by the comma, which suggests to the reader that the sentence would be perfectly sensible if it ended at "reckless driving" and that the clause following the comma simply adds additional, parenthetic information. The clause following the comma is nonrestrictive, or nondefining, because it does not purport to identify a subset of the general category of things within the term "reckless driving."

Even without any changes in wording, the second sample sentence suggests by the absence of a comma that only some forms of reckless driving rise to the level of a felony and that the statute applies only to those forms of reckless driving:

The new statute mandates a jail term only for reckless driving which ‖ constitutes a felony violation of the vehicle code.

The absence of a comma invites the reader to rush to the end of the sentence to discover what kind of reckless driving is covered, suggesting that the sentence could not sensibly stop at the term "reckless driving." In this sentence, the clause following "reckless driving" is restrictive, or defining, because it identifies a subset of the things in the general category of reckless driving.

Both sentences, however, use the relative pronoun "which" to introduce the restrictive or nonrestrictive clauses, leaving the burden of conveying the restrictive or nonrestrictive nature of the clause to the presence or absence of a comma. To partially relieve the comma of that burden, purists or traditionalists use the relative pronoun "that" in a restrictive clause to emphasize the restrictive nature of the clause and to more clearly distinguish it from a nonrestrictive clause:

The new statute mandates a jail term only for reckless driving that consti- ‖ tutes a felony violation of the vehicle code.

b. The Choice Between "That" and "Which"

Because most writers do not have a natural ear for the purist's use of "that," they tend to use "which" in both restrictive and nonrestrictive clauses. In fact, this practice is so widespread that it can be characterized as the popular approach. The few supervising attorneys who are purists on this matter will go "which hunting" when reviewing the work of associates, but they probably have limited effect on the writing habits of the general legal community.

In many cases, any ambiguity or uncertainty resulting from using "which" in a restrictive clause will be insignificant. For example, the difference in meaning between the following two sentences is insignificant to the analysis that the writer intends to convey:

(1) The court applied a fairness test, which inquires whether a transaction was consummated through fair dealing and at a fair price.

(2) The court applied a fairness test that inquires whether a transaction was consummated through fair dealing and at a fair price.

Because the sentence refers to only one of many possible formulations of a test that incorporates considerations of fairness, the final clause probably should be restrictive, as in the second example. However, because emphasis of the restrictive nature of the clause is not necessary for analytic clarity, the following popular construction would be inoffensive:

The court applied a fairness test which inquires whether a transaction was consummated through fair dealing and at a fair price.

Nonetheless, at least in those cases in which the choice of relative pronouns will affect clarity, you should follow the example of the Supreme Court, which clearly distinguished between restrictive and nonrestrictive clauses in the following excerpt from an opinion:

Although the Court of Appeals' construction of the Act and of Regulation Z is shared by three of the four other Courts of Appeals *that* have ruled on the question, this view, *which* is essentially a claim that the plain language of the statute and the regulation requires the result reached by the court below, has recently been challenged on several fronts.[8]

c. Procedural Labels

You may also raise questions about restrictive and nonrestrictive clauses when you join procedural labels, such as "plaintiff," to the names of parties to litigation. In that context, you need not worry about a choice between "that" and "which," but you may pause before choosing between the insertion or omission of a comma.

---

8. Anderson Bros. Ford v. Valencia, 452 U.S. 205, 211-212 (1981) (emphasis added).

For example, if Robert Jones is one of three plaintiffs in an action, then a phrase that uses his name to define "plaintiff" is restrictive and should omit any comma:

Plaintiff Robert Jones moves for summary judgment on the ground that . . . ‖

In this example, "Robert Jones" restricts the universe of "plaintiffs" to one of the three plaintiffs in the litigation.

In contrast, if Jones is the only plaintiff, you could treat a similar reference as nonrestrictive and include commas:

Plaintiff, Robert Jones, moves for summary judgment on the ground that . . . ‖

In this example, "Robert Jones" arguably supplies parenthetic information about a party who is already identified by the label "Plaintiff."

Alternatively, even if Jones is the only plaintiff, you could reasonably eliminate the commas by characterizing "Plaintiff" as a title that is joined with a name, as in "Dr. Long" or "Secretary-Treasurer Richard King":

Plaintiff Robert Jones . . . ‖

This is probably the least distracting stylistic option. However, you cannot adopt this usage of "plaintiff" as a title if you treat "plaintiff" as a common noun by preceding it with an article, such as "the." In that case, you must treat the party's name as a nonrestrictive modifier if he is the only plaintiff:

The plaintiff, Robert Jones, moves for summary judgment against the defendant, Cecelia Ynez . . . ‖

═══════════ E X E R C I S E   1 1 - 5 ═══════════

Relative Pronouns and Wealthy Relatives

Compare the following alternative provisions of a will:

I leave to my daughter my bank account that is in Western Savings.

or

I leave to my daughter my bank account, which is in Western Savings.

After drafting the will, but before death, the testator closed the bank account at Western Savings and used the funds from that account to open a new one at First Interstate Bank.[9] Which provision would most likely bequeath the First Interstate bank account to the daughter?

C. PRECISION

1. An Analytic Approach

Once you clearly understand the idea that you want to communicate, you must select the words and phrases that precisely convey your intended meaning. For example, Chapter 2 discusses the judicial interpretation of the phrase "because of . . . sex" in Title VII of the Civil Rights Act of 1964. A careless writer might state the conclusion of that discussion in the following manner:

‖ Title VII currently does not prohibit an employer from discriminating
‖ against homosexuals.

This overstates the conclusion, because it suggests that Title VII would provide no remedy to a victim of race discrimination simply because he also happened to be homosexual. A more precise statement of the statutory interpretation focuses on the basis of the discrimination rather than on the status of the discriminatee:

‖ Title VII currently does not prohibit an employer from discriminating
‖ on the basis of sexual orientation.

As suggested in Chapter 5, achieving precision in writing may require you to subordinate other potential goals, such as entertaining your reader. For example, many writers believe that they will bore their readers if they repeatedly use a single word or phrase to refer to the same idea throughout a passage. They often address this concern by engaging in "elegant variation": varying the word or phrase used to refer to the same idea. However, any entertainment value of the variation does not justify the confusion that typically results.

For example, perhaps to elegantly vary their phrasing, many legal writers intermittently use "while" as a synonym for "although," and they use "when" or "where" as a synonym for "if." The following construction is common:

‖ While the court declined to decide the issue of retroactivity in *Fleming*,
‖ its dictum in subsequent cases suggests that it has always assumed that
‖ the *Fleming* principle applies retroactively.

The primary meaning of "while" in this syntax is duration or simultaneity. But, of course, the writer does not mean that the court offered dictum in

---

9. The source of this problem is Rebecca W. Berch, Words That/Which Cause Problems in Legal Writing, 25 Ariz. Bar Briefs No. 9 (1987).

subsequent cases *at the same time* that it declined to decide the issue in a previous case. "Although" would more precisely convey the contrast or tension between the court's actions. In the context of the entire sentence, the less precise version does not cause serious confusion or inconvenience. By displaying care with details, however, the more precise wording strengthens the credibility of the writer on more substantive matters.

More substantial risks of confusion arise in the use of synonyms for "because." "Since" is particularly popular:

Since the employer invited the applicant to read the policy manual at the ‖
initial interview, the manual became part of their bargain. ‖

Although the multiple dictionary definitions of "since" typically include "because," the primary dictionary definition relates to time frame or sequence of events:

> From then till now; in the interval; before this; before now; ago; after that time. — *prep.* Continuously from the time of; as, *since* yesterday; subsequent to; after. — *conj.* In the interval after the time when, as: I have been ill twice *since* I saw you last. Without interruption, from the time when; as, *since* we saw you last; because; seeing that; inasmuch as.[10]

Therefore, most readers fail to recognize "since" as a signal for a causal relationship when they first encounter it in a sentence such as the example above. Although the reader undoubtedly later discovers the intended meaning of "since" from context, that process may produce momentary hesitation or even regression in reading. The ambiguity is more serious if the sentence otherwise refers to a time frame:

Since Rabin breached the contract on January 1, 1985, the three-year ‖
limitations period expired before Smith filed suit on January 10, 1988. ‖

This sentence will appear to some readers to make the marginally useful point that the limitations period expired after the breach of contract as well as before the filing of suit. The word "because" in place of "since" would more clearly convey the intended causal relationship: The breach of contract triggered the commencement of the running of the limitations period; therefore, the period expired before suit was filed.

You create an even greater risk of confusion if you replace "because" with "as," because causation is not a readily recognized connotation of "as":

Plaintiff is entitled to the equitable remedy of injunctive relief as his legal ‖
remedy is inadequate. ‖

One popular dictionary does not even clearly list "because" as a definition for "as"; the closest it comes is listing "since" as a definition of "as" in its

---

10. New Webster's Dictionary 902 (encyclopedic ed. 1981).

conjunctive form.[11] As explained above, even this reference to "since" is ambiguous.

In each of these three examples, "because" would more precisely and unambiguously convey the writer's intended meaning of causal relationship, because it has no other meaning.[12] Moreover, "because" is self-descriptive: The root word "cause" within it suggests its meaning.

2. Beyond Dogma

Popular use of synonyms for "because" illustrates the range of considerations that often influence nuances in writing style. Despite the precision that "because" permits, many writers depart from it in the interests of elegant variation, or they reject it altogether because they think that it has an unsophisticated ring to it. However, few readers demand variation or stimulation from every word in a sentence. As with many other words, such as "the," "with," and "a," "because" precisely and unobtrusively performs its function without diverting the reader's attention from more substantively important parts of the sentence. Indeed, the text of this section has used each of those words repeatedly, presumably without offending the average reader.

The most interesting reason that writers give for substituting "since" or "as" for "because" is their recollection of an admonition in grade school never to begin a sentence with "because." Of course, if beginning a sentence with "because" offended some principle of syntax or other consideration of composition, replacing it at the beginning of the sentence with a synonym, and a poor one at that, would not cure the defect. In fact, some grade school teachers may have invented or repeated such a rule in reaction to students' early tendencies to write incomplete sentences, such as: "Because I missed the bus." Those teachers probably should have explained the requisite components of a complete sentence rather than place undeserved blame on the word "because."

One defense of "as" and "since" as expressions of causal relationship has potential merit. Some writers believe that "as" and "since" are not synonymous with "because" in that context but express slightly different shades of causation. Those writers reasonably use "because" to refer to a direct causal relationship and "since" or "as" to refer to a more attenuated relationship.[13] A style that carefully recognizes such a distinction arguably enhances precision. Unfortunately, few writers use "since" or "as" to connote a causal relationship in such a principled manner. Moreover, to a greater extent than in literary writing, legal writing tends to describe causal

---

11. Id. at 58.
12. See, e.g., id. at 86.
13. See generally William Strunk, Jr. & E. B. White, The Elements of Style 24 (3d ed. 1979) ("because" presented as concise replacement for the verbose phrase "the reason why is that," and "since" presented as primary replacement for "owing to the fact that"); E. B. White, The Second Tree from the Corner 17 (1984) ("Parnell was not a playmate of mine, as he was a few years older. . . .").

relationships that are sufficiently direct to justify use of "because" in place of the softer "since" or "as."

This discussion illustrates once again the importance of avoiding unthinking adherence to inflexible and arbitrary rules of composition, such as a rule against starting a sentence with "because." If you understand the reasoning supporting a convention of writing style, you will be better equipped to evaluate that convention. You may then opt to apply the convention universally, reject it completely, or apply it selectively to those situations in which application furthers the reasoning.

=============== E X E R C I S E   1 1 - 6 ===============

Precise Prose

Rewrite the following passage so it more precisely summarizes some of the ideas discussed toward the end of Chapter 2. Feel free to use helpful terms of art, but avoid using unnecessary jargon to create a false sense of precision.

> While lawmakers can throw out laws that judges have developed on their own by enacting a bill, the judicial offices retain an important role, as they will decide what the enacted bill means as it relates to a legal battle. Moreover, the judiciary will toss the new law out of court if it goes against the federal or applicable state constitution.

II. CONCISENESS

A legal document that effectively conveys its message in 10 pages is more useful than one that rambles on for 20 pages to convey the same message. However, you must not achieve brevity in your writing at the cost of omitting important ideas or sacrificing clarity of expression. You should strive first to express all important ideas in sufficient detail to ensure reader comprehension. With that accomplished, you can trim the fat from your writing by omitting extraneous ideas and expressing the important ones efficiently.

To write concisely, you must control content, form, and style. You can control content primarily through the scope and depth of analysis. You can achieve concise form and style through efficient organization, sentence structure, and phrasing.

A. CONTENT—SCOPE AND DEPTH OF ANALYSIS

"Scope of analysis" refers to the range of issues or topics that you address in your legal document. "Depth of analysis" refers to the level of detail with which you address a topic.

1. Scope of Analysis

The range of ideas that you address in your document can dramatically affect the document's length. In analyzing a problem, you need not develop every theory that you have encountered in the library. Instead, you can (1) thoroughly discuss the most important and clearly relevant topics, (2) exclude distracting tangents that are unlikely to affect the outcome of the dispute, and (3) determine whether to discuss topics between the two extremes, perhaps in less detail than would be appropriate for a mainstream theory.

As discussed more fully in Chapter 4, in applying these standards, you may find that you tend to apply different scopes of analysis to different kinds of documents. The scope of analysis ordinarily can be quite broad in your examination answers, because most of your professors will specifically test your ability to identify a wide range of issues. The scope of analysis should be much narrower in a brief, because briefs generally are most persuasive if they focus only on the strongest available arguments. The scope of analysis in a typical office memorandum often is somewhere between that of an examination and a brief. An office memorandum should not fail to at least briefly discuss a theory or approach that may ultimately be helpful. On the other hand, to a greater extent than an examination answer, an office memorandum should focus on thorough development of the most helpful theories rather than on identification of every conceivable approach.

2. Depth of Analysis

By properly balancing varying depths of analysis in the discussion or argument section of your memorandum or brief, you can make the document more concise and readable. For convenience, this book will use the terms "light analysis" and "in-depth analysis" to refer to the opposite extremes on the spectrum. You engage in light analysis when you simply state a proposition of law and cite to supporting authority. You engage in in-depth analysis when you analyze legal authority more thoroughly, such as by discussing the facts, holding, and reasoning of case law. You may also control the depth of analysis by choosing between (1) expressing a full deductive argument or (2) expressing an incomplete syllogism, leaving a premise of your deductive argument implicit.

a. Depth of Analysis of Legal Authority

The sample memorandum on pages 185-188 provides an example of balance between light analysis and in-depth analysis of authority from the fictitious state of Calzona. The second paragraph of the discussion section briefly outlines fundamental principles, which provide helpful background information and which almost certainly will not be disputed by the parties. For this purpose, the author of the memorandum has used light analysis by simply stating propositions of law and citing to supporting authority:

An enforceable contract requires a bargained-for exchange in which a promisor exchanges his own promise for a return promise or performance. *Smith v. Newman*, 161 Calz. 443, 447, 667 P.2d 81, 84 (1984); Restatement (Second) of Contracts §71 (1981). The requirement of an exchange is not satisfied if one party gives only an illusory promise, which does not commit the promisor to any future performance. *See Atco Corp. v. Johnson*, 155 Calz. 1211, 627 P.2d 781 (1980).

However, the memorandum also raises the more difficult issue of whether a particular promise made by a lender was illusory, an issue the parties obviously dispute. An adequate discussion of that issue requires more thorough analysis of case law to determine which precedent is more nearly analogous to the facts of the current dispute. Such in-depth analysis explores the facts, holding, and reasoning of each significant case:

In *Atco Corp.*, the manager of an automobile repair shop promised to forbear "until I want the money" from asserting a claim against the owner of an automobile for $900 in repairs; in exchange, a friend of the owner promised to act as guarantor of the owner's obligation. *Id.* at 1212, 627 P.2d at 782. The word "want" stated no legal commitment, because it permitted the manager at his own discretion to refuse to perform any forbearance at all. Because the manager incurred no obligation, the guarantor's promise was gratuitous and unenforceable. *Id.* at 1213-14, 627 P.2d at 782-84.

In-depth analysis of *Atco*

On the other hand, even if a promise leaves open the possibility that the promisor will escape obligation, the promise is valid if the promisor does not have complete control over the events on which the promisor's obligation is conditioned. *Bonnie v. DeLaney*, 158 Calz. 212, 645 P.2d 887 (1982). In *Bonnie*, an agreement for the sale of a house provided that the buyer could cancel the agreement if the buyer "cannot qualify for a 30-year mortgage loan for 90% of the sales price" with any of several banks listed in the agreement. *Id.* at 213, 645 P.2d at 888. In enforcing the agreement against the seller, the court distinguished *Atco Corp.* on the ground that the word "cannot" referred to the buyer's *ability* to obtain a loan rather than to his *desire*. Because his ability to obtain a loan was partly controlled by events and decisions outside his control, the promises in the sale agreement were nonillusory and binding. *Id.* at 214-15, 645 P.2d at 889-91.

In-depth analysis of *Bonnie*

The light analysis in the first sample paragraph in this subsection quickly establishes noncontroversial points without weighing the reader down with unnecessary detail. The more detailed analysis in the second and third sample paragraphs provides the reader with a fuller understanding of a specific legal doctrine, the illusory promise, thus creating a solid legal foundation for the fact analysis that will follow. In some discussions, the in-depth analysis may explore such things as the legislative history of a statute or general policy considerations.

You must strike an effective balance between light and in-depth analyses to achieve the dual goals of clarity and conciseness. Unless the issue is extremely simple, if you use only light analysis to discuss or argue a point, you may not define the applicable legal principles with sufficient clarity to permit thoughtful fact analysis. On the other hand, if you use in-depth analysis excessively, you may cause the reader to grow weary and to lose sight of the general legal theory while wandering endlessly among individual cases.

To help strike this balance, you can use citations with parenthetic explanations as a middle ground between light and in-depth analyses. For example, the following passage uses parenthetic explanations to explain how the cited authorities support the proposition for which they are cited:

> In other decisions, Arizona courts have assumed that the statute of frauds may be mitigated to protect a party's reliance on the promise to perform, but they have refused to apply the doctrine because the normal requirements of estoppel were not satisfied. *E.g., Trollope v. Koerner,* 106 Ariz. 10, 17, 18, 470 P.2d 91, 98-99 (1970) (insufficient reliance); *Mac Enterprises v. Del E. Webb Development Co.,* 132 Ariz. 331, 336, 645 P.2d 1245, 1250 (Ct. App. 1982) (no promise).

The brief reference to facts or holdings in the parentheses following the citations provides helpful information for the reader. A full paragraph of in-depth analysis of each case, on the other hand, would simply distract from the fuller discussion of the cases that are more nearly on point.

Another example uses a parenthetic explanation to state the holding of nonbinding case law from another jurisdiction:

> The Arizona Statute of Frauds applies to ". . . an agreement which is not to be performed within one year from the making thereof." Ariz. Rev. Stat. Ann. §44-101(5) (1967) (copy of full text attached). The statute probably applies to any employment contract with a fixed term that exceeds one year without qualification. *See, e.g., Waddell v. White,* 51 Ariz. 526, 539-40, 78 P.2d 490, 495-96 (1938). *But cf. Doyle v. Dixon,* 97 Mass. 208 (1867) (holding that death of promisor could result in early full performance of promise not to compete for five years). Williams and Kramer agreed that their employment contract would remain in effect unconditionally for two years; therefore, it falls within the statute.

In this example, the author of the memorandum cited *Doyle* to help define the limits of the proposition for which *Waddell* is cited as affirmative support. *Doyle* does not warrant a full paragraph of in-depth analysis because it is a century-old case that interprets a different state's statute of frauds in a different factual context. The parenthetic explanation, however, takes up little space and helpfully warns of a possible limitation or counterargument to the main proposition.

b. Incomplete Syllogisms

So far, this section has discussed depth of analysis of legal principles. You may apply the same considerations to the complete deductive syllogism of major premise, minor premise, and conclusion. Normally, a memorandum or brief presents even a simple legal argument in a full syllogism with a discussion of the applicable legal rule, an application of the rule to the facts, and a conclusion:

> Under the Uniform Commercial Code (U.C.C.), the term "merchant" includes any person who "deals in goods of the kind." U.C.C. §2-104(1) (1980). Wilson deals in used cars because he regularly buys and sells used cars as an adjunct to his car rental business. Therefore, he is a merchant of used cars under the U.C.C.

Alternatively, particularly if the argument is minor or tangential, you can present it in an incomplete syllogism:

> Wilson is a "merchant" of used cars under the U.C.C. because he regularly buys and sells used cars as an adjunct to his car rental business. *See* U.C.C. §2-104(1) (1990).

A more detailed statement could mention the statutory definition, still without tying it directly to the statutory term "merchant":

> . . . because he regularly buys and sells used cars as an adjunct to his car rental business and thus "deals in goods of the kind." *See* U.C.C. §2-104(1) (1990).

In each of these examples of incomplete syllogisms, the single textual sentence states a conclusion and the facts supporting it. The legal rule that forms the major premise is implicit or incomplete; the reader assumes that the cited authority supplies an abstract rule that permits the conclusion to follow from the facts. In some cases, a brief parenthetic explanation after the citation helps to define the abstract legal rule and to show how the citation supports the fact analysis. With or without such an explanation, you can use this technique to make a minor point without disrupting the flow of the main analysis or distracting the reader's attention from more important discussions of authority.

B. FORM—EFFICIENT ORGANIZATION, SENTENCE STRUCTURE, AND PHRASING

1. Organization

By applying the principles of organization discussed in Chapter 10, you can write more concisely as well as more clearly. With good organization, you can eliminate unnecessary repetition and present ideas efficiently by building each subsection on the foundations laid in the previous ones.

You need not adopt an organizational framework that eliminates all repetition. Indeed, typical formats for office memoranda and briefs contemplate a form of repetition. Using an office memorandum format recommended in Chapter 9, for example, you can

(1) introduce your analysis in a statement of the issues and in brief answers at the beginning of the memorandum,
(2) explore your analysis fully in the discussion, and
(3) summarize your analysis and recommendations in a final conclusion.

In the same memorandum, you would

(1) state all the relevant facts near the beginning of the memorandum and
(2) analyze the facts relating to each issue in each corresponding section of the discussion.

This overlap in the elements of a legal document is not wasteful, particularly if you recognize the distinct purposes of the elements.

Nonetheless, needless repetition within such a framework may add pages without adding clarity. Good organization on all levels should minimize this problem.

2. Sentence Structure and Phrasing

You can often trace verbosity within a sentence to unnecessary repetition, loose verb structure, and expression of implicit information. In such sentences, the words expressing useful ideas are lost among words that convey marginally useful ideas or that simply connect substantive ideas to one another.[14] In editing surplus words from your writing, however, you must not shave your writing so close that you sacrifice clarity.

a. Repetition

As discussed in the previous section, some repetition is built into the general format of a legal document. Moreover, even at the level of words

---

14. Richard Wydick recommends that writers maximize the ratio of "working words" to "glue words" in a sentence. Richard C. Wydick, Plain English for Lawyers 7-21 (2d ed. 1985).

and phrases, carefully planned repetition may be justified on rare occasions as a guide to complex sentence structure or as a means of gaining unusual emphasis:

Jack Bailey has declared his guilt with his own actions. He declared his guilt when he fled the murder scene on the arrival of neighbors; he declared his guilt when he later tried to conceal the murder weapon; and he declared his guilt today by offering incredible and inconsistent testimony.

However, needless repetition of words or phrases serves only to add words that contribute nothing to the substance of a sentence. Even worse, it may cause the reader to pause and wonder whether the repetitive words are intended to convey slightly different ideas:

Section 24 of the lease is null, void, invalid, completely unenforceable, and of no legal force or effect whatsoever.

With a much shorter, cleaner sentence employing only one of the adjectives, you can precisely convey the intended meaning:

Section 24 of the lease is void.

On the other hand, even closely related terms are not repetitive if they convey meanings that are different in a way that is significant to the analysis. For example, state and federal statutes prohibit various kinds of discrimination based on "race, color, or national origin." Although the classes encompassed by these terms may overlap, they are not identical. Thus, an employer who discriminates against a dark-skinned African-American in favor of a light-skinned African-American arguably discriminates on the basis of color, even though not necessarily on the basis of race or national origin.[15]

b. Verb Structure

You will often add extra words to your sentences when you transform verbs into nouns or use verbs in the passive voice. For example, the author of the following clause added unnecessary bulk to his writing by transforming the verb "objected" into the noun "objection," and substituting "presented" as the verb:

Defense counsel presented an objection to the testimony on the ground that it was inadmissible[16] hearsay.

---

15. See generally Walker v. Secretary of Treasury, I.R.S., 713 F. Supp. 403 (N.D. Ga. 1989).
16. "Inadmissible" is not a superfluous modifier of "hearsay" if one adopts the approach that some testimony to out-of-court statements, although hearsay, is admissible pursuant to exceptions to the general rule.

You add further unnecessary bulk by using the passive voice, adding the words "was" and "by":

∥ An objection to the testimony was presented by defense counsel on the ground that it was inadmissible hearsay.

If you employ the verb "objected" to express the action in active voice, you can eliminate surplus words and lead the reader more directly to the main point:

∥ Defense counsel objected to the testimony on the ground that it was inadmissible hearsay.

c. Implicit Information

The clause following "objected" in the last sentence above reflects a different kind of verbosity: expression of implicit information. You can simply state the ground for objection; you need not expressly characterize it as a "ground":

∥ Defense counsel objected that the testimony was inadmissible hearsay.

Legal writers frequently express implicit information by referring to procedure when defining a substantive legal principle:

∥ If a party proves that a contract requires a performance that would violate a criminal statute, the court will strike down the contract as illegal and unenforceable.

Unless you really intend to emphasize burdens of proof and court procedures, you can convey all the necessary information in fewer words by focusing exclusively on substance:

∥ A contract is illegal and unenforceable if performance of its obligations would violate a criminal statute.

d. Tension Between Clarity and Conciseness

In your quest to eliminate surplus words, you should remain sensitive to the tension between clarity and conciseness, taking care to retain words and phrases that communicate important information. For example, the following sentences reflect each kind of verbosity cited at the beginning of this section:

∥ Robert Jones, who is the plaintiff, brought this action against Mary Smith, the defendant. In this action, Jones filed a complaint that alleges that

Smith committed a breach of the contract of employment between Smith ‖
and Jones.

You can combine these sentences into a single, much more concise sentence. At the margin, however, further revisions for conciseness may sacrifice important information, depending on your intended connotation and emphasis.

An initial revision reduces the number of words from 37 to 17, arguably without sacrificing clarity on any level:

Plaintiff Robert Jones brought this action against Defendant Mary Smith, ‖
alleging that Smith breached their employment contract.

Among other things, this revision eliminates the repetition of "this action," recognizes that the filing of a complaint is implicit in other phrases, uses "breached" as a direct verb, and replaces wordy clauses and phrases such as "who is the plaintiff" and "between Smith and Jones" with single but equally precise words.

By treating "Plaintiff" and "Defendant" as implicit, and by replacing "brought this action" with "sued," you can trim another five words from the sentence:

Robert Jones sued Mary Smith, alleging that Smith breached their em- ‖
ployment contract.

This revision, however, may achieve conciseness at the expense of other considerations of style. To many readers, "sued" carries the negative connotation of harassing litigation; therefore, counsel for Jones might prefer the softer, though less concise, phrase "brought this action." Also, if you wish to refer to the parties subsequently only as "Plaintiff" and "Defendant" or only as "Jones" and "Smith," you may prefer to emphasize the relationship of each party's name with his or her procedural title by initially using the full phrases "Plaintiff Robert Jones," and "Defendant Mary Smith."

If you do not object to the last revision above, you could trim one more word from the sentence and achieve a more direct flow by eliminating the reference to "alleging":

Robert Jones sued Mary Smith for breach of their employment contract. ‖

Sticklers for precision, however, might argue that you should use the preposition "for" to introduce a description of the requested relief rather than the ground for liability.

To summarize, revisions for conciseness are matters of judgment that require sensitivity to considerations of emphasis, precision, connotation, and other elements of clarity.

E X E R C I S E   1 1 - 7

1. *Verbosity*

Rewrite the following sentence to make it more direct and concise.

The Federal Rules of Civil Procedure, Rule 26(c), provides that the issuance of protective orders to the effect that certain matters ought not to be inquired into in the course of discovery is within the authorization of the court.

2. *Advanced Exercise*

Analyze the style problems in the following sentence, identify the nature of each problem, and rewrite the sentence to make it clearer and more concise.

With respect to time, the right to compensation for an injury, under the workmen's compensation acts is governed, in the absence of any provision to the contrary, by the law in force at the time of the occurrence of such injury.

Am. Jur. 2d Workmen's Compensation §89, at 772 (1976).

III. PRESENTATION OF AUTHORITY, USE OF QUOTATIONS, AND CITATION FORM

A. PRESENTATION OF AUTHORITY

1. Subordination of Citations

Authors of law journal articles or treatises can gracefully insert case names at the beginning or in the middle of textual sentences, because they customarily drop the remainder of the citations to footnotes. According to current convention, however, most citations in briefs and in office memoranda remain in the text. Consequently, when drafting a brief or an office memorandum, you should avoid citing to authority in full at the beginning or in the middle of a textual sentence. Instead, unless you intend to emphasize a particularly significant case name and citation, you should subordinate the citation to a separate citation sentence, permitting you to reserve the main text for the ideas for which the authority is cited.

Unfortunately, many legal writers draw their readers' attention first to the authority, and only then to the proposition for which the authority is cited:

In *Tucson Medical Center v. Zoslow,* 147 Ariz. 612, 614, 712 P.2d 459, 461 (Ct. App. 1985), the court held that, in the absence of an express restriction by contract or statute, a tenant generally has the unrestricted right to ‖ assign or sublet.

Because the case citation has no great independent significance in this example, you could improve this passage by moving the citation to a separate citation sentence. If you do not wish to emphasize the identity of the authoring court, you can make the strongest substantive statement by presenting the legal proposition as an unqualified statement of truth that at least one court has incidentally discovered:

In the absence of an express restriction by contract or statute, a tenant ‖ generally has the unrestricted right to assign or sublet. *E.g., Tucson Medical* ‖ *Center v. Zoslow,* 147 Ariz. 612, 614, 712 P.2d 459, 461 (Ct. App. 1985). ‖

On the other hand, if the decisions of the authoring court are controlling on the court adjudicating the current dispute, you may want to identify the authoring court in the textual sentence, while continuing to subordinate the case name and the rest of the citation:

The Arizona Court of Appeals has held that, in the absence of an express ‖ restriction by contract or statute, a tenant generally has the unrestricted ‖ right to assign or sublet. *Tucson Medical Center v. Zoslow,* 147 Ariz. 612, ‖ 614, 712 P.2d 459, 461 (Ct. App. 1985).

On rare occasions, you might appropriately retain a full citation to authority in a textual sentence if the citation itself has such great independent significance that it warrants such emphasis:

In *Brown v. Board of Education,* 347 U.S. 483 (1954), the Supreme ‖ Court unanimously held that segregated public school systems violate ‖ the equal protection guarantee of the fourteenth amendment.

In this example, the case name, the identity of the authoring court, and even the date of the decision all trigger recognition in most readers. Alternatively, you could refer to the instantly recognizable case name in the textual sentence, saving the remainder of the citation for a separate citation sentence:

In *Brown v. Board of Education,* the Supreme Court unanimously held that ‖ segregated public school systems violate the Equal Protection guarantee of ‖ the fourteenth amendment. 347 U.S. 483 (1954). ‖

This form, however, is unconventional if it represents the initial citation to this authority in the memorandum or the brief.

Subordination of citations is even more important in the presentation of an in-depth case analysis. The following introduction to the analysis of a fictitious case not only inappropriately begins a textual sentence with a full citation, it also begins exploring the details of the case without first explaining generally why the case warrants in-depth analysis:

> In *Bonnie v. DeLaney,* 158 Calz. 212, 645 P.2d 887 (1982), an agreement for the sale of a house provided that the buyer could cancel the agreement if the buyer "cannot qualify for a 30-year mortgage loan for 90% of the sales price" with any of several banks listed in the agreement. *Id.* at 213, 645 P.2d at 888. In enforcing the agreement against the seller, the court distinguished . . .

The reader trudges through such a passage with little interest and at least moderate irritation, because he doesn't discover the point of the case until the end of the passage. A series of such paragraphs presenting a laundry list of cases can produce a rambling effect that causes the reader to lose track of the principles that the cases are meant to illustrate.

You can greatly improve the passage quoted above by introducing it with an overview of the point that the in-depth case analysis will illustrate:

> On the other hand, even if a promise leaves open the possibility that the promisor will escape obligation, the promise is valid if the promisor does not have complete control over the events upon which the promisor's obligation is conditioned. *See Bonnie v. DeLaney,* 158 Calz. 212, 645 P.2d 887 (1982). In *Bonnie,* an agreement for the sale of a house provided that the buyer could cancel the agreement if the buyer "cannot qualify for a 30-year mortgage loan for 90% of the sales price" with any of several banks listed in the agreement. *Id.* at 213, 645 P.2d at 888. In enforcing the agreement against the seller, the court distinguished . . .

The preceding passage uses a topic sentence to present an overview of the case analysis. In more complex analyses, you might precede the case analysis with a paragraph that provides the appropriate overview in two or more sentences.

This method of presenting authority enables you to introduce the case citation in a separate citation sentence and to begin the in-depth case analysis with an unobtrusive, short-form reference to the case name:

> . . . is conditioned. *See Bonnie v. DeLaney,* 158 Calz. 212, 645 P.2d 887 (1982). In *Bonnie,* . . .

Moreover, if you intend to analyze several cases on the same issue, you can use the topic sentence or overview paragraph to help you to express your synthesis of the case law. Synthesis of authority is a critical component of legal method, warranting further exploration of writing techniques that effectively display synthesis.

2. Synthesis of Case Law

Many legal rules are the products of synthesis of two or more legal authorities. In an office memorandum or a brief, you should present such legal rules with clear guides to your synthesis rather than with independent and unconnected analyses of the authorities.

For example, suppose that a section of an office memorandum analyzes the issue whether a federal civil rights act addresses employment discrimination against a person because he is French Canadian. The following sample passage presents a "laundry list" of case briefs. It is ineffective because it provides insufficient guidance to the author's synthesis, or perhaps because it betrays the author's failure to synthesize:

I. RACIAL CLASSIFICATIONS UNDER SECTION 1981

Section 1981 of title 42 of the United States Code provides in part as follows:

All persons within the jurisdiction of the United States shall have the same right in every State and Territory to make and enforce contracts . . . as is enjoyed by white citizens . . .

General statutory rules

In *Runyon v. McCrary*, 427 U.S. 160 (1976), African-American applicants to private, commercially operated, nonsectarian schools sued the schools through their parents. They alleged that the schools refused to admit them because of their race in violation of section 1981. A divided Supreme Court ruled that the school's discriminatory admissions policy violated the statute. It held that the statute applied to private contracts and that application of the statute to the school's admissions policy did not infringe upon the constitutional interests of the students or their parents in association, privacy, and parental control.

In-depth analysis without topic sentence to express an overview

In *McDonald v. Santa Fe Trail Transportation Co.*, 427 U.S. 273 (1976), white employees sued their employer and their union under section 1981 and Title VII of the Civil Rights Act of 1964. They alleged that their discharge for misappropriation of property was racially motivated because an African-American employee similarly charged was not dismissed. The Supreme Court acknowledged that the "immediate impetus" for the 1866 predecessor to section 1981 was "the necessity for further relief of the constitutionally emancipated former Negro slaves." *Id.* at 289. Nonetheless, on the strength of legislative history indicating that the bill would protect all races, the Supreme Court held that section 1981 imposes liability for discrimination aimed at any race, including whites. *Id.* at 289-96.

In-depth analysis without topic sentence to express overview or synthesis

In-depth analysis without topic sentence to express overview or synthesis

In *St. Francis College v. Al-Khazraji,* 481 U.S. 604 (1987), a college professor of Arab ancestry sued his employer under section 1981 and other civil rights statutes. He alleged that the denial of his application for tenure was racially motivated because similarly situated Caucasians fared better in the tenure process. The trial court dismissed the section 1981 claim on the ground that it failed to state a claim of race discrimination because Arabs were not a race distinct from Caucasians. *Id.* at 606. The Court of Appeals reversed and remanded for further proceedings, and the Supreme Court affirmed the decision of the Court of Appeals.

The Supreme Court held that scientific knowledge and cultural attitudes at the time of enactment of the 1866 and 1870 predecessors to section 1981 shaped the racial classifications addressed by the statute. Legislative history and popular dictionary and encyclopedic sources of the era reflect the view that groups with relatively narrowly defined ancestral roots and ethnic characteristics, such as "Germans," "Greeks," "Jews," and "Gypsies," represent distinct races. The Supreme Court concluded that Arabs would be viewed as a separate race under those standards and that section 1981 therefore addresses discrimination based on Arab ancestry. *Id.* at 610-13.

In our case . . .

The preceding passage does not give adequate notice of the points or issues that each case brief is intended to illustrate, nor does it explain how the authorities relate to one another. The following passage provides a better guide to the author's synthesis. It uses a transition sentence or paragraph to provide a preview of the point illustrated by each case brief and to explain how each authority relates to previously analyzed authorities. The passage below also flows more coherently because it limits its in-depth analysis to the announced topic of the section and refers only tersely to other potential problems in the scope of the statute.

I. RACIAL CLASSIFICATIONS UNDER SECTION 1981

Federal civil rights legislation prohibits certain kinds of racial discrimination in contractual relations:

Statutory language

> All persons within the jurisdiction of the United States shall have the same right in every State and Territory to make and enforce contracts . . . . as is enjoyed by white citizens . . .

42 U.S.C. §1981 (1988).

As suggested by the statutory reference to rights "enjoyed by white citizens," the "immediate impetus" for the 1866 predecessor to section 1981 was "the necessity for further relief of the constitutionally emancipated former Negro slaves." *McDonald v. Santa Fe Trail Transportation Co.*, 427 U.S. 273, 289 (1976). Consequently, section 1981 applies most clearly to race discrimination against African-Americans. *See, e.g., Runyon v. McCrary*, 427 U.S. 160 (1976).

General guides from case law interpreting the statute

Section 1981's prohibition of discrimination, however, extends beyond discrimination against African-Americans and applies more generally to discrimination based on any racial classification. *McDonald v. Santa Fe Trail Transportation Co.*, 427 U.S. 273 (1976). In *McDonald*, white employees sued their employer and their union under section 1981 and Title VII of the Civil Rights Act of 1964. They alleged that their discharge for misappropriation of property was racially motivated because an African-American employee similarly charged was not dismissed. On the strength of legislative history indicating that the bill would protect all races, the Supreme Court held that section 1981 imposes liability for discrimination against members of any race, including whites. *Id.* at 289-96.

Topic sentence introducing in-depth analysis of *McDonald*

McDonald did not attempt to identify all the racial classifications protected under section 1981. More recently, the Supreme Court held that the applicable classifications are not those recognized by many contemporary scientific theories, but are the narrower and more numerous classifications generally recognized when Congress enacted the predecessors to section 1981. *St. Francis College v. Al-Khazraji*, 481 U.S. 604 (1987).

Transition paragraph expressing (1) relationship of *McDonald* to *St. Francis* and (2) overview of *St. Francis*

In *St. Francis*, a college professor of Arab ancestry sued his employer under section 1981 and other civil rights statutes. He alleged that the denial of his application for tenure was racially motivated because similarly situated Caucasians fared better in the tenure process. The trial court dismissed the section 1981 claim on the ground that it failed to state a claim of race discrimination because Arabs were not a race distinct from Caucasians. *Id.* at 606. The Court of Appeals reversed and remanded for further proceedings, and the Supreme Court affirmed the decision of the Court of Appeals.

In-depth analysis of *St. Francis*

The Supreme Court held that scientific knowledge and cultural attitudes at the time of enactment

> of the 1866 and 1870 predecessors to section 1981 shaped the racial classifications addressed by the statute. Legislative history and popular dictionary and encyclopedic sources of the era reflect the view that groups with relatively narrowly defined ancestral roots and ethnic characteristics, such as "Germans," "Greeks," "Jews," and "Gypsies," represent distinct races. The Supreme Court concluded that Arabs would be viewed as a separate race under those standards and that section 1981 therefore addresses discrimination based on Arab ancestry. *Id.* at 610-13.
>
> In our case . . .

The two passages quoted above illustrate the parallels between effective law school study techniques and techniques for preparing documents in a law office. The first passage resembles one of a series of only loosely connected case briefs, such as those you might prepare for class discussion. The case briefs contain useful information, but you can more effectively apply that information to an examination problem if you synthesize the cases and then reorganize them in a course outline that emphasizes controlling principles and that subordinates the discussion of cases to the role of illustrating those principles.

In a law office, you will use a similar analytic process in presenting case law in a memorandum or brief. As illustrated in the second passage above, topic sentences or paragraphs introducing each case discussion emphasize principles and often act as transitions that convey case syntheses. The detailed discussion of each case simply illustrates a principle or qualification to a principle that you have already identified in a topic sentence. You should construct such a topic sentence or paragraph to introduce each in-depth case analysis. Your reader can then make her way through the series of individual case briefs without losing sight of the broader outlines of the analysis.

In some analyses, you can state an overview of the complete synthesis in a single introductory sentence or paragraph rather than set it forth incrementally in the topic sentences of several paragraphs. For example, the third paragraph in the following passage from an office memorandum provides a synthesized overview of two cases that are subsequently discussed in detail:

> Federal civil rights legislation imposes liability for deprivation of constitutional rights by agents of the state:

General statutory rules

> Every person who, under color of [state law], subjects . . . any citizen of the United States . . . to the deprivation of any rights . . . secured by the Constitution and laws, shall be liable to the party injured. . . .
>
> 42 U.S.C. §1983 (1982).

Although section 1983 does not expressly limit its remedies, it implicitly incorporates a variety of common law immunity defenses. *City of Newport v. Fact Concerts, Inc.,* 453 U.S. 247, 258 (1981). A state judge, for example, is absolutely immune from liability for money damages even for allegedly unconstitutional judicial acts taken within the judge's subject matter jurisdiction. *Stump v. Sparkman,* 435 U.S. 349 (1978). This immunity defense protects the independence of the judiciary by encouraging judges to make controversial decisions to the best of their abilities, uninhibited by the fear of suit. *See id.* at 355-56, 363.

> General immunity rules from interpretive case law

Not all work-related tasks performed by a judge are judicial functions covered by absolute immunity. For example, a judge's hiring or firing a judicial employee may be a purely administrative act to which absolute immunity does not apply. *See, e.g., McMillan v. Svetanoff,* 793 F.2d 149 (7th Cir. 1986). In the Seventh Circuit, a judge's action relating to personnel is "judicial" rather than purely "administrative" only if the action implicates the judicial decisionmaking process that the immunity defense is designed to protect. *Compare id.* (holding that firing court reporter was an administrative act unprotected by absolute immunity) *with Forrester v. White,* 792 F.2d 647 (7th Cir. 1986) (holding that firing probation officer was judicial function protected by absolute immunity).[17]

> Specific immunity rules from case law

> Synthesis of *McMillan* with *Forrester*

In *McMillan,* a newly elected trial judge discharged his entire courtroom staff upon taking office and rehired only one of the dismissed employees. A discharged court reporter sued the judge under section 1983 and a related statute. She alleged that the judge had fired her because of her race and her political affiliation, in violation of her constitutional rights under the first and fourteenth amendments. The Seventh Circuit characterized the function of hiring and firing employees as "typically an administrative task." 793 F.2d at 155. It concluded that the act of firing a court reporter did not implicate the judicial decisionmaking process, because it did not involve judicial discretion requiring the exercise of the judge's "education, training, and experience in the law."

> In-depth analysis of *McMillan*

---

17. Two years after the Seventh Circuit issued its decision in *Forrester,* the United States Supreme Court overruled it. Forrester v. White, 484 U.S. 219 (1988). However, if you can imagine the passage in the main text as part of a memorandum written in 1987, it serves well to illustrate the process of synthesis.

In-depth analysis of *Forrester*

Id. at 154-55. The act was therefore unprotected by the defense of absolute immunity.

In contrast, in *Forrester,* the same court approved the defense of absolute immunity for a state appellate judge's allegedly discriminatory demotion and discharge of a juvenile and adult probation officer. 792 F.2d at 648. The probation officer's duties included preparing pre-sentencing reports, recommendations for disposition of juvenile cases, and recommendations for revocation of juvenile and adult probation and parole. *Id.* at 648-49. The information that the probation officer provided "directly implicated the exercise of the judge's discretionary judgment." *Id.* at 657. Thus, maintenance of judicial independence required absolute immunity to protect the judge's ability to demote and discharge the probation officer without fear of suit. *Id.* at 657-58.

In our case . . .

B. QUOTATIONS

1. Selective Use of Quotations

If the interpretation or application of a statute or contract is disputed by the parties, the starting point of your analysis is the actual language of the statute or contract. Accordingly, when presenting such an analysis in a memorandum or brief, you should quote the relevant statutory or contractual provisions.

You should generally quote more sparingly from case law. Supervising attorneys and judges are primarily interested in your original synthesis of case law and your analysis of the facts within the legal framework. They are not impressed by your demonstrated ability to cut and paste page-long passages written by others.

Occasionally, a passage from case law is so clear, concise, powerful, and narrowly tailored to your dispute that paraphrasing cannot improve on it. By quoting such a passage, you obviously will enhance the memorandum or brief. Often, however, a passage from case law will seem out of context if quoted, perhaps because it clashes with your writing style or because its relevant portions are unavoidably intermingled with distracting references to points not relevant to your dispute. In such a case, you can help focus the attention of your reader on important ideas, rather than on sudden shifts in style, by restating the rule or analysis of a case in your own words.

This general admonition against excessive quotation probably applies most strongly to appellate briefs. Most appellate judges or their law clerks have the luxury of sufficient time to study the important cases cited in appellate briefs. Moreover, appellate courts have the power to overrule at least some of the precedent likely to be cited in the briefs. Consequently, appellate judges in particular tend to look for original analysis, including policy analysis, rather than extensive quotation from authorities that a judge or a law clerk can easily secure from the library.

In contrast, busy trial judges preparing for hearings on motions may not have time to study carefully all the important cases cited in the briefs.[18] Additionally, they must follow, and cannot overrule, applicable appellate decisions within their jurisdiction. For both these reasons, some trial judges may appreciate passages in briefs that quote arguably controlling holdings from appellate case law. Similarly, some supervising attorneys ask their law clerks or associates to quote extensively from important case law in office memoranda, presumably because they want to second-guess the writer's analysis of the case law or because they want to determine whether portions of the quoted materials are suitable for quotation in their own briefs.

Still, when you do decide to quote authority in a brief or an office memorandum,

> you need not quote at epic length. Indeed, a sure way to induce skimming is the back-to-back employment of two quotes of more than ten lines each. . . . Select a short helpful quote, and show its application to your case. Give enough to make your point but not so much as to sink your brief from excess weight.[19]

If you believe that a trial judge or supervising attorney might want to read the full text of some statute or case law that is not readily available in her office or chambers, you need not clutter up the body of your document with lengthy quotation. You can simply attach photocopies of the authority as an appendix to your document.[20]

2. Presentation of Block Quotations

a. Basic Techniques

If you quote a substantial portion of any authority, you should set the quoted passage apart in a single-spaced, indented block, without quotation marks other than those that appear within the original quoted text. This blocking technique helps the reader to distinguish the lengthy quotation from the original text. The popular "Bluebook" citation manual requires block quotation only if the quoted passage exceeds 49 words.[21] The visual benefits of blocking, however, are evident in shorter passages. Therefore, you should consider blocking any quotation that runs for more than three lines of copy, even if it contains fewer than 50 words.

The principles stated in Section A above about subordinating citations and introducing case analyses with topic sentences apply equally to block

---

18. See generally Noel Fidel, Some Do's and Don'ts of Motion Writing, Ariz. Bar J., Aug. 1983, at 9.

19. Id. at 10-11.

20. See id.

21. The Bluebook R. 5.1(a) (15th ed. 1991) (published and distributed by the Harvard L. Rev. Ass'n).

quotations. Unless the citation to a block quotation has independent significance, you should relegate it to the end of the quote, or place it at the left-hand margin on a new line below the block. More important, you should introduce the quoted passage with a thesis statement, a substantive overview that summarizes the point that you intend the passage to convey to the reader.

The following passage inappropriately introduces a block quotation of a statutory provision with a citation that has little independent significance. Moreover, the absence of a substantive introduction induced the writer to convey the point of the quote with distracting underlining:

> Title 42 U.S.C. §2000e-2(a)(1) provides:
>
> It shall be an <u>unlawful</u> employment practice for an employer—
> (1) to fail or refuse to hire or to discharge any individual, or otherwise <u>to discriminate against any individual</u> with respect to his compensation, terms, conditions, or privileges of employment, <u>because of such individual's</u> race, color, religion, <u>sex</u> or national origin . . .

Using a substantive introduction, you could revise this passage to subordinate the citation, provide the reader with helpful orientation, and minimize the need for underlining as a means of emphasis:

> Federal law prohibits sex discrimination in employment:
>
> It shall be an unlawful employment practice for an employer—
> (1) to fail or refuse to hire or to discharge any individual, or otherwise to discriminate against any individual with respect to his compensation, terms, conditions, or privileges of employment, because of such individual's race, color, religion, sex or national origin . . .
>
> 42 U.S.C. §2000e-2(a)(1) (1988) [Title VII §703(a)(1)].

Alternatively, you may want to acknowledge that the name of the act in this example is familiar to most lawyers and therefore has independent significance. You can refer to the act in the introduction, while continuing to subordinate the code citation:

> Title VII of the Civil Rights Act of 1964 makes it unlawful for an employer to engage in sex discrimination:
>
> It shall be an unlawful employment practice for an employer—
> (1) to fail or refuse . . .
>
> 42 U.S.C. §2000e-2(a)(1) (1988) [Title VII §703(a)(1)].

Finally, if you want to refer repeatedly to this section of the statute throughout your brief or memorandum, you can emphasize the Act's section number, which is more familiar to most lawyers than the code number, by referring to it in the introduction:

Section 703(a) of Title VII of the Civil Rights Act of 1964 makes it unlawful for an employer to engage in sex discrimination:

> It shall be an unlawful employment practice for an employer—
>   (1) to fail or refuse . . .

42 U.S.C. §2000e-2(a)(1) (1988). Section 703(a) identifies two principal elements of unlawful discrimination . . .

Even after judicious editing, you may find that a quoted passage is exceptionally long or complex. Particularly if the quotation addresses multiple themes, you can lead the reader through such material by breaking the quotation into parts and preceding each part with a substantive introduction:

> Under the Uniform Commercial Code, a response to an offer may be an acceptance even though it varies the terms of the offer:

Introduction to U.C.C. §2-207(1)

>> A definite and seasonable expression of acceptance or a written confirmation which is sent within a reasonable time operates as an acceptance even though it states terms additional to or different from those offered or agreed upon . . .

Text of U.C.C. §2-207(1)

> U.C.C. §2-207(1) (1990). However, a proviso to the same statute provides that the offeree may avoid acceptance and state a counteroffer if "acceptance is expressly made conditional on assent to the additional or different terms." *Id.*

Introduction to proviso to U.C.C. §2-207(1)

Text of proviso

> If the original offeree's response is an acceptance, the statute provides that some of the new terms in the acceptance may be added to the contract without the express assent of the original offeror:

Introduction to U.C.C. §2-207(2)

>> The additional terms are to be construed as proposals for addition to the contract. Between merchants such terms become part of the contract unless:
>>   (a) The offer expressly limits acceptance to the terms of the offer;
>>   (b) they materially alter it; or
>>   (c) notification of objection to them has already been given or is given within a reasonable time after notice of them is received.

Text of U.C.C. §2-207(2)

U.C.C. §2-207(2) (1990).

b. Special Techniques for Advocacy

You can use a substantive introduction to a block quotation as effective preliminary advocacy in a brief. Your introduction will emphasize the point of the quote by presenting it in summary form. Indeed, because some judges tend to skim over block quotations, your substantive introduction may be the only statement of the point that the judge reads.

More important, quotations from contracts, statutes, or case law are often reasonably subject to varying interpretations, and a substantive introduction can encourage the reader to interpret the quoted passage in a favorable manner. For example, the following passage from an employment contract lists several grounds for discharging an employee, but it doesn't expressly state whether the list is exclusive:

> XI. Ajax Co. reserves the right to discharge any employee who
> (1) fails to perform satisfactorily,
> (2) commits gross insubordination, or
> (3) commits a criminal act on the work site.

Assuming that an employee hired under this contract is employed for an indefinite term, the traditional common law at-will rule would permit the employer to discharge the employee for any reason if the contractual list of grounds for discharge is not intended to be exclusive. On the other hand, if this section of the contract is interpreted to include an implicit promise by the employer to refrain from discharging an employee except for the listed reasons, then the contract would override the otherwise applicable common law rule.

When quoting this passage in the argument section of the brief for either the employer or a discharged employee, you will achieve the least impact with a stock introduction such as:

> Section XI of the Employment Contract provides, in relevant part, as follows:

Instead, as counsel for the discharged employee, you should use an argumentative introductory sentence to characterize the provision as a restriction on the employer's freedom to terminate the employment contract:

> The Employment Contract expressly identifies only three grounds for discharge, all relating to poor performance or serious misconduct:
>
> XI. Ajax Co. reserves the right to discharge any employee who
> (1) fails to perform satisfactorily,
> (2) commits gross insubordination, or
> (3) commits a criminal act on the work site.
>
> Employment Contract §XI. The parties obviously intended this list to be the exclusive . . .

Conversely, as counsel for the employer, you can use an argumentative introduction to characterize the provision as an affirmation of the employer's common law freedom to terminate:

> No provision of the contract expressly limits Ajax Co.'s common law right to discharge any employee at Ajax's will. Indeed, the only provision addressing termination selects three particularly strong grounds for illustration and emphasis:
>
> > XI. Ajax Co. reserves the right to discharge any employee who
> > (1) fails to perform satisfactorily,
> > (2) commits gross insubordination, or
> > (3) commits a criminal act on the work site.
>
> Employment Contract §XI.
> Vargas argues that the parties intended this list to be exclusive. On the contrary . . .

You can always begin arguing for a favorable interpretation after neutrally presenting the quoted passage. However, the reader is more likely to adopt your proposed interpretation if a substantive introduction biases him toward the interpretation before he reads the quoted passage.

═══════ E X E R C I S E   1 1 - 8 ═══════

Rewrite the following passage to subordinate citations and to introduce the block quotation with a brief substantive overview. You may assume that the case names are not sufficiently independently significant to warrant emphasis in textual sentences.

IV. DISCUSSION

A. Liability for Discrimination under Section 1981

• • • •

1. First Amendment Defense

Lilly Prep School has asserted in a letter to our client that it has a first amendment right to teach and practice racial segregation in its classrooms. We expect it to raise this as a defense in any lawsuit that we file.

In *NAACP v. Alabama*, 357 U.S. 449 (1958), the Supreme Court recognized a first amendment right "to engage in association for the advancement of beliefs and ideas." *Id.* at 460. In *Runyon v. McCrary*, 427 U.S. 160 (1976), however, the Court stated:

> From this principle it may be assumed that parents have a First Amendment right to send their children to educational institutions that promote the belief that racial segregation is desirable, and that the children have an equal right

to attend such institutions. But it does not follow that the *practice* of excluding racial minorities from such institutions is also protected by the same principle.

Id. at 176.

C. CITATION FORM

You must cite to authority in a manner that clearly and concisely identifies the source of the authority and that helps the reader find the authority in a library. A widely accepted citation form that meets these goals is presented in The Bluebook, A Uniform System of Citation, a citation manual published and distributed by the Harvard Law Review Association.

Below is a summary of citation form, most of it taken from the Bluebook, appropriate for legal memoranda and briefs. You may substitute underscoring for italics in any of the examples.

1. Constitutions and Codes

When citing to a specific constitutional provision, you should refer to the article or amendment number and, if appropriate, to a section number:

> U.S. Const. art. III, §1.
> U.S. Const. amend. XIV.
> Ariz. Const. art. VI, §1.

The first citation above refers to section 1 of article III of the United States Constitution. The second citation refers to the fourteenth amendment to that constitution. The third citation refers to section 1 of article VI of the Arizona Constitution.

You should cite to the title and section numbers of a codified statute:

> 42 U.S.C. §1983.
> Ariz. Rev. Stat. Ann. §47-2207.

The first citation above refers to section 1983 in title 42 of the official United States Code. The second refers to section 2207 of title 47 of the Arizona Revised Statutes Annotated, the title that encompasses Arizona's commercial code. Interestingly, almost all practicing attorneys in Arizona depart from the Bluebook by using the shortened abbreviation "A.R.S." when citing to the Arizona Revised Statutes Ann.

If you believe that the information will be useful to your reader, you should also include the date of publication of a statute:

> 42 U.S.C. §1983 (1988).
> 42 U.S.C. §1981a (1988 ed., Supp. III 1991).[22]

---

22. The Bluebook provides that the year is a mandatory part of the citation. The Bluebook R. 12.3, 12.3.2 (15th ed. 1991) (published and distributed by the Harvard L. Rev. Ass'n).

2. Case Law

a. Basic Citation Form

When citing to case law, you should specify the case name, the volume and page of the reporter, the court, and the year of decision:

Bell v. United States, 349 U.S. 81 (1955).
Bundy v. Jackson, 641 F.2d 934 (D.C. Cir. 1981).
Wagenseller v. Scottsdale Memorial Hospital, 710 P.2d 1025 (Ariz. 1985).
Tucson Medical Center v. Zoslow, 712 P.2d 459 (Ariz. Ct. App. 1985).

The first case cited above is a decision of the United States Supreme Court, found at page 81 of volume 349 of the official United States Reporter. The second is a decision of the District of Columbia Circuit of the United States Court of Appeals, found at page 934 of volume 641 of the federal reporter. The third is a decision of the Arizona Supreme Court, found at page 1025 of volume 710 of West Publishing Company's unofficial regional Pacific Reporter, second series. Because that regional reporter compiles decisions from several western states, the citation identifies the state of the deciding court with the abbreviation "Ariz." within the parentheses. The fourth citation also includes the notation "Ct. App." within the parentheses to identify the source of the authority as the Arizona Court of Appeals. The corresponding notation, "S. Ct." was unnecessary in the third citation, because a decision with the designation "Ariz." is assumed to be a decision of the Arizona Supreme Court unless the citation specifies otherwise.

Your case citation should include any relevant subsequent history:

Scott v. Sears, Roebuck & Co., 605 F. Supp. 1047 (N.D. Ill. 1985), *aff'd,* 798 F.2d 210 (7th Cir. 1986).

In the example above, the author of a memorandum has cited to a decision of the United States District Court for the Northern District of Illinois to support a proposition. She has noted in her citation that the United States Court of Appeals for the Seventh Circuit affirmed the district court's decision. We may assume that she cited primarily to the district court's opinion because it included some language or reasoning not expressed in the appellate court's opinion; otherwise, she could have cited directly to the appellate court's opinion to support her proposition.

b. Parallel Citations

Most judges and attorneys have easy access to library collections that include West's regional reporters, which together compile state court decisions from every state. On the other hand, many law library collections do not include the official reporters for states other than the state in which the library is located. For example, the central library for Division 1 of the Arizona Court of Appeals might offer all the regional reporters but only one official state reporter, the Arizona Reports. In addition, several copies of the official Arizona Reports and the regional Pacific Reports might be distributed throughout the court building, with each judge's chambers having one reporter system or the other on its shelves. Some large law firms may have a similar distribution of resources.

Accordingly, when citing to a decision of an Arizona court in a brief to an Arizona court, you should cite to both the official Arizona Reports and the regional Pacific Reporter:

‖ *Wagenseller v. Scottsdale Memorial Hospital,* 147 Ariz. 370, 710 P.2d 1025 (1985).

The decision cited above appears not only in the regional Pacific Reporter, second series, but also in volume 147 of the official Arizona Reports. Because the citation to the Arizona Reports identifies the state of the deciding court, no further identification of the state is needed within the parentheses.

This parallel citation is useful to the Arizona judge, because either one of the reporters may be within her reach. On the other hand, a citation to the official report of a decision of a Maryland court will not help the judge in Arizona, because she likely does not have easy access to the official Maryland Reports. Instead, you will serve her best by citing only to the regional Atlantic Reporter:

‖ *Kelley v. R.G. Industries,* 497 A.2d 1143 (Md. 1985).

The Bluebook advises legal writers to use parallel citations only in the circumstances described above: citation to a state decision in a brief to a court of that state.[23] However, practical realities suggest at least one other context in which parallel citations may be helpful: citation to a decision of the home state court in an office memorandum to a colleague within a law firm. Because large law firms sometimes have in-house library resources similar to those available to a state judge, the recipient of such a memo may have relatively easy access to either the official reporter or the regional reporter for the state in which the firm is located. Moreover, if the recipient is using the memo to help him prepare a brief to a court within the home state, he will appreciate parallel citations of that state's decisions in the memorandum, because he will need those full citations for the brief.

c. Specific Page Cites

When citing to a passage within a decision, you should cite to the specific page or pages on which the passage appears:

---

23. The Bluebook R. 10.3.1 (15th ed. 1991) (published and distributed by the Harvard L. Rev. Ass'n).

Bundy v. Jackson, 641 F.2d 934, 936-37 (D.C. Cir. 1981).
Wagenseller v. Scottsdale Memorial Hospital, 147 Ariz. 370, 380 n.5, 710
    P.2d 1025, 1035 n.5 (1985).

In the first citation above, the cited passage appears on pages 936 to 937. In the second citation, the cited passage appears in footnote 5, which is found on page 380 of the Arizona Reports and on page 1035 of the Pacific Reporter.

d. Short-Form Citation

If you have fully cited to a case in a legal document, you may refer to it within the subsequent few pages by a shortened case name, volume, reporter, and specific page cite:

Bundy, 641 F.2d at 938.
Wagenseller, 147 Ariz. at 381, 710 P.2d at 1036.

You may use "*Id.*" to refer to the immediately preceding citation, adding new specific page cites if necessary.

Wagenseller, 147 Ariz. at 381, 710 P.2d at 1036.
Id.
Id. at 380, 710 P.2d at 1035.

3. Books and Articles

You should cite to books or treatises by the full name of the author, followed by the title, the edition number if beyond the first edition, and the year of publication:

Richard C. Wydick, *Plain English for Lawyers* (2d ed. 1985).

You should cite to articles in law journals by the full name of the author, title, volume of the journal, page number on which the article begins, and year of publication:

Roscoe Pound, *Common Law and Legislation,* 21 Harv. L. Rev. 383
    (1908).

For either kind of authority, if you refer to a specific passage within the authority, cite to the specific page or pages on which the passage appears:

Richard C. Wydick, *Plain English for Lawyers* 53-55 (2d ed. 1985).
Roscoe Pound, *Common Law and Legislation,* 21 Harv. L. Rev. 383, 387
    (1908).

4. Citation Signals

Citation signals describe the relationship between the cited authority and either (1) the proposition for which it is cited or (2) other authority. An appropriate signal can take the place of a much longer phrase of equivalent prose. For example, the following sentence uses textual clauses after the first citation to describe the relationships among three cited authorities:

> Under the "mailbox rule," an acceptance is effective when mailed if mailing is a means of communication authorized by the offer. *Reserve Insurance Co. v. Duckett*, 238 A.2d 536 (Md. 1968). Another authority to the same effect is *Morrison v. Thoelke*, 155 So. 2d 889 (Fla. App. 1963). A contrary decision is found in *Rhode Island Tool Co. v. United States*, 128 F. Supp. 417 (Ct. Cl. 1955).

By replacing these clauses with the citation signals "*accord*" and "*contra*," you can communicate the same information in a more concise fashion:

> Under the "mailbox rule," an acceptance is effective when mailed if mailing is a means of communication authorized by the offer. *Reserve Insurance Co. v. Duckett*, 238 A.2d 536 (Md. 1968); *accord Morrison v. Thoelke*, 155 So. 2d 889 (Fla. Dist. Ct. App. 1963). *Contra Rhode Island Tool Co. v. United States*, 128 F. Supp. 417 (Ct. Cl. 1955).

Of course, such citation signals can effectively replace ordinary prose only if legal readers and writers agree on the meanings that they convey. The following propositions and examples, most of them inspired by The Bluebook,[24] can serve as a basis for such agreement. Publishers of journals and treatises may adopt different conventions in their use of Roman typeface or italics in case citations; however, in a typewritten document, you should underline or italicize both the case name and the citation signal.

a. No Signal

You should use no signal if the proposition is a quotation or paraphrase from one or more cited authorities:

> In Arizona, an employer is liable for breach of contract if it violates a promise in a company policy manual that has become incorporated into the contract. *Wagenseller v. Scottsdale Memorial Hospital*, 147 Ariz. 370, 381-83, 710 P.2d 1025, 1036-38 (1985); *Leikvold v. Valley View Community Hospital*, 141 Ariz. 544, 546, 688 P.2d 170, 172 (1984).

If a proposition directly quotes or refers to one authority, you may introduce additional direct support with "*accord*":

---

24. See The Bluebook R. 1.2 (15th ed. 1991) (published and distributed by Harvard L. Rev. Assn.).

In addition to establishing the tort of wrongful discharge, the *Wagenseller* court reaffirmed that an employer can be liable in some circumstances for breach of a promise in a company policy manual. *Wagenseller,* 147 Ariz. at 381-83, 710 P.2d at 1036-38; *accord Leikvold v. Valley View Community Hospital,* 141 Ariz. 544, 546, 688 P.2d 170, 172 (1984).

b. *See; See Also; See Generally*

You should use the signal *"see"* if the proposition does not appear in the cited authority but logically follows directly from it, as when you tailor the holding of the cited authority to the facts of your own case:

Johnson will be liable for breach of contract if he discharged Bailey in violation of a promise in the policy manual and if the manual was incorporated into the employment contract. *See Wagenseller v. Scottsdale Memorial Hospital,* 147 Ariz. 370, 381-83, 710 P.2d 1025, 1036-38 (1985).

If a signal applies to more than one citation, you can string the citations in succession after the signal, separating them with semicolons:

. . . into the employment contract. *See Wagenseller v. Scottsdale Memorial Hospital,* 147 Ariz. 370, 381-83, 710 P.2d 1025, 1036-38 (1985); *Leikvold v. Valley View Community Hospital,* 141 Ariz. 544, 546, 688 P.2d 170, 172 (1984).

In such a string, cite to the cases in descending order of strength of authority. Absent that or any other substantive criteria for ordering the citations, cite to cases decided by the same court in reverse chronological order.

In some circumstances, you may exercise discretion to introduce additional supporting authority with *"see also."* This signal is stylistically appropriate for additional authority when you have highlighted other authority by discussing it or otherwise citing it in a prominent manner:

. . . into the employment contract. *See Wagenseller v. Scottsdale Memorial Hospital,* 147 Ariz. 370, 381-83, 710 P.2d 1025, 1036-38 (1985). In *Wagenseller,* an employer . . . . The court held that . . . . *Id.* at 383, 710 P.2d at 1038; *see also Leikvold v. Valley View Community Hospital,* 141 Ariz. 544, 546, 688 P.2d 170, 172 (1984).

Finally, you can use *"see generally"* to signal a more attenuated relationship between the proposition and the supporting authority, as when the authority provides general background information:

The court held that . . . . *Id.* at 383, 710 P.2d at 1038; *see also Leikvold v. Valley View Community Hospital,* 141 Ariz. 544, 546, 688 P.2d 170, 172 (1984); *see generally* Michael A. Di Sabatino, Annotation, Modern status of rule that employer may discharge at-will employee for any reason, Annot., 12 A.L.R. 4th 544 (1982).

c. *E.g.; Accord*

You can use "*e.g.*" to show that the cited authority is simply an example of numerous cases that could support the proposition:

‖ *E.g., Barnes v. Costle,* 561 F.2d 983 (D.C. Cir. 1977).

You may combine "*e.g.*" with other signals:

‖ *See, e.g., Barnes v. Costle,* 561 F.2d 983 (D.C. Cir. 1977).

As an alternative to "*e.g.*," you may cite to multiple authorities without the "*e.g.*" signal:

‖ *Barnes v. Costle,* 561 F.2d 983 (D.C. Cir. 1977); *Bundy v. Jackson,* 641 F.2d 934 (D.C. Cir. 1981).

d. *Cf.; Compare . . . with*

You should use "*cf.*," along with parenthetic explanation, to introduce an authority that supports the stated proposition by analogy or distinction:

‖ The "Proposal to Purchase Real Estate" probably is not an offer to buy a lot within the subdivision, because it does not clearly identify which lot would be purchased. *Cf. Craft v. Elder & Johnston Co.,* 38 N.E.2d 416 (Ohio Ct. App. 1941) (holding that a newspaper ad for indefinite quantity of sewing machines was only an invitation to negotiate); *Lefkowitz v. Great Minneapolis Surplus Store,* 86 N.W.2d 689 (Minn. 1957) (holding that a newspaper ad was an offer because it was unusually specific and definite).

The first citation above supports the proposition by showing how analogous facts in a different context supported the same result as the one proposed. The second citation indirectly supports the proposition by explaining that a different result from the one proposed was justified by materially different facts. To directly compare these two different kinds of support, or to contrast different legal approaches, you can use "*compare . . . with,*" along with parenthetic explanations:

‖ A newspaper ad is an offer only if it is sufficiently complete and definite that it leaves no important terms open for further negotiation. *Compare Craft v. Elder & Johnston Co.,* 38 N.E.2d 416 (Ohio Ct. App. 1941) (newspaper ad for indefinite quantity of sewing machines was only an invitation to negotiate) *with Lefkowitz v. Great Minneapolis Surplus Store,* 86 N.W.2d 689 (Minn. 1957) (newspaper ad was an offer because it was unusually specific and definite).

e. *Contra; But*

You should introduce an authority that opposes your proposition with "*Contra*" or with "*But*" combined with another signal, such as "*But see*" or "*But cf.*":

The "Proposal to Purchase Real Estate" probably is not an offer to buy a lot within the subdivision, because it does not clearly identify which lot would be purchased. *Cf. Craft v. Elder & Johnston Co.,* 38 N.E.2d 416 (Ohio Ct. App. 1941) (newspaper ad for indefinite quantity of sewing machines was only an invitation to negotiate). *But cf. Buntz v. Great Calzona Surplus Store,* 251 Calz. 188 (1957) (newspaper ad may be an offer even though it leaves quantity and description of goods uncertain).

══════ E X E R C I S E 1 1 - 9 ══════

1. *Editing Citations*

Correct the errors in the following citations:

a. Article III, Federal Constitution, sec. 1.

b. U.S. Code, section 1983, title 42.

c. *Crane Co. v. American Standard, Inc.,* C.A.2d, 1973, 490 F.2d 332 at 335 through 336.

d. *Michigan Sugar Co. v. Jebavy Sorenson Orchard Co.,* Mich. Ct. App., 1976, 239 N.W.2d 693, 66 Mich. App. 642. {cited in a brief to a Michigan court}

2. *Constructing Citations*

Express the correct citation for the following authorities in a brief to a Connecticut court:

a. In 1980, the Connecticut Supreme Court issued a decision in *Cherwell-Ralli, Inc. v. Rytman Grain Co.* It appeared in volume 180 of the Connecticut Reporter, the official reporter for the Connecticut Supreme Court, beginning at page 714. It also appeared in volume 433 of the unofficial, regional Atlantic Reporter, second series, beginning at page 984.

b. You wish to cite in full to the decision described in *a* above at page 716 of the official reporter and page 986 of the unofficial reporter. After an additional sentence of text, you wish to cite to the same authority at page 715 of the official reporter and page 985 of the unofficial reporter. No other citations have intervened.

c. You wish to cite to the decision described in *a* above at page 717 of the official reporter and page 987 of the unofficial reporter. You last cited to this authority in the previous page of your document, as described in *b* above; since then, several citations to other authorities have intervened.

IV. REVIEW AND REVISION

To polish your writing, you must critically review and revise early drafts. The need for revision is particularly evident in first drafts dictated into a tape recorder. Moreover, you may need to revise successive drafts several times to produce the best possible final document.

To critically review and revise your own writing, you must approach writing analytically rather than purely intuitively: You must become sufficiently familiar with style problems that you can spot them in your own writing, even when the familiarity of your own prose tends to make you comfortable. You can best develop these editing skills by studying writing style in books or workshops, by reviewing and critiquing your own work and that of others, and by asking others to review and critique your writing.

Unfortunately, time pressures and limits on the client's resources will sometimes compel you to produce a final draft after only one or two opportunities for revision. The minimally acceptable level of review and revision is easily stated: At the very least, you must proofread your first draft and make necessary changes, particularly if you have dictated the draft. Every judge has a horror story about an atrociously written brief, one that obviously was dictated and never proofread. No limitation on time or resources justifies such shoddy work.

The appropriate level of review and revision beyond the minimum is a matter of priorities and economics. A client with ample resources and with a great deal at stake in an important pretrial motion or appeal might expect its legal counsel to spare no expense in writing the best possible brief. You and your colleagues undoubtedly would begin work on the brief as early as possible, subject it to particularly critical review, and polish it through many drafts.

In all but unusual cases, however, you would waste your client's money by spending as much time polishing a preliminary office memorandum or a letter to the client. Such a document should be clear, complete, and concise, but limits on resources may preclude more than one or two rewritings. Moreover, even if you ordinarily avoid procrastination, you will occasionally be stuck with an emergency "rush job" that leaves you little time for revision.

Consequently, you should strive to produce the best possible written product on the first draft. You can do this by learning to avoid style problems common to your writing and by devoting appropriate attention to the prewriting stage.

Ironically, to develop the ability to avoid common style problems on the first draft, you must identify and analyze your writing habits by initially devoting extra time and attention to multiple drafts. Perhaps with the aid of a colleague or a writing manual, you will gradually become sufficiently conscious of your writing problems and their solutions that you can begin to avoid those problems on first or second drafts, reducing the need for substantial editing.

For example, one summer associate in a major law firm learned from a writing consultant that he tended to overuse the passive, abstract verb form "there is." He resolved to use his word processing program to highlight this and related phrases in his first drafts, to revise the highlighted passages on second drafts, and eventually to become sufficiently sensitive to the problem to avoid it on first drafts.

You can further minimize the need for redrafting, and thus save time in the long run, by carefully formulating and organizing your analysis before beginning to write. You should prepare an outline of your document and consider discussing the outline with your supervising attorney or a peer. Because most people are less articulate when speaking than when writing, a careful outline is particularly important if you intend to dictate your first draft. Once satisfied with the broad outlines of your analysis, you can devote greater attention to the details when you begin writing or dictating.

V. SUMMARY

Your two most important goals in legal writing style are clarity and conciseness. These two goals ordinarily are consistent and complementary. When they conflict, you should give priority to clarity. More specifically:

(1) To write clearly, you should
  (a) use simple, plain English unless a legal term of art will inform more than distract;
  (b) flexibly use effective sentence structure and punctuation, with adequate closure and guides to structure;
  (c) use concrete verbs in the active voice, unless passive construction serves a specific purpose;
  (d) distinguish between restrictive and nonrestrictive clauses when necessary for clarity; and
  (e) select the word or phrase that precisely conveys your meaning.
(2) To write concisely, you should
  (a) maintain reasonable limitations on scope and depth of analysis; and
  (b) avoid verbosity by adopting efficient organization, sentence structure, and phrasing.
(3) To present authority effectively, you should
  (a) subordinate citations, emphasize ideas, and express your syntheses in topic sentences or paragraphs;
  (b) use quotations selectively, subordinate the citations to quotations, and introduce quotations with substantive overviews; and
  (c) use effective citation form and citation signals.
(4) To polish your writing, you should
  (a) revise early drafts; and
  (b) create the best possible product on first draft.

Finally, you should avoid applying conventions of composition mechanically. Instead, adopt an approach to writing that is analogous to legal method: Strive to understand the purposes and policies of conventions of composition, and apply those conventions flexibly to satisfy the purposes and policies.

ADVOCACY

12

Introduction to Advocacy

Written advocacy is a special branch of legal method and writing that combines creative analysis, persuasive writing, and attention to local rules, special formats, and ethical considerations. This chapter provides an overview of advocacy at all stages of litigation.

The remaining chapters in Part IV examine written advocacy in the context of four kinds of documents: (1) a complaint and an answer, (2) briefs on a motion for summary judgment, (3) briefs on a motion to exclude evidence, and (4) appellate briefs. Each of those chapters includes at least one full sample pleading or brief. By studying this chapter and the documents in the following chapters, you will develop a general grasp of the methods and purposes of brief writing, enabling you to prepare a brief for any stage of litigation.

On the other hand, if most of the documents in the following chapters are outside the scope of your course of study, you can simply combine this chapter with any of the others. For example, if you intend to draft only an appellate brief, you should study this chapter to gain a general overview of techniques of advocacy, and you can turn to Chapter 16 to master concepts and techniques that are peculiar to appellate advocacy. Even then, you may want to glance through one or more of the other chapters in Part IV to better appreciate the stages of litigation through which your dispute proceeded before reaching the appellate court.

I. OVERVIEW—GENERAL FORMAT AND PROCEDURE

A. PROCEDURE

In a typical dispute, you will advocate your client's case in various written documents through several stages of litigation. If correspondence between the parties fails to resolve the dispute in its early stages, the parties may commence formal litigation by filing pleadings, typically a complaint and an answer. Before trial, you might file or respond to "motions" that request the judge to take certain actions, such as to make advance rulings on the admissibility of evidence at trial or to dispose of some or all of the claims and defenses without a trial. During a trial with a jury, you may submit or respond to briefs that request the judge to instruct the jury on the law in a certain way or even to decide the case "as a matter of law" without the jury. At the outset of a trial without a jury, you may submit a trial brief that invites the judge to find certain facts and to apply your interpretation of the law to the facts to reach certain conclusions. Finally, if either party appeals the judgment of the trial court, you will draft one or more briefs to one or more appellate courts, inviting an appellate court to either affirm or reverse the judgment of the court immediately below it.

Throughout these proceedings, the pleadings, motions, and appeals will follow similar briefing schedules:

(1) The party seeking relief or seeking reversal of the judgment of a lower court files a complaint, petition, or opening brief.

(2) The opposing party responds with an answer, response, or answering brief.

(3) Finally, the party who filed the petition or opening brief generally has the opportunity to file a reply brief that addresses points raised in the opposing party's answering brief or response. Under federal pleading rules, the drafter of a complaint may file a reply to the answer only if the court orders a reply or if the defendant has asserted a counterclaim in the answer, in which cases the reply is mandatory.[1]

B. BASIC FORMATS

The format of a pleading differs significantly from that of a brief. Various pretrial, trial, and appellate briefs, however, have much in common. Each will include some statement of the background of the case, followed by an argument and a conclusion.

In some ways, an appellate brief may be more detailed and formal than a pretrial brief. By the time a case reaches an appellate court, the litigants have developed some record of the facts or factual allegations, and they have advanced the dispute through significant procedural steps. Accordingly, an appellate brief's description of the background of a case typically includes a formal statement of facts and a summary of the procedural history. On the other hand, when the parties litigate a pretrial motion, the facts may be sketchy and the procedural history brief. Consequently, many pretrial briefs may combine the procedural history and statement of relevant facts in a brief "Introduction," "Background," or "Statement of Facts." As explored in Chapter 14, briefs on a motion for summary judgment are exceptional in their unusually formal pretrial presentation of facts.

An appellate brief may be more formal than a pretrial brief in other

---

1. Fed. R. Civ. P. 7(a).

ways as well. For example, rules of procedure and local court rules typically require an appellate brief to include a table of contents, table of authorities, and formal statement of issues. These are customarily omitted from all but the most complex pretrial briefs.[2] Depending on the complexity of the case and the nature of the immediate ruling sought, a trial brief may be as relatively informal as most pretrial briefs, or it may include one or more of the formalities usually reserved for appellate briefs.

These differences, however, are relatively superficial in light of the universality of the heart of any brief: the argument. Unlike an office memorandum, your brief will not explore the strengths and weaknesses of both sides of the dispute. Instead, you will use the brief to advocate the legal and factual analysis that best supports the claims or defenses of your client.

This orientation is reflected not only in the subtler facets of writing style but also in fundamental elements of format such as section headings. In the discussion section of an office memorandum, a section heading may be a neutral phrase that generally describes a topic of discussion and helps your reader recall an issue stated more formally at the beginning of the memorandum. In contrast, you will use a "point heading" in the argument section of a brief to state the conclusion that you want the judge to adopt on each issue. In each point heading, you will assert a point in a complete sentence as a prelude to your full deductive argument on that issue.

Sections III and IV of this chapter address these and other techniques of written and oral advocacy in greater depth. First, however, Section II introduces you to a few of the many ethical obligations that you assume as an advocate.

II. GOOD FAITH, REASONABLENESS, AND FULL DISCLOSURE

A. ASSERTION OF CLAIMS AND DEFENSES

As an attorney, you owe a duty to your client to advocate her case vigorously.[3] In carrying out this duty, you will often argue for creative extension of existing law or for replacement of existing law with new rules.[4] Fundamental principles of professional responsibility, however, impose limits on your advocacy.[5] For example, as amended in 1993, Federal Rule of Civil Procedure 11 requires attorneys to certify that their written advocacy is reasonably supported by law and fact and is not advanced for an improper purpose:

---

2. Cf. Cal. R. Ct. 313(d) (1993) (motions brief exceeding 10 pages must include a table of contents and table of authorities).

3. E.g., Model Code of Professional Responsibility EC 7-4 (1982); id. at Canon 7.

4. See generally supra Chapter 4.

5. See, e.g., Model Rules of Professional Conduct Rule 3.3(a)(1) (1989) (proscribing knowingly false statements of material fact or law).

(b) Representations to Court. By presenting to the court (whether by signing, filing, submitting, or later advocating) a pleading, written motion, or other paper, an attorney or unrepresented party is certifying that to the best of the person's knowledge, information, and belief, formed after an inquiry reasonable under the circumstances,—

(1) it is not being presented for any improper purpose, such as to harass or to cause unnecessary delay or needless increase in the cost of litigation;

(2) the claims, defenses, and other legal contentions therein are warranted by existing law or by a nonfrivolous argument for the extension, modification, or reversal of existing law or the establishment of new law;

(3) the allegations and other factual contentions have evidentiary support or, if specifically so identified, are likely to have evidentiary support after a reasonable opportunity for further investigation or discovery; and

(4) the denials of factual contentions are warranted on the evidence or, if specifically so identified, are reasonably based on a lack of information or belief.[6]

The 1993 amendments to Rule 11 carry forward standards of conduct introduced in 1983. The 1983 amendments to the rule supplemented the original good-faith standard with a more stringent objective standard that requires reasonable prefiling inquiry into the facts and law supporting a pleading, motion, or other paper.[7] The history of the sanctions provisions in Rule 11 reveals continuing tension between the desire to deter unprofessional conduct and the fear of chilling creative advocacy. Prior to the 1983 amendments, Rule 11 granted federal judges discretion to punish violations of the rule by striking unfounded pleadings or bringing disciplinary proceedings. Those sanctions did not effectively deter abuses: Striking unfounded pleadings imposed no significant penalty for a frivolous filing, and the drastic measure of disciplinary proceedings was rarely invoked. The 1983 amendments to Rule 11 required courts to impose sanctions for violations of the rule, but they also introduced flexibility by authorizing a wider range of sanctions. Among other things, the sanction could include an order directing the certifying attorney to pay attorney's fees and other reasonable expenses incurred by the opposing party as a result of the violation of the rule.[8] The monetary sanctions in the 1983 amendments were thought to be effective precisely because they were both mandatory and flexible.[9]

The 1993 amendments strike a balance between the 1983 amendments and the earlier version of Rule 11. In a departure from the mandatory sanctions of the 1983 amendments, the 1993 amendments authorize, but do not require, a judge to impose "an appropriate sanction upon the attor-

6. Fed. R. Civ. P. 11(b), 113 S. Ct. 494 (orders) (1993).

7. Fed. R. Civ. P. 11 advisory committee note, 97 F.R.D. 198-199 (1983); Albright v. The Upjohn Co., 788 F.2d 1217 (6th Cir. 1986) (ordering sanctions against plaintiff's counsel for inadequate prefiling investigation of facts supporting claim against defendant); Kathleen M. Dorr, Comment Note—General principles regarding imposition of sanctions under Rule 11, Federal Rules of Civil Procedure, 95 A.L.R. Fed. 107 (1989).

8. Fed. R. Civ. P. 11, 97 F.R.D. 167-168 (1983).

9. See advisory committee note, supra note 7; see also Neal H. Klausner, Note, The Dynamics of Rule 11: Preventing Frivolous Litigation by Demanding Professional Responsibility, 61 N.Y.U. L. Rev. 300 (1986).

neys, law firms, or parties that have violated [Rule 11] or are responsible for the violation."[10] The 1993 amendments, however, retain the broad range of sanctions introduced by its predecessor:

> The sanction may consist of, or include, directives of a nonmonetary nature, an order to pay a penalty into court, or, if imposed on motion and warranted for effective deterrence, an order directing payment to the movant of some or all of the reasonable attorneys' fees and other expenses incurred as a direct result of the violation.[11]

The 1993 amendments also introduce a controversial "safe harbor" provision that permits a person responsible for a Rule 11 violation to escape sanctions by withdrawing the offending claim or defense after receiving notice of a motion for sanctions:

> A motion for sanctions under this rule . . . shall not be filed with or presented to the court unless, within 21 days after service of the motion . . . the challenged paper, claim, defense, contention, allegation, or denial is not withdrawn or appropriately corrected.[12]

Opponents of the 1993 amendments criticize this "safe harbor" provision, the discretion whether to grant sanctions at all, and the language suggesting that the new rule disfavors an award of fees to the moving party. A Supreme Court Justice has complained that the 1993 amendments "would render the Rule toothless."[13]

Undoubtedly, the debate will continue. The 1993 amendments are simply another chapter in a continuing effort to recognize the value of creative advocacy while discouraging claims or defenses that are intended solely to harass opponents or that reflect irresponsibly lax investigation. As explored more fully in the following sections, perhaps the best guide to responsible advocacy is the desire shared by most advocates to maintain their reputations for candor and quality work.

B. DISCLOSURE OF ADVERSE AUTHORITY

As an advocate, you have no duty to argue your opponent's case or even to present a balanced analysis such as would be appropriate in an office memorandum. Nonetheless, every advocate is also an officer of the court[14] and owes a general duty of candor and fairness to the court and to other lawyers.[15] Within this framework, the American Bar Association Model Rules

---

10. Fed. R. Civ. P. 11(c).
11. Id. at R. 11(c)(2).
12. Id. at R. 11(c)(1)(A).
13. Amendments to the Federal Rules of Civil Procedure, 113 S. Ct. 581 (orders) (1993) (Scalia, J., dissenting).
14. E.g., Ex parte Garland, 71 U.S. (4 Wall.) 333, 378 (1867) (cited in ABA Formal Opinion 146 (1935)).
15. See Model Rules of Professional Conduct Rule 3.3 (1983) (candor to court); ABA Formal Opinion 146 (1935).

of Professional Conduct specifically require every advocate to disclose significant authority adverse to the advocate's arguments:

> A lawyer shall not knowingly: . . .
> (3) fail to disclose to the tribunal legal authority in the controlling jurisdiction known to the lawyer to be directly adverse to the position of the client and not disclosed by opposing counsel.[16]

The scope of this duty depends in large part on the interpretation of the phrase "directly adverse." However, the most sensible approach to disclosure is one that maintains your credibility as an advocate. If adverse authority within the forum jurisdiction is sufficiently analogous that the court would consider it in deciding a case, the judge or the judge's law clerk likely will discover the authority sometime before the end of the proceedings, even if it has escaped the notice of the opposing counsel. You can minimize the impact of such adverse authority by acknowledging it early in the proceedings and distinguishing or discrediting it.[17]

The reference to "controlling jurisdiction" in the disclosure rule appears to flatly exclude authority from other than the forum jurisdiction, even if it is squarely on point. In some circumstances, however, your desire to maintain credibility may be a better guide than a specific ethical rule. For example, if the question before the court is so novel that no authority within the forum jurisdiction addresses it, and if adverse authority from another jurisdiction would be particularly persuasive, then the court might expect you to disclose the nonbinding adverse authority.

If an adverse authority does not meet these standards, you need not address it unless the other party relies on it or the court raises a question that encompasses it. In an opening brief, for example, you should not waste time by distinguishing marginally analogous adverse case law or by criticizing poorly reasoned persuasive authority on which the opposing counsel is unlikely to rely. Instead, you should concentrate on affirmatively presenting your own arguments and supporting authority, and you should attack only the most obvious adverse authority. Then, you can wait to see the authority on which the opposing counsel relies in the answering brief, and you can attack that adverse authority in your reply brief. Of course, if the court asks you broadly about adverse precedent, you "should make such frank disclosure as the question seems to warrant,"[18] regardless of the scope of ethical duties or strategic considerations that might otherwise apply.

C. MISLEADING LEGAL ARGUMENT

The ABA Model Rules of Professional Conduct prohibit a lawyer from knowingly making "a false statement of . . . law to a tribunal."[19] However,

---

16. Model Rules, Rule 3.3(a)(3) (1989) (taken from Model Code of Professional Responsibility DR 7-106(B)(1) (1969)).
17. Charles W. Wolfram, Modern Legal Ethics §12.8, at 682 (1986).
18. ABA Formal Opinion 280 (1949).
19. Model Rules, Rule 3.3(a)(1) (1989).

a legal analysis will not amount to a false statement about the law unless it clearly falls outside the range of plausible interpretations of the legal authorities.

For example, defining the holding of a judicial opinion and determining its effect as precedent is an exercise in legal realism that produces disagreement among able jurists. Thus, as an advocate, you often have room to take an aggressive stance in identifying facts that appear to have been material to a decision and in characterizing the holding and reasoning of the decision.

As with other ethical questions, practical considerations of effective advocacy may provide the best guide to responsible conduct. Published precedent on which you rely is readily accessible to the opposing counsel and to the court. Careless or fraudulent analyses that cross the line separating creative advocacy from misrepresentation almost certainly will be brought to the court's attention. Few things can damage your credibility and effectiveness more than a reputation for stretching legal authority beyond the limits of plausible interpretation.

III. THE ARGUMENT

Your statements of issues, facts, and procedural history will vary greatly in style and content depending on the stage of the litigation at which you draft a legal document. Consequently, this book separately examines those elements of a pleading or a brief in Chapters 13-16. Many techniques of argumentation, however, apply broadly to all kinds of briefs and are appropriately introduced in this overview chapter. Specifically, this chapter will examine methods of (1) organizing arguments, (2) introducing arguments, (3) developing the elements of a deductive argument, and (4) writing persuasively.

A. ORGANIZING LEGAL ARGUMENTS

As discussed in Chapter 10, you ordinarily should discuss or argue discrete issues in separate sections of your office memorandum or brief. Moreover, your section and subsection headings should show the proper relationships among your topics and subtopics.

Beyond this, when drafting the argument section of your brief, you must decide the order in which to present your arguments. If your brief includes a formal statement of the issues, the organization of that statement will mirror the organization of your arguments. To determine the most appropriate order of arguments, you may need to balance neutral analytic considerations against strategic considerations. Moreover, in a responsive brief, you must decide whether to adopt or depart from the organizational structure of the opposing counsel's preceding brief.

As discussed in Chapter 10, neutral analytic considerations will lead you to argue threshold issues first and then to argue the issues that are dependent on the outcome of the threshold issues. Strategic considerations, however, may lead you to place your strongest argument first, even if that organization requires you to depart from a purely logical ordering of arguments.

The strategic considerations are based on the varying levels of emphasis associated with different parts of the argument section of the brief. At the level of a sentence, an idea generally will receive greater emphasis if placed at the beginning than if placed in the middle, but the place of greatest emphasis in a sentence is the end. The same might be true of a short brief submitted to a judge who has plenty of time to study it. The first argument in such a brief would receive the emphasis associated with any initial encounter that makes a first impression. Ideas in the middle of the brief might capture slightly less attention, but they could help lay the foundation for a forceful climax. Presumably, the climactic argument would leave a lasting impression on the judge because it is the last argument that the judge would read.

Unfortunately, briefs are seldom brief, and judges almost never have enough time to read them. Indeed, a trial judge with a full pretrial motions calendar may have enough time only to skim through your motions brief before oral argument. Far from being the place of greatest emphasis, the end of your brief may not be read at all, or at least it may not be read with the same care that the judge devoted to the beginning of the brief.

Consequently, advocates usually begin their briefs with their strongest arguments. In fact, aware of this practice, judges have come to expect that the first argument in a brief is the strongest argument, and they accordingly may be tempted to prejudge an entire brief on the basis of the merits of the first argument. This phenomenon, of course, simply reinforces the belief among advocates that they should lead with their strongest arguments. Consequently, if one of your arguments is much stronger than the others, you can exercise discretion to present it before the others even though another issue is logically prior.

When you write a responsive brief, the organization selected by the opposing counsel for the preceding brief is yet another factor in your own deliberations about organization. In a complex case, you can conveniently respond to each point in a preceding brief by simply adopting the preceding brief's organizational structure and methodically knocking down each of your opponent's arguments. On the other hand, if you can more persuasively argue your case with a different organizational structure, you should not hesitate to depart from the structure adopted by your opponent.

For example, suppose that Maya Tortilla Co. has sued Bakeway Supermarkets, alleging that Bakeway (1) formed a contract with Maya; (2) breached its obligations, at least under Maya's interpretation of the contract; (3) and is liable to Maya for $40,000 in damages. Maya has filed a pretrial motion requesting the trial court to grant it summary judgment (judgment as a matter of law without a full trial on the facts). Maya has supported its motion with a preliminary showing of facts and with a brief that argues each of the issues in the order presented above. Bakeway can escape summary judgment on any issue by creating a genuine dispute of material fact on that issue, a dispute that must be resolved in a full trial.

As counsel for Bakeway, you could logically begin the argument of your answering brief with Maya's issue #1 because contract formation is a threshold issue: Bakeway did not assume any contractual obligations and consequent potential liability if it did not form a contract with Maya. Moreover, the opening brief begins with issue #1, and you could simplify your task by simply adopting the organizational structure of the opening brief.

However, suppose that you can most easily establish a genuine issue of fact on issue #2 because admissible evidence of contract negotiations creates a triable issue of fact about the meaning of the contract provision that states Bakeway's obligations. In those circumstances, you could reasonably begin your argument with issue #2, even though that organization departs from a purely logical ordering and from the structure of the opening brief. If you persuade the judge in your first argument that she should deny summary judgment on issue #2, she may then be more strongly disposed to order a trial on other issues as well.

B. INTRODUCING LEGAL ARGUMENTS

1. Point Headings

In the argument section of your brief, you ordinarily will follow the pattern of deductive reasoning introduced in Chapter 4: For each issue or subissue, you will discuss the law and apply the law to the facts to reach a conclusion. Before you begin your full argument, however, you should introduce it in a "point heading." In each section or subsection that addresses a discrete issue, your argumentative point heading previews the conclusion.

If a section or subsection of your argument develops a full deductive argument, its point heading should be tailored to the facts of your case, much like the statement of an issue or a full statement of the holding of a decision in a student case brief. Indeed, you may view your point headings as statements of the holdings in your case that you want the court to adopt:

II. ARGUMENT

    A. *O'Gorman Is Not Liable for Punitive Damages Because He Did Not Act with the Requisite "Evil Mind."*

• • • •

    B. *O'Gorman Is Not Liable for Medical Costs Associated with Wallace's Heart Failure, Because O'Gorman's Conduct Did Not Proximately Cause that Injury.*

In unusual cases, as discussed in Chapter 10, Section III.E.3, you may develop only one element of a deductive argument, such as an abstract legal principle, within a section or subsection. In such cases, of course, the point heading should be limited to stating a conclusion on the point developed in the section or subsection:

II. ARGUMENT

    A. *O'Gorman Is Not Liable for Punitive Damages unless He Acted with an "Evil Mind."*

• • • •

    B. *The Evidence at Trial Will Show that O'Gorman Did Not Act with an "Evil Mind."*

The advantages of point headings are obvious in multiple-issue briefs, in which you must divide the argument into sections and subsections. Even in a single-issue brief, however, you should begin your argument with a point heading. It will simply stand alone without any number or letter denoting division of the argument into sections:

II. ARGUMENT

    The UCC Requires the Alleged Agreement to Be in Writing, Because the Alleged Subject Matter Was Priced at More than $500.

Thus, your full argument should include four major elements, the first conveyed by the point heading: Conclusion, Rule, Application of the legal rule to facts, and Conclusion. The acronym "CRAC" may help you remember these elements. In contrast, "IRAC," introduced in Chapter 4, represents the elements of the more nearly neutral analysis of the discussion section of an office memorandum, beginning with a section heading: Issue, Rule, Application of the legal rule to facts, and Conclusion. Thus, a section heading in an office memorandum can neutrally denote the issue addressed in that section. In contrast, the point heading of a brief advocates a position by asserting a point and inviting the judge to reach a particular conclusion. It thus sets the tone for the full argument.

2. Introductory Paragraphs

Immediately after the point heading, and before discussing the legal authority, you may want to use an introductory sentence or paragraph to illuminate the issue and to expand on the point heading:

    A. *The UCC Requires the Alleged Agreement to Be in Writing, Because the Alleged Subject Matter Was Priced at More than $500.*

Scott Paper Supply alleges that Sun Printing Co. breached a contract to purchase a shipment of bond paper priced at $1,200. Sun Printing Co. denies that it ever agreed to such a purchase. This is precisely the kind of groundless contract claim that statutes of frauds are designed to bar.

The Uniform Commercial Code statute of frauds generally bars . . .

Such an introductory paragraph can be particularly helpful in a responsive brief. Rather than abstractly address the issues, an answering or reply brief should respond directly to each of the preceding brief's arguments. In a responsive brief, the introductory paragraph following a point heading can set up your full response by (1) summarizing the opposing party's argument and (2) explaining generally why the opposing argument lacks merit:

> A. *Scott Paper Supply's Timely Confirmation of the Agreement Satisfied the UCC Statute of Frauds, Because Sun Printing Co. Failed to Object to It.*
>
> Scott Paper Supply argues that the Uniform Commercial Code statute of frauds bars enforcement of the purchase agreement because the agreement is not memorialized in a written document signed or expressly adopted by Scott. Scott's argument is meritless because the confirmation signed by Sun Printing Co. satisfied the requirements of the statute and because the UCC deems Scott to have implicitly adopted that confirmation by failing to object to it.
>
> The UCC provides that . . .

This technique is consistent with the techniques of organizing an argument in a responsive brief: First, affirmatively present your own arguments and supporting authority, and only then discredit or distinguish the authority or interpretation on which your opponent has relied. The introductory paragraph in the preceding example does no more than emphasize and expand on the point heading by briefly placing it in context. It still permits you to exercise discretion to delay until the end of the section your full attack on the specific authority relied on by the opposing party.

Indeed, such an opening paragraph will accomplish its purpose only if it, as a whole, affirmatively advances your own argument. You will surely defeat its purpose if you simply lead with your opponent's argument and give it special emphasis. Accordingly, you should begin with a summary of your opponent's argument only as a means of putting your own argument in its best light. Specifically, after you summarize your opponent's argument, you must immediately and convincingly refute it with a summary of your response. The opening paragraph thus presents a condensed pattern of point and winning counterpoint that you hope the judge will see in the broader outlines of the competing briefs.

In some cases, you can use such an opening paragraph to particularly strong advantage by "setting up" your opponent's argument for an easy response. Specifically, you should try to restate your opponent's argument fairly and accurately but in a way that fully reveals its weaknesses. For example, suppose that your opponent's opening brief on appeal argues that the trial judge erred in denying injunctive relief, but it acknowledges the trial judge's broad discretion in such matters only in a vague passage buried within a lengthy passage. In your answering brief, you undoubtedly will emphasize the discretionary nature of such relief. You might begin that emphasis not only in your point heading but also in an opening paragraph that summarizes your opponent's argument in a way that reveals its weakness:

> *A. The Trial Court Properly Exercised Its Discretion to Deny the Extraordinary Remedy of Injunctive Relief.*
>
> Redrock Co. argues that Judge Norris abused her discretion by denying Redrock's demand for an injunction against further construction on the Big River Project. On the contrary, the record establishes a balance of equities that tip sharply against injunctive relief. Judge Norris's careful decision was a routine and proper exercise of discretion.
> Injunctive relief is . . .

C. DEVELOPING THE DEDUCTIVE ARGUMENT

1. Arguing the Law

Chapters 4, 10, and 11 have provided you with the legal method and the techniques of organization and writing with which you can construct an argument about the content of applicable law on a particular issue or subissue. An outline of these principles will illustrate the range of considerations that may enter into your strategic decisions when arguing the law within the argument portion of your brief.

a. Hierarchy of Authority

First, you must be sensitive to the hierarchy of authority. For example, suppose that (1) your client is not liable under common law standards for actions that he took as an employer, but (2) a federal statute will impose liability if it applies to your client's business. If applicable, the statutory law will supersede the common law. Therefore, you must analyze the statute and determine whether you can argue either that it is unconstitutional or that it does not apply to your case. This statutory analysis might include arguments concerning the statutory language, the legislative history, the policy underlying the statute, or the limitations imposed by constitutional provisions.

b. Strength of Case Law as Precedent

Second, in analyzing case law, regardless of whether it interprets a statute or applies common law, you must appreciate the relative strength of different kinds of authorities. Case law from a higher court within the forum jurisdiction is potentially a source of binding law, and you must argue for a broader or narrower interpretation of its holding, depending on whether it supports or undermines your position. For example, in the following passage, the counsel for Beatty, a lender, encourages an expansive interpretation of favorable precedent and encourages narrower application of adverse precedent:

Week cites to authorities from other jurisdictions to argue that Beatty's promise is illusory and therefore does not satisfy the consideration requirement. However, her position is inconsistent with Calzona Supreme Court authority. Applying the principles established in that authority, Beatty's promise is not illusory, and Week's promise is enforceable.	**Introduction to argument**
Even if a promise leaves open the possibility that the promisor will escape obligation, the promise is not illusory if the promisor does not have complete control over the events on which the promisor's obligation is conditioned. *See Bonnie v. DeLaney*, 158 Calz. 212, 645 P.2d 887 (1982). In *Bonnie*, an agreement for the sale of a house provided that the buyer could cancel the agreement if the buyer "cannot qualify for a 30-year mortgage loan for 90% of the sales price" with any of several banks listed in the agreement. *Id.* at 213, 645 P.2d at 888. In enforcing the agreement against the seller, the court emphasized that the word "cannot" referred to the buyer's ability to obtain a loan rather than to his desire. Because his ability to obtain a loan was partly controlled by events and decisions outside his control, the promises in the sale agreement were non-illusory and binding. *Id.* at 214-15, 645 P.2d at 889-91.	**In-depth analysis of favorable case law**
The *Bonnie* court distinguished its earlier decision, *Atco Corp. v. Johnson*, 155 Calz. 1211, 627 P.2d 781 (1980). In *Atco Corp.*, the manager of an automobile repair shop promised to forbear "until I want the money" from asserting a claim against the owner of an automobile for $900 in repairs. In exchange, a friend of the owner promised to act as guarantor of the owner's obligation. *Id.* at 1212, 627 P.2d at 782. The word "want" stated no legal commitment because it permitted the manager at his own discretion to refuse to perform any forbearance at all. Because the manager did not incur even a conditional obligation, the guarantor's promise was gratuitous and unenforceable. *Id.* at 1213-14, 627 P.2d at 782-84.	**In-depth analysis of adverse case law**

Synthesis that emphasizes favorable case law	Together, these cases show that any limitation on the promisor's freedom will validate his promise. A promise is illusory only if it leaves the promisor complete control over his actions.

In this example, counsel for Beatty has synthesized the case law by applying a form of inductive reasoning in which he generalized from particular cases. The final paragraph represents this advocate's characterization of the legal rule. The argument can now proceed with a fact analysis that either (1) directly applies this legal rule to the facts, or (2) employs another form of inductive reasoning to analogize the favorable precedent to Beatty's case and to distinguish the adverse precedent.

Authority from a lower court or from a court in another jurisdiction will have only persuasive influence. If persuasive authority undermines your client's position, you can try to distinguish it from the facts of your case or to discredit its reasoning as unworthy of adoption as the rule of law in the forum jurisdiction. Conversely, if persuasive authority supports your position, you should argue that its reasoning is sound and is consistent with the policy of the forum jurisdiction.

For example, in the following passage, an advocate attempts to persuade a court in the imaginary state of New Maine to adopt the reasoning of California case law and to reject precedent from Washington and Florida:[20]

Complimentary in-depth analysis of favorable case law	The Federal Gun Control Act (FGCA) preempts more stringent state gun control legislation. *California v. Biggs*, 567 P.2d 765 (Cal. 1987). In *Biggs*, state officials sought to confiscate a private collection of automatic pistols under the authority of a California statute that bans private ownership of all automatic guns. The California Supreme Court found that the FGCA's registration requirements for most varieties of automatic guns implicitly authorizes private, registered ownership of such guns. It therefore held that the FGCA barred the state from prohibiting such ownership.
	In reaching its decision, the California Supreme Court exhaustively analyzed the legislative history of the FGCA. It noted that . . .
Critical analysis of adverse case law	Two courts had previously rejected the preemption argument adopted in *Biggs*, but each of them overlooked the critical legislative history so carefully analyzed in *Biggs*. *See Arzani v. Matlock*, 332 So. 2d 234 (Fla. 1986); *Washington v. Smedley*, 558 P.2d 777 (Wash. 1986). For example, in *Arzani*, the Court summarily held that . . .

---

20. All the arguments, authorities, and citations in this example are fictitious.

The advocate obviously hopes that the preceding passage will persuade the court to adopt the reasoning of *Biggs*. In the fact analysis, the advocate can argue further that *Biggs* is analogous to the facts of her case and that the rule of law it represents thus applies to those facts.

c. Depth of Analysis

Third, in presenting legal authority, you should exercise firm control over depth of analysis. As discussed in Chapter 11, Section II.A.2, you may use

(1) "light analysis" to present fundamental and undisputed propositions with direct statements of law and citation to authority,

(2) in-depth analysis of statutes or case law to explore policy and reasoning, and

(3) direct statements of law and citation to authority with parenthetic explanations for an intermediate level of analysis.

d. Presentation of Authority

Finally, you must lead your reader through your argument on a particular issue or subissue. Three techniques explored in Chapter 11, Section III are particularly important: You should

(1) express your syntheses of authorities´ or other thesis statements in topic sentences or paragraphs;

(2) unless the citations are independently significant, focus attention on your ideas and relegate citations to subordinate citation sentences; and

(3) introduce quotations with substantive overviews that invite the judge to adopt your interpretation of the quoted material.

2. Analyzing the Facts

As discussed in greater detail in Chapter 16 in the context of appellate briefs, the opening statement of facts in a brief is most effective if it does not prematurely argue the law or the application of the law to the facts. In contrast, when you analyze the relevant facts in the argument section of a brief, you should explicitly reach a conclusion by relating the facts to the previously discussed legal standards. You may accomplish this by (1) directly applying the law to the facts or (2) using a form of inductive reasoning to analogize or distinguish precedent by comparing the facts and reasoning of the precedent to your own case.

To illustrate the first technique, suppose that you have established in your discussion of the law that a state police officer can be liable for punitive damages for recklessly depriving a citizen of her right to be free from arrest without probable cause. In the fact analysis of your argument, you could directly apply that rule of law to the facts. In the following sample passage, the notations within brackets refer to pages of the trial court reporter's transcript on which critical testimony of witnesses is found.

> Substantial evidence in the record supports the jury's finding that Officer Mullins acted with at least reckless disregard for Wong's clearly established fourth amendment rights. Mullins's actions show that even he did not believe that Wong fit the dispatcher's description of the robbery suspect. According to his own testimony, when he initially spotted Wong moments after receiving the robbery report, he passed by her and continued looking for the suspect. [RT 324.] Only after failing to find a suspect who fit the dispatcher's description did he relocate Wong and summarily arrest her. [RT 326.] An experienced officer such as Mullins obviously knew that he didn't have probable cause to arrest Wong.
>
> The jury could infer from these facts that Officer Mullins felt compelled to arrest somebody for the robbery and that he recklessly gambled that Wong might have been involved simply because of her proximity to the robbery. This is precisely the kind of reckless disregard for constitutional rights that an award of punitive damages is designed to deter. . . .

Alternatively, your discussion of the law may include in-depth case analysis and synthesis of arguably controlling, analogous, or distinguishable authority. If so, you may want to use the second technique to compare those cases directly to your dispute in your fact analysis:

Analogizing favorable case law on the facts

> *Bonnie* is closely analogous to our case and thus supports the conclusion that Beatty's promise was not illusory. In both *Bonnie* and our case, the promised performance was conditioned on events not entirely within the control of the promisor. In *Bonnie,* the buyer could escape his obligations only if market conditions rendered him *unable* to obtain a satisfactory mortgage loan. Similarly, in our case, Beatty could terminate his obligation to refrain from collecting on the debt only if economic conditions affected his income and expenses so as to create a *need* for the money.

Distinguishing adverse case law on the facts

> Conversely, *Atco Corp.* is distinguishable from our case. The promisor in that case retained the freedom to escape all contractual obligations if, at his own discretion, he *wanted* to. In contrast, the Guarantee Agreement in this case did not permit Beatty to demand his money whenever he *wanted* it. Instead, . . .

3. Conclusions

Immediately after your fact analysis in each argument of your brief, you should briefly repeat the conclusion that you previewed in the point heading for that section or subsection:

Scott Paper Supply timely objected to Sun Printing Co.'s written confirmation of the alleged agreement. Therefore, the confirmation does not satisfy the requirements of the statute of frauds.

Additionally, every brief should end with a formal conclusion section. Many attorneys squander this opportunity to summarize their analyses. The following boilerplate is typical:

CONCLUSION

For the foregoing reasons, appellant respectfully requests this court to reverse the judgment of the Superior Court.

Although this style is conventional, a more substantive conclusion ordinarily is more satisfying, particularly if the brief presents more than one argument.

A substantive conclusion need not take up much space. If your arguments are simple, your conclusion need only briefly and generally repeat the request for relief and the supporting grounds, as in this closing to a brief in support of a motion to exclude evidence before trial:

III. CONCLUSION

Under Rule 403, Powell is entitled to pretrial exclusion of all evidence of his membership in the Black Panther's organization. The prejudicial effect of the evidence substantially outweighs its probative value, and the prejudice can be avoided only through exclusion of the evidence before trial.

In a more complex case, the conclusion might briefly summarize multiple arguments:

III. CONCLUSION

Yazzi's statement to the police officer is inadmissible on three grounds. First, it is not relevant to any issue in this suit. Second, even if it were relevant, it would be excludable because its prejudicial value substantially outweighs its probative value. Finally, it is inadmissible hearsay not falling within the exception for statements for purposes of medical treatment. This evidence should be excluded before trial to avoid exposing it to the jury and causing irremediable prejudice.

D. PERSUASIVE WRITING STYLE

Supervising attorneys often complain that law students or recent graduates from law school do not use sufficiently strong language to write persuasively. Admittedly, advocacy calls for a writing style different from the more nearly neutral style appropriate for an office memorandum. Unfortunately, many supervising attorneys equate persuasive writing style with hyperbole, and they advise their writers to pepper every sentence of a brief with exaggerated modifiers. Such a style may grab a judge's attention, but it does not often persuade. Judges recognize overstatement and tend to take everything in such a brief with an extra pinch of salt. Even worse, a writing style that is too obvious in its advocacy tends to divert the judge's attention from the substance of the argument and to focus it on the style itself.

The most persuasive writing style may be one that the judge never notices, one that keeps her attention riveted on the substance of the arguments and that presents those arguments so clearly as to give her the impression that the brief merely confirms her own independent conclusions. The most important element of such writing is good substantive analysis; a few extra hours of research and reflection may lead to an argument that is easily written in a persuasive manner. Beyond that, persuasive legal writing is distinguished by (1) strong, but not exaggerated, language and (2) effective emphasis through sentence structure, specificity, and concreteness.

1. Persuasive Language

a. The Adversarial Approach

To clearly communicate your legal analysis to a supervising attorney in an office memorandum, you must candidly reveal uncertainties in the law and weaknesses in your client's case. In contrast, a brief in the same litigation generally should not explore the weaknesses of a client's case except as necessary to satisfy ethical duties or maintain credibility. The adversary system ensures that opposing counsel will test your arguments.

Thus, in an office memorandum, you might candidly admit the weakness of the support for a client's argument, as with the following fictitious analysis of a client's preemption argument:

> Only one state court has held that the Federal Gun Control Act preempts more stringent state gun control legislation. *See California v. Biggs,* 567 P.2d 765 (Cal. 1987). Two other courts have interpreted the act to permit, or even encourage, more stringent state controls that are consistent with its policy. *See Arzani v. Matlock,* 332 So. 2d 234 (Fla. 1986); *Washington v. Smedley,* 558 P.2d 777 (Wash. 1986). To support our argument that the federal act preempts the New Maine gun registration legislation, we should emphasize the thorough reasoning of *Biggs* and try to discredit or distinguish *Arzani* and *Smedley.*
>
> In *Biggs,* . . .

In a brief to the court in the same case, you must state your client's argument more positively, while acknowledging and attempting to distinguish or discredit the contrary authority:

> The Federal Gun Control Act preempts more stringent state gun control legislation. *California v. Biggs,* 567 P.2d 765 (Cal. 1987). In *Biggs,* state officials sought to confiscate . . .

Two courts had previously rejected the preemption argument adopted in *Biggs*, but each of them overlooked the critical legislative history so carefully analyzed in *Biggs*. *See Arzani v. Matlock*, . . . ; Washington v. Smedley. . . . For example, in *Arzani*, . . .

The proposition for which *Biggs* is cited in the second example illustrates the power of the simple, unqualified statement:

The Federal Gun Control Act preempts more stringent state gun control legislation.

You should avoid unnecessary qualifiers that weaken arguments, such as the following introduction to the argument of your client, Mason:

Mason contends that the Federal Gun Control Act preempts more stringent state gun control legislation.

Because the argument section of your brief obviously comprises a series of legal contentions, specific introductions to that effect are superfluous. You may set up a response to your opponent's propositions by referring to them as "arguments" or "contentions," but such a characterization of your own conclusions or statements of law tends to weaken them.

b. Cliches That Weaken or Offend

Ironically, modifiers that are designed to reinforce a proposition sometimes sap the strength from an otherwise powerful statement. For example, comments such as "It is abundantly clear that" have become such cliches that they have little effect on the judge except to make him wonder whether the words were added to shore up a shaky proposition that in fact is subject to great debate. Along with other forms of exaggeration, cliches such as these tend to make the advocacy in the writing too obvious and distracting. Most judges will accept your conclusions more readily if you offer persuasive arguments than if you invoke stock phrases that describe your arguments as persuasive.

The line between strong advocacy and overstatement is most delicate when referring directly to a matter within the court's discretionary power. For example, the word "should" in the following argument reflects lack of confidence in the argument:

This court should exclude evidence of Jenkins' subjective intentions regarding the lease.

On the other hand, a stronger verb suggests a presumptuous challenge to the power of the court:

This court must exclude evidence of Jenkins' subjective intentions regarding the lease.

On reading such an argument, the judge might be subconsciously inclined to demonstrate that she does indeed have the discretionary power to admit the evidence, the exercise of which would not likely be overturned on appeal. Restating the proposition in passive voice tends to soften and depersonalize the challenge:

‖ Evidence of Jenkins' subjective intentions regarding the lease must be ‖ excluded.

Nonetheless, the challenge to the judge's power remains implicit in this construction. Perhaps the best statement is one that focuses directly on the character of the evidence rather than on the power of the judge:

‖ Evidence of Jenkins' subjective intentions regarding the lease is inad- ‖ missible.

This proposition is strong and unqualified, yet it avoids expressing or directly implying a personal challenge to the judge.

c. Personal Attacks

Equally important to avoid are personal attacks on opposing counsel. Although you may become exasperated with apparently unreasonable or offensive conduct by your opponent, judges generally do not appreciate being caught in a crossfire of personal insults. Unless misconduct by a party or his attorney are properly the subject of a motion, judges are far more interested in your response to the opposing counsel's arguments than in your personal opinion of his intelligence, research skills, or personality. Thus, you may safely characterize the opposing counsel's argument as internally inconsistent, but you should not comment that he is unable to write a coherent brief. Similarly, if your statement of the procedural history unemotionally records events that reflect the opposing counsel's intransigence or bad faith, the judge will undoubtedly draw negative conclusions about him without any further comment from you.

2. Sentence Structure

To preserve your credibility and ethical standards, you often must candidly acknowledge law that is adverse to your client's case and that you can neither discredit nor distinguish. You can minimize the resulting damage by using techniques of persuasive writing style to deemphasize the adverse law and to focus attention on more helpful points.

One such technique consists of placing helpful information in the main clause and relegating adverse information to a dependent subordinate clause, a clause that cannot stand by itself as a complete sentence. For example, as counsel for the plaintiff in a contract action, you can deemphasize the general rule against damages for emotional distress by disposing of it in an opening subordinate clause:

Although damages for emotional distress are not often awarded for breach of contract, Jones is entitled to such an award in this exceptional case because the central purpose of his contract with Runyon Pet Cemetery was to alleviate his grief over the loss of his dog.

You maintain credibility with this passage by facing, rather than evading, the general rule. Moreover, by placing the general rule in a subordinate clause, you invite the reader to give it only brief pause, as you might invite a guest at a restaurant to dine lightly on appetizers in anticipation of the main course.

Location of information within a sentence also affects emphasis. Generally, the end of a sentence conveys the greatest emphasis, the beginning of a sentence conveys secondary emphasis, and a parenthetic phrase or clause at a natural breaking point in the middle of the sentence conveys the least emphasis. For example, if you represent the defendant in the example above, you can emphasize the general rule by placing it at the end of the sentence:

On the strength of his assertion that the contract was intended to alleviate his grief over the loss of a dog, Jones demands an award of damages for emotional distress, despite the general rule that such damages are not awarded for breach of contract.

In this example, as in the first, the general rule is stated in a subordinate clause. Nonetheless, the order of clauses within the sentence emphasizes the general rule.

Generally, you will emphasize the general rule least by placing it in a parenthetic clause at a natural breaking point in the middle of the sentence:

Jones is entitled to an award of damages for emotional distress in this exceptional case, even though such awards are rare in contract actions, because the central purpose of his contract with Runyon Pet Cemetery was to alleviate his grief over the loss of his dog.

This passage may be the best of the three for the plaintiff because it places favorable information in the positions of greatest emphasis.

Of course, if you are willing to sacrifice other style objectives, you can create unusual emphasis in the middle of the sentence with an abrupt, dramatic, or unnatural interruption of the sentence:

Jones demands—and he admits that such awards are rare in contract actions—an award of damages for emotional distress.

IV. ORAL ARGUMENT TO THE COURT

In most appeals and in many pretrial and trial motions, you will argue your client's case orally to the court after submitting your written brief. Generally, your written brief will influence a judge more strongly than will your oral argument. Indeed, before oral argument, most judges read both parties' briefs and come to a tentative decision on the merits.

Nonetheless, oral argument is not yet a meaningless formality in our courts. It provides you with a final opportunity to emphasize critical points, respond to judges' questions, and perhaps change the mind of a judge who had tentatively decided to rule in favor of the opposing party.

A. GENERAL FORMAT

The typical oral argument follows a pattern similar to that of a briefing schedule: The advocate seeking relief or reversal of a judgment in a lower court argues first, the opposing advocate responds, and the first advocate has an opportunity for rebuttal. In some courts, the advocate arguing first must tell the court before she begins her argument whether she wishes to divide her time between opening argument and rebuttal.

Rebuttal is a powerful weapon. It provides the advocate who opens the oral argument with an opportunity to respond directly to the oral argument of the opponent. It also permits the advocate with the opening argument to have both the first and last word on the issues. Therefore, if you give the opening oral argument, you should always preserve the opportunity for rebuttal.

B. FORMALITY AND DEMEANOR

Appropriate courtroom attire is mandatory for any oral argument. Beyond that, the level of formality of the proceedings will vary among courts.

For pretrial and trial motions, some state trial court judges hold oral arguments in their chambers rather than in the courtroom. After friendly, informal introductions, all are seated. As the judge listens from behind his desk, you and the opposing counsel will deliver your arguments while seated in office chairs.

Other trial judges and virtually all appellate panels of judges, however, conduct oral arguments with greater formality. In those courts, you deliver your oral argument from a lectern in the courtroom.

If you are uncertain about the customs in a court or the expectations of a particular judge, you should not hesitate to seek advice from the staff of the clerk's office or from the judge's personal law clerk. To consult with them, you can use the telephone or simply arrive early on the day of the argument.

Your demeanor in oral argument should be as formal as your attire. You should be confident and relaxed but respectful of the judge. If you disagree with a judge during the argument, you need not make him defensive by being disagreeable. For example, if he asks you whether your formulation of a legal rule will have certain adverse policy ramifications, you should answer the question confidently but without arrogantly suggesting that the question is silly.

Thus, you should not respond to a judge's question or assertion with a challenge to his analytic skills, such as the following:

No, your Honor, that is incorrect. ‖

Instead, you should answer the question without casting doubt on the questioner:

Your Honor, the court should be able to avoid those potential prob- ‖ lems of line-drawing by stating its holding in this appeal narrowly. I ‖ suggest the following formulation: . . .

In some cases, you may even want to validate the question before answering it:

That question has occupied the attention of a number of courts and ‖ scholars, Your Honor. To answer it, I must review the rationale for the ‖ exclusionary rule.

C. CONTENT OF THE ARGUMENT

1. Introduction of the Argument

In a formal courtroom argument, you should begin your presentation by introducing yourself and your representative capacity:

Good morning, Your Honors. I am Terry Malloy. I represent Bakeway ‖ Stores, the appellant on this appeal and the defendant in the trial court. ‖

Many advocates still begin their arguments with the traditional phrase

May it please the court, I am . . . ‖

Unless this language suits your personal style or that of the judges you are addressing, you ought to feel safe replacing it with something more natural, like "Good morning . . ." or "Good afternoon . . ." Unfortunately, silly as it sounds, the traditional opening phrase still suits the tastes of many judges. When in doubt, you probably should introduce yourself with the cliche that suggests that you hope your name "pleases the court."

After the personal introduction, you can capture the judges' attention with a brief characterization of the motion or appeal. If the facts are compelling, you can describe the general nature of the case in a sentence or two.

For example, suppose that a state is prosecuting prison inmates for possessing weapons materials in prison in violation of prison regulations and the state criminal code. The attorney for the defendant inmates has filed a motion to exclude from trial evidence obtained in an allegedly illegal search. He might introduce his oral argument at the suppression hearing with the following characterization of the case:

> Your Honor, the evidence in question is the product of a series of intrusive, physically brutal, and medically unsound body cavity searches of nearly a dozen unconsenting inmates, some of whom sustained permanent injuries as a result.

Alternatively, you can introduce your advocacy strongly by stating the issue in a way that invites a favorable response. In the criminal prosecution of the prison inmates, the prosecutor might begin her oral argument with the following:

> Your Honor, this motion presents the question of whether prison officials may constitutionally conduct emergency searches to maintain prison security against the threat of a planned, armed insurrection by inmates.

2. Body of the Argument

a. General Strategy

Many courts impose a time limit on each oral argument. Although the limits in some courts of last resort may be as long as 60 minutes for each side, 15 to 30 minutes is more typical, and arguments on simple pretrial motions may be limited to 5 minutes. In most motions or appeals, you will not have time to address every issue in the depth that the parties have examined in the briefs. Consequently, you should carefully study the arguments presented in both parties' briefs to determine the most effective strategy for oral argument.

Your strategy will differ depending on the circumstances of each case. In one appeal, for example, you may rely on multiple arguments that are both complex and interdependent. You may fear that, even with a well-organized brief to guide them, the judges may not fully appreciate how the arguments fit together to form the larger picture. You may thus decide to present an oral outline of all the arguments and their relationships, leaving the detail of each to your brief. More commonly, you can identify an argument in your brief that you wish to emphasize, perhaps because it addresses a critically important threshold issue, because it is your strongest theory, or even because it is the weakest link in your argumentative chain and needs extra support.

Whatever strategy you choose, you should communicate your intentions immediately after the introduction to your argument. For example, at a hearing to suppress evidence obtained in an allegedly illegal search, the prosecutor may try to justify the search on several grounds. Although she will introduce evidence at the hearing supporting each of the grounds and will advocate each ground in her brief, she might use her oral argument to focus on the determinative issue of consent to search. If so, she should reveal her plans to the court:

> This hearing presents three major issues, all of which the briefs examine in detail. I will be happy to answer questions on any of the issues. However, I would like to focus my presentation on the issue of consent to search. If the facts show that the inmates consented to the searches, this court need not address the more difficult questions related to expectations of privacy in prison and to reasonableness of the search methods.

b. Use of Facts

Many judges will advise oral advocates before argument that the judges are familiar with the facts of the case and that the advocates should proceed with their legal analyses. Even absent such an instruction, you ordinarily should not begin your argument with a recitation of the facts beyond a general characterization of the nature of the case. You might depart from this advice if the facts are particularly compelling and your legal arguments are not. In most cases, however, you will make better use of your limited time by arguing the law and applying the law to the facts without a separate introductory recitation of facts.

Whenever you rely on facts in an oral argument, be certain of the source of the facts. Be prepared to cite to the portion of the record that establishes the facts.

c. Responding to Questions

Questions from the bench constitute the most uncertain variable in oral argument. They ensure that oral advocacy in most cases is not a series of speeches but a dialogue, primarily between each advocate and the judges, and secondarily between the advocates as they respond to one another. Ironically, oral argument also permits judges on a panel to establish a coy dialogue among themselves, as they attempt to persuade each other with comments and questions ostensibly directed to the advocates.

You should genuinely welcome the opportunity to respond to questions. A judge's questions may reveal areas in which she has confusion or doubts, permitting you to directly influence her thinking on those points.

Occasionally, a judge will press you for a concession on your weakest among several alternative arguments. Your waiving the argument might be the most effective way to turn the judge's attention to your stronger arguments. However, you should be reluctant to waive a point that you had earlier determined was sufficiently meritorious to warrant discussion in your brief. If you are arguing before a panel of judges, the other panel members may not share the doubts of the questioning judge; yet, if you waive the controversial point during oral argument, none of the judges will take up your cause on that theory. Thus, when pressed for a concession on an argument, you should first try to shift to a more productive topic of discussion without making the concession:

> Your Honor, I prefer not to waive our argument that the prison officials lacked probable cause to search, but I admit that our other arguments are stronger. Both in the trial court and on appeal, the defendant inmates have most strongly complained of the unreasonable method of the searches. On this issue the law is clear: . . .

Except when trying to avoid a waiver of an argument, you should not give the appearance of evading questions from the bench. Confront and answer the questions directly. To answer judges' questions effectively, you must come to the argument thoroughly prepared. In particular, you should be ready to

(1) discuss the facts, holding, and reasoning of any case that you seek to rely on or to distinguish;
(2) cite to the record to identify the source of facts on which you rely; and
(3) discuss the policy implications of alternative holdings among which the court must choose.

An excellent method of preparing for the oral argument is to hold practice sessions with colleagues acting as judges. Your colleagues can give you constructive criticism on your performance. Moreover, the questions they ask during the practice rounds will help you anticipate the questions likely to be asked by the judges in the actual oral argument.

Even with excellent preparation, you may not always anticipate every question that a judge may ask you. If you cannot formulate a satisfactory answer to a question, do not be afraid to say that you are unprepared to respond.

Because you cannot always predict the number of questions from the bench, you must build maximum flexibility into your argument. You should be prepared to do either of the following or anything in between:

(1) present your arguments uninterrupted until your time elapses or you otherwise finish your argument; or
(2) present a brief introduction, respond without break to a series of questions that takes up all your allotted time, and request that the court permit you to end with a prepared conclusion no longer than a few sentences.

3. The Conclusion

You should end your argument on a strong note, perhaps with a summary of your strongest points. A carefully planned conclusion will be particularly helpful if persistent questioning from the bench prevents you from covering all the points that you had planned to address in your oral argument. Faced with the impending expiration of your allotted time, you can fall back on the conclusion as a quick means of stating your points, if only in summary fashion.

D. NERVOUSNESS AND VERBAL STUMBLING

All but the most experienced oral advocates experience some anxiety at the prospect of facing an inquisitive panel of judges in a public setting. If you feel such anxiety, you may be concerned that your nervousness will interfere with your speech patterns, causing your voice to shake or causing you to stumble over your words or to pause to collect your thoughts. You need not worry excessively about such problems. First, as long as the judge can understand you, the substance of your arguments and of your responses to questions will be more important than your charisma and stage presence. Second, you can take some simple measures to control your nervousness.

Some law school moot court programs may exalt form over substance: You may earn points if you can glibly respond to a judge's questions without pause, or lose points if you occasionally stumble over a difficult word. In actual oral arguments, however, judges will be more concerned with establishing a genuine dialogue with you. They will not be uncomfortable with a few moments of silence from you; indeed, most will expect you to pause to think deeply before answering a particularly difficult question. Moreover, if you speak sufficiently slowly and clearly to make yourself understood, most judges will forgive you for the occasional verbal stumbling that nervousness may produce.

For example, a few months after the 1989 massacre of Chinese demonstrators near Tiananmen Square in Beijing, China, President Bush responded to a question in a news conference about the resulting tensions between the Chinese and American governments. President Bush rejected the Chinese government's suggestion that the United States should take the next step toward improving relations:

> The Chinese have a slogan: "He who ties the knot must untie it." They think we tied the knot. I don't see it that way.

President Bush's delivery was far from perfect: He stuttered and stumbled several times while groping for the word "slogan." Yet the substance of his response compensated for his lingual fumbling. He had deftly borrowed a rhetorical technique from another culture to concisely portray the two governments' disagreement about responsibility for the deterioration in relations. His response thus was infinitely more satisfying than the slickly articulated but evasive or vacuous responses often heard in political press conferences. The same will be true of your responses to a judge's questions.

Of course, your argument will be all the more effective if you can minimize distracting imperfections in your delivery caused by nervousness. Perhaps the best way to bring such nervousness under control is to approach your oral argument with the confidence that comes from thorough preparation. If you have carefully prepared your analysis and have rehearsed your argument, you can confidently assume that you will bring an expertise to the courtroom that the judge will appreciate.

To deal with nervousness at the beginning of your argument, you can prepare a carefully worded introduction that you can commit to memory, so that you will not find yourself groping for words at the outset. Then, after you have warmed up your speaking voice, you can speak more flexibly from a rough outline of your main argument before closing with a carefully planned conclusion.

V. SUMMARY

Effective advocacy requires sound analysis, sensible organization, and effective writing style. Specifically, you should:

(1) satisfy ethical duties in asserting claims and defenses, disclosing adverse authority, and representing the content of legal authority;
(2) organize your legal arguments in logical order, subject to overriding considerations of strategy;
(3) introduce each of your arguments with an effective point heading and introductory paragraph;
(4) present your analysis of the law, apply the law to the facts, and state the conclusion that you want the court to reach;
(5) apply principles of persuasive writing; and
(6) carefully prepare an oral argument that strategically supplements your brief.

The following chapters examine further techniques of persuasive writing in the context of particular legal documents.

CHAPTER

13

Pleadings

I. THE COMPLAINT

"A civil action is commenced by filing a complaint with the court."[1] One might suppose that any lawyer would graduate from law school with a solid grasp of the mechanics of such a fundamental and significant document. However, few law students draft a complaint before leaving law school, and many graduate without having seen one. Not surprisingly, when faced with the task of preparing a complaint, you may be tempted to turn for guidance to the forms in formbooks or in your office files.

Forms may provide general guidance in some cases. In fact, many jurisdictions have officially authorized pleading forms for certain kinds of suits. The California Judicial Council has even approved pleading forms that invite the user to choose among standard allegations by checking boxes.[2]

Nonetheless, you will more quickly and thoroughly master the skills of artful pleading if you understand the components of a complaint well enough to draft one "from scratch." Your primary tools in such a task are the results of your investigation of facts and your knowledge of the applicable law. Beyond that, rules of procedure and local court rules provide the necessary guidance.

---

1. Fed. R. Civ. P. 3.
2. See Barbara Child, Drafting Legal Documents: Principles and Practices 10-14 (2d ed. 1992).

A. FORMAT

Local court rules on pleading often specify a form for a caption that identifies the case and the nature of the document. For example, the Rules of Practice for the United States District Court for the District of Arizona specify the precise location in the caption on the cover sheet for, among other things, the following information: (1) the name, address, state bar attorney number, and telephone number of the representing attorney; (2) the title of the court; (3) the names of the parties; and (4) a designation of the nature of the document.[3]

More substantively, the Federal Rules of Civil Procedure require a complaint, or any other pleading setting forth a claim for relief, to contain three elements:

1. a short and plain statement of the grounds upon which the court's jurisdiction depends . . .
2. a short and plain statement of the claim showing that the pleader is entitled to relief, and
3. a demand for judgment for the relief the pleader seeks.[4]

Each of these elements warrants further examination.

1. Jurisdictional Statement

The jurisdictional statement is particularly important in a complaint filed in federal court, because the subject matter jurisdiction of federal courts is limited to that authorized by Article III of the United States Constitution and by federal statutes.[5] Therefore, in the initial paragraphs of a complaint in federal court, you should allege facts establishing subject matter jurisdiction based on a federal question,[6] diversity of citizenship,[7] or a special statutory grant of jurisdiction.[8] Although the jurisdictional statement is sufficient if it alleges facts that support the court's exercise of jurisdiction,[9] federal pleaders customarily cite to the specific statutes that grant jurisdiction:

> 3. This claim arises under Title VII of the Civil Rights Act of 1964; therefore, this court has subject matter jurisdiction under 42 U.S.C. §2000e-5(f)(3) and 28 U.S.C. §1331.[10]

Some jurisdictional statements in federal complaints also include allegations that establish that the court has personal jurisdiction over the defendant,

---

3. U.S. Dist. Ct. D. Ariz. R. 10(a).
4. Fed. R. Civ. P. 8(a).
5. See, e.g., Mayor v. Cooper, 73 U.S. (6 Wall.) 247, 252 (1868).
6. 28 U.S.C. §1331 (1988).
7. 28 U.S.C. §1332 (1988).
8. E.g., 42 U.S.C. §2000e-5(f)(3) (1988) (granting jurisdiction of actions brought under Title VII of the Civil Rights Act of 1964).
9. Aguirre v. Automotive Teamsters, 633 F.2d 168, 174 (9th Cir. 1980).
10. See also Fed. R. Civ. P., app. Form 2 ¶¶(b), (c).

if that is not apparent from the body of the complaint. Assuming that lack of personal jurisdiction is treated as an affirmative defense for pleading purposes, however, a complaint will not be insufficient for failure to affirmatively plead personal jurisdiction over the defendant.

Pleading subject matter jurisdiction is less important in state court than in federal court, because most state trial courts are courts of general jurisdiction. When state pleaders address subject matter jurisdiction at all, it is often with perfunctory introductory allegations that the amount in controversy exceeds that reserved for state courts of limited jurisdiction, perhaps coupled with a citation to the state constitutional or statutory provision that authorizes the court's exercise of general trial jurisdiction. Even this is usually unnecessary, because the request for relief ordinarily satisfies any jurisdictional amount in controversy.

Interestingly, perhaps without noting the difference between the subject matter jurisdictions of state and federal courts, some state legislatures have adopted all the elements of the governing federal rule of civil procedure, thus requiring a jurisdictional statement in state court complaints.[11] Pleaders in such states recognize that a special allegation of subject matter jurisdiction should be unnecessary in a state court complaint, but they appropriately feel compelled to satisfy the rule's express requirement by including some kind of jurisdictional statement. Consequently, even though the original federal rule almost certainly was not intended to impose on a plaintiff in federal court the burden of affirmatively pleading personal jurisdiction, state pleaders often begin their complaints with allegations of personal jurisdiction over the defendants. Such statements typically introduce the parties and allege in fairly conclusory fashion that the defendant has engaged in conduct in the state out of which the claim arises or has otherwise established the requisite contacts with the state.

2. Claim for Relief

Early state pleading codes that required allegations of "material facts" or "ultimate facts" supporting a cause of action generated considerable controversy over the intended meaning of the word "facts."[12] Perhaps to avoid that controversy, Federal Rule of Civil Procedure 8(a)(2) omits any reference to "facts" in its requirement of a statement of the claim for relief. Nonetheless, "Rule 8(a)(2) envisages the statement of circumstances, occurrences, and events in support of the claim presented."[13] Most people would use the word "fact" to describe allegations of that nature. Similarly, this book will use "fact" in this context while attempting to avoid the historical confusion surrounding the term.

---

11. See, e.g., Ariz. R. Civ. P. 8(a).

12. See, e.g., Walter W. Cook, "Facts" and "Statements of Fact," 4 U. Chi. L. Rev. 233, 233-234, 235-239, 241-242, 246 (1937), *reprinted in* William R. Bishin and Christopher D. Stone, Law, Language, and Ethics 277-281 (1972).

13. Advisory Committee on Rules for Civil Procedure, Report of Proposed Amendments to the Rules of Civil Procedure for the United States District Courts 18-19 (1955), *reprinted in* Richard H. Field & Benjamin Kaplan, Materials for a Basic Course in Civil Procedure 439 (5th ed. 1984).

Thus, in the main body of the complaint, you will allege facts and conclusions of liability that establish entitlement to relief. This may require preliminary legal research as well as fact investigation. Your knowledge of the law enables you to identify legally significant facts, and your knowledge of the case helps you to determine what facts you can allege in good faith.

To draft your claim for relief artfully, you must determine

(1) the extent, if any, to which you should supplement fact allegations with references to the law;
(2) the specific content of the fact allegations; and
(3) the appropriate level of specificity of the allegations.

a. Allegations of Fact and Citations to Law

Your complaint should allege facts and ultimate conclusions establishing a claim for relief; you need not cite to supporting legal authority.[14] This can be illustrated with the model of the syllogism of deductive reasoning:

Major premise—Rule of Law
Minor premise—Allegations of Fact
Conclusion—Allegation of Liability or Other Ultimate Conclusion

A complaint with the minimum necessary elements will explicitly set forth the minor premise and the conclusion, and it will leave the major premise implicit. Some complaints even omit an explicit statement of the ultimate conclusion of liability, on the theory that it is implicit in the request for relief.

For a simple example, a form complaint appended to the Federal Rules of Civil Procedure states a claim for debt that alleges subsidiary facts and the ultimate conclusion that the defendant "owes" money to the plaintiff:

2. Defendant on or about June 1, 1935, executed and delivered to plaintiff a promissory note . . . whereby defendant promised to pay to plaintiff or order on June 1, 1936 the sum of _____ dollars with interest thereon at the rate of six percent. per annum.
3. Defendant owes to plaintiff the amount of said note and interest.[15]

These sample allegations do not explicitly state the major premise that a promise to pay money expressed in a written promissory note is enforceable under the common law of contracts or under some other legal authority. Whether the alleged facts state a claim for relief under applicable legal authority can be addressed in subsequent proceedings, such as on a motion to dismiss.[16]

Thus, in practice, citation to specific legal authority is much less common in the claim for relief than in the jurisdictional statement. The only references to legal authority commonly found in claims for relief are descriptive headings

---

14. E.g., Doss v. South Central Bell Tel. Co., 834 F.2d 421 (5th Cir. 1987).
15. Fed. R. Civ. P., app. Form 3 (brackets and footnote deleted).
16. See Fed. R. Civ. P. 12(b)(6).

that introduce counts with general legal theories of relief, such as "Negligence," "Wrongful Discharge," "Employment Discrimination," or "Breach of Contract."

Nonetheless, a pleader will sometimes cite to authority in the claim for relief for a strategic purpose. For example, in cases in which the plaintiff wants a settlement at the outset of litigation, his attorney may briefly cite to authority in the complaint to demonstrate to the defendant that the claim is substantial and that further litigation is unlikely to reduce the risk of liability. In most cases, however, the attorney could achieve the same result less subtly, and perhaps more effectively, with a demand letter that explains the merits of the claim. Such a letter could either precede or accompany the complaint.

In one exceptional case, the primary drafter of a state complaint preceded her first claim for relief with a special statutory section that included more than a page of quotations from, and citations to, state statutes that she alleged established a duty on the part of state officials to provide health care for the chronically mentally ill:

XIX
APPLICABLE STATE LAW

Pursuant to A.R.S. §36-104.17, the Director of D.H.S. has the mandatory obligation to:

> Take appropriate steps to provide health care services to the medically dependent citizens of this state.

Furthermore, under A.R.S. §36-204.A.1, the director has the responsibility to "[a]dopt rules and regulations for outpatient services" at Arizona State Hospital. . . .

XXIII

Pursuant to the foregoing statutes, D.H.S., Arizona State Hospital, and the Board have the duty to provide medical and health care to the needy sick, including the chronically mentally ill. . . .[17]

Because the theory of relief in this complaint was novel, the drafter probably wanted to introduce the major premise of the claim into the complaint to minimize the risk that the judge or the opposing counsel would conclude at the outset that the claim was frivolous. In this case, the drafter's purpose was not to encourage an early settlement but to enhance the chances that the claim would survive pretrial challenges so that the theory of the claim could be developed on a full record at trial. The strategy worked: The claim survived to trial, the trial court granted extensive injunctive relief, and the state supreme court affirmed.[18]

---

17. Complaint in Arnold v. Sarn, No. C432355, ¶¶XIX-XXIII (Ariz. Super. Ct. March 26, 1986) (filed by the Arizona Center for Law in the Public Interest).
18. Arnold v. Arizona Dept. of Health Servs., 775 P.2d 521 (Ariz. 1989) (en banc).

The analysis of statutes in that complaint illustrates an exception to the general rule. Under the federal rules, citation to legal authority in a claim for relief is never mandatory and is only rarely strategically advantageous.

b. Substance of Allegations

One writer has recommended that pleaders pay heed to the journalist's five Ws when stating a claim for relief: who, what, where, when, and why.[19]

Who—In many complaints, you will introduce the parties in the jurisdictional allegations. Otherwise, your statement of the claim for relief should identify them and their relationship to one another. It should also identify any other significant actors.

What, Where, When—The statement of the claim should describe the events that give rise to the claim. You should take care to allege all facts or conclusions needed to support the request for relief. For example, you should support a request for specific performance with an allegation that the legal remedy is inadequate.

Why—You should allege any state of mind that is material to the claim or to the availability of special relief. For example, a request for punitive damages in a common law tort claim must be supported by an allegation of malice, willful misconduct, or at least recklessness, depending on the jurisdiction.

You need not allege all matters that may ultimately be in dispute; you need allege only the elements of your client's prima facie case. Affirmative defenses must be pleaded in the answer,[20] and the complaint need not anticipate them. The federal rules list 19 affirmative defenses;[21] statutes and case law may help you define the burdens of pleading on other matters. In case of doubt, you should plead a matter as part of the claim for relief.

For example, suppose that the jurisdiction in which the complaint is filed recognizes a cause of action for intentional infliction of emotional distress on proof of four elements: (1) The defendant engaged in extreme and outrageous conduct (2) with the intent to cause severe emotional distress or with reckless disregard for the possibility of those consequences, and (3) the conduct caused the plaintiff to suffer (4) severe emotional distress.[22] After introductory allegations establishing personal jurisdiction and identifying Jansen as the plaintiff and Bostich as one of the defendants, the count for this claim should allege facts supporting each of the four elements of the prima facie case:

---

19. Delmar Karlen, Procedure Before Trial in a Nutshell 41-42 (1972).
20. Fed. R. Civ. P. 8(c).
21. Id.
22. See, e.g., Watts v. Golden Age Nursing Home, 619 P.2d 1032, 1035 (Ariz. 1980) (citing Restatement (Second) of Torts §46).

COUNT I
Infliction of Emotional Distress

3. Jansen worked on an assembly line at the Zydeco Radio factory under the direct supervision of Bostich. As Jansen's supervisor, Bostich had the authority to impose production quotas on Jansen and to impose discipline, including termination, for failure to meet quotas. — **Relationship of parties**

4. From April 1 to June 10, 1993, Bostich engaged in the extreme and outrageous conduct of imposing impossible production quotas on Jansen and causing Jansen to believe that his job security depended on his meeting the quotas.[23] — **Conduct**

5. Bostich maliciously engaged in this conduct for the purpose of causing Jansen to suffer severe emotional distress. Alternatively, Bostich recklessly disregarded the likelihood that Jansen would suffer such distress.[24] — **State of mind**

6. As a direct result of Bostich's conduct, on June 10, 1993, Jansen suffered a complete nervous breakdown requiring bed rest for three weeks and extensive medical care. Jansen continues to suffer from insomnia, headaches, inability to concentrate at work, general nervousness, and other emotional distress as a result of Bostich's conduct. In an effort to address these symptoms, Jansen has frequently consulted a general physician and a psychological counselor, incurring substantial medical expenses. — **Causation and distress** / **Injuries**

Jansen therefore requests the following relief: . . .

In contrast, even if the allegations raise some question of whether the statute of limitations has expired, the complaint need not affirmatively allege that the statute of limitations has not expired or has been tolled. Instead, expiration of the statute of limitations is an affirmative defense that the defendant has the burden of pleading.[25]

c. Specificity of Fact Allegations

Modern rules of procedure abolish the rigid common law forms of action.[26] The federal rules and those of most states approve pleadings that

---

23. Whether the allegations of paragraphs 3 and 4 establish "extreme and outrageous conduct" will depend on the law of that jurisdiction and could be litigated on a motion to dismiss for failure to state a claim. See, e.g., Fed. R. Civ. P. 12(b)(6).

24. This allegation of scienter should suffice not only to satisfy the second element of the tort but to support a request for punitive damages as well.

25. Fed. R. Civ. P. 8(c).

26. "There shall be one form of action to be known as 'civil action.'" Fed. R. Civ. P. 2.

give the court and opposing party only general notice of most claims and defenses.[27] Revelation of more specific evidentiary details is left to the discovery and disclosure process, motions practice, and the pretrial conference.[28]

A bare allegation of liability without any supporting facts would be insufficient even under the federal rules:

> [Rule 8(a)(2)] requires the pleader to disclose adequate information as the basis of his claim for relief as distinguished from a bare averment that he wants relief and is entitled to it.[29]

Nonetheless, the rules permit fact allegations that are fairly general and conclusory.

The appropriate level of generality can be illustrated by a continuum that represents varying degrees of specificity in fact allegations. The continuum begins with allegations of conclusions based on the analysis of implicit subsidiary facts. It gains steadily in specificity until it presents specific evidence that establishes subsidiary facts:

CONCLUSION	**SPECIFIC EVIDENCE**
negligence	**eyewitness estimate of speed; analysis of skid marks**

As an example of extreme specificity, a complaint could state a claim for negligent operation of an automobile by alleging each bit of evidence with which the plaintiff hopes to prove negligence at trial:

> 3. . . . Jill Graham and Ben Cooper were standing at the corner of 7th Avenue and Washington Street at noon and observed the defendant driving his automobile at high speed west on Washington Street toward 9th Avenue. Each of them estimated that the defendant was traveling at approximately twice the posted speed limit of 35 miles per hour. An expert who examined skid marks at the accident scene estimated that the defendant's automobile was traveling at more than 60 miles per hour when it entered the intersection of Washington Street and 9th Avenue. . . .

Nearer to the other extreme, the complaint could allege the ultimate conclusion of negligence with only general supporting factual information:

> 2. On January 1, 1987, defendant negligently drove a motor vehicle in the intersection of Washington Street and 9th Avenue, striking plaintiff in the crosswalk.
> 3. As a result, . . .

---

27. Cf. Fed. R. Civ. P. 9 (requiring specificity in allegations of certain matters).
28. See Fed. R. Civ. P. 12, 16, 26-37, 56.
29. Advisory Committee on Rules for Civil Procedure, Report of Proposed Amendments to the Rules of Civil Procedure for the United States District Courts 18-19 (1955), *reprinted in* Richard H. Field and Benjamin Kaplan, Materials for a Basic Course in Civil Procedure 439, 440 (5th ed. 1984).

This second example is adapted from a sample form in the Federal Rules of Civil Procedure,[30] illustrating the acceptability of general, conclusory allegations on most matters.

In those states that retain the more traditional "code pleading" requirements, the appropriate level of specificity probably would lie somewhere in the middle of the continuum. The complaint in such a state would allege the "ultimate facts" supporting the conclusions of liability, but it would not give a detailed account of all the evidence from which the facts and conclusions are derived. For example, the complaint might allege that the defendant operated the car negligently by exceeding the speed limit and by weaving between lanes, but it would not require allegations of the subsidiary evidence of speeding, such as the analysis of skid marks.[31]

Whether your complaint is governed by the federal standard of notice pleading or by more traditional rules, you may reap strategic advantages from alleging your claim for relief with the maximum generality allowable. Unnecessarily specific allegations might prematurely commit the plaintiff to a particular factual theory of the case or might reveal information helpful to the opposing party. For example, in one suit to recover a commission, an attorney specifically alleged that her client, the plaintiff, acted as agent for the defendant in a real estate transaction. That allegation was unnecessary to the client's claim for relief, which would have been supported by a more general allegation of contractual liability. Subsequent discovery revealed that the plaintiff probably did not act as the defendant's agent. The plaintiff's earlier allegations of agency, however, supported a defense and counterclaim for the defendant based on breaches of an agent's fiduciary duties. The plaintiff was forced to move to amend the complaint to delete the allegation of agency, an amendment necessary to avoid summary judgment for the defendant.

Despite the potential pitfalls of detailed allegations, few complaints are as conclusory as the passage above quoted from the sample federal negligence pleading. In some cases, greater specificity is required by applicable rules. For example, the Federal Rules of Civil Procedure provide that allegations of certain "special matters," such as fraud or mistake, shall state the circumstances with particularity.[32]

Even when particularity is not required, few pleaders achieve the generality reflected in the federal sample complaints. Some may include greater detail out of excessive caution; they may erroneously fear that less specific allegations would fail to state a proper claim. Many pleaders simply prefer to present a clearer, more sympathetic story than would be told with minimal notice pleading. In some cases, the pleader may hope that detailed allegations will more forcefully display the merits of the claim and will persuade the opposing party to settle quickly. In others, the pleader may hope to use the pleadings as a preliminary discovery device by eliciting specific answers to

---

30. Fed. R. Civ. P., app. Form 9 ¶¶2, 3.
31. See generally Richard H. Field & Benjamin Kaplan, Materials for a Basic Course in Civil Procedure 440-442 (5th ed. 1984).
32. E.g., Fed. R. Civ. P. 9(b); see Stern v. Leucadia Nat'l Corp., 844 F.2d 997 (2d Cir. 1988) (allegations of fraud based on information and belief must be accompanied by statement of facts on which belief is founded).

detailed allegations in the complaint or by triggering mandatory disclosure requirements with detailed allegations.[33]

In summary, the specificity of your allegations is partly a matter of style and strategy. As long as you take care to allege facts supporting every element of your prima facie case, you can tailor the specificity of your allegations to your strategic needs.

3. Request for Relief

Your complaint should end with a simple statement of the relief sought by your client. The main request for relief typically is for an injunction, an award of money damages, or both. Additionally, you should request an award of reasonable costs and attorney's fees if your client has a legal basis for such an award. Finally, you can retain flexibility by closing the request for relief with a catch-all request for "other appropriate relief":

> Jansen therefore requests judgment granting the following relief:
> (1) an award of compensatory damages in an amount to be set at trial;
> (2) an award of punitive damages in an amount to be set at trial;
> (3) an award of costs and attorney's fees; and
> (4) such other relief as the court deems appropriate.

B. STYLE AND ORGANIZATION

1. Writing Style

Some of the lawyer's stuffiest jargon can be found in antiquated pleadings:

> Comes now the plaintiff before this honorable court and, through his attorneys, Jenkins, Brown, and Little, alleges, pleads, and avers as follows: . . .
> 3. That the defendant did employ said plaintiff as a designer of clothes . . . ;
> 4. That on July 6, 1927, said defendant did . . .
> Wherefore, the plaintiff prays that this honorable court grant judgment for the plaintiff and award . . .

The Federal Rules reject jargon in favor of plain English: "Each averment of a pleading shall be simple, concise, and direct."[34] Stated in plain English, the allegations in the preceding example are unquestionably simpler and more concise:

---

33. See Fed. R. Civ. P. 26(a)(1)(A), 113 S. Ct. 505 (orders) (1993) (mandatory disclosure rule approved by U.S. Supreme Court).
34. Fed. R. Civ. P. 8(e)(1). Ironically, the sample forms in the appendix to the Federal Rules contain their share of jargon.

Plaintiff alleges: . . .
3. The defendant employed the plaintiff as a designer of clothes . . .
4. On July 6, 1927, the defendant . . .
Plaintiff requests the following relief: . . .

Among other things, plain English avoids pretentious cliches. For example, one fairly recent complaint alleged that "Plaintiff and Defendant discussed their marriage agreement from time to time and on a great many occasions too numerous to mention herein." A more concise version achieves simplicity without loss of material substance: "Plaintiff and Defendant discussed their marriage agreement regularly and frequently."

2. Organization

To facilitate analysis of the claims by the court and the parties, you should set forth the allegations of your complaint in consecutively numbered paragraphs. Separation of the statements of different claims for relief into separate counts may be permissible or required, depending on the circumstances.

If you have joined separate claims for relief based on different transactions, federal rules require a statement of the claims in separate counts "whenever a separation facilitates the clear presentation of the matters set forth."[35] Otherwise, presentation of allegations in separate counts appears to be discretionary.

Even if your client's claims arise out of a single transaction, separate counts may be helpful if you rely on distinct legal theories that are based on different fact allegations. For example, a consumer injured by a faulty electrical appliance may have a cause of action against the retailer on two legal theories: products liability in tort, and breach of a contractual warranty. If you divide the allegations into separate counts, you can identify which fact allegations are material to each theory of relief. If some facts are common to both theories, one count can incorporate some of the allegations of the other:

COUNT I
Products Liability

4. On January 1, 1987, Green purchased a microwave oven from Retailer.
5. The microwave oven had an unreasonably dangerous defect . . .

• • • •

COUNT II
Breach of Warranty

8. Green realleges the allegations in paragraphs 4-7.
9. Babcock Appliance Center warranted the microwave oven to be free of defects. . . .

---

35. Fed. R. Civ. P. 10(b).

You must also exercise discretion to determine whether to follow each count with a separate request for relief or to consolidate them in a single request after presentation of all counts. As with separation of theories into counts, separation of requests for relief to accompany different counts may be helpful if the available remedies vary with each count. For example, if punitive damages are available only on the products liability count and if attorney's fees are available only on the count for breach of warranty, separate requests for relief after each count may facilitate subsequent analysis of the claims. On the other hand, if the requests for relief on different counts are identical, consolidation in a single request obviously avoids pointless repetition.

II. THE ANSWER

To avoid judgment against him by default, the defendant must respond to a complaint by filing an answer or other appropriate response.[36] The answer must admit or deny each allegation of the complaint.[37] In addition, the answer may set forth affirmative defenses,[38] assert counterclaims against the plaintiff,[39] or both.[40] If the answer asserts a counterclaim, the original plaintiff must file a reply that admits or denies each allegation of the counter-claim and that may set forth affirmative defenses to the counterclaim.

A. ADMISSIONS AND DENIALS

If a defendant contests liability, he obviously is prepared to deny in good faith some of the material allegations of the complaint. On the other hand, nearly every complaint will contain some allegations that the defendant admits. Therefore, when drafting an answer, you should not generally deny all allegations of the complaint; instead, you should address each paragraph of the complaint and identify areas of dispute. For example, an answer to the complaint partially set forth earlier in this chapter might admit and deny allegations in the following manner:

ADMISSIONS AND DENIALS

1. Defendant Bostich admits the allegations in paragraphs 1-3 of Plaintiff Jansen's complaint.
2. Bostich denies the allegations in paragraph 4 of the complaint that

---

36. See Fed. R. Civ. P. 12(a). The defendant may move to dismiss the complaint on its face before filing an answer. Fed. R. Civ. P. 12(b).
37. Fed. R. Civ. P. 8(b).
38. Fed. R. Civ. P. 8(b), 8(c).
39. Fed. R. Civ. P. 7(a), 8(a).
40. An answer may also assert a cross-claim against an originally named co-defendant or a third-party claim against a new "third-party defendant" that the defendant impleads. See id.

he set impossible goals for Jansen and that he intimidated Jansen in his work. Bostich admits that he warned Jansen of the possibility of termination for failing to meet goals.

3. Bostich denies the allegations in paragraph 5 of the complaint.

4. Bostich has no information on which to form a belief in the truth of the allegations in paragraph 6 of the complaint, and he therefore denies them.[41]

B. AFFIRMATIVE DEFENSES

In a separate section of your answer, you should allege facts and conclusions supporting any affirmative defenses that your client, the defendant, may reasonably assert.[42] Even if the allegations of the complaint are true and are legally sufficient to state a claim for relief, a meritorious affirmative defense to the prima facie case will justify judgment for the defendant.

For example, in the litigation between Jansen and Bostich, suppose that the statute of limitations for tort actions in the jurisdiction is one year, that Jansen filed his complaint on June 10, 1994, and that Bostich last communicated a supervisory ultimatum to Jansen on Thursday, June 7, 1993. Bostich may be prepared to argue that the statute of limitations has expired on the ground that Jansen's cause of action accrued at the latest on June 7, 1993, the date of Bostich's last act, rather than on Monday, June 11, 1993, the date of Jansen's nervous breakdown. If so, Bostich could assert this in fairly conclusory fashion as an affirmative defense:

AFFIRMATIVE DEFENSE

5. Bostich last exercised any supervisory control over Jansen on June 7, 1993. Therefore, Jansen's cause of action accrued more than one year before the filing of his complaint, and the statute of limitations bars his action.

C. COUNTERCLAIMS

The defendant named in a complaint may himself wish to assert an independent claim for relief against the plaintiff. If so, the roles of the parties are reversed for purposes of the counterclaim, and the principles of pleading discussed in Section I above apply to the counterclaim.[43]

For example, in the litigation between Jansen and Bostich, additional facts might support a claim against Jansen for battery:

---

41. See generally Fed. R. Civ. P. 8(b) (form of denials).
42. See Fed. R. Civ. P. 8(b), 8(c).
43. See Fed. R. Civ. P. 8(a).

COUNTERCLAIM
Battery

6. On the evening of Friday, July 16, 1993, Jansen struck Bostich over the head with a baseball bat as Bostich left the Zydeco Radio factory.

7. Jansen acted maliciously and for the specific purpose of causing serious injury to Bostich.

8. As a result of Jansen's malicious attack, Bostich lost consciousness, required treatment in a hospital emergency room, and suffered debilitating pain for 24 hours.

Therefore, Bostich requests the following relief: . . .

III. SUMMARY

When drafting pleadings, you should carefully follow the format prescribed by applicable rules. For example, federal rules require the drafter of a complaint to allege

(1) jurisdiction,
(2) a claim for relief, and
(3) a demand for judgment.

In an answer, you

(1) must admit or deny the allegations of the complaint, and
(2) may also assert affirmative defenses or a counterclaim.

Generally, pleadings should allege ultimate conclusions and supporting facts but not legal standards. Although the claim for relief must allege all elements of the prima facie case, most allegations may be general and need not develop specific, evidentiary facts.

═══════ E X E R C I S E   1 3 - 1 ═══════

Compare and critically evaluate the following three versions of a complaint in the same wrongful discharge action. Which level of specificity of allegations do you prefer? What other differences in style do the complaints reflect? Which styles do you prefer?

Thomas Sanchez
Simpson, Sanchez & Summers
303 North Central Avenue
Phoenix, Arizona 85002
(602) 229-1111
Bar No. 28371
Attorney for the plaintiff

IN THE SUPERIOR COURT
MARICOPA COUNTY, ARIZONA

GEORGE BRYANT, Plaintiff, v. MARIE JARDON, d.b.a. Chez Marie, Defendant.	No. _____ COMPLAINT

Plaintiff alleges:

COUNT 1

I

Plaintiff George Bryant is a resident of Phoenix, Arizona. Defendant Marie Jardon owns and operates Chez Marie, a restaurant located in Phoenix, Arizona.

II

Bryant worked for Jardon as a waiter at Chez Marie from August 16, 1992, to September 28, 1993.

III

At the time of his discharge on September 28, 1993, Bryant had an employment contract with Chez Marie that imposed substantive and procedural restrictions upon Jardon's right to terminate Bryant's employment.

IV

Acting through her agent, Mario Prieto, Jardon discharged Bryant September 28, 1993, in breach of her employment contract with Bryant.

335

V

As a result of Jardon's breach of contract, Bryant has suffered lost wages and other incidental and consequential losses.

COUNT 2

VI

Bryant realleges and incorporates paragraphs I-V above.

VII

Acting through her agent, Jardon maliciously and unlawfully discharged Bryant for reasons that violate public policy, causing Bryant lost wages and other injuries.

Bryant therefore requests judgment granting the following relief:

(1) an order reinstating Bryant to his position as waiter at Chez Marie;
(2) an award of compensatory and punitive damages;
(3) an award of costs and attorney's fees; and
(4) other appropriate relief.

Dated _____

by _____ ,
Thomas Sanchez
Simpson, Sanchez & Summers
303 North Central Avenue
Phoenix, AZ 85002
Attorneys for Plaintiff

Thomas Sanchez
Simpson, Sanchez & Summers
303 North Central Avenue
Phoenix, Arizona 85002
(602) 229-1111
Bar No. 28371
Attorney for the plaintiff

ARIZONA SUPERIOR COURT
MARICOPA COUNTY

GEORGE BRYANT, Plaintiff, v. MARIE JARDON, d.b.a. Chez Marie, Defendant.	No. _____ COMPLAINT

Plaintiff alleges:

I
BREACH OF PROMISE

1. Plaintiff George Bryant is a resident of Phoenix, Arizona. Defendant Marie Jardon owns and operates Chez Marie, a restaurant located in Phoenix, Arizona.

2. Bryant worked for Jardon as a waiter at Chez Marie from August 16, 1992, to September 28, 1993. Mario Prieto acted as the maitre d' and supervisor of waiters at Chez Marie during Bryant's employment at Chez Marie. In all the events alleged below, Prieto acted on behalf of Jardon.

3. At the time of his discharge on September 28, 1993, Bryant had an employment contract with Chez Marie that included the terms of an "Employee Handbook." Bryant foreseeably relied to his detriment on promises contained in the Handbook.

4. The Employee Handbook contains promises of job security, including promises that (i) Jardon will not discharge any waiter except for inadequate performance and (ii) any waiter recommended for discharge has the right to meet with Jardon and Prieto to persuade them that the waiter should not be discharged. The Handbook also provides that Jardon will make the final determination in the event of disagreement between Prieto and Jardon on a discharge matter.

5. At all times during his employment at Chez Marie, Bryant performed his job in a manner that met the highest standards at Chez Marie. Despite the adequacy of Bryant's performance, Prieto discharged Bryant September 28, 1993. Although Bryant immediately requested a meeting with Prieto

and Jardon to discuss the discharge, both Prieto and Jardon refused to convene such a meeting.

6. As a result of Jardon's breach of promises in the Handbook, Bryant has suffered lost wages and other incidental and consequential losses.

7. Jardon's breach of promises in the Handbook constitutes a breach of her employment contract with Bryant and has created an injustice that can be avoided only by enforcing the promises.

II
WRONGFUL DISCHARGE

8. Bryant realleges and incorporates paragraphs 1-7 above.

9. In discharging Bryant, Prieto was motivated by malice, by an invidiously discriminatory animus, and by concerns unrelated to the successful operation of Chez Marie. Jardon's termination of Bryant's employment therefore violated public policy.

III
REQUEST FOR RELIEF

10. Bryant requests an order reinstating Bryant to his position as waiter at Chez Marie; an award of compensatory damages in an amount to be set at trial; an award of punitive damages in an amount to be set at trial; an award of costs and attorney's fees; and such other relief as the court deems appropriate.

Dated _____

by _____,
Thomas Sanchez
Simpson, Sanchez & Summers
303 North Central Avenue
Phoenix, AZ 85002
Attorneys for Plaintiff

Thomas Sanchez
Simpson, Sanchez & Summers
303 North Central Avenue
Phoenix, Arizona 85002
(602) 229-1111
Bar No. 28371
Attorney for the plaintiff

IN THE SUPERIOR COURT OF THE STATE OF ARIZONA
IN AND FOR THE COUNTY OF MARICOPA

GEORGE BRYANT, Plaintiff, v. MARIE JARDON, d.b.a. Chez Marie, and MARIO PRIETO, Defendants.	No. _____ COMPLAINT (JURY TRIAL REQUESTED)

Plaintiff George Bryant, by and through his attorneys, Simpson, Sanchez and Summers, alleges the following:

1. This is an action for injunctive relief and for compensatory damages exceeding $30,000. This court has original jurisdiction pursuant to the Arizona Constitution, Article 6, §14(3).

2. Plaintiff is a resident of Phoenix, Arizona. Defendant Marie Jardon owns and operates Chez Marie, a restaurant located in Phoenix, Arizona. Defendant Mario Prieto acted as the maitre d' and supervisor of waiters at Chez Marie during Bryant's employment at Chez Marie. All material events alleged below took place in Maricopa County.

I
FIRST CLAIM FOR RELIEF
(Breach of Contract)

3. Plaintiff worked for Defendants as a waiter at Chez Marie from August 16, 1992, to September 28, 1993. In all the events alleged below, Defendant Prieto acted on his own behalf as well as on behalf of Defendant Jardon.

4. On January 1, 1993, Defendants modified Plaintiff's employment contract to include promises of job security contained in the terms of an "Employee Handbook" and in oral assurances.

5. Among other things, the Employee Handbook contains the following promises of job security: (i) Defendants will not discharge any waiter except for inadequate performance and (ii) any waiter recommended for discharge has the right to meet with Defendants to persuade them that the waiter should not be discharged. The Handbook also provides that Defendant

339

Jardon will make the final determination in the event of disagreement between Defendants on a discharge matter. (Copy of text of excerpts of Handbook are attached and incorporated by this reference.)

6. At all times during his employment at Chez Marie, Plaintiff performed his job in a manner that met the highest standards at Chez Marie. Despite the adequacy of Plaintiff's performance, Defendants discharged Plaintiff on September 28, 1993. Although Plaintiff immediately requested a meeting with Defendants to discuss the discharge, Defendants refused to convene such a meeting.

7. As a result of Defendant's breach of contract, Plaintiff has suffered lost wages and other incidental and consequential losses.

THEREFORE, Plaintiff demands judgment granting the following relief:

  (i)   an order reinstating Plaintiff to his former position at Chez Marie;
  (ii) an award of compensatory damages for all consequential and incidental losses;
  (iii) an award of costs and attorney's fees; and
  (iv) such other relief as the court deems appropriate.

II
SECOND CLAIM FOR RELIEF
(Promissory Estoppel)

8. Plaintiff realleges paragraphs 1-7 above and incorporates them by this reference.

9. On January 1, 1993, Defendants gave Plaintiff promises of job security by making oral assurances and by distributing the Employee Handbook. Plaintiff relied to his detriment on those promises by performing extraordinary services and by forbearing from taking other job opportunities. That reliance was reasonably foreseeable by Defendants.

10. Defendants' termination of Bryant's employment on September 28, 1993 constituted a breach of their promises of job security and has created an injustice that can be avoided only by enforcing the promises.

THEREFORE, Plaintiff demands judgment granting the following relief:

  (i)   an order reinstating Plaintiff to his former position at Chez Marie;
  (ii) an award of compensatory damages for all consequential and incidental losses;
  (iii) an award of costs and attorney's fees; and
  (iv) such other relief as the court deems appropriate.

III
THIRD CLAIM FOR RELIEF
(Wrongful Discharge)

11. Plaintiff realleges paragraphs 1-10 above and incorporates them by this reference.

12. Defendants maliciously discharged Plaintiff because of his sexual orientation and because Plaintiff's exemplary performance made Defendant Prieto jealous. Those reasons for discharge reflect bad faith and violate the public policy of state laws.

THEREFORE, Plaintiff demands judgment granting the following relief:

  (i)   an order reinstating Plaintiff to his position as waiter at Chez Marie;

  (ii) an award of compensatory damages in an amount to be set at trial;

 (iii) an award of punitive damages in an amount to be set at trial;

 (iv) an award of costs and attorney's fees; and

  (v) such other relief as the court deems appropriate.

Dated _____

by _____,
Thomas Sanchez
Simpson, Sanchez and Summers
1303 North Central Avenue
Phoenix, AZ 85002
Attorneys for Plaintiff

CHAPTER 14

Motion for Summary Judgment

I. PROCEDURAL CONTEXT

Summary judgment is a popular means of pretrial disposition. In most cases, you will have no difficulty alleging facts that state a claim for relief; therefore, your complaints will seldom be susceptible to attack for failure to state a claim. On the other hand, even if you allege a claim or defense in good faith, you may fail to gather substantial admissible evidence supporting the claim or defense. In such cases, the opposing party's motion for summary judgment exposes the absence of a triable issue of fact. It compels you to choose between making at least a preliminary showing of the evidence supporting your allegations or suffering adverse judgment before trial. In other cases, both parties concede the absence of any dispute of fact, stipulate to the facts, and use the motion for summary judgment to argue unsettled questions about the law and its application to the stipulated facts.

Summary judgment litigation often takes place only after each party has thoroughly investigated the case through the discovery and disclosure process.[1] Indeed, the trial judge may delay resolution of a motion for summary judgment if further discovery is needed to permit the nonmoving party to support its opposition. Nonetheless, if you successfully move for summary judgment, you will avoid the greater burdens of a full trial.

On the other hand, if the trial court denies your motion for summary judgment, your unsuccessful motion may hamper your ability to settle the case before trial. If the opposing counsel initially expected to settle the case,

---

1. The procedures for discovery are set forth in Federal Rules of Civil Procedure 26-37. The Arizona Rules of Civil Procedure have partly replaced the adversarial discovery process with mandatory disclosure requirements. See, e.g., Ariz. R. Civ. P. 26.1 (1991). See also Fed. R. Civ. P. 26(a) (1993) (proposed mandatory disclosure rules approved by U.S. Supreme Court).

he may have only minimally prepared the case prior to summary judgment litigation. Your motion for summary judgment, however, will have forced your opponent to organize his facts and legal arguments. If the motion fails, he likely will be much more demanding in settlement negotiations for three reasons. First, the denial of the motion will strengthen his belief in the potential merits of his client's claims or defenses. Second, he will be more nearly prepared for trial after researching the law and gathering the facts to oppose your motion for summary judgment. Finally, his client will have invested significant resources in opposing the motion, expenditures that his client will likely incorporate into its new settlement position.[2] Consequently, you should not move for summary judgment unless you have a reasonable chance of success.

Summary judgment litigation provides you with a stimulating vehicle for developing brief-writing skills. You must remain constantly sensitive not only to the merits of the underlying claims or defenses but also to the standards for summary judgment. Moreover, the local rules of many courts prescribe a special format for summary judgment briefs, providing you a valuable opportunity to examine the role of procedural rules in written advocacy.

II. STANDARDS FOR SUMMARY JUDGMENT

The federal rules authorize a court to grant summary judgment if the parties do not genuinely dispute any material facts and if the moving party is entitled to judgment as a matter of law.[3] In some cases, the court may use summary judgment proceedings to grant final judgment "as to one or more but fewer than all of the claims or parties,"[4] or to identify some uncontested material facts without granting any final judgment.[5]

When moving for summary judgment, you have the initial burden of showing that the pretrial record supports judgment in your favor. If you move for summary judgment on the strength of a claim or defense on which you would have the burden of proof at trial, you must support your motion for summary judgment with credible evidence tending to prove all the elements of the claim or defense.[6] You could make such a showing with deposition testimony, answers to interrogatories, admissions, or other information and documents obtained during discovery or disclosure, or with affidavits prepared specifically for the motion.[7]

---

2. See, e.g., Raymond L. Ocampo, Jr., Moving Violations, California Lawyer, August 1984, at 47, 48.

3. Fed. R. Civ. P. 56(c), 56(e). Beyond the scope of this discussion are state standards for summary disposition that deviate from the federal rules. Many states follow the federal standards closely. See, e.g., Orme School v. Reeves, 802 P.2d 1000 (Ariz. 1990) (en banc) (interpreting Ariz. R. Civ. P. 56).

4. Fed. R. Civ. P. 54(b).

5. Fed. R. Civ. P. 56(d).

6. See Celotex Corp. v. Catrett, 477 U.S. 317, 331 (1986) (Brennan, J., dissenting).

7. See Fed. R. Civ. P. 56(c).

As an alternative basis for summary judgment, you may demonstrate the absence of factual support for an element of a claim or defense relied on by the opposing party. If so, you need not affirmatively produce evidence tending to negate that element. Instead, you may satisfy your initial burden simply by reviewing the existing record and demonstrating that it contains no evidence supporting the critical element.[8]

Once you have satisfactorily supported your motion, the opposing party can avoid summary judgment by setting forth "specific facts" that establish a genuine issue of material fact for trial.[9] She may not rely on the allegations or denials in her own pleading but must point to facts in affidavits, deposition testimony, or other documentary evidence or fruits of discovery.[10]

Moreover, to warrant a trial, the factual issue must be both genuine and material.[11] For an illustration of the materiality requirement, suppose the record on summary judgment establishes without dispute that the defendant intentionally struck the plaintiff with a baseball bat. The defendant could not successfully respond to the plaintiff's motion for summary judgment by establishing even a genuine dispute of fact about the color of the shoes worn by the defendant on the day of the attack. Once the identity of the attacker and the nature of the attack have been established, a factual dispute about the attacker's footwear would not be material to the plaintiff's tort claim, because it would have no bearing on liability.

The court must not resolve genuine issues of material fact on summary judgment. To determine the genuineness of a factual issue, however, the court may undertake a limited evaluation of the strength of the facts presented by the nonmoving party. A factual issue is not genuine if the nonmoving party's factual support is so trivial that "the record taken as a whole could not lead a rational trier of fact to find for the non-moving party."[12] In short, the nonmoving party "must do more than simply show . . . some metaphysical doubt as to the material facts."[13]

If the materials establish grounds for summary judgment, the court ordinarily will grant judgment to the moving party, but the rules do not require it to do so.[14] For example, if a case presents a difficult and novel issue of law, the appellate courts may be better equipped to review the case and develop the new legal standard in the context of a full record after trial. In such a case, the trial court might exercise discretion to deny summary judgment even though the moving party has established grounds for judgment as a matter of law.[15]

---

8. Celotex Corp. v. Catrett, 477 U.S. 317, 322-324 (1986) (majority opinion); id. at 329-331 (Brennan, J., dissenting).

9. Fed. R. Civ. P. 56(e). Alternatively, the nonmoving party may concede the absence of any issue of material fact and simply argue that it, rather than the moving party, is entitled to judgment. In such a case, the parties typically file cross-motions for summary judgment, and each party asserts entitlement to judgment as a matter of law.

10. Fed. R. Civ. P. 56(e). See Southern Rambler Sales, Inc. v. American Motors Corp., 375 F.2d 932, 937 (5th Cir.) ("Rule 56 [is] saying in effect, 'Meet these affidavit facts or judicially die.' "), cert. denied, 389 U.S. 832 (1967).

11. Fed. R. Civ. P. 56(c).

12. Matsushita Elec. Indus. Co. v. Zenith Radio Corp., 475 U.S. 574, 587 (1986).

13. Id. at 586.

14. Orme School v. Reeves, 802 P.2d 1000, 1008 n.11 (Ariz. 1990) (en banc).

15. See generally Haydon v. Rand Corp., 605 F.2d 453, 455 (9th Cir. 1979).

III. FORMAT FOR SUMMARY JUDGMENT BRIEFS—OVERVIEW

Rules of procedure, local court rules, and custom suggest that materials supporting a motion for summary judgment should include the following:

(1) a motion requesting action by the court;

(2) a statement of facts;

(3) affidavits, or other materials not already in the record, that support the fact statement and the motion; and

(4) a supporting brief, sometimes referred to in court rules as a "memorandum of law" or "memorandum of points and authorities."

The requirements for the response are similar except that the nonmoving party need not file a formal motion opposing the motion for summary judgment. At most, the nonmoving party may wish to file a cover page that announces the response and briefly introduces the supporting brief and other materials. The moving party's reply, if any, consists solely of a brief that replies to the arguments raised in the nonmoving party's response.

Some local rules describe parts of the required format in surprising detail. For example, local rules for some United States District Courts specify the information required on designated lines of the caption of the title page of each document filed in support of the motion.[16] The most interesting of the local rules addressing summary judgment, however, are those specifying formats for the statements of facts.

IV. STATEMENTS OF FACTS

Before the advent of local rules governing motions for summary judgment, briefs and supporting materials often failed to pinpoint areas of factual dispute. Often, counsel for the moving party summarized the materials supporting the motion in a general narrative fact statement, and counsel for the nonmoving party summarized supporting materials in a general counterstatement of the facts. Worse yet, in some cases, one or both advocates omitted any consolidated statement of the facts and simply referred to the record in fact analyses dispersed throughout the argument section of the brief.

To help trial judges identify the potential areas of factual dispute, many courts have enacted local rules specifying special formats for briefs on motions for summary judgment. Among the best of these are the Uniform Rules of Practice of the Superior Court of Arizona, which require the moving party to state the facts in numbered paragraphs, similar to allegations in a complaint:

---

16. E.g., U.S. Dist. Ct. D. Ariz. R. 10(a).

> Any party filing a motion for summary judgment shall set forth, separately from the memorandum of law, the specific facts relied upon in support of the motion. The facts shall be stated in concise numbered paragraphs.[17]

Unlike allegations in a complaint, this fact statement must include citations to supporting materials: "As to each fact, the statement shall refer to the specific portion of the record where the fact may be found."[18] If you represent the moving party, you could reasonably entitle this section "Statement of Material Facts."

The local rules instruct the nonmoving party to identify areas of factual dispute in much the same way that an answer sets forth denials of allegations in a complaint:

> Any party opposing a motion for summary judgment shall file a statement in the form prescribed by this Rule, specifying those paragraphs in the moving party's statement of facts which are disputed, and also setting forth those facts which establish a genuine issue of material fact or otherwise preclude summary judgment in favor of the moving party.[19]

If you represent the nonmoving party, you might reasonably entitle this section "Statement of Undisputed and Disputed Material Facts," because you obviously hope that the court will rule that your documents establish a dispute with respect to at least some of the material facts.

Fact statements following this format provide the court with a clear guide to the opposing parties' positions on summary judgment. For example, the following represents excerpts from the plaintiff's statement of facts on his motion for summary judgment in a suit alleging race discrimination in violation of federal law:

> 1. Defendant, Irma Barnes, owns and operates "Irma's Diner," a restaurant and bar located in Mesa, Arizona. Barnes employs more than 15 employees in this business. (Exh. D, Deposition of Irma Barnes at 3-4).
> 2. Plaintiff, Michael Powell, is African-American. He worked as the night manager of the bar at Irma's Diner from January 1, 1993 to June 17, 1994. (Exh. B, Personnel Record for Michael Powell). . . .
> 3. . . .
> 4. On June 17, 1994, Barnes confronted Powell about Powell's selection of a soul band as musical entertainment for the bar. After using several racial slurs in the ensuing discussion, she fired Powell solely because of his race. (Exh. A, Affidavit of Michael Powell at 2). . . .

Barnes's response to the motion for summary judgment should specifically identify which portions of Powell's statement of facts she disputes:

---

17. Ariz. Super. Ct. Unif. R. Prac. IV(f).
18. Id.
19. Id. The rules also permit the nonmoving party to join with the moving party in stipulating to facts not in dispute. Id.

1. Barnes does not dispute paragraphs 1-3 of Powell's Statement of Facts.

2. Barnes does not dispute the assertions in paragraph 4 that Barnes fired Powell on June 17, 1994, after confronting Powell about his selection of musical entertainment. Barnes disputes that she used racial slurs or that race played any factor in her termination of Powell's employment. . . .

In addition, Barnes should set forth the specific facts that reflect a genuine factual dispute on the material issue of Barnes's racial animus. Barnes's counsel may accomplish this in either of two ways. First, in simple cases she might state her version of the events in the same paragraph in which she rejects Powell's version:

2. Barnes does not dispute the assertions . . . musical entertainment. Barnes disputes . . . Powell's employment. In fact, Barnes never used racial slurs in Powell's presence, and she fired Powell solely because he displayed insubordination in the face of direct instructions by Powell to replace the band that Barnes had hired. (Plaintiff's Exh. D, Deposition of Irma Barnes at 24-25).

Alternatively, Barnes could assert her version of the events in a separate section that follows her identification of areas of dispute:

STATEMENT OF UNDISPUTED AND DISPUTED FACTS

1. Barnes does not dispute . . .
2. Barnes does not dispute the assertions . . . musical entertainment. Barnes disputes . . . Powell's employment.

ADDITIONAL FACTS

1. Barnes never used racial slurs in Powell's presence, and she fired Powell solely because he displayed insubordination in the face of direct instructions by Powell to replace the band Barnes had hired. (Plaintiff's Exh. D, Deposition of Irma Barnes at 24-25).

This second format appears to be the more popular, particularly in more complex cases.

The local rules quoted above probably permit you to attach the statement of facts under the same title sheet that states the motion and that covers the supporting brief, as long as you set forth the statement of facts separately from the brief itself. Nonetheless, attorneys operating under those and similar local rules customarily file the formal statement of facts under a caption as a separate document. This custom may have been inspired by local rules that restrict the length of motions briefs.[20] Because such rules usually exclude the formal statement of facts and other attachments from

---

20. See, e.g., Ariz. Super. Ct. R. of Prac. 3.2(f) (Maricopa County) (limiting motion and supporting memorandum to 15 pages).

the page limit,[21] litigants prefer to file the statement of facts separately to more easily demonstrate that the brief by itself does not exceed the page limit.

V. SUPPORTING EVIDENTIARY MATERIALS

Each assertion in your statement of facts should be supported by admitted alleged facts from the opposing party's pleading or by facts reflected in affidavits, materials generated through discovery and disclosure, or other evidence. Rule 56 specifically provides that the affidavits must "be made on personal knowledge"[22] and must "set forth such facts as would be admissible in evidence."[23] More broadly, you should assume that the determination of whether all the materials supporting and opposing summary judgment create a genuine issue of fact for trial will be based only on evidence that would be admissible at trial.[24] Therefore, even though your opponent may overlook this matter,[25] the materials supporting your fact statements in summary judgment litigation should preliminarily establish the admissibility of the evidence in the materials.

For example, the following excerpt from an affidavit asserts the admissibility of other documents under the "business records" exception to the "hearsay rule" of evidence:[26]

5. The Payroll Action forms in Exhibits B and C are true copies of records that I prepared and kept in the course of my regularly conducted business activity, which includes maintaining such employment records as a uniform practice. Those forms include information within my own knowledge and information that my supervisor transmitted to me on matters within his knowledge.

Some attorneys separately file supporting affidavits and other evidence. If those materials are not voluminous, however, you can more conveniently and appropriately attach them to the formal statement of facts.

---

21. E.g., id.

22. See Sherman v. Community Consol. School Dist. 21, 758 F. Supp. 1244, 1250 (N.D. Ill. 1991) (rejecting father's affidavit because it did not assert father had personal knowledge of retaliation against his son because of his son's refusal to pledge allegiance to the flag).

23. Fed. R. Civ. P. 56(e). The Federal Rules of Evidence and their state counterparts govern the admissibility of evidence at trial.

24. See Tigg Corp. v. Dow Corning Corp., 822 F.2d 358 (3d Cir. 1987) (on review of partial summary judgment in contract dispute, discussing admissibility of extrinsic evidence of parties' intended meaning); see also Olympic Ins. Co. v. H. D. Harrison, Inc., 418 F.2d 669, 670 (5th Cir. 1969) (document produced in ordinary course of business was sufficiently reliable to form basis for summary judgment).

25. See, e.g., Catrett v. Johns-Manville Sales Corp., 826 F.2d 33, 37 (D.C. Cir. 1987) (regardless of whether letter qualified as a business records exception to the hearsay rule, trial court properly considered it on summary judgment because other party failed to object to its use).

26. Fed. R. Evid. 803(6).

VI. THE MOTION

As with every document that you separately file with the trial court, you should begin your motion with a caption identifying the case and the nature of the document. In the motion itself, you should simply and clearly state your request for action and briefly introduce the grounds supporting the request.

Unfortunately, many lawyers have developed a tradition of loading motions with abstract boilerplate that says almost nothing about the motion or the dispute:

> Defendant, Sun Printing Co., by and through its undersigned attorneys, Jenkins, Powell, and Smith, P.C., hereby moves, pursuant to the Federal Rules of Civil Procedure, Rule 56, for an order granting summary judgment against Plaintiff, Scott Paper Supply, on the grounds that there exists no genuine issue of material fact and that Defendant is entitled to summary judgment as a matter of law. This motion is supported by the attached memorandum of law, the Statement of Material Facts separately filed with this court, and the documents and exhibits filed with this court.

A judge skims such boilerplate with glassy eyes. She does not need a superfluous reference to the legal representation; your identity as legal counsel is revealed at the top of the cover page and in your signature at the end of the motion. In addition, the judge is well aware of the basic abstract standards for summary judgment;[27] repeating those standards in the motion adds nothing to her knowledge about your case.

The judge will read your motion with greater interest if you clearly and concisely state what relief your client wants and why he is entitled to it. In particular, you should convey new information to the court by tailoring the abstract standards to the facts:

> Pursuant to Federal Rule of Civil Procedure 56, the defendant, Sun Printing Co., moves for summary judgment against the plaintiff, Scott Paper Supply. Sun Printing Co. is entitled to judgment under the U.C.C. Statute of Frauds because Scott Paper Supply cannot genuinely dispute that the agreement alleged by Scott was for paper priced at more than $500 and was never reduced to writing.
>
> This motion is supported by the attached memorandum of law, by the separately filed Statement of Undisputed Facts and accompanying exhibits, and by the record in this case.

An even crisper motion could state the first paragraph more concisely:

> Defendant, Sun Printing Co., moves for summary judgment against Plaintiff, Scott Paper Supply. See Fed. R. Civ. P. 56. Sun Printing Co. is

---

27. See Fidel, Some Do's and Don'ts of Motion Writing, Ariz. Bar J., August 1983, at 8, 9 (advising legal writers to omit "canned" recitations of basic summary judgment standards).

entitled to judgment because the oral agreement alleged by Scott Paper Supply is unenforceable under the U.C.C. Statute of Frauds as a matter of law.

As terse as this passage may sound, it contains more useful information than the longer string of boilerplate in the first example.

When opposing a motion, you should not state a formal countermotion in the title page of your opposition materials. You may follow the caption immediately with your responsive brief. At the most, you might include in your title page a brief statement of opposition parallel to the motion:

Plaintiff, Scott Paper Supply, opposes Defendant's motion for summary judgment. Defendant, Sun Printing Co., is not entitled to judgment as a matter of law, because Scott Paper Supply has established a genuine factual dispute about the written documentation of the sale agreement.

This opposition is supported by the attached memorandum of law, by the . . .

VII. THE BRIEF

Your brief, or legal memorandum, is your tool of persuasion. With it, you argue for a favorable interpretation of the law and analysis of the facts. A motions brief typically includes three sections:

(1) an introduction,
(2) an argument, and
(3) a conclusion.

A. THE INTRODUCTION

Because local rules of many courts require a separate, formal statement of facts in summary judgment materials, your brief need not begin with any introductory statements; you can launch immediately into your legal argument. In most cases, however, you can enhance the persuasiveness of your brief by beginning with an introductory section, perhaps entitled "Introduction" or "Summary of Facts," which precedes the argument section. In this introductory section, you can summarize the facts in a more concise and less formal manner than is possible in the separate, formal statement. If you emphasize facts favorable to your client, you can make the judge more receptive to the argument that follows.

Alternatively, you may use an introductory section to present a summary of your argument or a combination of facts, procedural history, and summary of your argument. Chapter 16 advises against premature legal argument in a statement of facts in an appellate brief. However, this admonition applies with less force in the introduction to your summary judgment brief, because you will separately file a formal statement of facts for summary judgment. For the same reason, you can exercise discretion whether to cite to the record in a brief introduction to the facts; the separate, formal statement of facts will carefully document each assertion of fact.

Finally, you should consider preceding your argument with a formal statement of the issues, either in place of another form of introduction or in addition to it. Although motions briefs do not customarily state the issues, a formal statement would almost never detract from your brief and might be helpful in a complex case.

B. THE ARGUMENT

Chapters 4 and 12 discuss techniques of legal argument. Indeed, some of the examples in Chapter 12 are taken from sample summary judgment briefs. This section will address techniques of persuasion peculiar to summary judgment briefs.

Argument of nearly purely legal questions can be crucial in some summary judgment litigation: If the court determines that material facts are not in dispute, or if the parties have stipulated to the absence of factual dispute, the court will decide whether a moving party is entitled to judgment as a matter of law.

More typically, the parties will also argue about the presence or absence of a genuine dispute of fact. In such a case, once you have established the law on an issue or subissue, you should thoroughly analyze the facts. In arguing the facts, you should remember to cite to the record or to the formal, separately filed statement of facts. The samples in this chapter suggest several ways to cite to the record; any reasonable citation form is acceptable.

Also, you should incorporate the standards for summary judgment into your argument. For example, if you are moving for summary judgment, you should not argue that "the preponderance of the evidence shows that Sun Printing Co. objected to the contents of the confirmation within ten days after receipt." Such an argument gives the impression that you are inappropriately asking the judge to resolve a factual issue without a trial. Instead, your brief should refer to the "undisputed evidence" and the inferences that can be drawn from it, thus properly asserting the absence of a factual dispute.

Conversely, if you are opposing summary judgment, your brief should remind the judge periodically that nothing more than a genuine and material question of fact is needed to defeat summary judgment. In making this point, you should not simply reiterate the abstract standard; rather, you should identify issues of fact that make summary judgment inappropriate:

Opposition facts   Scott Paper Supply's letter confirming the purchase agreement is dated September 1 [Exh. 2], and Scott's Distribution Manager personally mailed it that day [Exh. 3, Affidavit of Rosa Connor ¶3]. Scott Paper Supply never received any objection to the terms of the confirmation. [*Id.* at ¶4]. Moreover, Sun Printing Co. concedes that it has no record of making any such objection. [Exh. 4, Sun's Answer to Scott's First Set of Interrogatories, No. 23].

In direct opposition to Sun Printing Co.'s assertions, this evidence shows that Sun Printing Co. received the confirmation and failed to object to it. At the very least, this evidence raises a genuine dispute of fact that must be resolved at trial.

Dispute of fact

C. THE CONCLUSION

You should end each section of the argument of your brief with a conclusion about the topic of that section, similar to the conclusion stated in the point heading that introduces the argument. Together, the point heading and the conclusion provide maximum emphasis in their positions as the first and last things the judge reads within a section. Finally, as illustrated in Chapter 12, the entire brief should end with a section entitled "Conclusion" that encompasses all the arguments of the brief.

VIII. SUMMARY

To prepare a motion for summary judgment, you should:

(1) draft a motion that requests summary judgment and briefly introduces the judge to the grounds for your motion;
(2) prepare evidentiary materials that will support your statement of facts, if they are not already in the record;
(3) draft a separate statement of facts that cites to the supporting materials; and
(4) draft a supporting brief that
    (a) summarizes the facts and procedural history,
    (b) argues the law and facts relating to the issues, with attention to the standards for summary judgment, and
    (c) states your conclusions.

When opposing a motion for summary judgment, you should prepare a brief and a separate statement of facts with supporting materials. To oppose a motion or to reply to an opposition brief, you need not file a separate motion. Instead, you should submit a brief that responds to the arguments presented in the preceding brief.

Lisa Hall
Kendricks, Hall, & Oats, P.C.
3310 Alma School Rd., Suite 200
Mesa, Arizona 85283
(602) 839-0365
Bar No. 0076089

ARIZONA SUPERIOR COURT
MARICOPA COUNTY

CHARLOTTE REMBAR, Plaintiff, v. ALEXANDER HART d.b.a. COMCON, Defendant.	No. C732431 Defendant Hart's Motion for Summary Judgment (Judge Wisdom)

Defendant Alexander Hart d.b.a. Comcon moves for summary judgment on all claims in this action. Under Arizona Rule of Civil Procedure 56, Hart is entitled to judgment as a matter of law because the undisputed facts show that Hart did not promise Rembar job security and did not discharge Rembar for an unlawful reason or in a wrongful manner.

This motion is supported by the attached Memorandum of Law, the separately filed Statement of Material Facts, and the entire record before the court.

March 3, 1994

Lisa Hall for
Kendricks, Hall, & Oats, P.C.
3310 Alma School Rd., Suite 200
Mesa, Arizona 85283

MEMORANDUM OF LAW IN SUPPORT OF
MOTION FOR SUMMARY JUDGMENT

I. INTRODUCTION

As set forth more fully in the Statement of Undisputed Facts, Alexander Hart employed Charlotte Rembar as a computer systems consultant for Hart's sole proprietorship, Comcon. Although Hart distributed an employment manual to Rembar, their employment contract permitted either party to terminate the contract at will.

On October 29, 1993, Hart discharged Rembar because of her "negative attitude." During her employment, Rembar often flirted with Hart, and Hart sometimes returned the flirtations; however, Hart and Rembar did not have a romantic relationship, and Hart never made any unwelcome advances toward Rembar.

Rembar has asserted four claims for relief in her complaint: breach of an alleged promise of job security, breach of an implied duty of good faith and fair dealing, wrongful discharge in violation of public policy, and intentional infliction of emotional distress. Because the record shows that Hart employed Rembar at will and that Hart discharged Rembar for a legitimate business reason, Hart is entitled to judgment as a matter of law on the contract claim. Rembar has no basis for relief on her claim for breach of the implied duty of good faith and fair dealing, because that duty does not limit an employer's freedom to terminate an at-will contract. Finally, Hart is entitled to judgment on the tort claims because he discharged Rembar for a legitimate business reason and in a proper manner.

II. ARGUMENT

A. Hart Did Not Breach His Employment Contract with Rembar by Discharging Rembar for Her Negative Attitude.

Generally, "an employment contract of indefinite duration is terminable at will," permitting either party to "terminate the contract at any time for any reason or for no reason at all." *Leikvold v. Valley View Community Hospital,* 141 Ariz. 544, 546, 688 P.2d 170, 172 (1984). In some circumstances, an employee manual can become part of the employment contract, and promises of job security in the manual can restrict the employer's freedom to terminate the contract even though the term of the contract remains indefinite. *Id.* at 548, 688 P.2d at 174; *Wagenseller v. Scottsdale Memorial Hospital,* 147 Ariz. 370, 381, 710 P.2d 1025, 1036 (1985). Nonetheless, even assuming for purposes of summary judgment that Hart and Rembar's employment contract included the terms of the Comcon Policy Manual, Hart did not breach those terms for two reasons. First, neither the Policy Manual nor any other term of the contract imposed any restriction on Hart's freedom to terminate Rembar's employment. Second, even if the contract permitted Hart to fire Rembar only for unsatisfactory performance, her negative attitude created such grounds for discharge.

Because the terms of the contract "are clear and unambiguous, the construction of the contract is a question of law for the court" and thus is appropriate for summary judgment. *Leikvold*, 141 Ariz. at 548, 688 P.2d at 174.

1. The Employment Contract Remained Terminable at Will.

Even assuming the Comcon Policy Manual was incorporated into the employment contract, it did not change the at-will nature of the contract because it contained no "provisions of job security." *Id.* at 547, 688 P.2d at 173 (quoting *Pine River State Bank v. Mettille*, 333 N.W.2d 622, 628 (Minn. 1983)).

The terms of Comcon's Policy Manual unambiguously left Hart free to terminate his contract with Rembar at his will. No provision of the Policy Manual purports to restrict the grounds for discharge of an employee. Instead, the only provisions relating to termination affirmatively reserve Hart's right to discharge employees. Policy Manual (Exh. A) §IV.

Because Rembar had worked at Comcon for more than 60 days, she was classified as a nonprobationary employee at the time of her discharge. *See id.* (Exh. A) §IV(A). Under the heading "Nonprobationary Employment," the Policy Manual especially emphasizes a particular ground for discharge: "Comcon reserves the right to terminate the employment of any employee who is not performing satisfactorily." *Id.* at §IV(B). However, it does not state or even suggest that unsatisfactory performance is the exclusive ground for discharge. Absent such a stated restriction, Hart remains free under the general rule to terminate the contract for any reason or for no reason at all.

Hart's employment contract with Rembar was terminable at will.

2. Hart Validly Fired Rembar for Unsatisfactory Performance.

Even if the Policy Manual had identified unsatisfactory performance as the sole ground for discharging nonprobationary employees, Hart would not have breached such a provision.

Hart discharged Rembar because of her "negative attitude." Nov. 1, 1993 Payroll Action (Exh. C); Affidavit of Alexander Hart ¶4 (Exh. D). Because Rembar's position required her to work closely with clients, a pleasant personality and a positive attitude were indispensable qualities for satisfactory job performance. *Id.* Therefore, even assuming that the employment contract provided for job security, Hart did not breach the contract because the undisputed facts show that he discharged Rembar for unsatisfactory performance.

B. *Hart Did Not Breach the Implied Duty of Good Faith and Fair Dealing Because That Duty Did Not Limit Hart's Freedom to Terminate His Contract with Rembar.*

Implied in an employment contract is a duty of good faith and fair dealing that prohibits the employer from denying benefits already earned an employee. *Wagenseller*, 147 Ariz. at 385, 710 P.2d at 1040 (1985). However, prospects of continued employment are not among the benefits of a contract that is terminable at will. Therefore, so long as an employer does not discharge an employee to avoid paying benefits already earned, the duty does not limit an employer's freedom to terminate an at-will contract. *Id.*

Rembar has not alleged that Hart failed to pay her the salary that she earned up to the time of her discharge. Moreover, as established in section A of this memorandum, Hart's contract with Rembar was terminable at the will of either party. As a matter of law, therefore, Hart could not have breached the implied duty of good faith and fair dealing.

C. Hart Did Not Wrongfully Discharge Rembar in Violation of Public Policy.

1. Hart's Alleged Sexual Harassment Does Not Violate Arizona Public Policy, Because Employment Discrimination Laws Do Not Apply to Comcon.

The tort of wrongful discharge requires proof of a violation of an important public policy reflected in the state's constitution, its statutes, or, in limited circumstances, its judicial decisions. *Wagenseller*, 147 Ariz. at 378-379, 710 P.2d at 1033-1034 (1985). Rembar's allegations of sexual harassment suggest that she relies on the employment discrimination provisions of the Arizona Civil Rights Acts as her source of public policy.

However, those provisions apply only to employers with at least 15 employees. Ariz. Rev. Stat. Ann. §41-1461(2); *see also* 42 U.S.C. §2000e(b) (identical limitation in Title VII of the Civil Rights Act of 1964). Even if Hart is included in the total number of Comcon employees, Comcon has never employed more than nine employees. Affidavit of Alexander Hart ¶1 (Exh. D).

As a matter of law, therefore, the Arizona Civil Rights Act is not a source of public policy with respect to Rembar's employment and discharge.

2. Even if the Arizona Civil Rights Act Were a Source of Public Policy in This Case, Hart Would Not Have Violated Its Policy, Because He Did Not Make Unwelcome Sexual Advances.

The state policy against sexual harassment is defined in the Arizona Civil Rights Act in its prohibition of sex discrimination in employment. Ariz. Rev. Stat. Ann. §41-1463. An employer engages in sexual harassment by either (1) making submission to demands for sexual favors a condition of employment benefits, or (2) making unwelcome sexual advances that by their nature and frequency create a discriminatory work environment. *See, e.g., Meritor Savings Bank, FSB v. Vinson*, 477 U.S. 57 (1986) (applying identical provisions of Title VII); *see also Higdon v. Evergreen International Airlines, Inc.*, 138 Ariz. 163, 165 n.3, 673 P.2d 907, 909 n.3 (1983) (case law interpreting Title VII is persuasive authority for questions of interpreting the Arizona Civil Rights Act).

Even if Arizona's statutory policy against sexual harassment applied to Comcon, Hart would not have violated that policy, because he made no sexual advances toward Rembar. Rembar's own frequent flirtations with Hart showed that she welcomed Hart's harmless flirtations and attentions. Hart never made advances that were not welcomed by Rembar, and he never conditioned benefits of employment on Rembar's acquiescing to his flirtations. Affidavit of Alexander Hart (Exh. D). Most important, Rembar's discharge had nothing to do with any flirtations between Hart and Rembar; Hart discharged Rembar solely because of her unsatisfactory job performance. *Id.* at ¶4.

In short, even if Hart were an employer covered by the Arizona Civil Rights Act, the undisputed facts show that he would not have violated its prohibitions. Therefore, Hart did not contravene public policy.

D. Hart Did Not Engage in Extreme and Outrageous Conduct and Therefore Is Not Liable for Infliction of Emotional Distress.

An employer cannot be liable for infliction of emotional distress for an otherwise lawful termination of employment. *Daniel v. Magma Copper Co.,* 127 Ariz. 320, 324, 620 P.2d 699, 703 (App. 1980). The means by which an employer terminates might be independently tortious, but it would amount to intentional infliction of emotional distress only if the conduct was "extreme and outrageous." *Watts v. Golden Age Nursing Home,* 127 Ariz. 255, 258, 619 P.2d 1032, 1035 (1980). Conduct that is "extreme and outrageous" falls "within that quite narrow range" of conduct "at the very extreme edge of the spectrum." *Id.*

Hart is entitled to summary judgment on Rembar's claim for emotional distress for the same reasons that he is entitled to judgment on the claims for breach of contract and wrongful discharge. As discussed above, Hart's termination of Rembar's employment did not breach the contract or violate public policy. Therefore, the termination itself cannot be a basis for a claim of infliction of emotional distress.

Likewise, Hart did not accompany the termination with any extreme and outrageous conduct. Rembar's allegations of sexual harassment are simply not supported by the record. Hart discharged Rembar for a legitimate business reason and communicated his decision in a professional manner. Affidavit of Alexander Hart ¶¶3, 4 (Exh. D).

Because of its economic consequences, termination of employment is often an extremely distressing event for the discharged employee. However, discharge for business reasons is an economic fact of life and hardly amounts to the kind of extreme and outrageous conduct that results in tort liability. As a matter of law, Hart is not liable for intentional infliction of emotional distress.

III. CONCLUSION

Rembar cannot genuinely dispute Hart's showing on the facts that Hart promised Rembar no job security, that Hart discharged Rembar for performance, and that Hart did not engage in sexual harassment. Therefore, Hart is entitled to summary judgment on all claims.

March 3, 1994

Lisa Hall for
Kendricks, Hall, & Oats, P.C.
3310 Alma School Rd., Suite 200
Mesa, Arizona 85283

COPY OF THE FOREGOING MAILED
March 3, 1994 to:

Roberts and Cray
101 E. Washington St.
Suite 600
Phoenix, Arizona 85001

Hall
Kendricks, Hall, & Oats, P.C.
3310 Alma School Rd., Suite 200
Mesa, Arizona 85283
(602) 839-0365
Bar No. 0076089

ARIZONA SUPERIOR COURT
MARICOPA COUNTY

CHARLOTTE REMBAR, Plaintiff, v. ALEXANDER HART d.b.a. COMCON, Defendant.	No. C732431 Defendant Hart's Statement of Material Facts and Exhibits Supporting Motion for Summary Judgment (Judge Wisdom)

For purposes of summary judgment only, Defendant Alexander Hart d.b.a. Comcon presents the following material facts:

1. Alexander Hart is the sole owner and manager of Comcon, a firm that provides expert consulting on computer systems to businesses in the Phoenix metropolitan area. From January to November 1993, Comcon employed eight employees other than Hart himself; Comcon has never employed a greater number of employees before or since. Affidavit of Alexander Hart ¶1 (Exh. D).

2. On January 1, 1993, Hart hired Charlotte Rembar for the position of Comcon consultant at a salary of $4,000/month. Jan. 1, 1993 Payroll Action (Exh. B). The only written record of Rembar's contract with Comcon is a Payroll Action form that states her date of hire and her salary. *Id.*; Affidavit of Alexander Hart ¶2 (Exh. D). The term of Rembar's employment was left indefinite. *Id.*

3. At or before the time of Rembar's hiring, Alexander Hart gave Rembar a Policy Manual that summarizes many of the personnel procedures at Comcon. Policy Manual (Exh. A).

4. From the beginning of her employment at Comcon, Rembar sought to attract Hart's attentions with casual flirtations, such as references to his appearance and suggestive smiles. Hart returned the flirtations in a similar manner, but no sexual relationship developed between them. Any flirtations directed by Hart toward Rembar were welcomed, and even invited, by her. Hart never demanded sexual favors from Rembar, and he never conditioned any benefits of employment on Rembar's submitting to a sexual demand or otherwise reacting to a flirtation. Affidavit of Alexander Hart ¶3 (Exh. D).

5. In the fall of 1993, Hart became dissatisfied with Rembar's performance. Specifically, she displayed a negative attitude in her work. Because

Comcon consultants must work closely with their clients, a consultant with a negative attitude severely hampers Comcon's business relationships. Affidavit of Alexander Hart ¶4 (Exh. D).

6. Effective November 5, 1993, Hart terminated Rembar's employment because of her negative attitude. Nov. 1, 1993 Payroll Action (Exh. C). Hart communicated the discharge to Rembar in a normal, professional manner. Affidavit of Alexander Hart ¶4 (Exh. D).

March 3, 1994

Lisa Hall for
Kendricks, Hall, & Oats, P.C.
3310 Alma School Rd., Suite 200
Mesa, Arizona 85283

EXHIBIT A

I. INTRODUCTION

The success of Comcon lies in its ability to recruit and retain the best employees available nationally. To promote a stable and productive workforce, Comcon endeavors to provide attractive terms and conditions of employment, as reflected in the following policies.

II. SALARY

A. Initial Salary . . .

B. Change in Salary . . .

III. HOLIDAYS, VACATIONS, SICK LEAVE

A. Holidays . . .

B. Personal Leave . . .

IV. TERMINATION

A. Probationary Employment

Each employee will work on probationary status during his or her first 60 days of employment. During this probationary period, Comcon reserves the right to terminate the employee for any reason or for no reason at all.

B. Nonprobationary Employment

Comcon reserves the right to terminate the employment of any employee who is not performing satisfactorily.

E X H I B I T B

PAYROLL ACTION

NATURE OF ACTION

__X__ New Hire _____ Change in Pay _____ Termination

PREVIOUS PAY __N.A._____

NEW PAY ___$4,000/mo_____

EFFECTIVE DATE __Jan. 1, 1993_____

REASON FOR CHANGE OR TERMINATION

COMMENTS

　　　Consultant

DATE __Jan. 1, 1993_____

PROCESSED BY __Leslie West_____

EXHIBIT C

PAYROLL ACTION

NATURE OF ACTION

——— New Hire   ——— Change in Pay   _X_ Termination

PREVIOUS PAY ___$4,000/mo_____

NEW PAY ___N.A._____

EFFECTIVE DATE ___Nov. 5, 1993_____

REASON FOR CHANGE OR TERMINATION

   Negative Attitude

COMMENTS

DATE ___Nov. 1, 1993_____

PROCESSED BY ___Leslie West_____

E X H I B I T   D

AFFIDAVIT OF ALEXANDER HART
IN SUPPORT OF MOTION FOR SUMMARY JUDGMENT

Maricopa County
Arizona

Alexander Hart, under oath, swears to the following information from personal knowledge:

1. I am the sole owner and manager of Comcon, a firm that provides consulting services to businesses on the development and use of computer systems. From January to November 1993, I employed eight employees, the largest workforce that I have employed since I formed Comcon in 1991. Specifically, during that period I employed a secretary, an accountant, and six consultants. Comcon participates in the Arizona Worker's Compensation program.

2. On January 1, 1993, I hired Charlotte Rembar for the position of consultant. The Payroll Action form identified in this motion as Exhibit B is the only written record of Rembar's hiring and her terms of employment. Rembar and I understood at the time of hiring that her term of employment was indefinite. On or before the time of her hiring, I gave her a Comcon Policy Manual, which reaffirms that Rembar had no definite term of employment.

3. From the beginning of her employment at Comcon, Rembar sought to attract my attentions with casual flirtations such as suggestive smiles and compliments on my grooming and appearance. She made it clear that she welcomed reciprocation, and I often returned her flirtations with similar smiles and comments. Our personal relationship never advanced beyond these casual flirtations. Specifically, we never had a sexual relationship, and I never made any unwelcome sexual advances toward Rembar, nor did I ever condition any benefits of employment on Rembar's submitting to any sexual demands or otherwise reacting in any way to my flirtations.

4. Sometime in the fall of 1993, I began to notice that Rembar displayed a negative attitude about me, about herself, and about her work. I find it extremely important to maintain a workforce with positive attitudes and pleasant personalities, because the consultants work closely with clients, and our business thus depends on maintaining good personal relationships with clients. To ensure that we maintained those relationships, I discharged Rembar effective November 5, 1993, to rid our workforce of her negativism. I communicated the discharge to Rembar in a normal, professional manner in an office meeting on November 1, 1993.

5. The Payroll Action forms in Exhibits B and C are true copies of records that were prepared and kept by my personal secretary, Leslie West, in the course of her regularly conducted business activity, which includes

maintaining such employment records as a uniform practice. Those forms include information within Ms. West's own knowledge and information that I transmitted to her on matters within my knowledge. The Policy Manual in Exhibit A is a true copy of a manual that I drafted and printed in June 1992 and have since distributed to all employees.

I swear under oath that the foregoing is true:

_____

Alexander Hart

_____

Date

15

Motion to Exclude Evidence Before Trial

To most law students or new associates, the term "motion in limine" is mysterious and a little intimidating. It will cease to be so once the legal profession replaces this Latin phrase with plain English. Black's Law Dictionary defines "in limine" as: "On or at the threshold; at the very beginning; preliminarily."[1] Simply put, the typical motion in limine is a motion to exclude evidence before trial. Conversely, but much more rarely, an advocate may use it to move for admission of evidence before trial if she anticipates an objection to the evidence.

Thus, in contrast to the typical motion for summary judgment, a motion to exclude evidence seeks to define the scope of the trial litigation rather than finally dispose of the case before trial. It generally is simpler than a motion for summary judgment. If you can strip the mystery away from the popular Latin phrase, you should have little trouble supporting or opposing the motion.

I. PRETRIAL EXCLUSION OF EVIDENCE

The Federal Rules of Civil Procedure expressly authorize "advance rulings from the court on the admissibility of evidence" in pretrial conferences.[2] Additionally, those Rules and the Federal Rules of Evidence implicitly authorize a trial court to rule on pretrial motions to exclude evidence other

---

1. Black's Law Dictionary 896 (5th ed. 1979).
2. Fed. R. Civ. P. 16(c)(3).

than in pretrial conference, or they at least leave undisturbed the court's inherent power to do so.[3]

Attorneys can and do object to evidence offered for admission during trial.[4] However, pretrial rulings on complex, potentially prejudicial, or particularly significant evidentiary matters tend to improve the efficiency and quality of the trial proceedings.[5]

For example, suppose a visitor to your client's factory sues your client for injuries sustained at the factory. At trial, the plaintiff's counsel asks a defense witness in front of the jury to confirm that your client offered to pay the plaintiff's medical expenses. You can immediately object that the question seeks a response that may lead the jury to find liability on an improper ground.[6] In most jurisdictions, the judge will sustain your objection and will order the witness not to provide the solicited testimony.[7] However, the damage to your client's case may be irreparable if the question alone improperly influences the jury's deliberations, despite the court's admonishments to the jury to ignore it. You could have protected your client more effectively had you earlier persuaded the judge to exclude the evidence before trial and to order the parties to refrain from referring to the evidence in any way at trial.

Additionally, pretrial litigation of complex evidentiary matters permits more thorough written and oral argument by the parties and more considered deliberation by the court, all without disrupting an ongoing trial. Moreover, pretrial disposition of objections to particularly significant evidence gives the parties an opportunity to modify their trial strategies or to reassess their settlement positions.[8]

II. FORMAT—OVERVIEW

Local rules addressing motions typically provide for a motion and supporting brief, an opposing brief, and an optional reply brief.[9] However, unlike local rules that require a special format for some parts of a motion for summary judgment,[10] rules of procedure and local court rules of most jurisdictions specify no detailed format for a motion to exclude evidence. Instead, the common format is a product of custom and common sense. As with any legal document, you can best support or oppose a motion to

---

3. See generally Charles W. Gamble, The Motion *In Limine*: A Pretrial Procedure That Has Come of Age, 33 Ala. L. Rev. 1, 2 & n.6 (1981).
4. See generally Fed. R. Evid. 103.
5. See Fed. R. Civ. P. 16(a) (stating objectives of pretrial conference).
6. See Fed. R. Evid. 409 advisory committee's note. Exclusion of such evidence also promotes a generally humanitarian policy of encouraging such assistance, regardless of liability. Id.
7. See Fed. R. Evid. 409.
8. See Gamble, supra note 3, at 8-10.
9. See, e.g., U.S. Dist. Ct. R. Prac. 11(b), (c), (d), (e), (h) (D. Ariz.).
10. See Chapter 14.

exclude evidence if you understand the purposes of your document and draft it accordingly.

III. THE MOTION

In a motion to exclude evidence, you should simply and clearly state the action requested and briefly summarize the grounds for the motion. In describing the relief requested, you probably should go beyond generally asking for exclusion of certain evidence. To ensure effective protection, you should describe the objectionable evidence as inclusively as possible and should request an order specifically prohibiting the opposing party from referring to the evidence:

> The defendant, Axxon Corp., moves for pretrial exclusion of all evidence that Axxon Corp. offered to provide medical care and pay the medical expenses of the plaintiff, Herb Taylor. The evidence is inadmissible under Federal Rule of Evidence 409.
>
> Specifically, Axxon Corp. requests an order directing Taylor and his counsel (1) to refrain from referring to such an offer in any way in the presence of the jury and (2) to take all necessary steps to ensure that their witnesses avoid such references.

To oppose a motion to exclude evidence, you need not file a separate motion; you can simply file a brief that opposes the original motion. At the most, you might want to draft a cover page for your brief that parallels the motion in summarizing the ruling you seek and the supporting grounds:

> Plaintiff Herb Taylor opposes Defendant Axxon Corp.'s motion to exclude evidence of Axxon Corp.'s offer to provide and pay for medical care. The evidence is admissible to show the extent of Taylor's injuries. The court should not exclude the evidence for this purpose.

IV. THE BRIEF

A brief supporting or opposing a motion to exclude evidence, or any other motion, is sometimes referred to as a "memorandum of law" or a "memorandum of points and authorities." When preparing a brief supporting a motion to exclude evidence, you ordinarily should follow the familiar pattern of Introduction, Argument, and Conclusion. The party opposing your motion should file a responsive brief that directly answers the contentions of your supporting brief. Similarly, in your reply brief, if any, you should respond to the points made in the opposing brief.

On a motion for summary judgment, you will address at least some of the claims or defenses of the litigation on their merits. In contrast, on a motion to exclude evidence, you will typically focus more narrowly on the admissibility of certain evidence. Consequently, in your supporting or opposing briefs, you should address the merits of claims or defenses only to the extent necessary to address some element of admissibility, such as relevance. This narrow focus affects the scope of the introduction and argument sections of the briefs.

A. THE INTRODUCTION

In the introductory section of a brief supporting a motion to exclude evidence, you need not include a full statement of facts and procedural history. In light of the motion's focus on an evidentiary issue, your introduction need summarize only those portions of the facts and procedural history necessary to an understanding of that issue. You should accompany your motion with any necessary factual support for your assertions, such as affidavits or documents. Additionally, you should cite to such attachments or to other parts of the record. Any reasonable citation form is acceptable; two examples are presented below.

In addition, your introduction may include a statement explaining why you expect the nonmoving party to attempt to introduce the evidence at trial. It may also include a fairly conclusory statement of the need to resolve the matter before trial, although that point can be left to the argument section.

For example, the brief supporting the motion might begin with the following introductory points:

MEMORANDUM IN SUPPORT OF
MOTION TO EXCLUDE EVIDENCE

I. INTRODUCTION

Nature of the case

Herb Taylor, a sales representative for Corbin Heavy Equipment Co., brought this tort action against Axxon Corp. He alleges negligence in the maintenance of the Axxon manufacturing plant in Albuquerque, New Mexico.

Facts

Specifically, Taylor alleges that, while touring the Axxon plant in January 1994 with Axxon General Manager Jerry Olshon, Taylor lost his footing, fell backwards, and struck his head against a forklift. [Complaint at ¶¶3, 4.] According to Olshon's deposition testimony, as a humanitarian gesture, Olshon immediately offered on behalf of Axxon to provide transportation to the nearest hospital and to pay for Taylor's medical expenses. [Deposition of Jerry Olshon at 18.] Taylor later developed difficulties with his eyesight, which he alleges are the result of his accident at the Axxon plant. [Complaint at ¶6.]

    The critical issue in this case is whether Axxon negligently maintained its plant, causing Taylor to fall. Taylor's counsel has examined Olshon extensively during deposition about Olshon's offer to pay medical expenses, leading Axxon to believe that Taylor's counsel will attempt to introduce that evidence at trial.

    Evidence of Olshon's offer to pay medical expenses is inadmissible to establish Axxon's liability, and Axxon will not introduce it for other purposes. The evidence must be excluded before trial, because reference to it even in a question to a witness would indelibly and improperly influence the jury.

Belief that evidence will be introduced

Need for pretrial exclusion

    When opposing a motion, you should state any facts and procedural history that are material to your argument and that are not fairly stated in the opening brief:

I. INTRODUCTION

    Plaintiff Taylor is prepared to prove that Defendant Axxon Corp.'s negligence proximately caused Taylor to lose nearly all sight in his right eye. Axxon apparently seeks to show that Taylor's injuries at the Axxon factory were slight and that Taylor's partial blindness must be unrelated. *See* Answer ¶6. Thus, the extent of Taylor's injuries at the factory are in issue.

    Taylor plans to introduce Axxon Corp.'s offer to provide and pay for medical care as evidence that Axxon's agent at the scene of the accident determined Taylor's injuries to be serious. The evidence is admissible for this purpose and should not be excluded.

Issues for trial

Relevance of evidence on particular issue

B. THE ARGUMENT

1. Legal Rules

    The argument section of a motion to exclude evidence follows the same general pattern discussed in Chapters 4 and 12. Each section or subsection within the argument should state a contention in a point heading, analyze the law and the facts, and restate or summarize the contention in a conclusion.

    In the statement of legal standards in the opening brief supporting a motion to exclude evidence, you typically will focus on rules of evidence that restrict admissibility. If you prefer a thorough analysis, you may choose to develop the legal standards carefully:

> Even relevant evidence is inadmissible "if its probative value is substantially outweighed by the danger" that it will cause "unfair prejudice." Fed. R. Evid. 403. Evidence presents such a danger if it has "an undue tendency to suggest a decision on an improper basis, commonly, though not necessarily, an emotional one." *Id.*, advisory committee note.
>
> In this case, evidence of Powell's membership in the Black Panthers organization more than 20 years ago has little, if any, probative value . . .

On the other hand, the general standards for some of the more commonly invoked evidentiary rules are familiar to judges and attorneys. Therefore, you could exercise stylistic discretion to present those standards summarily, or even implicitly, and to move more quickly to the fact analysis:

> Evidence of Powell's former membership in the Black Panthers organization should be excluded because it presents a danger of unfair prejudice that greatly outweighs its probative value. *See* Fed. R. Evid. 403.
>
> The F.B.I. file report shows that Powell was a member of the Black Panthers nearly 30 years ago for the brief period of eight months. During that time, Powell participated in peaceful demonstrations and political rallies, and he met with other members in "strategy meetings." . . .

2. Application of Rules to Facts

As in any legal argument, the fact analysis should lead to a conclusion by relating the facts to the legal standard:

Little relevance	Purely political and social activities such as these have little or no probative value on the question of the likelihood that Powell provoked Beatty's assault. As a member of the Black Panthers organization, Powell did not espouse violence or engage in any violent activities.
Unfair prejudice	The primary effect of the evidence would be to inflame the passions of the jury. Despite the nonviolent role that Powell played as a member of the organization, many view the Black Panthers as a radical organization that actively sought violent confrontation with established institutions such as police agencies. Conservative jurors undoubtedly would react emotionally to the controversial image of the Black Panthers.
	The evidence of Powell's membership in the

Black Panthers organization therefore should be excluded on the ground that it presents a danger of unfair prejudice that substantially outweighs its probative value.

The argument section of an opposing brief or a reply brief will contain similar elements, except that each will be narrowly tailored to respond directly to contentions advanced in the brief that preceded it.

C. THE CONCLUSION

Chapter 12's discussion of conclusions uses examples from sample motions in limine. In summary, you should

(1) end each argument in a brief with a conclusion on that argument, and
(2) end the entire brief with a general summary of all the arguments and of your request for relief.

V. SUMMARY

To prepare a motion to exclude evidence before trial, you should

(1) draft a motion that simply and clearly requests the court to exclude specified evidence and to order the parties from referring to the evidence at trial;
(2) draft a supporting brief that
    (a) introduces the facts and procedural history relevant to the motion,
    (b) argues the law and facts relating to the evidentiary issues, and
    (c) states your conclusions; and
(3) attach any documentary evidence or affidavits necessary to support your motion, or refer to evidence already in the record.

To oppose a motion to exclude evidence, or to reply to an opposition brief, you need not file a separate motion. Instead, you should submit a brief that responds to the arguments presented in the preceding brief.

Deborah E. Driggs
State Bar No. 6081
David L. Keily
State Bar No. 12345
SACKS, TIERNEY, KASEN & KERRICK, P.A.
3300 North Central Avenue, Suite 2000
Phoenix, Arizona 85012-1576
Telephone: (602) 279-4900
Attorneys for Defendants Rayner

SUPERIOR COURT OF ARIZONA
MARICOPA COUNTY

AGUA FRIA SAND & ROCK,
INC.,
    an Arizona corporation,
        Plaintiff,

    v.

Estate of DALE FAY RAYNER,
    Deceased; JACK RAYNER,
    JR., Personal Representative of
    the Estate of DALE FAY
    RAYNER, Deceased; Estate of
    JACK RAYNER, JR., Personal
    Representative of the Estate of
    JACK RAYNER, SR.,
    Deceased; JACK RAYNER,
    JR.,
        Defendants.

No. C-531100

MOTION IN LIMINE TO
    EXCLUDE TESTIMONY AS
    TO TRANSACTIONS WITH
    OR STATEMENTS BY JACK
    M. RAYNER, SR. AND DALE
    FAY RAYNER

(Oral Argument Requested)

(Hon. Gloria G. Ybarra)

Defendants Rayner move for an order excluding testimony by the principals of Agua Fria, George R. Mutschler, Sr., and George R. Mutschler, Jr., about transactions with or statements by Jack M. Rayner, Sr., and Dale Fay Rayner. This motion is made pursuant to Arizona's Deadman's statute, A.R.S. §12-2251, and is supported by the attached Memorandum of Points and Authorities.

DATED December 29, 1986.

        By _____
            Deborah E. Driggs
            David L. Keily, for
            SACKS, TIERNEY, KASEN & KERRICK, P.A.
            Attorneys for Defendants

MEMORANDUM OF POINTS AND AUTHORITIES

I. FACTUAL BACKGROUND

Plaintiff Agua Fria Sand & Rock, Inc. (Agua Fria) brought this suit against defendants for fraud, breach of a duty of due care, and breach of a lease. Agua Fria was the assignee of a leasehold interest in certain real property owned by defendants. On this property, Agua Fria operated a sand and gravel mine. In February 1980, Agua Fria's plant and equipment were destroyed by a flood. After the flood, Agua Fria moved its operations to a new site on the property.

Agua Fria alleges that the defendants wrongfully evicted them from the new site. Although Agua Fria occupied the land as a tenant at will, it alleges that the defendants promised to execute and deliver a written lease for a term of twenty years.

The defendants deny that they had promised to execute and deliver a written lease for a term of 20 years to Agua Fria. They allege that Agua Fria was evicted because it had failed to make rental payments and to satisfy other lease obligations.

Jack M. Rayner, Sr., died on October 14, 1982. Dale Fay Rayner died on April 17, 1984. Jack M. Rayner, Jr., is the Personal Representative of the Estates of Jack M. Rayner, Sr., and Dale Fay Rayner. Agua Fria has sued Jack M. Rayner, Jr., in his capacity as Personal Representative of the estates of Jack M. Rayner, Sr., and Dale Fay Rayner.

II. ARGUMENT

The Arizona Deadman's Statute Bars Admission of Testimony of Transactions with, or Statements by, Jack M. Rayner, Sr., and Dale Fay Rayner.

To reduce the danger of fraudulent testimony, the Arizona Deadman's statute restricts the admission of testimony about transactions with, or about statements made by, the testator in certain suits:

> In an action by or against personal representatives, administrators, guardians or conservators in which judgment may be given for or against them as such, neither party shall be allowed to testify against the other as to any transaction with or statement by the testator, intestate or ward unless called to testify thereto by the opposite party, or required to testify thereto by the court. The provisions of this section shall extend to and include all actions by or against the heirs, devisees, legatees or legal representatives of a decedent arising out of any transaction with the decedent.

Ariz. Rev. Stat. Ann. §12-2251 (Supp. 1985).

The statute clearly applies to this case. First, Agua Fria has filed suit against Jack M. Rayner, Jr., in his capacity as personal representative of the estates of Jack M. Rayner, Sr., and Dale Fay Rayner. Judgment may be granted for or against Jack M. Rayner, Jr., in his capacity as personal representative. Finally, Agua Fria plans to introduce evidence of an alleged oral agreement by the deceased, Jack M. Rayner, Sr., and Dale Fay Rayner, to execute a written lease with a term of 20 years.

The statute authorizes admission of testimony of transactions with or statements by the deceased if "required . . . by the court." Therefore, such admission ultimately lies within the discretion of the trial court. *Mahan v. First National Bank*, 139 Ariz. 138, 140, 677 P.2d 301, 303 (App. 1984). The trial court's determination to admit testimony of transactions with or statements by the decedent will be upheld only if (1) independent evidence corroborates the transaction with the decedent, and (2) an injustice will result if the testimony is rejected. *Id.*

Agua Fria has no independent evidence to support its claims that the deceased promised to execute and deliver a written lease of the premises for a term of 20 years. Instead, Agua Fria rests on the bald assertion that the deceased made such promises. This type of uncorroborated testimony is exactly what the statute was intended to proscribe.

Second, no injustice will result from exclusion of testimony of transactions with or statements by Jack M. Rayner, Sr., and Dale Fay Rayner. The exclusion will apply equally to both parties. Moreover, exclusion of the testimony comports strongly with public policy to render incompetent as witnesses persons who will gain from distortion of transactions with the decedent when death has rendered the decedent incapable of refuting these inaccuracies. *See Carrillo v. Taylor*, 81 Ariz. 14, 299 P.2d 188 (1956). The exclusion will simply preclude Plaintiff Agua Fria from evading the statute of frauds by making use of self-serving, uncorroborated declarations about what the deceased supposedly said. Agua Fria should not be able to manufacture lease obligations out of the alleged representations of those who are no longer able to refute them.

III. CONCLUSION

The objectionable testimony in this case is uncorroborated and will not result in an injustice if excluded. Therefore, this testimony should be excluded under the applicable Deadman's statute.

December 29, 1986.

SACKS, TIERNEY & KASEN, P.A.

Deborah E. Driggs
David L. Keily
3300 North Central Avenue
Phoenix, Arizona 85012-1576
Attorneys for Defendants

16

Appellate Briefs

Briefwriting on appeal differs from most pretrial briefwriting in three respects. First, if you have fully tried your case before appeal, you will analyze the appellate issues on a more complete factual record than was available during the litigation of pretrial motions. Second, in developing your arguments on appeal, you must consider standards of appellate review, which require varying levels of deference to trial court rulings and findings. Third, rules of procedure and local rules typically prescribe a more formal and detailed format for appellate briefs than for pretrial or trial briefs.

I. THE RECORD ON APPEAL

The proceedings in the trial court are recorded in two records: the trial court clerk's record and the reporter's transcript.[1] The trial history of a case can usually be most easily traced in the trial court clerk's record, which contains all the documents filed with the trial court, from the initial pleadings to the notice of appeal. It also includes the written judgment of the court, along with orders reflecting the court's rulings on procedural and other preliminary matters. A docket sheet attached to the clerk's record contains a brief entry for each document in the record. This provides a convenient index to the record and a summary of the history of the litigation. The reporter's transcript is a record of all the statements made in court during the litigation process. It includes oral arguments of the parties on motions, testimony of witnesses, rulings from the bench, and instructions to the jury.

Shortly after a disappointed litigant has filed notice of appeal from the

---

1. See, e.g., U.S. Ct. App. 9th Cir. R. 10-2.

judgment of the trial court, the parties on appeal designate the portions of the clerk's record and reporter's transcript that are necessary for the appeal.[2] At least in some court systems, physical exhibits remain with the trial court clerk until requested by the appellate court.[3]

Before writing an appellate brief, you must master the record on appeal, because the evidence and arguments presented to the trial court help to define the scope of the appellate court's inquiry. Indeed, when referring in your brief to testimony, arguments, rulings, or other portions of the trial history, you should carefully cite to the pages of the clerk's record or reporter's transcript that reflect that information. Common abbreviations for citation to page 134 of the clerk's record are "CR 134," for "clerk's record" or "CT 134," for "clerk's transcript." The reporter's transcript is commonly cited as "RT 383." If either record is bound in multiple volumes, you must also cite to the volume number in some reasonable fashion. For example, you might cite to page 115 of the third volume of the reporter's transcript as "III RT 115" or "3 RT 115."

II. STANDARDS OF REVIEW

A. OVERVIEW

As introduced in the chapter on briefing cases, an appellate court will apply different standards of review to different kinds of trial court findings or rulings. For example, on a motion for summary judgment or a motion to dismiss an action for failure to state a claim, a trial court does not resolve any factual disputes; instead, it decides as a matter of law whether alleged or undisputed facts satisfy the applicable legal standards. When reviewing a trial court's granting of such a motion, the appellate court will place itself in the position of the trial court and decide, without deference to the trial court's analysis, whether the moving party satisfied its burden on the motion.[4]

In contrast, a jury's verdict or a trial judge's findings of fact rendered after trial represent the factfinder's resolution of factual disputes. When reviewing such findings, an appellate court will restrict its review, deferring to the factfinder's resolution of conflicting evidence.

Thus, to effectively argue your case on appeal, you must consider the standard of review, or the degree to which the appellate court will defer to a finding or ruling made in the trial court. Indeed, the outcome of some

---

2. E.g., id. at Rule 10-3. Indeed, the court reporter normally will not prepare a transcript of his or her shorthand trial notes until this designation. Id.; Fed. R. App. P. 10(b).

3. E.g., U.S. Ct. App. 9th Cir. R. 11-4.2.

4. Experimental Eng., Inc. v. United Technologies Corp., 614 F.2d 1244, 1246 (9th Cir. 1980) (reviewing dismissal of action for failure to state a claim); Heiniger v. City of Phoenix, 625 F.2d 842, 843-844 (9th Cir. 1980) (discussing standards of review for summary judgment).

appeals will depend directly on the standard of review that the appellate court chooses to apply.[5]

Appellate standards of review in the federal court system are typical of those in other court systems and will serve as general examples. Under the two most important standards, an appellate court restricts its review of questions of fact but not of questions of law.

B. RESTRICTED APPELLATE REVIEW OF FINDINGS OF FACT

The seventh amendment to the United States Constitution guarantees the right to a jury trial "in suits at common law," and it provides that "no fact tried by a jury shall be otherwise re-examined in any court of the United States, than according to the rules of the common law." Under the common law rules, an appellate court will not overturn the factual findings of a jury unless those findings are not supported by "any substantial evidence."[6] Federal statutes prescribe the same standard of review for the findings of some administrative agencies.[7] Similarly, an appellate court will restrict its review of a jury's findings of fact resulting in conviction in a criminal case. Specifically, an appellate court may constitutionally uphold a criminal conviction if "the record evidence could reasonably support a finding of guilt beyond a reasonable doubt."[8]

For example, consider a jury's verdict that the defendant in a civil suit negligently caused the plaintiff to suffer injuries valued at $150,000. Assuming that the trial court properly instructed the jury on the law, the appellate court will affirm the jury's verdict if substantial evidence in the record supports the finding of negligence[9] and the calculation of damages, even if the appellate judges might have reached a different verdict had they evaluated the same evidence as jurors.

In civil suits in which the parties have no constitutional or statutory right to a jury, or in suits in which the parties have waived their right to a jury, the trial judge will both find the facts and rule on the law. Under Federal Rule of Civil Procedure 52(a), a federal court of appeals will not overturn the factual findings of a federal trial judge unless the findings are "clearly erroneous." Although Rule 52(a) applies only to civil proceedings and does not directly apply to a trial judge's factual findings on preliminary

---

5. See, e.g., Chaline v. KCOH, Inc., 693 F.2d 477, 480 n.3 (5th Cir. 1982); Walsh v. Centeio, 692 F.2d 1239, 1241 (9th Cir. 1982).

6. E.g., Aetna Life Ins. Co. v. Kepler, 116 F.2d 1, 4 & n.1 (8th Cir. 1941).

7. E.g., 29 U.S.C. § 160(f) (appellate review of findings of the National Labor Relations Board).

8. Jackson v. Virginia, 443 U.S. 307, 318 (1979).

9. Interestingly, a finding of negligence is not a pure finding of fact, because it requires the jury to define and apply a standard of care, resulting in a mixed conclusion of law and fact. For purposes of appellate review, however, such jury verdicts are treated as findings of fact. Cf. McDermott Int'l v. Wilander, 498 U.S. 337, 342 (1991) (stating that question of who is a "seaman" under the Jones Act is a mixed question of law and fact for the jury). Appellate courts distinguish more finely between a trial judge's findings of fact and conclusions of law.

rulings in a criminal trial, some courts have adopted Rule 52(a)'s clearly-erroneous standard by analogy for that context.[10]

Under Rule 52(a), a trial judge trying a case without a jury will divide his findings into findings of fact and conclusions of law. For example, he may state as a conclusion of law that a federal antidiscrimination statute requires proof of intent to discriminate, and he may state as a finding of fact that the evidence shows no discriminatory intent. On appeal, the appellate court could review without restriction the trial judge's interpretation of the statute to require proof of intent to discriminate, and it would reverse the trial court's conclusion on that question if it interpreted the statute differently. In contrast, the appellate court would not overturn the trial judge's factual finding of absence of discriminatory intent unless the record showed that finding to be clearly erroneous,[11] even if the appellate judges might have found discriminatory intent had they been the initial factfinders.

At least in theory, the clearly-erroneous standard of review of a trial judge's factual findings permits broader appellate review than does the substantial-evidence standard mandated by the seventh amendment for review of a jury's findings and mandated by statute for review of the findings of some administrative agencies:[12]

> Under the substantial-evidence standard, a reviewing court must uphold the findings of a jury or administrative agency if the record contains sufficient evidence to permit a reasonable person to make those findings. In contrast, the clearly-erroneous standard permits the reviewing court to review the entire record, and to overturn a finding of fact if it is convinced that the finding is clearly wrong, even though a reasonable person could have made the finding.[13]

An appellate court's deference to factual findings made in the trial court is supported by practical and policy considerations that recognize distinctions in the roles of trial and appellate courts. The factfinder in the trial court, either the judge or the jury, is generally in a better position than the appellate court to evaluate the evidence. This advantage is strongest when factual findings are based partly on the factfinder's evaluation of the credibility of witnesses: The mannerisms of the witness on the stand may be much more revealing than the cold print of the reporter's transcript. Accordingly, Rule 52(a) specifically directs appellate courts to give "due regard" to "the opportunity of the trial court to judge of the credibility of the witnesses."

Conversely, the trial court's advantage is weakest when factual findings are based largely on documentary evidence that is available in identical form to both the trial and appellate courts. Nonetheless, Rule 52(a) applies to "[f]indings of fact, whether based on oral or documentary evidence,"[14]

---

10. E.g., United States v. Page, 302 F.2d 81, 85-86 (9th Cir. 1962) (en banc) (appellate review of trial judge's finding of consent to search). Of course, the defendant has a right to a jury determination of the ultimate facts regarding criminal liability. U.S. Const. amend. VI.

11. See Pullman-Standard v. Swint, 456 U.S. 273, 287-288 (1982).

12. E.g., Loehr v. Offshore Logistics, Inc., 691 F.2d 758, 760-761 (5th Cir. 1982).

13. Charles Calleros, Title VII and Rule 52(a): Standards of Appellate Review in Disparate Treatment Cases—Limiting the Reach of Pullman-Standard v. Swint, 58 Tul. L. Rev. 411 n.40 (1983) (citations omitted).

14. Fed. R. Civ. P. 52(a).

suggesting that restrictions on appellate review must be at least partly based on policies other than a practical advantage enjoyed by the trial court.

In fact, restricted appellate review of findings of fact is independently justified by the importance of an appellate court's role in developing general principles of law relative to its role of correcting error in the judgment in a particular case. Admittedly, appellate courts should perform a limited "corrective" function by subjecting each trial judgment to some review for error and thus reducing the risk of injustice.[15] At least as important, however, is the appellate court's "institutional" function of "developing and declaring legal principles that will have application beyond the case that serves as the vehicle for expression of the principles."[16] This institutional function is strongest in the highest appellate court in a jurisdiction.[17] It emphasizes the development of a cohesive body of legal standards rather than the review of evidence supporting findings of fact.

C. CONCLUSIONS OF LAW; MIXED CONCLUSIONS OF FACT AND LAW

In contrast to restricted appellate review of findings of fact, appellate review of a trial judge's conclusions of law is unrestricted. The appellate court may freely correct the trial court's formulation of legal standards.[18]

Often, however, classifying a finding as more nearly one of law than of fact in a nonjury trial is a difficult task.[19] Without doubt, Rule 52(a)'s clearly-erroneous standard applies to appellate review of a trial judge's findings of historical fact, such as findings about events and actions.[20] It also applies to review of "factual inferences" drawn by a trial court from "undisputed basic facts."[21] However, some trial court determinations fall between the two extremes of formulation of abstract legal standards and findings of historical fact or factual inference. For example, a trial judge's determination of whether the historical facts satisfy an abstract legal standard is a mixed finding of fact and law, which may contain elements of both factual inference and refinement of the legal standard.

Appellate review of a narrow class of such mixed findings is restricted under a special standard of review. Specifically, an appellate court will restrict its review of certain "discretionary" rulings of a trial judge, such as the determination to grant or deny an injunction.[22] Assuming that the trial judge formulated the correct legal rule before applying it to the facts, the appellate

---

15. See Calleros, supra note 13, at 421-422.

16. Id. at 420-421.

17. Indeed, under its "two-court rule," the United States Supreme Court will give particular deference to a finding of fact made by a trial judge and upheld on appeal in the intermediate court of appeals. See, e.g., Rogers v. Lodge, 458 U.S. 613, 622-627 (1982).

18. Pullman-Standard v. Swint, 456 U.S. 273, 287 (1982).

19. Id. at 288.

20. E.g., Washington v. Watkins, 655 F.2d 1346, 1352 (5th Cir. 1981), *cert. denied,* 456 U.S. 949 (1982).

21. Commissioner v. Duberstein, 363 U.S. 278, 291 (1960) (citing United States v. United States Gypsum Co., 333 U.S. 364, 394 (1948)).

22. E.g., Los Angeles Memorial Coliseum Comm'n v. National Football League, 634 F.2d 1197, 1200 (9th Cir. 1980).

court will not overturn such a mixed finding of the trial judge unless she abused her discretion.

Most mixed findings, however, do not fall within this narrow class of discretionary rulings. Instead, for purposes of appellate standards of review, appellate courts must classify the findings under Rule 52(a) as findings of fact or conclusions of law. The proper means of accomplishing this classification is a matter of continuing debate.[23] However, the practical and policy considerations underlying restrictions on appellate review provide some guidance in the debate.

If a mixed question of fact and law requires the application of a simple, noncontroversial legal rule to complex historical facts, its resolution may primarily require the trial judge to refine her understanding of the facts rather than to engage in substantial legal reasoning. The trial judge is in the best position to make such a determination, and review of the resulting mixed finding requires exercise primarily of the appellate court's corrective function. Therefore, an appellate court should view the finding as more nearly a finding of factual inference than a conclusion of law.

Consider, for example, a dispute about whether numerous statements and actions by an employer cumulatively created a hostile working environment for female employees, in violation of Title VII. Although resolution of that question inevitably requires some refinement of the statutory language "conditions . . . of employment,"[24] it primarily requires an analysis of the facts. Thus, an appellate court undoubtedly would treat it as a question of fact for purposes of restricted appellate review.

Conversely, if a mixed question of fact and law requires the application of complex, uncertain, or highly controversial legal standards to simple historical facts, the trial judge's resolution of the question may primarily reflect refinement of her understanding of the content of the legal rules. The appellate court is at least equally capable of making such a determination, and it will primarily exercise its institutional function on review. Therefore, an appellate court should view the finding as more nearly a conclusion of law than one of factual inference.[25]

Consider, for example, the question in one United States Supreme Court case of whether the government presented "clear, unequivocal and convincing" proof that a naturalized citizen had fraudulently procured his certificate of naturalization during World War II by falsely renouncing his allegiance to Nazi Germany and falsely swearing allegiance to the United States. The technical nature of the special standard of proof and the uncertainty and political sensitivity of the legal concept of "allegiance" made this mixed question primarily one of law. Therefore, the appellate courts could review the trial court's determination without restriction.[26]

---

23. See Pullman-Standard v. Swint, supra note 18.

24. 42 U.S.C. §2000e-2(a)(1).

25. See generally United States v. McConney, 728 F.2d 1195, 1204 (9th Cir.), *cert. denied*, 469 U.S. 824 (1984) (in a criminal case, adopting a "functional analysis that focuses on the nature of the inquiry required when we apply the relevant rule of law to the facts as established"); Calleros, supra note 13, at 425-432 (using different definitional framework to develop similar analysis).

26. Baumgartner v. United States, 322 U.S. 665 (1944).

TRIAL COURT DETERMINATION	APPELLATE STANDARD OF REVIEW
Finding of fact by jury and some administrative agencies	Affirmed if supported by substantial evidence
Findings of jury in criminal conviction	Affirmed if rational basis or reasonable support in the evidence for a finding that prosecution met its burden of proof
Trial judge's exercise of discretion	Affirmed unless judge abused discretion
Trial judge's finding of fact	Affirmed unless clearly erroneous
Trial judge's ruling on the law	Reviewed without restriction and rejected if appellate court disagrees on the merits
Trial judge's mixed finding of law and fact	Treated as finding of fact or finding of law by trial judge, depending on whether legal or factual questions predominate

III. THE BRIEF—EFFECTIVE APPELLATE ADVOCACY

A. FORMAT—OVERVIEW

Rules of procedure and local court rules typically prescribe formats for appellate briefs that are more formal and detailed than those for motions memoranda and other briefs. When you represent the "appellant," the party bringing the appeal, you will file the opening brief. Typical rules will require this brief to include the following substantive components:

(1) a statement of the issues raised on appeal;
(2) a statement of the procedural history of the case, usually entitled "Statement of the Case";
(3) a statement of the facts relevant to issues raised on appeal;
(4) an argument; and
(5) a conclusion.

In addition, rules usually impose limitations on length and require formal components such as a table of contents and alphabetically arranged tables of authorities.[27]

Some rules may modify the organization of the components listed above, specify subcomponents of one or more of the components, or add other required components. For example, the Federal Rules of Appellate Procedure

---

27. E.g., Ariz. R. of Civ. App. P. 13(a), 14(b).

require the components listed above but combine the statements of procedural history and facts into a single section, referred to as "a statement of the case."[28] Supplementing those rules, the local rules for the United States Court of Appeals for the Ninth Circuit require the statement of the case to address jurisdictional matters, including the subject-matter jurisdiction of the trial court, the statutory basis for the appellate jurisdiction of the Court of Appeals, the right to appeal the order appealed from, and the timeliness of the notice of appeal. The Ninth Circuit local rules also require separate sections that address such matters as the standard of appellate review and the identity of any related cases pending before the court.[29]

If you represent the "appellee," the party seeking affirmance of the judgment of the trial court, you must file an answering brief. This brief will contain the same components as that of the opening brief. However, to the extent that you do not contest the statement of the procedural history, facts, or issues, your answering brief need not repeat the substance of that portion of the opening brief; you may simply state that the appellee adopts all or part of the opening brief's statement.[30]

Finally, if you represent the appellant, you may file a reply brief. This brief should confine itself to rebutting points made in the appellee's answering brief.[31]

Rules of procedure or local court rules often specify a form for the cover sheets for appellate briefs, even assigning different colors for the covers of opening, answering, and reply briefs.[32] The specified form for the information on the cover of an appellate brief varies in different jurisdictions. In some jurisdictions, the cover sheet includes the caption of the case in the same basic format as it appeared in trial pleadings and briefs.[33] In other jurisdictions, the caption and other critical identifying information is presented on several widely spaced lines that are centered on the cover page.

B. STATEMENT OF ISSUES

The art of stating issues in a student case brief or an office memorandum is discussed in detail in Chapters 6 and 9. You should review those principles as a starting point for your drafting the statement of issues in your appellate brief. When drafting an issue statement in a brief, however, you should additionally strive to phrase the issue in a way that suggests a favorable response or otherwise serves to advocate your client's case.

1. Issue Statements as Preliminary Advocacy

Your statement of the issue can invite the court to apply an analytic framework or standard of review that best suits your client's arguments. Of

28. Fed. R. App. P. 28(a)(3).
29. U.S. Ct. App. 9th Cir. R. 28-2.
30. See, e.g., Ariz. R. Civ. App. P. 13(b).
31. See, e.g., Ariz. R. Civ. App. P. 13(c).
32. E.g., Fed. R. App. P. 32(a).
33. For examples of this format, see the sample pleadings and briefs at the ends of Chapters 13-15 and this chapter.

course, you should develop that strategy primarily in the argument section of the brief. In addition, however, you can make the judge more receptive to your approach by initially exposing her to your strategy in your statement of the issues.

For example, suppose that you represent an appellant who appeals from a trial judge's decision to deny a preliminary injunction. You know that the appellate court will overturn that decision only if the trial judge abused her discretion, provided that the trial judge applied the proper legal standards to the facts.[34] However, you believe that her ruling leaves some room for question about the content of the legal rules governing injunctions that she applied to the facts. Accordingly, you might use the statement of the issue to invite the appellate court to find error in the trial judge's formulation of the legal rules, which formulation would be subject to unrestricted review:

I. In denying Surge Corp.'s request for a preliminary injunction, did the trial judge apply an incorrect legal rule by requiring a showing of likelihood of success on the merits, rather than using a "sliding scale" test that would justify a preliminary injunction upon a showing of especially great irreparable harm and at least substantial questions on the merits?

The opposing counsel may argue that the trial judge in fact applied a sliding-scale test and that the judge's balancing of the facts does not reflect an abuse of discretion under the most flexible of legal rules. Nonetheless, he might frame the issue so that it emphasizes the restricted standard of review of the ultimate ruling and refers only abstractly to potential questions about choices among legal rules:

I. Did the trial judge properly exercise her discretion to deny preliminary injunctive relief on the ground that Surge Corp. failed to make the requisite showing on the merits under applicable legal rules?

Of course, the nature of the opportunity to promote a favorable approach in the statement of the issue will vary with the circumstances of each appeal. For example, an appeal might raise a purely legal question about whether the court should recognize a special exception to the general common law contract requirement of consideration to suit the peculiar facts of an exceptional case. If so, the parties might use their statements of the issue, as well as their arguments, to appeal either to the appellate judges' senses of fairness and justice or to their beliefs in the virtue of certainty in the law.

In those circumstances, if you represent the party who would benefit from an exception to the principle, you might use the statement of the issue to vividly and concretely emphasize the peculiar facts of the case:

I. Does McGowin's moral obligation to perform his promise to pay Webb for past services give rise to a legal obligation in light of the serious

---

34. See, e.g., Los Angeles Memorial Coliseum Comm'n v. National Football League, 634 F.2d 1197, 1200 (9th Cir. 1980).

> physical injuries suffered by Webb and the immeasurable benefit he gave
> to McGowin in heroically saving McGowin's life?

This statement of the issue focuses the judges' attention on the appellate
court's corrective function: reaching a just result on the unique facts of the
particular case before it, even if that requires a departure from general
principles.[35]

In contrast, if you represent the party who would benefit from application of the general principle, you might use the statement of the issue to
promote the consideration rule in its abstract form or to emphasize the
general policies supporting the rule:

> I. Did the trial court correctly reject a "moral obligation" exception
> to the fundamental principle that a promise made in recognition of past
> services lacks consideration and therefore is unenforceable?

This issue focuses the judges' attention on factors related to the appellate
court's institutional function: the wisdom of applying the rule in nearly
every context, the importance of maintaining the vitality of a long-standing
rule, and the need for certainty in the law.[36]

2. Credibility of the Advocate

In phrasing the statement of the issue to advocate an approach or a
conclusion, you should not be so anxious to invite a favorable response that
you state a false issue. For example, assume that you represent a criminal
defendant who appeals from a state conviction for illegal possession of cocaine. The applicable criminal statute defines "possession" as contemporaneous intent and ability to exercise physical control over the substance. If the
trial judge correctly instructed the jury on the applicable legal rules and
definitions, you might still argue that substantial evidence did not support
the jury finding of ability to exercise control over the cocaine. If so, the
following statement of the issue would not effectively advance your client's
cause:

> I. Is proof of ability to control an illegal substance a requisite element
> of a conviction for illegal possession of that substance?

Under currently accepted legal definitions in the state, an appellate judge
would readily agree that the question presented by this statement of the
issue must be answered affirmatively. However, she would object that the
question does not fairly characterize any nonfrivolous issue on appeal. Be-

---

35. See generally Webb v. Mcgowin, 168 So. 196, 199 (Ala. Ct. App.) (Samford, J.,
concurring) (departing from "strict letter of the rule" in the interests of justice), *cert. denied,*
168 So. 199 (Ala. 1936).

36. See generally Mills v. Wyman, 3 Pick. 207 (Mass. 1825) (rejecting "moral obligation"
exception in the interests of maintaining universal application of the consideration doctrine).

cause the trial judge correctly instructed the jury on the applicable legal standards, your implicit attack on the completeness of the instructions would be futile. Instead, your issue statement must fairly address your client's true contention on appeal:

> I. Is the jury's finding of Wade's ability to control the cocaine unsupported by substantial evidence in light of undisputed testimony that the officers found Wade standing outside the locked automobile containing the cocaine without a key to the automobile?

Thus, you must recognize limits to your efforts to invite a favorable response to a statement of the issue. Specifically, you must maintain credibility and must fairly link the statement of the issue to your genuine argument on appeal.

C. STATEMENT OF PROCEDURAL HISTORY

Rules of procedure or local court rules will specify whether you must state the procedural history in a separate section or combine it with the historical facts. If the rules require you to state the procedural history in a separate section, they typically designate the section as the "Statement of the Case." If the rules instead require you to combine the facts and procedural history, they typically designate the combined section as either the "Statement of the Case" or the "Statement of Facts." With either format, the essential elements of a statement of procedural history are brief descriptions of "the nature of the case, the course of the proceedings, and its disposition in the court below."[37]

In the opening paragraph of the statement of procedural history, you should introduce the parties and generally describe the claims and defenses that they presented in the trial court. Next, you should chronologically recite the portions of the trial history and the rulings of the court that are relevant to the issues on appeal, including the trial court's final judgment and the appellant's filing notice of appeal. In a brief to a second-level court of appeal, you should also summarize the ruling of the intermediate appellate court. As described in Section III above, court rules in some jurisdictions may require you to discuss additional matters.

D. STATEMENT OF FACTS

1. Format

Your statement of facts on appeal is subject to two limitations. First, except for matters within common knowledge or otherwise subject to judicial

---

37. Fed. R. App. P. 28(a)(4).

notice,[38] the appellate court and the litigants are constrained by the trial court record as the exclusive source for the facts of the dispute. In a fully tried case, those facts are reflected in testimony recorded in the reporter's transcript, in documentary evidence admitted at trial, and in any physical evidence admitted at trial and retained by the trial court clerk. If the trial court disposed of the case on the pleadings or on summary judgment, the facts are reflected in the allegations of the pleadings or in the preliminary presentation of evidence on the motion for summary judgment.[39]

Second, if findings of fact are made by a jury or by the trial court, those findings take on greater significance than the underlying record of testimony and other evidence because of the restricted appellate review of such findings. If the appellant wishes to challenge the findings of fact, then the appellant should refer to the underlying record of evidence to support the challenge; however, the findings will stand unless clearly erroneous or unsupported by substantial evidence. If the appellant instead chooses to limit the attack to a challenge of the trial judge's formulation of legal standards or the judge's application of those standards to facts, the appellant must rely on the findings of fact, perhaps with supplementary references to illuminating evidence that is consistent with the findings. The appellee, of course, should focus on either the findings or the underlying evidence supporting the findings, depending on which response most appropriately meets the appellant's challenge. These strategic considerations are illustrated in Section E.2 below.

2. The Power of Facts

The opening statement of facts in a brief can play a surprisingly important role in persuasion. In many cases, applicable legal standards are sufficiently general, flexible, or unclear to support any of several conclusions on the application of the law to facts. Indeed, a judge's determination of whether the facts satisfy the applicable legal standard helps to further refine the legal standard.

In making this determination, a judge tries to reach a just result in the case before her while performing the separate institutional function of developing a coherent body of law that will satisfy general policy considerations and will provide useful precedent for the resolution of other disputes. Developing a coherent body of precedent is primarily the task of appellate courts and is particularly important in the highest court in a jurisdiction. A trial judge, on the other hand, will be most concerned about reaching a just result within the parameters of existing precedent.

A persuasive statement of facts near the beginning of your brief may incline a judge to rule in favor of your client even before the judge has considered the legal analysis. If so, the judge may take advantage of the flexibility or uncertainty in the legal principles to reach the result that the facts have persuaded her to define as just, provided that she can do so

---

38. See, e.g., Fed. R. Evid. 201 and advisory committee note on subdivision (f) (judicial notice of adjudicative facts in trial and on appeal); United States v. Pink, 315 U.S. 203, 216 (1942) (appellate judicial notice of record in other case).
39. See generally Ariz. S. Ct. R. 5(b)(5).

without departing from clearly controlling precedent or otherwise upsetting the orderly development of a coherent body of law. A persuasive opening statement of facts will help make the judge receptive to the legal and factual analyses in the argument section of your brief.

3. Persuasive Presentation of Facts

To present the facts persuasively, you may be tempted to slant the record misleadingly in favor of your client's case or to introduce legal arguments and conclusions in the statement of facts. Neither technique is likely to succeed.

a. Advocacy with Credibility

If you riddle your statement of facts with exaggerations or misleading omissions, you will simply diminish your credibility. Instead, your statement of facts should display your client in a favorable light while reflecting a concern for completeness and accuracy. If the judge is convinced that your statement is accurate and complete, she may repeatedly consult it as a fair summary of the record, resulting in maximum exposure of the subtle advocacy of your statement.

Rather than omit unfavorable facts, you should simply deemphasize them, while emphasizing favorable ones. In addition to the techniques of persuasive writing discussed in Chapter 12, you can use the organization of the entire fact statement to emphasize the favorable facts. Chronological order of facts may be the clearest and most logical. However, you can increase the impact of favorable events by describing them in the places of greatest emphasis: the beginning and end of the fact statement. If you can do so without unduly sacrificing clarity and continuity, you can justify departing from chronological order.

You can also emphasize favorable facts by using specific and concrete descriptions and strong verbs in active voice. Conversely, you can lessen the impact of unfavorable facts by describing them in general, abstract terms. For example, suppose that Samuel Hughes, the defendant in a prosecution for first-degree murder seeks to mitigate the offense by showing that he was intoxicated at the time of the crime and therefore could not have premeditated the killing. As the prosecutor, you can deemphasize his intoxication by referring to it generally, and you can emphasize his aggressive conduct by describing it in gruesome detail:

> While under the influence of self-induced intoxication, the defendant murdered Grace Smith by bludgeoning her from behind with a baseball bat.

This statement relegates the defendant to anonymity by referring to him with a procedural label. In contrast, it names the victim, thus inviting the reader to recognize her as a person, rather than a statistic. Moreover, the description of the attack as one from behind tends to portray the victim as particularly sympathetic and defenseless. The statement not only refers to the defendant's impaired state of mind abstractly and in a subordinate phrase, it invites the reader to reject the intoxication as a mitigating factor by characterizing it as self-induced. Finally, strong, vivid words such as "murdered" and "bludgeoning" convey the horror of the assault.

As counsel for the defendant, you might refer to the same incident with converse emphasis:

‖ When the victim was killed by a blow to the head, Samuel Hughes was
‖ staggering from the effects of nearly three pints of whiskey.

In contrast to the prosecutor's statement, this one refers to the killing and the victim in abstract terms, in passive voice, and in a subordinate clause. Moreover, it humanizes the defendant by referring to him by name, and it describes his intoxication vividly.

b. Premature Legal Argument

If you prematurely introduce legal or factual argument into your statement of facts, you may undermine the effectiveness of your fact statement as a vehicle for making the judge receptive to your main argument. A judge knows that the legal argument of a brief will be one-sided, and he generally reserves judgment on legal conclusions until he has read both briefs. But he may be more willing to draw his own conclusions from an apparently complete and accurate statement of facts.

For example, if your statement of facts specifically characterizes a driver's operation of an automobile as negligent, it may produce a defensive reaction in the judge; he may warn himself that he should resist such a mixed conclusion of law and fact until he has thoroughly studied the arguments in both briefs. On the other hand, if your statement of facts vividly describes the automobile veering from lane to lane at an excessive speed, it will implicitly invite the judge to draw his own conclusion that the driver acted negligently. Even if tentative or subconscious, that conclusion will predispose the judge toward accepting your explicit legal arguments and conclusions in the argument section of your brief.

Thus, when the judge reaches the argument section of the brief, he may resist arguments supporting conclusions that you had bluntly attempted to force on him in the statement of facts. He will be more comfortable with arguments that seem to confirm conclusions he had reached on his own after reading apparently nonargumentative facts.

4. Summary and Perspective

To ensure that your opening statement of facts makes the judge more receptive to your main argument, you should

(1) state the facts completely and accurately;
(2) emphasize favorable facts and deemphasize unfavorable ones through sentence structure, varying levels of specificity and concreteness, and general organization; and
(3) avoid premature argument.

E. THE ARGUMENT

Earlier chapters have provided you with the basic information and skills you need to formulate, organize, and express your arguments in any brief. In summary, for each issue you should

(1) state your contention in an argumentative point heading,
(2) argue for a favorable interpretation of legal authority,
(3) apply the legal rules to the facts, and
(4) state the conclusion that you want the appellate court to reach.

This section will supplement the earlier chapters by examining some characteristics of argumentation that are peculiar to appellate briefs.

1. Arguing the Law—The Role of Policy Analysis

Appellate briefs differ in style from pretrial and trial briefs in the greater extent to which they examine the underlying policies of legal standards. Depending on the procedural posture and other circumstances of a particular appeal, this difference in approach may reflect such factors as the restrictions on appellate review of factual findings, the appellate court's institutional function of developing a cohesive body of law, and the varying degrees to which stare decisis controls decisions at various levels of the court system.

For example, suppose that after the presentation of evidence to the jury in a contract dispute, a party requests the trial judge to rule on the merits as a matter of law on the ground that the jury could reasonably reach only one conclusion on the evidence. In considering such a motion for a "directed verdict," the trial judge has no authority to modify or overrule appellate precedents that establish the applicable contracts law or the standards for a directed verdict. Rather, the trial judge must seek to understand and to apply those rules to the evidence. Of course, the trial judge can engage in creative legal analysis to the extent that the content of the legal rules or their application to facts is uncertain, but that opportunity is relatively limited in many cases at the trial level. Accordingly, the briefs on such a motion likely will summarize the appellate precedent on the legal questions and will focus attention on the evidence and the inferences to be drawn from it.

On appeal from a final judgment, the emphasis often shifts from analysis of the factual record to the content of the legal rules, particularly if the trial judge or jury has made findings of fact after a full trial. Unless the appellant assumes the difficult burden of challenging such factual findings, the appellate briefs likely will explore questions about the content of legal rules, either in the abstract or in the process of determining whether the accepted facts satisfy the rules. Because the appellate court can overrule its own precedents, it will consider policy arguments that favor or oppose extending, modifying, or overruling those precedents.

The institutional function of the appellate courts further encourages policy analysis in appellate briefwriting. For two reasons, this effect is greatest in the highest court of a jurisdiction. First, unlike an intermediate court of appeals, the highest court is not bound by the precedent of any court within that jurisdiction.[40] Second, the highest courts in many jurisdictions will accept review of some kinds of lower court decisions only after a discretionary determination that the decision raises important questions about the development of a cohesive body of law or that it otherwise would significantly affect the outcome of many cases other than the one that serves as the vehicle for addressing the questions.

These qualities of courts of last resort are illustrated by the hearings in 1987 of the Senate Judiciary Committee on Judge Robert Bork's unsuccessful bid for confirmation to the United States Supreme Court. Some who actively opposed Judge Bork's confirmation to the Court had not opposed his earlier appointment to the United States Court of Appeals for the District of Columbia Circuit. They explained that Judge Bork's perceived extremist views on constitutional law could work little mischief on the Court of Appeals because that court is constrained by Supreme Court precedent. However, they feared that his presence on the Supreme Court, which is not absolutely bound by even its own precedent, might hasten that Court's retreat from hard-won advances in civil rights.[41]

Thus, more often than in trial briefs, appellate advocates will allocate substantial portions of their arguments to the policies underlying legal rules and to the social and jurisprudential consequences of retaining or abandoning those rules. Moreover, these characteristics typically will be even more pronounced in a court of last resort than in an intermediate court of appeals.

For example, the following two passages are excerpts of arguments about the proper application of precedent of the state supreme court, the highest court in the state. The first argument could be addressed to the trial court or even to the intermediate court of appeals. Because neither court can overrule the state supreme court precedent, the argument focuses on the applicability of the law of the precedent to the facts of the dispute:

Introduction to argument	*B. The trial judge erred in instructing the jury that Bramwell could be liable for the tort of wrongful discharge if he discharged Kirkeide in "bad faith" rather than in violation of public policy.* The trial court's instruction on the tort of wrongful discharge fails to distinguish between conduct that violates a public policy and conduct that is simply unfair or retaliatory in the context of a

---

40. Of course, decisions of a state court of last resort on a question of federal law could be reviewed by the United States Supreme Court, and the state court would be bound by United States Supreme Court precedent on such questions.

41. See, e.g., The United States Senate Judiciary Committee Chairman's Consultants, Response Prepared to White House Analysis of Judge Bork's Record §VI(D) (Sept. 2, 1987), *reprinted in* 9 Cardozo L. Rev. 219, 293 (1987).

particular employment relationship. This instruction permitted the jury to award damages against Bramwell for conduct that is not tortious in this state.

The New Maine Supreme Court has recently recognized a cause of action in tort for wrongful discharge. However, it carefully limited its holding to discharges that violate public policy:

> Thus, an employer is liable in tort for wrongful discharge if it discharges an employee for a reason that violates an important public policy of the state. Pronouncements of public policy will most often be found in our state's constitution and its legislation.

General legal rule

Blass v. Arcon Co., 337 N. Me. 771, 776 (1988).

In *Blass,* the employer discharged a truck driver in retaliation for the driver's refusal to transport toxic wastes in unsafe containers. The employer was liable in tort for wrongful discharge because its conduct violated the policies of state environmental and occupational safety statutes. *Id.* at 777.

In-depth case analysis

In contrast to *Blass,* Bramwell's discharge of Kirkeide in this case did not violate any public policy. At most, Bramwell acted arbitrarily and exercised poor business judgment, but not in a way that implicates public policy. Yet, the trial court's instruction permitted the jury to impose liability. . . .

Application to facts

In the preceding illustration, the *Blass* decision did not need to address whether a discharge can be tortious for reasons other than a violation of public policy; therefore, it does not preclude future extensions of the new tort of wrongful discharge. Nonetheless, the briefwriter has reasonably assumed that a trial court or intermediate court of appeals would not readily extend a newly recognized tort beyond the terms of the Supreme Court's holding. Thus, the briefwriter concentrates on explaining the holding of the *Blass* decision and distinguishing it.

In contrast, the following passage is addressed to the New Maine Supreme Court, the mythical author of the *Blass* decision. Because that court can overrule, limit, or extend its own precedent, the argument spends more time on policy analysis. Specifically, it argues that, as a matter of policy, the court should not broaden the tort of wrongful discharge beyond the holding of the *Blass* decision.

B. The trial judge erred in instructing the jury that Bramwell could be liable. . . .

The trial court's instruction on the tort of wrongful discharge fails to distinguish between conduct that violates a public policy and conduct that . . .

Introduction to argument

General legal rule	Although this court has recently recognized a cause of action in tort for wrongful discharge, it carefully limited its holding to discharges that violate public policy:
	Thus, an employer is liable . . . *Blass v. Arcon Co.*, 337 N. Me. 771, 776 (1988).
In-depth case analysis	In *Blass*, the employer discharged a truck driver in retaliation for the driver's refusal to transport toxic wastes in unsafe containers. . . .
Policy analysis	This court should reject Kirkeide's invitation to extend the tort of wrongful discharge beyond the holding of *Blass*. This state has long promoted the policy of freedom of contract, permitting contracting parties to shape their own rights and obligations. *E.g., Snell v. Abundes*, 128 N. Me. 217, 221 (1970). Even if limited to violations of public policy, the tort of wrongful discharge effectively limits the parties' freedom to create a contract that is terminable at will. This court should not restrict the freedom to contract any further. Therefore, this court should narrowly tailor the tort of wrongful discharge to impose liability only for discharges that offend the values of society as a whole, and not for discharges that merely reflect ill will between two private parties.
Policy analysis	If tort liability can be based on simple "bad faith," courts and juries will be forced to second-guess every discharge to determine whether it was motivated by legitimate business considerations or personal spite. . . .
Application to facts	In our case, the trial court's instruction, approved by the court of appeals, extended the tort of wrongful discharge beyond the holding of *Blass*. By permitting an award of damages for a bad-faith discharge, . . .

2. Arguing the Law and the Facts

a. Strategic Choices

The appellant will seek to overturn unfavorable findings or conclusions of the trial court. Thus, as explained in Section II above, the appellant will benefit from unrestricted appellate review of such findings or conclusions. Accordingly, if you represent the appellant, you should try to characterize unfavorable mixed findings of fact and law in a nonjury trial as conclusions of law, which are reviewable on appeal without restriction. On this matter, neither party is bound by the trial court's characterization of a finding as one of fact or law. In a jury trial, on the other hand, a jury's mixed finding of fact and law will always be treated as a finding of fact for purposes of restricted appellate review.

If an unfavorable finding is undeniably one of fact, you must make some strategic choices among alternative approaches on appeal. As counsel for the appellant, you must decide whether to challenge the unfavorable finding of fact under a restricted standard of review, argue that the trial court applied the wrong legal rule to the facts, or both.

For example, suppose the plaintiff in a federal civil rights suit successfully sought compensatory and punitive damages against your client, a police officer, for false arrest in violation of the fourth amendment. At trial, the trial judge gave the following instructions to the jury over your objection:

> If you find that Officer Mullins arrested Ms. Wong without probable cause, you must find that Officer Mullins violated Ms. Wong's constitutional rights, and you must award Ms. Wong compensatory damages in the amount of her actual injuries. Furthermore, if you find that Officer Mullins was grossly and inexcusably careless with regard to Ms. Wong's constitutional rights, you may exercise discretion to award Ms. Wong punitive damages in an amount that will punish Officer Mullins and discourage him and others from similar violations.

Applying these instructions to the facts, the jury found Officer Mullins liable and awarded Ms. Wong $5,000 in compensatory damages and $25,000 in punitive damages. The trial court also awarded Ms. Wong her reasonable attorney's fees.

Your client, Officer Mullins, has appealed. As one of your arguments on appeal, you wish to challenge the award of punitive damages, which is necessarily premised on a jury finding that Officer Mullins was "grossly and inexcusably careless." You can attack the award in either or both of two ways.

First, to take advantage of unrestricted appellate review of matters of law, you can try to persuade the appellate court that the trial judge incorrectly instructed the jury on the law:

Officer Mullins is entitled to a new trial, because the trial judge erroneously instructed the jury that it could award punitive damages for conduct less culpable than reckless disregard for constitutional rights.

The United States Supreme Court has established a recklessness standard for punitive damages in federal civil rights actions:

General legal rule

> We hold that a jury may be permitted to assess punitive damages in an action under §1983 when the defendant's conduct is shown to be motivated by evil motive or intent, or when it involves reckless or callous indifference to the federally protected rights of others.

Smith v. Wade, 461 U.S. 30, 56 (1983).

Related legal rules	A standard based on reckless misconduct requires a greater showing of culpability than simple negligence. *See Johnson v. Lundell* . . . In *Johnson,* . . .
Policy analysis	The extraordinary nature of punitive damages justifies close scrutiny of the trial judge's instructions to ensure that they recognize even fine distinctions in culpability. Otherwise, . . .
Application to facts; the instruction	In this case, the trial court instructed the jury that it could award punitive damages if it found that Officer Mullins was "grossly and inexcusably careless." This instruction did not adequately convey the requisite standard: reckless or callous disregard of constitutional rights.
Further analysis of instruction	Even when coupled with the adjective "grossly," the word "careless" connotes only a breach of duty rising to the level of negligence. . . .
Conclusion	The trial court improperly instructed the jury on the standard for punitive damages. Officer Mullins is entitled to a new trial so that the jury may apply the proper legal standard to the facts.

Alternatively, if you are prepared to labor against a restricted standard of review, you can try to persuade the appellate court to overturn the jury's implicit finding that Officer Mullins was "grossly and inexcusably careless." Under that approach, you must review the underlying evidence, such as the testimony at trial, and explain why the jury's finding is not supported by substantial evidence:

	D. This court should vacate the award of punitive damages, because substantial evidence does not support the jury's finding that Officer Mullins acted with the requisite culpability to justify punitive damages.
Introduction to argument	Even if the trial court's instructions adequately conveyed the culpability required for an award of punitive damages, the jury did not properly find such culpability on the part of Officer Mullins. At most, the evidence supports the conclusion that Officer Mullins made a reasonable mistake in judgment in chaotic circumstances. Therefore, the trial judge erred in denying Mullins's Motion for Judgment Notwithstanding the Verdict on the issue of punitive damages, and this court should overturn the jury's award of punitive damages.
Rules governing review of jury's findings	This court may overturn a finding of the jury if the finding is unsupported by substantial evidence in the record so that no reasonable juror could have made the finding on the evidence. *See* . . . This

substantial-evidence standard permits appellate courts to review jury findings to guard against verdicts based on bias, passion, or incompetence. *See* . . . . To satisfy the purposes of such review, this court should scrutinize the record for . . .

Officer Mullins's uncontradicted testimony establishes the reasonableness of his actions. He testified that the report over his squad car radio identified the robbery suspect only as a young man of slight build with dark, shoulder-length hair. II RT 335-36. One block from the robbery site, Officer Mullins spotted Ms. Wong walking at a very brisk pace away from the robbery site. *Id.* at 336. He initially passed her by because he was looking for a male suspect. *Id.* at 337. However, when he found no other suspects in the vicinity, he realized that Ms. Wong fit the description of the robbery suspect except for her gender. *Id.* at 339. He remembered that Ms. Wong was wearing jeans and a sweatshirt, and he realized that an agitated witness might have been mistaken about her gender. *Id.* at 339-440. Consequently, he turned his squad car around, found Ms. Wong again, and stopped her for questioning. *Id.* at 440.

Other testimony supports Officer Mullins's version of the events. Ms. Wong herself testified that she had been walking at an unusually brisk pace. I RT 327. She also admitted that she had trouble answering Officer Mullins's questions. *Id.* at 331. Although in her testimony Ms. Wong offered innocent explanations for her hurried pace and her inability to communicate effectively with Officer Mullins, nothing in the record shows that these explanations were apparent to Officer Mullins at the time of the arrest. . . .

In sum, the evidence leads inescapably to one conclusion: In his eagerness to fulfill his duties as a police officer, Officer Mullins mistakenly arrested the wrong person, but he did not recklessly disregard anyone's constitutional rights in doing so. Quite the contrary, he took steps at several stages to safeguard Ms. Wong's rights.

The record simply does not contain substantial evidence supporting the jury's finding of sufficient culpability to justify an award of punitive damages. Apparently, the jurors misunderstood or ignored the trial court's instructions and based their verdict on irrelevant factors.

For these reasons, even if this court affirms the

Examination of facts: The testimony

Analysis of testimony: Permissible inferences

Conclusion

> jury's finding of lack of probable cause, it must overturn the jury's award of punitive damages. The evidence does not support this extraordinary award.

Counsel for the appellee can respond to either of these arguments directly. In response to the first sample argument, she can argue either that (1) the law permits an award of punitive damages for culpability less than recklessness, or (2) the trial judge's instructions adequately conveyed the requisite standard of recklessness. In response to the second sample argument, she can (1) emphasize the restricted standard of appellate review, (2) describe evidence in the record that supports a jury finding of recklessness, and (3) explain why that evidence should be viewed as "substantial."

b. Varieties of Fact Analysis

As illustrated in the preceding subsection, the appropriate nature and depth of fact analysis on appeal will depend in part on two factors: (1) the nature of the appellant's challenge to the trial court's judgment, and (2) the procedural posture of the case when the trial court disposed of it.

(1) Nature of Appellant's Challenge. For an example of the first factor, suppose that you represent the appellant and that you choose to challenge not the jury's findings of fact but only the trial judge's instructions on the law, as in the first sample passage in Subsection a above. Your arguments on such a challenge will often focus on the law and include only modest fact analysis. Specifically, even if "fact" is expansively defined to include the trial judge's actual instructions, your application of the law to the facts could include no more than a comparison of the correct legal rule to the actual instruction and a statement about the need for a new trial with proper instructions to the jury:

> In this case, the trial court instructed the jury that . . . . This instruction did not adequately convey . . . .
> . . . Officer Mullins is entitled to a new trial so that the jury may apply the proper legal standard to the facts.

Even when asking for a new trial, you could analyze the facts in much greater detail if you or the opposing counsel further invited the appellate court to examine the record and reach its own conclusion about the application of the proper rule to the facts. Ordinarily, however, the factfinder in the trial court should have the first opportunity to evaluate new, material evidence or to apply new, materially different instructions to the facts. Therefore, a more detailed fact analysis would contemplate an appellate procedure that is not mandatory and is not even clearly appropriate.

In contrast, detailed fact analysis will be mandatory if the appellant challenges the factfindings of the trial judge or jury. As illustrated in the second sample passage in Subsection a above, the parties then must review the record and argue whether the evidence supports the finding of fact under the applicable standard of review:

> Officer Mullins's uncontradicted testimony establishes the reasonableness of his actions. He testified that . . .
>
> Other testimony supports Officer Mullins's version of the events. Ms. Wong herself testified that . . .
>
> In sum, the evidence leads inescapably to one conclusion: . . .
>
> The record simply does not contain substantial evidence supporting the jury's finding. . . .

(2) Procedural Posture. Your fact analysis may also vary with the second factor: the procedural posture of the case at the time of trial disposition. Specifically, dispositions at different pretrial and trial stages will lead to appellate analyses of different kinds of facts.

For example, suppose that the trial court dismissed the action for failure of the complaint to state a claim for relief. On appeal, you can argue the law, but you will have no findings of fact or even underlying evidence in the record to which to apply the law. Instead, you must argue whether the factual allegations of the complaint state a claim for relief under the correct interpretation of the law.

In summary judgment litigation, on the other hand, you ordinarily will develop a record of preliminary showings of fact with documents, affidavits, and discovery materials. Therefore, on appeal, you can argue whether the evidentiary materials submitted by both parties create a genuine issue of fact for trial under the applicable law.

Finally, the record will include formally introduced evidence if either party has appealed from the trial judge's denial of a motion for a directed verdict or for a judgment notwithstanding the verdict after presentation of the evidence in a jury trial. Moreover, on appeal from judgment after a full trial, the record will include both the evidence and the findings of the judge or jury. As explored above, the record in either case provides a fertile source for fact analysis if the appellant chooses to challenge the role of the factfinder under a restricted standard of review. On the other hand, if the appellant chooses to accept the findings of fact, his arguments will focus on analysis of the law.

F. THE CONCLUSION

Chapter 12's discussion about the conclusion section of a brief applies with full force to appellate briefs. At the least, your conclusion must briefly restate the action that your client requests the appellate court to take. In a complex case, your conclusion may also include a brief summary and synthesis of the arguments presented in your brief.

======= E X E R C I S E   1 6 - 1 =======

In addition to responding to the appellant's arguments on appeal, an appellee may file its own "cross-appeal" to affirmatively challenge aspects of a lower court's decision. The following appellate briefs are the Opening Brief, Answering Brief, and Reply Brief on a cross-appeal filed by the appellee of the main appeal. The briefs reproduced below appear in their original form, with the exception of corrections of minor typographical errors, the deletion of some references to the main appeal, and the omission of a procedural issue.

The briefs depart in many ways from the techniques suggested in Chapter 11 of this book, perhaps illustrating that a variety of styles can effectively communicate or persuade. As you read these briefs, consider what changes you would make to conform the writing to your own style, and consider the following questions.

1. *Statements of the Case*

Study the procedural history traced in the statements of the case in the opening brief and the answering brief. Identify the trial court rulings challenged by each party. Is it clear why both Koepnick and Sears were dissatisfied, resulting in cross-appeals? What standard did the trial court apply in reaching its decision on the point appealed from on the cross-appeal? What standard of review should the appellate court apply?

2. *Statements of Fact*

Study the statements of fact in the opening and answering briefs. Could you identify the author of each statement if you read no other parts of the briefs? Does each fact statement successfully present an apparently complete and neutral summary of the facts while placing the advocate's client in the best possible light?

Consider the points of conflict between the two fact statements. In what instances is the apparent conflict simply a reflection of each advocate using techniques of writing style to emphasize some facts and deemphasize others? In what instances is the conflict rooted in genuine disagreement about the factual conclusions that find support in the record? What is the legal significance on appeal of conflicting evidence in the record on a material point, given the procedural posture of this case?

3. *Statements of Issues*

Study the statements of the issues in the opening and answering briefs. Does each advocate successfully phrase each issue in a way that invites a favorable response for his client? Does either state a false issue that easily invites a favorable response but that does not fairly pinpoint the real issue on appeal?

4. *Arguments*

Study the arguments in all three briefs. How important is fact analysis to the arguments in each brief? Would the allocation of resources between fact analysis and discussion of legal rules be different if the appellant were appealing from the trial court's rejection of a novel legal theory of recovery?

5. *Responsive Arguments*

Does the answering brief effectively respond to the opening brief? Does the reply brief effectively respond to the answering brief?

6. *Writing Style*

How would you change the writing style or presentation of authority in any of the briefs? Explain the reasons for your editing.

7. *Format*

How well do the briefs conform to the following formats for appellate briefs prescribed by the Arizona Rules of Civil Appellate Procedure?

Rule 13. Briefs
13(a) Brief of the Appellant. The brief of the appellant shall concisely and clearly set forth under appropriate headings and in the order here indicated:

1. A table of contents with page references.
2. A table of citations, which shall alphabetically arrange and index the cases, statutes and other authorities cited, with references to the pages of the brief on which they are cited.
3. A statement of the case, indicating briefly the basis of the appellate court's jurisdiction, the nature of the case, the course of the proceedings and the disposition in the court below.
4. A statement of facts relevant to the issues presented for review, with appropriate references to the record. . . .
5. A statement of the issues presented for review. . . .
6. An argument, which shall contain the contentions of the appellant with respect to the issues presented, and the reasons therefor, with citations to the authorities, statutes and parts of the record relied on. The argument may include a summary. . . .
7. A short conclusion stating the precise relief sought.
8. An appendix if desired.

13(b) Brief of the Appellee. The brief of the appellee shall conform to the requirements of the preceding subdivision, except that a statement of the case, a statement of the facts or a statement of the issues need not be included unless the appellee finds the statements of the appellant to be insufficient or incorrect.

13(c) Reply Brief. The appellant may file a reply brief, but it shall be confined strictly to rebuttal of points urged in the appellee's brief. No further briefs may be filed except as provided in Rule 13(e) or by leave of court. . . .

13(e) Briefs in Cases Involving Cross-Appeals. A party who files a cross-appeal may combine in one brief his brief as appellee and his brief as cross-appellant. If the appellant wishes to file a further brief, he may combine in one brief his reply brief as appellant and his brief as cross-appellee. The cross-appellant may file a reply brief on the issues of the cross-appeal.

Ariz. R. Civ. App. P. 13.

Fred Cole
Roger W. Perry
Gust, Rosenfeld, Divelbess & Henderson
3300 Valley Bank Center
Phoenix, Arizona 85073
Attorneys for Defendant-Appellee/Cross-Appellant

IN THE
COURT OF APPEALS
STATE OF ARIZONA
Division One

MAX KOEPNICK,
    Plaintiff-Appellant
    Cross-Appellee,
 	
v.
 	
SEARS, ROEBUCK & COMPANY,
    Defendant-Appellee
    Cross-Appellant.
	1 CA-CIV 9147
	
	MARICOPA County
	Superior Court
	No. C 502081

OPENING BRIEF ON CROSS-APPEAL

TABLE OF CONTENTS

TABLE OF AUTHORITIES

APPELLEE'S OPENING BRIEF ON CROSS-APPEAL

STATEMENT OF THE CASE

Plaintiff-appellant Max Koepnick ("Koepnick") commenced this action by filing a complaint on December 5, 1983 (C.T. 1). The defendants named in the complaint were defendant-appellee Sears, Roebuck & Company ("Sears") and the City of Mesa ("Mesa"). The complaint set forth claims in six counts, which were all alleged to have arisen out of an incident that occurred at the Sears store at Fiesta Mall in Mesa, Arizona on December 6, 1982. Sears was named as defendant in only four of the counts. These were Count One for false arrest, Count Four for trespass to chattel, Count Five for invasion of privacy and Count Six for malicious prosecution. Mesa was named as defendant in Count Two for false arrest and Count Three for assault and battery. Mesa was also named as a co-defendant with Sears in Counts Five and Six.

Prior to trial, Mesa moved for summary judgment on Count Two for false arrest (C.T. 55). The court granted Mesa's motion on that count based on the court's determination that probable cause existed for Mesa to detain Koepnick (Minute entry dated January 9, 1986).

Trial to a jury on the other counts of Koepnick's complaint commenced on January 10, 1986. At the close of Koepnick's case-in-brief, Sears moved for a directed verdict on all counts asserted against it (7R.T. 13). Plaintiff stipulated to the dismissal of Count Six for malicious prosecution against Sears, and the court granted Sears a directed verdict on Count Four for invasion of privacy (Minute entry dated January 21, 1986). Mesa made a similar motion and was granted directed verdicts on Count Two for false arrest, Count Five for invasion of privacy, Count Six for malicious prosecution and all plaintiff's claims for punitive damages (Minute entry dated January 21, 1986).

At the close of evidence, Sears and Mesa again moved for directed verdicts on all the remaining claims against them. These motions were denied (8R.T. 84-92). The remaining claims were submitted to the jury. The jury returned verdicts against Sears for $25,000.00 in compensatory damages and $500,000.00 in punitive damages on Count One for false arrest and $100.00 in compensatory damages and $25,000.00 punitive damages on Count Four for trespass to chattel (9R.T. 101-03). The jury also returned verdicts against Mesa for $50,000.00 on Count Three for assault and battery and $100.00 on Count Four for trespass to chattel (9R.T. 101-03). Judgment was entered on the verdicts on February 25, 1986 (C.T. 97; Appendix A).

Sears filed motions for judgment notwithstanding the verdicts and for a new trial on Counts One and Four on March 11, 1986 (C.T. 100). Mesa filed a motion for a new trial on March 11, 1986 (C.T. 101) and a motion for judgment notwithstanding the verdict or, in the alternative, for a new trial and for remittitur on March 12, 1986 (C.T. 104). An amended motion for judgment notwithstanding the verdicts and for new trial was filed by Sears on April 16, 1986 (C.T. 113).

A hearing on the post-trial motions was held on April 17, 1986. Upon consideration of the motions, the court granted Sears' and Mesa's motions for judgment N.O.V. on Count Four for trespass to chattel and granted Sears' motion for new trial on Count One for false arrest. The court granted judgment N.O.V. for defendants on the trespass to chattel claim as Koepnick failed to present evidence that the alleged trespass caused any damage or injury, which is an essential element of an actionable claim. The court granted a new trial on the false arrest claim as the court determined that reasonable cause to detain Koepnick existed as a matter of law and that, therefore, it had erred in instructing the jury on the issue of reasonable cause (Minute entry dated May 14, 1986; Appendix B).

A second hearing occurred on June 24, 1986 pertaining to further post-trial motions, and the court clarified its minute entry of May 14, 1986 (Minute entry dated June 27, 1986; Appendix C). (The trial court's attempt at clarification did not completely succeed in that the minute entry repeatedly refers to the "assault" claim when the court actually means to refer to the false arrest claim.) The final order setting forth the court's disposition of the post-trial motions, including the granting of judgment on Count Four for trespass to chattel and the granting of Sears' motion for new trial on Count One for false arrest, was entered July 23, 1986 (C.T. 125; Appendix D).

Koepnick filed a notice of appeal on July 24, 1986, with respect to the trial court's order granting Sears' motion for judgment notwithstanding the verdict on Count Four for trespass to chattel and for a new trial on Count One for false arrest (C.T. 124). Sears filed a notice of cross-appeal with respect to the portions of the judgment dated February 24, 1986, granting judgment in favor of Koepnick and the portions of the order dated July 18, 1986, denying Sears' motion for judgment notwithstanding the verdict on Count One for false arrest and conditionally denying defendant Sears' motion for new trial on the Count Four for trespass to chattel (C.T. 128). No appeal was taken by either Koepnick or Mesa with respect to the adjudications of the claims asserted by Koepnick against Mesa. Accordingly, Mesa is not a party to this appeal.

The parties stipulated to waiving the posting of cost bonds on the appeals. This court has jurisdiction of the appeal and cross-appeal pursuant to A.R.S. §12-1201 B and F.

STATEMENT OF FACTS

On December 6, 1982, Koepnick drove to the Sears store located at Fiesta Mall to get some screwdrivers (4R.T. 145-47). He arrived at approximately 5 P.M. (4R.T. 145). Once in the store, he was assisted by Mara Thomas, a sales clerk in the hardware department (4R.T. 147; 8R.T. 36). After Koepnick selected the tools he wanted, Thomas carried them to the cash register (4R.T. 148). Koepnick was waited on at the cash register by Bruce Rosenhan, another sales clerk, who rang up the tools for Koepnick (4R.T. 150-51; 7R.T. 88). These tools consisted of a set of screwdrivers, a wrench set, a nut-driver set, an open-end wrench set and a set of pliers (7R.T. 88-89; Ex. 11). Koepnick asked Rosenhan for an itemized receipt

(4R.T. 151; 7R.T. 88). Rosenhan bagged Koepnick's purchases, stapling the bag closed with the receipts on the outside (4R.T. 151; 7R.T. 89). Koepnick left the cash register area (4R.T. 171; 7R.T. 89).

After waiting on Koepnick, Rosenhan went out to work on the sales floor (7R.T. 90). Rosenhan saw Koepnick again in the hardware department approximately 15 minutes after he had waited on him (7R.T. 90-91). Koepnick came over to where he and Thomas were in the back of the department (7R.T. 90). Rosenhan saw Koepnick speak to Thomas and pull a large wrench out of the shopping bag Rosenhan had earlier stapled closed (7R.T. 91). At that time, Koepnick's bag was open and there were no receipts in view on it (7R.T. 91). Rosenhan realized that the wrench Koepnick pulled out of the bag was not one of the wrenches from the sets that he sold to Koepnick (7R.T. 91). When Rosenhan finished with the customer he was helping, he asked Thomas if Koepnick put the wrench back in his bag and whether she had sold it to him (7R.T. 92). Thomas told him that Koepnick put it back in his bag and that she had not sold that wrench to him or had anything to do with it (7R.T. 92). Rosenhan asked all the other employees present in the department whether they had sold that particular wrench to Koepnick and learned that none of them had either (7R.T. 92).

Rosenhan went to the front register and used the phone to call security (7R.T. 92). He spoke with Steve Lessard, one of the security agents on duty at that time in the store (4R.T. 77). It was approximately 5:35 to 5:40 when Lessard received the call from Rosenhan (4R.T. 83). He informed Lessard that he believed that there was a customer in the store who was a shoplifter (4R.T. 77). Lessard told him to meet in the sewing machine department, which is located next to hardware (4R.T. 77-78). When Rosenhan and Lessard met, Rosenhan explained what had occurred with the purchase of the tools and the subsequent incident of the large wrench being observed in the bag (7R.T. 93; 4R.T. 78-79). Lessard radioed to Dave Pollock, another security agent on duty at Sears, and requested that he come and assist him (4R.T. 79).

When Pollock arrived, Lessard explained what he had learned from Rosenhan and asked him to watch Koepnick while he spoke with the other employees (4R.T. 79-80). Lessard went around the hardware department and spoke with each of the employees present there (4R.T. 80). Among the employees he spoke with was Mara Thomas, who informed Lessard of her contacts with Koepnick and confirmed the fact that she did not sell or help Koepnick with the large wrench he had in his bag (4R.T. 80-81; 8R.T. 41).

After Lessard had spoken with all of the employees in the hardware department and confirmed that none of them sold the wrench in question, he observed Koepnick in the socket aisle (4R.T. 82). Koepnick picked out some sockets and then put the bag he was carrying down at the cash register (4R.T. 82). Koepnick went back to the socket aisle and picked up another socket (4R.T. 82). While Koepnick was away from the cash register area, Lessard instructed Pollock to go by the shopping bag and confirm that the large wrench in question was still in it (4R.T. 82). When Pollock went over to the bag, he observed that the bag was pulled open and the wrench was inside (7R.T. 41). No receipts were seen in or on the bag by Pollock (7R.T.

41, 84). Pollock reported back to Lessard and told him what he saw (7R.T. 41).

Lessard and Pollock observed as Koepnick returned to the cash register and purchased some sockets (7R.T. 42; 4R.T. 82-83). As Koepnick began to leave the store, Lessard went to the clerk at the cash register and asked what items had been purchased, verifying that Koepnick had not paid for the crescent wrench in question at that time (7R.T. 83-84). Lessard and Pollock followed Koepnick out of the store (4R.T. 84). At no time did either observe Koepnick take any receipts off the shopping bag he was carrying (4R.T. 84). As they followed Koepnick out of the store, they discussed the information they had and decided to stop Koepnick with respect to the large wrench in question (4R.T. 84).

Koepnick estimated that it was approximately 6:15 P.M. when he exited the east door of the store (5R.T. 72). Lessard approached Koepnick as he walked into the parking lot area approximately 20 to 25 feet from the door of the store (4R.T. 87). Koepnick refused to stop when Lessard first spoke to him (5R.T. 178; 4R.T. 87-88). Koepnick testified that Lessard then came around in front of him, pulled the wrench in question out of the bag and told him that he did not have a receipt for it (4R.T. 178). Koepnick was also told he was under arrest for shoplifting (4R.T. 178). Both Koepnick and Lessard testified that Koepnick was shown identification by Lessard, although Koepnick testified that he did not see it clearly (4R.T. 179-80; 4R.T. 87-88). Koepnick did not show a receipt for the wrench when Lessard stopped him (4R.T. 91; 5R.T. 63).

Koepnick initially refused to return to the store with Lessard and Pollock (4R.T. 179). Koepnick was informed that he had to return to the store with them (4R.T. 180). After some further discussion, Koepnick was escorted up to the security office in the Sears store (4R.T. 179-81; 5R.T. 70-72). He was not handcuffed or physically injured in any way by the Sears employees (5R.T. 70, 72). Once in the security office, Koepnick was instructed to sit down to wait for the police to arrive (4R.T. 183).

In the security office, Lessard examined the shopping bag Koepnick had been carrying and found receipts for the purchase of the sockets (4R.T. 94; 5R.T. 72-73). No other receipts were found in or on the bag (4R.T. 95). Although Koepnick had the receipts for his other purchases in his front shirt pocket, he never attempted to show them to the Sears employees (5R.T. 63, 66). While waiting for the police to arrive, Koepnick asked if he could get a drink of water or go down to his truck, but those requests were refused (4R.T. 183).

While Pollock watched Koepnick, Lessard continued his investigation and began to prepare his report of the incident (4R.T. 97-98). Lessard telephoned the hardware department and spoke to Kim Miller, the hardware department manager. Lessard called the hardware department as he needed the stock number for the wrench in question (8R.T. 72). He also wanted to have the audit tape on the cash register checked as there were no receipts in the shopping bag for the tool sets that Rosenhan had told him he had rung up for Koepnick (8R.T. 72).

Officer Michael Campbell of the Mesa Police Department arrived at 6:30 P.M., approximately 15 minutes after Koepnick had been brought to the security office (6R.T. 67; 4R.T. 186). Campbell and Lessard stepped across the hall to permit Lessard to inform the officer as to what he had observed (4R.T. 186; 4R.T. 101-02). As Lessard was talking with Officer Campbell, Koepnick attempted to walk out of the security office (4R.T. 187; 4R.T. 58). Officer Campbell came out into the hallway and met Koepnick at the door to the security office (4R.T. 187; 4R.T. 59). Koepnick and Officer Campbell became involved in an altercation, resulting in Koepnick striking his head against the back wall of the security office (4R.T. 187-88; 4R.T. 60-64). After that occurred, Officer Campbell was able to handcuff Koepnick (6R.T. 96-98).

Officer Campbell had made the decision to arrest Koepnick when the altercation started (6R.T. 93). While he was being handcuffed by Officer Campbell, Koepnick took the receipts that had been in his shirt pocket and stuffed them inside his shirt (4R.T. 189; 6R.T. 96-97). Once Koepnick was handcuffed, Officer Campbell removed the receipts he had observed Koepnick stuffing inside his shirt (4R.T. 66; 6R.T. 100). The receipts that were found on Koepnick were examined and matched to the various tools Koepnick had in his shopping bag (4R.T. 191; 4R.T. 68).

During the altercation, Officer Campbell had instructed Pollock to use his radio to call for assistance (6T. 981). Sergeant Reynolds and Officer Gates came to the Sears security office in response to the request (6R.T. 108).

Lessard learned after the altercation that another sales clerk, Jeff Ward, had also been working in the hardware department that day (4R.T. 103-04). Ward, however, had left the sales floor before Rosenhan observed Koepnick with the wrench in the shopping bag and called Lessard down to investigate the situation (8R.T. 9-10). When Ward later returned to the hardware department, Miller informed him of the call from Lessard and that security had some questions about whether a customer paid for a certain wrench (8R.T. 110). Ward told Miller that he had rung up such a wrench for a customer (8R.T. 11). Miller took Ward up to the security office (8R.T. 11). They arrived about the time the altercation occurred between Koepnick and Officer Campbell (4R.T. 103; 8R.T. 12).

Once Lessard became aware of Ward's contact with Koepnick, he interviewed Ward (4R.T. 104). Ward stated that he had first observed Koepnick as Koepnick walked up to the cash register and pulled the receipt off a shopping bag that was lying on the counter (4R.T. 104; 8R.T. 6). Ward asked him if that was his package and Koepnick said it was (4R.T. 104; 8R.T. 6). Koepnick had a large combination wrench and a smaller set of wrenches with him to purchase (4T. 104; 8T. 6). Ward rang these items up, and Koepnick paid for them (4R.T. 104). Ward then bagged these wrenches in a smaller brown bag, which Koepnick placed inside the larger shopping bag he already had (4R.T. 104; 8R.T. 104; 8R.T. 8). Koepnick then placed the receipts Ward had prepared for the wrenches in his shirt pocket and left (8R.T. 8).

Ward did not see Koepnick again on the sales floor that night (8R.T. 9). After Ward finished ringing up the other customers at the cash register, he left the sales floor (8R.T. 9, 24). Ward told Lessard he had been on a break (4R.T. 72). Ward could not recall at trial exactly where he went when he left the sales floor (8R.T. 9).

After questioning Ward, Lessard discussed with the police officers the possibility that Koepnick had taken the wrench he purchased from Ward out to his truck and brought the shopping bag back in and put another wrench in it (4R.T. 69-70). Lessard was familiar with this method of shoplifting through his work as a security agent (4R.T. 105). The information Lessard had that caused him to believe that this was a possibility was (1) Ward's statement that he had bagged the large wrench in a separate brown bag that was not present in the large shopping bag Koepnick had when he was stopped, (2) Rosenhan's statement that there was a period of 15 minutes from the time he last saw Koepnick after his first purchase until he saw him again in the hardware department with the wrench, and (3) Koepnick's actions in not exhibiting the receipts for his purchases when he was detained (4R.T. 105-06, 111).

The police officers made the decision to search Koepnick's truck (6R.T. 101-02; 6R.T. 128). Officer Campbell testified that he asked Koepnick for permission to search the truck and Koepnick consented (6R.T. 130). Koepnick testified that he consented to the search only on the condition that he be allowed to go with them (4R.T. 194). Lessard accompanied Officer Gates down to Koepnick's truck (4R.T. 107). Officer Gates opened the vehicle and Lessard assisted him in looking in the truck (4R.T. 107). No Sears merchandise was found (4R.T. 107). The search of the truck lasted about two minutes (4R.T. 72-73). Nothing was taken or damaged in the search (4R.T. 110-11, 197).

Once Officer Gates and Lessard returned to the security office, the police officers discussed what action they would take (4R.T. 197-98). Sergeant Reynolds made the decision to cite Koepnick for disorderly conduct for his actions in striking Officer Campbell (6R.T. 130). After Koepnick received the citation, he was released by the Mesa Police Department (4R.T. 198).

ISSUES PRESENTED

1. Did the trial court err in denying Sears' motion for judgment notwithstanding the verdict on the claim for false arrest when the evidence is insufficient to support a finding by the jury that plaintiff was detained by Sears in an unreasonable manner or for an unreasonable length of time?

2. Did the trial court err in denying Sears' motion for judgment notwithstanding the verdict on the punitive damage claims where the evidence fails to establish a *prima facie* case for such damages?

ARGUMENT

I. SEARS' MOTION FOR JUDGMENT NOTWITHSTANDING THE VERDICT ON THE CLAIM FOR FALSE ARREST SHOULD HAVE BEEN GRANTED BY THE TRIAL COURT.

A. *Applicable Standard of Review.*

The standard of review for determining the appropriateness of the granting of a judgment N.O.V. is whether the evidence is sufficient that reasonable men could discern facts to support the verdict. *Rancho Pescado, Inc. v. Northwestern Mutual Life Insurance Co.*, 140 Ariz. 174, 680 P.2d 1235 (App. 1984). In reviewing a judgment N.O.V., the appellate court views the evidence most favorably to sustaining the verdict. *Lerner v. Brettschneider,* 123 Ariz. 152, 598 P.2d 515 (App. 1979). When the evidence is insufficient to meet the burden of proof to establish the claim, entry of judgment N.O.V. is proper. *Rancho Pescado, Inc. v. Northwestern Mutual Life Insurance Co.,* 140 Ariz. at 186, 680 P.2d at 1247; *Lerner v. Brettschneider,* 123 Ariz. at 155, 598 P.2d at 518.

B. There Was Insufficient Evidence to Justify Any Finding of Liability on the Claim of False Arrest.

A.R.S. §13-1805C sets forth the statutory shopkeeper's privilege for detaining a suspected shoplifter. A detention is deemed privileged under this statute if it is made with reasonable cause for a proper purpose and done in a reasonable manner and for reasonable time. *Gortarez v. Smitty's Super Valu, Inc.*, 140 Ariz. 97, 680 P.2d 807 (1984). The undisputed evidence established the existence of all the elements necessary for this privilege. Therefore, Sears' motion for judgment notwithstanding the verdict on plaintiff's claim of false arrest should have been granted by the trial court.

1. Reasonable Cause.

The existence of reasonable cause and the reasonableness of the detention, both as to time and manner, are for the court to decide as a matter of law where there is no conflict in the evidence. *Id.* at 104. The trial court determined as a matter of law that reasonable cause did exist for plaintiff's detention in granting of the motion for new trial. The propriety of that decision is discussed in Section I.E of Sears' response brief, which is incorporated herein by reference to avoid duplication.

The remaining elements of A.R.S. §13-1805C that must be established for the privilege to exist are (1) a proper purpose for the detention, (2) the reasonableness of the time of the detention, and (3) the reasonableness of the manner of the detention. *Id. Gortarez,* 140 Ariz. at 104.

2. Proper Purpose.

A.R.S. §13-1805C sets forth two purposes for which a privileged detention may be made under the statute. They are (1) questioning the subject, or (2) summoning a law enforcement officer. Given Koepnick's testimony at trial, which must be accepted for the purposes of deciding a motion for judgment N.O.V., there is plainly a dispute in the evidence as to what questioning, if any, occurred during Sears' detention of him. Koepnick's testimony was that he was not questioned at all (4R.T. 184-85). There is, however, no question about the existence of the alternative purpose authorized by the statute for Koepnick's detention—summoning a law enforcement officer. It is undisputed that the Mesa Police Department was contacted by Sears and requested to respond to where plaintiff was being detained (Opening brief, p. 8). Thus, this element of the privilege is unquestionably present in this case.

3. The Length of Detention.

The reasonableness of the length of Koepnick's detention is also undisputedly established by the evidence. There is no evidence in the record that creates any issue of fact as to the reasonableness of the length of Sears' detention of Koepnick. The undisputed evidence is that plaintiff was taken to the Sears security office and the police called without any undue delay on the part of Sears. No evidence of anything to the contrary is present in the record. Upon Officer Campbell's arrival, Lessard immediately began to explain the situation to him. Even before he could even finish, the altercation between Koepnick and Officer Campbell occurred. At that time, Koepnick was placed under arrest by Officer Campbell independently of any shoplifting and taken into the custody of the Mesa Police. From that point on plaintiff was no longer in Sears' custody.

These facts are undisputed. There is nothing in the evidence which would permit the jury to conclude that the length of Koepnick's detention by Sears for the express statutory purpose of summoning a law enforcement officer was unreasonable. Indeed, there was no way Sears could make Koepnick's detention for that purpose any shorter. The length of that detention was determined by the amount of time it took the Mesa Police to respond to the Sears store. This is something that Sears had no control over; in any event, there is no evidence to permit a jury to find that the actual amount of time it took the officer to respond was in any way unreasonable. Accordingly, the trial court should have determined that the length of Koepnick's detention by Sears was reasonable as a matter of law.

4. The Manner of Detention.

Neither is there any evidence in the record that creates any issue of fact as to the reasonableness of the manner of Koepnick's detention by Sears. The evidence is again undisputed that Koepnick was stopped by Lessard, escorted up to the Sears security office and detained there until the police arrived. The Arizona Supreme Court in *Gortarez* stated that reasonable force may be used to detain a suspected shoplifter. 140 Ariz. at 104, 680 P.2d at 814. There is no evidence that any unreasonable force was ever used on plaintiff by Sears employees. Sears employees never struck or fought with Koepnick (5R.T. 70-72). They did not even handcuff or search him (4R.T. 96; 5R.T. 70). Koepnick confirmed in his testimony that he was not physically injured in any manner by Sears employees (5R.T. 72). In short, there is absolutely no evidence to indicate that the manner of plaintiff's detention by Sears was unreasonable.

As indicated above, the reasonableness of the detention, both as to time and manner, is one for the court to decide as a matter of law where there is no conflict of the evidence. *Id.* As there was no conflicting evidence presented at trial as to these elements that would support a finding that the manner and length of Sears' detention of Koepnick was unreasonable, the trial court should have determined that the detention was reasonable as a matter of law and not submitted any issue of this claim to the jury. Accordingly, Sears' motion for judgment notwithstanding the verdict on the claim of false arrest should have been granted by the trial court.

414 ‖ Part IV. Advocacy

II. SEARS' MOTION FOR JUDGMENT NOTWITHSTANDING THE VERDICT ON THE CLAIMS OF PUNITIVE DAMAGES SHOULD HAVE BEEN GRANTED BY THE TRIAL COURT.

A. The Applicable Standard.

The Arizona Supreme Court has recently modified the standard for determining whether there has been a *prima facie* showing permitting the assessment of punitive damages. The decisions discussing and applying this new standard include *Filasky v. Preferred Risk Mutual Insurance Co.*, No. CV-86-0237-T (filed March 2, 1987); *Gurule v. Illinois Mutual Life and Casualty Co.*, No. CV-86-0488-PR (filed March 2, 1987); *Rawlings v. Apodaca*, 151 Ariz. 149, 726 P.2d 565 (1986); and *Linthicum v. National Life Insurance Co.*, 150 Ariz. 326, 723 P.2d 675 (1986). The portion of the *Linthicum* decision setting forth the new standard is quoted at length in Section IV.B of Appellee's response brief, which is incorporated herein by reference to avoid duplication.

Although the trial court denied Sears' motion for judgment N.O.V. with respect to punitive damages before the Supreme Court announced the more stringent standard in *Linthicum v. National Life Insurance Co.*, that standard applies to cases upon appellate review. *See, e.g., Hawkins v. Allstate Insurance Co.*, No. CV-86-0010-PR (filed February 26, 1987) (applying standard announced in *Linthicum* to trial court's pre-*Linthicum* ruling on motion for judgment notwithstanding the verdict).

Under the new standard, plaintiffs are not automatically entitled to an instruction on punitive damages upon the showing of a *prima facie* intentional tort. To recover punitive damages, something more is required over and above the "mere commission of a tort." *Rawlings v. Apodaca*, 151 Ariz. at 162, 726 P.2d at 587. There must be a showing of either an intent to injure the plaintiff or a conscious pursuit of a course of conduct knowing that it creates a substantial risk of significant harm to others. *Linthicum v. Nationwide Life Insurance Co.*, 150 Ariz. at 330, 723 P.2d at 679. The requirement of this "something more" or "evil mind" is to assure that punitive damages are awarded only where the purposes of deterrence are furthered. *Gurule v. Illinois Mutual Life and Casualty Co.*, slip op. at 3. The punishment resulting from punitive damage is appropriate only where there is "some element of outrage similar to that usually found in crime." *Rawlings v. Apodaca*, 151 Ariz. at 161, 726 P.2d at 578, *quoting* Restatement (Second) of Torts, §908, comment b (1979).

B. The Evidence Fails to Show a Prima Facie *Case for Punitive Damages with Respect to the Claim of False Arrest.*

As discussed in Section I.B of this cross-appeal brief, the evidence in the record is insufficient to make out a *prima facie* case of false arrest, let alone rise to the level necessary to permit the assessment of punitive damages. There is absolutely no evidence that suggests that Sears intended to injure Koepnick or that it consciously pursued a course of conduct knowing that it created a substantial risk of tremendous harm to him. As the trial court determined, the facts are uncontradicted that Lessard actually and reasonably believed that when Koepnick left the store he had merchandise for which he had not paid. Acting on that reasonable belief, Lessard stopped Koepnick, had him return to the Sears security office and detained him there until the police arrived. As discussed above, Koepnick was not physically injured by Sears in any manner. Sears' detention of Koepnick ended when Koepnick was arrested by Officer Campbell at the time of the altercation in the security office. While Koepnick was injured in that altercation, there is nothing in the record that would permit a jury to find that the Sears employees could even foresee, let alone intend, that Koepnick would become involved in a fight with the police and be injured. In the absence of evidence that Sears acted with an "evil mind" as required under the new standard, Sears is entitled to judgment notwithstanding the verdict on the issue of punitive damages on the false arrest claim.

C. The Evidence Fails to Establish a Prima Facie Case for Punitive Damages with Respect to the Claim of Trespass to Chattel.

Steve Lessard's conduct with respect to the claim of trespass consists of accompanying a police officer out to plaintiff's truck in the parking lot and assisting him in searching the vehicle. No inference of "evil mind" can be reasonably drawn from these actions. The evidence fails to suggest any risk of significant harm or an intent to injure. The *police officers* made the decision to search the truck. Lessard's conduct in assisting the police officers in their investigation only evidences his intent to aid the police officers in their investigation. No other *reasonable* inference is to be drawn from such conduct.

How are the purposes of punishment and deterrence served by an award of punitive damages in this case? The evidence, even when viewed in a light most favorable to Koepnick, indicates that the Sears employees simply stopped someone whom they had reasonable cause to believe had shoplifted, detained him without injury until the police arrived and arrested him, and then accompanied the police in the search of his vehicle. As the record is devoid of any evidence that the Sears employees acted with an "evil mind," the issue of punitive damages on both the false arrest and trespass claim should never have been submitted to the jury. Sears is entitled to judgment notwithstanding the verdicts on the claims for punitive damages.

CONCLUSION

The trial court was correct in finding that reasonable cause existed as matter of law for Sears' detention of Koepnick. The court erred, however, in ruling that there was sufficient evidence to submit to the jury the issues of the reasonableness of the time and manner of the detention. Accordingly, the trial court's order of July 23, 1986 should be reversed to the extent that it provides for a new trial on these issues. The trial court should be instructed to enter judgment notwithstanding the verdict in favor of Sears on the false arrest claim.

The evidence was also insufficient to submit the issue of punitive damages to the jury on either the claims of false arrest or trespass to chattel. Accordingly, Sears is entitled to judgment notwithstanding the verdict on the issue of punitive damages as well.

Respectfully submitted this 13th day of April, 1987.

GUST, ROSENFELD, DIVELBESS & HENDERSON

By _____
    Fred Cole
    Roger W. Perry
    Attorneys for Defendant-Appellee/Cross-Appellant

Thomas J. Quarelli, Esq.
1832 E. Thomas
Phoenix, Arizona 85016

William J. Monahan, P.C.
340 E. Palm Lane, Suite 130
Phoenix, Arizona 85004

Paul G. Ulrich, P.C.
3030 N. Central, Suite 310
Phoenix, Arizona 85012

Attorneys for Plaintiff-Appellant/Cross-Appellee

IN THE COURT OF APPEALS
STATE OF ARIZONA
DIVISION ONE

MAX KOEPNICK, 　　　　Plaintiff-Appellant, 　　　　Cross-Appellee, 　v. SEARS ROEBUCK & COMPANY, 　　　　Defendant-Appellee, 　　　　Cross-Appellant.	No. CA-CIV 9147 MARICOPA County Superior Court No. C-502081

APPELLANT'S CROSS-APPEAL ANSWERING BRIEF

TABLE OF CONTENTS

418

TABLE OF AUTHORITIES

APPELLANT'S CROSS-APPEAL ANSWERING BRIEF

STATEMENT OF THE CASE

On December 5, 1983, Plaintiff/cross-appellee Max Koepnick sued Defendant/cross-appellant Sears, Roebuck & Co. ("Sears") and the City of Mesa ("Mesa") for false arrest, assault, trespass to chattel (by further detaining him while searching his truck), invasion of his right of privacy and malicious prosecution. These claims all arose out of Koepnick's arrest for alleged shoplifting on December 6, 1982 (Appendix A, C.T. 1). The counts in Koepnick's complaint alleging invasion of privacy against both defendants and malicious prosecution, false arrest and punitive damages against Mesa were all disposed of by directed verdicts (Appendix B, C.T. 97). Those issues are not involved in this appeal.

The remaining portions of Koepnick's complaint were tried to a jury on January 13-22, 1986. The jury awarded Koepnick $25,000 in compensatory damages and $500,000 in punitive damages against Sears for false arrest. It awarded him $100 in compensatory damages against both Sears and Mesa and $25,000 in punitive damages against Sears for trespass to Koepnick's personal property. The jury also awarded Koepnick $50,000 in compensatory damages against Mesa for assault (9R.T. 101-03). Judgment was entered against both defendants pursuant to those jury verdicts on February 25, 1986 (Appendix B, C.T. 97).

On March 11, 1986, Sears filed motions for judgment notwithstanding the verdicts and for new trial (C.T. No. 100). Mesa also filed a motion for a new trial on March 11, 1986 (C.T. 101). Mesa then also moved for judgment notwithstanding the verdict and, in the alternative, for new trial and for remittitur on March 12, 1986 (C.T. 104). Sears thereafter filed an amended motion for judgment notwithstanding the verdicts and for new trial on April 16, 1986 (C.T. 113). Koepnick filed responses to Mesa's and Sears' motions on March 20 and 25, 1986, respectively (C.T. 107, 108, 109). Both Sears and Mesa filed reply memoranda in support of their respective motions on April 16, 1986 (C.T. 114, 115).

On May 14, 1986, the trial court entered the following minute orders: (1) granting Sears' motion for new trial on Koepnick's false arrest claim; (2) granting Sears' and Mesa's motions for judgment N.O.V. with respect to Koepnick's claim of trespass to personal property; and (3) denying Mesa's motion for new trial or for judgment N.O.V. with respect to Koepnick's assault claim. On June 27, 1986, the trial court clarified its May 14, 1986 minute order by denying Sears' motion for judgment N.O.V. on Koepnick's false arrest claim to the extent it granted Sears' motion for a new trial concerning that issue. Having granted a new trial on Koepnick's false arrest claim, the trial court also vacated his judgment against Sears for punitive damages. A formal written order incorporating all those rulings and directing that it be entered as a final judgment was filed on July 23, 1986 (C.T. 124).

On July 24, 1986, Koepnick filed a notice of appeal only from the portions of the trial court's order granting Sears' motion for new trial on his false arrest claim and for judgment N.O.V. on his claim of trespass to chattel (C.T. 124). The portion of the litigation involving Mesa has been settled. Mesa is therefore not a party to this appeal and has not filed a cross-

420

appeal. Sears filed a notice of cross-appeal with respect to other portions of the judgment on August 5, 1986 (C.T. 128). The parties have stipulated that the cost bonds for their respective appeals are waived. This Court has jurisdiction concerning this appeal pursuant to A.R.S. §12-2101(F)(1).

STATEMENT OF FACTS

I. KOEPNICK AND HIS PURCHASES.

A. Max Koepnick was a manager, foreman, and mechanic for a large Queen Creek farming operation whose assets exceed $2,500,000 (4R.T. 145, 6R.T. 21). His lawsuit resulted from his detention and arrest for shoplifting while he was purchasing tools for the farm at the Sears store in Fiesta Mall, Mesa, Arizona, on December 6, 1982 (4R.T. 145-47). Koepnick paid cash for those tools and had the receipts for all of them in his possession when he was arrested, including the receipt for a $1\frac{5}{16}''$ open-end crescent wrench. That wrench was the precipitating cause of his arrest.

Koepnick drove to Sears in the farm pickup truck he used for business purposes (4R.T. 145-46). He entered the store at approximately 5:00 P.M. (4R.T. 145, 5T 68). Business in the Sears store happened to be slow at that particular time (3R.T. 13). Koepnick proceeded to the hardware department. He first purchased a five-wrench set, a nut-driver, an open-end wrench set, a plier set, and a set of screwdrivers (Ex. 11). Bruce Rosenhan, Sears hardware department manager, rang up those purchases on a cash register and stapled portions of the Sears seven-part handwritten receipt used at customers' requests for cash purchases to the outside of the bag (4R.T. 149, 173). Sears' policy was to staple the register receipt and the original of the seven-part receipt to the outside of the bag (3R.T. 22, 4R.T. 45). The customer's purchases were also recorded automatically on the cash register tape (3R.T. 18-19). The other six copies of the handwritten receipt may have been placed in a trash can on one of the shelves below the cash register (3R.T. 21).

Koepnick then left his purchases at the cash register counter to look for a wrench (4R.T. 151). During this time he flirted with a sales person, Mara Thomas, who showed him various tools. Ms. Thomas then escorted him to the register where he purchased a $1\frac{5}{16}''$ open-end crescent wrench. Sales clerk Jeff Ward made this sale. At that time, Ward prepared another handwritten seven-part form, since this sale was also for cash (8R.T. 8-9, Ex. 12). As had occurred with Koepnick's first purchases, the crescent wrench was bagged and stapled together with the receipt. This bag was placed inside the first, with the wrench handle sticking out (4R.T. 173). At trial, Koepnick denied the wrench was ever put into a separate brown bag (4R.T. 173, 174). He also testified all the receipts were stapled onto the original bag (4R.T. 17). Jeff Ward then left the hardware department to take a break (3R.T. 12, 8R.T. 9).

Koepnick picked up the bag from the register counter and started to leave. However, he then remembered he needed some spark plug sockets (4R.T. 174). He therefore went back to the register, set the bag down and proceeded to look for the sockets (4R.T. 175).

During this time, manager Rosenhan contacted Sears security guards Steve Lessard and Dave Pollack, who began observing Koepnick. Lessard spoke with all four hardware department employees then on the floor about whether there was a receipt for the open-end crescent wrench (3R.T. 9). None could remember ringing it up. However, Lessard failed to ask those employees if anyone else was then on a break (*id.*). He simply assumed those four employees were the only ones on duty (3R.T. 10-11). Moreover, no one checked either the register tape or the receipts tray behind the counter (3R.T. 34). Doing so would have confirmed that Koepnick had in fact paid for the crescent wrench, since the cash register tape could have been checked against the wrench's stock number (3R.T. 19-20). Lessard also admitted at trial that he also could have searched for the six discarded copies of Koepnick's three sets of receipts that were probably in the trash container below the cash register (3R.T. 21-22).

Meanwhile, Lessard had Pollack walk past the bag on the counter to confirm visually that the wrench in the bag was a Sears product (3R.T. 28). Pollack could see a price tag sticker on the end of the wrench. However, although the stapled receipts on the bag were also in plain view, they were not checked against the merchandise (4R.T. 175). Lessard himself admitted that Pollack had an "easy view" of the receipts (3R.T. 29-30).

Lessard himself also saw the bag on the counter. However, he did not notice the handwritten receipts and cash register tape stapled to the top of the bag (3R.T. 27). He also testified at trial he could not dispute testimony that the register receipts and handwritten receipts were stapled to the top of the bag (*id.*). He "didn't recall" whether anyone bothered to look for those receipts on the bag before Koepnick was stopped, although he conceded that it would have been a "fairly reasonable thing to do" (3R.T. 30).

While this "investigation" was occurring, Koepnick located and purchased the sockets, returned to the register counter, picked up his bag from the counter, tore off all the receipts, placed them in his shirt pocket and left the store. Lessard and Pollack followed him (4R.T. 177). Lessard estimated that he had between 20 and 25 minutes to make his investigation before he stopped Koepnick outside the store (3R.T. 14). He even had time to discuss with Pollack that they had "done a thorough investigation" (3R.T. 34).

II. KOEPNICK'S DETENTION, ARREST, ASSAULT, AND EVENTUAL RELEASE.

Koepnick placed the time and location of his stop and arrest by Lessard and Pollack at 6:15 P.M., in a dark, dimly lighted area of the Sears parking lot (5R.T. 72). Koepnick's version of the facts was that in that dimly lighted area two punks accosted him, yelled "Hey," and positioned themselves on each side of him (4R.T. 178). They then jerked the wrench out of the bag stating, "You don't have a receipt, do you?" (4R.T. 180-81).

Koepnick thought he was being hustled. He asked who his captors were. Their response was, "We're security guards." (4R.T. 179). Koepnick asked them to "prove it." In response, one of the guards flashed his badge (*id.*). However, Koepnick could not see it clearly (4R.T. 179-80). Koepnick was then told that he was going with the guards and that he was under arrest for shoplifting (4R.T. 180).

Koepnick was escorted to an upstairs security room, denied a drink of water, and seated, with no inquiry as to whether he had a receipt for the wrench (4R.T. 180). The Mesa police were called. When Koepnick attempted to enter the hallway to obtain a drink of water, he and Officer Campbell (who was wearing a bulletproof vest) got into a pushing match. As a result, Koepnick fell or was thrown head first through the wall of the security room, causing him to incur neck and other injuries (4R.T. 60-64).

Koepnick was then handcuffed. While he was recovering from the blow to his head, the Mesa police and the Sears security staff verified every item he had purchased against every receipt on the table of the security room (4R.T. 68). Lessard had also verified with Jeff Ward that Koepnick had in fact purchased the crescent wrench. The bag which supposedly contained the wrench had already been accounted for in the security office. However, despite all of Koepnick's purchases being fully accounted for, the Mesa police continued to detain him at Sears' insistence while Lessard conducted a non-consensual, unescorted search of his truck, looking for an alleged "brown bag" (4R.T. 71). Koepnick had approximately $1,200-1,400 in cash and all of his business records in the truck (4R.T. 197). The search, which required approximately 15 to 20 minutes, proved fruitless (4R.T. 197-98). During this time, Koepnick remained under detention. Had Lessard not decided to search Koepnick's truck, Koepnick would simply have been cited immediately for disorderly conduct and then released (6R.T. 115). Instead, after the search, Koepnick was then freed of his handcuffs and cited for disorderly conduct (4R.T. 198). He was finally permitted to leave the Sears security room at about 7:00 P.M. (4R.T. 199).

ISSUES PRESENTED

1. Did the trial court properly deny Sears' motion for judgment notwithstanding the verdict on Koepnick's false arrest claim where the evidence, viewed most favorably to him, was disputed as to each element of the statutory shopkeeper's privilege, A.R.S. §13-1805(C)?

2. Did the trial court properly deny Sears' motion for judgment notwithstanding the verdict on Koepnick's false arrest punitive damage claim where the evidence presented reasonably established a *prima facie* case for such damages?

3. Was the evidence supporting punitive damages as to Koepnick's trespass to chattel claim sufficient to submit that issue to the jury as well?

ARGUMENT

I. THE TRIAL COURT PROPERLY DENIED SEARS' MOTION FOR JUDGMENT NOTWITHSTANDING THE VERDICT WITH RESPECT TO KOEPNICK'S FALSE ARREST CLAIM.

A. Applicable Standards of Review.

In reviewing the trial court's denial of a motion for judgment notwithstanding the verdict, the appellate court will review the evidence to determine whether it was of sufficient character that reasonable minds could differ as to inferences to be drawn from the facts. *Adroit Supply Co. v. Electric Mutual Liability Insurance Co.*, 112 Ariz. 385, 542 P.2d 810 (1975); *Marcal Limited Partnership v. Title Insurance Co. of Minnesota*, 150 Ariz. 191, 722 P.2d 359 (App. 1986). In doing so, this Court will view the evidence in the light most favorable to sustaining the verdict. It then must review the evidence to determine whether the evidence would permit a reasonable person to reach the challenged verdict. *Maxwell v. Aetna Life Insurance Co.*, 143 Ariz. 205, 693 P.2d 348 (App. 1984).

When the sufficiency of evidence to sustain the jury's verdicts is questioned on appeal, every conflict in the evidence and every reasonable inference therefrom will be resolved in favor of sustaining the verdict and judgment. *See McNelis v. Bruce*, 90 Ariz. 261, 367 P.2d 615 (1962). On appeal, a reviewing court must take the evidence in the light most favorable to upholding the jury's verdict. *Miller v. Schaffer*, 102 Ariz. 457, 432 P.2d 585 (1967). Applying these standards to the evidence in this record, Koepnick submits the trial court properly denied Sears' motion for directed verdict with respect to his false arrest claim.

B. Requirements to Sustain the Statutory Shopkeeper's Privilege.

A.R.S. §13-1805(C) provides that a merchant "with reasonable cause may detain on the premises in a reasonable manner and for a reasonable time any person suspected of shoplifting . . . for questioning or summoning a law enforcement officer." The statute thus states four elements, all of which must be established to sustain the shopkeeper's privilege: (1) reasonable cause for detention; (2) reasonable manner for detention; (3) reasonable time; and (4) proper purpose (for questioning or summoning a law enforcement officer). Koepnick submits that a directed verdict in Sears' favor with respect to his false arrest claim would not be justified unless the evidence satisfied the applicable standard of review previously stated with respect to all four elements required to establish the statutory privilege. Viewing the evidence most favorably to Koepnick, this record simply does not permit that conclusion.

Each of the elements of Sears' defense also required Sears to prove the affirmative of the issue. *E.g., Black, Robertshaw, Frederick, Copple & Wright, P.C. v. United States*, 130 Ariz. 110, 634 P.2d 298 (App. 1981); *Yeazell v. Copins*, 98 Ariz. 109, 402 P.2d 541 (App. 1965). Unless Sears could persuade a jury by a preponderance of the evidence and reasonable inferences therefrom that each statutory element had been satisfied, Sears thus could not prevail.

1. Reasonable Cause.

Given the facts and reasonable inferences therefrom most favorable to Koepnick, he was clearly entitled to have the reasonable cause issue submitted to the jury. In the first place, Lessard testified he had 20 to 25 minutes to make an investigation before Koepnick left the Sears store and stated that he had made a thorough investigation. He therefore did not have to make a "snap" decision based on incomplete evidence to detain someone who might be hurriedly leaving. Koepnick testified that all of the handwritten receipts for the tools he bought were stapled to the outside of his shopping bag in plain view. However, neither Lessard nor Pollack ever attempted to read them to determine whether the open-end crescent wrench was listed. Lessard was also unable to dispute Koepnick's testimony in this regard, and admitted that looking at the receipts would have been a reasonable thing to do.

Lessard also failed to make the basic inquiry whether there were other hardware department employees then on duty other than the four he interviewed. The possibility that another employee might have been on a break was certainly a reasonable one to be explored. The security guards also never looked for the extra copies of the seven-part receipt, although they might well have been found either in the receipts tray behind the counter or in a trash container on one of the shelves below the cash register. No one ever checked the register tape which would have shown the stock number for the open-end wrench Koepnick had paid for. Given all these deficiencies in the security guards' investigation, there was certainly a reasonable basis for disputing Sears' position that it had reasonable cause to detain Koepnick. Moreover, pursuant to A.R.S. §13-1805(d), "reasonable cause" is a defense to a false arrest claim. Sears therefore had the burden of proving the affirmative of this issue. *E.g., Black, Robertshaw, Frederick, Copple & Wright, P.C. v. United States,* 130 Ariz. 110, 634 P.2d 298 (App. 1981); *Yeazell v. Copins,* 98 Ariz. 109, 402 P.2d 541 (1965). Unless it could persuade a jury by a preponderance of the evidence and reasonable inferences therefrom that the nature and extent of its investigation was appropriate under the circumstances, Sears could not prevail. Given all the deficiencies in the security guards' investigation and in view of the relatively lengthy time available for them to pursue the simple additional inquiries that could have been made, the trial court could not properly remove the "reasonable cause" issue from the jury in Sears' favor.

2. Proper Purpose.

Sears' Cross-Appeal Opening Brief at p. 3 concedes there was a factual dispute concerning what questioning, if any, occurred during Sears' detention of Koepnick. The statutory purpose of "questioning the subject" was thus admittedly not satisfied for purposes of obtaining a directed verdict.

The other possible proper purpose permitted by A.R.S. §13-1805(C) for privileged detention is "summoning a law enforcement officer." Koepnick acknowledges that Sears did contact the Mesa Police Department, but only after he was detained by Sears employees. He was not necessarily detained for that purpose. Moreover, after Officer Campbell's investigation, the officer testified he would simply have cited Koepnick immediately for disorderly conduct and then let him go (6R.T. 115). Instead, Lessard, Sears employee, insisted that Sears search Koepnick's truck even after all the receipts for his purchases had been accounted for (6R.T. 101, 102). Koepnick remained in detention for at least 15 to 20 minutes more while Lessard and Officer Gates searched his truck (4R.T. 197). His handcuffs were not removed until this search had been completed (4R.T. 197). Koepnick submits that this continuation of his detention was improper because it was motivated by Lessard's desire to search his truck, not for any legitimate reasons connected with the police officers' investigation. There was therefore an issue presented as to whether a proper purpose existed throughout the entire period of time in which Koepnick was detained.

3. Length of Detention.

Koepnick contends that the length of his detention was reasonable only until the Sears employees and Mesa police officers had completed their investigation. Once that occurred, Koepnick should have been released immediately. Instead, he was then detained for an additional 15 to 20 minutes at Lessard's request so Lessard could search his truck. Although Koepnick technically may have been in the police officers' custody during that additional period of time, the evidence clearly established that this additional period of detention would not have occurred but for Lessard's request. Under these circumstances, there is also a factual issue as to the propriety of the length of time Koepnick was detained so far as Sears is concerned.

4. Manner of Detention.

Factual disputes were also presented as to the manner in which Koepnick was detained by Sears. To begin with, he was accosted by Lessard and Pollack in an accusatory manner. Koepnick testified they stated, "You don't have a receipt, do you?" (4R.T. 180-81) rather than asking to see a receipt. Then, although Koepnick responded that he had a receipt, he was nevertheless detained for shoplifting without further questioning on that subject. Koepnick submits the manner of his initial detention was thus improper for that reason.

Koepnick was then escorted to an upstairs security room where he was denied a drink of water and seated with no inquiry as to whether he had a receipt for the wrench (4R.T. 180). When Koepnick entered the hallway to obtain a drink of water, he and Officer Campbell got into a pushing match which resulted in Koepnick falling or being thrown head first through the wall of the security room, causing him to incur neck and other injuries (4R.T. 60-64). Koepnick was then handcuffed. However, had Koepnick been offered a drink of water and had the proper inquiries been made by Sears employees initially, his injuries arguably would not have occurred.

Koepnick submits these facts all raise factual issues as to whether the manner of his detention was reasonable. Based on these facts, a jury could reasonably have found that Sears security guards did not handle his detention in a reasonable manner.

II. THE TRIAL COURT PROPERLY DENIED SEARS' MOTION FOR JUDGMENT NOTWITHSTANDING THE VERDICT AS TO KOEPNICK'S PUNITIVE DAMAGES BASED ON HIS FALSE ARREST CLAIMS.

A. *The Applicable Standards of Review.*

The recent Arizona appellate decisions modifying the standard for determining whether there has been a *prima facie* showing permitting the assessment of punitive damages do not necessarily require that all prior jury verdicts awarding such damages be reversed. For example, *Filasky v. Preferred Risk Mutual Insurance Co.*, 152 Ariz. 591, 734 P.2d 76 (1987), instead recognizes that "a jury's decision to award punitive damages should be affirmed if any reasonable evidence exists to support it." *Gurule v. Illinois Mutual Life and Casualty Insurance Co.*, 152 Ariz. 600, 734 P.2d 85 (1987), also states that the appellate court must review the facts in a light most favorable to the party obtaining a punitive damage award and affirm the jury's verdict if a reasonable juror could conclude that the defendant either intended to violate his rights or consciously pursued a course of conduct knowing that it created a substantial risk of doing so. 734 P.2d at 88.

Of the various recent decisions, both *Hawkins v. Allstate Insurance Co.*, 152 Ariz. 490, 733 P.2d 1072 (1987), and this Court's Opinion in *Carter-Glogau Laboratories, Inc. v. Construction, Production & Maintenance Labors Local 383*, (1 CA-CIV 8107, 8128 filed October 30, 1986, *review denied*, May 12, 1987), have affirmed punitive damages awards where the evidence presented met the standards stated in *Linthicum v. Nationwide Life Insurance Co.*, 150 Ariz. 326, 723 P.2d 675 (1986). *Rawlings v. Apodaca*, 151 Ariz. 149, 726 P.2d 565 (1986), also remanded for further proceedings as to punitive damages where it was uncertain whether the trial judge had applied the appropriate standards.

According to *Gurule, supra*, the "evil mind" required for punitive damages may be satisfied by "defendant's conscious and deliberate disregard of the interests and rights of others." 152 Ariz. at 602, 734 P.2d at 87. It may also be established by defendant's expressed statements or inferred from his expressions, conduct or objectives. *Id.* If a defendant conducts himself in an outrageous or egregiously improper manner, the inference is permitted that he intended to injure or consciously disregarded the substantial risk that his conduct would cause significant harm. The "evil mind" may also be inferred if a defendant "deliberately continued his actions despite the inevitable or highly probable harm that would follow." *Id.*

B. *Applying These Standards, the Evidence Demonstrated a* Prima Facie *Case for Punitive Damages with Respect to Koepnick's False Arrest Claim.*

Numerous deficiencies in Sears' investigation support a jury's finding that its employees acted with conscious and deliberate disregard of Koepnick's rights and interests. The "bottom line" of Lessard's investigation at the time Koepnick left the Sears store was that he and Pollack "felt we had done a thorough enough investigation for us to ask [Koepnick] if he had a receipt for the wrench" (3R.T. 35). Significantly, Lessard himself apparently did not then believe he had sufficient cause to detain Koepnick for shoplifting at that time without further questioning. Yet Lessard and Pollack accosted Koepnick in a hostile and threatening manner in a dark corner of the parking lot and accused him of not having a receipt, instead of asking in a more normal manner whether he had a receipt. Then, even though Koepnick told Lessard and Pollack in response to their accusations that he *did* have a receipt, he was ordered under arrest for shoplifting without further discussion or inquiry (4R.T. 178-81). These facts clearly could support a reasonable conclusion that Sears employees had the required "evil mind" in making their initial decision to detain Koepnick without adequate investigation or proper inquiry concerning whether he in fact had the receipts they should be seeking.

Further evidence supporting a *prima facie* case for punitive damages existed with reference to Sears' decision to continue to detain Koepnick even though the Mesa police officers were then willing to release him. By that time, all of the receipts in Koepnick's possession had been checked against his purchases and found to be satisfactory (4R.T. 68). Lessard had also verified with Jeff Ward that Koepnick had in fact purchased the crescent wrench, and the bag which supposedly contained the wrench had been accounted for in the security office. However, despite all these facts, the Mesa police officers continued to detain Koepnick at Sears' request while Lessard conducted a nonconsensual search of his truck, looking for an alleged "brown bag" (4R.T. 71). This search, which required approximately 15 to 20 minutes, predictably proved fruitless (4R.T. 197-98). During this time, Koepnick remained under detention and in handcuffs (4R.T. 197). Lessard's conduct is thus arguably precisely the sort of continuing wrongful conduct by Sears employees that would support a jury verdict for punitive damages under the new "evil mind guiding an evil hand" standard.

C. The Evidence Supporting Koepnick's Punitive Damages with Respect to His Trespass to Chattel Claim Was Sufficient to Submit That Issue to the Jury as Well.

The evidence previously stated with respect to Lessard's insistence that Koepnick continue to be detained further while his truck was searched, even though by then there was absolutely no objective basis to do so, also supports the reasonable conclusion that Lessard continued in his wrongful conduct, despite the continuing harm to Koepnick's liberty interests resulting from his continued detention: Koepnick remained in handcuffs while the search of his truck was occurring, and there had by then been demonstrated to be no objective basis whatsoever for any belief that Koepnick had been shoplifting. The facts discussed in the preceding section of this argument are here repeated and incorporated by reference. In short, on the merits, the jury here could reasonably find that Lessard had the requisite "evil mind" to meet the *Linthicum* standard for a *prima facie* case of punitive damages as to the trespass to chattel issue based on that conduct as well.

CONCLUSION

For all the foregoing reasons, the trial court properly denied Sears' motions for judgment notwithstanding the verdict as to Koepnick's claim for false arrest claim, for punitive damages with respect to the false arrest, and for punitive damages with respect to Koepnick's trespass to chattels claim. The trial court's rulings concerning the issues properly before this Court should therefore be affirmed.

DATED this _____ day of May, 1987.

Respectfully submitted,

THOMAS J. QUARELLI, ESQ.
WILLIAM J. MONAHAN, P.C.

By _____
William J. Monahan

and

PAUL G. ULRICH, P.C.

By _____
Paul G. Ulrich
Attorneys for Appellant
Cross-Appellee

Fred Cole
Roger W. Perry
Gust, Rosenfeld, Divelbess & Henderson
3300 Valley Bank Center
Phoenix, Arizona 85073
Attorneys for Defendant-Appellee/Cross-Appellant

IN THE COURT OF APPEALS
STATE OF ARIZONA
DIVISION ONE

MAX KOEPNICK,
    Plaintiff-Appellant
    Cross-Appellee,
 	
    v.
 	
SEARS, ROEBUCK & COMPANY,
    Defendant-Appellee
    Cross-Appellant.
	1 CA-CIV 9147
	
	MARICOPA County
	Superior Court
	No. C 502081

APPELLEE'S REPLY BRIEF ON CROSS-APPEAL

TABLE OF CONTENTS

TABLE OF AUTHORITIES

432

ARGUMENT

I. SEARS IS ENTITLED TO JUDGMENT NOTWITHSTANDINGTHE VERDICT ON THE FALSE ARREST CLAIM.

Koepnick fails to demonstrate any valid issue of fact that would preclude the granting of judgment in favor of Sears on the false arrest count. All four of the necessary elements for a privileged detention under A.R.S. §13-1805 C are undisputedly established in the record. On the element of reasonable cause, the trial court, after hearing all the evidence, determined that reasonable cause existed for Koepnick's detention. This ruling was a proper exercise of the trial court's discretion and is fully justified by the evidence. There is no basis for this court to reverse the trial court's determination on this issue. To avoid duplication, Sears incorporates all its proper arguments on this issue by this reference.

The evidence also undisputedly establishes a proper purpose for Koepnick's detention pursuant to the statute. It is uncontroverted that Sears detained Koepnick to summon the Mesa police concerning the suspected shoplifting. Indeed, Koepnick never made any claim or offered any jury instruction with respect to some other purpose for his detention by Sears. For Koepnick to now make the bald, totally unsupported statement in his response brief that "He was not necessarily detained for that purpose" is ridiculous (Cross-appeal answering brief, p. 5). Koepnick does not even suggest any other purpose in support of this statement. As for the period of time after the police arrived, the evidence is also undisputed that Koepnick was legitimately in the Mesa police department's custody, not Sears. Probable cause existed for the police to detain Koepnick during this period, and Sears had no control over whether or how Koepnick was kept in detention by the police.

There is also no dispute concerning the reasonableness of the length of time Sears detained Koepnick. Koepnick concedes that the length of his detention in Sears' custody until the police arrived and investigated was reasonable (Cross-appeal answering brief, p. 6). As stated above, from that point on, Koepnick was in the Mesa police department's custody, not Sears. Koepnick was under arrest for his altercation with Officer Campbell. Prior to trial, the trial court ruled that probable cause existed for the Mesa police department's detention of Koepnick during that period for the alleged assault on Officer Campbell. (*See* Minute entry dated January 9, 1986.) Koepnick has never raised any issue or objection with respect to that ruling.

Although Koepnick repeatedly states that Steve Lessard "requested" his continued detention by the Mesa police department during this period, such statements have no support in the record. Koepnick fails even to cite to the record when making such assertions of "fact." (*See*, e.g., cross-appeal answering brief, p. 6.) The uncontroverted evidence is that Lessard simply told the police the information and knowledge he had in his possession (4R.T. 105-06). This information included the fact that the bag Jeff Ward stated he had wrapped the wrench in before placing it in the larger shopping bag was missing (4R.T. 104-05). Contrary to Koepnick's statements in his briefs, that bag was never accounted for in the security office (4R.T. 104-05). It was the police officers who made the decision to search Koepnick's truck (6R.T. 128). Lessard had no control over whether Koepnick was detained or released by the police during that period (8R.T. 59-60).

Finally, the element of the reasonableness of the manner of Sears' detention of Koepnick is also undisputedly established by the record. Koepnick's arguments in trying to explain why Sears' detention of him should be viewed as unreasonable are nothing less than frivolous. Koepnick's first argument revolves around the fact that, according to Koepnick's testimony, Lessard approached him and said, "You don't have a receipt, do you?" rather than asking to see his receipt. Even accepting all of Koepnick's testimony as true, as we must on this appeal, there is still no evidence of any abusive conduct that would rise to the level of a tortiously unreasonable specific manner of detention. If the court were to accept Koepnick's argument, potential liability would exist any time a subject stopped pursuant to A.R.S. §13-1805 did not like the manner in which he was addressed. It is inconceivable that the legislature intended such a result when referring to a "reasonable manner" of detention in A.R.S. §13-1805 C. Much more substantial conduct is required for liability to exist for false arrest.

Koepnick further argues that the manner of his detention was unreasonable in that he should have been questioned by Sears. A.R.S. §13-1805 C, however, indicates that store personnel are not required to question a subject; they can simply detain for the purpose of summoning a law enforcement officer to handle the investigation.

Finally, Koepnick stretches so far as to attempt to attribute the injuries he received in his altercation with Officer Campbell in the hallway to the fact that the Sears employees declined to give him a drink of water. Koepnick's need for such a nonsensical argument makes readily apparent the total lack of any factual basis for any claim that Sears detained Koepnick unreasonably. The undisputed facts show that Koepnick was simply stopped outside the store and then taken to the security office to await the arrival of the police. According to even Koepnick's testimony, he was not physically or verbally abused by the Sears employees. As such, there is no evidence that would warrant submitting this issue to the jury.

As all the elements for a privileged detention under A.R.S. §13-1805 C are undisputedly established in the record, Sears is entitled to have judgment entered in its favor on the false arrest claim.

II. SEARS IS ENTITLED TO JUDGMENT NOTWITHSTANDING THE VERDICTS ON THE PUNITIVE DAMAGE CLAIMS.

As Koepnick acknowledges in citing *Filasky v. Preferred Risk Mutual Insurance Co.*, 152 Ariz. 591, 734 P.2d 76 (1987), and *Gurule v. Illinois Mutual Life and Casualty Co.*, 152 Ariz. 600, 734 P.2d 85 (1987) (en banc), a punitive damage award will only be sustained on appeal when there is reasonable evidence to support it. In discussing the nature of an act necessary to permit punitive damages, the Arizona Supreme Court observed that "[p]unishment is an appropriate objective in a civil case only if the defendant's conduct or motive involves 'some element of outrage similar to that usually found in a crime.' " *Gurule*, 434 P.2d at 86 (quoting *Rawlings v. Apodaca*, 151 Ariz. 149, 162, 726 P.2d 565, 578 (1986). Where a trial court submits the issue of punitive damages to the jury on slight and inconclusive evidence of such conduct, an appellate court may correct the error. *Filasky*, 734 P.2d at 84. In both *Filasky* and *Gurule*, the Supreme Court found that the evidence did not measure up to the requisite standard and reversed the awards of punitive damages. The same conclusion should be reached in this appeal.

A. *The False Arrest Claim.*

Koepnick attempts to support the punitive damage award on the false arrest claim based on alleged "deficiencies" in the initial investigation and Lessard's alleged "request" that the Mesa police officers continue to detain Koepnick while his truck was searched. Both of these arguments ignore the uncontroverted facts in the record and fail to demonstrate a level of conduct sufficient to justify an award of punitive damages. First, Koepnick's assertion that the investigation by Lessard was inadequate and unreasonable is belied by the trial court's ultimate determination that reasonable cause existed for Sears' detention of Koepnick. Inherent in the trial court's ruling that reasonable cause existed for Koepnick's detention is the determination that the pre-stop investigation conducted by Lessard was reasonable. If the facts and investigation relied on by Sears were unreasonable, reasonable cause could not exist for the detention. It would be completely illogical for the same evidence that the trial court found to establish reasonable cause for the detention to also be deemed sufficient to support an award of punitive damages for the same detention.

Koepnick's second argument for supporting the punitive damage award also fails to find justification in the record. There is no evidence to support Koepnick's contention that it was "Sears decision to continue to detain Koepnick even though the Mesa police officers were then willing to release him" (Cross-appeal answering brief, p. 10). Koepnick repeatedly asserts in his brief that Lessard "requested" that the police officers continue to detain Koepnick while his truck was searched. Koepnick, however, fails to cite any portion of the record for that proposition. He cannot; none exists.

Steve Lessard's role in the decision to search Mr. Koepnick's truck was simply that of providing information to the police concerning the possibility of merchandise being in the truck (4R.T. 105-06). It was the police who made the decision to search the truck (6R.T. 128). There is nothing in the record to permit a finding that Lessard requested or suggested that Koepnick continue to be detained by the police during this period. At that time, Koepnick was under arrest for his role in the altercation with Officer Campbell. The Mesa police department had reasonable cause for Koepnick's detention. Sears is not responsible for the manner or the length of time that a person is legitimately detained in police custody. Indeed, Lessard could not have required the Mesa police to release Koepnick even if he had thought the detention was improper (8R.T. 59-60).

Moreover, even if Lessard's actions could be considered as the cause of Koepnick's continued detention, his conduct was not the reprehensible, outrageous sort that would warrant punitive damages. Again, all he did was inform the police of certain facts and knowledge in his possession. The police made the final decision on what action would be taken with respect to such information. Such conduct by Lessard does not evidence an evil mind; it is not even tortious conduct. Sears is entitled to have judgment entered in its favor on the claim for punitive damages on the false arrest count.

B. Trespass to Chattel Claim.

Koepnick's argument for punitive damages on the trespass to chattel claim is identical to his second argument presented on the false arrest claim. The same comments made in response to Koepnick's position on the false arrest claim are applicable here. Koepnick's argument that Steve Lessard's conduct is responsible for the Mesa police officers' continued detention of Koepnick is just as meritless on this claim as it is on the false arrest claim. Moreover, Koepnick is again confusing his trespass to chattel claim with the false arrest claim. Koepnick's detention does not constitute an element of the tort of trespass to chattel. In essence, Koepnick is attempting to assert some kind of claim for double punitive damages for the same conduct on which he bases his claim for false arrest. Koepnick offers no authority to support his position, and it should be rejected accordingly.

CONCLUSION

The trial court properly granted Sears' judgment notwithstanding the verdict on the claim of trespass to chattel. The trial court erred, however, in not doing the same on the claim of false arrest. There are no issues of fact present to justify submitting this claim to the jury. This court should therefore reverse the trial court's ruling that denied Sears' motion for judgment N.O.V. on this count.

Furthermore, there was no evidence to justify the submission of the claims for punitive damages on either of the two counts submitted to the jury. Thus, regardless of the ultimate decisions on the trespass to chattel and false arrest counts, Sears is entitled to have the trial court instructed to grant it judgment N.O.V. on the punitive damage claims.

Respectfully submitted this 8th day of June, 1987.

GUST, ROSENFELD, DIVELBESS & HENDERSON

By _____

Fred Cole
Roger W. Perry
Attorneys for Defendant-Appellee/Cross-Appellant

V

WRITING TO PARTIES: CONTRACTS AND CORRESPONDENCE

Parts III and IV examined advocacy to a court and written communication between members of a law firm. As a practicing attorney, however, you will communicate not only with judges and other attorneys but also with your clients and other parties.

For example, you may draft a written contract that the parties adopt as the final and complete expression of their negotiated agreement. If your client later complains that the other party has breached the contract, you may draft an "advice letter" to your client, advising her of her legal rights and recommending certain action. Depending on your client's assessment of her options, you might then send a "demand letter" to the opposing party, demanding that he take certain action to satisfy your client's claims.

Part V examines contracts and letters as examples of drafting directed to parties. It does not proceed on the premise that your immediate audience will invariably be the parties themselves. On the contrary, if you know that the opposing party is represented by counsel, you will ordinarily address your contract proposal or your demand letter to the opposing counsel. Similarly, if you or your law firm is the outside counsel for a corporation, you may address your advice letter to the corporation's in-house counsel. Nonetheless, more so than with office memoranda and briefs, contracts and letters are directed ultimately to the parties themselves.

Contracts and letters may be useful at various stages of litigation. For example, a contract may precede a dispute, or it may express the parties' agreement to settle a dispute that has already proceeded through pretrial, trial, or even appellate litigation. Similarly, although you will often draft advice and demand letters at the earliest stages of litigation, you may use them at any stage of the litigation that raises new questions or that creates a new opportunity to state your demands.

CHAPTER

17

Contracts

I. BASIC APPROACHES

With some limits, parties can privately shape their legal rights and obligations by exchanging enforceable promises in a contract. Each party's promises impose contractual duties on that party and create contractual rights in the other.

The authors of one contracts casebook believe that the contractual promise is the greatest human invention, even greater than the wheel, the lever, and the pulley:

> [F]or it is the promise that breaks the ultimate physical restraint. It permits us to live a bit of the future today. When two or more employ the tool of promise in concert, they create a unique social engine—the *bargain*.[1]

Although this claim may provoke some debate between lawyers and engineers about the relative merits of the promise and the pulley, none will dispute that enforceable contracts are indispensable to modern commerce.

As with pleadings, you can readily find forms for contracts in a formbook or in a dusty file cabinet of a law office. However, many such forms are as antiquated as the parody of a contract presented in Exercise 11-1, page 230. You will produce a much better contract if you throw away the outdated forms, understand the purposes of each section of a contract, and express the agreement of the parties in plain, simple, clear English.

On the other hand, you need not reinvent the wheel with every contract. Some law firms produce high-quality form contracts for common transac-

---

1. Daniel W. Fessler & Pierre R. Loiseaux, Contracts, Morality, Economics and the Marketplace (Cases and Materials) 1 (1982).

439

tions that require similar provisions. For example, some firms have created and maintain a series of provisions for real estate contracts on computer disk. An attorney assigned to a real estate transaction can (1) leaf through a hard copy of the available provisions, (2) select the paragraphs that are best suited to the current transaction, (3) use a word processor to create a document with the selected paragraphs, and (4) tailor the document to the particular facts and requirements of the current transaction. Such a system can be highly successful if its users ensure that the forms are well written and if they avoid complacency in tailoring the forms to particular transactions.

For contracts that do not lend themselves to a computerized form system, you should feel comfortable drafting "from scratch" without reliance on an antiquated form. You can draft with confidence if you understand the fundamental components of a contract.

II. FUNDAMENTAL COMPONENTS

A. GENERAL FORMAT

A contract should always contain the following provisions:

(1) an introduction identifying the parties to the transaction,
(2) a section describing the rights and obligations of the parties, and
(3) signature lines showing the parties' agreement to the terms of the contract.

A contract may also include:

(1) a statement of "recitals," which describes the background of the transaction and the parties' reasons for entering into the contract,
(2) a glossary of defined terms, or
(3) a section of miscellaneous provisions addressing such topics as termination or modification of the contract and the relationship of the contract to other transactions.

B. INTRODUCTION TO THE CONTRACT

In the first lines after the title of a contract, you should identify the parties as simply and clearly as possible. If more than two parties join in the transaction, or if at least one of the parties is a complex entity, you should set the parties' names apart from each other on the page.

For example, you can start with a descriptive section heading and use paragraphing to separate the parties' names:

I. PARTIES

The parties to this contract for the purchase and sale of sand are:
1. SOONER SAND CO., a general partnership consisting of Harley T. Price and W. M. McMichael, general partners, and

2. BASSI DISTRIBUTING CO., a joint venture of Bassi Trucking ‖ Co. and Hardcore Rock & Gravel, Inc.

If you use this format for the introduction, you can refer to the parties throughout the contract by the formal names of their business entities: SOONER SAND CO. and BASSI DISTRIBUTING CO. Alternatively, you can assign descriptive labels to the parties, such as Seller and Buyer:

1. Sooner Sand Co. (SELLER), a general . . . ‖
2. Bassi Distributing Co. (BUYER), . . .

Many drafters also like to assign a label to the contract itself and to include the date of the agreement in the introductory sentence:

This contract for the purchase and sale of sand (the "Agreement") ‖ is entered into on _____ by the following parties:
1. Sooner Sand Co. (SELLER), a general . . . ‖

C. RECITALS

Although not essential to an enforceable contract, a statement of the factual background of the transaction can help a neutral party interpret the contract if the parties dispute its meaning. Such recitals can even help establish consideration for the contract by showing the parties' reciprocal inducements or by providing a basis for implying obligations. For example, in the celebrated contracts case *Wood v. Lucy, Lady Duff-Gordon*,[2] Justice Cardozo of the New York Court of Appeals relied partly on the recitals of a written contract to imply an obligation by an exclusive agent to use reasonable efforts, thus satisfying the consideration requirement.

You should not confuse the recitals with the contract's statement of mutual promises. In the recitals, you should state only the background of the transaction and the motivations of the parties, not the actual obligations that the parties have assumed by their agreement.

Recitals in an outdated contract are easy enough to spot. Each recital of a background fact appears in a clause beginning with the word "Whereas" and is strung together with other recitals in a single, unmanageably long run-on sentence. To provide better guidance to your reader, you should (1) introduce the recitals with a section heading, such as "Recitals," "Background," or "Preamble," and (2) state your recitals in conventional sentences within numbered paragraphs:

II. RECITALS ‖

1. SELLER is engaged in the business of selling and shipping sand ‖ from Phoenix to various customers in the State of Arizona but has not

---

2. 118 N.E. 214 (N.Y. 1917).

developed markets outside of Arizona. SELLER desires to supply sand wholesale to a distributor with customers outside the state.

2. BUYER has an established business . . .

D. STATEMENT OF RECIPROCAL PROMISES

The heart of any contract is the parties' statement of their reciprocal promises. Those promises define the parties' mutual rights and obligations, which form the consideration for the agreement.

1. Introductory Clause; Recital of Consideration

Perhaps in an excess of caution, many drafters still begin their statements of reciprocal promises with outdated recitals of consideration such as the following:

> NOW, THEREFORE, in consideration of the mutual covenants herein contained, and other good and valuable consideration the receipt of which is hereby acknowledged, the parties hereby agree . . .

Aside from displaying an antiquated writing style, such passages fail to establish consideration in many jurisdictions. In some states, stating a promise in a signed writing raises a presumption of consideration,[3] but a recital of consideration has no additional legal effect.[4] In most transactions, moreover, the reference to "other . . . consideration" is simply false. Instead, the consideration consists of the mutual promises stated in the written contract. Rather than pompously recite the existence of consideration, you should simply state the mutual promises under a descriptive section heading and a simple introductory clause:

> III. MUTUAL RIGHTS AND OBLIGATIONS
>
> SELLER and BUYER agree to the following exchange:
> 1. *Supply.* For a period of five years from the date of formation of this contract, SELLER will supply BUYER with all the sand that BUYER requires . . .
> 2. *Delivery.* . . .
> 3. *Quality.* . . .
> 4. *Price.* For each ton of sand delivered, BUYER will pay SELLER a sum equal to . . .

Some drafters are tempted to begin each statement of an obligation with a phrase such as "SELLER promises to supply" or "SELLER agrees

---

3. See E. Allan Farnsworth & William F. Young, Cases and Materials on Contracts 117 (4th ed. 1988) (citing to Cal. Civ. Code §1614 (West 1954) as typical statute).

4. See John D. Calamari & Joseph M. Perillo, The Law of Contracts §4-6 at 198 n.85 & accompanying text (3d ed. 1987).

to supply." The reference to "promises" or "agrees," however, is unnecessary. If you begin your statement of mutual promises with an umbrella statement such as "SELLER and BUYER agree to the following exchange:", you need not repeatedly invoke the word "agree" in each statement of a promise. Moreover, to state a promise, you need not use the word "promise." Words such as "will" and "shall" appropriately convey a party's intent to commit herself to a future performance.

2. Precision in Drafting

a. Simplicity; Terms of Art

The terms of the exchange are a matter of negotiation between the parties. If you represent your client in the negotiations, you can participate in shaping the substance of the bargain. As part of that process, you may draft proposed contract provisions to serve as offers or counteroffers to the other party. In other cases, your client may ask you to prepare a formal written document expressing a bargain that the parties have previously negotiated. In either case, one of your primary tasks as drafter of the final document is to express the parties' negotiated rights and obligations as precisely as possible to reduce the risk of misunderstanding and costly disputes during performance of the contract.

To draft precisely, you should take advantage of helpful terms of art but avoid unnecessary jargon. For example, the provisions below refer to the buyer's "requirements," a legal term of art that has special meaning and legal consequences under the Uniform Commercial Code.[5] Otherwise, however, the provisions contain plain, simple English:

1. *Supply.* For a period of five years from the date of formation of this contract, SELLER will supply BUYER with all the sand that BUYER **requires** for BUYER's business of selling and shipping sand to customers outside the State of Arizona.

2. *Delivery.* BUYER may order sand as BUYER's **requirements** arise by sending a written purchase order to SELLER. . . .

Some legal terms are not necessarily terms of art but may be generally helpful and inoffensive. In the following passage, for example, the seller makes a special kind of promise by "warranting" the quality of the goods:

3. *Quality.* SELLER **warrants** that the quality of the sand that is delivered to BUYER will be at least equal to that of sand of corresponding grades sold by other sand companies in the City of Phoenix, Arizona.

The word "warrants" in this passage is not a necessary term of art under the Uniform Commercial Code. The seller would assume the same legal obligation by simply promising that

---

5. U.C.C. §2-306(1) (1990).

‖ SELLER will deliver to BUYER sand of a quality that is at least equal . . .[6]

Nonetheless, drafters typically and reasonably use the term "warrants" or "warranty" to draw attention to the special nature of a promise that goods or services will meet certain standards.

Similarly, many drafters use special phrases to draw attention to statements of "conditions," which qualify or limit contractual duties. For example, in a standard insurance contract, the insured will assume an absolute obligation to pay premiums to the insurer, but the insurer will pay money to the insured only if the insured suffers a loss of the type covered by the insurance contract. You could introduce the insurer's conditional promise with the simple word "if":

‖ If the insured suffers a covered loss as defined in section VI above, the ‖ insurer will reimburse the insured for . . .

Many insurers, however, like to emphasize the conditional nature of their promises with special phrases, such as "on the condition that" or "in the event that":

‖ In the event that the insured suffers a covered loss as defined in section ‖ V above, the insurer . . .

Such language may catch the eye, but it is no more precise than "if." Therefore, if special emphasis is not your aim, you need not use the special phrase.

An even less defensible example of legal terminology in contracts is the use of "such" or "said" to refer to a particular thing that the contract has previously specifically identified:

‖ On execution of this Employment Agreement, the Company will ‖ transfer to Executive an option to purchase 100 shares of preferred stock ‖ at the price of $100/share on or before June 1, 1991. . . . Executive ‖ may not transfer the rights to **such** stock option at any time before January ‖ 1, 1991.

Before attending law school, you probably never considered using "such" or "said" in this way. In traditional nonlegal usage, the word "said" is not an adjective at all. In its primary nonlegal usage, "such" acts as an adjective, but it refers to a general class of persons or things with common characteristics:

‖ The "Profit-sharing Agreement" requires the parties to share the proceeds ‖ of illegal gambling. Such contracts are unenforceable.

"Such" is only secondarily recognized as a means of referring to a specific, previously identified thing. Nonetheless, many legal drafters contend

---

6. U.C.C. §2-313(1)(a), (2) (1990).

that "such" and "said" have taken on a special meaning in the legal community and that they therefore qualify as useful terms of art in contracts. However, if this special meaning is simply "previously mentioned," then "such" or "said" is really no more precise than the simpler and less distracting "the," "this," or "that":[7]

> . . . the Company will transfer to Executive an option to purchase 100 shares. . . . Executive may not transfer the rights to **this** stock option at any time before January 1, 1991.

Of course, this level of precision would be inadequate to identify a particular stock option if the document had previously referred to several. In those circumstances, you can identify a particular stock option most precisely by giving it a special label:

> . . . the Company will transfer to Executive two stock options: (1) an option to purchase 500 shares of common stock at $50/share on or before June 1, 1996 (the Common Option), and (2) an option to purchase 100 shares of preferred stock at the price of $100/share on or before June 1, 1995 (**the Preferred Option**). . . . Executive may not transfer the rights to the **Preferred Option** at any time before January 1, 1995.

Some legal drafters tenaciously insist that "such" and "said" have become legal terms of art that satisfy even this higher standard of precision. They ascribe to "such" and "said" the special meaning "the one last referred to in this document." Thus, they interpret "said stock option" or "such stock option" to mean "the stock option last referred to above." But this argument strains the capacity of these simple words. In particular, the word "such" does not gracefully convey this level of precision, because this peculiar legal usage of "such" conflicts with its primary nonlegal usage as an adjective that refers to a general class of things.

For example, in the following excerpt from an employment contract, it is not clear whether an employer may discharge an employee for any violent acts on the premises or only for the particular violent acts of fighting and of damaging property:

> Employer may discipline Employee for any violent acts on the factory premises, such as fighting with other employees or maliciously damaging Employer's property. **Such** conduct constitutes grounds for immediate discharge.

If the reader ascribes the primary nonlegal meaning to the word "such" in the second sentence, that sentence could refer to a class of conduct describing any violent acts, of which fighting and damaging property are only two examples. If the reader ascribes some special legal meaning to the word "such" in the second sentence, that sentence arguably refers only to the particular violent acts of fighting and damaging property; under that interpre-

---

7. See Richard Wydick, Plain English for Lawyers 54 (2d ed. 1985) (analyzing "said").

tation, the employer could discipline an employee for other violent acts, but not by discharging the employee. Thus, unless the reader knows precisely what meaning to ascribe to "such," the provision does not clearly state whether the employer may discharge an employee for violently destroying the employee's own property on the factory premises in a fit of anger.

Unfortunately, along with trusts and wills, contracts seem to be among the last refuges for marginally useful or even counterproductive legal jargon. You will serve your client and the profession well if you have the courage to use plain English and only truly helpful terms of art, even at the cost of ruffling some feathers within your law firm or the legal community.

b. Deliberate Imprecision

Occasionally, precision is neither feasible nor desirable. In some cases, for example, the parties may have failed to reach precise agreement on some point. If so, you may be forced to express their general agreement on that point in terms that are sufficiently imprecise to encompass the range of interpretations that describe their divergent positions.

For example, the buyer of factory equipment may demand during negotiations that the seller agree to repair or replace defective parts within 10 days after receiving notice of the defect. The seller might counteroffer to repair or replace defective parts within 45 days after receiving notice of the defect. If the parties cannot agree on a time period measured by a specific number of days, they may instead agree on the vague language "within a reasonable time in light of all the circumstances," realizing that they might not share the same interpretation of that language in particular applications.

Language such as this may save the deal if negotiations are stalled on the sticky point. Moreover, if performance of the contract proceeds smoothly, the parties may never test their divergent interpretations of the language. On the other hand, if adverse circumstances place a strain on performance, the lack of perfect agreement on the precise meaning of the provision may erupt into a serious dispute. Thus, during the negotiation of such a deal, you must help your client weigh the benefits of reaching general agreement against the risks of subsequent disputes over the meaning of vague language.

3. Termination, Modification, and Merger Clauses

Substantive rules of contract law create special challenges for you when you draft either of two kinds of miscellaneous provisions: (1) restrictions on the parties' powers to orally terminate or modify a written contract, and (2) "merger clauses" designed to identify the signed contract as the complete and exclusive statement of the parties' agreement. These are certainly not the only kinds of provisions that present drafting challenges, but they serve to illustrate some interesting problems and helpful principles.

a. Restrictions on Termination or Modification

In many cases, parties to a written contract will seek to prevent their agents from casually entering into a subsequent oral agreement to modify or terminate the original written contract. A typical clause in the written contract states:

This agreement cannot be terminated or modified except in a signed, ‖ written agreement executed by the authorized agent of each party. ‖

Unfortunately, such a clause may not have the intended effect. Many courts hold that parties can orally agree to modify or terminate a written contract and that one of the parties can orally waive a specific contract right. Many of those courts will apply these principles to a specific provision requiring a writing for modification or termination. Under that approach, the parties can orally agree to "rescind," or eliminate, the clause that prohibits them from modifying the contract without a writing. Once they orally rescind that provision, the parties are free to orally modify or terminate the remainder of the agreement. A court can reach the same result by holding that a party effectively orally waived rights under a provision prohibiting oral modification or termination. Under that approach, the waiving party may be precluded from challenging a subsequent oral agreement to modify or terminate the substantive provisions of the contract.[8]

In a jurisdiction that is friendly to oral modifications or waivers, you may find it impossible to draft a restriction that absolutely precludes oral modification or waiver. You can start by adding an extra layer of prohibition in the clause:

The parties cannot terminate or modify this contract except in a signed, ‖ written agreement executed by the authorized agent of each party. More-over, this section's requirement of a writing is not subject to oral waiver ‖ or modification. ‖

Of course, even this careful language may not successfully curb persistent attempts to orally modify or terminate the agreement. The parties presumably can orally rescind or waive the second sentence of the provision, paving the way for oral rescission or waiver of the main restriction, which in turn paves the way for oral termination or modification of the substantive terms of the agreement. Indeed, some courts might not even require the multiple layers of waivers or rescissions to take place in separate steps.[9]

Thus, in some jurisdictions, careful drafting may not be enough. If your client is troubled by the prospect of unauthorized oral modifications or terminations, you should research your state's law on this point. If you

---

8. See generally C.I.T. Corp. v. Jonnet, 214 A.2d 620 (Pa. 1965); Wagner v. Graziano Constr. Co., 136 A.2d 82 (Pa. 1957); 6 Arthur L. Corbin, Corbin on Contracts §1295 (1962).

9. See generally Universal Builders, Inc. v. Moon Motor Lodge, Inc., 244 A.2d 10 (Pa. 1968).

conclude that you cannot contractually avoid the risk of unauthorized changes, you should candidly explain the limits of your drafting powers. So informed, your client can take other steps to avoid the risk, such as by increasing its administrative control over its agents.

b. Merger Clauses and Parole Evidence

When drafting a written contract, you will often want to include a "merger clause," which states that the written contract is the exclusive statement of the parties' agreement. If the other party subsequently asserts that the total agreement includes rights and obligations not expressed in the written contract, you can refer to the merger clause and seek to exclude evidence of the alleged unwritten obligations under the "parol evidence rule."

A typical merger clause refers only generally to the subject matter of the agreement:

> XXV. Prior Agreements Superseded—This written contract constitutes the parties' complete and exclusive statement of their agreement on the subject matter covered by this contract, and it supersedes all previous agreements, promises, or representations regarding that subject matter.

Unfortunately, such a clause does not eliminate the risk of litigation of a common question under the parol evidence rule: Does the alleged additional agreement address topics within the subject matter of the main written contract so that the main contract supersedes it, or does the additional agreement address unrelated topics so that it can stand separately as an independent, enforceable contract?[10]

For example, suppose that on July 1, 1994 the parties signed a written contract for the lease of empty restaurant space. The lessee later asserted that the lessor also orally agreed on June 28, 1994 to sell dining tables and chairs to the lessee at a discounted rate. The lessor denies the oral agreement. He also points to the merger clause and argues that, assuming he did tentatively agree on June 28 to sell the dining furniture, the agreement was simply part of continuing negotiations that the parties abandoned and superseded in their July 1 agreement.

However, to successfully invoke the merger clause to exclude evidence of the oral agreement, the lessor must demonstrate that the alleged agreement to sell dining furniture falls within the subject matter of the July 1 contract; otherwise, the alleged June 28 agreement can stand outside the field occupied exclusively by the July 1 contract. Unfortunately, the merger clause cannot help the lessor much, because it fails to define the subject matter of the contract.

If you intend a written contract to broadly supersede prior agreements or promises on related transactions, you must describe the subject matter

---

10. See, e.g., Gianni v. R. Russell & Co., Inc., 126 A. 791 (Pa. 1924).

of your contract expansively so that the merger clause can have the intended effect. If you anticipate particular problems stemming from failed negotiations on collateral matters, you can address those matters explicitly:

XXV. Prior Agreements Superseded—This written contract constitutes the parties' complete and exclusive statement of their agreement on all matters relating to the lease of the Scottsdale premises, the operation of a restaurant on those premises, and the equipment needed for the operation. This contract supersedes all previous or contemporaneous agreements, promises, or representations regarding that subject matter.

This merger clause expresses the parties' intent to abandon any prior agreement for the sale of restaurant equipment and to replace it with the terms of the lease agreement.

E. SIGNATURE LINES

You may end your contract with any reasonable means of presenting the parties' signatures as evidence of their agreement to the terms of the contract. You do not need to invoke formalistic jargon such as:

In witness whereof, the said parties have hereunto set their hands and seals the day and year first above written.

Instead, you may simply precede the signature lines with the single word "Signed." At most, you might introduce the signatures with a clause such as "The undersigned parties agree to these terms."

If you have not already dated the contract at the beginning, you can include a space for the date next to each party's signature. The latest date on a signature line will represent one party's acceptance of the other party's offer and will mark the date of contract formation.

III. SUMMARY

To draft a simple contract, you should

(1) identify the parties in an introductory provision,
(2) recite the background facts, if helpful,
(3) state the reciprocal promises of the parties as precisely as possible, and
(4) provide signature lines as a means for the parties to express their assent to the terms of the contract.

===== E X E R C I S E 1 7 - 1 =====

1. *Sample Requirements Contract*

Study the following contract. Compare it with the antiquated version presented in Exercise 11-1, page 230, and with your revision of that contract.

REQUIREMENTS CONTRACT

I. PARTIES

The parties to this contract for the purchase and sale of sand are:
1. Sooner Sand Co. (SELLER), a general partnership consisting of the general partners Harley T. Price and W. M. McMichael, and
2. Bassi Distributing Co. (BUYER), a joint venture of Bassi Trucking Co. and Hardcore Rock & Gravel, Inc.

II. RECITALS

1. SELLER is engaged in the business of selling and shipping sand from Phoenix to various customers in the State of Arizona but has not developed markets outside of Arizona. SELLER desires to supply sand wholesale to a distributor with customers outside the state.
2. BUYER has an established business in Phoenix selling and shipping sand to various customers in several states outside Arizona, including California, Nevada, Utah, and Colorado. BUYER desires a stable source of supply of sand for that business.

III. MUTUAL RIGHTS AND OBLIGATIONS

SELLER and BUYER agree to the following bargained-for exchange:
1. *Supply.* For a period of five years from the date of formation of this contract, SELLER will supply BUYER with all the sand that BUYER requires for BUYER's business of selling and shipping sand to customers outside the State of Arizona.
2. *Delivery.* BUYER will order sand as BUYER's requirements arise by sending a written purchase order to SELLER. On receipt of such a purchase order, SELLER will deliver the ordered sand within a reasonable time to BUYER's facility at 1531 Range Road in Glendale, Arizona.
3. *Quality.* SELLER warrants that the quality of the sand that is delivered to BUYER will be at least equal to that of sand of corresponding grades sold by other sand companies in the City of Phoenix, Arizona.
4. *Price.* For each ton of sand delivered, BUYER will pay SELLER a sum equal to sixty percent (60%) of the market price per ton of concrete in the City of Phoenix at the time of SELLER's delivery to BUYER.
5. *Term of Payment.* SELLER may give an invoice to BUYER for sand

on or after SELLER delivers the sand to BUYER. BUYER will pay the full amount of such an invoice within thirty (30) days of its receipt of the invoice.

Signed:

_____   _____

SELLER—Authorized Agent for Sooner Sand Co.   Date

_____   _____

BUYER—Authorized Agent for Bassi Distributing Co.   Date

2. *Format for More Complex Agreement*

a. Compare the following outline of a sample contract with the sample contract in problem 1 above. The sample below displays an alternative introductory section, and it contemplates more complex provisions that must be subdivided into more numerous subsections.

b. In §4.2 of the contract, draft a merger clause that identifies your document as the complete and exclusive statement of the parties' agreement. In particular, be certain to supersede prior failed negotiations in which SELLER proposed to lease trucks to BUYER for the transportation of the sand to other states.

REQUIREMENTS CONTRACT

This contract for the purchase and sale of sand (the Agreement) is entered into on _____ by the following parties:

1. SELLER—Sooner Sand Co., a general partnership consisting of Harley T. Price and W. M. McMichael, general partners, and

2. BUYER—Bassi Distributing Co., a joint venture of Bassi Trucking Co. and Hardcore Rock & Gravel, Inc.

RECITALS

1. SELLER is engaged . . .
2. BUYER has an established . . .

MUTUAL RIGHTS AND OBLIGATIONS

SELLER and BUYER agree to the following bargained-for exchange:

ARTICLE I
Definitions

1.1 *Grades of sand*— . . .
1.2 *Market price*— . . .

ARTICLE II
Supply of Sand

2.1 *Quantity—* . . .
2.2 *Quality—* . . .
2.3 *Delivery—* . . .

ARTICLE III
Payment

3.1 *Price* . . .
3.2 *Terms of Payment—* . . .
• • • •

ARTICLE IV
Miscellaneous Provisions

4.1 *No Oral Modification—* . . .
4.2 *Prior Negotiations Superseded—* . . .
• • • •

SIGNED

_____

_____

Advice and Demand Letters[1]

As counselor and advocate, you will draft many kinds of letters to your client or to others on your client's behalf. Two of the most important are advice letters and demand letters. These letters are closely related to two kinds of documents examined in previous chapters: office memoranda and briefs. Like an office memorandum, an advice letter communicates a balanced legal analysis of a dispute or proposed action. In contrast, like a brief, a demand letter advocates a position, and it usually requests the addressee to take specific action.

I. ADVICE LETTERS

A. ADVICE LETTERS DISTINGUISHED FROM OPINION LETTERS

Many attorneys and commentators use the term "opinion letter" to refer to any letter addressed to a client that offers a legal analysis, opinion, or recommendation. Within this general class of letters, however, are two important subcategories, each of which warrants a narrowly descriptive label. The term "opinion letter" best describes only a small subcategory of letters in which you will provide your clients formal opinions on certain kinds of legal questions. The term "advice letter" accurately describes the far more common kind of letter in which you will more generally analyze a legal

---

1. Many of the ideas in this chapter are taken with permission from lecture materials prepared by Frank M. Placenti and Mark Hileman, partners in the Phoenix law firm Streich, Lang, Weeks & Cardon, P.A.

problem and advise your client about the relative merits of alternative courses of action.

More specifically, an opinion letter is a highly specialized and formal document that expresses your opinion or that of your law firm that a specified act is legally valid. For example, you might issue to a corporate client your formal opinion that the corporation has validly issued certain stock under applicable laws and under the articles and bylaws of the corporation. Because the client will significantly rely on such an opinion, the standards for an opinion letter are high, and its format is fairly rigid. Indeed, if you have any doubts about the legal validity of the action in question, you ordinarily will issue no opinion letter at all.

In contrast, in an advice letter, you will communicate your analysis of a legal problem to a client in much the same way that you would use an office memorandum to communicate the analysis to a supervising attorney. Even if you cannot definitively resolve the legal issues in the analysis, you can evaluate the relative merits of the parties' claims and defenses and estimate the probability of success on the merits. You can thus provide your client with valuable advice short of giving a definite opinion of the legality of certain actions.

In many law firms, only designated attorneys are authorized to issue formal opinion letters on behalf of the firm. Moreover, those attorneys tend to follow carefully developed forms when drafting their opinion letters, leaving little room for flexibility in format or creativity in analysis. Further examination of opinion letters is beyond the scope of this book. Instead, this chapter will explore the more common advice letter before addressing demand letters.

B. PURPOSE, AUDIENCE, AND WRITING STYLE

The writing style that you adopt for a document is partly a function of your intended audience and the purpose of your document. When you draft an office memorandum, you can easily identify your audience and purpose: You will communicate a balanced legal analysis to an experienced attorney. When you draft an advice letter, however, your audience and purpose may be less clear.

For example, the legal experience and general sophistication of your audience may vary greatly from one letter to the next. One client may be new to his business, have no legal training, and have learned English only after recently emigrating from a foreign country. Another client may be a sophisticated, experienced businessperson with at least a rudimentary knowledge of the laws that affect her business. Still another client may be a corporation with an in-house counsel to whom you will direct your advice letter. Obviously, you should adapt your writing style to suit the experience and sophistication of your audience. In a letter to the inexperienced client described above, you should take particular care to use plain, simple English and to avoid or explain even rudimentary legal terms. In letters to other, more experienced and legally knowledgeable clients, you can safely use more sophisticated language and legal terminology. In each case, however, your goal is the same: to communicate, not to impress.

One advice letter drafted by an associate in a major law firm provides a humorous example of the unintended effect you may have on your client if you fail to adapt your writing style to the client's needs. In the early 1980s, this law firm represented a man who had emigrated from Iran shortly after the Islamic revolution and the rise to power of the Ayatollah Khomeini. This client had violated a federal regulation in his business dealings in the United States, and he asked the law firm to advise him about the nature of the penalties and the possibility of avoiding them. In a letter, an associate of the law firm advised the client that he might avoid a fine if he "executed" a certain document. Unfortunately, the client had only a limited command of English, was painfully conscious of the executions by firing squad occurring daily in his homeland, and was anxious to skim the advice letter to determine what kinds of penalties an agency of the United States imposed for violation of its regulations. In these circumstances, the associate probably should have avoided the term "executed," which has a relatively innocuous legal meaning but which might have caused this client's heart to skip a beat or two when he first glanced at the letter.

In some cases, you may have multiple audiences, thus complicating your task of choosing a suitable writing style. In one case, for example, an attorney anticipated that a federal regulatory agency would ultimately seek a copy of his advice letter to a client. Accordingly, rather than present a neutral, balanced analysis, the attorney advocated his client's position in a manner designed to persuade the regulatory agency to approve his client's actions. In essence, he wrote a brief that was packaged as an advice letter.

In other cases, your client may wish to share your advice letter with customers, partners, or other attorneys. If so, you should draft the letter with the needs of the secondary audience in mind. For example, if your law firm's client is a corporate manager, she may intend to discuss your advice letter with the corporation's separate, in-house counsel. If so, you may want to provide a full explanation of your underlying legal analysis or even attach a copy of the formal office memorandum on which the advice letter is based.

C. FORMAT

You should flexibly adopt any format that suits your audience and the purpose of your advice letter. As a starting point, you can follow the basic elements of a reasonable format for an office memorandum:

Issues
Brief Answers
Facts
Discussion
Conclusion

With this format, your advice letter would

(1) restate the questions that your client posed to you,
(2) briefly summarize your conclusions,
(3) state the facts on which your analysis is based,

Clay Franks

(4) summarize your analysis of the law and the facts, and
(5) state your conclusions and your strategic recommendations.

If your advice letter is simple and brief, you need not use formal section headings to display the transitions between elements of your format. Instead, you can simply use sensible paragraphing to lead the reader from one element to the next. On the other hand, if your letter is long and complex, you should use section headings, just as you would in an office memorandum or a brief. You need not use precisely the same format headings as you would for an office memorandum. One attorney used the following primary headings in an advice letter to introduce the issues, brief answers, facts, discussion, and conclusion:

Issues Addressed
Executive Summary of Conclusions
Background
Analysis (divided into subsections)
Recommendations

D. INTRODUCTION AND STATEMENT OF ISSUES

Immediately after the address and before the salutation of your advice letter, you should concisely state the general subject matter of the letter:

Clay Franks
Vice-President, Construction
GRT Developers
1212 Central Ave, Suite 2201
Boomtown, Calzona 81717

RE: TRI Corp.'s possible breach of contract on the Westcourt project.

Dear Mr. Franks,

Then, in the first paragraph after the salutation, you should refer to your client's inquiry on this subject matter and state the issues that your letter addresses.

In some cases, your client will pose a general question that asks for strategic advice rather than legal conclusions: "Should we fire TRI and sue it for breach of contract?" If so, you may want to inform your client of the legal issues on which your strategic advice will depend:

Dear Mr. Franks,

You have asked us to advise you whether you should fire TRI from the Westcourt project and sue it for breach of contract. In formulating our advice on this matter, we have analyzed the following questions:

(1) Did TRI breach the construction contract by using Cohoes pipe rather than the Reading pipe called for in the architect's plans?

(2) If so, was TRI's breach "material," thus permitting you to cancel the construction contract and fire TRI from the project?

(3) If TRI has breached the contract, to what remedies is GRT entitled?

If you decide to introduce the primary parts of your letter with formal section headings, you could begin with "*Issues*":

Dear Mr. Franks,

You have asked us to advise you whether you should fire TRI from the Westcourt project and sue it for breach of contract.

I. Issues

In formulating our advice on this matter, we have analyzed the following questions:

A. Did TRI breach the construction contract by using Cohoes pipe rather than the Reading pipe called for in the architect's plans?

B. If so, was TRI's breach "material," thus . . .

E. BRIEF ANSWERS

Some attorneys will discourage you from summarizing your conclusions in brief answers near the beginning of your advice letter. They fear that your client will fail to appreciate or will even misinterpret your conclusions if he has not read your full analysis first. However, like a supervising attorney reading an office memorandum, a client reading an advice letter is anxious to reach the bottom line. You should not lightly withhold it from him out of some misplaced concern that he is not ready to face it. Moreover, mindful that he has paid for the entire letter, the client is nearly certain to read beyond the brief answers and to appreciate your full analysis. Thus, unless the letter is very short, or unless exceptional circumstances compel you to lay unusual groundwork before revealing an unfavorable conclusion,[2] you should satisfy your client's curiosity early in the letter.

If you use a simple format without section headings, you may briefly summarize your conclusions in a sentence or two immediately following your statement of the issues in the opening paragraph:

Dear Ms. Price,

You have asked us whether you would be liable for damages if you discharged your head chef in retaliation for his testifying against you in

---

2. See Henry Weihofen, *Legal Writing Style* 178, 199 (2d ed. 1980).

a hearing of the state Food and Beverage Commission. As discussed more fully below, we conclude that such a discharge would not constitute a breach of your employment contract, but it would render you liable under the state tort law of "wrongful discharge."

In a more complex letter, you could state your brief answers under some appropriate heading, such as "Brief Answers" or "Summary of Conclusions":

Dear Mr. Franks,

You have asked us to advise you whether you should fire TRI from the Westcourt project and sue it for breach of contract.

I. Issues

In formulating our advice on this matter, we have analyzed the following questions:

A. Did TRI breach the construction contract by using Cohoes pipe rather than the Reading pipe called for in the architect's plans?
B. If so, was TRI's breach "material," thus permitting you to cancel the construction contract and fire TRI from the project?
C. If TRI has breached the contract, to what remedies is GRT entitled?

II. Summary of Conclusions

A. TRI breached the construction contract, because the architect's plans clearly call for Reading pipe and do not permit substitutes.
B. TRI's breach almost certainly is not material, because Cohoes pipe is nearly identical to Reading pipe in all important specifications. Therefore, you cannot cancel the contract.
C. GRT is entitled to the difference between the value of the Reading pipe and that of the Cohoes pipe, a difference that may be insubstantial.

In addition to providing these answers to the specific legal issues that you have formulated, you might add a sentence to your overview paragraph that summarizes your response to the client's general strategic question:

Dear Mr. Franks,

You have asked us to advise you whether you should fire TRI from the Westcourt project and sue it for breach of contract. In this letter, we summarize our legal analysis and advise you not to fire TRI or withhold its payments.

F. FACTS

In every advice letter, you should state the facts on which your analysis is based. By making a record of the factual premises of your analysis, you can protect yourself against criticism or liability if subsequently discovered facts render your legal analysis obsolete. Indeed, if your client has supplied you with the facts, you may want to disclaim responsibility for any fact investigation:

III. Facts

The advice in this letter is premised on the following facts, which you have supplied and which we have not independently investigated. If the following facts prove to be incomplete or incorrect, you should not rely on the advice in this letter without first consulting us.

G. LEGAL ANALYSIS

In the body of your letter, you should reach a conclusion on each issue by applying the relevant law to the facts. In a letter to a corporate client's in-house counsel or to a sophisticated client who has some legal knowledge, you can develop your legal analysis and cite to authority in much the same way that you would in an office memorandum. Other clients, however, will have little use for your in-depth analysis of authority. They would rather read a simplified summary of your legal analysis, and they are willing to assume that your underlying research and analysis has been thorough.

Thus, even if you have more fully expressed your analysis in another document, you may want to simplify the discussion in your advice letter. For example, as an initial reaction to a client's inquiry, you often will draft a full office memorandum addressed to a supervising attorney. The memorandum will then serve as a basis for formulating advice to the client. In the advice letter, however, you need not analyze the legal authority with the same depth and formality that you found useful in the memorandum. Instead, you can more simply and briefly convey your analysis of each issue by (1) abstractly summarizing the law with little or no citation to authority, (2) identifying the relevant facts, and (3) stating your conclusion:

Under state tort law, you are liable for damages if you discharge an employee for a reason that violates public policy. Legislation of this state establishes public policies of maintaining health standards in restaurants and encouraging witnesses to testify at state administrative hearings. Therefore, if you discharge Chef Boyardi in retaliation for his testifying about violations of hygiene standards in your restaurant, you will be liable for violation of public policy.

In some cases, you can even leave the legal rule implicit by simply stating a conclusion, after identifying the facts on which it is based:

Your contract with Chef Boyardi does not commit the parties to a definite term of employment, and it does not restrict your right to terminate the contract. Therefore, under state contract law, you can discharge Chef Boyardi at any time and for any reason without breaching the contract.

If your client has some legal training or expects to share your letter with another attorney, you may want to analyze authority to an extent that approaches the depth of analysis in your office memorandum. Alternatively, you can summarize your analysis in the letter and simply attach the office memorandum on which the advice in your letter is based. In this way, the client can rely primarily on the more accessible information in the letter, but he also has access to your more thorough and formal memorandum if the need for it arises.

H. CONCLUSION; STRATEGIC RECOMMENDATIONS

In a final paragraph or section of your advice letter, you should summarize your subsidiary conclusions and offer your ultimate advice. If your client's legal rights and obligations are unclear, do not hesitate to convey the uncertainty with words and phrases that permit you to hedge. Even so, you should reach a conclusion, even if only a qualified one:

Although the question is a close one, TRI's breach probably is not material. . . .

Your ultimate advice likely will be strategic, such as a recommendation to file a lawsuit, communicate a settlement offer, or refrain from discharging an employee. If the ultimate decision for the client is essentially a business decision, such as whether to purchase property for development, you should outline the legal consequences of the purchase but leave the actual business decision to the client. On the other hand, if the ultimate decision is more clearly tied to the legal merits of a claim or defense, such as whether to settle a legal dispute, you can more strongly recommend a particular course of action.

Nonetheless, in all cases, you should invite the client to make the final decision. For example, when advising a client to settle, you should recommend a range of settlement offers within which your client can exercise some judgment to choose a particular position or to reject settlement altogether.

E X E R C I S E   1 8 - 1

1. *Advice Letter Without Section Headings*

The following advice letter is addressed to a restaurant owner with no legal training. The author has used only paragraphing to signal the transition from one element of the letter to the next, and he has not cited to authority.

a. Identify the purpose or purposes of each paragraph in the letter.

b. Research the problem and rewrite the letter so that it conveys additional information to a client with legal training. Specifically, cite to authority and briefly analyze the authority. If appropriate, divide the expanded letter into sections with section headings.

August 1, 1990

Leona Price
Hep Crepe Restaurant
123 Washington St.
Spinach Village, New Maine 10307

Dear Ms. Price,

You have asked us whether you would be liable for damages if you discharged your head chef in retaliation for his testifying against you in a hearing of the state Food and Beverage Commission. As discussed more fully below, we conclude that such a discharge would not constitute a breach of your employment contract, but it would render you liable under the state tort law of "wrongful discharge."

Our analysis is premised on the following facts, as you have supplied them. The state Food and Beverage Commission has recently held hearings on violations of state health and hygiene regulations at various restaurants within the Village. The Commission requested your head chef, Anthony Boyardi, to testify at the hearings. Under examination by Commissioners, Chef Boyardi testified that employees have failed to control rat and insect infestations, resulting in continuing violations of state regulations. Because you view Chef Boyardi's act of testifying as disloyal conduct, you wish to fire him.

Your contract with Chef Boyardi does not commit the parties to a definite term of employment, and it does not restrict your right to terminate the contract. Therefore, under state contract law, you can discharge Chef Boyardi at any time and for any reason without breaching the contract.

However, under state tort law, you will be liable for damages if you discharge an employee for a reason that violates public policy, regardless whether the discharge would constitute a breach of contract. Legislation of this state establishes public policies of maintaining health standards in restaurants and encouraging witnesses to testify at state administrative hearings. Therefore, if you discharge Chef Boyardi in retaliation for testifying at the administrative hearings, you will be liable for violation of public policy. Your liability may extend to damages designed to compensate Chef Boyardi for his losses and to additional damages designed to punish you for your intentional misconduct.

In conclusion, if you discharge Chef Boyardi in retaliation for his testimony, he will have a valid claim against you for damages. We advise you not to discharge him unless you are prepared to justify the discharge on other grounds.

If you have any questions on this matter, please call me at 123-4567.

Sincerely,

Robert Linzer
for Avila and Celaya, P.C.
222 N. 3d St.
Spinach Village, New Maine 10307

2. *Advice Letter with Section Headings*

a. Compare the following letter with the one above. Describe each way in which the letters differ in style and format.

b. Assume in the letter below that your client, Clay Franks, is an Anglo-American with racist tendencies and that the opposing party's representative, Cal Dunlap, is African-American. Do those facts affect your analysis of the problem? Does the letter below adequately address the problems potentially caused by your client's racism without unduly offending him? Should you be worried about offending him?

c. The letter below is addressed to a client who has at least a basic knowledge of the law relating to performance and breach of construction contracts. Rewrite the letter so that it is appropriate for a client who has no legal training or knowledge. Specifically, summarize your analysis without citing to specific authority. If appropriate, eliminate the section headings and guide your reader through the simpler letter with good paragraphing and transition sentences.

Marcia Todd
Todd, Brown & King
1212 Central Ave., Suite 401
Boomtown, Calzona 81717
July 5, 1990

Clay Franks
Vice-President, Construction
GRT Developers
1212 Central Ave, Suite 2201
Boomtown, Calzona 81717

RE: TRI Corp.'s possible breach of contract on the Westcourt project.

Dear Mr. Franks,

You have asked us to advise you whether you should fire TRI from the Westcourt project and sue it for breach of contract. In this letter, we summarize our legal analysis and advise you not to fire TRI or withhold its payments.

I. Issues

In formulating our advice on this matter, we have analyzed the following questions:

A. Did TRI breach the construction contract by using Cohoes pipe rather than the Reading pipe called for in the architect's plans?

B. If so, was TRI's breach "material," thus permitting you to cancel the construction contract and fire TRI from the project?

C. If TRI has breached the contract, to what remedies is GRT entitled?

II. Summary of Conclusions

A. TRI breached the construction contract, because the architect's plans clearly call for Reading pipe and do not permit substitutes.

B. TRI's breach almost certainly is not material, because Cohoes pipe is nearly identical to Reading pipe in all important specifications. Therefore, you cannot cancel the contract.

C. GRT is entitled to the difference between the value of the Reading pipe and that of the Cohoes pipe, a difference that may be insubstantial.

III. Facts

The advice in this letter is premised on the following facts, which you have supplied. We have not independently investigated the facts. If the following facts prove to be incomplete or incorrect, you should not rely on the advice in this letter without first consulting us.

GRT Developers is constructing a shopping center at the southwest corner of 27th Ave. and Marconi Way in Boomtown. As Vice-President of the Construction Division, you have hired TRI to install the plumbing system. GRT's contract with TRI incorporates the architect's plans, which you first transmitted to TRI in a letter soliciting its bid on the project. Those plans clearly call for the plumbing subcontractor to use Reading brand pipe for all plumbing:

> All pipes in the plumbing system must be Reading pipe, in the sizes and grades specified in these plans, and no other brand pipe.

From the beginning, you have had difficulty working with TRI's foreman, Cal Dunlap. When TRI had completed about half the plumbing on the project, you discovered that TRI had installed Cohoes-brand pipe rather than Reading pipe. In a heated conversation with Dunlap, you demanded that TRI remove the Cohoes pipe, install Reading pipe, and compensate GRT for the resulting delay in construction. Dunlap agreed to install Reading pipe in the remainder of the plumbing, but he refused to replace the previously installed pipe. You now want to know whether you can fire TRI if Dunlap does not meet your demands.

Your own engineers have concluded that Cohoes pipe is equal to Reading pipe in durability and other relevant specifications. You do not know why the architect required Reading pipe, but you know that his brother-in-law is a sales manager for Reading Manufacturing Co.

IV. Analysis

If TRI has breached the construction contract, GRT may sue it for all foreseeable damages caused by the breach, provided that GRT can prove the damages with reasonable certainty. *See Johnson v. Coombs Construction Co.*, 345 Calz. 2d 331, 334 (1979). However, you may not fire TRI from the project unless TRI's breach is so substantial that a court would characterize it as "material," rather than "minor." *See Lehman Brothers, Inc. v. Steenhook Enterprises*, 401 Calz. 2d 112, 115 (1985). If a breach is only minor, you may not terminate the contract; instead, you must permit TRI to complete its performance, while reserving GRT's claim for damages resulting from its minor breach. *See id.* If you terminate the construction contract for only a minor breach, GRT will itself be guilty of the first material breach and will be liable to TRI for damages. *See id.*

A. Breach of Contract

The construction contract plainly requires TRI to use Reading pipe and no other. TRI has admitted that it used Cohoes pipe in approximately half of the plumbing. Therefore, TRI has breached the contract, and it is liable to GRT for foreseeable damages that GRT can prove with reasonable certainty.

B. Materiality of Breach

TRI's breach is material if it is so substantial that it either (1) robs GRT of the primary benefit that it expected from the contract, or (2) demonstrates that the TRI is not competent to perform the work and therefore should not be allowed to continue. *See id.* at 116. Stated conversely, the breach is minor if TRI is competent to complete the contract and GRT can be fully compensated for its losses by an award of money damages that is small in proportion to the value of the entire contract. *See id.*

In this case, TRI's breach probably is not material under either branch of the test of materiality. First, GRT's primary benefit from the plumbing contract presumably is high-quality durable plumbing. Cohoes pipe is equal to Reading pipe in durability and other relevant specifications. The architect apparently required Reading pipe for personal reasons and not because it is superior to Cohoes pipe. Therefore, unless GRT has some special need for Reading pipe, it will get its primary benefit from the contract even though half of the plumbing consists of Cohoes pipe.

Second, although TRI's use of Cohoes pipe shows that Dunlap departed from the architect's plans, we have no evidence that he has failed to follow more important specifications of the plans or that his crews have performed poorly in the actual installation. Dunlap probably knows that Cohoes pipe is equal to Reading pipe, and he may have simply not taken the architect's requirement seriously. Therefore, the events do not suggest that TRI is incompetent to perform Dunlap's promise to complete the installation of plumbing with Reading pipe.

In summary, a court likely would infer that your unhappiness with TRI stems more from your personal dislike for Dunlap than from problems caused by TRI's use of Cohoes pipe. Therefore, a court almost certainly will find that TRI's breach is not material.

C. Remedies

Assuming TRI's breach was only minor, you have no right to fire TRI from the project. Instead, you must permit TRI to complete its performance, and you may demand that it compensate GRT for any damages that result from its minor breach. If you are reasonably certain about the breach and the extent of damages, you may collect the damages yourself by withholding an appropriate amount of payments that GRT otherwise would owe to TRI. *See Johnson,* 345 Calz. 2d at 335. On the other hand, if you wrongfully withhold a substantial portion of TRI's payments above any amount that it owes GRT for breach, GRT may itself be liable for breach. *See id.*

Unfortunately, without further evidence that the choice between Reading pipe and Cohoes pipe will affect the value of your project in any way, you will have difficulty proving any damages. Therefore, we advise you not to withhold any payments owed to TRI.

V. Conclusion

Although TRI has breached its contract with GRT, the breach almost certainly is not material, and it may not have caused any damages. In these circumstances, if you fire TRI from the project, GRT will be liable to TRI for breach of contract. Indeed, even withholding TRI's payments to cover damages caused by its breach is risky, because we have difficulty identifying any such damages.

We recommend that you cooperate with Dunlap to ensure the best possible performance of TRI's remaining duties under the contract. In the meantime, you may want GRT's engineers to determine what damages, if any, the installation of Cohoes pipe has caused. If you find any damages, we will be happy to advise you about the best possible means of demanding compensation from TRI.

Please do not hesitate to call me if you have any questions about this matter. My direct line is 232-3232.

Sincerely,

Marcia Todd
for Todd, Brown & King

II. DEMAND LETTERS

A. PURPOSE, AUDIENCE, TONE, AND WRITING STYLE

With a demand letter, you may seek to achieve any one or more of three purposes. First, you may seek to persuade another party to take or cease some action. For example, you may send a demand letter to your client's tenant in an office building, demanding that it stop entering into unauthorized subleases and that it pay past rent due.

Second, you may seek to revoke a waiver of rights to permit your client to assert those rights in the future. For example, even though your client's lease agreement clearly requires payment of rent on the first of each month, your client may have implicitly waived his right to demand timely payment by frequently accepting late rent payments over the previous year without complaint. If so, you can help your client reassert his rights by sending a demand letter that (1) revokes any implied consent, (2) demands prompt payment of rent strictly according to the contract for the remainder of the lease, and (3) warns of your client's resolve to pursue legal remedies for future breaches of the lease.

Third, you may seek to obtain information or concessions from the opposing party to help your client assert rights in the future. In such a letter, you do not really expect the opposing party to accede to your client's demand; rather, you hope to provoke a reaction that you can use to your client's advantage. For example, suppose that your client orally agreed to purchase goods from a supplier for a total price of $10,000, but the supplier has balked at performing. You know that your client will have trouble enforcing the oral agreement, because the Uniform Commercial Code generally requires such agreements to be evidenced in a writing signed by the party against whom enforcement is sought.[3] You might nonetheless send a letter to the supplier setting forth the terms of the oral agreement and demanding performance pursuant to those terms. In so doing, you may hold out little hope that the supplier will immediately perform as promised; instead, you hope that the supplier will either (1) respond by repeating its decision not to perform but admitting that it entered into the oral agreement or (2) fail to respond within ten days of receiving the letter, thus implicitly adopting your letter's description of the agreement.[4] Either reaction to the demand letter will satisfy the Uniform Commercial Code's requirement that the oral agreement be evidenced by a signed writing, thus enabling your client to assert a contract claim.[5]

The audience for your demand letter is the opposing party, her attorney, or both. Because your purpose is to persuade the other party to take or cease some action or to otherwise modify his relationship to your client, you will advocate your client's position in a demand letter in much the same way that you would advocate her position in a brief to a court. Indeed, you will often adopt an even stronger tone of advocacy in a demand letter than

---

3. U.C.C. §2-201(1) (1990).
4. See U.C.C. §2-201(2) (1990).
5. U.C.C. §2-201(1, 2) (1990).

in a brief, because a self-interested adversary may be more difficult to persuade than a disinterested judge.

Of course, you should adopt a tone that will most likely achieve your goals. Your task is complicated, however, by the multiplicity of audiences and goals. For example, although your primary audience is the opposing party, her attorney, or both, your own client is an important secondary audience. Even if you think that a conciliatory tone will achieve the best results with the opposing party, your client may make it clear that she has hired you to take the strongest possible stance and to intimidate the opposing party. On the other hand, the community as a whole is a possible tertiary audience, because the opposing party may seek to gain public support by airing the dispute in the news media. If your demand letter is excessively strident, adverse public reaction may hinder your client's ability or willingness to assert her claims. Thus, you should adopt a tone that is firm and precise, but not nasty.

Aside from tone, your style should be straightforward, businesslike, and professional. As is true in a brief, the most persuasive style in a demand letter is one that the reader does not notice, one that focuses the reader's attention on your demands, justifications, and threats. Thus, you should write in plain English and avoid legal jargon or florid, distracting prose.

B. FORMAT

You may flexibly adopt any reasonable format that will achieve the goals of your demand letter. At a minimum, your demand letter should include

(1) an introductory sentence or overview paragraph,
(2) a statement of the legal and factual support for your demands, and
(3) a specific statement of the demands and the consequences of the opposing party's failure to satisfy the demands.

You need not divide a simple demand letter into sections; good paragraphing will suffice. If you divide a long or complex demand letter into sections, you should use whatever section headings suit the purposes of your letter.

C. OVERVIEW

Immediately below the address and before the salutation of your demand letter, you should identify the general subject matter of the letter:

Arnold G. Hooper
Maxine C. Hooper
4094 East Laurel Lane
Fairbanks, New Maine 10713

RE: Eastern Savings and Loan Association Loan No. 082168

Dear Mr. and Mrs. Hooper,

In the first paragraph of your demand letter, you should provide any introductory information necessary to orient your reader. If this is your initial correspondence to the addressee, your opening paragraph should identify your representative capacity. Beyond that, the opening paragraph can provide such information as a general description of the relationships of the parties and an overview of your client's demands.

For example, the following, unusually direct opening sentence states the author's representative capacity and captures the reader's attention with a threat:

Dear Mr. and Mrs. Hooper,

Our client, Eastern Savings and Loan Association, has directed us to prepare to foreclose your interest in the above loan. . . .

In contrast, the following opening paragraph in a settlement proposal develops the background and purpose of the letter more deliberately, and it introduces the demand for payment in a more conciliatory fashion:

RE: *Araiza v. Udave*

Mr. Phillips,

I met last Wednesday night with my clients, the plaintiffs in the suit against Max and Josephine Udave. All the plaintiffs are keen to press their claims. Nonetheless, they have agreed to make the following settlement offer: They will withdraw their suit if Max and Josephine Udave pay them a total of $4,500, conditioned on actual payment by noon on October 31, 1988. In light of my following evaluation of the case, I think you will find this offer to be quite reasonable.

D. FACTUAL AND LEGAL BASIS FOR THE DEMANDS

Your explanation of the factual and legal justification for your client's demands may take many forms. In a routine collection letter, you can simply state the amount that is past due under an identified loan agreement or installment contract. In such a demand letter, the opposing party ordinarily will not dispute the general enforceability of such contracts, and you need not discuss the legal principles that make contractual obligations enforceable:

You are now delinquent in the installments due for the months of January and February, 1989. The total amount that you must pay Eastern Savings to bring your loan payments current is $1,103.72. Also, your next payment of $501 will be due on March 5, 1989. Therefore, after March 5, the amount necessary to bring your loan payments current will be $1,604.72.

In other cases, the fact or amount of the opposing party's liability may be more doubtful, prompting you to more thoroughly explain the legal basis for your client's demands. Such an explanation may look very much like the legal analysis and application to facts in a brief. For example, the following passage justifies a demand for consequential damages stemming from a breach of contract:

> In addition, the plaintiffs will be entitled to foreseeable consequential damages stemming from the breach. *Southern Arizona School for Boys, Inc. v. Chery,* 119 Ariz. 277, 280, 580 P.2d 738, 741 (1978). Those will include the plaintiffs' expenditures on specialized accessories that were suitable only for the wedding and that some plaintiffs were unable to use. *See A.R.A. Manufacturing Co. v. Pierce,* 86 Ariz. 136, 341 P.2d 928, 932 (1959) (victim of breach entitled to award of damages for wasted promotional expenditures). Those members of the wedding party who could not fully participate in the wedding, the sole event for which the specialized gowns were ordered, can also recover damages for that lost opportunity. *See, e.g., Mieske v. Bartell Drug Co.,* 593 P.2d 1308 (Wash. 1979) (in UCC case, upholding award of $7,500 for emotional value associated with contracting parties' loss of home movies of significant events). Indeed, the opportunity to participate in the wedding formed the basis for the contracts for the gowns.
>
> All of these losses are itemized in Count I of the complaint. They total approximately $9,000. Because the plaintiffs will certainly prove a breach of contract and will establish at least some of their alleged damages, they will also be entitled to an award of attorney's fees, which could add thousands more to the total recovery.

The appropriate level of formality of your legal analysis will depend on the sophistication of your audience. If you address your demand letter to the opposing party's attorney, or if you are certain that the opposing party will consult an attorney, you can reasonably cite to legal authority, as in the immediately preceding example. On the other hand, if the opposing party does not have legal training, and if you can appropriately address your letter directly to that party, then you should express your arguments in terms that the party can understand. If you try to intimidate the opposing party with formal citations to authority, you might simply confuse or antagonize rather than persuade.

For example, the following excerpt of a demand letter to an insurance company's subrogation analyst assumes that the analyst has a sophisticated knowledge of business practices but has no formal legal training. The excerpt refers to three legal concepts: waiver, offer, and the "mailbox rule" governing the timing of acceptance. The author of the letter has tried to use these concepts in a persuasive manner without diverting the reader's attention to distracting citations:

> Even if Mr. Upton's premium had arrived after expiration of the grace period, his rights were preserved in the conversation between him and Diane Campbell, assistant to Dee Boston, on March 12. In that

conversation, Ms. Campbell notified Mr. Upton that his claim would be covered but that she would delay processing his claim until he paid his late premium. Mr. Upton stated over the phone that he would mail his premium. In effect, Ms. Campbell waived any condition to coverage that would require Mr. Upton to deliver the premium to her within the grace period. She thus made the date of her receipt of the premium relevant only to the matter of processing his claim. At worst, Ms. Campbell may have communicated a new offer of coverage that invited Mr. Upton's return promise to pay the premium. If so, Mr. Upton accepted the offer either over the phone or under the "mailbox rule" when he placed his premium in the mailbox.

A demand letter is not the proper place to make concessions or admissions that may come back to haunt you later. Therefore, if you choose to adopt a conciliatory tone, do so in a way that does not preclude you from taking a stronger position in the future. For example, suppose that your client demands compensation on the basis of a strong contract claim and a weak tort claim. To maintain credibility and to avoid antagonizing the opposing party, you might invoke only the contract claim to justify your client's demands in a demand letter. If so, you should remain silent about the weaker tort claim or refer to it only vaguely. If you affirmatively concede the weakness of that claim in writing, you may hinder your ability to pursue it later if newly discovered facts enhance its potential merit.

You should also avoid ambiguous conciliatory language that might grant unintended rights to the opposing party. For example, in a letter demanding payment of amounts past due on a loan agreement, you should exercise caution before inviting the opposing party to apply to your client for an extension of the loan. If you state the invitation in a way that raises reasonable expectations in the opposing party of receiving the extension, you may obligate your client to grant such an extension.

E. DEMANDS AND THREATS

You should not send a demand letter unless your client has a well-defined goal that you can formulate into a straightforward demand to the opposing party. Moreover, to maximize the chances of achieving that goal, you must provide the opposing party with an incentive to satisfy your client's demand. If the opposing party is fair-minded and your demand is just, your persuasive presentation of the legal and factual bases for the demand may help induce him to accede to the demand. In most cases, however, you can provide the greatest incentive to the opposing party by threatening to take actions that would be less pleasant for the opposing party than acceding to the demand.

Thus, you must clearly state both your client's demand and the actions your client will take if the opposing party rejects the demand. To ensure prompt action, you should set a specific date by which the opposing party must satisfy your client's demand or suffer the adverse consequences of the threatened action. If the relief to which your client is entitled is uncertain, your objective may simply be to initiate settlement negotiations. More specifically, you may desire to induce your opponent to advance the first settlement offer, which might reveal something about her evaluation of the case or her client's interests. If so, your demand letter might state the maximum possible liability and threaten formal action unless the opposing party takes action to reach a settlement.

In other cases, your client may seek payment of a certain sum of money. For example, if your client is demanding the payment of amounts past due on a loan or an installment contract, you should

(1) state the precise payment that your client demands;
(2) set a date by which the opposing party must deliver the payment to a particular address; and
(3) depending on the circumstances, threaten to foreclose on secured property, to sue on the contract, or to take other appropriate legal action if the demand is not satisfied.

The following excerpt from a loan collection letter illustrates the clarity, specificity, and directness for which you should strive:

. . . Therefore, after March 5, the amount necessary to bring your loan payments current will be $1,604.72.

If you desire to avoid legal proceedings, you must submit the above sum on or before March 17, 1989, in cash, cashier's check, or certified funds made payable to Eastern Savings and Loan Association. You must mail or deliver the payment directly to:

Eastern Savings and Loan Association
Suite 11000, Financial Plaza
1901 South Alma School Road
Fairbanks, New Maine 10701
Attention: Kathy Growl

Take notice that time is of the essence. . . .

If Eastern Savings has not received the above amount on or before March 17, 1989, it will accelerate the principal balance of the loan and will immediately commence foreclosure proceedings. These proceedings could result in a sale of the property securing the loan. . . .

You should ensure that your letter satisfies any applicable statutory prerequisites to making the demand, such as requirements that the demand be made in a certain form or that it contain certain information:

Pursuant to the terms of the deed of trust, you have the right to challenge any such acceleration or to assert the absence of a default or any other defense in court. Under the laws of New Maine, however, a court will presume the debt to be valid unless you dispute the validity of the indebtedness, or any portion of it, within 30 days of your receipt of this notice.

Also, to avoid any dispute about the opposing party's receipt of your demand letter, you should always send the demand letter by registered mail. Finally, to preserve your credibility in future correspondence, you must confirm that your client is willing and able to back up its threats with action.

======== E X E R C I S E   1 8 - 2 ========

1. *Collection Letter*

Study the following collection letter and explain the purpose or purposes of each paragraph.

> Scott L. Short
> Stanley, Leeds & Cardon
> 100 W. Central Ave., Suite 2100
> Fairbanks, New Maine 10701
> February 15, 1989

CERTIFIED MAIL
RETURN RECEIPT REQUESTED

Arnold G. Hooper
Maxine C. Hooper
4094 East Laurel Lane
Fairbanks, New Maine 10713

RE: Eastern Savings and Loan Association Loan No. 082168.

Dear Mr. and Mrs. Hooper,

Our client, Eastern Savings and Loan Association, has directed us to prepare to foreclose your interest in the above loan. You are now delinquent in the installments due for the months of January and February 1989. The total amount that you must pay Eastern Savings to bring your loan payments current is $1,103.72. Also, your next payment of $501 will be due on March 5, 1989. Therefore, after March 5, the amount necessary to bring your loan payments current will be $1,604.72.

If you desire to avoid legal proceedings, you must submit the above sum on or before March 17, 1989, in cash, cashier's check, or certified funds made payable to Eastern Savings and Loan Association. You must mail or deliver the payment directly to:

> Eastern Savings and Loan Association
> Suite 11000, Financial Plaza
> 1901 South Alma School Road
> Fairbanks, New Maine 10701
> Attention: Kathy Growl

Take notice that time is of the essence on this matter. Eastern Savings will strictly adhere to the above deadline and future due dates despite any past acceptance of late or partial installment payments, any prior reinstatement, any prior negotiations, or any other actual or implied forbearance of any nature by Eastern Savings.

If Eastern Savings has not received the above amount on or before March 17, 1989, it will accelerate the principal balance of the loan and will immediately commence foreclosure proceedings. These proceedings could result in a sale of the property securing the loan.

Pursuant to the terms of the deed of trust, you have the right to challenge any such acceleration or to assert the absence of a default or any other defense in court. Under the laws of New Maine, however, a court will presume the debt to be valid unless you dispute the validity of the indebtedness, or any portion of it, within 30 days of your receipt of this notice.

Very truly yours,

Scott L. Short
Stanley, Leeds & Cardon

2. The Bad Example

Study the following collection letter and explain why it is less effective than the letter in Exercise 1 above. Identify and describe each defect.

Green and Gain
120 West Washington
Phoenix, AZ 85003
April 4, 1989

Mr. and Mrs. Joe Smith
5555 North 55th Street
Phoenix, AZ 85055

RE: Delinquent Loan #9-1403726-841

Dear Borrower:

We are counsel of record for the Bank of Phoenix (hereinafter referred to as the Bank). Our client has informed us that you are behind in your loan payments, and has asked that we write you on its behalf to request that you take some action to bring your loans current. We understand that you presently are approximately $2,500.00 behind in your payments.

Over the past several months, the few loan payments you have actually made have been consistently late. While the Bank was happy to take whatever it could get from you, it would prefer that you try to make payments on time. If you are having difficulty making your payments, the Bank would be happy to consider and, if reasonable, would agree to an extension of your loan, a modification of its terms, or the extension of additional monies to see you through whatever difficulties you may be experiencing. If you desire to pursue this offer, please call your loan officer or some other authorized representative of the Bank.

Please be advised, however, that the Bank has no intention of waiting forever for you to make good on your commitments. Frankly, in our experience the Bank has very little patience with deadbeat borrowers such as you appear to be. The Bank has ruined the credit of thousands of borrowers who, like you, did not take their obligations seriously. Hundreds more have been forced into bankruptcy. Moreover, the Bank is a large, powerful institution which can afford to hire big law firms such as this one, against which the average debtor has little chance of prevailing. We sincerely hope that you will take the hint and pay up.

The Bank therefore suggests that you make arrangements to bring the aforementioned loan current by paying the amount hereinbefore stated or making such other arrangements as you and said Bank may subsequently agree upon.

Sincerely,

Bob Jenkins
Green & Gain

3. Settlement Letter

a. The settlement letter below was written several months after suit was filed and shortly before a scheduled arbitration hearing. Explain the purpose or purposes of each paragraph. Precisely what does the letter demand? What action does the author of the letter threaten to take if the demand is not met?

b. The letter below is addressed to the opposing party's attorney in response to preliminary settlement discussions. Rewrite the letter so that it is appropriate for a client who has no legal training or knowledge. Summarize your analysis without citing to specific authority.

Charles Rehnquist, Esq.
333 S. Central Ave.
Phoenix, Arizona 85001
(602) 849-0101
September 6, 1988

Robert M. Phillips, Esq.
Kim, Phillips, Burley & Stewart
3301 E. Bethany Home Road, Suite B-111
Phoenix, Arizona 85012

RE: *Araiza v. Udave*

Mr. Phillips,

I met last Wednesday night with my clients, the plaintiffs in the suit against Max and Josephine Udave. All the plaintiffs are anxious to press their claims. Nonetheless, they have agreed to make the following settlement offer: They will withdraw their suit if Max and Josephine Udave pay them a total of $4,500, conditioned upon payment by noon on October 31, 1988. In light of my following evaluation of the case, I think you will find this offer to be quite reasonable.

I have no doubts about our ability to prove the claim for breach of contract. Indeed, your early correspondence and the defendants' answers to the complaint and interrogatories admit that Josephine failed to perform as promised. Even if she had acted in good faith and with best efforts, that would be no excuse for breach of the contract. Therefore, the defendants have essentially admitted to their breach of contract. The direct loss in value is easily computed: the difference between the value of each gown as promised ($550-$600 by your own correspondence) minus the value of the dress as delivered (we can prove that some are total losses).

In addition, the plaintiffs will be entitled to foreseeable consequential damages stemming from the breach. *Southern Arizona School for Boys, Inc. v. Chery,* 119 Ariz. 277, 280, 580 P.2d 738, 741 (1978). Those will include the plaintiffs' expenditures on specialized accessories that were suitable only for the wedding and that some plaintiffs were unable to use. *See A.R.A. Manufacturing Co. v. Pierce,* 86 Ariz. 136, 142, 341 P.2d 928, 932 (1959) (victim of breach entitled to award of damages for wasted promotional expenditures). Those members of the wedding party who could not fully participate in the wedding, the sole event for which the specialized gowns were ordered, can also recover damages for that lost opportunity. *See, e.g., Mieske v. Bartell Drug Co.,* 593 P.2d 1308 (Wash. 1979) (in UCC case, upholding award of $7,500 for emotional value associated with contracting parties' loss of home movies of significant events). Indeed, the opportunity to participate in the wedding formed the basis for the contracts for the gowns.

All of these losses are itemized in Count I of the complaint. They total approximately $9,000. Because the plaintiffs will certainly prove a breach of contract and will establish at least some of their alleged damages, they will also be entitled to an award of attorney's fees, which could add thousands more to the total recovery.

Josephine's own theory of the case is that she breached the contract because she lost the ruffles. Coupled with her failure to warn the plaintiffs to obtain gowns from an alternative source, those facts should easily support the negligence claim in Count II. That claim provides even stronger support than Count I for an award of general compensatory damages, including damages for emotional distress.

Also solid are the claims for promissory fraud and consumer fraud in Counts III and VI. The consumer fraud statute prohibits use of deception, fraud, false promises, or suppression of material fact with intent that others rely, in connection with the sale of any merchandise. A.R.S. §44-1522. "Merchandise" includes services. A.R.S. §44-1521(5). Like the common law tort of promissory fraud, a claim under the consumer fraud statute will support an award of punitive damages. *Schmidt v. American Leasco,* 139 Ariz. 509, 512, 679 P.2d 532, 535 (Ct. App. 1983). We should have little trouble proving a claim under either theory: The plaintiffs will offer abundant and vivid testimony describing the way in which Max and Josephine deliberately misrepresented that many of the gowns would be ready on time, thus inducing many of the plaintiffs to wait until the last minute and beyond, when in fact Max and Josephine knew that the gowns could not possibly be completed on time. In light of the "evil minds" associated with such actions, these claims potentially could add thousands of dollars in punitive damages to the compensatory damages detailed in Count I.

In sum, the plaintiffs are angry and confident. They are anxious to go to an arbitration hearing, and they are ready to enforce their judgment by attaching the Udaves' property. Indeed, I experienced some difficulty getting them to agree to propose this settlement offer. I can assure you that it is not a bargaining posture; it represents their current bottom line. Despite their passionate views on this matter, however, they have compromised their full claims substantially. The $4,500 figure represents 50% of the compensatory damages for Count I, without costs or attorney's fees, and without any punitive damages.

This offer remains open until noon, September 22. Please call or write to me before then if your clients wish to settle.

Sincerely,

Charles Rehnquist, Esq.

4. *Response to Demand Letter: Demand for Withdrawal of Claim*

The following letter responds to a demand letter from an attorney for Framer Insurance Co. addressed to Michael Upton. Mr. Upton caused an automobile accident, resulting in injuries to Eileen Bradley, who was insured by Framer. Framer paid Ms. Bradley's claim for $10,000 in losses and medical expenses arising out of the accident. Framer then demanded that Mr. Upton reimburse Framer for Framer's payment to Ms. Bradley. Mr. Upton, however, claimed that he had liability insurance from Framer and that Framer thus was obligated to assume the cost of his liability to Ms. Bradley. The primary matter of dispute between Framer and Mr. Upton was whether Mr. Upton had validly renewed his insurance contract with Framer despite Framer's assertion that it received his late premium payment only after expiration of the policy's grace period.

a. Although it responds to a demand letter, the letter below is itself a demand letter, albeit a subtle one. What does it demand? What action does it implicitly threaten if the demand is not met? Should the author have stated the demand and threat more strongly?

b. Who is the audience for this letter? Assuming that Marilyn Branscomb is not a lawyer, would she likely consult with Framer's attorney, Jon Drake, before deciding whether to drop Framer's claim against Mr. Upton? If so, should the author have advanced a more formal legal analysis with citation to authority?

> Charles Rehnquist, Esq.
> 333 S. Central Ave.
> Phoenix, Arizona 85001
> (602) 849-0101
> December 1, 1987

Marilyn Branscomb
Subrogation Analyst for Framer Insurance
P.O. Box 3108
Mesa, Calzona 89211

Policy No. 881347 94

Dear Ms. Branscomb,

I represent Michael Upton in his claim for coverage under the above policy. I write in response to Jon C. Drake's letter dated October 30 to Michael Upton, in which Mr. Drake requests Mr. Upton to indemnify Framer for Framer's payment of claims to Eileen Bradley. I address this letter to you because Mr. Drake directed Mr. Upton to contact you. I'm sure that everyone hopes to resolve this matter before either party must incur the enormous legal expenses associated with litigation.

Mr. Upton is unwilling to pay the claim for two reasons. First, he claims liability coverage under his policy and thus expects Framer to satisfy Ms. Bradley's claims. Second, he challenges the damages claimed by Ms. Bradley.

The confusion about the possible lapse of Mr. Upton's insurance coverage stems from his not receiving Framer's bill or notice of grace period, apparently because of his change of address. Although I haven't seen a copy of the policy, I assume that it requires actual receipt of a late premium before expiration of the grace period. Even so, Mr. Upton suspects that the post office in fact delivered his premium within the three days remaining in the grace period, and he doubts Framer's claim that it received the premium a full week after it was posted two miles away. A jury would have the same doubts. Once Mr. Upton proves to a jury with his testimony and that of a witness that he posted the letter three days before expiration of the grace period, Framer would be hard pressed to prove that the letter took longer than the standard one to three days for delivery.

Mr. Upton is confident of his ability to prove his version of events before a jury, particularly in light of his previously communicated willingness to submit to a lie detector test. Of course, if litigation or other inquiry reveals that anyone within the Framer organization sought in bad faith to deny Mr. Upton coverage by covering up the facts, the resulting issues would transcend the relatively small dispute now before us. Thus, you should consider the possibility of a counterclaim to any claim that Framer might consider pursuing against Mr. Upton.

Even if Mr. Upton were not covered under this policy, it is highly unlikely that he would be liable for the full amount of Ms. Bradley's claim. Initially complaining of an injury to her finger, Ms. Bradley used the occasion of the accident to take advantage of chiropractic treatment, including vibratory massage, that required time away from work. As a matter of common knowledge, the chiropractic profession holds that countless persons suffer routinely from physical stresses that can be alleviated through chiropractic therapy as a supplement to other medical care. Mr. Upton thus suspects that Ms. Bradley's medical bills and time off from work represent an extravagant reaction to the accident. The medical bills and report do not conclusively resolve the question whether the chiropractic therapy was used to treat conditions suffered by Ms. Bradley that preexisted the accident. Nor do they resolve doubts about how much, if any, of the chiropractic care and resulting lost wages were reasonably necessary to treat any injuries that did stem from the March 12 accident. Thus, Framer acted unreasonably in paying Ms. Bradley's claim in full. Mr. Upton should not have to reimburse Framer for anything more than Ms. Bradley's actual damages.

In sum, even if Mr. Upton were not covered, he would not be inclined to indemnify Framer for anything but a small fraction of Ms. Bradley's extravagant bills. More than that, Mr. Upton is prepared to prove that he owes Framer nothing because Framer had a contractual duty to provide him insurance coverage for his liability to Ms. Bradley stemming from the March 12 accident.

If Framer drops its claim, Mr. Upton will be happy to cease any further inquiry into possible claims he might have against Framer based on bad faith or other misconduct that Framer may have engaged in. Please contact me by January 15, 1988, with your response.

Sincerely,

Charles Rehnquist, Esq.

cc Jon C. Drake

III. SUMMARY

In an advice or demand letter, you should

(1) use plain English whenever possible, and
(2) adapt your format and depth of legal analysis to your audience and your purpose.

In an advice letter, you should

(1) restate the questions that your client has posed to you and identify the legal issues that they encompass,
(2) briefly answer the issues,
(3) state the facts on which your analysis and advice are premised,
(4) discuss the law and apply the law to the facts to reach a conclusion for each issue, and
(5) summarize your subsidiary conclusions and state your advice.

In a demand letter, you should

(1) use an introductory sentence or paragraph to identify your representative capacity, provide an overview of the purpose of your letter, or orient the reader in some other fashion,
(2) state the legal and factual bases for your demand, and
(3) state your demands, including the time and place for satisfaction of the demands, and threaten to take action if the demands are not met.

APPENDICES

In a legal method and writing course, you can best master a challenging writing assignment by preparing for and accomplishing your task in at least three separate steps. First, you should acquire information about the topic of your assignment by reading assigned portions of a descriptive text, such as the main text of *Legal Method and Writing,* and by attending classes in which an instructor lectures and leads class discussion. Second, you must become an active participant in the educational process by analyzing assigned problems and preparing legal documents, such as case briefs, office memoranda, and briefs. Third, you should welcome constructive criticism from instructors or peers, and you should thoughtfully react to their editorial comments by deciding which have merit and by revising your draft accordingly.

Along with the exercises in the main text, the Appendices provide you with the problems and other materials you need for the second step of the educational process—your active participation in research, analysis, and writing. The exercises in the main text are suitable for class discussion or for in-class writing exercises. They include policy questions, invitations to critique sample documents, an essay examination, and composition problems.

The Appendices include "problems" that are similar to the "exercises" in the main text: They provide further opportunities to think about and discuss fundamental questions of legal method and writing. Although an instructor could make these problems the subjects of formal writing assignments, they are primarily designed for individual review or for class discussion.

The "assignments" in the Appendices on the other hand, are take-home assignments requiring formal written documents. They ask you to analyze a problem and draft a document such as an office memorandum or a pretrial brief. Many of the assignments requiring formal documents provide all necessary materials and require no supplementary research. Others, particularly the more complex ones, provide you with little or no authority and require you to perform all necessary research in the library.

The assignments that require research will inspire different analyses depending upon when you perform them and what authorities have been issued at that time. For example, statutes or judicial decisions issued after the publication of this book might radically alter the nature of the issues originally intended to be raised. Similarly, one of the office memorandum assignments is set in the state in which your law school is located. Because your analysis of the problem in that assignment will depend upon the law of your particular state, the assignment may be more interesting in some law schools than in others. For all these reasons, your instructor may perform some "fine tuning" of some of the assignments by modifying the facts or otherwise adjusting the problems to avoid unintended difficulties raised by intervening laws or the laws of a particular state.

Introduction to Legal Method: Problems for Part I of the Main Text

Analyze Problem 1 below after you have completed your study of Chapter 2 and Chapter 3, Section II of the main text. Analyze Problems 2-4 after you have studied Chapters 2-4 of the main text.

Problem 1. Sources and Limits of Lawmaking Powers

Examine each government action described in the sections below. Which represents a legitimate exercise of legislative, judicial, or executive authority?

a. The Flag-Bashing Bill

The first amendment to the United States Constitution provides in part that "Congress shall make no law . . . abridging the freedom of speech, or of the press." Shortly before July 4, however, Congress sought to override the first amendment by restricting speech critical of the American flag. Offended by a wave of public criticism of the American flag and the values for which it stands, Congress enacted the "Flag-Bashing Bill," which the President signed into law. Section 1 of that statute makes it an "unlawful publication practice for any person to publish any oral or written statement critical of the flag of the United States of America." Section 2 provides for fines of up to $5,000 for each violation of the statute.

Section 3 of the statute created the Flag Protection Commission (FPC), a federal agency, and granted it powers to investigate violations of the statute, to hold hearings on alleged violations, to impose fines for violations, and to issue rules and regulations to aid in its investigative and enforcement activities. Section 4 of the statute grants jurisdiction to the United States

Courts of Appeals to review the FPC's actions, subject to further appeal to the United States Supreme Court.

b. The FPC Flexes Its Muscle

As the chief officer of the executive branch of the United States government, the President appointed several staunch flag enthusiasts to the FPC. Without delay, the FPC issued rules and regulations that, among other things, (1) describe procedures for FPC hearings, (2) authorize FPC hearing officers to impose fines of $1,000 to $10,000 for various kinds of violations of the Flag-Bashing Bill, and (3) define the statutory phrase "unlawful publication practice" to include any public criticism of the flag or the President's wardrobe.

c. Judicial Review

In the FPC's first major hearing, an FPC hearing officer found that a Washington, D.C., newspaper publisher had violated the Flag-Bashing Bill by publishing a critical commentary entitled "The Stars and Stripes—Do the Colors Clash?" The hearing officer fined the publisher $2,000. The publisher appealed to the United States Court of Appeals for the District of Columbia Circuit.

On appeal, the Court of Appeals overturned the hearing officer's decision. Contrary to the plain language, legislative history, and clear purpose of the Flag-Bashing Bill, the court found that the bill prohibited only oral criticism of the President's foreign trade policies.

The FPC appealed to the United States Supreme Court. The Supreme Court upheld the Court of Appeals' overturning of the hearing officer's decision, but on different grounds. The Supreme Court concluded that (1) the FPC had validly issued the rules and regulations upon which the hearing officer had relied in this case, and (2) the hearing officer's findings and imposition of a fine were consistent with a proper interpretation of the Flag-Bashing Bill. However, the Court held that the statute was unenforceable because it violated the first amendment to the United States Constitution.

Problem 2. Developing the Common Law and Interpreting Statutes That Modify the Common Law

In each of the sections below, fully explain the reasons for your conclusions. Express each step of your analysis.

a. Survival of the Fittest and the Common Law

Imagine that you are deciding cases in the nineteenth century as the Chief Justice of a state's highest appellate court. Your state has no criminal statutes; instead, the criminal law of the state is exclusively common law.

Before you is an appeal from a murder conviction in the case of *State v. Blight*. After a full trial, the jury found that Fletcher Blight, the defendant and appellant, had killed Davie Jones by pushing him off a life raft and into the ocean.

The trial record shows that both men boarded the life raft after their sailing vessel had sunk on the high seas. After days of drifting, and with no ship or land on the horizon, it became apparent that the water rations would not sustain both men until a rescue ship arrived. Blight, the stronger of the two, decided to (1) save the remaining water supply for himself; (2) stop administering water to Jones, who was too weak to move; and (3) allow Jones to die. Jones suffered great pain as he slowly died of dehydration. To end Jones's misery and to spare himself the pain of watching Jones suffer, Blight tearfully pushed the helpless Jones into the sea, where Jones quickly died. When Blight was rescued by a passing ship a few days later, he was near death himself. Physicians testified at trial that, if Blight had continued sharing the water rations with Jones until the water was exhausted, both men undoubtedly would have died before the rescue ship arrived.

In your state, the courts have defined the common law crime of murder as the "unlawful killing of a human being without justification." At the time of Blight's appeal, your court has recognized only one justification for killing another person: self-defense in the face of a potentially deadly attack from the other person. On appeal, Blight asks your court to expand the common law justifications to cover the circumstances of his case.

Precisely what new common law rule or rules would justify Blight's deeds? Draft Blight's proposed rule or rules in the form of a trial court's instructions to the jury: "You must acquit the defendant of the charge of murder if he was justified in killing Jones. In this case, the defendant was justified in killing Jones if you find that . . ."

As Chief Justice of the appellate court, would you recognize the proposed rule? What reasons would you give for supporting or opposing an extension of the common law doctrine of justification that would result in Blight's acquittal?

Would you support a new common law rule that would not necessarily result in acquittal for Blight? Describe the rule and explain your reasons for proposing it.

b. The Justification of Self-Preservation

Assume that your court responded to *State v. Blight* by adopting the following common law rule and by remanding to the trial court for a new trial with jury instructions consistent with the new rule:

> A defendant is justified in killing another human being if the defendant is reasonably certain at the time of the killing that the killing is necessary to preserve his own life and that failure to kill the other will result in the death of both.

Do you support the rule? Apply this rule to the facts of *State v. Blight*. Should the jury acquit if instructed to apply this rule? Explain your answer in detail.

c. Mercy Killing and the Criminal Code

One hundred years after *State v. Blight,* your state has largely replaced the common law crimes with a comprehensive criminal code: a collection of statutes that defines criminal conduct and penalties, incorporating some common law principles and modifying or rejecting others. Section 101 of the criminal code defines the crime of murder as "the killing of another human being without justification." Section 101.A provides that "premeditated murder" constitutes first-degree murder, which carries a maximum penalty of life in prison. Section 101.G, enacted just last year, provides that "a desire to ease the suffering of a terminally ill person is not justification for ending the person's life prematurely." A state legislative committee report explained the purpose of the bill that later was codified as §101.G:

> This bill makes it clear that euthanasia, popularly known as "mercy-killing," is not "justified" under §101 of our criminal code and therefore is not excluded from our definition of murder. With this bill, the state declares its policies to promote the use of life-sustaining measures and to preserve the life of even a terminally ill patient for as long as possible, in the hope that a cure for the illness may be found before the patient dies. The physical and emotional suffering of terminally ill patients should be relieved through counseling and the prescription of pain-relieving drugs rather than the termination of life-sustaining medical equipment or treatment. Thus, even well-meaning friends or relatives who "pull the plug" on a terminally ill patient may be charged under our murder statute.

(1) *Blight* Revisited

Review Sections a and b above. If facts identical to those of *State v. Blight* were presented to a jury today, should the jury convict the defendant of first-degree murder under the criminal code? How should the trial judge instruct the jury? If the state appellate courts have not yet interpreted §101's reference to "justification," should the trial judge attempt to define that term for the jury? On what would it base its definition? Suppose that Blight has argued that the trial judge should not instruct the jury according to §101.G, on the ground that §101.G does not apply to his case. How should the trial court rule and why?

(2) The Pact

Emma Padilla was losing her battle against cancer. Although she continued to receive chemotherapy, it made her quite ill and offered her almost no hope of remission. Preferring to live her final days in familiar surroundings, she arranged for full-time nursing care in her home. She often spoke to her nurses about her desire to die and about her wish that no one prolong her life with heroic lifesaving measures.

One evening, Padilla suffered a seizure; her heart stopped beating, and she ceased breathing. Her night nurse, Jim Murrow, rushed to Padilla's side to administer cardiopulmonary resuscitation and to hook up a portable respirator and other lifesaving equipment. He stopped short, however, remembering Padilla's wish to die naturally. Murrow allowed Padilla to die, notified the hospital that had been treating Padilla with chemotherapy, and admitted to several colleagues that he had honored Padilla's wishes that he refrain from prolonging her life.

Is Murrow guilty of murder under §§101 and 101.G of the criminal code? Fully analyze the law and the facts, taking care to advance arguments for both the defense and the prosecution.

Problem 3. Analogy, Distinction, and Precedent

Read the materials for Office Memorandum Assignment 1 in Appendix IV. The only two Arizona cases provided in the materials, *Henderson* and *Fogleman,* deny any award of damages for emotional distress. The only case in your materials that approves of such an award for breach of contract is *Browning,* an early decision from another jurisdiction. Fully explain how you could distinguish the facts of *Henderson* and *Fogleman* from Araiza's case, and explain how you could analogize the facts of her case to those of *Browning.*

Problem 4. Economic Analysis

Read the following problem and use it to construct an economic rationale for a general rule disallowing punitive damages for even intentional breaches of commercial contracts. If a policy supports application of a general rule in most cases, should courts apply the rule without exception to promote certainty in the law, or should they recognize exceptions to the general rule to reach a fair result in exceptional cases? Consider the ethical problems, if any, of advising a client to intentionally breach a clearly binding contract.

Problem

Uptown, Inc., is a chain of department stores. It owns the Uptown Mega Mall, a sprawling shopping mall in Bonneville. An Uptown department store is the anchor store at the shopping mall, attracting shoppers to dozens of other retail outlets at the mall. The mall employs 400 Bonneville residents. Brisk business at the Uptown Mega Mall put pressure on the store's ground-level parking lot during peak hours. In January, the Board of Directors of Uptown committed funds to construct a three-level underground parking facility at the Bonneville store. On January 25, Uptown contracted with the largest excavator in Bonneville, Pierce Excavation Co., to excavate the site for the new parking facility. In the written contract, Pierce Excavation Co. promised to begin excavation on July 1 and to complete the work by August 15, and Uptown promised to pay Pierce Excavation Co. $100,000. John Pierce, owner of Pierce Excavation Co., estimated that he would earn about $15,000 profit from the project and that it would use about half the capacity of his firm; he did not have any other offers for work beyond the last week of May.

On June 10, the City Council of Bonneville unexpectedly broke a year-long deadlock and approved the plans of a developer, Lynn Mullins, to construct an enormous and lavish convention center near the Bonneville airport. Once completed, the convention center will employ 800 Bonneville residents and contribute millions of dollars annually to the Bonneville economy. Pierce Construction Co. is the only excavator in Bonneville with sufficient equipment to efficiently excavate the convention center site. Anxious to begin construction of the long-delayed project, Mullins offered to pay Pierce Construction Co. $240,000 to perform excavation and other earth moving at the convention center site if Pierce agreed to begin work immediately and complete work sometime in August. Pierce estimated that he would earn $60,000 profit from the project and that it would use the full capacity of his firm for approximately eight weeks beginning in mid-June.

On June 11, John Pierce met with officers of Uptown and discussed the possibility of modifying their contract to delay excavation until mid-August. The Uptown officers refused to modify the contract; a six-week delay in excavation would extend the construction period into the holiday shopping season, disrupting even the existing ground-level parking. Another Bonneville excavator was available to perform the Uptown work in July, either as an independent contractor or as a subcontractor to Pierce Construction Co. However, in light of market conditions caused by the approval of the convention center plans, the substitute excavator insisted on a price of $120,000 for the Uptown project. Moreover, even if the substitute excavator acted nominally as Pierce's subcontractor, Pierce would not have the capacity during the month of July to supervise the Uptown project full time. Uptown had hired Pierce Construction Co. partly for its reputation for high quality work, and it was reluctant to replace it with a substitute. Uptown represented that it would suffer $30,000 in damages if it were forced to hire a substitute excavator or delay excavation until mid-August.

On June 12, John Pierce met with his attorney, Patricia Ruiz, to discuss his options. Ruiz advised Pierce to repudiate the Uptown contract, accept Mullins's offer, and pay the consequences of his breach of the Uptown contract. Ruiz knew that Pierce would not be liable for punitive damages, and she was confident that she could negotiate a reasonable settlement of Uptown's claim. What terms should Pierce authorize Ruiz to accept in settlement negotiations?

Case Briefs:
Assignments for Chapter 6
of the Main Text

Assignment 1. Case Brief with Synthesis

Exercise 6-1(1, 2) in Chapter 6 of the main text includes excerpts and a sample case brief of *White v. Benkowski*. Review those materials now. Then read the following excerpt from the appellate opinion in *McKibben v. Mohawk Oil Co., Ltd.*, and prepare a case brief for a contracts class that includes a synthesis of this case with *White v. Benkowski*.

McKIBBEN v. MOHAWK OIL COMPANY, LTD.
Supreme Court of Alaska
667 P.2d 1223 (1983)

BURKE, Chief Justice.

Plaintiffs Harley McKibben, Adolph Vetter, and Roudolph Vetter are the owners of the Christina mining claim located near Fairbanks. On December 2, 1977, plaintiffs entered into a mining lease agreement with Joseph Taylor and Paul Rice, giving Taylor and Rice the right to mine the land in a workmanlike manner until March 15, 1978. The lease also provided that the plaintiffs would receive forty-five percent of the value of all ores and minerals mined and extracted from the claims after deducting smelting and refining costs. Taylor and Rice would bear the entire costs of mining and milling the ore.

Taylor and Rice assigned their interest in the lease to Tri-Con Mining, Inc. [Tri-Con] with plaintiffs' consent. Plaintiffs and Tri-Con entered into an addendum of the lease, which provided that whenever the lessee's ore shipments had a specified low assayed value, plaintiffs' royalty interest would be reduced to ten percent. Soon after Tri-Con began mining the Christina claim, Tri-Con entered into a joint venture with Mohawk Oil and Gas, Inc. [Mohawk Inc.], a wholly owned subsidiary of Mohawk Oil Company, Ltd. [Mohawk Ltd.]. With only two weeks remaining in the term of the lease, Tri-Con and Mohawk Inc. engaged in a bulk mining program during which some 12,000 to 15,000 tons of ore were mined from the property and shipped to the nearby Fox Mill. Tri-Con and Mohawk Inc. processed and milled approximately 6,000 tons of the stockpiled ore. The percentage recovery of precious metals from the ore was extremely low. . . .

On March 21, 1980, plaintiffs filed a complaint against Tri-Con, Mohawk Ltd., and Mohawk Inc. First and second amended complaints were filed on September 18, 1980. As amended, the complaint alleges that defendants breached the lease; committed waste and conversion; engaged in unworkmanlike mining; and intentionally diluted the ore. Plaintiffs also requested punitive damages for the "purposeful and outrageous conduct" committed by defendants.

Defendants subsequently moved for partial summary judgment to dismiss plaintiffs' claims for intentional dilution, unworkmanlike mining, punitive damages, and waste. . . . [T]he superior court . . . denied defendants' motion to dismiss plaintiffs' claims for waste, intentional dilution, and unworkmanlike mining, but dismissed plaintiffs' punitive damages claim. . . .

VII. PUNITIVE DAMAGES

In their complaint, plaintiffs requested punitive damages for the defendants' purposeful and outrageous conduct, which apparently consisted of intentionally diluting the ore. Defendants moved for summary judgment on the punitive damages claim on the ground that punitive damages are not available in Alaska for a breach of contract. The motion was granted by the superior court.

In *Lull v. Wick Construction Co.*, 614 P.2d 321, 325-326 (Alaska 1980), we stated that it was an open question whether punitive damages may be awarded in a contract action, and noted that some states permit punitive damages when the breach is maliciously or grossly reckless or when the conduct associated with the breach also constitutes an independent tort. We refused to decide the issue in *Lull* because the breach in that case was neither malicious nor tortious in character. *Lull*, 614 P.2d at 326. However, in the case at bar, plaintiffs' claim that defendants intentionally diluted the ore is clearly tortious in character, since the alleged act is the basis of plaintiffs' claim for conversion. *See* Part III supra. Thus, the issue is now squarely before us.

According to the Restatement, punitive damages are recoverable for a breach of contract if the conduct constituting the breach is also a tort for which punitive damages are recoverable. *See* Restatement (Second) of Contracts §355 (1981). We now adopt this view[1] because it furthers our policy of allowing punitive damages for certain tortious acts. *See Bridges v.*

---

1. We do not now reach the issue of whether punitive damages are recoverable for a breach of contract if the conduct constituting the breach is malicious but not tortious in character.

Alaska Housing Authority, 375 P.2d 696, 702 (Alaska 1962). Since defendants' alleged conduct also constituted a tort for which punitive damages might have been recoverable, the superior court erred in dismissing plaintiffs' punitive damages claim.

Accordingly, the judgment below is affirmed in part, reserved in part, and remanded for proceedings consistent with this opinion.

Assignment 2. Case Brief with Synthesis

Read the following excerpt from the appellate opinion in *Davies v. Bradley.* Prepare a case brief for a contracts class that includes a synthesis of this case with both *White v. Benkowski* and *McKibben v. Mohawk Oil Co.*

DAVIES v. BRADLEY
Colorado Court of Appeals
676 P.2d 1242 (1983)

KELLY, Judge.

This case involves the sale of a house built and sold by defendants Bobby and Mary Lee Bradley to the plaintiffs, James and Judith Davies. Citing the existence of 11 defects, including the failure to obtain a certificate of occupancy, all in violation of the county building code, the trial court found that the house was unsuitable for habitation and ruled that the Bradleys had breached the implied warranty of habitability.

. . . We affirm.

The Bradleys worked full time on the construction of the house for almost a year. It was the third house which they had built and lived in, and subsequently sold. When the house was put on the market, it appeared to be complete with the exception of a partially completed deck on the exterior of the house. The Bradleys obtained a building permit prior to construction of the house, but did not obtain a certificate of occupancy. The Bradleys performed substantially all the work on the residence themselves.

The plaintiffs submitted an offer to purchase the house which was accepted by the Bradleys, who added a clause to the standard form contract stating that "the buyers agree to accept said property as-is with the exception of the deck which will be completed by (illegible) 1978." The plaintiffs agreed to the inclusion of this clause. The trial court found that the purpose of this clause was to relieve the Bradleys of the obligation of performing further work on the house except as specified in the contract. The court further found that the parties did not intend for the clause to waiver or limit any implied or express warranties of workmanlike construction or habitability.

After closing, the plaintiffs took possession of the house and discovered it to be in violation of the Uniform Building Code of Pitkin County. An inspection revealed 11 distinct defects in quality and workmanship rendering the house unsuitable for habitation. The trial court found that the plaintiffs had no knowledge of the defects at the time of the closing, and that the Bradleys knew or should have known of their obligation to obtain periodic building inspections and a certificate of occupancy under the Uniform Building Code.

The trial court held that the Bradleys' failure to disclose that no such inspections or certificate had been obtained was done willfully and with a wanton and reckless disregard for the rights and interests of the plaintiffs. Therefore, the court awarded the plaintiffs the actual costs of making the house habitable and bringing it into compliance with the county's building code, and exemplary damages in an amount equal to the legal fees incurred by the plaintiffs because of the Bradleys' willful and wanton failure to disclose. . . .

IV

The Bradleys argue that the trial court erred in awarding exemplary damages. . . . We disagree.

Exemplary damages are not ordinarily a proper remedy in breach of contract cases. *Williams v. Speedster, Inc.,* 175 Colo. 73, 485 P.2d 728 (1971); *Sams v. Curfman,* 111 Colo. 124, 137 P.2d 1017 (1943). This is because the allegations in an action for breach of contract do not ordinarily bring the case within the confines of the statute. *See* §13-21-102, C.R.S. 1973.[2] Where, however, as here, the facts alleged and proved establish willful and wanton conduct and reckless disregard for the rights of the plaintiff, the maleficent intent on which exemplary damage awards in tort are based is present, and exemplary damages may be awarded though the action sounds in contract. The punitive and deterrent purposes of the statute authorizing exemplary damages in civil cases are thereby effected. . . .

The judgment is affirmed.

Smith and Van Cise, JJ., concur.

---

2. Author's Note: At the time of the Court of Appeals' decision in Davies v. Bradley, §13-21-102 provided:

Exemplary damages. In all civil actions in which damages are assessed by a jury for a wrong done to the person, or to personal or real property, and the injury complained of is attended by circumstances of fraud, malice or insult, or a wanton and reckless disregard of the injured party's rights and feelings, the jury, in addition to the actual damages sustained by such party, may award him reasonable exemplary damages.

Course Outline: Assignment for Chapter 7 of the Main Text

Imagine that you have studied the doctrine of quasi-contract in your contracts class and that you are ready to summarize your case briefs and to express your understanding of the subject in outline form. Further imagine that the notes reproduced below represent your briefs of principal and note cases on the topic. To prepare your outline, classify the holdings of the cases according to topic and subtopic, synthesize the holdings to arrive at an understanding of general legal rules, and develop a logical organization of the rules or problem areas. Then, summarize your ideas about them in outline form, using summaries of your case briefs as illustrations of legal rules.

Boswell v. Weldon (Texarkana S. Ct. 1958), CB 201.

Issues and Holdings:

I. Did a bank employee enrich an accident victim by rendering nonprofessional but competent first aid that nonetheless failed to save the victim's life? Yes.

II. Was the enrichment unjust even though the bank employee did not expect compensation at the time that he rendered aid? No; judgment for Defendant Estate affirmed.

Facts:

Bank robbers shot and critically wounded Boswell, a security guard. Weldon, a bank loan officer, attempted to stop the guard's bleeding and to revive him with CPR. The loan officer had no medical training other than

493

a single CPR class sponsored by the bank for all employees. He had never charged for first-aid services and had never expected to. Although he rendered competent first aid, the guard died of his wounds before an ambulance could arrive.

Procedural History:

The loan officer sued the guard's estate for compensation for the emergency first-aid services. The trial court granted the estate's motion for summary judgment on the grounds that (1) the loan officer provided no benefit to the security guard, and (2) any benefit provided by the loan officer to the guard did not unjustly enrich the guard. The loan officer appealed, and the state's only appellate court affirms.

Reasoning on Each Issue:

I. Quasi-contract permits recovery upon proof of unjust enrichment. Summary judgment cannot be based on lack of enrichment, because the record raises a genuine fact dispute about whether the loan officer transferred an actual benefit with measurable value to the guard. Even though the guard died, a jury could find that he received services with a market value that increased his chances of surviving.

II. On the undisputed facts, the loan officer could not reasonably have expected compensation at the time he rendered the emergency services; he is presumed to have rendered them gratuitously, and no facts rebut that presumption. Therefore, as a matter of law, it was not unjust for the guard and his estate to retain the benefit of the loan officer's services without compensating him for them.

Evaluation:

I find it odd to recognize enrichment in a person who dies soon after services are rendered. However, I agree with the ultimate disposition—it is reasonable to presume that emergency services would be rendered without expectation of compensation in a case such as this.

Cutter v. Noble (Texarkana S. Ct. 1982), CB 205.

Issues and Holdings:

I. Was it unjust for the victim of an auto accident to retain emergency lifesaving medical services from a physician without compensating the physician? Yes.

II. Did the trial court correctly instruct the jury that it must award compensation based on the results of the emergency services, as valued by someone in the position of the recipient? No.

Facts:

The victim of an automobile accident lay in the street near the office of a physician who engaged in the general practice of medicine. Alerted by a witness to the accident, the physician ran to the accident site with medical instruments, and she stabilized the unconscious victim until an ambulance could transport the victim to a hospital. The victim fully recovered. He almost certainly would have died had not the physician rendered emergency aid before arrival of the ambulance. The physician sent a bill of $300 to the victim, which the victim refused to pay.

Procedural History:

The physician sued the victim on the theory of quasi-contract. After a trial before a jury, the victim moved for a directed verdict on the ground that no reasonable juror could find that the enrichment was unjust. The trial court denied the motion and instructed the jury that, if it found unjust enrichment, it could award the physician the full value of the benefit received by the victim. The jury awarded the physician $500,000. The victim appealed, and the appellate court reverses.

Reasoning on Each Issue:

I. Because the physician ordinarily charged for such services, and because the services she rendered were nontrivial, a reasonable jury could find that the physician reasonably expected compensation when she rendered the services. Therefore, the question whether the enrichment was unjust was properly before the jury.

II. Full restitution of the benefit received by the victim would be disproportionately high if measured by the value of the life saved. To put practical limits on such awards more consistent with the quasi-contractual basis for relief, the trial court should have specifically instructed the jury that the benefit in such a case is measured by the general market price of the medical services rendered, or by some other measure that incorporates the physician's costs plus reasonable profit.

Evaluation:

I agree with the results on both issues, but the reasoning of the second holding is analytically unsatisfying. If measured by the physician's costs, the interest protected is more like reliance than restitution.

Valenzuela v. Rose (Calzona S. Ct. 1942), CB 209.

Issue and Holdings:

When a house painter enriched a homeowner by painting the owner's newly constructed house pursuant to a contract between the painter and the general contractor, was it unjust for the owner to retain the benefits of the paint job without compensating the painter for it? No.

Facts:

The owner, Rose, hired a general contractor to build a custom home, but the owner omitted painting from the tasks covered by their contract because a friend of the owner, Tierney, had separately agreed to paint the interior and exterior at a bargain price. The general contractor months later mistakenly hired Valenzuela to paint the interior and exterior of the owner's new house. When Valenzuela completed the painting according to his contract with the general contractor, the owner reminded the general contractor that painting was omitted from their contract, and the owner refused to pay either the general contractor or Valenzuela for the painting. In turn, the general contractor refused to pay Valenzuela for the work.

Procedural History:

Valenzuela sued the owner in quasi-contract for the reasonable value of the paint job. On the owner's challenge to the sufficiency of the complaint, the trial court dismissed the action. Valenzuela appealed, and the intermediate court of appeals affirmed. Here, the Supreme Court also affirms.

Reasoning:

In contracting with Valenzuela, the general contractor acted independently and not as the agent of the owner. At the time of painting, the painter expected compensation from the general contractor, not from the owner. The court sympathizes with the painter's fear that local contractors would exclude the painter from bid lists if he sued the general contractor. Nonetheless, the painter's proper remedy is against the general contractor for breach of their contract. Given the posture of the case, it was not unjust for the owner to retain the benefit of the painting without paying the painter for it.

Evaluation:

It seems unfair that the owner is permitted to enjoy this windfall; perhaps the owner ought to pay the painter the same bargain rate that the owner's friend had agreed to charge, even if that would be less than the normal market rate. Also, I wonder whether the general contractor could recover against the owner if the general contractor were liable to the painter. If so, why not permit the painter to sue the owner directly and bypass the general contractor?

Note Cases, CB 213-214:

1. *Cirankowitz v. Pastorini* (New Maine Ct. App. 1957). On facts similar to those of *Valenzuela v. Rose,* the court permitted a carpenter's suit against the owner, because the general contractor with whom the carpenter contracted had declared bankruptcy by the time of suit.

2. *Firello v. Combs* (W. Dakansas Ct. App. 1975). While the owner of a new structure solicited bids directly from painters, an unemployed painter painted the exterior of the structure without the prior knowledge of the owner and demanded that the owner pay him the amount of the lowest bid that the owner received from other painters for the job. Although the paint job was exactly as the owner specified in the job solicitation, the owner refused to pay. The court affirmed dismissal of the painter's action against the owner, ruling that the owner was not unjustly enriched.

3. *Spencer's Distributing Co. v. Hometown Appliances* (New Maine S. Ct. 1981). A distributor sent 10 microwave ovens to a retailer that had not ordered the ovens. The court held that the retailer was unjustly enriched, because the distributor had sent the microwave ovens under a reasonable mistake to which the retailer had contributed. The distributor was entitled to restitution of the value of the benefit bestowed upon the retailer measured by the wholesale price at which the retailer normally could buy such ovens rather than by the retail price at which it sold them to the public or the relatively high wholesale price that the distributor usually offered to retailers.

Office Memoranda: Assignments for Chapter 9 of the Main Text

The five assignments below vary in their complexity and in the extent to which they require research in your law library.

Each of the first two assignments presents a single issue for analysis. Assignment 3 is identical to Assignment 2 except that it adds a second issue for analysis. Assignments 4 and 5 present one or more issues for analysis, some of which may break into subissues. To some extent, precisely which and how many issues you discuss in Assignments 4 and 5 is a matter of judgment.

The first three assignments are "closed universe" problems: All the necessary authority is provided at the end of each assignment. In contrast, Assignments 4 and 5 are "open library" problems: You must conduct your own research in the law library to find authorities that will help you analyze the problems. Of course, your instructor can modify these problems by (1) asking you to conduct research to supplement the materials provided to you in Assignment 1, 2, or 3, or (2) providing you with some or all of the authorities that you will need for Assignment 4 or 5. Even if you are restricted to the authorities supplied in an assignment below, you will notice that some of the judicial opinions set forth at the end of an assignment cite to other decisions. In your memorandum, you may refer to such cited decisions, but only to the extent appropriate in light of your limited knowledge of the content of those cited decisions. For example, *Consolidated Edison*, the second judicial opinion set forth at the end of Assignment 2, cites to *Ben Construction Corp. v. Ventre* for the proposition that New York courts look to "the main objective sought to be accomplished by the contracting parties." In discussing *Consolidated Edison* in your memorandum, you might want to cite to *Ben Construction Corp.* as further support for the point made in *Consolidated Edison* or perhaps as the original source of language that you quote from *Consolidated Edison*. However, you should not rely more heavily on *Ben Construction Corp.*, because you do not have the benefit of the full text of that decision in your materials.

The page numbers within the opinions in the original reporters appear in brackets in the reproductions of the opinions at the end of Assignments 1 and 2.

Finally, the assignments are set in different jurisdictions. Assignments 1 and 5 are set in actual states, including the state of residence of your law school. In those assignments, you can use both mandatory case law from the forum state and persuasive case law from other states. Assignments 2-4 are set in the fictitious states of Calzona and New Maine. In those assignments, the forum state has some relevant statutes but no helpful case law; all case law, therefore, is from other states and is persuasive only.

Assignment 1. Office Memorandum
Single Issue
Jurisdiction: Arizona
Closed Universe

You are an associate in a firm that represents 15 young women and their mothers who complain that a seamstress intentionally breached a contract to provide gowns for their use in a Quinceanera ceremony in Phoenix, Arizona. As part of its professional responsibility to provide free legal services, your firm agrees to represent them without charge.

A Quinceanera ceremony is a traditional "coming out" party for a woman on her fifteenth birthday. It is celebrated in the Mexican and Mexican-American communities throughout Mexico and the southwestern United States. The celebration consists of a Catholic mass, followed by a formal reception that includes a dinner and dance. The celebrant, known as the "Quinceanera," traditionally wears a gown that is nearly as formal and ornate as a wedding gown. She is attended by relatives, by godmothers and godfathers, and by 14 maids of honor. The maids of honor are typically peers and close friends of the Quinceanera. The maids traditionally wear fancy gowns that match each other either in color or in pattern. Along with their male attendants, they participate in both the mass and the reception.

Your primary client, Trina Araiza, turned 15 last July 10. She and her 14 chosen maids of honor hired Ramona Udave to sew gowns of a particular pattern for the Quinceanera celebration. Trina's mother, Cristina, negotiated the contract with Udave. Because the Quinceanera and her maids of honor were minors, their parents cosigned the contract to ensure enforceability. On March 15, the Quinceanera participants provided Udave with material for the gowns and met with Udave so that she could take measurements. On May 5, Udave met with each participant for final fittings. At that meeting, each gown was only partially sewn, was partially held together with pins, and was not wearable.

Throughout May and June, Udave repeatedly assured all the participants that she was making normal progress on the gowns and that the gowns would be ready on time. In early July, Udave represented that she was putting the finishing touches on the gowns and that they would all be ready by the morning of the Quinceanera. Although some of the participants were anxious to see the gowns, Udave said that she never let her clients see her work until the last stitch was in place.

On the morning of the Quinceanera celebration, the participants arrived at Udave's shop to pick up their gowns. Udave repeatedly assured each of them that her gown was minutes away from completion and that each one should wait for the gown in the front room of Udave's shop. Udave kept the participants waiting for varying periods of time, some beyond 1:00 P.M., the time for commencement of the mass. Araiza herself received her gown at 12:30. At that time, she was nearly ill with anxiety. She dressed quickly and arrived at the site of the mass by 1:10 P.M. However, her maids of honor were still waiting for their gowns and therefore could not yet participate in the formal procession that begins the mass. By 1:30 P.M. five of the maids of honor had arrived with their gowns. Although the gowns were unfinished and looked terrible, Araiza and her five maids of honor walked in the processional and began the mass. Araiza was emotionally distraught during the mass, partly because of the absence of two maids of honor who were designated to recite prayers with her; those maids of honor were still waiting at Udave's tailoring shop on Udave's representations that their gowns were nearly complete.

In fact, the remaining gowns were in the same condition as they had been during the March fitting, and Udave never completed them. Although Udave continued to represent that the gowns were nearly completed, the remaining Quinceanera participants left her shop shortly after the mass and attended the reception in casual or semi-formal clothes. Although they participated in the traditional reception procession and waltz, they felt humiliated because of their inappropriate attire.

Araiza and the maids of honor suffered embarrassment and other forms of emotional distress as a result of Udave's actions. Based on information they acquired after the Quinceanera ceremony, they are convinced that Udave intentionally ruined the Quinceanera because of her friendship with a bitter rival of the Araiza family.

Your supervising attorney, Daniel Adams, intends to explore various potential claims, including breach of contract, fraud, and intentional infliction of emotional distress. He wants you to assume that he can establish only the contract claim, and he wants you to analyze the question whether the Quinceanera and her maids of honor can recover damages for emotional distress on their claims for breach of their collective contract with Udave. He knows that they can recover damages for other kinds of losses stemming from the breach, but he thinks that the damages for emotional distress may be problematic. Using only the following research materials, prepare an office memorandum, four to seven pages in length, discussing this question. In reciting the facts of this dispute, summarize only the facts material to your analysis. You may assume that the Quinceanera and her maids of honor are parties to an enforceable contract and that any dispute regarding the contract will be governed by Arizona law. Because Mr. Adams intends to use your memorandum to help him prepare a brief that he will submit to an Arizona tribunal, he wants you to use parallel citations when citing to either of the two Arizona decisions. When citing to the Alabama decision, you may cite only to the regional reporter.

Research Materials

CONTRACTS

E. Allan Farnsworth
(Little, Brown & Co. 2d ed. 1990)
(p. 934, footnotes omitted)

§12.17 Other Limitations, Including Emotional Disturbance . . .

A limitation more firmly rooted in tradition is that generally denying recovery for emotional disturbance, or "mental distress," resulting from breach of contract, even if the limitations of unforeseeability and uncertainty can be overcome. It could be argued that the real basis of this rule is that such recovery is likely to result in disproportionate compensation, and that the rule could therefore be subsumed under the more general rule of Restatement Second §351(3). Whatever the basis of the limitation, courts have not applied it inflexibly. Some courts have looked to the nature of the contract and made exceptions where breach was particularly likely to result in serious emotional disturbance. . . .

FARMERS INSURANCE EXCHANGE v. HENDERSON
82 Ariz. 335, *313 P.2d 404* (S. Ct. 1957)

[**pg. 337**, *pg. 405*] WINDES, Justice.

The appellant, Farmers Insurance Exchange, issued to appellee, George Henderson, a public liability insurance policy insuring him against claims for death or bodily injury and property damage resulting from the operation of Henderson's car. The limits of the policy for death or bodily injury was $5,000 for one person and $10,000 for one accident and $5,000 for property damage. There was a collision between the Henderson car when operated by his employee, one Whitehead, and an automobile operated by Charles Breesman. Three actions were filed for damages resulting from the accident. One action was by . . . Breesman against Henderson and Whitehead. This . . . action was tried in the superior court. The present case is a suit by Henderson against the company for damages claimed to have resulted from the failure to settle the Breesman claim for an amount within its policy limits when opportunity was presented for such settlement. A jury trial resulted in a verdict and judgment against the company in the sum of $45,000. The company appeals. The appellant will be referred to as the company and individuals by name.

The principal questions presented for solution are the extent of the obligations of the insurer to the insured to settle within the policy limits a claim against the insured and, if liability is established, the correct measure of the insured's damages. . . .

[**pg. 342**, *pg. 408*] On the question of damages Henderson submitted and the court gave instructions that if the jury found the company breached its contract, it could assess damages for the following items: loss of the property as a going business and interest from time of loss, humiliation, pain and suffering, attorney fees incurred by Henderson, loss of earnings, expenses of seeking employment [*pg. 409*] including traveling expenses to that end, and his loss of business reputation and credit. Over the company's objection evidence on these items was admitted. Except as to the value of the business as a going concern and interest thereon from the time of its sale, the court erred in the admission of evidence and giving instructions on the foregoing items of damages.

The wrong involved is causing the destruction or conversion of insured's business property in satisfaction of the [**pg. 343**] company's obligation. The court correctly instructed that as a general rule the damages for the loss or destruction or conversion of a going business is its value at the time and place of destruction with interest. This is in accord with the pronouncements of this court. Jones v. Stanley, 27 Ariz. 381, 233 P. 598. The humiliation, mental pain, suffering and anguish incurred by the Hendersons was the direct result of the pecuniary loss suffered. If it is to be considered a breach of contract, to recover for these items the contract must be of such a nature that its breach would cause mental suffering for reasons other than the pecuniary loss. Restatement of Law, Contracts, section 341. . . .

[**pg. 344**, *pg. 409*] The judgment is reversed with instructions for a new trial on the entire case as to all issues.

FOGLEMAN v. PERUVIAN ASSOCIATES
127 Ariz. 504, *622 P.2d 63* (App. 1980)

[**pg. 505**, *pg. 64*] OPINION

HATHAWAY, Chief Judge.

In August of 1973, appellants were residents of Tucson, Arizona, and Mr. Fogleman was employed as a welder at a copper mine near Tucson. Appellees offered him employment at a mine operated by appellees at Quajone, Peru, and he accepted. The contract of employment was dated September 24, 1973, and was for a two-year period, employing Mr. Fogleman as welding supervisor at $1,700 per month plus housing allowance and other benefits.

Appellees terminated Fogleman's employment on March 8, 1974. Appellants brought this action alleging wrongful termination of the employment contract and seeking damages. After trial to the court, without a jury, judgment was entered in favor of appellants in the amount of $14,989.33, plus costs, together with interest commencing on the date of judgment. The trial court entered findings of fact and conclusions of law.

On appeal, appellants contend that they were entitled to an award of consequential general damages. . . .

[**pg. 506**, *pg. 65*] Appellants first contend that the trial court erred in not awarding consequential general damages because the evidence and findings support such an award. Specifically, the court found that appellees could terminate appellants' employment contract only for cause and that they did not have cause. This breach caused appellants economic loss of $14,989.33. In finding of fact number 10, the court found:

10. The wrongful conduct of the Defendants S.P.C.C., Fluor Utah and Peruvian Associates also caused Plaintiffs to suffer general damages, including emotional distress, anxiety, embarrassment, humiliation and other items listed on page 14 of Plaintiffs Post-Trial Memorandum.

The court refused to award consequential damages, perceiving the rule to be that such damages are not allowed in a breach of contract action, and so stated in conclusion of law number 15.

Appellants argue that consequential damages are allowable in a breach of contract action and that appellees' wrongful conduct was both a breach of contract and a tort, therefore such damages were allowable. The trial court's first finding of fact stated that the action was for breach of contract, rejecting appellants' proposed finding that the appellees had a fiduciary relationship to appellants involving "special trust and confidence." We do not have before us an appeal from a tort action, and appellants' citations for the proposition that damages for mental anguish are allowable in actions which sound both in contract and in tort, are not applicable. The appropriate measure of damages for an employee who has been wrongfully discharged is the unpaid balance of the salary less the sums earned during the remainder of the contract period. . . .

In *Browning v. Fies,* 4 Ala. App. 580, 58 So. 931 (1912), cited by appellants, a special situation was presented where the plaintiff had hired a carriage to transport him to church for his wedding. The defendant was aware of the reasons and the time frame for performance and that the failure of performance would, under the circumstances, expose plaintiff to particular consequences, alluded to by the court and for which the plaintiff was allowed damages. This case is inapplicable to the facts herein. . . .

[**pg. 507,** *pg. 66*] Affirmed as modified.

BROWNING v. FIES
4 Ala. App. 580, **58 So. 931** (1912)

[**pg. 932**] Appeal from City Court of Birmingham; Chas. A. Senn, Judge.

PELHAM, J. This is a suit for damages for the breach of a contract entered into between the appellant, who was the plaintiff below, and the appellees. Under the terms of the contract, the defendants, for the consideration of $5 paid to them by the plaintiff, agreed to furnish a carriage and team for the special purpose of carrying the plaintiff, his friends, and relatives from the home of the plaintiff near Rising Station to a church in Birmingham, Ala., a distance of about three miles, at which church the plaintiff on this particular occasion was to be married. The damages claimed and sought to be recovered were for the actual financial loss arising out of a breach of the contract, and damages for mental suffering, physical pain, humiliation, mortification, etc.

Demurrers were filed to each count of the original complaint, setting up as grounds of demurrer, among others, that damages for mental suffering and humiliation, etc., were not recoverable under the allegations of the complaint. The plaintiff amended his complaint by withdrawing the second count and filing an additional count designated as count No. 4. Demurrers having been refiled and sustained to the complaint as thus amended, the plaintiff again amended by adding count No. 5 and making certain amendments to counts 1, 3, and 4, making more certain the allegations of such counts as to the parties with whom the plaintiff entered into the contract. The demurrers interposed to counts 1, 3, 4, and 5, as last amended, were overruled, and defendants thereupon filed two motions to strike from each count of the complaint as amended the averments as to the plaintiff's having suffered great mental anguish, humiliation, distress, etc., on the ground that such allegations did not set up matters constituting proper elements for the recovery of damages. The defendants also separately moved to strike from each count of the complaint any claims for damages based on delay in reaching the place appointed for the marriage ceremony, for being compelled to ride to the church in a public street car, and for physical and mental pain and suffering, for humiliation, etc., etc., in consequence thereof, on the grounds that such damages were speculative, too remote, and not recoverable in an action of this nature. The court granted the defendants' motion to strike from the complaint these elements as claims of damage as to each count, and the plaintiff reserved exceptions to the court's ruling. On the pleadings as thus framed, the issues were tried before a jury. . . .

The evidence without conflict showed that the plaintiff, on the day of the evening upon which he was to be married, went to the defendants' place of business in Birmingham, Ala., and entered into a contract with the defendants, who were engaged in conducting a public livery business, to furnish the plaintiff, for the use of himself, friends, and family, a carriage and team which was to be sent to the plaintiff's residence at or near Rising Station at 7:30 o'clock P.M. on that day to carry plaintiff and his wedding party to the church in Birmingham, three miles distant, where the plaintiff was to be married at 8 o'clock on that evening. The defendants made a charge of $5 for this specified use of the carriage and team, which amount was paid to the defendants by the plaintiff, who at the time of making the contract informed the defendants of the purpose [pg. 933] for which the same was to be used and the hour appointed for the ceremony, and the defendants agreed and contracted to furnish the carriage and team to be used by the plaintiff for this specific purpose. It was also shown without conflict in the evidence that the defendants made default and breached the contract and failed to send the carriage at the time and place as they contracted to do, and no excuse whatever was offered upon the part of the defendants for having failed to perform the contract. The plaintiff, on account of the defendants' breach of the contract, was compelled, in order to reach the church where his prospective bride and friends were awaiting his coming, to resort to a public street car in which plaintiff and his family and friends, at the expenditure of 30 cents for street car fare, attended the wedding appareled in "dress" or "evening" clothes. The plaintiff and the lady members of his family, unsuitably attired for riding in a street car and for walking along the public streets, had to walk for several squares from the place necessary to leave the car line in going to the church, and the wedding ceremony was delayed for 45 or 50 minutes on account of the failure of the plaintiff to reach the church on time. During this period of delay, the bride, family, minister, and friends in attendance at the church were kept waiting upon the delayed arrival of the prospective groom.

On the trial the plaintiff offered in varying forms questions to elicit evidence going to show that he suffered mental and physical pain, mortification, and humiliation, but on objection of the defendants he was not allowed to make such proof or to show any elements of damage of this nature. At the instance of the defendants, the court gave the following charge in writing to the jury: "If the jury believe the evidence, they can only find a verdict for the plaintiff for $5.30 with interest thereon from the 26th day of April, 1906." The plaintiff requested charges in writing, which were refused by the court, to the effect that the plaintiff was entitled to recover for any mental suffering and physical pain caused as a proximate consequence of the defendants' breach of the contract. The jury returned a verdict for plaintiff for $6.55, and, from the judgment entered on this verdict, the plaintiff prosecutes this appeal.

The main contention of appellant is that the court was in error in its ruling on the pleading and on the evidence, and its rulings on the charges in refusing to allow mental suffering and physical pain as an element of recoverable damages for breach of the contract.

The plaintiff's special or ulterior purpose in making the contract was disclosed at the time it was entered into and thereby became incorporated into it and thus afforded a substantial basis for the assessment of special damages. The special circumstances having been known and assented to by each of the contracting parties, each is deemed to have contracted with reference to them, and the party who breaches the contract may be justly held to make good to the other whatever damages, general or special, he has sustained which are the reasonable and natural consequences of the breach under the known circumstances with reference to which the parties acted in making the contract.

When a contract is entered into under special circumstances within the knowledge of both parties, the natural and proximate consequences of a breach of which will entail special damages upon the party not in default, the larger amount of damages may be recovered as having been in the contemplation of both parties. *Bixby-Theirson Lumber Co. v. Evans*, 167 Ala. 431, 52 South. 843, 29 L.R.A. (N.S.) 194, 140 Am. St. Rep. 47. This was also the English rule and the rule at common law. Damages recoverable for the breach of a contract are measured, not only by the actual loss sustained that naturally results as the ordinary consequence of the breach, but extend to consequences which may, under the circumstances of entering into the contract, be presumed to have been in the contemplation of both parties as the probable result of a breach. 6 Eng. Rul. Cas. 617. And, if the special circumstances are communicated, they become an element of the contract. *Daugherty v. Am. U. Tel. Co.*, 75 Ala. 168, 51 Am. Rep. 435.

But are damages for mental suffering an element of the special damages recoverable? "Injury to the feelings—mental harassment—is an element of actual damages. 'Wounding a man's feelings is as much an element of actual damages as breaking his limb.' *Head v. Georgia Pac.*, 79 Ga. 358 [7 S.E. 217, 11 Am. St. Rep. 434]." *Birmingham Water Wks. Co. v. Martini*, 2 Ala. App. 652, 56 South. 833.

The right to recover special damages for mental anguish growing out of a breach of contract to send and deliver a telegram, as said in the recent case of *W. U. Tel. Co. v. Cleveland*, 169 Ala. 131, 135, 53 South. 80, 82, "has been settled in this court," citing the cases sustaining this proposition.

If damages for mental suffering are actual damages and recoverable as compensatory damages when proximately resulting from a breach of the contract, because of the nature of a telegram and the relationship disclosed bringing this consequence of the breach within the contemplation of the parties, as was held in *W. U. Tel. Co. v. Haley*, 143 Ala. 586, 39 South. 386, we cannot perceive under what rule or by what sound reason such *actual* damages can be excluded as a proper measure of recovery in connection with the pecuniary loss sustained in any case where they flow naturally and as a direct consequence from the infraction [**pg. 934**] of a contract entered into under special circumstances known to both parties, and with reference to which they contracted. . . .

This court has also held (*C. of G. Ry. Co. v. Knight*, 57 South. 253) that, for a breach of contract for transportation, a woman may recover for mental distress and worry due to having been prevented and delayed in securing stateroom accommodations while on her bridal trip.

In this particular case, considering the subject matter of the contract, the special purpose and exceptional use to which plaintiff intended to put the carriage, which was communicated and well known to the defendants, and with reference to which they contracted, it would seem that it was in the reasonable contemplation of the parties when the contract was entered into under the special known circumstances, that the immediate effect and proximate result ensuing from a breach of the contract by the defendants would cause the plaintiff inconvenience, annoyance, mental harassment, or distress, and make him to suffer physical delay with the attendant discomfort, as well as mental pain in consequence thereof. Certainly it is but common knowledge that some distress of mind must be the natural and proximate consequence of being delayed and not having proper conveyance to meet an appointment of such delicate nature.

The plaintiff by proper averments claimed damages in different counts of the complaint for physical discomfort in consequence of being delayed and not having proper conveyance to meet the special and particular appointment (undoubtedly of great moment to him), and for mental distress attendant upon and suffered in consequence of these physical inconveniences, delay, etc. The court was in error in not submitting these questions to the jury as a proper element of recoverable damages, and in limiting the recovery to the actual financial loss sustained.

A detailed discussion of the various assignments of error is unnecessary. The main proposition involved in each of all of them goes to the question we have considered and determined in what has been said.

Reversed and remanded.

Assignment 2. Office Memorandum
Single Issue
Jurisdiction: Fictitious State of New Maine
Closed Universe

You work as a law clerk for attorney Susan Corleone. This morning she called you into her office and initiated the following conversation with you:

Corleone: I just finished an interview with Bob Carson, a new client. He spent 10 years working as a plumbing subcontractor on construction sites. Now he owns and manages Carson Plumbing Supply, and he sells and installs pipe and plumbing fixtures in Sweetwater, New Maine, and surrounding areas.

Law Clerk: What's Mr. Carson's problem?

Corleone: John King, owner of King Enterprises, Inc., is suing him for breach of a written contract. Here's a copy of the contract. King is the owner of an office building currently under construction in Sweetwater; King alleges that Carson breached a contract to supply and install the plumbing in the new building.

Law Clerk: Did Carson try to perform at all?

Corleone: No. He took on a different job instead. He says that he revoked his bid over the telephone August 11, 10 days after he submitted it and five days before King tried to accept; in other words, Carson asserts that he never formed a contract with King in the first place. It looks like Carson clearly notified King of his intent to revoke the bid before King accepted it. Unfortunately for Carson, the bid form supplied by King included a promise by Carson to hold the bid open for 30 days; Carson used and signed that form, and King accepted Carson's bid within 30 days.

Law Clerk: Did King give any consideration for Carson's promise to hold his bid open and irrevocable for 30 days?

Corleone: I don't see any.

Law Clerk: Doesn't that end the inquiry? Carson's promise to hold his bid open was gratuitous and unenforceable; therefore, Carson validly revoked his bid before King accepted it.

Corleone: That's good analysis under common law, but the Uniform Commercial Code provides that, in some circumstances, "firm offers" like the one that Carson gave are irrevocable even though the offeree gave no consideration for the offeror's promise to hold the offer open.

Law Clerk: Does the UCC apply to this case?

Corleone: That's what I want you to tell me. Give me your analysis and conclusions in memorandum form. New Maine has adopted the UCC as part of the New Maine Commercial Code, but no New Maine court decisions have addressed the issue in this case. You'll have to rely on the UCC provisions and on interpretive case law from other jurisdictions.

Law Clerk: Do you want me to discuss the question whether the parties successfully formed a contract under either the UCC or the common law?

Corleone: Not at this point. Just address the question of choice of law; tell me whether the UCC or the common law will apply to the dispute.

Law Clerk: Did Carson tell you anything about the negotiations leading up to the bidding?

Corleone: Yes. King especially wanted Carson to do the job because Carson is the exclusive distributor of patented pipe fittings designed by Carson himself. Carson's pipe fittings reduce the difficulty and expense of installation. King had originally asked Carson to submit only a bid for the parts; it had planned to hire another subcontractor to install them. However, Carson insisted that he install any parts that he sold.

Law Clerk: Why is that? Does Carson make most of his profit on the installation?

Corleone: I don't know what his profit margins are. I do know that Carson quoted prices over the phone to King of $35,000 for all the parts and $39,700 for installation. However, the bid form simply calls for a total price, which Carson filled in for $74,000. When Carson refused to perform, King had to use another supplier and installer at a higher cost.

AGREEMENT FOR SUPPLY AND INSTALLATION
OF PLUMBING

I
PARTIES

The parties to this agreement are:

King Enterprises, Inc. (OWNER), and
Bob Carson, d.b.a. Carson Plumbing Supply (CONTRACTOR).

II
MUTUAL RIGHTS AND OBLIGATION

OWNER and CONTRACTOR agree to the following bargained-for exchange:

1. . . .

2. . . .

3. CONTRACTOR will supply and install all pipe and plumbing fixtures in accordance with the specifications in the architect's plans (attached and incorporated). All fixtures so installed will be incorporated into OWNER's building and will become the sole property of OWNER.

4. Within 30 days of the architect's certifying satisfactory installation of the plumbing, OWNER will pay CONTRACTOR the total sum of _$74,000_ .

5. . . .

6. . . .

7. The parties understand that CONTRACTOR will use this document as a bid form to make an offer to OWNER. This document becomes a contract when OWNER accepts CONTRACTOR's bid by notifying CONTRACTOR orally or in writing of OWNER's decision to use CONTRACTOR's services. *By signing this document immediately below, CONTRACTOR promises to hold its offer open and irrevocable for 30 days from the date of CONTRACTOR's signature below.*

Signed

Bob Carson _____
Contractor

_____ _8-1_ 199x[3]
Date

John King _____
Owner

_____ _8/16_ 199x
Date

_____

3. In place of "199x" after each signature, write in the year of the August immediately preceding your work on this assignment.

Research Materials

UNIFORM COMMERCIAL CODE (1990)
ARTICLE 2. SALES

§2-102. Scope; certain security and other transactions excluded from this article

Unless the context otherwise requires, this article applies to transactions in goods; . . .

§2-105. Definitions: transferability; "goods"; "future" goods; "lot"; "commercial unit"

A. "Goods" means all things (including specially manufactured goods) which are movable at the time of identification to the contract for sale other than the money in which the price is to be paid, investment securities (article 8) and things in action. "Goods" also includes the unborn young animals and growing crops and other identified things attached to realty as described in the section on goods to be severed from realty (§2-307).

COAKLEY & WILLIAMS INC. v. SHATTERPROOF GLASS CORPORATION
706 F.2d 456 (4th Cir. 1983) [footnotes omitted]

[**Pg. 457**] Before HALL, MURNAGHAN and SPROUSE, Circuit Judges:

MURNAGHAN, Circuit Judge:

On appeal from a dismissal under 12(b)(6) the accepted rule is "that a complaint should not be dismissed for failure to state a claim unless it appears beyond doubt that the plaintiff can prove no set of facts in support of his claim which would entitle him to relief." . . . Liberal construction in favor of the plaintiff is mandated. . . . We state as "facts" the allegations and inferences most favorable to the plaintiff. . . .

Washington Plate Glass Company had a contract to "furnish and install aluminum and glass curtain wall and store front work" on a building located in Lanham, Maryland being built by Coakley & Williams, Inc., the plaintiff. To accomplish its contractual undertaking, Washington purchased the glass spandrel required from the defendant, Shatterproof Glass Corp. Still other materials needed for the project, predominantly aluminum, it appears were acquired in part at least elsewhere.

The contract price under the Coakley and Washington agreement amounted to $262,500, subsequently increased by amendment to $271,350. The glass purchased by Washington from Shatterproof cost $87,715.00, [**pg. 458**] with the proviso that units were "to be properly marked for field installation."

The work progressed and the contract for the aluminum and glass curtain wall and storefront work was completed in March of 1974. Discoloration of the glass ensued, and Coakley complained. To remedy the situation, Washington agreed to replace the glass at no cost to Coakley, and did in fact replace a substantial portion of the glass. Shatterproof supplied the replacement glass and reimbursed Washington for the cost of re-installation, accomplished in April of 1977.

By December of 1977, the glass had again discolored, and complaints began to flow from Coakley to Washington and Shatterproof in or about December 1978. Shatterproof declined to replace a second time. On January 14, 1981, Coakley filed suit against Shatterproof in the Circuit Court for Montgomery County, Maryland alleging breach of implied warranties of merchantability and fitness for a particular purpose. Reliance was placed on certain provisions of the Maryland Uniform Commercial Code, Annotated Code of Maryland, §1-101 et seq. Removal to the United States District Court for the District of Maryland followed, and Shatterproof sought dismissal under Fed. R. Civ. P. 12(b)(6).

A hearing on the 12(b)(6) motion followed at which Shatterproof contended (1) that the U.C.C. was inapplicable, (2) that lack of privity was fatal to the claim, and (3) that the statute of limitations had run prior to commencement of the action. We now have the case before us on appeal from an order granting the 12(b)(6) motion and dismissing the case solely on the grounds that the U.C.C. was not applicable.

Whether the U.C.C. applies turns on a question as to whether the contract between Washington and Coakley involved principally a sale of goods, on the one hand, or a provision of services, on the other. U.C.C. §2-314 creates an implied warranty "that the *goods* shall be merchantable" to be "implied in a contract for their sale." Section 2-315 establishes an implied warranty "that the *goods* shall be fit" for a [**pg. 459**] particular purpose, "[w]here the seller at the time of contracting has reason to know [the] particular purpose." (Emphasis added.)

Consequently, unless there has been a buyer of goods, the U.C.C. warranties of merchantability and of fitness for a particular use do not apply. Furthermore, unless there has been a buyer of goods, the elimination of a requirement of privity would not have been achieved. Accordingly, both questions (1) as to the availability of the warranties and (2) as to the amenability of Shatterproof, who was not in privity with Coakley, to suit by Coakley, come down to whether the transactions between Washington and Coakley was a sale of goods or the provision of services.

To resolve that question, we must address ourselves to a welter of cases reaching varying results depending on the considerations deemed to predominate in each particular case. It should not pass unnoticed that all were decided at summary judgment [**pg. 460**] or beyond. No case involving the issue appears to have been disposed of at the rule 12(b)(6) or demurrer stage. They emphasize, in particular, three aspects which may, or may not, constitute indicia of the nature of the contract: (1) the language of the contract, (2) the nature of the business of the supplier, and (3) the intrinsic worth of the materials involved.

A distillation of the cases outlined in the foregoing notes 11-14 [omitted by editor] produces an inescapable conclusion that, on the facts in their present pro-plaintiff posture, a reasonable viewing of them would permit a factfinder to conclude that the contract between Washington and Coakley predominantly concerned a sale of goods, and consequently was governed by the U.C.C. A Rule [**pg. 461**] 12(b)(6) motion simply cannot serve to dispose of the case.

As to the first of the emphasized aspects, the contract between Washington and Coakley speaks in terms of furnishing and installing a wall and performing storefront work. Clearly, at the very outset of performance Washington had the responsibility to bring to the affected premises the materials which ultimately would form the glass curtain wall and storefront. The U.C.C. in §2-105 defines "goods" as "*all* things (including specially manufactured goods) which are movable at the time of identification to the contract for sale other than the money in which the price is to be paid, investment securities (Title 8) and things in action." (Emphasis added.) That at least creates an uncertainty to be resolved only by a full factual presentation to determine whether the nature of the Washington business was predominantly the provision of goods or the furnishing of services. The fact that Coakley was a building contractor specializing in construction is not sufficient to provide a completely definitive answer. While often, and perhaps customarily, a contractor is engaged in the provision of services, the scope of a contractor's work is not necessarily monolithic and, in the present circumstances, it becomes a question of unresolved fact whether Coakley, for the purposes of the single relationship to which we are restricted, was a buyer of goods.

In this connection, it is not irrelevant that Coakley has alleged that the purchases by Washington from Shatterproof included anchor clips and field fasteners. At the early stage at which we find ourselves, the allegation requires us to indulge the inference urged by counsel for Coakley that putting the glass in place was a simple snap-on process requiring little expenditure of time or labor. One can readily imagine, without the advantage of specificity deriving from a full trial on the merits, that the contract largely contemplated the provision of precast panels as goods, without the installation being nearly so extensive or significant as the supplying of the glass itself.

The fact that the contract does not follow a standard, routine or regularized form, coupled with the plaintiff's contention that standard form contracts are virtually universal for construction (i.e., generally, service) contracts, operates to leave open the possibility of a finding that the contract is more one for goods than would be the customary construction contract.

Turning to the second point, the nature of Washington's business, the fact that Washington was a dealer and not a manufacturer does not have any particularly dispositive significance. Many retailers of goods function in the role of middleman. Shatterproof sold Washington materials in a transaction which unquestionably, on the sparse record before us at the preliminary stage at which we find ourselves, was a sale of goods, and the question comes down essentially to whether those materials or the services which Washington also provided under its contract with Coakley predominated. Without full consideration of as yet unascertained facts that question is simply not ripe for resolution. It is one of fact, not law; at least it is at this early stage.

Third, the complaint affords no realistic, and certainly no dispositive, information as to the value of the spandrels et al. in case of breakup into the component parts of the glass curtain wall and storefront work. That can only be determined by further development of the record, and is, in all events, but one of several factors which must be evaluated in conjunction with all the others in resolving the ultimate factual issue: Did Washington and Coakley deal primarily with goods or services?

Accordingly, Coakley has alleged enough to survive a motion to dismiss under Fed. R. Civ. P. 12(b)(6). [pg. 462] Nor, at the other extreme, has it alleged too much, permitting sure ascertainment that services, not goods, were the gravamen of the transaction. Coakley should, therefore, be permitted to show, unless the statute of limitations bars recovery, that it was a buyer of goods and, therefore, entitled to proceed under the U.C.C. provisions. . . .

[pg. 463] Accordingly, the judgment is reversed and the case remanded for further proceedings not inconsistent with this opinion.

Reversed and remanded.

CONSOLIDATED EDISON COMPANY OF NEW YORK, INC. v. WESTINGHOUSE ELECTRIC CORPORATION
567 F. Supp. 358 (S.D.N.Y. 1983)

[pg. 360] LASKER, District Judge.

On December 3, 1971, Westinghouse Electric Corporation ("Westinghouse") entered into an agreement (the "Agreement") with Consolidated Edison Company of New York, Inc., ("Con Ed") calling for Westinghouse to "furnish and construct a complete and operable nuclear power plant (excluding, however, the nuclear fuel assemblies) built to Westinghouse commercial utility standards and specifications. . . ." (Agreement, Article I) (Def. Ex. A). The facility, since built, is known as the Indian Point Power Plant Unit Number 2 (IP 2 Plant) and is located in Buchanan, New York.

Con Ed's complaint alleges that, following completion of the plant, and beginning in 1975, defects began to appear in various components of the plant that, *inter alia,* have required extensive monitoring, repairs and modifications, have impeded Con Ed's ability to obtain maximum output from the IP 2 Plant, and may in the future require a complete shutdown of the plant for the replacement of defective equipment. The complaint divides the defects into three groups: (1) denting, corrosion and cracking of the tubes and tube support plates contained in the plant's steam generators; (2) cracks in certain turbine rotating components known as discs; and (3) defects in "other equipment," including low pressure turbine blades, the high pressure turbine casing joint, condenser tubes, cross-under piping, and circulating water pumps.

The complaint alleges seven causes of action. The first through sixth allege breach of express warranty and implied warranties of merchantability and fitness for intended purpose (first, second and third causes of action), breach of contract (fourth cause of action), negligence (fifth cause of action), and strict products liability (sixth cause of action). . . .

Westinghouse moves to dismiss various causes of action pursuant to Fed. R. Civ. P. 12(b)(6). It argues that (1) all seven causes of action are barred in whole or in substantial part by the applicable New York statutes of limitation, . . .

[pg. 361] I. Applicable Statute of Limitations—Counts One
through Four (Warranty and Contract Claims)

. . . Under New York law, a four-year statute of limitations applies to causes of action based on contracts for the sale of goods, which are governed by the New York Uniform Commercial Code ("N.Y.U.C.C."), while a six-year statute of limitations applies to causes of action based on service or construction contracts, which are governed by the common law. *See* N.Y.U.C.C. §2-725; New York Civil Practice Law & Rules ("C.P.L.R.") §213(2). Thus, although Con Ed's contract claims with respect to the steam generators are timely under either measure, the timeliness of its contract claims with respect to the steam turbines and other equipment depends upon whether the IP 2 Agreement is "in essence" a contract for the sale of goods under the N.Y.U.C.C., or whether instead it is a service contract—a "work, labor and materials contract." *Schenectady Steel Co., Inc. v. Bruno Trimpoli General Construction Co.,* 43 A.D.2d 234, 237, 350 N.Y.S.2d 920, 923 (3rd Dep't), *aff'd on other grounds,* 34 N.Y.2d 939, 359 N.Y.S.2d 560, 316 N.E.2d 875 (1974). In deciding whether a contract is one for the sale of goods or for the rendition of services, New York courts look to "the main objective sought to be accomplished by the contracting parties," *Ben Construction Corp. v. Ventre,* 23 A.D.2d 44, 45, 257 N.Y.S.2d 988, 989 (4th Dep't 1965).

Westinghouse argues, in favor of the applicability of the N.Y.U.C.C., that the primary object of the agreement was the purchase by Con Ed of Westinghouse-manufactured and designed component parts—the steam generators, turbines, and other components of the IP 2 Plant. Indeed, Westinghouse asserts, Con Ed's lawsuit complains of defective equipment, not of the structural soundness of the plant; since Con Ed's claims relate in fact to the goods that Westinghouse sold Con Ed, Con Ed should not be heard to contend that the law governing construction contracts is the applicable law. Westinghouse further contends that the U.C.C. has become the "operative law" applicable to agreements between utilities and suppliers of power plant equipment, even though services are required for construction and installation of the equipment. *E.g., Florida Light & Power Co. v. Westinghouse Electric Corp.,* No. 78-1896, slip op. (S.D. Fla. June 22, 1982) (nuclear steam supply systems); *Ebasco Services, Inc. v. Pa. Power & Light Co.,* 460 F. Supp. 163 (E.D. Pa. 1978) (steam turbine generator and boiler feed pump turbines); *American Electric Power Co. v. Westinghouse Electric Corp.,* 418 F. Supp. 435 (S.D.N.Y.1976) (steam turbine generator); *Royal Indemnity Co. v. Westinghouse Electric Corp.,* 385 F. Supp. 520 (S.D.N.Y.1974) (turbine generator).

In answer Con Ed points out that the IP 2 Agreement is a contract not simply for the sale of specific items of power plant equipment, but for the construction of a complete nuclear power plant. The Agreement, [pg. 362] Con Ed argues, not only required Westinghouse to provide all architectural and engineering services necessary to the construction of the plant, along with the labor required for its construction, but also provided that Westinghouse would take all necessary steps to assure that the plant would be granted an operating license under the requirements established by the United States Atomic Energy Commission. Con Ed contends that the scope of Westinghouse's responsibilities under the Agreement, which continued throughout several years of design, construction, testing and licensing, differentiates the Agreement from typical "goods" contracts involving the one-time installation of a specific item of equipment. Con Ed also argues that, because "goods" by definition must be "movable at the time of identification to the contract for sale," see N.Y.U.C.C. §2-105(1), a contract for the furnishing and construction of a nuclear power plant cannot be considered a contract for the sale of goods. Finally, although Con Ed asserts that the IP 2 Agreement is in essence a service contract as a matter of law, it contends, in the alternative, that at most Westinghouse has raised a question of fact as to the nature of the contract that cannot be resolved on the basis of the pleadings.

The New York cases exploring the distinction between sales and services contracts provide no clear answer to the proper classification of the IP 2 Agreement. In several instances New York courts have held that contracts as to which "service predominates and the transfer of title to personal property is an incidental feature of the transaction" are outside the scope of the U.C.C. *Schenectady Steel, supra,* 43 A.D.2d at 237, 350 N.Y.S.2d at 922 (contract to furnish and erect the structural steel for a bridge), *citing Perlmutter v. Beth David Hospital,* 308 N.Y. 100, 104, 123 N.E.2d 792, 794 (1954) (action for strict liability against hospital that supplied impure blood plasma in course of blood transfusion); *see also Ben Construction Corp., supra* (sale and installation of a swimming pool); *Milau Associates, Inc. v. North Avenue Development Corp.,* 42 N.Y.2d 482, 398 N.Y.S.2d 882, 368 N.E.2d 1247 (1977) (installation of a sprinkler system). In the present case, however, on the record as it stands, neither the goods nor the services aspect of the Agreement can reasonably be characterized as "incidental." Just as Con Ed plainly could not have considered the power generating equipment to be an incidental feature of its contract with Westinghouse, so also the architectural, engineering and testing services provided by Westinghouse, and the labor necessary to carry them out were crucial to the Agreement's objective.

Moreover, contrary to Westinghouse's rationale, the applicable law cannot be determined simply by looking to the matters about which Con Ed is seeking relief—primarily, defects in various items of equipment supplied by Westinghouse. The New York courts appear to have rejected an approach of applying sales law to the sales aspect of a transaction which combines both sales and service features, requiring instead that the applicable law be determined by looking to the essential nature of the underlying contract. *Compare Schenectady Steel, supra,* 43 A.D.2d at 238, 350 N.Y.S.2d at 924 (concurring opinion of Greenblott, J.) *with Milau Associates, supra,* 42 N.Y.2d at 485, 398 N.Y.S.2d at 884, 368 N.E.2d at 1249. Where, as here, the question is closely balanced, factual development is necessary before the issue is resolved. *See Back O'Beyond, Inc. v. Telephonic Enterprises, Inc.,* 76 A.D.2d 897, 429 N.Y.S.2d 250 (2nd Dep't 1980); *Schulman Investment Co.*

v. Olin Corp., 477 F. Supp. 623 (S.D.N.Y.1979); *cf. Stafford v. International Harvester Co.*, 668 F.2d 142 (2d Cir. 1981); *Triangle Underwriters v. Honeywell, Inc.*, 604 F.2d 737 (2d Cir. 1979). The pleadings do not reveal the allocation of contract price as between construction and equipment costs, the precise nature and scope of the services undertaken by Westinghouse, or other matters that may contribute to a proper resolution of the question. It may be, as Westinghouse argues, that the "essential" nature of the contract will not be significantly clearer [**pg. 362**] following development of the record, but the accuracy of this prediction cannot be determined in advance of obtaining the facts. . . .

[**pg. 369**] . . . [T]he motion to dismiss is denied without prejudice. It is so ordered.

OSTERHOLT v. ST. CHARLES DRILLING COMPANY, INC.
500 F. Supp. 529 (E.D. Mo. 1980)

[**pg. 530**] *Memorandum*

FILIPPINE, District Judge.

This matter is before the Court for a decision on the merits, after a trial to the Court, of plaintiff's two-count complaint. Count I of the complaint alleges a breach of contract; Count II alleges misrepresentation. After consideration of the testimony of the witnesses, the exhibits, and the stipulations of the parties, the Court makes the following findings of fact and conclusions of law.

Findings of Fact

Plaintiff is a resident of the City of Collinsville, Illinois, and a citizen of the State of Illinois. Defendant Osage Homestead, Inc., d/b/a St. Charles Drilling Co., Inc., is a Missouri corporation with its principal place of business in St. Charles County, Missouri.

In November, 1974, plaintiff contacted the defendant to inquire about the possibility of defendant installing a well and water system on plaintiff's property in Illinois. Plaintiff's property consists in twenty acres located on Kosten Hill Road in Collinsville, Illinois, east of Illinois Highway 157. . . .

[**pg. 531**] . . . On July 11, 1975, plaintiff and Bob Torrance [defendant's salesman] executed an agreement for the installation by defendant of the well and water system. The agreement, plaintiff's Exhibit 9, was signed on plaintiff's Illinois property.

The agreement itself contained no description of the items which were to be included in the water system. It did show a maximum total price of $4,620.00 for the well and water system. Among the general terms and conditions contained in the agreement were a one-year guarantee on labor and parts, and the statement "[n]o agreements, expressed or implied, other than stated herein shall be considered as part of this contract." Next to the quoted statement was written "See Supplement Letter 7-11-75."

In the "Supplement Letter," dated July 11, 1975, plaintiff specified certain items which he wanted to be certain were part of the agreement; he would have allowed no work to be done by defendant on his property had the defendant not agreed to the terms in the "Supplement Letter." Defendant sent a letter to plaintiff, dated July 18, 1975, in which it confirmed the terms of the plaintiff's supplement letter; but defendant added a qualification. Part of defendant's letter to plaintiff, plaintiff's Exhibit 12, reads as follows: "1¼ pipe is large enough to supply 12 homes at 12 GPM each, total 144 GPM (30 # to 50 # pressure at houses); with proper sized pump and accumulator system." (Emphasis added). The underlined words or their equivalent were not contained in plaintiff's supplement letter. Defendant's letter also confirmed plaintiff's understanding that the "[w]ater line [was] to be buried 36 inches deep." . . .

Plaintiff was ultimately billed for $4,778.39; the billing included certain authorized extra items. Plaintiff has paid the defendant the full amount billed. . . .

[**pg. 532**] The system did not function perfectly from the date of its installment, and defendant made numerous service calls to plaintiff's property in an attempt to correct the problems. Defendant has replaced the pressure controls at the squat tank four times. The squat tank operates at a significantly higher pressure than its rating.

The pump in the well short-cycled from the day of installation, but it has not been replaced. The shortcycling has since been rectified by plaintiff's installation of a time-delay, but this is only a temporary solution. . . .

Conclusions of Law

. . . [**pg. 533**] The parties have not addressed the possibility that the Uniform Commercial Code, as adopted by Illinois, governs this case. The Court has given strong consideration to that possibility, but has concluded that the contract at issue was primarily a service contract, with a sale of goods incidental thereto, rather than vice versa. See *generally* 1 Anderson, Uniform Commercial Code §§2-102:5 and 2-102:6 (1970 and Supp. 1979). At least one Illinois appellate court has adopted a "predominate factor in the contract" test, developed in *Bonebrake v. Cox,* 499 F.2d 951 (8th Cir. 1974), to determine the applicability of the U.C.C. *Executive Centers of America Inc. v. Bandon,* 62 Ill. App. 3d 738, 19 Ill. Dec. 700, 703, 379 N.E.2d 364, 367 (1978). . . .

This Court finds that the transaction between the parties in the instant case falls on the "service" side of the *Bonebrake* test, for two reasons: With two exceptions discussed below, the parties had no agreement specifying the various component parts of the "water system" which were to be installed. The defendant was not bound to use specified items of "goods" in the water system. Neither party has suggested that the estimate sheet (plaintiff's Exhibit 8) prepared by defendant the day before the contract was signed, was a part of the parties' contract. Essentially, defendant undertook to install a "water system" of indefinite description but with a certain warranted capacity, rather than to install a detailed list of specific "goods." Therefore, not only was the contract essentially for defendant's services, but the component parts did not become identified to the contract until they were actually installed on plaintiff's property, and thus it is doubtful that they fell within the definition of "goods" contained in Ill. Rev. Stat., ch. 26, para. 2-105.

Secondly, the language of the instant contract is unmistakably that of service rather than of sale. Defendant is identified as the "contractor," and the contract acknowledges "an express mechanics lien . . . to secure the amount of contract or repairs." Plaintiff's Exhibit 9, General Terms & Conditions no. 9.

Thus, the Court concludes that the U.C.C. does not, strictly speaking, govern this case. . . .

Assignment 3. Office Memorandum
Two Issues
Jurisdiction: Fictitious State of New Maine
Closed Universe

Assume that you have had the conversation with your supervising attorney, Susan Corleone, that is set forth in Assignment 2 above. Assume further that Corleone approached you in your office a few hours later with the following additional assignment:

Corleone: I would like you to address a second issue in your memorandum in the *Carson* case. After discussing whether the UCC or common law applies to this dispute, I would like you to assume that the UCC applies and to discuss whether the parties formed a contract under the UCC. Specifically, you can assume that Carson's bid was a valid offer, that Carson expressed his intent to revoke that offer 10 days later, and that King expressed his intent to accept the bid five days after that. I want to know whether Carson's offer was irrevocable under the UCC.

Law Clerk: Are we certain that King gave no consideration for Carson's promise not to revoke the bid for 30 days?

Corleone: Yes. At least, I want you to assume for purposes of this memo that King cannot prove such consideration.

In addition to the statutory materials provided in Assignment 2, you may use the following provision of the Uniform Commercial Code (1990):

§2-205. Firm Offers
An offer by a merchant to buy or sell goods in a signed writing which by its terms gives assurance that it will be held open is not revocable, for lack of consideration, during the time stated or if no time is stated for a reasonable time, but in no event may such period of irrevocability exceed three months; but any such term of assurance on a form supplied by the offeree must be separately signed by the offeror.

You have found no case law, in New Maine or any other jurisdiction, that interprets the relevant language of §2-205. You may assume that Carson is a merchant of plumbing supplies for purposes of the statute. On other matters of statutory interpretation, advance your own interpretation of the relevant language based on your understanding of (1) the ordinary meaning of the statutory language and (2) the apparent purpose of the provisions. For general background information on option contracts and the enforceability of a promise not to revoke an offer, you may consult the following excerpt from a secondary source:

CONTRACTS

E. Allan Farnsworth
(Little, Brown & Co. 2d ed. 1990)
(pp. 185-186, 188; footnotes omitted)

§3.23 Irrevocable Offers. An offeree may need time to decide whether to accept the offer and, during that time, may need to spend money and effort in deciding. Even if the offeror is willing to assure the offeree that the offer will be held open for that time, the traditional common law rules make it difficult to protect the offeree against the offeror's power of revocation. Not only does the common law posit that offers are generally revocable, but the offeror's mere promise not to revoke the offer—or its mere statement that the offer is not revocable—is traditionally unenforceable unless under seal or supported by consideration. The doctrine of consideration, combined with the principle of free revocability, makes it impossible for the offeror to give the offeree the desired protection merely by saying so. The result has been increasingly subjected to criticism, especially where irrevocability does not expose the offeror to a substantial risk of speculation by the offeree.

Before the abolition of the seal, the offeror could make the offer irrevocable by promising under seal not to revoke it. Such promises were called *options*. Now that the seal has been generally abolished, the offeror can still make the offer irrevocable if its promise not to revoke is supported by consideration. The consideration may consist of either a promise or a performance. Often it consists of a sum of money that is small in relation to the opportunity that speculation affords the offeree and the risk that speculation imposes on the offeror. . . .

Uniform Commercial Code §2-205 goes further in providing for "firm offers," as the Code calls irrevocable offers. The offer need only be "in a signed writing which by its terms gives assurance that it will be held open." It is then irrevocable "during the time stated or if no time is stated for a reasonable time." In keeping with the policy of shielding the offeror from excessive risk of speculation, the period of irrevocability may not exceed three months. In order to prevent imposition on consumers, only a merchant can make a firm offer. Even a merchant must separately sign the firm offer clause if it is on a form supplied by the other party. These Code provisions are, of course, limited to the sale of goods.

Assignment 4. Office Memorandum
One or More Issues
Jurisdiction: Fictitious State of Calzona
Open Library

The following problem is set in the fictitious state of Calzona. Study the problem, research and analyze it using resources available in your library, and draft an office memorandum to your supervising attorney. In this problem, fill in "199y" with the year of the summer immediately preceding your work on this assignment, and fill in "199x" with the year previous to 199y.

You are an associate in Simpson, Sanchez, and Summers, a law firm in Lennox, Calzona. Last week, firm partner Mark Simpson asked you to (1) interview a potential new client, George Bryant, who complains that his employer unlawfully fired him, and (2) draft an office memorandum to help Simpson determine whether the firm should take Bryant's case. You arranged to meet Bryant in your office, and you instructed him to bring any employment documents that he has. Following are excerpts of your interview with Bryant.

Associate: I understand that you have a grievance against your former employer.

Bryant: Yes. I worked as a waiter at Chez Marie for more than a year, from September 199x through August 8, 199y. That's when the maitre d' fired me—at the end of the dinner shift.

Associate: Did he give you any reason for firing you?

Bryant: You bet, and one of the other waiters heard the whole thing. He said right to my face that he wouldn't have a gay waiter on his staff. When I protested that my sexual orientation had nothing to do with my job, he got pretty ugly—he said I probably had AIDS and might give it to the customers. In case you're wondering—Yes, I am gay; no, I don't have the H.I.V. virus; and even Mario will admit that I'm the best waiter in the state.

Associate: Who's Mario? Is he the one who fired you?

Bryant: Yes, Mario Prieto. He is the maitre d' at Chez Marie. Marie Jardon owns the restaurant, and she supervises the kitchen, but she delegates to Mario all the hiring, firing, assignment, and supervision of the waiters and other table staff. Oh, he's smooth with the customers, all right; he's been a popular institution at Chez Marie for six years. But to his employees, he's arrogant, demanding, and almost unbearably macho.

Associate: Did Mario know that you were gay when he hired you?

Bryant: No, why would he? That's one question the application form doesn't ask, and I don't advertise it to the customers or other employees at the restaurant. You see, I've lived with the same man, Larry, for more than a year, and he used to come to the restaurant near closing time every now and then to have coffee and dessert and to go on the town with me when I got off work. A couple of weeks ago Mario asked some of my closer friends on the staff about Larry, and he discovered our relationship.

Associate: I see that you have brought some documents with you. What are they?

Bryant: This is a copy of my employment application; I think they give a photocopy to all the employees to remind them of the clause at the bottom that shows that Mario has complete control over their lives.

Associate: Yes, that shows that you were hired as an "at-will" employee. That gives Mario a lot of discretion.

Bryant: Does that mean that he can fire me because of my sexual orientation?

Associate: Well, that's a question I intend to answer. In the meantime, are you certain he fired you because of your sexual orientation? Is it possible that you simply didn't meet his exacting standards in your work?

Bryant: Oh no, my performance as a waiter was impeccable. Quite simply, I'm the best. A distinguished restaurant like Chez Marie requires waiters with the charm of a diplomat, the grace of a ballet dancer, and the timing of a stand-up comic; add to those qualities a pleasing voice, a computer-like memory, and the proper balance between confidence and humility, and you have the package that I've perfected during my years in the profession. Mario never complained about my work; instead, he put me on the best weekend shifts because of my popularity with important customers. His discovery of my sexual orientation is the only possible explanation for his change in attitude.

Associate: Has this whole affair upset you emotionally in any serious way? Has it made you nervous? Have you suffered insomnia, headaches, anything like that?

Bryant: No, not at all. I got another job right away. And I learned to accept my sexuality a long time ago; I've learned to roll with the punches when guys like Mario treat me like some kind of freak. Why do you ask that?

Associate: I'm just trying to identify potential claims. Where are you working now?

Bryant: L'Orangerie. As soon as word got around that I was fired, I got offers from three top restaurants to start working immediately. They didn't even care that I was fired; they know my reputation for excellence, and they know Mario's reputation for impulsive and arbitrary action. I took a waiter's position with L'Orangerie; it's not a headwaiter's position, but it's a job.

Associate: So, what are you seeking from our law firm?

Bryant: To get even with Mario. I want to see him squirm a little. But that's not all; it's the principle of the thing. I don't think that I should be pushed around because of my sexual orientation; I want to show everyone that gays have a right to employment just like everyone else. Besides that, you've got to understand: Chez Marie is one of the top 20 restaurants in the country, and it's in a class all by itself in Lennox. No other restaurant in the state can come close to matching the pay and prestige enjoyed by Chez Marie's staff. And its clientele is the wealthiest and most sophisticated that the Valley can offer. In my year at Chez Marie I earned a base salary of $30,000 and tips of $25,000; even at L'Orangerie I'll pull in only about $30,000 per year in salary and tips combined, and the prestige is much lower. I've saved up quite a bit of money, and I'm willing to pay you your normal fees to see this through.

Associate: Okay. Thank you for visiting with me today. I'll get back to you as soon as the firm decides whether to take your case.

After interviewing one of the other waiters at Chez Marie over the telephone, you are convinced that Bryant's version of the facts is generally accurate and that Mario at all times acted with full authority on behalf of Marie, Bryant's ultimate employer.

Your preliminary research shows that the City of Lennox has adopted an antidiscrimination ordinance:

> It is contrary to the policy of the City and unlawful to discriminate against any person because of sex, age, physical disability, marital status, sexual orientation, race, color, creed, national origin, or ancestry in places of public accommodation, in employment, or in housing.

Lennox, Calz. City Code ch. 18, art. I, §7(a) (as amended 1987). The ordinance provides for a $500 fine, payable to the City for violation of the ordinance. Id. at §7(b). A state statute makes it a misdemeanor to engage in certain kinds of sexual conduct between members of the same sex. Calz. Rev. Stat. §13-1411. A section of comprehensive state legislation guaranteeing equal opportunity in employment, Calz. Rev. Stat. §22-3202, is identical to §703(a) of Title VII of the 1964 Civil Rights Act, 42 U.S.C. §2000e-2(a).

Bryant's application form is reproduced on the next page.

APPLICATION FOR EMPLOYMENT

Bryant, M. George   _658-80-2240_
Name: Last, Middle Initial, First   Social Security Account #

721 E. Culver St., Apt. #23
Address

Lennox   _85209_   _253-7821_
City   Zip Code   Phone Number

Waiter, headwaiter, maitre d'
Positions for which you are applying

Experience—Describe all prior employment in the restaurant industry. Identify the employer, the employer's location, and your position with the employer.

Waiter at La Chaumiere, Scottsdale, Calzona, Sept. 1987– present

Waiter at Narsi's, Berkeley, CA, Sept. 1985–August 1987

Waiter at various casual restaurants 1971–85.

To the best of my knowledge, all of the above information is accurate. I understand that this application constitutes an offer to work in any of the positions listed above at the standard salary for that position at the time of hire plus gratuities. I also understand that, if the employer accepts this offer by approving the application, the resulting employment contract is one for indefinite duration and may be terminated at the will of the employer.

George Bryant   _Sept. 10, 199x_
Applicant's signature   Date

FOR OFFICE USE ONLY

Mario Prieto   _9-16-199x_
Application approved by   Date of hire

Chez Marie, 112 W. Camelback, Lennox, Calzona 85272

Assignment 5. Office Memorandum
Multiple Issues
Jurisdiction: State in which your law school
is located
Open Library

You are an associate with the law firm of Roberts and Cray. Partner Susan Cray asks you to prepare an office memorandum analyzing the claims of Charlotte Rembar, a potential client. The following is a transcript of your interview with Rembar. Fill in "199Z" with the current year, "199Y" with the year before the current year, and "199X" with the year before "199Y."

Associate: I understand that you have a problem with your employer.

Rembar: My ex-employer—he fired me November 199Y; that's my problem.

Associate: Did he tell you why he fired you?

Rembar: It was pretty obvious—he cut me off because I wouldn't go to bed with him.

Associate: Start from the beginning. Tell me about your job and your employer.

Rembar: I worked for Alexander Hart. He owns Comcon, a local computer consulting firm; they help businesses determine the best computer system for their needs, and they create custom computer programs for them. Alex is a real genius, and he hires the best consultants to work for them, so his business is booming. I started working there January 1, 199Y.

Associate: What was your position with the firm?

Rembar: I was one of his consultants; I designed computer systems and developed programs. I graduated from Stanford with honors in May 199X with a degree in computer programming; this was my first decent job in the computer industry.

Associate: How many of you work at the firm?

Rembar: Alex works in the field himself as a consultant, and he had six of us working also as consultants. Other than that, he's got a secretary and a part-time accountant.

Associate: Is that his full work force? Has it ever been bigger?

Rembar: As far as I know, that work force represented substantial expansion for him from previous years; his firm has never been bigger.

Associate: Tell me about your termination.

Rembar: Well, Alex had an eye for me since the day he hired me. He was always flirting and asking me out on dates. I always thought of some polite excuse not to go out with him; I didn't want to offend him, but I don't like him that much and I didn't think it would be good for our working relationship to get involved in dating. It started getting worse last fall, and near the end of October, 199Y he called me into his office at the end of the day and flatly propositioned me. I refused, and he fired me.

Associate: Precisely what did he say, and how did you respond?

Rembar: First he asked me how I liked my job and my pay; I said I liked it fine. Then he said that he was in love with me and that he wanted me to go home with him that night and sleep with him and that I wouldn't regret it if I did. I didn't know what to say—I was so shocked. I think I just stood there with a stupid expression on my face for a few seconds; then I told him I had to go to a Halloween party, and I ran out of his office.

Associate: Did he fire you then?

Rembar: Not at that meeting. I was so distressed, I could hardly eat or sleep the whole weekend. I was worried about how we were going to maintain a decent working relationship if he was infatuated with me. I decided to talk to him about it on Monday morning, but I never got a chance. When I arrived at work, Alex called me into his office and told me that he didn't need my services any longer and that I had one week to clean out my office. I was literally speechless. I just walked out to my car and cried and cursed him. I got my last paycheck a week later.

Associate: Were you upset for a long time?

Rembar: Oh yes. I had trouble sleeping for a month. I was so nervous and depressed that I couldn't attend normal social functions. And I felt guilty—and stupid. I thought that I could have avoided all this if I had been more assertive in the beginning and told Alex more clearly that I wasn't interested. I started seeing a doctor and a counselor so that I could cope with it. I guess you've probably handled bigger problems than this, but I felt like my world was coming apart. This was my dream job—I was making $4,000 a month doing work that I love. When Alex fired me, I didn't know how I would ever explain it to other employers in job interviews. Luckily, I told the truth to the Personnel Manager at IBM, and she believed me. I started working there at the same salary in early January, 199Z.

Associate: How was your performance at Comcon?

Rembar: Great. I was the newest consultant, but I was better than two or three of the more experienced ones.

Associate: Did Alex ever praise your work, either orally or in writing?

Rembar: Sure. In my first month, he said I was learning fast. And in August, he complimented me on a particularly good job I did with one account. But he never put anything like that in writing.

Associate: Did he ever complain about your work, either orally or in writing?

Rembar: Never.

Associate: Do you want your job back at Comcon?

Rembar: No. I'm happy at IBM, and I don't want to ever work for that worm again. But I went through a lot of pain, and I think he owes me something for it.

Associate: Did you have a written contract of employment with Comcon?

Rembar: No, we just orally agreed that I would provide the consulting services for a starting salary of $48,000 a year. But he gave me a little policy manual to look at when I interviewed for the job. I've got a copy of it right here.

Associate: Did he say anything when he gave it to you?

Rembar: Yeah, he said that he believed in treating his consultants like professionals and that he could offer me better benefits and working conditions than I would get at the bigger firms. He encouraged me to read the policy manual to confirm that. He obviously wanted to give the appearance of a class operation so that he could attract the best consultants; he made a lot of money off of us.

Associate: I think that's all I need. I don't have authority to take your case; I'll have to report to the partners and get a decision from them. I'll get back to you by the end of the month. If we don't take the case, I'll help steer you toward some other attorneys who may be interested. In the meantime, read this explanation of our fee system and call me if you have any questions.

POLICY MANUAL
for Employees of Comcon

I. INTRODUCTION

The success of Comcon lies in its ability to recruit and retain the best employees available nationally. To promote a stable and productive work force, Comcon endeavors to provide attractive terms and conditions of employment, as reflected in the following policies.

II. SALARY

. . . .

III. HOLIDAYS, VACATIONS, SICK LEAVE

. . . .

IV. TERMINATION

A. Probationary Employment

Each employee will work on probationary status during his or her first 60 days of employment. During this probationary period, Comcon reserves the right to terminate the employee for any reason, or for no reason at all.

B. Nonprobationary Employment

Comcon reserves the right to terminate the employment of any employee who is not performing satisfactorily.

Legal Writing Style: Problems for Chapter 11 of the Main Text

Problem 1. Conventions of Punctuation: Policy and Style

Described below are several conventions for use of commas, semicolons, and colons.[4] For each convention of usage,

(1) describe the policies of composition that support the rule; alternatively, critique the rule or comment on it in some other fashion;
(2) explain what practical problems may arise if the rule is ignored;
(3) determine whether the rule should be viewed as sufficiently flexible
to permit exceptions when adherence to the rule is not necessary
to satisfy important policies or to avoid significant problems; and
(4) consider alternatives to the approach described in the rule.

If helpful, illustrate your points with examples.

a. Independent Clauses

An independent clause is a clause with a subject and verb, structured so that it could stand alone as a complete sentence. You should separate independent clauses either with a period, thus creating two sentences, or with the following punctuation:
(1) In the absence of a conjunction, use a semicolon, not a comma:

The roughest American team sport is football; basketball and baseball are comparatively gentle.

---

4. For further examples, see William Struck, Jr., and E. B. White, The Elements of Style 1-9 (3d ed. 1979).

(2) Use a comma if the second independent clause begins with a coordinating conjunction, such as *and, but, yet, for, so, or, nor*:

> For two weeks after the earthquake, the tap water in the Sarah's house was contaminated, **but** potable water was available in plastic containers at a nearby Red Cross outpost.

(3) Use a semicolon if the second independent clause begins with a conjunctive adverb, sometimes called an adverbial connective, such as *therefore, however, moreover, consequently, accordingly, nevertheless, thus.* Follow the connective with a comma:

> Basketball is not intended to be a contact sport; **nonetheless,** basketball players often deliver crushing blows to one another without incurring penalties.
> For two weeks after the earthquake, the tap water in the Sarah's house was contaminated; **however,** potable water was available in plastic containers at a nearby Red Cross outpost.

(4) Multiple verbs of the same subject do not create independent clauses and therefore should not be separated with a comma:

> Joanie dribbled the ball past a defender and drove to the basket.

b. Lists or Illuminations

After an independent clause, use a colon to introduce a list or illumination of the first clause:

> A claim under the due process clause requires proof of three elements: a protectable interest, deprivation of the interest by a state official, and the state's failure to afford procedural protections appropriate in the circumstances.

When the clause following the colon is independent, you may exercise discretion to begin it with a capital letter:

> Judge Crowder looked forward to oral argument: He learned much from well-prepared advocates, and he took a perverse pleasure in grilling those who were ill-prepared.

c. Parenthetic Words, Phrases, or Clauses

Use a comma or commas to set off parenthetic words or phrases and nonrestrictive clauses:

> One disgruntled patron in the back row, **however,** complained bitterly about the acoustics of the concert hall.

Carlos Nakai, **the flutist and leader of the band,** had composed the finale while visiting the Yucatan peninsula.

The audience stood and cheered for Carlos Nakai, **who had composed the finale while visiting the Yucatan peninsula.**

The court held that, **in light of the predominance of service activities,** Article 2 of the U.C.C. did not apply to the transaction.

Problem 2. Prehistoric Prohibitions

The following questionable cliches of composition are outdated; indeed, some never rose to the level of an accepted rule. Nonetheless, they still have currency among some editors. If you accept any of these "rules," justify it according to the directions in Problem 1 above. If you reject a rule or would limit it significantly, explain the reasons for your more flexible approach.

(1) Never start a sentence with "because," "however," "and," or "but."

(2) Never split an infinitive, as in "to severely limit his use of water."

(3) Do not insert a comma between the last two elements of a series of three or more elements joined by a conjunction, as in "red, white, and blue."

c. You wish to cite to the decision described in Paragraph a above at page 717 of the official reporter and page 987 of the unofficial reporter. You last cited to this authority within the last page of your document, as described in Paragraph b above; since then, several citations to other authorities have intervened.

VI

Assignments for Part III of the Main Text

Assignment 1. Format—Trial Brief

Review Office Memorandum Assignment 1 in Appendix IV. Assume that (1) you have filed a complaint on behalf of the plaintiffs against Ramona Udave and (2) the trial court has assigned the case to mandatory arbitration because of the relatively low amount in controversy.

The arbitrator has set the case for a hearing, but she is concerned about your claim for damages for emotional distress based on breach of contract. She has asked you to write a trial brief explaining why the plaintiffs would be entitled to such relief under the facts that you intend to prove at the hearing. She has specifically asked both parties to limit their briefs to that issue.

Without referring to a sample trial brief, draft the document requested by the arbitrator, and argue your clients' case persuasively. You are limited to the authorities reproduced in the office memorandum assignment. You may begin with the caption on the next page; otherwise, use any reasonable format that satisfies the purpose of the document and the needs of your audience. Although you may never have seen a trial brief before, have confidence in your common sense.

ARIZONA SUPERIOR COURT
MARICOPA COUNTY

Trina ARAIZA, et al.,
Plaintiffs,

v.

Ramona UDAVE,
Defendant.

No. CIV-9X-1279

OPENING TRIAL BRIEF

Before Elena Long,
Arbitrator

Assignment 2. Revision of Sample Complaint

Critically evaluate the following sample complaint for substance and style.

a. Specificity of Allegations

Identify the fact allegations that are especially detailed and redraft them to achieve greater generality. What are the advantages and disadvantages of each version?

b. Simplicity

Discard cliches or jargon in the sample complaint and replace them with simple, plain English.

c. Request for Relief

Each count in the sample complaint includes a request for punitive damages, as well as compensatory damages. Would a court be likely to instruct a jury that it could award punitive damages on the first count? See the main text at Chapter 2, Exercise 1-1(2). Does that question help explain the importance of a second count stating a claim in tort? What tort, if any, does the second count allege?

IN THE SUPERIOR COURT OF
THE STATE OF ARIZONA
IN AND FOR THE COUNTY OF MARICOPA[5]

Georgia Anne TUCKER, Plaintiff,	No. _____
v.	C O M P L A I N T
Harry Joe CLYDE, Defendant.	(Breach of Promise; Tort, Non Motor Vehicle)

Plaintiff alleges:

I

This is an action for money damages exceeding $1,000.

---

5. A few years after the filing of this complaint, local court rules were amended to require identification of the authoring attorney at the beginning of the pleading as well as at the end. Ariz. Super. Ct. Maricopa County R. 2.15 (as amended 1987).

II

Plaintiff is a resident of Cushing, Oklahoma. Defendant is a resident of Morris, Oklahoma. Defendant has caused an act to occur in Maricopa County, Arizona, out of which this cause of action arises.

COUNT ONE
(Breach of Promise)

III

At all relevant times, both Plaintiff and Defendant were over the age of 18 years, and in all respects capable of entering into a marriage contract.

IV

Plaintiff and Defendant were introduced and became acquainted with each other in September 1983. On or about December 8, 1983, Defendant proposed marriage to Plaintiff, and Plaintiff accepted. On January 17, 1984, the proposal and acceptance of marriage were reaffirmed when Defendant purchased a diamond engagement ring for Plaintiff.

V

Plaintiff and Defendant discussed their marriage agreement from time to time and on a great many occasions too numerous to mention herein. In the course of these discussions, Plaintiff and Defendant confirmed plans to be married in Hawaii on March 10, 1984.

VI

In January and February of 1984, Plaintiff and Defendant came to Phoenix, Arizona, for the purpose of locating and purchasing a home for their future marital residence. Defendant purchased a house located at 6052 East Cortez Drive, Scottsdale, Arizona. In addition, in preparation for the marriage, Defendant opened bank accounts, charge accounts, and utility service accounts in the names of Harry Joe Clyde and Georgia Anne Clyde.

VII

At the insistence of Defendant and in reliance on the agreement to marry, Plaintiff gave up a profitable business as a hair stylist in Cushing,

Oklahoma; borrowed and spent the sum of $12,000.00 to refurbish her residence in order to facilitate its sale; listed her residence for sale with a real estate agency; leased her residence to Defendant's son; withdrew her children from school; and moved her household possessions and her children from Cushing, Oklahoma to Scottsdale, Arizona, at great expense and inconvenience.

VIII

On March 1, 1984, after having moved to Scottsdale, Arizona, Defendant presented to Plaintiff a prenuptial agreement that, among other things, listed the State of Arizona as the domicile of the parties and that provided for execution of the agreement in Maricopa County, Arizona. Plaintiff refused to sign the prenuptial agreement as written; however, despite Plaintiff's refusal to sign the prenuptial agreement, Defendant again renewed his promise to marry Plaintiff.

IX

On March 8, 1984, Defendant, Plaintiff, and three of Plaintiff's four children flew to Hawaii for the purpose of consummating the marriage, which was scheduled for March 10, 1984.

X

At approximately 8:00 A.M. on the morning of March 9, 1984, Defendant informed Plaintiff that he would not go through with the wedding. Since that date, Defendant has refused to carry out his promise to marry Plaintiff.

XI

On March 9, 1984, Defendant, Plaintiff, and Plaintiff's three children returned to Scottsdale, Arizona, where Defendant left Plaintiff and her three children in the house that was to have been the marital residence. On March 22, 1984, Defendant demanded that Plaintiff and her three children vacate the Scottsdale residence; for lack of other accommodations, Plaintiff was forced to return to Cushing, Oklahoma.

XII

By reason of Defendant's breach of promise to marry, Plaintiff has been deprived of Defendant's support and care for herself and her children, and of the commensurate standard of living that she would have enjoyed had the marriage been consummated. In addition to the foregoing, Plaintiff has suffered, and will continue to suffer, the following damages: a loss of past and future income as the result of Defendant's insistence that she give up her business; economic loss as the result of monies expended for refurbishing her residence in preparation for sale; economic loss resulting from the move from Cushing, Oklahoma to Scottsdale, Arizona, and from Scottsdale, Arizona back to Cushing, Oklahoma; and mental pain and anguish, wounded pride, mortification, humiliation, shame, and disgrace, which has directly impaired Plaintiff's health.

XIII

Defendant's actions in breaching his promise to marry were intentional or taken with reckless disregard for the rights of Plaintiff.

Plaintiff therefore requests judgment as follows:
1. past and future lost income in an amount to be determined at trial;
2. out-of-pocket expenses in an amount to be determined at trial, but not less than $2,000;
3. mental pain and anguish in an amount to be determined at trial, but not less than $10,000;
4. other compensatory damages in an amount to be determined at trial;
5. reasonable attorney's fees;
6. punitive damages in an amount to be determined at trial; and
7. such other and further relief as the Court deems just and proper.

COUNT TWO
(*Tort*)

XIV

Plaintiff realleges and incorporates into this count paragraphs I through XIII.

XV

Defendant stated to friends, relatives, and acquaintances of Plaintiff that Plaintiff and Defendant were engaged, that Plaintiff and Defendant were moving to Scottsdale, Arizona, and that Plaintiff and Defendant would be married on March 10, 1984.

XVI

After Defendant informed Plaintiff that he would not go through with the marriage, Defendant promised Plaintiff that he would provide her with the financial means to relocate wherever she desired so that she would not have to return to Cushing, Oklahoma, where she would experience the humiliation, shame, disgrace, pain, and anguish of explaining Defendant's failure to fulfill his marriage promise.

XVII

Defendant, after making the above-described promise to Plaintiff, forced Plaintiff to move out of the residence located in Scottsdale, Arizona, and refused to provide any financial assistance except transportation expenses to Cushing, Oklahoma.

XVIII

Defendant's actions in providing only transportation expenses for Plaintiff's return to Cushing, Oklahoma were extreme and outrageous, were intentional, and were done with full knowledge of the emotional consequences to Plaintiff.

XIX

Plaintiff has suffered grievous mental pain, anguish, mortification, humiliation, shame, and disgrace; Plaintiff's mental and physical health has been impaired.

Plaintiff therefore prays for judgment as follows:

1. compensatory damages in an amount to be determined at trial, but not less than $12,000;

2. punitive damages in an amount to be determined at trial; and

3. such other and further relief as the Court deems just and proper in the premises.

Dated May 21, 1984   TICKER, STRANGER & NEAR

                                  By _____
                                  James R. Near
                                  Joseph A. Hammer
                                  900 East Camelback Road
                                  Suite 1010
                                  Scottsdale, AZ 85281
                                  Attorneys for Plaintiff

Assignment 3. Drafting an Answer

Review the sample complaint in Assignment 2 above or the revised version prepared by you or by a classmate. The defendant, Harry Joe Clyde, is prepared to prove that Georgia Anne Tucker repudiated the marriage agreement when she refused to sign a written prenuptial agreement, that he never renewed his promise after Tucker's repudiation, that Tucker called off the wedding, and that he suffered severe disappointment as a result. Draft an answer on behalf of Clyde.

Assignment 4. Drafting a Complaint

Review Office Memorandum Assignment 5 at the end of Appendix IV. Based on the analysis in your office memorandum, determine what claims you could allege in good faith, and draft a complaint for an action in state court on behalf of Charlotte Rembar.

Assignment 5. Opposition to Motion for Summary Judgment

Review Office Memorandum Assignment 5 in Appendix IV, Assignment 4 above, and the sample motion for summary judgment at the end of Chapter 14 of the main text. Prepare and file materials opposing Hart's motion. Your instructor may ask you to change the dates on the materials in the motion and in Paragraph b below, so that you can more accurately simulate summary judgment litigation in the current year. Additionally, your instructor may ask you to change the setting of the motion from Arizona to some other state, real or fictitious.

In preparing your opposition, you may assume the following developments:

a. Your firm filed a complaint alleging four claims for relief: (1) breach of a promise of job security, (2) breach of an implied promise of good faith and fair dealing, (3) wrongful discharge in violation of public policy, and (4) infliction of emotional distress. In his answer, Hart denied that Rembar's contract contained any provisions for job security and denied the allegations of sexual harassment. He alleged that he discharged Rembar for poor performance.

b. Rembar stands by the information she provided in the initial interview, and she is willing to swear to it in an affidavit. Your independent fact investigation has revealed some corroborating evidence from Leslie West, Alex Hart's secretary during Charlotte Rembar's tenure at Comcon. In a recent interview, West revealed that she and Rembar developed a close friendship and that she was distressed to learn of Rembar's discharge. After Rembar filed suit, Hart became irritable and unpleasant to work for; West voluntarily quit her job two weeks ago and immediately offered to support Rembar with trial testimony and statements in an affidavit. The following is an excerpt from the March 3 interview:

> *West:* That was near Halloween last fall. I saw Charlotte run out of the office in tears just before quitting time. The following Monday afternoon, Mr. Hart told me to process the paperwork to terminate Charlotte's payroll

at the end of the week. When I said that I had thought Charlotte was one of his best consultants, he said "Her consulting isn't my problem—it's her stuck-up attitude." I asked him what I should put down on the paperwork as the reason for her termination, and he said something like, "I don't care what you put—just say that she has a negative attitude."

Through discovery requests, you have obtained copies of the contents of Rembar's employment file at Comcon. The file includes only a few insignificant notes and the two Payroll Action forms attached to Hart's motion for summary judgment.

Assignment 6. Motion to Exclude Evidence

Review Office Memorandum Assignment 5 in Appendix IV and Assignments 4 and 5 above. Assume that you have successfully opposed Hart's motion for summary judgment and that the trial judge has scheduled a pretrial conference.

You are concerned about some embarrassing evidence that Hart has obtained through the discovery process. While a freshman at Stanford University, Rembar posed nude for a two-page spread in *Hustle and Bustle*, an adult magazine; some of the poses would strike the average juror as lewd and tasteless. Rembar explained that she posed for the pictures on a dare and that she didn't realize until later how lewd and revealing they would be. She regrets her decision to pose, and she insists that the pictures do not reflect her current personality or style of relating to friends or colleagues.

Hart probably learned of the magazine spread through one of Rembar's freshman college classmates or instructors. In a discovery request, Hart requested confirmation of the event, along with a copy of the magazine. Pursuant to your state's counterpart to Federal Rule of Civil Procedure 26(c), you objected to the request on the ground that the information requested would be inadmissible at trial and that its production would result in annoyance, embarrassment, and oppression. The trial judge, however, compelled discovery on the ground that the information sought, whether or not admissible itself, might lead to the discovery of admissible evidence. *See* Fed. R. Civ. P. 26(b)(1).

You now seek an advance ruling barring any reference to the magazine spread at trial. Draft a motion to exclude the evidence before trial.

‖ INDEX ‖

Page numbers in italics indicate principal discussion.